Don Lively

University Publishing Company

THE
REVOLUTIONARY WAR MEMOIRS
OF
GENERAL HENRY LEE

EDITED
WITH A BIOGRAPHY OF THE AUTHOR
BY
ROBERT E. LEE

NEW INTRODUCTION BY
CHARLES ROYSTER

DA CAPO PRESS • NEW YORK

Library of Congress Cataloging-in-Publication Data

Lee, Henry, 1756-1818.
[Memoirs of the war in the Southern Department of the United States]
  The Revolutionary War memoirs of General Henry Lee / edited, with a
biography of the author, by Robert E. Lee; new introduction by Charles
Royster.
     p.   cm.
  Originally published: Memoirs of the war in the Southern Department
of the United States. 1812.
  ISBN 0-306-80841-2 (alk. paper)
  1. Southern States—History—Revolution, 1775–1783—Personal narratives. 2. United States—History—Revolution, 1775–1783—Personal narratives. 3. Southern States—History—Revolution, 1775–1783—Campaigns. 4. United States—History—Revolution, 1775–1783—Campaigns.
5. Lee, Henry, 1756–1818. 6. Generals—United States—Biography. 7.
United States. Army—Biography. I. Lee, Robert E. (Robert Edward),
1807–1870. II. Title.
E230.5.S7L494 1998
975′ .02—dc21   97-34561
                                                                     CIP

First Da Capo Press edition 1998

This Da Capo Press paperback edition of *The Revolutionary War Memoirs
of General Henry Lee* (originally titled *Memoirs of the War in the Southern
Department of the United States*) is an unabridged republication of the
third edition published in 1869 in New York, with the addition of a
new introduction by Charles Royster.

New introduction copyright © 1998 by Charles Royster

Published by Da Capo Press, Inc.
A Subsidiary of Plenum Publishing Corporation
233 Spring Street, New York, N.Y. 10013

Manufactured in the United States of America

INTRODUCTION

A large part of the handwritten manuscript of Henry Lee's *Memoirs* is preserved in the library of the Virginia Historical Society. Much of it was written in the Spotsylvania County jail during 1809 and 1810. Lee was insolvent. His many investments and loans had not prospered. Neither city lots in the new District of Columbia nor vast tracts of land west of the Allegheny Mountains had turned the sure profits once predicted for them. Lee was imprisoned at the suit of his creditors. He could have gained release by declaring himself insolvent and surrendering control of all his property, but he shrank from this final admission of failure. After a year of confinement he took the necessary steps. During that year, though importuned by creditors seeking payment, he spent his time not sorting out his tangled finances but reliving his years as commander of Lee's Legion in the Southern states during the Revolutionary War. He was writing his *Memoirs*.

Since its publication in two volumes in 1812, Henry Lee's *Memoirs of the War in the Southern Department of the United States* (retitled for this paperback edition) often has been cited and quoted by historians. Lee was not always a reliable storyteller, but he made his narrative irresistible. For many dramatic episodes his account is the only surviving one or the one with the most vivid details. The passion and violence of the war, including the violence he perpetrated, troubled him afterward. His intense feelings about these events emerged in his text. As a young officer in the Continental Army he found himself unable to make war a series of elegant victories. As an author in his later years he could not always sustain the ironical tone of Edward Gibbon or of the ancient historians he and Gibbon had read. Lee wanted to sound magisterial, authoritative, detached—writing for posterity. Yet the story he was telling aroused the old emotions of a participant. He could not resist commentary, showing how episodes might have been handled better. The opportunities he and others had missed in war he could reclaim in history.

In the eyes of some of his fellow officers during the war, Henry Lee was a spoiled brat. In 1781 he was 25 years old. Many officers older than he, with more experience of hard combat, served without special fame in regiments of the Continental Army, while Lee attracted attention by commanding a special "legion" that combined infantry and cavalry, undertaking conspicuous assignments. He had won the favor of the commander of the Southern Department, Nathanael Greene, and the commander of the Continental Army, George Washington. Lee represented a prominent Virginia family. He was a graduate of the College of New Jersey in Princeton. The president of the college, John Witherspoon, who taught good republican principles and politics, supported the American Revolution vigorously. All but a few of the young men at Princeton in Lee's day sided with American independence. Lee, though, never acquired—never tried to acquire—the popular touch. He expected to be obeyed by soldiers and honored by citizens because he was braver, smarter, and better than they were.

Almost thirty years passed between Lee's service in the war and his work on his *Memoirs*. During those years he held a wide variety of public offices. Soon after the war, he represented Virginia in the Continental Congress. More than ten years later, he won a term in the United States House of Representatives. He served in the convention that gave Virginia's ratification to the Constitution of the United States, supporting this cause vehemently, meeting Patrick Henry in debate. He served as governor of Virginia early in the 1790s. Except for a brief period during which he criticized policies of President George Washington's first administration, Lee was a dedicated Federalist, devoted to strengthening the union of states by enhancing the power of the national government. He had seen internecine war among Americans in the Southern Department during the American Revolution. He did not want to see it again. In later years, he reminded readers of his *Memoirs* how cruel it had been.

In the years between the war and his *Memoirs*, Lee married twice. First, at the end of the war, he married his cousin Matilda Lee, granddaughter of one of his uncles. She died eight years later, leaving him and their children at Stratford Hall, the Lee family mansion she had inherited on the south bank of the Potomac River. Three years afterward, while he was governor, Henry Lee married Ann Hill Carter. They began another family at Stratford. Two years before he went to jail for debt, his wife gave birth to a son they named Robert Edward.

Although Henry Lee was attached to his family and ardent in public service, he repeatedly lost the trust of others in private and in public life. He lived beyond his means. He lent money freely, spent money freely, borrowed money freely. He acquired more and more land—or claims to land. Winning independence gave Americans a western boundary on the Mississippi River. Even before the Revolution, land speculators had foreseen huge profits in fertile fields west of the Allegheny Mountains. In the 1780s and 1790s the rush to get rich grew feverish. No one was more eager than Lee. Like others, he failed. He hoped that a Potomac River canal could make the new federal capital, Washington, D.C., not only the center of government but also the great metropolis of commerce between the American west and the transatlantic world. George Washington had similar hopes. The outcome disappointed Washington. It ruined Lee. In the year his *Memoirs* appeared, a hostile newspaper called him "The Swindling Harry Lee." His critics and creditors said that he had been deceptive and dishonest in his failed dealings, not just unlucky or unwise. If Lee was a swindler, he was not a good one, and he paid a high price for his crimes. He *was* a good dreamer, and paid a high price for that, too.

As he contemplated writing his *Memoirs*, thinking about the lesson he wished to teach, as well as the story he could tell, Lee's mind fixed on Thomas Jefferson. In 1809, while Lee faced bankruptcy, Jefferson was retiring to Monticello after having served two terms as president of the United States. Lee deplored Jefferson's policies. He had tried to prevent Jefferson's election. The Republicans led by Jefferson, not content with defeating Lee and other Federalists in elections, claimed also to be the true heirs of the American Revolution—the real patriots who saved the republic. They called Federalists "tories" and "monarchists." Amid the ruin of his fortunes Lee believed that Jefferson had tried to rob him of his greatest distinction—his achievements as a patriotic fighter on behalf of American independence and self-government.

Such an attempt by Jefferson galled Lee even more because he found Jefferson's public record so weak. He had, Lee thought, turned against and betrayed George Washington in the political contests of the 1790s. Lee often stressed his own close ties to

Washington, most notably in his funeral oration in 1799, which called Washington "First in war—first in peace—and first in the hearts of his countrymen." War was the subject of Lee's *Memoirs*. He set out to show that Jefferson had failed the test of war in which Washington and Lee had excelled.

Thomas Jefferson served as governor of Virginia during the British Army's incursions into the state in 1779, 1780, and 1781. Lee fought in South Carolina and North Carolina, as Lord Cornwallis moved his British force northward into Virginia. Lee did not witness Jefferson's conduct, but in his *Memoirs* he wrote about it. At that point in his manuscript he added a note instructing his copyist: "Take care how you copy here." If his narrative could demonstrate that Governor Jefferson had fled Richmond rather than confront the traitor Benedict Arnold and a detachment of British troops, and then had run away from Monticello to escape Banastre Tarleton and a British raiding party, Lee could fix in his reader's mind a conviction that Jefferson—for all the good words in the Declaration of Independence and elsewhere—lacked courage. If Lee's narrative could persuade his reader that courage was the test of character and that courage had won American independence, he could reclaim his stature as a man of character and as a leading patriot.

Upon publication Lee's *Memoirs* received favorable reviews, especially in Federalist periodicals. He hoped that sales of the work would yield a steady revenue for his family, but it did not make money. Lee's account of the British invasions of Virginia made Thomas Jefferson angry for the last fourteen years of his life. Jefferson encouraged and assisted rival accounts: Louis Girardin's history of Virginia during the war years and William Johnson's biography of Nathanael Greene. During the last week of his life Jefferson was still working to prove Lee wrong.

Henry Lee spent the last five years of his life in self-imposed exile. During the summer of the year his *Memoirs* appeared, he and other Federalists went to Baltimore to defend the office of a Federalist newspaper against assault by violent supporters of America's declaration of war against Britain, which Federalists opposed in 1812. Lee and the other defenders were attacked and beaten severely. Lee never recovered his health. Leaving his wife and children in Alexandria, Virginia, he wandered among the Caribbean islands. Growing ever weaker, in March 1818 he made his way back to the United States in time to die on Cumberland Island, Georgia in the house built by the widow of his commanding officer in the Southern Department, Nathanael Greene.

In 1827 Lee's son by his first marriage, also named Henry Lee, brought out a second edition of the *Memoirs*, with additions and corrections. The fiftieth anniversary of American independence, as well as a triumphal tour of the United States two years earlier by George Washington's friend and fellow soldier, the Marquis de Lafayette, stimulated renewed interest in the history of the Revolutionary War. Americans already looked back upon those years as the remote past, a time of almost legendary heroism.

The third edition of the *Memoirs* appeared in 1869, edited by Robert E. Lee. After his surrender of Confederate forces at Appomattox Court House and the close of the Civil War, Lee accepted the presidency of Washington College in Lexington, Virginia. He often said that Southerners should put the war behind them and look to the future. By linking his name with his father's *Memoirs*, he could remind people in both sections of the country that Southerners—including, especially, the Lee family—had played crucial parts in winning the independence of the United States. The first 68 pages were a biography of Henry Lee. Although Charles Carter

Lee prepared this material for his brother, a reader can find the message Robert E. Lee wanted to convey. It is clear in the last paragraph—one sentence, describing the burial of his father's body. Henry Lee had deplored the War of 1812, but his son evoked the United States Navy's successes in that war to close his contribution to the *Memoirs* on a patriotic note: "A ship of war being anchored near, her captain and crew assisted at the funeral, and paid all honors that could be given by the American flag and those guns which had lately won for it so much glory on the ocean."

Although Henry Lee failed in many ways, he succeeded as a writer. His success lay not in producing a book which sold many copies, only to be soon forgotten. Instead, he wrote a work which even his harshest critics never accused of dullness, a work which still is read and used. He put his own tension into his story—a tension between vivid memories of youthful enthusiasm in a daring campaign and mature reflection, from which arose a deep aversion to war.

CHARLES ROYSTER

Baton Rouge, Louisiana

August 1997

Charles Royster, Boyd Professor of History at Louisiana State University, is a noted expert in the fields of the American Revolution and the Civil War. His books include Light-Horse Harry Lee and the Legacy of the American Revolution, A Revolutionary People at War: The Continental Army and American Character, *and* The Destructive War: William Tecumseh Sherman, Stonewall Jackson, and the Americans.

PREFACE.

The favorable reception of Lee's Memoirs evinced by the exhaustion of two editions, seems to justify the issue of a third. The corrections and the additions to the original text made in the edition of 1827 have been retained; and a short biography of the author has been added in the hope of giving increased interest to the work. The incidents from which the biography has been prepared were furnished to the editor of the present edition by his eldest brother, Charles Carter Lee, so that he had only to select from the materials prepared for him what he deemed appropriate for the purpose.

On one point some explanation may be necessary. In the series of letters written to his son from the West India Islands by the author of the Memoirs in the latter days of his life, some repetition of his sentiments occurs, owing to his declining health, his distance from home, and the slow and uncertain communication of that period, and there are some topics discussed more interesting to his family than to the general reader; these have been omitted, though without affecting the sense of the letters.

The maps and plans accompanying the work have been prepared from sketches made by the engineers attached to the British army, for which I am indebted to Mr. H. B. Dawson.

R. E. LEE.

Lexington, Va., *June* 1, 1869.

CONTENTS.

CHAPTER IX.

CHAPTER X.

CHAPTER XI.

CHAPTER XII.

CHAPTER XIII.

CHAPTER XIV.

CHAPTER XV.

CHAPTER XVI.

CHAPTER XVII.

CHAPTER XVIII.

CHAPTER XIX.

CHAPTER XX.

CHAPTER XXI.

CHAPTER XXII.

CHAPTER XXIII.

CHAPTER XXIV.

CHAPTER XXV.

CHAPTER XXVI.

CHAPTER XXVII.

CHAPTER XXVIII.

CHAPTER XXIX.

CHAPTER XXXVI.

CHAPTER XXXVII.

APPENDIX.

STEEL ENGRAVINGS.

MAPS AND PLANS.

LIFE OF GENERAL HENRY LEE.

THE Lee family in Virginia* is the younger branch of one of the oldest families in England. Launcelot Lee, the founder, was originally from Loudon, in France, and went to England with William the Conqueror. After the battle of Hastings, when the estates of the native English nobility were divided among the followers of William, a fine estate in Essex was bestowed upon him. Lionel Lee, first Earl of Litchfield, raised a company of gentlemen cavaliers, at the head of which he accompanied Richard Cœur de Lion in the third Crusade, in 1192. For gallant conduct at the siege of Acre, he was made Earl of Litchfield, and another estate was bestowed on the family, called Ditchley. The armor worn by Lionel Lee was placed in the Horse Armory in the Tower of London. (See "Guilliam's Complete Heraldry.") Richard Lee accompanied the unfortunate Earl of Surrey in his expedition against the Scotch Borders in 1542. Two of the family were Knights Companions of the Garter, and their banners surmounted by the Lee arms were placed in St. George's Chapel, Windsor Castle. The arms consisted of a shield, band sinister, battled and embattled; crest, a closed visor surmounted by a squirrel holding a nut; the motto, *Non incautus futuri*. Richard Lee, a younger son of the house of Litchfield, emigrated to America in the year 1600.

Richard Lee, of Shropshire, whose picture, in 1771, was at Coton, near Bridgenorth, the seat of Launcelot Lee, Esq., during the reign of Charles I. came over to the colony of Virginia as secretary and one of the king's privy council. He is described as a man of good

---

* This pedigree of the Lee family is abridged from a narrative written by Mr. William Lee in London, September, 1771, and obtained from his daughter, Mrs. Hodgson. He was American Minister at the Hague during the Revolution.

stature, comely visage, enterprising genius, a sound head, and generous nature. When he reached Virginia, at that period not much cultivated, he was so pleased with the country that he made large settlements with the servants who accompanied him. After some years he returned to England, and at his departure bequeathed to his followers all the lands on which he had settled them at his own expense. Some of their descendants thus became possessed of considerable estates in the colony. After remaining some time in England, he again visited Virginia with a fresh band of followers, whom he also settled there.

During the civil war in England, Sir William Berkeley was Governor of Virginia. He and Lee, being Loyalists, held the colony to its allegiance, so that after the death of Charles I., Cromwell was forced to send armed vessels of war and troops to reduce it to subjection. Unable to resist, they made a treaty with the "Commonwealth of England," wherein Virginia was styled an "Independent Dominion." This treaty being ratified as with a foreign power, Sir William Berkeley, of the same family as the subsequent Earl of Berkeley, was removed, and another governor appointed. Oliver Cromwell, to punish Virginia and other parts of America for adhering so firmly to the royal cause, after he had obtained supreme power established the famous Navigation Act, by which the American Colonies were deprived of many of their ancient and valuable privileges. After the Restoration this act was never repealed, and at two other periods taxes were imposed upon American commodities under the pretext of "Regulations of Trade."

While Prince Charles II. was at Breda, Richard Lee went over from Virginia to ascertain if he would protect the colony, should it return to its allegiance to the royal line. Finding no support could be obtained, he retraced his steps and remained quiet until the death of Cromwell, when, with the aid of Sir William Berkeley, Charles II. was proclaimed in Virginia, King of England, Scotland, France, Ireland, and Virginia, two years before his restoration. In consequence, the motto to the Virginia arms was "*En dat Virginia quintam*," until after the union of England and Scotland, when it was changed to "*En dat Virginia quartam*." * This

* The territory granted to Virginia when first established as a British Colony extended from the river St. Croix, in Maine, to Cape Fear, in North Carolina, and from the Atlantic to the Pacific Ocean. Out of this domain were formed colonies north and south, which are now great States. When Virginia be-

Richard Lee had several children; the two eldest, John and Richard, were educated at Oxford. John took a degree as Doctor of Physic, and returning to his father, died young. Richard was so distinguished for talent and learning that he was offered the highest dignities of the church, if his father would permit him to remain in England; but he had determined to establish his children in Virginia, and was so fixed in this purpose that he ordered an estate near Stratford by Bow, in Middlesex, worth eight or nine hundred pounds per annum, to be sold and the money divided among his heirs. He died on his much-loved soil and left many children, whose names are generally unknown.

His eldest son was Richard, who spent his time in study, writing his notes in Greek, Latin, and Hebrew, and did not improve his paternal estate, which might have produced a princely revenue. He was of the Council in Virginia, filled other offices of honor, and married a Miss Corbyn or Corbyne, of the same family into which his predecessor had married in England, and left five sons and one daughter at his death, which occurred in Virginia some time after the Restoration. The names of the sons were Richard, Philip, Francis, Thomas, and Henry. Richard settled in London as a Virginia merchant, in partnership with his uncle Thomas Corbyn, married in England an heiress named Silk, left one son, George, and two daughters, Lettice and Martha, who all lived in Virginia. George married a Miss Womley, who died leaving one daughter. His second wife was Miss Fairfax, nearly allied to Lord Fairfax of Yorkshire, who outlived him, and had three sons who were placed at school in England under the care of Mr. James Russell. Lettice married a Corbin; and her sister a Turbeville. Their eldest children intermarried, from which union sprung George Lee Turbeville. Philip, the second son, went to Maryland, where he married and became one of the Proprietors' Council. He left a numerous family, that branched out largely over the whole province, and were in affluent circumstances, his eldest son Richard being also a member of the Proprietors' Council. Francis, the third son, died a bachelor; Thomas, the fourth, with few advantages of education, by the force of his own

came a State, her limits extended indefinitely westward, and one of her first acts was to grant to Kentucky its present area. She subsequently threw into the common territory all of her northwest possessions, out of which have been created the rich States beyond the Ohio River.

genius and industry acquired Latin and Greek. He married a Ludwell.

The Ludwells, though the name is now extinct, were an old and honorable family of Somersetshire, and came originally from Germany. Philip Ludwell and John Ludwell, brothers, the sons of Miss Cottington, heiress of Jean Cottington, brother and heir of the famous Lord Francis Cottington (of whom a full account may be found in Clarendon's History of the Rebellion), were in court favor after the Restoration of Charles II. John was appointed Secretary and one of the Council of Virginia, where it is said he died without issue. Philip was sent to America as Governor of Carolina; whence he went to Virginia and married the widow of Sir William Berkeley, by whom he had a daughter who became the wife of Colonel Daniel Parke, and one son named Philip. The father returned to England, where he died and was buried at Bow Church, Stratford. The son had a fine estate in the "Independent Dominion," and married Miss Harrison, by whom he had two daughters—Lucy, who married Colonel Grymes, of the Council of Virginia, and Hannah, who married the before-mentioned Thomas Lee, and one son, Philip, who became also a member of the Council. This last married a Miss Grymes, and had a number of children, most of whom died in infancy, and in the year 1753 his wife died. Returning to England for his health in 1760, he expired in1767, when the male line of Ludwell became extinct. There were three daughters, Hannah Phillippa, Frances, and Lucy. The second died unmarried. Thomas Lee acquired a handsome fortune, and was also of the Council; and though he had but few friends in the mother country, was so well known by reputation, that upon suffering some losses by fire, Queen Caroline sent him a present from her privy purse. When Sir William Gooch, the governor, was recalled, he became president and commander-in-chief in the Colony, in which station he continued until the king appointed him governor; but he died in 1750, before the commission reached him. He had by his marriage with Miss Ludwell six sons—Philip Ludwell, Thomas Ludwell, Richard Henry, Francis Lightfoot, William, and Arthur—and two daughters, all well provided in point of fortune. Philip Ludwell, a member of the Council, married, and had two daughters; he lived at Stratford on the Potomac River. Thomas Ludwell married, had several children, and lived at Bellview, on the Potomac River, Virginia.

Richard Henry married, had several children, and lived at Chantilly, on the Potomac River. Francis Lightfoot married a daughter of John Taylor, had no children, and lived at Manokin, Rappahannock River. William, the writer of this account, in 1769 married in London, Miss Hannah Phillippa Ludwell, co-heiress of Philip Ludwell, and remained a merchant on Tower Hill, London. Arthur studied physic at Edinburgh and took his degree, but disliking the profession became a student of law at Lincoln's Inn, No. B, Essex Court. The two daughters, Hannah and Alice, married well and settled in America.

Henry, the fifth brother and next to Thomas, married Miss Bland; had three sons—John, Richard, and Henry—and a daughter Lettice. John died without issue. Richard lived a bachelor at Lee Hall on the Potomac. Henry married Miss Grymes, had several children, and dwelt at Leesylvania, on the same river. The only sister of these five brothers was united to a Fitzhugh, a family of note in Virginia, and had several children.

Henry Lee, of Leesylvania, and Lucy Grymes were married at Green Spring, on James River, Saturday, December 1, 1753, by the Rev. William Preston, of James City. She was a daughter of the Colonel Grymes and Lucy Ludwell mentioned above, and a favorite niece of Bishop Porteus, whose correspondence with her after he became Bishop of London has been lost, but is said by the members of her family who read it, to have been interesting and beautiful. Those who have seen his notes on the Bible, especially on the Gospel of St. Matthew, will conceive what a sacred light may have been shed upon her mind by that great luminary of the Church of England.

The first child of this marriage was a daughter, who lived but ten months; the second, Henry Lee, the subject of this memoir, was born on the 29th of January, 1756, at Leesylvania, which is situated on a point of land jutting into the Potomac, three miles above Dumfries, then the county town of Prince William. This village, chiefly built by the enterprise of Scotch merchants, was enriched by a tobacco inspection, and enlivened by a theatre.*

---

* Mr. Grigsby, in his discourse on the Virginia Convention of 1776, note to page 187, says: "Henry Lee, of Prince William, was an old member of the House of Burgesses, of all the Conventions, of the Declaration Committee, and of the General Assembly. His standing was of the first, before and after the Revolution."

Mr. Lee was apparently a favorite in the community, and represented the county, either as a burgess or delegate, for more than twenty years. His sons Henry and Charles (the latter subsequently attorney-general in Washington's second cabinet) were sent to Princeton College. Dr. William Shippen wrote concerning them to Richard Henry Lee from Philadelphia, 25th August, 1770: "I am persuaded there is not such a school as Princeton on this continent. Your cousin Henry Lee is in college, and will be one of the first fellows in this country. He is more than strict in his morality, has a fine genius, and is diligent. Charles is in the grammar school, but Dr. Witherspoon expects much from his genius and application." *

Henry was preparing himself for the profession of law and about to embark for England to pursue that study under the direction of Bishop Porteus, when the commencement of hostilities with the mother country changed his destiny. Soon after the battle of Lexington, he entered the army as captain of cavalry, at the age of nineteen. Besides being present at other important actions in the Northern Department, he was at the battles of Brandywine, Germantown, and Springfield, and early became a favorite of Washington. In the difficult and critical operations in Pennsylvania, New Jersey, and New York, from 1777 to 1780 inclusive, he was always placed near the enemy, intrusted with the command of outposts, the superintendence of scouts, and that kind of service which required the possession of coolness, address, and enterprise. During the occupation of Philadelphia by the Royal forces, his activity and success in impeding their communications, cutting off their light parties, and intercepting their supplies, drew on him the particular attention of the enemy.† In consequence of this continual annoyance they resolved to cut him off, and their attempt to surround him resulted in driving him into the Spread Eagle tavern.

This affair is narrated by Marshall in his "Life of Washington" (vol. iii., page 377), and by Major Garden in his "Anecdotes" (page 67). General Weedon, in a letter to R. H. Lee, dated Valley Forge, 1st February, 1778, states that a surprise was attempted by two

---

* Excerpts from the Lee Papers in "Southern Literary Messenger," December, 1858, page 443.

† Lee's Observations on Jefferson's Writings, and the authorities there cited.

hundred British light horse against Captain Harry Lee, who was quartered about six miles below Valley Forge. The enemy, on the night of the 20th January, set out upon this expedition by a circuitous route of twenty miles, eluded the vigilance of his vedettes, and reached his quarters at daylight. With great activity Lee first secured the doors, which they made fruitless attempts to force; then mustered his garrison, consisting of a corporal and four men, Lieutenant Lindsay, Major Jamieson, and himself, amounting to eight in all; and by judiciously posting them, though not sufficient in number to man each window, he obliged the enemy to retire after an action of half an hour. Lieutenant Lindsay received a slight wound in the hand; four or five of his men, who were out of the house, were captured. Five of the attacking party were killed and several wounded. When foiled in their attempt to force the doors, they endeavored to take off the horses from a stable near the house, which was enfiladed by the end window. To this place Lee immediately drew his force, and, to deceive the enemy, cheered loudly, exclaiming, "Fire away, men, here comes our infantry; we will have them all!" This produced a precipitate retreat. He then sallied, mustered his troops, and pursued; but to no purpose. Garden adds, "He assured the dragoons under his command, who gallantly joined in defending the house, that he should consider their future establishment in life as his peculiar care, and he honorably kept his word. They were all in turn commissioned, and by their exemplary good conduct increased their own renown, and the reputation of their regiment."

"The event of this skirmish gave great pleasure to the commander-in-chief. Throughout the late campaign Lee had been eminently useful to him, and had given proofs of talent as a partisan from which he had formed sanguine expectations for the future. He mentioned this affair in his orders with strong marks of approbation, and in a private letter to the captain testified the satisfaction he felt at the honorable escape that officer had made from a stratagem which had so seriously threatened him. For his merit throughout the preceding campaign, Congress promoted him to the rank of major, and gave him an independent partisan corps, to consist of two troops of horse, and by a subsequent resolution another troop was added to this corps.* When the distress of the army for

---

* Marshall's Life of Washington, vol. iii., page 378.

provisions reduced General Washington to the necessity of foraging for supplies, as if he had occupied the.country of an enemy, a measure which excited the greatest discontent among the inhabitants, Lee, being employed, managed to execute this painful but necessary duty without causing the smallest disapprobation." *

"Captain Lee found large droves in the marsh meadows of the Delaware, preparing for Philadelphia, which he had the address to procure, without giving to the body of the people any additional irritation." "He co-operated, as far as cavalry could act, in General Wayne's attack on Stony Point, and procured the intelligence upon which it was projected." † Indeed, from a portion of his correspondence with General Washington, which has been preserved, it seems not improbable that Major Lee suggested that enterprise. In a letter to the commander-in-chief of the 21st June, 1778, he observes :—

MAJOR HENRY LEE TO GENERAL WASHINGTON,

"21st June, 1778.

"SIR,—Since my last, no movement has taken place among the enemy encamped on this side of the river. Two very intelligent deserters, this morning from Stony Point, mentioned that yesterday a body of troops (number unknown) embarked from the east side of the river, between the hours of 12 and 2. They confirm the information contained in my last, concerning the sixty-third and sixty-fourth regiments being about to move from Stony Point. They also say that two days since the sick and aged soldiers, the women with children, and the baggage belonging to both officers and soldiers, were shipped for New York. The following is not a very accurate statement of their naval force at King's Ferry :—

"One 50-gun ship, the Rainbow, armed sloops and schooners, floating batteries, gun-boats, bomb-ketches, row-galleys, transports, and victuallers—numbers not ascertained.

"Their chief work on Stony Point is a triangular fort on the summit of the eminence, exceedingly strong and doubly abatised. On every spot in the camp which admits of it they have erected batteries. They talk also of opening a canal, and forming drawbridges. They have in their several works seven twenty-fours, two

---

* Marshall's Life of Washington, vol. iii., page 372.   † Ibid., vol. iv., p. 73.

medium-twelves, two long-twelves, and two threes—all brass. They have also one howitzer and two mortars, and six iron sixes, not mounted. General Clinton has not yet returned from New York; General Vaughan commands in chief. Colonel Johnston, of the seventeenth, commands at Stony Point. It is reported in their camp that Lord Cornwallis has arrived at the Hook with a re-enforcement under convoy of Admiral Arbuthnot. They do not credit the news from the southward. I begin to apprehend that General Clinton has designs on the East River. He certainly means to draw off all the troops but a sufficient garrison to possess the ferry. This he keeps to distress us in the conveyance of support to our troops, should your Excellency follow him to the eastward, as expected. Your Excellency will pardon me for the intrusion of my opinion; it proceeds only from a desire to exhibit every probable object that may engage the enemy's attention. Many deserters get in from your Excellency's army. The manner of sending scouts by detail from divisions affords them good opportunity—a detachment seldom comes down without losing several of its men before they return. There can be no object in reach of these parties adequate to their certain loss. Good intelligence cannot be obtained by flying parties. The enemy continue so close within their lines that there can be no hope of meeting with marauders, and protecting the people from their depredations. Pickets of armies, stationary and under cover of works, cannot be easily carried. Officers in command, anxious to perform some service, are apt to engage in improbable attempts. Accidents happen, and soldiers are lost without venture of service. I lay these observations before your Excellency, because they originate from what I see and know.

"I am, &c., &c.,

"H. LEE, Jr." *

In a letter, dated Stony Point, 11 o'clock at night, July 18, 1779, he thus writes to Governor Reed:—

MAJOR H. LEE TO GOVERNOR REED.

"DEAR SIR,—I wrote your Excellency by Mr. Gordon, since which the object which has engaged our attention from the commencement of the campaign is no more. Previous to this an official account of the enterprise on the night of the 15th must

* Observations on Jefferson's Writings, by H. Lee.

have reached Congress. For your satisfaction I furnish the partic
ulars. Early on the morning of the 15th I received orders from
General Wayne to join the light infantry with my corps. The
general was so polite as to show me his disposition of attack, and
as my station was the post of intelligence, he also consulted with me
on the lines of approach. The right column, under the command
of General Wayne, took the route along the beach, crossed the
morass up to their knees in mud and water, and moved on to the
enemy's left. Colonel Butler commanded our left column, and made
his way through the marsh over the relics of the bridge, although
the passage was very difficult and defended by a work in twenty
steps of it. A fence was made in the centre. My corps of infantry,
annexed *pro tem.* only, followed in the rear of the two columns as
a reserve.

" The troops rushed forward with a vigor hardly to be paralleled,
and with a silence which would do honor to the first veterans on
earth. A spirit of death or victory animated all ranks. General
Wayne has gained immortal honor ; he received a slight wound,
one proof that Providence decreed him every laurel in her gift.
Every other officer acquired fame proportionate to his opportunity.
The storm was more rapid than can be conceived, and in fifteen minutes the works were carried, with the loss only of eleven killed on
the spot, which every officer engaged reckoned would be purchased
by the sacrifice of nothing less than every third man. Lieutenant-
Colonel Fleury led on the right, Major Stewart the left. Captain
Lawson and Lieutenant Gibbons, who conducted the vans of the
columns, distinguished themselves by their valor and coolness. We
captured the whole garrison, excepting a few who got off in boats.
One hundred of them were killed and wounded ; 444, inclusive
of 18 officers, have marched on toward Lancaster. The humanity
of the Americans, perhaps, never was more conspicuous than on
this occasion. Although the repeated cruelties of the enemy exercised on our countrymen were known by all and felt by many, as
the nature of assaults by storm, particularly in the dead of night, also,
yet I can venture to affirm, the moment a surrender was announced
the bayonet was laid aside. The British officers are candid enough
to declare their gratitude for the lenity of their treatment. May
this fresh proof of the magnanimity of our soldiers tend to civilize
our foe ; if it does not, it must and will be the last. Fifteen can-
nons, mortars, cohorns, howitzers, &c., were found in the fort, an

abundance of military stores and a quantity of baggage. The most valuable of these are safe, the rest are now burning. Some unfortunate accidents prevented, till too late, the intended attack on Verplank's Point. General Clinton is at hand, and we have evacuated Stony Point. I fear the consequences of this signal success will not be adequate to moderate expectations. Our not possessing both sides has compelled us to relinquish the one. It is probable it will be repossessed by the British; and, of course, our old position will be reassumed, a position which both policy and comfort conspire to reproach. To-morrow, perhaps, Mr. Clinton's intentions will begin to show themselves; should any thing turn up, and I should be among the fortunate, you may expect to hear from me, provided you assure me that my hasty, incorrect epistles are not disagreeable. I have long wished my corps was legionary. The event of the 15th makes me more anxious on this head. His Excellency has been pleased to flatter me with McLane's incorporation; it is now before Congress. I shall be very unhappy if it does not succeed, as the mode of carrying on the war now renders infantry absolutely necessary for the accomplishment of any thing clever. I wish you would think of me on this occasion. Two companies of. infantry, besides McLane's, are now under my command; but as it is but a temporary annexation, I conceive it useless to establish the police most advantageous to partisan officers, and do not, therefore, receive their full use. Please make my most respectful compliments to your lady, and believe me to be, with great sincerity,

" Your affectionate humble servant,

" HENRY LEE, Jr." *

In the course of this severe campaign, when desertions from the American army became so frequent as to threaten its dissolution, Major Lee was authorized by General Washington to inflict summary punishment on such deserters as he should take *flagrante delicto*. Being in command of the outposts, and always close to the enemy, these offenders often fell into his hands, and he commenced by hanging one of the party, which produced a most salutary effect.

" The orders he received and the reports he transmitted during the campaigns of 1779 and 1780, were daily, and showed that

---

* I am indebted to the Honorable William B. Reed for the original of this and the other letters addressed to his distinguished ancestors.

General Washington relied on him peculiarly for intelligence respecting the enemy's force and movements. It appears, in short, that at this early period he had so completely engaged the confidence of that great commander, that in an official letter of the 9th October, 1779, he was directed in future to mark his communication, '*private*,' so that they should not be examined even by the officers of the general's family.

" When compassion for the impending fate of Major André" (and consideration for the public interest) " induced General Washington to make extraordinary exertions to capture Arnold, he consulted Lee, who planned the scheme and selected the agent for that purpose, which are both described in his Memoirs. He projected and executed the surprise of Paulus Hook, a service for which the thanks of Congress, with an emblematical medal of gold, were voted him, a distinction which no other officer below the rank of general received during the war." *

" Paulus Hook is a long, low point of the Jersey shore, stretching into the Hudson, and connected to the mainland by a sandy isthmus. A fort had been erected on it, and garrisoned with four or five hundred men, under the command of Major Sutherland. It was a strong position ; a creek, fordable only in two places, rendered the Hook difficult of access—within this, a deep trench had been cut across the isthmus, traversed by a drawbridge with a barred gate ; and still within this a double row of abatis, extending into the water. The whole position, with the country immediately adjacent, was separated from the rest of Jersey by the Hackensack river, running parallel to the Hudson, at the distance of a very few miles, and only traversable in boats, excepting at the new bridge about fourteen miles from Paulus Hook." † The order of attack on Paulus Hook contains the following address :—

" Major Lee is so assured of the gallantry of the officers and men under his command, that he feels exhortation useless; he therefore only requires the most profound secrecy. He pronounces death as the immediate fate of any soldier who may violate in the slightest degree the silence he has ordered to be observed. He recommends to his officers to add to the vigor of their attacks the advantage of surprise ; therefore to continue occult till the moment of action.

---

* Observations on Jefferson's Writings.
† Irving's Life of Washington, vol. iii., p. 473.

Success is not at the will of mortals; all they can do is to deserve it. Be this our determination and this our conduct, and we shall have cause to triumph, even in adversity. Watchword ' Be firm.'   HENRY LEE, Jr."

Strung to the achievement of their enterprise by this address, with Major Lee at their head, the forces, consisting of 300 men of Lord Stirling's division, and one troop of dismounted dragoons under Captain McLane, set out the 25th August upon their dangerous expedition. The chief impediment to success was not the long and secret march, but to gain an entrance when they reached the fort. Irving represents that this difficulty was overcome in consequence of their having been mistaken for a foraging party sent out the day before, which was supposed to be returning. This may have facilitated their approach, but could not have been foreseen by the planners of the expedition. The stratagem relied on was to have eight or ten soldiers disguised as countrymen carrying provisions for sale, who procured the gate to be opened by the sentinel, and held it, until the rest of their party, concealed near, rushed in. They were thus enabled to capture all the garrison, except Major Sutherland and about sixty Hessians, who threw themselves into a small block-house on the left of the fort, and opened an irregular fire. Time could not be spared to dislodge them. Alarm guns from the forts in New York and from the ships in the river were firing, and relief might be momentarily expected. "Having made one hundred and fifty prisoners, among whom were three officers, Lee commenced his retreat without tarrying to destroy either barracks or artillery. He had achieved his object, a *coup de main* of signal audacity. Few of the enemy were slain, for there was but little fighting and no massacre. His own loss was two men killed and three wounded."* "Congress passed resolves highly complimentary to Major Lee, thanking him for the remarkable prudence, address, and bravery displayed by him in the attack on the enemy's fort and works at Paulus Hook. Much praise was likewise bestowed on the officers and soldiers of his party. A medal of gold, emblematical of the affair, was ordered to be struck and presented to Major Lee. The brevet rank and pay of a captain

---

* Washington Irving.

were given to Lieutenants McAllister and Rudolph, respectively, and $15,000 in money were voted to be distributed among the non-commissioned officers and privates, in such a manner as the commander-in-chief should direct." *

The following letters will exhibit the service intrusted to Major Lee, his attention to the efficiency of his corps, and the estimation in which he was held by his immediate commander, Lafayette, who shares with Washington the love and veneration of America:—

MAJOR HENRY LEE TO GOVERNOR REED.

"ADVANCED POST, *June* 20, 1780.

" MY DEAR SIR,—Since my junction, which was the second day after we passed Philadelphia, every measure with us seemed to be in consequence of something from them. The arrival of Sir Henry from Charleston has urged us to motion. The main body of the army under his Excellency decamped last night, pointing its march toward the North River. A secondary body remains in this*country ; General Greene commands. My corps continues here, and with a detachment of infantry form the advance. On my reaching the army I was immediately ordered to the front, and honored with the command on the lines, in consequence of which line of life I know the springs of action in both armies. Be assured that the enemy conduct themselves with much wisdom ; not only are their movements matured and military, but their positions are circumspect and their discipline rigid. A very different chief is Mr. Clinton from Sir William Howe. They have made two fruitless excursions on my post ; we have made prisoners one lieutenant and his party ; every day we kill and are killed. I have proposed this day to make an attempt on Mr. Kniphausen with 300 men. My object is to bring off a picket, and oblige him either to extend his pickets or to contract his lines. His caution has worked so far on him as to induce him to proximate his pickets to his camp, lest the former might be taken off. I am now speaking of his right flank ; his left is secured by the Elizabethtown Creek. It is on his left I mean to strike seriously, and to alarm his right. The alarm on his right, I expect, will show him the impropriety of having his pickets so near his lines, as it is certain that in such a position his army is lia

---

* Sparks, note on page 376, vol. vi., of Washington's Correspondence.

ble to surprise. He will, therefore, extend his pickets on his right; if he does, the prosecution of my plan orders them to be cut off at some opportune moment. This being done, he will necessarily contract his lines or re-enforce his army.

"Either of these objects will be very important to us. The first liberates Elizabethtown; the second prevents any important move· ment in another quarter. How this reasoning will be relished I do not know; but fear the general will not consent, because it must produce the loss of twenty or thirty lives in the operation of the plan. But to have done with these matters; I cannot but express my happiness in the movement taking place toward the North River.

"The enemy are about one-third superior to us in numbers. Wisdom on our side will effectually prevent any injury to us. The succor we expect from our countrymen will give us in time the ability of offence. In the interim, while the main body preserves a position capable of relieving West Point if besieged, or of striking on the enemy's right should they advance on General Greene, we shall be safe. The moment we lie under cover of the mountains in one body, the enemy will sensibly hurt us by their manœuvres. I should not have written thus in a hurry, but for my wish to add to the gratification of a gentleman who struggles with such ardor and wisdom *pro bono publico*. May your efforts be properly seconded; we look to you and your State. I have the honor to be

"Your friend and servant,

"HENRY LEE, JR."

HENRY LEE TO HIS EXCELLENCY JOSEPH REED.

"EASTON, *August* 6, 1780.

"DEAR SIR,—When I wrote your Excellency last I had not received any particular instructions, and only knew what I then expressed. On the 3d, General Greene's orders, inclosing a warrant for the impress of such a number of wagons as the transportation of ordnance, military stores, and provisions from Easton and Sussex County might render necessary, reached me; since which I have been engaged in waiting on the magistrates of this county. I have experienced from them the utmost zeal; and yesterday the quotas of the several townships were fixed for the furnishing of one hundred four-horse wagons, including the eleven already in service. I have made a requisition for the same number from Berks, and flatter myself my application to the magistrates will meet with equal success. To-morrow I mean to move into Bucks County, where I shall also require one hundred wagons. My requisition will extend to the upper part of the county only. Having accomplished this business, I then rejoin the army. My efforts in Jersey are successful; so much so that probably the Bucks teams will not have objects for employment on this route. Of this I shall be able to speak more accurately by toward the close of my business. In the execution of my orders, I have as yet been only in the service of the magistrates. No occurrence will influence me to act otherwise, unless something remarkable; and then I shall follow the advice of the people. In my letter to your Excellency on the subject of the existence of my corps, I stated the just claims of my officers. I did it with candor and respect, nor do I see where or how it was exceptionable. I continue to think that the Pennsylvania officers under me have the same right to their proportion of the drafts as the officers of the Pennsylvania Division. I must be satisfied with the answer the Council has been pleased to give me. I have but one way to redress myself, and I presume my countrymen will justify me in so doing; when they know that I conceived it injurious to honor to serve in an army where distinctions were established repugnant to that equality which by compact was the basis of the American service. I cannot be happy when I am told you may draw support to your body, but shall not command your proportion of men. The small number due from this State can advantage us but little. Of course it is not the loss of the men, so much as the establishment of the principle, which hurts me. Other States, I suppose, will treat us in the same manner, and at the close of this campaign my small corps will be reduced to a mere party. However, I have learned the art of being happy under distress. I have done my duty, so far as I know how, faithfully. My letters to the several governments will show my officers my endeavors to procure soldiers for them, and my conscience will acquit me if forced to relinquish a command I most sincerely love.

"I have the honor to be, with the most perfect respect and esteem,
"Your Excellency's most obedient servant,
"H. LEE, Jr."

General Lafayette to Major Henry Lee.

"LIGHT CAMP, *August* 27, 1780.

"DEAR SIR,—All motives of esteem and friendship contribute to my happiness on hearing that you are directed to join the light infantry, and I assure you that I wish to do every thing·in my power to procure what you and your corps will like the best, viz., fighting and glory. I think, my dear sir, that your present employment is very necessary, and ought not to be interrupted. I wish, therefore, you would stay where you are until it is finished; and afterward join the Light Camp, where I shall be happy to see you. In case there should be any hope of doing something I will immediately give you notice, so that you may not be deprived of the honor you will certainly gain, nor I of the help I expect to derive from such a corps as yours and such an officer as Major Lee. But unless you hear from me, you may very quietly employ these three days in your preparations. I request, my dear sir, that you will please send me a return of the officers, non-commissioned officers, and men under your command, which, for a particular purpose, I want to have before your arrival. After what I have once told you, you will easily guess what my object is. With the highest esteem and sincere affection, I have the honor to be, dear sir, your most obedient, humble servant,

"LAFAYETTE.

"P. S.—The more I have considered the situation of Paulus Hook, the more I have admired your enterprising spirit and all your conduct in that business."

General Lafayette to Major Henry Lee.

"LIGHT CAMP, *half-past* 10.

"I am very sorry, my dear sir, that it was not in my power to be here by the appointed time; but was detained by the general on public business. We are at a loss to know, with some degree of exactness, how many men have sailed, how many have arrived. The general has particularly requested that I should get certain intelligence on those two points, and to you I have recourse for obtaining that end. The numbers of the enemy and the disposition of their forces will serve to fix our uncertainties, and at the same time to let us know by how many men, in how many hours, * * * may be re-enforced. I wish therefore, my dear sir, you may send into New York all the people that may give you intelligence Inclosed you will find the questions which I wish to be answered. Could you not send to your new friend, lay before him a copy of the inclosed note, and if he gives a good account of the truth, promise him one hundred guineas? In dispatching your several spies, I wish you would give them orders to return to us, to have full intelligence by Monday in the forenoon, and such of them as may be acquainted with the roads or circumstances might be left with us. We will be glad to hear, also, about the shipping; but though your friend is employed that way, he must not forget his principal business. Will you come and breakfast with us to-morrow about 9 o'clock? I will then speak with you about our common affairs. I wish your man of this day may have found the means of escaping the two water sentries. As to that article which you know to be scarce in camp, we pick it up in the neighborhood.

"Adieu, yours,

"LAFAYETTE."

LAFAYETTE TO MAJOR LEE.

"You will see that orders are given for the boats, and I don't believe we can remedy it. The * * * must certainly be had, but how can we stop the directions that are given by the quartermaster-general? The only way, then, is to use every means in our power to get it done, which I leave to you, my dear sir, in all confidence that if it can be done by any human being it will be executed by Major Lee.   LAFAYETTE."

A letter from the same source dated 29th October, 1780, thus concludes:—

"From my soul, my dear sir, I wish you all possible success; and I shall not only ever rejoice, but glory in any advantage that may add to your laurels. Let me often hear from you, and be sure that the moment when we meet again will be a happy one for me. Present my best compliments to the officers of your Legion, and tell them, as well as your soldiers, that I shall ever preserve the most perfect esteem and affection for them. I wish you would direct the bearer, the other men, and all the spies to come to me immediately.   Adieu, yours forever,

"LAFAYETTE."

The separation contemplated in the foregoing letter was caused by Lee's departure with his Legion for the South, as will be seen by the following communication to Governor Reed.

MAJOR LEE TO GOVERNOR REED.

"PHILADELPHIA, *November* 17, 1780.

"MY DEAR SIR,—The period has at length arrived when I must move for the Southern army; want of cash detains us for a day, to-morrow we are to receive it, the day following we are to march; as we pass through the city I mean to gratify myself with a personal adieu, but my feelings command me to separate with more solemnity, therefore I honor and please myself with wishing you in writing every public success and private felicity; I do it not only from my individual attachment, but, sir, because I rate you as one of the instruments selected by Providence to extricate this unhappy country from its very pressing embarrassments. I have the honor to be, with singular attachment and respect,

"Your obedient servant,
"HENRY LEE, Jr."

Washington, on the 11th October, wrote to the President of Congress: "Major Lee has rendered such distinguished services, possesses so many talents for commanding a corps of this nature, and deserves so much credit for the perfection in which he has kept his corps as well as for the handsome exploits he has performed, that it would be a loss to the service and a discouragement to merit to reduce him. I do not see how he can be introduced into one of the regiments in a manner satisfactory to himself." *

Congress in November, 1780, promoted him to a lieutenant-colonelcy of dragoons; and added to his corps three companies of infantry. Judge Johnson remarked " it was, perhaps, the finest corps that made its appearance on the arena of the Revolutionary war. It was formed expressly for Colonel Lee, under an order of General

---

* General Charles Lee, who was an accomplished soldier and had a genius for war, had said before, in his " proposals for the formation of a body of light troops," that " Major Lee, who seems to have come out of his mother's womb a soldier," should be incorporated in this Legion, with the rank of lieutenant-colonel, and command specifically the whole cavalry.—*Life of General Charles Lee*, page 116.

Washington, while the army lay in New Jersey. It consisted, at this time, of about 300 men, in equal proportion of infantry and horse. Both men and officers were picked from the army; the officers with reference only to their talents and qualities for service, and the men by a proportionable selection from the troops of each State enlisted for three years or for the war." *

Washington, in a letter to John Matthews, member of Congress from South Carolina, October 23, 1780, says: "Lee's corps will go to the southward. I believe it will be found very useful; the corps is an excellent one, and the officer at the head of it has great resources of genius." Colonel Lee states in his Memoirs, in reference to his corps at this time, that "it consisted of three troops of horse and three companies of infantry, giving a total of 350 effectives." But it was not complete, and after its arrival at the South, it gradually diminished. Such was the debilitated condition of our military force, that only this trifling re-enforcement could be spared to a general charged with the arduous task of saving Virginia and North Carolina, and of re-annexing to the Union the States south of them.

The cares and embarrassments attending this march will be understood from the following letters from Mr. George Mason and two officers of the Legion :— ·

George Mason to Lieutenant-Colonel Lee.

"Gunston Hall, *December* 13, 1780.

"Dear Sir,—I received your favor of the 30th November, and have the warmest sense of your very friendly offer to my son William, whose inclination I well know would strongly incline him to accept it, in which I would most cheerfully indulge him if I had any thought of continuing him in the military line, as in that case it would give me great satisfaction to place him under the direction of a gentleman who has rendered such important services to our country, and in whose friendship I could so thoroughly confide. But I have ever intended him for civil and private life; his lot must be that of a farmer and country gentleman, and at this time there is a particular domestic circumstance which will require his return as soon as his present time of service expires.

---

* Life of Greene, vol. i., page 344.

Permit me, sir, to return you my thanks for the very friendly part
you have acted, and to assure you that I am, with the greatest
esteem and regard,

"Your most obedient servant,

" G. Mason."

Captain James Armstrong to Lieutenant-Colonel Lee.

" Head of Elk (supposed to be), 17th Nov., 1780.

" Sir,—We arrived here last night, after an agreeable passage, but
could find no one willing to give a soldier a night's quarters.
After many entreaties and some threats, we got our men tolerably
quartered. This morning boats are ready to take us any moment,
and a sufficiency of provisions for our passage. I must beg leave
to tell you that I think it is impossible we can subsist without
utensils, as the people here deny us every thing; and I suppose it is
to be the case wherever the Maryland troops have been in their
march to the southward. You may rely upon it, canteens are very
important things with us, and it is very inconvenient to proceed
further south without them. We cannot move without a little
cash.

" I am, with respect, your obedient servant,

" James Armstrong."

Henry Peyton to Lieutenant-Colonel Lee.

(No date.)

"Dear Sir,—I have been studiously engaged, ever since the
receipt of your letter by Bristol, in effecting the completion of its
instructions. I never could dispatch him till this morning. I have
influenced Mr. Walker to aid the business of your address to Governor Jefferson by a letter with yours which left here yesterday
noon. His confidence in the governor's immediate concurrence
with your proposition has induced me to trouble no more of the
delegates on the subject. You have an answer to your address to
Governor Reed. That to Rodney is in the hands of McLean, who,
I suppose, has told you when he shall attend to its execution. That
to Lee is waiting Handy's arrival at Elk, in the care of Mr. Rudolph, who will have it delivered. I have sent you two bottles, six
cups and saucers, and twelve knives and forks. Charles Lee cannot
get your silver cups, for the want of money, and I am destitute.

Stoddart has not procured the loans, and, I fear, will not. Nathan is almost distracted about money, and says if he does not get some in a few days he shall be obliged to send to Virginia purposely to obtain it. He is dunned hourly.

"Henry Peyton."

The difficulties with which Colonel Lee had to contend in his march through this friendly country arose from the exasperated feelings of the population caused by the calamities of war; but they did not diminish his efforts to recruit his Legion, as is shown by his applications to the governors of the States of Pennsylvania, Delaware, Maryland, and Virginia. He also expended his own patrimony in furnishing suitably his brave followers.*

On his arrival in South Carolina these efforts were renewed, as will be shown by the following letter from the heroic governor of that State:—

"Meraws, 11th January, 1781.

"Colonel Lee being desirous of raising about one hundred and fifty cavalry on a regular and permanent establishment, to be attached to his Legion, I not only consent to his so doing, but recommend to active and spirited young men in this State to join him upon that footing, whereby they may signalize themselves and render important services to their country.

"J. Rutledge."

All these efforts, however, to increase the numbers of the Legion were unavailing, for its commander states that "it gradually diminished;" the losses by hard service being greater than its recruits.

The following letters are introduced as having a special bearing upon the condition of affairs in the South:—

Colonel Henry Lee to General Wayne.

"Camp on Pedee River, South Carolina,
January 7, 1781.

"Full of affection for my friends North, and for you among the first, my very dear sir, I pay this early tribute of friendship. I well

---

* On this occasion "his patriotism was exalted by the misfortunes of his country. He expended in the purchase of horses for his dragoons, and in equipping his corps, a considerable part of the fortune given him by his father, a contribution for which, though it proved of essential service to his country, he never received, or even asked, remuneration."—Lee's Observations on the Writings of Jefferson, page 151.

know your anxiety for a true representation of the position of
affairs in this part of the world. I also very well know from what
I heard when in the Northern army, and from what I see now,
that truth very seldom reaches either Congress, the general, or
the public. When Gates threw the die on the 16th August, the
countenance of affairs looked propitious. This unfortunate general
has been most insidiously, most cruelly traduced. Happy, on all
occasions, to support the injured, I feel it my duty as an honest
soldier to give you an account of that action. The impartial and
sensible part of the army here are the persons from whom I have
my communications. General Gates advanced from Rudgely's Mill
to seize an advantageous camp near Camden. He wished to have
accompli-hed this in peace. He moved in the night of the 15th,
and issued the orders you may have seen published, to prepare for
every contingency. Lord Cornwallis moved the same night, with
the intention to force General Gates from his camp at Rudgely's,
and to fight him. The armies very unexpectedly met about two
o'clock in the morning. The vanguard of each fell back, and the
two generals arrayed their troops in line of battle, waiting the
dawn of day. General Gates consulted his officers whether he
should fight or retire. It passed in the affirmative. An action
took place on advantageous terms: we were very completely routed.
Those of our army who escaped went off by ones, twos, and threes.
Gates pushed on himself to Hillsborough, as the only place where
he had the least resource, and the most probable spot to reassemble.
As to the retreat, there was none. General Smallwood had not
thirty men with him till he got to Charlotte, where the poor fellows who had escaped re-collected in small parties. The Mary
land line fought with superior gallantry; and had the militia
not given way, we must have been completely victorious. The
defeat of Ferguson at King's Mountain was very important
in its consequences. The conduct of this action does great
honor to the three colonels of militia, but the course of the North
Carolina government has in a great degree baffled the fruits of that
victory. The tories captured were enlisted into the militia or draft
service, and have all rejoined the British. General, I heard General
Greene say yesterday that his last return made out sixty in jail, and
his intelligence from the enemy declares that two hundred of them
were actually in arms against us. Since this affair there has been
some skirmishing with the tories, and they are taken and killed

daily. * * * Colonel Washington, with his regiment and some militia cavalry, cut a party to pieces the other day. Colonel Marion has done the same. * * * But these petty advantages do not tend to the promotion of grand designs. Not a single post of the enemy has yet been broken up; their communication with Charleston is uninterrupted, not a convoy taken or destroyed, unless some trifling tory's baggage or stores; not a single British regiment has been struck at; whenever they strike they succeed. The affairs of Sumter have been against us, except the last, in which we were victorious. Major Weymiss was taken with twenty-five privates. What is worse, I am confident nothing important can be accomplished by this army in its present state. * * * *Inter nos* the following calculation is large : Eight hundred Maryland line ; eight hundred Virginia levies; six hundred Virginia militia, whose time of service expires in twenty days; and my Legion, two hundred and fifty, with one hundred North Carolina militia. General Morgan has one hundred regular horse, three hundred Maryland regulars, and eight hundred militia under him. General Sumter and General Marion have also flying parties. The Virginians are destitute of every article of clothing. Their only covering is an old shirt and trousers; the whole are without shoes, nor can any sort of manufactory be established in this country, therefore our hides are useless to us. Our two regiments of horse are reduced to half a regiment, and illy supplied with accoutrements. Our provisions are from hand to mouth. The present camp affords good support of every kind; but when we are forced from this, Heaven only knows how we are to employ our teeth. General Greene has conducted himself with the greatest wisdom and assiduity, and I verily believe, was he tolerably supported by the States, he would oblige his antagonist to retire to Charleston. * * * I feel most sensibly for the situation of the refugees from South Carolina, their distresses are only equalled by their virtue. No situation of any inhabitant of the above description in the Northern States can give you even a faint idea of what these people suffer. This is a necessary preface to a letter of this date, which I mean to write to Governor Reed, wherein you will see the reasons why North Carolina may easily be reduced. You will know the state and position of the enemy's army, and you will observe with what facility they may be forced to relinquish their present vast possessions. I must beg you to give my affectionate assurances of friendship to Delaney, Wilkinson, and other city friends, and to Butler, and my dear brother officers.

"I have the honor to be your obedient servant,

"H. LEE, Jr."*

HENRY LEE TO GOVERNOR REED.

"ON PEDEE RIVER, SOUTH CAROLINA,
January 9, 1781.

"I not only discharge a debt which my friendship owes by this address, but execute, in some degree, that duty which my country has a right to exact from me as their servant. I have lamented through the progress of this war the imperfect manner in which all wants are communicated to those whose station calls for the most accurate account of every material transaction. One characteristic is applicable to most of our public relations, and is particularly applicable to those from this quarter; exaggeration of successful operations, diminution of adverse; from hence arise those false hopes which influence our councils, and operate on the exertions of the people. This single consideration ought to influence a perfect communication between those in the field and those at the head of affairs, and indeed I think if the printers would refuse the publication of reports, it would have a happy issue on the temper of the people. I wrote to General Wayne yesterday, and I beg to refer you to him for the relation of past occurrences in the Southern army. The two letters will present you with a comprehensive view of the general face of affairs in the Southern District. Lord Cornwallis, consummate in the art of war, his decision and conduct on the 16th of August will ever do him honor. On returning from Charlotte he made a most masterly disposition of his army; comprehending within his post the rich western country of South Carolina, Camden, Ninety-six, and Georgetown are his most important posts. He is nursing his army, recruiting his horse, augmenting his cavalry, and establishing a traitorous correspondence with the inhabitants of North Carolina. From the best accounts, I reckon the British army, exclusive of the garrison at Charleston, and including General Leslie's re-enforcement, will amount to five thousand effectives. Add to this computation a numerous cavalry, perhaps one

---

* I am indebted to the Honorable William B. Reed for the original of this letter.

thousand on the legionary plan. With this army he can   *   *
through North Carolina, provided he takes the lower route.
* * * In my opinion a very different policy must be pursued
by the General commanding the Southern army from what was
pursued in the Northern States. There it was our interest to keep on
the country flank of the foe. Here it is our plan (in my humble
opinion) to move in the lower country, keeping an army of observation on the left flank. You must know that only on the rivers is
there the least attention to agriculture among these people, unless
high up in the country. The settlements on the river are rich and
populous; the intermediate lands barren and unsettled. Therefore
the motions of the army must be from river to river, striking at
the head of navigation, and receiving by boats the produce.
* * * * Should Cornwallis take the upper route, it will be
in General Greene's power to preserve himself in the lower country,
and subsist his army on its retrograde, while General Morgan, with
the aid of our back friends, may harass and disturb the enemy's
progress. Should he take the lower route, the difficulty of subsisting the flank detachment will be very great; nor can the army support itself comfortably during its retreat. The enemy are making
preparations to move out, though from the impoverished state of
their horse, I flatter myself we shall not be disturbed for three or
four weeks. If you hear that the enemy move on the Salisbury
route, and there is no corresponding operation from Virginia or *via*
Cape Fear River, be assured we shall baffle them, unless the country deprives us of every assistance. If they move on the lower
route they will succeed in * * * this army * * properly
clothed * * * fed regularly. This representation is very different from what you have from the civil characters of North Carolina. Rely on it, the zeal of those gentlemen leads them into mistakes. * * * * * It is natural to good men to wish that their
countrymen should act with propriety; but it is a public misfortune that this disposition should create opinions and issue information, which, in their consequences, are injurious to the public good.
I remember well when I was in Philadelphia, and Cornwallis' retreat from Charlotte was announced, some gentlemen, high in
office, from the Southern world, spoke confidently of the capture of
the British army. Our regular force in the field was not adequate to
the capture of a British regiment, nor had this little force supplies of
provisions to support them three days. How horrid it is that the

public * * * * . Every little * * * * * is cried up
into a victory ; when a British chief will readily sacrifice a thousand of those poor wretches, to destroy one hundred of our regular
troops. Indeed, such an exchange would hardly be accepted by us.
General Greene is exerting himself with great wisdom. His movement from Charlotte was most judicious. His camp on this river
abounds with supplies for man and horse, procured by his personal
efforts. He has wisely declined the aid of one class of the North
Carolina militia, who were ordered out, and is assiduous in his attempts to clothe and discipline his little brigade. I very well know
that irregulars are completely unfit for the war in this country,
notwithstanding Campbell's glorious success at King's Mountain.
They will do on the flank of the enemy, and will suit Morgan's detachment exactly. His business is to harass, our business to force
the enemy from their posts. Irregulars will do very well for the
one, but will not answer where much patience is required in the
operations, and where want of correspondence in motion may blast
the best concerted plan. Were we equal to the enemy in regulars,
and clad, a position on the Santee River would oblige Cornwallis to
relinquish his possessions. Indeed, there is nothing so easy as to
restore the country of South Carolina, had we but an army of 5,000
regulars. This army must be had and well supplied, or our allies
must assist the operations in the country. If neither is done, I pronounce, without any pretension to the gift of prophecy, that North
Carolina will be added to the British dominions in America before
'82. The Marquis Lafayette and General Wayne would be of infinite service to this country. I wish to God they were sent here
forthwith. I hope to hear from you whenever leisure will permit,
and beg you to accept my most earnest wishes for your public and
private prosperity.

"I have the honor to be your most obedient servant,

"HENRY LEE, Jr." *

As soon as Lee joined Greene, he was detached toward the Santee
to co-operate with Marion, and these officers speedily engaged in the
surprise of Georgetown. From this period, the operations of the
Legion are so fully narrated in the memoirs that they need not be
repeated. How they, together with his services, were estimated,
the reader may judge from the following extracts :—In a letter from

* This letter is much mutilated.

General Greene, 25th June, 1781, it is stated, " some of the South-ern army are much wished for (in Va.), I mean the Legion of the gallant Colonel Lee ;" on the 19th of August, 1781, Greene writes : " It will be more necessary for you to be particular (in pressing the State government of South Carolina to furnish the means of clothing the Legion), than any other officer, for the inhabitants are so sensi-ble of the merit and services of your corps, that they will be much more embarrassed to speak to you upon a matter of this sort, than to any person. Gratitude and every other consideration would induce them to be silent, when they may feel sensibly; your anxiety for the honor of your corps and your zeal for the service are truly laud-able, but they must be bounded by considerations of a higher nature ; and I am persuaded you will be no less attentive to the harmony of the State than to the interest of your corps." The tes-timony of Marshall is also inserted :* " The continued labors and exertions of all were highly meritorious, but the successful activity of one corps will attract particular attention. The Legion, from its structure, was peculiarly adapted to the partisan warfare of the Southern States, and by being detached against the weaker posts of the enemy, had opportunities for displaying with advantage all the energies it possessed. In that extensive sweep which it made from the Santee to Augusta, which employed from the 15th of April to the 5th of June, this corps, acting in conjunction first with Ma-rion, afterward with Pickens, and sometimes alone, had constituted the principal force which carried five British posts and made up-ward of 1100 prisoners," about four times its own number.

GENERAL NATHANIEL GREENE TO LIEUTENANT-COLONEL LEE.

HEAD-QUARTERS, *January 27th*, 1782.

" DEAR SIR,—I have beheld with extreme anxiety, for some time past a growing discontent in your mind, and have not been without my apprehensions that your complaints originated more in distress than in the ruin of your constitution. Whatever may be the source of your wounds, I wish it was in my power to heal them. * * * * From our earliest acquaintance, I had a partiality for you, which progressively grew into friendship. I was under no obligations to you until I came into this country ; and yet I believe you will do me

* Life of Washington, vol. iv., p. 536.

the justice to say, I never wanted inclination to serve you. Here I have been under the greatest obligations,—obligations I can never cancel. * * * I am far from agreeing with you in opinion, that the public will not do you justice. I believe few officers, either in America or Europe, are held in so high a point of estimation as you are. Substantial service is what constitutes lasting reputation; and your reports this campaign are the best panegyric that can be given of your actions. * * *. It is true, there are a few of your countrymen, who from ignorance and malice are disposed to do injustice to your conduct, but it is out of their power to injure you. Indeed, you are ignorant of your own weight and influence, otherwise you would despise their spleen and malice. * * * Everybody knows I have the highest opinion of you as an officer, and you know I love you as a friend; whatever may be your determination, to retire or continue in service, my affection will accompany you. * * * *

"I am, with esteem and affection,
"Your most obedient humble servant,
"Nathaniel Greene."

Notwithstanding his successes and the eulogies contained in these letters, Colonel Lee left the army at the close of the campaign, in sickness and sorrow. The broken health produced by his long and arduous services depressed his spirits, and caused the melancholy so apparent in his farewell letter. "The reply is too full of the finest feelings, to be altogether omitted. It professes the most ardent and inviolable friendship for his commander." * "I candidly told you that I read some of your public reports with distress, because some officers and corps were held out to the world with a lustre superior to others, who to say the least deserved equally. But this I attributed to accident of expression, or to the temper of the moment, and therefore regarded it as naught. My attachment to you will end only with my life. I am bold to use this expression, from my confidence that your conduct will always claim the support of those who try to be virtuous. Could I suppose my leaving the army now was a breach of private friendship, I would not hesitate in my decision a moment, although increasing affliction would be my portion. But the prosperous train of your affairs puts this matter beyond a

* Johnson's Life of Greene, vol. ii., p. 322.

doubt. I communicated to Major Pearce the causes of my distress. I am candid to acknowledge my imbecility of mind, and hope time and absence may alter my feelings: at present my fervent wish is for the most hidden obscurity; I want not private or public applause; my happiness will depend on myself; and if I have but fortitude to persevere in my intentions it will not be in the power of malice, outrage, or envy to affect me. Heaven knows the issue. I wish I could bend my mind to other decisions. I have tried much, but the sores of my wounds are only irritated afresh by such efforts. My poor soldiers are dear to me, most dear. I pray your patronage to them if I must part. Through them I am open to feelings of pleasure, and their woes will add to my misery. The subject of this letter is so affecting that I can not be correct or hardly consistent." It concludes with "pressing Captain Egleston's request for leave of absence, though he should himself be obliged to remain until no inconvenience should arise from want of officers. Several other matters passed, equally creditable to the heads and hearts of the correspondents; but, finally, both Lee and Egleston took their leave of absence from camp together."

General Greene's parting letter to him of February 12, 1782, concludes thus: " You are going home and you will get married, but you cannot cease to be a soldier; should the war rage here, I shall call for you in a few months, unless I should find your inclinations opposed to my wishes. I thank you most affectionately for your attachment and good wishes, and beg leave to assure you that I shall always be happy to do you every friendly office in my power."

It seems impossible that the idea of injustice, even when acting upon a temper enfeebled by ill health, could so painfully have affected the spirits of one who must have known what Burke has impressed upon mankind, that it is "in the nature and constitution of things for calumny to accompany triumph;" and this truth was confirmed by General Greene, who tells him in a letter of March 12, 1782: " You have this consolation, that prevailing envy is the best evidence in the world of great merit." It is probable that some domestic trouble was mingled with those already mentioned, and that the disease of his body was aggravated by care and anxiety of mind.

Very soon after his return to Virginia he visited Stratford, the residence of Colonel Philip Ludwell Lee, in Westmoreland, on the bluffs of the Potomac.

STRATFORD HOUSE.—The Author's Home.

The approach to the house is on the south, along the side of a lawn, several hundred acres in extent, adorned with cedars, oaks, and forest poplars. On ascending a hill not far from the gate, the traveller comes in full view of the mansion; when the road turns to the right and leads straight to a grove of sugar-maples, around which it sweeps to the house. The edifice is built in the form of an H and of bricks brought from England. The cross furnishes a saloon of 30 feet cube, and in the centre of each wing rises a cluster of chimneys, which form the columns of two pavilions connected by a balustrade. The owner, who before the Revolution was a member of the king's council, lived in great state, and kept a band of musicians, to whose airs his daughters, Matilda and Flora, with their companions, danced in the saloon or promenaded on the house-top. Their young kinsman, attended by his military servant, was recognized as he rode past the grove of maples, and was welcomed with joy; and he, who had recently left the Southern army overwhelmed with grief and despondency, was soon happily restored by his union with the eldest daughter, Matilda.

But in the midst of his happiness he did not forget the brave men he had left in Carolina. His correspondence with General Greene, continued to the end of the war, is filled with evidences of the solicitude he felt for his soldiers and the veneration he cherished for his general. The latter had written to the President of Congress, 18th February, 1782 : " Lieut.-Col. Lee retires for a time for the recovery of his health. I am more indebted to this officer than any other for the advantages gained over the enemy in the operations of the last campaign, and should be wanting in gratitude not to acknowledge the importance of his services, a detail of which is his best panegyric." In a long letter to this officer of the 7th of October, of the same year, about the troubles of the Legion, the general says: " No man in the progress of the campaign had equal merit with yourself, nor is there one so represented." He also wrote to Colonel Lee in April, 1782: " I find the war will continue. * * * I am not pleased by any means with our prospects. I would it were over and I at supper." When it was over, he wrote to Colonel Lee from Philadelphia, Oct. 27th, 1783 : " It is now quite uncertain how fortune will dispose of me, or whether I shall have the happiness of meeting you in this city next May. The army is disbanded, and both duty and necessity will oblige me to attend to my family affairs. My circumstances are far from being easy, and my family have not where to put their heads. They have been like the wandering Jews all the war. It is men in my situation in the progress of this war who have had feelings which exceed description. Alas! few know what I have felt; my fondness for my family has increased my distress. Men of affluence have been in quite different circumstances. Public virtue is best proved by private sacrifices; but enough of this."

Soon after the peace, Colonel Lee was a member of the Virginia delegation to Congress, where he devoted himself to forwarding those measures that prepared the way for the adoption of the Constitution. " He was also among those of Gen. Washington's friends who most earnestly persuaded him to undertake the all-important duties of the first presidency. Happening to be in the vicinity of Mount Vernon, when Washington was about to fill for the first time the office of President, on the impulse of the moment he prepared the address, which was presented to that illustrious man by his neighbors, and was so well adapted to the occasion as to be thought by Marshall worthy to be transferred to the pages of history." *

" The sentiments of veneration and affection which were felt by all classes of his fellow-citizens for their patriot chief, were manifested by the most flattering marks of heartfelt respect; and by addresses which evinced the unlimited confidence reposed in his virtues and talents. Although a place cannot be given to these addresses generally, yet that from the citizens of Alexandria derives such pretensions to particular notice from the recollection that it is to be considered as an effusion from the hearts of his neighbors and private friends, that its insertion may be pardoned. It is in the following words: ' Again your country commands your care, obedient to its wishes, unmindful of your ease, we see you again relinquishing the bliss of retirement; and this, too, at a period of life, when nature itself seems to authorize a preference of repose. Not to extol your glory as a soldier; not to pour forth our gratitude for past services; not to acknowledge the justice of the unexampled honor which has been conferred upon you by the spontaneous and unanimous suffrage of three millions of freemen, in your election to the supreme magistracy; nor to admire the patriotism which directs your conduct, do your neighbors and friends now address you.

---

* Marshall's Life of Washington, vol. v., p. 154.

Themes less splendid, but more endearing, impress our minds. The first and best of citizens must leave us; our aged must lose their ornament; our youth their model; our agriculture its improver; our commerce its friend; our infant academy its protector; our poor their benefactor; the interior navigation of the Potomac (an event replete with the most extensive utility, already by your unremitted exertions brought into partial use) its institutor and promoter. Farewell! go, and make a grateful people happy, a people who will be doubly grateful when they contemplate this recent sacrifice for their interest. To that Being who maketh and unmaketh at His will, we commend you; and after the accomplishment of the arduous business to which you are called, may He restore to us again the best of men, and the most beloved fellow-citizen.'" Not long after, "Colonel Lee represented the county of Westmoreland in the Convention of Virginia which ratified the Federal Constitution, and was distinguished for zeal and eloquence in support of that measure." *

The contest which rendered the old Confederacy intolerable was continued under the new government. Mr. Hamilton's measures of finance and his plans to introduce and encourage manufactures were opposed by the agricultural sections of the country, and Colonel Lee's correspondence with Mr. Madison at that period shows that he retained the opinions in which he was educated and which he shared with his neighbors and his distinguished correspondent. While condemning the measures of the secretary of the treasury, he still approved the man and styled him "My friend Hamilton, of whose head and heart I entertain the highest sentiments of respect." (Letter to Mr. Madison, 4th April, 1792.)

He was at this time governor of Virginia, but before he attained that honor, in a letter to Mr. Madison, June, 1789, he informed him of the death of his mother-in-law, and how that affliction had aggravated the malady under which his wife was suffering. From Stratford, March 4th, 1790, he writes to him again: "Mrs. Lee's health is worse and worse. She begs you will present her most cordially to her friends, Mrs. Colden and Mrs. Hamilton, and unites with me in best wishes for your health and happiness." This was her last message. She is mentioned no more in their correspondence. A few days after this, he suffered a second calamity, in the death of his eldest son, a beautiful boy of ten years old. He was devoted to

* See debates of that body, published by Elliott.

the child, and found some consolation in wearing his miniature, which is still preserved in the family. He had previously lost a son, who died in infancy, named Nathaniel Greene. Two other children remained to him : a daughter, Lucy ; and a son, Henry, who so eloquently defended his memory, and who died in Paris in 1837.

To return from this brief sketch of Lee's domestic life ; Mr. Madison had written to him from Philadelphia, January 21, 1792: "The House of Representatives has been engaged for several days with shut doors, on the communications from the President relating to the western frontier. There is a general disposition to make the protection effectual, but nothing like unanimity as to the means. It is probable that much will be left to the judgment of the President, at the same time that the military command will be made of more consequence than heretofore. Tell me truly (for it will be in due confidence) what, in case your name should be in consideration, ought to be the language of your friends with regard to your inclinations ? * * * I wish it also to be understood that in asking the question, I mean not to insinuate any decided opinion or bias as to the answer it may receive. I am deeply impressed with the magnitude of the trust alluded to ; but I am not less so with that of the one you now hold. The latter has, doubtless, its unimportant aspects ; it has others, however, which make it extremely desirable that it should be in good hands. One is particularly presented by the interior improvements of the State, which are promised by your auspices and energy ; and I have contemplated them with equal pleasure and hope, from the moment your election was announced."

To this Governor Lee replied on the 29th of the same month :—

" The latter part of your letter affects my mind very sensibly ; as indeed you will presume. There are very few to whom I could say a word upon the subject, but there is no question you can propound to me which will not receive a frank and full answer."

" Were I called upon by the President to command the next campaign, my respect for him would induce me to disregard every trifling obstruction which might oppose my acceptance of the office, such as my own repose, the care of my children, and the happiness I enjoy in attention to their welfare, and in the execution of the duties of my present station. As a citizen, I should hold myself bound to obey the will of my country, in taking any part her interests may demand from me.. Therefore, I am upon this occasion under a bias in favor of obedience to any claim which may be made on me. Yet, I profess I should require some essential stipulations,— stipulations only to secure a favorable issue to the campaign." After speaking of how formidable the enemy was, he adds : " One objection I should only have (the above conditions being acceded to), and that is, the abandoning my native country, to whose goodness I am so much indebted. *No consideration on earth could induce me to act a part, however gratifying to me, which could be construed into disregard or forgetfulness of this Commonwealth."* Although Governor Lee was thought of to command the western frontier, after St. Clair's defeat had caused his removal, he was not appointed, though considered eminently competent by many, and especially by Washington,* because it might have been mortifying to the officers of the old army to serve under one whom they had formerly ranked, and their feelings were entitled to great considera- tion. As General Wayne was entirely qualified for the command, and all things were harmonized by his appointment, he very prop- erly received it, and triumphantly fulfilled its duties. These ex- tracts, however, show that immediately after the adoption of the Federal Constitution, and during the administration of Washington, men who had distinguished themselves for their zeal in promoting it, were deeply sensible of the obligations they owed both to the State and general governments, their native commonwealths and the adopted community into which these commonwealths had been formed. Mr. Madison's authorship of the Virginia Resolutions of '98 and '99, leaves no doubt of his views on this subject. Lee's cor- respondence with that statesman, at this time, evinces that he felt sensibly those measures of Hamilton, which had irritated his State and section. Yet, in a letter to Mr. Madison from Richmond, January 8, 1792, he writes : " I deeply lament the sad event (the financial legislation), but I really see no redress, unless the govern- ment itself be destroyed. This is risking too much, because great evils must indubitably flow from discord ; and the people must suffer severely, whatever be the event of such an experiment." In another letter, nine days later, he says : " While we deprecate and lament the obnoxious event, we must submit to it, because effectual opposition may beget civil discord and civil war." Although his correspondence at this time, as well as the course of his life, proves

* Spark's Washington, vol. x., page 243.

his devotion to the Federal Government, yet he recognized a distinction between his "native country" and that which he had labored to associate with it in the strictest bonds of union.

While he was governor, that part of Virginia lying under the Cumberland Mountains and projected between Kentucky and Tennessee was formed into a separate county and named after him, Lee. It has since been divided into two; the eastern portion, called after the late General Scott, is said to contain a natural bridge equal to that which gives to a county the name of Rockbridge, while Lee was remarkable for a cave crowded with bees from which swarms were annually scattered through the surrounding forests.

LETTER FROM GENERAL HAMILTON TO GOVERNOR LEE.

August 25, 1794.

" My Dear Lee,—This accompanies an official letter inviting you to the command of the whole force to be employed against the insurgents. The invitation is given on the presumption that it will not be unacceptable to you. But there are reasons which render it expedient for the present to keep the matter *sub silentio.* A proposal has been made to Carrington, if consistent with his other duties, to take charge of the quarter-master's and commissary's departments. As an inducement to him, you may mention in confidence the call upon you. But it had best go no further. I may be one of your aids-de-camp. It is important, as well from the opinion the insurgents have of him as from his real value, that General Morgan should be with you. A fear has started (though his good sense is counted upon to take off its force), that he might feel some reluctance to your command on the score of former relative military situation. But Irvin is to go from Pennsylvania. Irvin would command him, being a senior militia-officer; and we cannot doubt, that on public and personal accounts, he will prefer your command, which, as commander-in-chief of the Virginians, he may submit to on the strictest military principles. Let this matter be so managed as that Morgan's services may be secured. Adieu,

"Yours truly,

" A. Hamilton."

The appointment was conferred on him ; and as General Mifflin, the governor of Pennsylvania, had reported that the militia of the State would not be competent to put down the insurgents, and requisitions had been made upon the governors of New Jersey, Maryland, and Virginia for quotas from those States to compose an army of 15,000 men, the governor of Virginia sacrificed no duty by complying with the wishes of the administration. The insurgents resisted by force of arms not only the authority of the United States but that of Pennsylvania, their "native country." This resistance grew out of irritation produced by a tax laid on distilled spirits, and was called "The Whiskey Boys' Insurrection."* "It advanced through all the stages of seditious violence, from loud discontent to frequent acts of treason, and from these to open and general insurrection," which took root and acquired tenacity in the trans-montane counties of Pennsylvania. So tender was the government toward its citizens, that for more than three years it made offers of conciliation, and repeatedly introduced alterations in the offensive act to render it more acceptable. This failing of the desired effect, "a deputation, consisting of Judge Yates of the Superior Court, Mr. Ross, senator from Pennsylvania (a gentleman of great popularity in the disaffected country), and the Attorney-General of the United States, also a citizen of Pennsylvania, were dispatched by General Washington to offer them a general amnesty, upon the sole condition of future submission to the laws; and at the request of the Executive, and for the purpose of giving success to this last effort to avoid the employment of military force, the Governor of Pennsylvania appointed commissioners to act in concert with these deputies." This proving unavailing, the President proceeded to effect by force that which persuasion could not accomplish; but even then Washington, in a letter of Oct. 20, 1794, dated "United States (Bedford)," and addressed, to "Henry Lee, Esq., commander-in-chief of the militia army on its march against the insurgents," says, "there is but one point on which I think it proper to add a special recommendation; it is this, that every officer and soldier will constantly bear in mind that he comes to support the laws, and it would be peculiarly unbecoming in him to be in any way the infractor of them. That the essential principles of free government confine the province of the military when called forth on such occasions to these two objects: 1st, to combat and subdue all who may be found in arms in opposition to the national will and authority; 2d, to aid and

---

* For a full account, see Marshall, vol. v., from page 286 to 293, and 575 to 590, confirmed by Ramsay, vol. iii., p. 74.

support the civil magistrate in bringing offenders to justice. The dispensation of this justice belongs to the civil magistrate ; and let it ever be our pride and our glory to leave this sacred trust there unviolated." This wise injunction, so accordant with the spirit of the free and tolerant institutions of our forefathers was faithfully observed ; and as the magnitude of the force employed was too great to be resisted, the rebellion was crushed without the shedding of blood or a single act of devastation.

" Several of the leaders who had refused to give assurances of future submission to the laws were seized, and some of them detained for legal prosecution ;" and the only two persons prosecuted to a conviction of treason, received pardon. This clemency was peculiarly acceptable to the commander of the expedition, who, when urged to recall for punishment a Mr. Bradford who had fled to Spain, and " had manifested peculiar violence—and had openly advocated an appeal to arms," replied,* " that the dignity of the laws was vindicated by his flight from them, and that he could never countenance a proposal which had for its object the hunting of an American citizen to death."

From the office of governor, General Lee retired to private life. It is probable that it was his preference for its enjoyments that prevented his accepting a high position in the armies of France ; fighting, as they were supposed to be, in that great cause of liberty which had just triumphed on our shores. His relative, Mr. Wm. Lee, in a letter from Green Spring, April 20, 1793, says : " I once wrote to you on a very interesting subject, and though my letter had little effect, I shall not be discouraged from doing what I conceive to be my duty. It is reported that you intend to quit your present honorable and dignified situation to go in search of adventures among the savage cannibals of Paris. To this report I give not the least credit, having a high idea of your profound sagacity and judgment, for it is impossible but you must see the hand of Divine vengeance uplifted upon that city." * * * General Washington's opinion on the same subject had, no doubt, an effect proportionate to the regard he felt for that illustrious man.† A letter from Mr. Charles Carter, dated Shirley, May 20, 1793, furnishes conclusive evidence that whatever might have been his intentions, they were abandoned.

---

* See Marshall.   † Spark's Washington, vol. x., page 343.

" The only objection we ever had to your connection with our beloved daughter is now entirely done away. You have declared upon your honor that you have relinquished all thoughts of going to France, and we rest satisfied with that assurance. As we certainly know that you have obtained her consent, you shall have that of her parents most cordially, to be joined together in the holy bonds of matrimony, whenever she pleases; and as it is determined on, by the approbation and sincere affection of all friends, as well as of the parties immediately concerned, we think the sooner it takes place the better."

The concluding remark is very characteristic of this excellent man, whose hospitality and benevolence were commensurate with his opulence. His merchant in London, Mr. Maine, had instructions to give yearly a certain amount of the sales of his tobacco to the poor of that city, Mr. Carter giving as a reason that there were not indigent persons enough in Virginia to enable him to fulfill the great Christian duty of charity; and he was accustomed, when crops were light on James River, to bring corn from his estates on the Chickahominy, Pamunkey, or Rappahannock, wherever they were most abundant, and sell to the suffering farmers at the ordinary instead of the inflated price. The old mansion was always filled to overflowing with his numerous family and guests, and no small portion of it was occupied by the suitors to his fair daughters, nieces, and grand-daughters.* On the 18th June, in accordance with the consent given in her father's letter, Miss Anne Hill Carter was married to General Henry Lee.

Their first child was born in April, 1795, and lived not eighteen months; and though his mother preserved among her jewels, as more precious than them all, a rich curl of his golden hair, he might have been unmentioned except for his name, which was indicative of the spirit of the times—Algernon Sydney, after the

---

* "Died, on Saturday, 28th June, 1806, Charles Carter, Esq., of Shirley, aged 70 years. His long life was spent in the tranquillity of domestic enjoyments. From the mansion of hospitality his immense wealth flowed like the silent streams, enlivening and refreshing every object around. In fulfilling the duties of his station, he proved himself to be an Israelite, indeed, in whom there was no guile. He has gone to receive from the Saviour of mankind the blissful salutation, 'Come, thou blessed of my Father, inherit the kingdom prepared for you from the foundation of the world; for I was a stranger and you took me in, naked and you clothed me, sick and in prison and you ministered unto me.'" This obituary of her father was found among Mrs. Lee's papers after her death.

great martyr of liberty and, according to family tradition, of the kindred of the Lees.

The political excitements of the country, soon after this period, became too portentous for men of prominence to remain quietly at home. The "throes and convulsions" of Europe had reached even this peaceful shore, and assumed a shape so menacing that the Federal Government deemed it necessary to pass the alien and sedition laws as measures of self-defence. These, instead of abating, increased the agitation, by which, as Washington said in a letter to Patrick Henry, urging him to resume his place in the councils of his country, "every thing dear and valuable to us was assailed;" "and which," he remarked in a previous letter, "threatened to destroy the great pillars of all government, and of social life, virtue, morality, and religion." It was to lend his aid to avert such evils that General Lee became a member of the General Assembly, from Westmoreland, in the winter of '98 and '99, and carried into the debate on Mr. Madison's famous resolutions a spirit which, had it been fully sustained by others, might have saved the country from a world of woe. He contended that the laws in question were not unconstitutional, but admitted the right of interposition on the part of the General Assembly if they were so. He repeated, in the close of his remarks, the sentiment he had expressed in the letter to that eminent man already quoted, viz., that the State of Virginia was his country, whose will he would obey, however lamentable the fate to which it might subject him. He complied with a sense of duty, stimulated by a request from Washington, in becoming again a candidate for Congress, to which he was elected, notwithstanding the tide of opposition then running against the Federalists. In the midst of a session embittered by party contests, he was informed of the death of the great leader, whose career he had followed from youth to manhood.

Washington, who had been inured to hardship by a life in the wilderness and the exposure incident to Indian warfare, and who seemed even more robust after the toils of the Revolution, rode to his mill on Dogue Creek, about three miles from Mt. Vernon, on a cold day. A slight but driving snow which was falling, insinuated itself among the wrappings encircling his throat. When he reached home he was oppressed with a severe cold, which resulted in the disease then called quinsy, and which soon proved fatal. But it was not until the "Father of his Country" had become the glory

of the world that it pleased Providence to remove him to a higher
sphere.   Lord Brougham styles him " the greatest man of our own
or any age; the only one upon whom an epithet so thoughtlessly
lavished by men to foster the crimes of their worst enemies, may be
innocently and justly bestowed."   He states it to be "the duty of
the historian and the sage of all ages to let no occasion pass of com-
memorating this illustrious man, and until time shall be no more
will a test of the progress which our race has made in wisdom and
virtue be denied from the veneration paid to the immortal name of
Washington."   It must have been a consolation to Genesal Lee, in
his individual grief, to have been appointed by Congress the public
organ of his country's sorrow, on which occasion he pronounced
those memorable words : " *First in war, first in peace, first in the
hearts of his fellow-citizens.*"

It was at the close of his public career that the following en-
comium appeared in the Boston *Commercial Gazette :* "It is with
the highest pleasure we insert the elegant and truly poetic notice
of one of the best and most active officers of the Revolution, and one
of the most correct and influential statesmen in the Congress of the
late administration :—

"TRIBUTARY LINES INSCRIBED TO GENERAL HENRY LEE.

" Yes : thou wert born beneath the hero's star,
   Triumphant leader in a patriot war ;
   Like Amnon's son, ere manhood's ripening grace
   Nerved the young limbs and stamped the blooming face,
   Supreme in arms, a veteran foe thy claim,
   Thy dazzling valor won the prize of fame ;
   Or at thy country's call, her powers to join,
   Where listening senates felt thy voice divine,
   As round her great deliverer's trophied bier
   Awakened memory gave the hallowed tear,
   Warm from the heart, and glistening with its flame,
   Endeared by thee its best libation came.
   Brave was that arm which taught a Briton fear,
   And sweet that voice which charmed a nation's ear ;
   But not the forum nor the battle claim
   Alone thy homage and divide thy fame ;
   For all the graceful charities that blend
   Round social life, the husband, father, friend,
   Are *thine ;* and thine a generous breast that glows

With every worth the noblest nature knows;
In council honored and in arms renowned,
By fortune followed and by victory crowned,
Fame is thy own, nor can a muse like mine
One flower of fragrance with thy chaplet twine;
Blooming and bright the eternal green shall cheer
The closing winter of each future year:
With thriftiest germ shall brighten unsubdued
By faction's blight or chill ingratitude;
Amid the wreath no bosomed worm shall feed,
Nor envy taint it with one mingling weed.
This to thy deeds doth patriot virtue give
That with thy *country* shall thy *glory* live,
Bright as her rivers, as her hills sublime;
Shall pierce her clouds and glitter through her clime,
Like a rich gem, with beam unquenched by age;
Wear through all time and light a nation's page."

In one particular Lee may be said to have excelled his illustrious contemporaries, Marshall, Madison, Hamilton, Gouverneur
Morris, and Ames. It was in a surprising quickness and talent, a
genius sudden, dazzling, and always at command, with an eloquence which seemed to flow unbidden. Seated at a convivial
board, when the death of Patrick Henry was announced, Lee called
for a scrap of paper and in a few moments produced a beautiful
and striking eulogium upon the Demosthenes of modern liberty.

His powers of conversation were also fascinating in the extreme,
possessing those rare and admirable qualities which seize and hold
captive his hearers, delighting while they instruct. That Lee was
a man of letters,—a scholar who had ripened under a truly classical
sun,—we have only to turn to his work on the Southern war, where
he was indeed the *"magna pars fui"* of all which he relates—a
work which well deserves to be ranked with the commentaries of the
famed master of the Roman world, who like our Lee was equally
renowned with the pen as the sword. But there is a line—a single
line—in the works of Lee which would hand him over to immortality, though he had never written another. *First in war, first in
peace, and first in the hearts of his countrymen* will last while
language lasts. What a sublime eulogium is pronounced in this
noble line; so few words, and yet how illustrative are they of the
vast and matchless character of Washington; they are words which
will descend with the memory of the hero they are meant to honor

to the veneration of remotest posterity, and be graven on colossal statues of the Pater Patriæ in some future age.

"The attachment of Lee to Washington was, like that of Hamilton, pure and enthusiastic—like that of the chivalric Laurens, devotional. It was in the praise of his ʻhero, his friend, and country's preserver,' that the splendid talents of Lee were often elicited with a force and grandeur of eloquence wholly his own. The fame and memory of his chief was the fondly cherished passion to which he clung amid the wreck of his fortunes—the hope which gave warmth to his heart when all else around him seemed cold and desolate * * * * His eloquence in her senates and his historical memoirs of her times of trial, shed a lustre on his country in the young days of the Republic; and when the Americans of some future date shall search amid the records of their early history for the lives of illustrious men who flourished in the age of Washington, high on a brilliant scroll will they find inscribed Henry Lee—a son of Virginia—the patriot, soldier, and historian of the Revolution, and orator and statesman of the Republic." *

The retirement of General Lee was devoted to recording the events of his military life, including those of Marion, Sumter, Pickens, Howard, William Washington, the gallant Kirkwood, and the operations of his Legion.

In the year 1811 he removed with his family to Alexandria for the purpose of educating his children, when the war with England occurred. After the first disastrous campaigns in Canada, he was offered and accepted a major-general's commission in the army.†

While making his arrangements to leave home, business called him to Baltimore, and being in Mr. Hanson's house for the purpose of transacting it, he was detained there so long, that when about to leave, he found it so surrounded by a mob, as to prevent his departure. The results of that night, fatal to General Lingan, nearly fatal to General Lee, and disgraceful to party spirit, are too well known to need repetition. The injuries he received prevented his taking part in the war of 1812 and eventually terminated his life. It was thought a voyage to the West Indies and the influence of that mild climate might restore him; the following correspondence will show

---

* Recollections of Washington, by J. W. P. Custis, pp. 361, 362, 363.
† Statement of President Monroe, who was, at the time alluded to, a member of Washington's cabinet, to C. C. Lee, during a visit to him at his residence in Loudon.

how the difficulties in accomplishing it were overcome and the temporary benefit he at first received.

CHARLES CARTER LEE TO MR. MADISON.

"NEW YORK, *May* 9, 1831.

"MY DEAR SIR,—I have been so fortunate as to obtain to-day some letters and papers sent by my father from the West Indies many years ago. The trunk which contained them and all the letters were opened before they fell into my hands, and I took the liberty of reading that which I now send you, as it was inclosed to my brother unsealed. I despair of ever being able to find the wine alluded to, but assure you that I relinquish with sincere regret the hope of being instrumental in procuring for you any thing which might be conducive to your health; yet I am sure you will be gratified to receive, as it were from the grave, thanks from an old friend for benefits of which you cannot but be pleased to be reminded—I can conceive of nothing so refreshing to the evening of life as those long shadows of memory, which reach to acts of kindness attended with gratitude, and I beg you to believe that much of that the grave extinguished, survives in me. I shall never forget the very agréeable day I passed with you a few summers since. To converse familiarly with any of the great founders of the Republic is an era in the life of one who venerates them and adores their work as I do, and it was scarcely a less interesting event to me to meet for the first time with Mrs. Madison and to be charmed with that affability, and won with that graciousness of which I had so often heard; pray present me to her with the most cordial respect, and believe me, my dear sir, with affectionate veneration,

"Your most obedient humble servant,

"C. C. LEE."

The following is the letter which was inclosed in the above:—

HENRY LEE TO PRESIDENT MADISON, U. S.

"BARBADOES, *August* 24, 1813.

"MY DEAR SIR,—I feel daily and hourly the effect of yours and Admiral Warren's goodness to me, and my heart constantly avows a grateful sense of your kindness. Had I not escaped from my country, the climate must have finished me ere now; as it is, I am much bétter, and have the agreeable prospect of being restored to health and strength. Although a state of war interposed obstacles to the execution of my views, which seemed insurmountable, yet they were overcome as soon as they were communicated to you and the British admiral.   It cannot but follow that, as long as I live, I shall seize every opportunity to testify my personal respect and gratitude. The cartel going from here to the Chesapeake enables me to send you some very fine Madeira five years old, with a green turtle, the largest I can procure; and the character of Captain Randlet assures me that he will with great pleasure safely deliver them. I embrace the opportunity with delight, happy when I can in any way administer to your accommodation. Accept my prayers for your health and prosperity.

"Your faithful friend and much obliged servant,

"H. LEE.

"P. S. I cannot yet see accurately, and must beg you to excuse mistakes and errors in writing."

JAMES MADISON TO C. C. LEE.

"MONTPELIER, *May* 17, 1831.

"DEAR SIR,—I have received your letter of the 9th, inclosing a long latent one from your father. My acquaintance with him commenced at a very early stage of our lives, and our friendly sympathies never lost their force, though deprived for long periods of the nourishing influence of personal intercourse, and exposed occasionally to the disturbing tendency of discordance in political opinions. I could not fail, therefore, to be of the number of sincerest mourners, when it was announced that he was no more, and to be gratified now, by the evidence of his letter, that his affectionate recollections had undergone no change. It is not strange that a tempting article like selected wine, should disappear in such a lapse of time and its changes of place. Had it reached its destination, it would have derived its best flavor from the feelings of which it was a token. I thank you, sir, for your kind sentiments and good wishes, as Mrs. Madison does for her share in them ; and I beg you to accept in her behalf as well as mine a cordial return of them.

"JAMES MADISON."

When General Lee went to the West Indies, he cherished the hope that his health might be sufficiently restored to enable him to perfect his memoirs, and add to them biographies of his two beloved commanders, Greene and Washington; but, except a few unimportant additions, which appeared in the second edition by his son, Major Henry Lee, his ill health prevented him from accomplishing any part of that design. How great his sufferings were, and the manner in which he employed his time, will best appear from his letters to the eldest son of his second marriage, then at Harvard University, Cambridge. Besides being the record of the close of an eventful life, they are interesting as portraying the tastes and studies of the preceding generation, and may animate the rising one to pursue those which so exalted their ancestors of the revolution.

Letter from C. C. Lee, Esq., to R. E. Lee.

"Fine Creek, Powhatan County, *July* 25, 1866.

"My Dear Brother,—I send you, for the work you are engaged upon, as the best history that can be furnished of the close of our father's life, his letters to me at that sad period. How much of them it may be necessary to publish I leave to you; for I should reproach myself did I not overestimate such evidences of his affection. I have endeavored to clear my judgment of partiality, * * * to write about them with as much calmness as I can command. I think they show how well-directed studies in our youth operate to bless our declining years. What consolation he must have felt, to be enabled to inculcate wisdom and virtue in those, in elevating whom he raised himself above his sufferings. I think too, they are peculiarly valuable for inspiring a love of truth as the basis of all excellence. Of course I do not limit that inculcation, merely to correct narration and faithful testimony; but to that enlarged view, which in all its aspects regards Truth as the daughter of God, and as such to be preferred, no matter how much she may frown upon us and our preferences, to all the erroneous though smiling offspring of the brain of man. This is the most difficult of our achievements in religion, in manners, and even in science. * * * As to his praises of myself, no one will imagine, I presume, that I regard them in any other light than as proofs of affection; and therefore, the more I am impressed with their extravagance, the more precious they become to me. I send you full copies of the letters, twelve in number, from which you must use your own discretion to take what you deem proper, to record the melancholy close of a life whose dawn

I am very truly yours

R E Lee

University Publishing Company

was so brilliant, whose meridian was devoted to promote the best interests of his country and of mankind, and whose career was shortened and end darkened by forebodings of the failure of these exertions. It is most gratifying to us to perceive how the innate grandeur of his soul, exalted by the noblest studies and sanctified by the holiest affections, shed a glory on the close of his day, which the clouds that surrounded it seemed rather to enrich than obscure, and which, I pray, may render its last teachings so dear to his descendants as to make them blest in themselves, and by their beneficial influence a blessing to others.

" Your affectionate brother,

" C. C. LEE. "

LETTERS OF GENERAL HENRY LEE TO C. C. LEE.—LETTER 1.

" PORT-AU-PRINCE, ST. DOMINGO, June 26, 1816.

"MY DEAR CARTER,—I have just heard by a letter from Henry that you are fixed at the University of Cambridge, the seminary of my choice. You will there have not only excellent examples to encourage your love and practice of virtue, the only real good in life, but ample scope to pursue learning to its bottom, thereby fitting yourself to be useful to your country and to be an ornament to your friends.

" You know, my dear son, the deep and affectionate interest I have taken in you from the first moment of your existence, and your kind, amiable disposition will never cease enjoying and amplifying your father's happiness to the best of your ability. You will do this by preferring the practice of virtue to all other things; you know my abhorrence of lying, and you have been often told by me, that it led to every vice and cancelled every tendency to virtue. Never forget this truth, and disdain the mean and infamous practice. Epaminondas, the great Theban, who defended his country when environed by powerful foes, and was the most virtuous man of his age, so abhorred lying that he would never tell one even in jest. Imitate this great man and you may equal him in goodness, infinitely to be preferred to his greatness. I am too sick to continue this discussion; though I begin to hope I may live to see you, your dear mother, and our other sweet offspring. I only write now to require that you write monthly to me. Send your letters by vessels from Boston which go to Turk's Island for salt;

and inclose them to Mr. Daniel Bascombe, merchant. He will send them to me wherever I may be, though I shall not get them as expeditiously as my heart desires. This goes to Mr. Wm. Sullivan, a gentleman of Boston, who will send it to you, and do you any necessary favor, should sickness or accident render such favor requisite. He is, too, an exemplary gentleman, worthy of your imitation. There is a little boy, James Smith, son of a Mr. Smith of these islands, at school at Westfield, not far from Cambridge; should you ever go that way call and see this boy, and assist him by your advice and countenance. He is in a strange land and far from his relatives. My prayers are always offered to Almighty God for the protection of my darling Carter, and especially for establishing in his heart and conduct virtue in all its power. I pray you never to forget that virtue is our first good and lying its deadly foe.

'Your father,

"H. Lee."

General Henry Lee to C. C. Lee.

"Turk's Island, on my voyage to New Providence,
"*August* 8, 1816.

" My Dear Carter will have received one letter written as soon as I knew he was settled at Cambridge, and which was sent to the care of Mr. Sullivan, in Boston. Having this moment an opportunity to send to New York, I use it to repeat my love and prayers for his health and advancement in the acquisition of knowledge from its foundation, not on the surface. This last turns man into a puppy, and the first fits him for the highest utility and most lasting pleasure. I requested you to write monthly to me, giving to me with clearness and brevity a narrative of your studies, recreations, and your relish for the occupations which employ you in and out of college. Never mind your style; but write your first impressions quickly, clearly, and honestly. Style will come in due time, as will the maturity of judgment. Above all things earthly, even love to the best of mothers and your ever-devoted father, I entreated you to cherish truth and abhor deception. Dwell on the virtues, and imitate, as far as lies in your power, the great and good men whom history presents to our view.

> " Minerva! Let such examples teach thee to beware,
> Against Great God thou utter aught profane;

And, if perchance, in riches or in power
Thou shinest superior, be not insolent;
For, know, a day sufficeth to exalt
Or to depress the state of mortal man.
The wise and good are by our God beloved,
But those who practise evil he abhors.' *

" You have my favorite precept, instilled from your infancy by
my lips, morning, noon, and night, in my familiar talks with you,
here presented to your mind in the purity and elegance of the
Grecian tragedian. You never, I trust, will forget to make it the
cardinal rule of your life. It will, at least, arrest any tendency to
imitate the low, degrading usage, too common, of swearing in conversation, especially with your inferiors. My miserable state of
health improves by the occasional voyaging in this fine climate,
with the sage guidance of a superior physician to whom I am now
returning. When Boston fails to give you opportunities to write
as before directed, send your letters to Mr. William Goddard, in
Providence, who will forward them to me.

" May God ever protect you, &c.,

" H. LEE."

GENERAL HENRY LEE TO C. C. LEE.

" CAICOS, September 30, 1816.

" October is near at hand, and no letter from my beloved Carter;
notwithstanding I have been writing to you ever since I learned
that you were at Cambridge, and the salt vessels are weekly arriving
at the adjacent island, and I had asked my friends, Mr. Sullivan
and Mr. Goddard, to forward your letters. What can this mean?
Any thing, I know, my dear son, but your lukewarmness of devotion
and love to your father. I have been detained three months on my
way to my Spanish doctor in Nassau, the chief town of Providence,
where I hope to be partially restored or to die in the attempt;
why, then will you not give me the delight of reading your letters?
Write, I entreat, your thoughts just as they come, and in the order
and fashion in which they arise. * * * I am very serious in
this requisition; and if your letters exhibit labor, instead of negligent ease, I shall be unhappy. Never show those for me to your
preceptor or any one else. Speak from your heart to my heart;

* From the Ajax of Sophocles.

that is what I want, and want only. In Barbadoes, where I
landed from Alexandria, and where I resided six months, I often
wrote to you and sometimes to Anne, but never heard from either.
One of these letters treated on the subject of your advance and
progress through life, and I will here repeat some of its contents
* * * * Important as it is to understand nature in its range
and bearing, it is more so to be prepared for usefulness, and to
render ourselves pleasing by understanding well the religious and
moral knowledge of right and wrong, to investigate thoroughly
the history of mankind, and to be familiar with those examples
which show the loveliness of truth, and demonstrate the reasonable-
ness of our opinions by past events. Providence and justice
manifest their excellence at all times and in all places; we are
called to moralize daily, but we seldom turn to geometry;
with intellectual nature we have constant intercourse, but specula-
tions upon matter are rare, and when much at leisure, we know
little of the skill of our acquaintance in astronomy, though we
daily see him, but his integrity, his benevolence, his truth and
prudence instantly appear. Read therefore the best poets, the
best orators, and the best historians; as from them you draw principles of moral truth, axioms of prudence and material for conversation. This was the opinion of the great Socrates. He labored
in Athens to turn philosophy from the study of nature to the
study of life. He justly thought man's great business was to learn
how to do good, and to avoid evil. Be a steady, ardent disciple of
Socrates; and regard virtue, whose temple is built upon truth, as
the chief good. I would rather see you unlearned and unnoticed,
if virtuous in practice as well as theory, than to see you the equal
in glory to the great Washington; but virtue and wisdom are not
opponents; they are friends and coalesce in a few characters such
as his. A foolish notion often springs up with young men as they
enter life, namely, that the opinion of the world is not to be
regarded; whereas, it is the true criterion, generally speaking, of
all things that terminate in human life. To despise its sentence,
if possible, is not just; and if just, is not possible. So think now,
and be confirmed as you advance. Tell me about my dear Smith
and Robert; their genius, temper, their disposition to learn, their
diligence and perseverance in doing what is assigned to them. Tell
me the whole truth; and be virtuous, which will render you happy.

"H. LEE."

GENERAL HENRY LEE TO C. C. LEE.

"NASSAU, NEW PROVIDENCE, *Dec.* 1, 1816.

"MY DEAR CARTER has never answered one of the many letters to him from the day I understood he was placed by his dear mother at Cambridge; my misfortune, not your fault. I have confidence in your heart, not to be shaken; and I well know, ardent and constant as has been my love for you, correspondent at least has been your affection and respect for me * * * I occasionally sent you a book, which I commended to your serious study, but whether any have ever reached you I do not know. Now I must urge you, as the library of Cambridge will present to your discrimination a large collection, to avoid all frivolous authors; such as novel writers, and all skeptical authors, whether religious, philosophic, or moral. Adhere to history and ethical authors of unrivalled character; first of the latter description is John Locke; do not only read him, but study him; do not only study, but consult him as the Grecians did the Delphic oracle. Make him the director of your mind and the guide of your lucubrations. Francis Bacon (Viscount of St. Albans, I believe) is wonderfully instructive; though of cowardly, despicable character.

"The Earl of Shaftesbury, Locke's patron, is like Locke himself, in another way. Dean Swift commands your high admiration and is truly instructive, as well as infinitely agreeable. David Hume is at the head of English historians, and his essays abound with shining informationto the mind, as do Johnson's works. Among the English poets prefer Pope; he is worthy of universal applause, far superior to Milton, as his Iliad compared with Paradise Lost evinces.*

"I trust you are a good classic, and then among the ancients pore over Tacitus, Xenophon, Julius Cæsar, and Polybius in prose, and Homer and Sophocles in verse. Virgil is Homer's excellent imitator, but far below the transcendant Greek. Lucretius, '*de naturâ rerum*,' is full of marks of superior genius; but he supports atheism, and incites in the mind wonder at his folly and compassion for his error, with indignation for the possible injury he might do to the human race. If I had not partly read him, I never could have

---

* "Of Pope himself, he (Lord Byron) spoke with extravagant admiration. He did not venture directly to say that the little man of Twickenham was a greater poet than Shakespeare or Milton, but he hinted pretty clearly that he thought so."—*Macauley's Miscellanies*, p. 124.

believed there had ever lived a man who was in judgment an atheist. If you have not Locke in your college library, tell me, and I
will furnish you; as I will with the meditations of Marcus Aurelius, the great and good emperor, adopted by Antoninus, his equal
in excellence, whose name he bears in history. In the first of his
meditations, he thus speaks of himself, which I give summarily,
to excite your desire to become intimate with him and to emulate
him,—'From the example of my grandfather I acquired a virtuous
disposition and an habitual command over my temper. From my
own father I learned to behave with modesty, yet with a manly
firmness on all occasions. My mother I have imitated in piety,
and have been taught not only to abstain from vice, but to abhor
the thought of it, and she taught me to be simple and abstemious
in diet. To my great grandfather I am indebted for the best masters; and from the governor of my early days I learned to avoid
races, games, and such diversions; substituting for them hardships
and fatigue; to reduce the conveniences of life into a narrow com-
pass, to wait upon myself; never to listen to calumny, or to meddle with the business of others. Dignetus stopped me from pursuing
trifles and from believing the vulgar tales of prodigies, spirits, and
such kinds of follies. He taught me to bear patiently the admonitions of my friends; to sleep on a hard couch; and, while a boy,
to write dialogues. From Rusticus I learned, not to assume any
state in my deportment; to write letters in a plain, unornamented
style; to be readily reconciled to all who had injured me, when
they seemed inclined to do right; to read with care and attention;
not to be content with a general, superficial view of the subject,
nor to recede from my opinion only when convinced it was error.
Apollonius taught me to maintain the freedom of mind; a constancy independent of fortune; and to keep a steady eye in the most
minute instances to the dictates of reason; to preserve an even
temper always, even in joy or pain; and to be like him, rigid in
principle, but easy and affable in manners. In Sextus I had an
example of a truly benevolent disposition, and of a family governed
with paternal care and affection. Like him, I determined to live
according to nature, simple and unaffected; and, like him, to acquire reputation without noise, and deep learning without ostentation. I imitate my relative, Severus, in love of my relations and of
truth and justice; and from Claudius I learned to be always master
of myself, and never to yield to passion.'

" You will agree that a boy thus reared must turn out good and great when a man ; and you will, I hope, hold before your eyes as a model, Marcus Aurelius. It is a small book, and its precepts should be engraved upon your mind and habituated in your conduct. You write, I hope, regularly to your dear mother, and to Henry, also to your sister Anne, and your brother Sydney. This will improve them and cement your mutual affection. My letters you must keep, and give them to Smith to read. * * * My health is better. I hope to leave this place in April, if I live. Farewell, my dear son.

"Your affectionate father,

"H. LEE."

GENERAL HENRY LEE TO C. C. LEE.

"NASSAU, February 9, 1817.

" My beloved Carter's letter of July 25th came to hand, not on the birth day of the great and good Washington, but in his birth month, and infused into his father's heart an overflow of delight, in defiance of the torturing pains of disease. Always dear to me, always the source of delicious anticipations, I see, from your first performance, ample evidence that my fond hopes will not be disappointed. Go on in the road of truth to the temple of virtue, where dwell her handmaids, modesty, temperance, benevolence, fortitude, and justice. Fame in arms or art, however conspicuous, is naught, unless bottomed on virtue. Think, therefore, of fame, only as the appendage to virtue; and be virtuous, though poor, humble, and scorned.

" Remember how often I have prayed you to imitate Epaminondas in his regard for truth, if you cannot aspire to follow him in his trail of true glory. He is my favorite Grecian ; and next to him Aristides, whom you place as second to Alcibiades. To bring the reasoning home to you, your dearest mother is singularly pious from love to Almighty God and love of virtue, which are synonymous; not from fear of hell,—a low, base influence. Your dear mother recalls to my mind our dear Anne, Smith, Robert, and my unknown. You ought to have said something of them all, their growth, their health, their amusements, their occupations, their progress in literature, their tempers as they open, and last not least their love and devotion to their good mamma. * * * Your brother

delineates to me your character with all the affection of his generous heart. * * * My dear Lucy, too, her excellent husband
and sweet progeny, ought not to have escaped your attention. Two
sheets, instead of one and a half, might have been so employed ;
and the more I read from my darling son, the more I feast. *. * *
I cannot answer your query concerning Washington's charger,*
nor withhold my admiration for your tender regard for useful animals, with gratitude to those from whom we have derived services.
You know that I am almost an Egyptian in my love for the cow
and ox; yet after their daily service through life, after the third
year I always fatten, kill, and eat them. The subject which you
touch, has been decided rather from feeling than judgment; we
will discuss it when we meet. Your panegyric on Shakespeare is all
just, but when you read the Athenian, Sophocles, you will find his
superior, at least his equal, in all the requisites of tragedy.

"Eloquence is our first gift in civic walks, nor is it without
great advantage in war. To be eloquent, you must understand
thoroughly your subject ; out of the abundance of knowledge the
tongue uttereth just ideas ; voice, gesticulation, manner may be acquired with care, but knowledge cannot be acquired but by labor,
and that by night as well as by day. In every distinguished character, nature gives the turn and scope; art and study polish and
spread. * * * Tell me in your reply what are your expenses
in toto, designating every item, and the sum it demands. Tell me
your diversions, amusements, and bodily exercises ; whether at ball,
long bullets, &c. The climate of Cambridge is much colder
than that of your native country. How does it agree with you?
Pray guard against cold; it is the stepping-stone to other diseases ;
I repeat my entreaty to save yourself from its injuries, and I pray
you also to cherish your health by temperance and exercise. It is
hard to say whether too much drinking or too much eating most un-
dermines the constitution; you are addicted to neither, and will, I am
sure, take care to grow up free from both. Cleanliness of person
is not only comely to all beholders, but is indispensable to sanctity
of body. Trained by your best of mothers to value it, you will
never lose sight of it. To be plain and neat in dress, conforms to
good sense and is emblematic of a right mind. Many lads, who

---

* Whether he was shot in his old age, as is said to be customary in England,
or as some one asserted Washington did with his war-horse.

avoid the practices mentioned, fall into another habit which hurts only themselves and which certainly stupefies the senses—immoderate sleeping. You know how I love my children; and how dear Smith is to me. Give me a true description of his person, mind, temper, and habits. Tell me of Anne; has she grown tall? and how is my last in looks and understanding? Robert was always good, and will be confirmed in his happy turn of mind by his ever-watchful and affectionate mother. Does he strengthen his native tendency?

"You speak of the 'soul' in your letter, I trust you mean by the word the faculty which the Almighty has indued us with, of thinking, reasoning, and concluding; as he has given to our eyes the faculty of seeing, our ears of hearing, and our nerves of feeling. You do not mean by the soul, a being connected with the body. Mr. Locke will put you right on all subjects of this sort, and ought to be revered by all who love truth and seek knowledge. When you study natural philosophy, and admire, as you must, Sir Isaac Newton, forget not Pythagoras; he announced and taught the principle that Newton has so profoundly explained,—the earth turning on its axis, and all the planets turning around the sun. I have a book which I wish to send you for your constant perusal—Bacon. It is most edifying, and worthy of your exact acquaintance: and yet superb in genius and profound in knowledge as was Sir Francis Bacon, he was, almost proverbially, base and mean; a rare example of debasement of mind, with richness of knowledge.

"Did you ever get a gun and letters from me, more than six months ago? Do you ride and shoot well? These are secondary, but they are agreeable, useful, and manly. ' Unde derivatus? ' is a scholastic interrogatory; be assured, it is all important to correct literature; and you will, I hope, thoroughly meet it. When you have the derivation of every word, you never can forget the language, nor be at loss for its purest use. Your letter has been four days in my possession, and is always before me, when capable of diverting my attention from my body. Mr. McIntosh, whose father was an officer in a corps against which I was employed when in the Southern war, has made my house his home, and with his daughter, bestowed every effort in their power, to soften my pains. She was as kind, and as tender, and as constant, as would have been my daughter, and read all the letters I received; among them one from Henry. She admired his heart and filial love. Being here at present, I sent her your letter, acquainted as she was with my affection and hopes for my Carter. You have her note returning the letter. My Spanish doctor has done me good, and sometimes inspires hopes of partial restoration. I leave here as soon as spring arrives, whatever may be my condition, and land in the South, to graduate my experience of change of climate. * * * * May God Almighty cherish, bless, and guide my dear son, is and ever will be the prayer of his loving father,

"H. LEE."

GENERAL HENRY LEE TO C. C. LEE.

"NASSAU, NEW PROVIDENCE, *April* 19, 1817.

" I answered your second letter, my dear Carter, directly after its receipt; and now repeat, so fond am I of cultivating acquaintance with my beloved boy. In my last I told you that my disease had at length yielded in a degree, and that I hoped still to mend; but whether or not, my return home would take place in a few weeks, directing my course to the South, as a warm climate still continues necessary for me. Before this day month, I expect to find a vessel to South Carolina or Georgia, when I shall embark. Mr. Goddard will be informed where to address your letters. But at all events, after May, send them by the various vessels going to Charleston from Boston, to the care of General Pinckney; indeed you might inclose them in a short epistle, asking his attention, and telling him you took the liberty in consequence of my directions. Send always by vessels, as thus General Pinckney will be put to no expense. His Christian name is Thomas; and his title Major-General. Tell me all about your dear mother and my children; for scarcely do I ever hear from Henry, although I am sure he writes every two weeks.

" I find your mind is charmed with eloquence, and I infer that the bar is the theatre selected for its display. The rank of men, as established by the concurrent judgment of ages, stands thus: heroes, legislators, orators, and poets. The most useful and, in my opinion, the most honorable is the legislator, which so far from being incompatible with the profession of law, is congenial to it. Generally, mankind admire most the hero; of all, the most useless, except when the safety of a nation demands his saving arm. Confessedly, Alexander, Cæsar, and Hannibal stand on the summit, in the days of Greece and Rome. Much as the two first will be admired for their magnanimous conduct, and loved for their mental excellency, the correct mind can never applaud the object for which they wasted human life, and will ever mingle with its admiration, execrations bitter and degrading.

"Hannibal, whom I am inclined to consider the first soldier of the three, and whom I believe to be the equal of the other two in all the qualities which endear individuals to those around them, had a justifiable cause of war against the Romans. Their enmity to Carthage was known ; and his father, as well as himself, and all other enlightened and honest Carthaginians, long before his crossing the Alps, had been convinced by past events that the safety of Carthage hung upon the humbling of Rome; which this prince of soldiers would have completely effected, had not Hanno's envy and malice, supported by his faction in the Senate, crossed and stunted all Hannibal's plans and means. It has ever been a cause of regret with me that the history of this superior man has never reached us. We know him only from the records of his enemies; and these, notwithstanding Roman hatred and prejudice, leave him first of antiquity in cabinet and field. Polybius, being a Grecian, may be considered impartial ; but his personal intimacy and almost dependence on Scipio Africanus may justly beget suspicions that he did not display candor on the virtues and exploits of Hannibal. Lycurgus, Solon, Numa, the second king of Rome, attract universal admiration as legislators ; and how can Alexander, Cæsar, and Hannibal be compared with them in the promotion of human good ; the only way in which man can, however humbly, imitate Almighty God and merit our love. Greece, before the grand military exploit of taking Troy, was, like the northern nations of Europe of that day, barbarous ; but after their expedition against the Trojans their advance was rapid to the high reputation which they preserved until their subjugation by the Macedonians. Petty states, always fighting with each other, with Persia, or Philip, or Alexander, they nevertheless rose to the summit of improvement in the arts of peace and war ; emphatically demonstrating that the constant exercise of the mind, struggling to maintain freedom and independence of the State, brings forth that superb display of genius which attains in a little time the highest rank in literature and the arts. This is not exemplified by Greece alone ; for the same result was produced by the perpetual wars among the small states of Italy, until Rome succeeded in conquering all. From the settlement of Italy by the

Pelasgi, who inhabited Arcadia in the Peloponnesus, now Morea, nearly four centuries passed before the time of Numitor, predecessor of Romulus ; but as the history of that period is traditional, we know but little save that the different little republics were always contending for mastership, which at last settled on Rome. Covetous of dominion and military in habit, after haying subdued Italy, they went to Africa, Asia, and the contiguous regions of Europe, in quest of additional subjugation, till they brought under their dominion nearly all the world then known to them.   In such continuation of wars at home and abroad, the mind was always on the stretch, and heroes, statesmen, orators, and poets, in abundance, were the certain consequence.   In England, too, we find the same cause producing the same effect.   During the civil wars, when the mind was in constant excitement, genius was resplendent, especially in enjoying the tranquillity of peace, which is always the case. Refer to the history of Charles I., the Protector, and Charles II. ; again to James, and the Revolution, which was achieved by his expulsion, and the elevation of William and Mary, when British liberty, always the first object of our British ancestors, was fully established.   The extraordinary philosopher, Roger Bacon, a friar, flourished long before this period, having been born in 1214 ; but Francis, Lord Bacon, a man of singular mental powers, died not long before Charles's accession to the throne ; he was followed by Harvey, who was succeeded by Boyle, after whom came Sir Isaac Newton.   In poetry, Milton, Jonson, Waller, Denham, Otway, and Dryden, adorned too the above-mentioned period.   In our own day we have experienced the display of genius during the convulsions of France, begun for the purpose of ameliorating the political condition of the country ; in which laudable work the virtuous Louis XVI. embarked with truth and zeal.   Even our own country never exhibited such a display of genius before or since as she did during her eight years' war.

" It may therefore be considered as a truth demonstrated by the history of man, that a continuous and ardent excitement of the mind, especially in regaining lost or defending menaced rights, places man in that train of mind and body which brings forth the greatest display of genius ; especially after the storm has subsided, and the mind, reposing with security in the sweets of tranquillity, meditates without fear.

" When you answer, be sure to tell me what is your general state of health, what your hours of sleep, whether you eat copiously or sparingly, and your age; and be sure to take up in life the custom of fasting two or three days, living on bread and water, when disordered, rather than swallow drugs. Adieu, my dear son.

"H. LEE."

GENERAL HENRY LEE TO C. C. LEE.

"NASSAU, *May* 5, 1817

"Having within a few days, my dear Carter, received letters from home, yours of February last was inclosed by your dear mother. Your defence of your favorite Milton is entitled to much consideration, although it approaches to literary impiety, when you approximate him so close to Homer; but it cannot remove the objections I have to your poet, nor arrest my preference of Pope. '*Homo sum; humani nihil a me alienum puto.*' Had Milton condescended to treat of men,—and their history affords untried subjects fit for epic poetry in abundance,—I should have perused his works with delight, though not with Homeric rapture, and might have classed him with the first of English poets; but as he has preferred angels to men, my ignorance of that order of beings and their theatre of action deprives me of the capacity to perceive the poet's beauty and to decide upon the merits of his poem. Indeed, travelling with him, *terrâ incognitâ,* I become weary, and shut up the book, to be opened only by those who can comprehend celestial personages and celestial battles.

"I never could read a novel, because it was the narrative of imaginary action; and yet I have seen many grave men and pious ladies bedew their cheeks and exclaim, 'How natural, how affecting!' with Fielding in their hand. Paradise Lost is to me alike distasteful; and I must adhere to Pope, because he treats of man and his ways. In one of my letters I urged you to acquire French, not only to read, but to speak; and I now renew my advice with anxious zeal. If you could only thereby be benefited with the perusal of Racine, you would be liberally rewarded. Sophocles, Euripides, in Greek; Racine, and Voltaire's Henriade, in French; are enough to invest your young mind with true taste, even had the immortal Homer and his coadjutor Virgil been lost to man.

"But there is another matter which very much affects my heart, and which I have glanced at in some of my letters, the acquirement of complete self-command. It is the pivot upon which the character, fame, and independence of us mortals hang. Turn your attention steadily and closely to this cardinal quality, and habituate yourself at once to reject with disdain every temptation which may assail your self-dominion. Thus are the passions, the appetites, the cravings subjected to reason, and thus does weak man humbly assimilate himself to his Almighty Creator. Encircled as were Alexander and Scipio by the glories of the field and the cabinet, their self-command evinced on the most trying occasions,—when even beauty, the most captivating, and in their power by the right of conquest, was sheltered from the rude touch of passion,—threw around their names the splendor of virtue which overshadowed all their glory.

"What breast is so callous to noble feelings as not to pant to be called their rivals? In one road only is the youth to walk whose mind is thus ennobled. He must begin with himself when young, and as his occupations at that period are of the inferior sort, he can only become a true disciple of future glory by watching his tongue and his purse. Let not the first utter a word injurious to truth, decency, or to another's peace; and never suffer want or temptation to induce the wanton disbursement of the last, but take up the determination to spend only what is absolutely necessary, and thus assume the habit of retaining part of your pecuniary allowance for casualties to which your own body is liable, and another part to enable you to help a friend when afflicted with distress. That you may at once begin and travel on to the goal under your father's guidance, ascertain exactly the sum necessary for your next year, specifying the several items; and record from week to week every expression actuated by passion, and its consequences to truth, decorum, and another's peace. * * *

"Thank you for Henry's address to his district; it does honor to his political principles, as well as to his literary talents. By a letter lately from him, he is married and I hope happily. I shall have another daughter to embrace and admire when I get home. Lucy also wrote to me; by which I learn the fate of Woodstock, and Mr. Carter's removal to Philadelphia.

"But all those dear to me,—all thanks to great God,—were well, unstained by follies even, much less by offences against morality. Adieu, my beloved son. Your affectionate father,

"H. LEE."

GENERAL HENRY LEE TO C. C. LEE.

"NASSAU, *June* 18, 1817.

" MY DEAR CARTER will receive this additional letter, though I never expected to write again from hence; this is, too, the day of the month when your dear mother became my wife, and it is not so hot in this tropical region as it was then at Shirley, though situated in the temperate zone. Since that happy day, marked only by the union of two humble lovers, it has become conspicuous as the day that our war with Great Britain was declared in Washington; and the one that sealed the doom of Bonaparte on the field of Waterloo. The British general rising *gradatim* from his first blow struck in Portugal, climbed on that day to the summit of fame and became distinguished by the first of titles, ' Deliverer of the civilized world.' Alexander, Hannibal, and Cæsar among the ancients; Marlborough, Eugene, Turenne, and Frederick, among the moderns; opened their arms to receive him as brother in glory. I scarcely believe that Hannibal and Frederick would claim him as theirs especially. There is a similitude in the leading circumstances of my three heroes : the first contended against Rome, the greatest nation then on earth ; Frederick, against Austria, in that day like Rome; and Wellington, against France, the colossal power in late days. The first and the last fought, too, at the head of troops, partly their own countrymen and partly Spaniards ; Frederick may be said to have commanded Prussians only, an advantage never to be doubted in war. Frederick and Wellington succeeded completely in their objects ; Hannibal was lost, because the senator Hanno, great in influence in Carthage, withheld, more or less, supplies of men, money, and munitions; preferring the gratification of his personal hatred to the prosperity of his country, which in the issue became ruined. The two first resembled each other in two points of character replete with weight in all the affairs of man, viz., foresight and economy ; Wellington certainly equals them in the first, and, for aught I know, may in the last. Both are essential to perfection, and the last is indispensable ; as without it, the first power penetrated must be crushed in its efforts for want of means, which the last affords in a constant adequate current. This admirable habit grows out of reflection and love of personal independence, and happy the youth, whether in high or low condi-

tion, who clings to it as his palladium. Frederick, whose character
I so much admire, was remarkable for his frugality, or rather
economy and assiduity. I wish to hold him up to your imitation.
* * * He rose at four ; went to bed at ten; was temperate in all
things ; knew every thing to be done; and saw every thing done
in due season. He was liberal in his gifts to the deserving, but
he measured them by his fiscal ability and his fiscal wants; thus
he never wanted money, and never missed the opportunity of advancing his nation's prosperity, because the means were not ready.
He had early habituated himself to keep his wants within his
means, and this habit became confirmed as he grew up, and
adhered to him till his death. You may acquire the same; and in
your little affairs, alike important to you as his great affairs were
to him, it will be sure to produce the same effects. That it should
begin at once, I learn by letters from your dear mother, is indispensable, as your expenses transcend your allowance. Do think
seriously and constantly on this subject. Write to me frankly, and
you shall hear from me in the spirit of love and desire to gratify
all requisite claims. I find the vessel in which I expected to embark to-morrow has changed its destination. I am disappointed
and must embrace any favorable opportunity, without regard to
place of arrival. Do not write to me until you hear from me after
my arrival.

" H. Lee."

General Henry Lee to C. C. Lee.

"Nassau, *August* 25, 1817.

" When I was about embarking, my dear Carter, for Alexandria,
the middle of last month, I was detained by the seizure of the vessel, in which I had a small interest. I have been vainly trying to
get another opportunity, and can find none suitable, but one per
Savannah, where I may be compelled to go, far as it is out of my
way. I have been reading Raynal daily. * * * I hope you will
give this French author a deep reading. I have for you Quintius
Curtius, whose history of Alexander is most instructive; 'Newton's Principia,' in 3 vols., the foundation of Natural Philosophy,
and the ' Asiatic Researches ' so often recommended to you. * * *
Again I beg you to send me a correct statement of your pecuniary
affairs. * * * If any debts hang on you, tell me the amount, and I
will enable you to deliver yourself from a state abhorrent to a noble

mind and sure to degrade the most chosen. Knowing, as you do, how dearly I love you, how precious truth is to me, I am sure your letter will display the virtue which only leads to true glory. Tell me always all you know of your dear mother, and your dear sisters and brothers; three of each you had, and I hope still have. Farewell, my son, more dear to me as you become more virtuous.

"H. LEE."

GENERAL HENRY LEE TO C. C. LEE.

"NASSAU, *Sept.* 3, 1817.

"MY DEAR CARTER,—I wrote a few days since to the care of Mr. Goddard to tell you that my only chance of getting to the United States is in a vessel destined to Savannah, to sail in twelve or fifteen days. I conclude to embrace the opportunity, malgre season and distance from home. Relieved much from my long torture of pain, my mind is refreshed, and I can calmly meet difficulty. You must write from Boston, under cover to Mr. Joseph Thorne, merchant, in Savannah; and detail to me your expenses, and the sum necessary to defray them. * * * Avoid debt, the sink of mental power and the subversion of independence, which draws into debasement even virtue, in appearance certainly, if not in reality. 'A man ought not only to be virtuous in reality, but he must also always appear so;' thus said to me the great Washington. I have the following books for you, to be sent only when I have a sure conveyance:— 'Newton's Principia,' 3 vols.; 'Asiatic Researches,' 5 vols.; and 'Quintius Curtius,' the historian of Alexander Magnus; valuable, all of them, and will I trust be prized by you, not because they come from me, but from their own superior worth. I hope and beg, you will read well and speak better the French language. * * * Begin a grammar; a dictionary and two hours per day will give you the reading; a French family's acquaintance will give you the speaking. Farewell, my ever dear son.

"H. LEE."

GENERAL HENRY LEE TO C. C. LEE.

"NEW PROVIDENCE, NASSAU, *Nov.* 20, 1817.

"I am unfortunately still here, as I have never been able to obtain a passage with a cabin to myself, which my disease, much mended as I am, still demands; and I shall be obliged to get a small vessel, like John Randall's at Stratford, and pass the ocean. To freight this will cost little; and to get the cabin entirely, I shall be forced to go to the expense of freighting. While here, I indulge every hour I am able in reading, more with a view of yours, Smith's, and Robert's good than any satisfaction to myself. * * * You have been told that I have for you 'Newton's Principia.' This great and good man, like man, has erred evidently in some important facts, in which a great and good Frenchman has set him right,— St. Pierre. His book has been promised me; if the promise is fulfilled you shall have both. Newton had the great honor to put down all previous systems of philosophy from Aristotle to his own time; by introducing a system founded on observation, and experiments geometrically demonstrated, giving to the sun its pre-eminence which Pythagoras had established. Sir Isaac admits not hypothesis; but proceeds analytically and synthetically, deducing from the appearances of nature, the forces of nature; and thence demonstrating the character of the rest. He was the first who showed the existence of gravity, although its cause remains hidden; and has made it the foundation of his wonderful system, the principle of which others before him had suspected. Sir Isaac has not only been an eminent benefactor to the human mind in opening to its view the frame of the universe and the action of all the primary parts, but by so doing has contributed more than any other man, to knock down fate and confirm Providence, destroying atheism and upholding theism; thus crowning his labors by enabling and guiding man to limit his misery and extend his happiness. Indeed, the man must be blind, who, after understanding Sir Isaac's works, cannot discover the infinite goodness and wisdom of Almighty God; and he must be a brute or an idiot, who can hesitate in believing that the Deity is the Alpha and Omega of the universe, the Ruler and Benefactor of all beings, to whom we men can only be acceptable by the practice of virtue and abhorrence of vice. I tire, my dear Carter, and must stop.

" A week has passed; I seize an hour comparatively free from pain to resume, and will give specimens of ·St. Pierre, whose morality I admire as much as I do his luminous correction of philosophic error. He is a profound and devoted servant of the Most High, in all his labors when pointed to natural or moral philosophy; and he greatly honors the great Newton.

"Admiration is not a relation of the understanding or a perception of our reason ; but a sentiment of the soul, which arises in us from a certain, indescribable instinct of Deity, at sight of extraordinary objects, and from the very mysteriousness in which they are involved. All the works of nature have the wants of men for their end, as all the sentiments of men have God for their principle. The final intentions of nature have given to man the knowledge of all her works, as it is the instinct of Deity which has rendered man superior to the laws of nature. It is this instinct, which differently modified by the passions, engages the inhabitants of Russia to bathe in the ices of the Neva, during the severest cold of winter, as well as the natives of Bengal, in the waters of the Ganges ; which, under the same latitude, has rendered women slaves in the Philippine Islands, and despots in the Isle of Formosa ; which makes men effeminate in the Moluccas, and intrepid in the Macaria ; and which forms in one and the same city, tyrants, citizens, and slaves. ' The sentiment of Deity is the first mover of the human heart.' St. Pierre gives to the word ' sentiment ' a fuller meaning than I am used to give, and I vainly have struggled to find it out. Do so, for then this high and novel first-principle of man will be understood, and the sequent system can be fairly judged of. It charms me. ' It was the instinct of the Deity which first assembled men together, and which became the basis of the religion and of the laws whereby their union was to be cemented. On this, virtue found support in proposing to itself the imitation of the Divinity ; not only by the exercise of the arts and sciences, which the Greeks for this effect denominated the petty virtues, but in the result of the Divine power and intelligence which is beneficence. It consisted in efforts made upon ourselves for the good of man, in the view of pleasing God only. It gives to man the sentiment of his own excellence by inspiring him with the contempt of terrestrial and transient enjoyments, and with a desire of things celestial and immortal. It was this sublime attraction which exalted courage to the rank of virtue, and which made man intrepidly advance to meet death amidst the many anxieties to preserve life. * * Religion places all on a level. She humbles the head of the mighty by showing the vanity of their power, and she raises up the head of the unfortunate by disclosing the prospect of immortality.' * * * ' If I manifest a disregard for religion, I enfeeble the hope which sustains us under the pressure of misery.'

" I must quit my pen, and I leave you in good company, two of the most virtuous, as well as learned, of philosophers. Be like them, virtuous, and as far as you can, like them, useful. * * * I seldom have an opportunity to write to your dear mother,—often to you. Tell me how she is, and how my sweet girls and good boys are. Farewell, my son.

" H. LEE."

GENERAL HENRY LEE TO C. C. LEE.

"NASSAU, January 24, 1818.

" MY DEAR SON,—

> ' Learn from yon orient shell to love thy foe
> And store with pearls the hand that brings thee woe :
> Free, like you rock, from base vindictive pride,
> Emblaze with gems the wrist that rends thy side ;
> Mark, where yon tree rewards the stony shower
> With fruit nectareous or the balmy flower ;
> All nature cries aloud, shall man do less
> Than heal the smiter and the railer bless ?'

" Where, my dear Carter, think you, the above delightfully-conveyed cardinal moral axiom was indited ? In Arabia, and by a Mussulman, the poet of Shiraz—the immortal Hafiz. The two great maxims of right taught by our religion were, happily for the human race, ages before our era, the themes of enlightened legislators. Thales, Pittacus, and many others in Greece taught the doctrines of morality, which these maxims inculcate, and repeated them almost in our words : ' Do unto others as you would they should do unto you,' and instead of returning evil for evil confer benefits on those who injure you. Long before their day, and before the Christian era some centuries, Confucius taught the same doctrines. The beautiful Arab couplet written three centuries before Christ announces the duty of a good man, even in the moment of destruction, not only to forgive but to benefit the destroyer ; as the sandal-tree, in the instant of its overthrow sheds perfume on the axe that fells it. The verse of Vadi, of the same day, represents the return of good for good as a slight reciprocity ; and enjoins the virtuous man to confer benefits on his injurer. Why these ancient scraps ? only to bring you in love with oriental books, the store-houses of human knowledge obscured,—too much obscured for our happiness by their fashion of conveying wise precepts in allegory. * * * In all my letters I urge you to habits of virtue in mind and body as the only path to happiness in this life, and as the most probable security to happiness in another world. But, my dear Carter, what is happiness? *Hoc opus, hic labor est.* Peace of mind based on piety to Almighty God, unconscious innocence of conduct with good will to man; health of body, health of mind, and prosperity in our vocation; a sweet, affectionate wife; *sana mens in corpore sano;* children devoted to truth, honor, right, and utility, with love and respect to their parents; and faithful and warm-hearted friends, in a country politically and religiously free;—this is my definition. We see it around us in various instances; but as Solon, the Athenian legislator, told the king of Lydia, upon being asked, if he did not reckon him happy, ' Wait till you die,' deducing as a positive truth that such are the changes of mortal condition as long as life continues, that sentence must be suspended until death. You know the last scene of the king, and never can forget Cyrus's magnanimity.

"Weeks have passed since the above; such is your poor father's condition. Now it is Shrove-Tuesday, and to-morrow will be Ash-Wednesday. To-day men, women, lads, and lasses are all with joy, singing, kissing, and dancing. To-morrow our holy religion reminds us of death, and dust to dust,—two days in each year giving to Christians the enjoyments congenial to nature, and reminding them of their humility and nothingness. * * *

"*February 9th,* I resume my pen, and add more scraps from oriental authors, showing that the immortality of the soul has been generally believed by all nations from our first records of man; so also has been the belief in an Almighty God; two truths so fixed in the mind of man, that I cannot believe there ever was, or ever will be, an atheist, unless some poor being unsound in mind. Homer, Virgil, Lucan, and other poets recognize both principles, as do Pythagoras, Plato, Empedocles, and other ancient philosophers. Cæsar and Strabo tell us that the Greeks believed the soul imperishable. Of the Indian Brahmins, Strabo quotes from their creed as follows: ' We are to think of this life as of the state of a child before it is born, and of death as a birth to that which is truly life and happiness to wise men.' Herodotus, concerning the Egyptians, says especially, they believed in the immortality of the soul; and Tacitus in his history, speaking of the Jews, ' they buried, rather than burned their bodies, after the manner of the Egyptians; they having the same regard and persuasion concerning the dead.' Mata and Socinus writing of the Thracians, mention, ' some of them think the souls of those who die, return again ; others that they do not die, but are made more happy.' As to our God, when every thing we see, hear, or know, assures us of His real existence, it is ridiculous to dilate on the subject; I will therefore only recite the opinions of the wise men of antiquity, to show how they concur with Moses and the learned of modern times. Sophocles says:

> 'There is really but one God,
> The maker of Heaven and Earth
> And sea and wind.'

So sing Homer, Hesiod, and Ovid, &c. Maximus Tyrius, on the same subject, says : ' Great as is the discord, debate, and confusion among men, the whole world agree in this one opinion, that God is the sole Father of all ; but there are many other gods, his sons, who share in his government.' * * * Confucius, Plato, Varro, Cicero, and hundreds of others, hand down the same opinion ; though pagans, and admitting secondary gods, one Supreme they avow as the Almighty Father. * * *

"I send this letter to Mr. Goddard, and with it two books for you, worthy of your best attention ; one of them the inimitable Cervantes. At length I get off. The ship Betsey is in harbor, taking in her cargo, and is destined to some Southern port; which, not yet decided. In her, I go; and shall be landed, I dare say, as soon as you get this letter. I fear you will be puzzled to read it, but it cannot be altered by one afflicted as I am daily.

"God bless my dear Carter.　　　　　　　　　　"H. LEE."

Thus ended these letters of love and wisdom, in establishing the sublime doctrine of the immortality of the soul; and soon after, ended the life of the writer. Instead of landing at Savannah, he only reached Cumberland Island, on the coast of Georgia, where he was received by Mrs. Shaw, the daughter of General Greene, at the last home of his beloved commander.

This lady met in Boston the son to whom these letters were addressed, in the autumn following the death of his father, and gave him an account of his last moments. One incident is worth recording, as showing how his veneration for Washington and his fondness for expressing it, clung to him to the last. "A surgical operation was proposed, as offering some hope of prolonging his life ; but he replied, that the eminent physician to whose skill and care during his sojourn in the West Indies he was so much indebted, had disapproved a resort to the proposed operation. The surgeon in attendance still urging it, his patient put an end to the discussion, by saying : 'My dear sir, were the great Washington alive, and here, and joining you in advocating it, I would still resist.' "

After this he sank rapidly ; and his last effort at communication with this world, was to send a message, which, after many attempts, he failed to make comprehensible. " Mrs. Shaw said she could only gather that it was sent to some one of the name of Carter. It may reasonably be conjectured that its object was to impress upon him with his latest breath the lessons he had been so earnestly inculcating with his pen, and that thus he faded from the world, like the sun from the horizon, in a last lingering radiation of life and love." It was doubtless a consolation to him, as he could not reach his home, to have his last hours soothed by the tender care of the daughter of one he so much revered, and to know that his remains would be placed by his side. He died, March 25, 1818.

A ship of war being anchored near, her captain and crew assisted at the funeral, and paid all the honors that could be given by the American flag and those guns which had lately won for it so much glory on the ocean.

University Publishing Company

MEMOIRS OF THE WAR

SOUTHERN DEPARTMENT OF THE UNITED STATES.

CHAPTER I.

INTRODUCTORY.

THE determination of the mind to relinquish the soft scenes of tranquil life for the rough adventures of war, is generally attended with the conviction that the act is laudable; and with a wish that its honorable exertions should be faithfully transmitted to posterity. These sentiments lead to the cultivation of virtue; and the effect of the one is magnified by the accomplishment of the other. In usefulness to society, the difference is inconsiderable between the conduct of him who performs great achievements, and of him who records them; for short must be the remembrance, circumscribed the influence of patriotic exertions and heroic exploits, unless the patient historian retrieve them from oblivion, and hold them up conspicuously to future ages. "Sæpè audivi, Q. Maximum, P. Scipionem, præterea civitatis nostræ præclaros viros, solitos ita dicere, cùm majorum imagines intuerentur, vehementissimè sibi animum ad virtutem accendi. Scilicet non ceram illam, neque figuram tantam vim in sese habere; sed memoriâ rerum gestarum eam flammam egregiis viris in pectore crescere, neque priùs sedari, quàm virtus eorum famam atque gloriam adæquaverit."*—*Sall Bell. Jugur.*

---

* "Often have I heard, that Quintus Maximus, Publius Scipio, and other renowned men of our commonwealth, used to say, that whenever they beheld the images of their ancestors, they felt their minds vehemently excited to virtue. It could not be the wax or the marble that possessed this power; but the recollection of their great actions kindled a generous flame in their breasts, not to be quelled till they also by virtue had acquired equal fame and glory."

Regretting, as we all do, that not one of the chief actors in our camp or cabinet, and indeed very few of our fellow-citizens, have attempted to unfold the rise, or to illustrate the progress and termination of our revolution, I have been led to this my undertaking with a hope of contributing, in some degree, to repair the effects of this much lamented indifference.   With this view I am about to write memoirs of the Southern campaigns, being that part of the war with which I am best acquainted, and which in its progress and issue materially contributed to our final success, and to the enlargement of our military fame. Desirous of investing the reader with a full and clear understanding of the operations to be described, I shall commence these memoirs at the beginning of the third year of the war; for the principal events which occurred thereafter, laid the foundation of the change in the enemy's conduct, and turned the tide and fury of the conflict from the North to the South.

When I first engaged in this undertaking, many of my military comrades, capable and willing to contribute their aid to the fulfilment of my design, were living; whose minute knowledge of various scenes, all of which they saw, in some of which they led, would have rendered it peculiarly interesting and valuable.   After postponing, as is common to man, what for various reasons ought not to have been delayed, I have experienced in my progress abundant cause for self-reproach ; since in many instances I have been deprived of this important assistance, which no effort or application has been able fully to supply. Discouraged by this privation, I should, though reluctantly, have receded from my purpose, had not the injurious consequences of my dilatoriness been repaired in a measure by the animated and friendly exertions of the few survivors among my martial companions.   To these individuals I owe a heavy debt of personal gratitude; and should the following sheets be deemed worthy of general approbation, to their ready and unwearied assistance, more than to the author's care and diligence, may be justly ascribed the pleasing result.   I have, nevertheless, been compelled to abridge considerably my first design; not having been able to obtain the documents necessary to its full accomplishment.

It was my intention to present the public, not with a narrative of the Southern operations only, but with the life of Major-General Greene, our distinguished leader.   The two subjects appeared to be closely connected; and the latter is strongly claimed by my intimate knowledge of the military plans and measures of that illustrious man, by the homage due to his superior virtue, and the grateful remembrance, which I hold in common with all who served under him, of his benignity and justice.

Apprehending that longer delay might eventuate in leaving altogether unexecuted my design, I resolved for the present to confine myself to these memoirs, deferring to some future day, or to more adequate abilities, the completion of my original plan.

CHAPTER II.

The campaign of 1777 and forces employed.—Its termination by the surrender of Burgoyne.

THE campaign projected by the British for seventy-seven, announced in its commencement a system portentous of much evil to the United States. It contemplated the annihilation of resistance in all the country between the lakes and Albany, undisturbed possession of the Hudson River (thus severing the Union), and the conquest of Pennsylvania, whose capital (Philadelphia) was the metropolis of the American States. This extensive plan of operations was supported by coextensive means.*

Lieutenant-General Burgoyne, a leader of renown, conducting the British army in the North, undertook his part with zeal and gallantry. Entering from Canada, he pressed forward with impetuosity. Ticonderoga, with its various dependencies, fell without a

---

* British force under Sir William Howe.	In 1776.	American force under General Washington.
August, 24,000		16,000
November, 26,900		4,500
December, 27,700		3,300
	In 1777.	
March, 27,000		4,500
June, 30,000		8,000

Force under Sir William Howe when he landed at Elkton, horse, foot, and artillery, amounted in toto, to 18,000.

Force under General Washington at the battle of Brandywine, including militia, 15,000.

At which time the British force in Rhode Island and New York, under Sir Henry Clinton, was 12,000.

And the American force under General Putnam at West Point, &c., exclusive of militia, which he was authorized to call to him as he chose, from the States of Connecticut, New York, and New Jersey, 2,000.

Force under Lieutenant-General Burgoyne, excluding Canadians and Indians, 7,000.

Force under Major-General Gates (Continentals), 9,000
 "   "   "   "   (Militia),   4,129

                              Total,   13,129
                    See Appendix, A and B.

blow; and the victorious army, pursuing its·success with ardor gained repeated advantages over our broken and dispirited troops, commanded by Major-General St. Clair. This promising beginning did not long continue. Major-General Gates, bred to arms in the British school, and much respected by Congress, was appointed to the chief command in the Northern Department. His reputation produced confidence; our vanquished army was reanimated; the East poured forth her hardy sons; and chosen troops were detached by the commander-in-chief from the main body. Gates soon found himself at the head of a sufficient force to face his enemy, whose advance had been fortunately retarded by the usual incumbrances of European armies, increased by the uncommon difficulties which the face of the country presented, improved as they had been by the skill, diligence, and zeal of Major-General Schuyler, then commanding in that quarter. This delay reduced the provisions of the enemy; and the first attempt to replenish them terminated in the destruction of a considerable body of Germans, detached on that service, under Lieutenant-Colonel Baum.* Brigadier Starke, at the head of a force, mostly militia, attacked this corps on the heights of Wal-loomsack, and destroyed it : a dreadful blow to the assailing army, and the mirror of its future fate. Burgoyne, however, persuaded that victory alone could retrieve him, sought for battle with perti-nacity and keenness. The American leader was not disinclined to the appeal, apprehending a serious movement * from New York to

---

* Brigadier-General Starke had fortunately reached Bennington with a body of militia from New Hampshire, where was established a depot of provisions for the use of the Northern army, at the time Lieutenant-Colonel Baum made his appearance with 500 Germans. Starke, uniting his militia to the remains (200) of a Continental regiment under Colonel Warner, judiciously decided to strike Baum before he could complete intrenchments, begun for the purpose of strength-ening his position. The assault was immediate and vigorous; and the enemy was completely routed, most of the detachment being killed, wounded, and taken. Starke's conduct was not only justified by his success, but by the disclosure that a re-enforcement under Lieutenant-Colonel Brecknam was hastening to join Baum. The united force under Starke amounted to 2,000.

† This important operation was conducted by Sir Henry Clinton, second in command of the British army. He left New York early in October at the head of 3,000 men ; and by masterly manœuvres entirely deceived General Putnam, the American commander. On the 6th he carried the Forts Clinton and Mont-gomery by storm, which produced the immediate evacuation of the Forts Inde-pendence and Constitution. Thus with an inferior force did the British general in a few days dispossess us of the Hudson River, believed to have been in a condition impregnable to any force then at the enemy's disposal. The military conduct of Sir Henry during this expedition, carried with it manifesta-tions of genius far above the common order ; but he stained his laurels, so gallantly won, by the cruel conflagration of the defenceless town of Esopus, then the depot of women and children.

dislodge him from his posts on the Hudson, and to occupy Albany, his place of deposit. Two actions were fought, in which great courage was displayed. Both armies felt the magnitude of the stake; every officer and every soldier acted as if on his single arm the fate of the day depended. The slaughter was great, especially of the British : the glory was equal; to the enemy, for having sustained himself through two long and sternly contested battles against superior numbers; to America, for having with raw troops, chiefly undisciplined militia, checked a veteran army, conducted by a gallant and experienced chief, seconded with skill and ardor by his officers, and heroically supported by his soldiers. The second action was speedily followed by the surrender of the British force.* Conditions more favorable than the relative situation of the armies authorized were granted by the conqueror; who in this act, as in all its appurtenances, manifested an immutable attachment to the claims of humanity. Conduct so estimable gave new lustre to the splendid victory, where heroism was adorned by clemency ; illustrating the edifying truth, that glory is inseparable from virtue.

General Burgoyne in his official report bestowed great praise on his troops; but especially on the able and active support derived from the Generals Philips, Reidezel, and Frazier, the last of whom fell in the second action, lamented and admired. Brigadier Arnold and Colonel Morgan, among a host of distinguished associates, took the lead on the side of America, and were particularly regarded by Congress and the nation, in the burst of applause which resounded throughout the United States on the happy conclusion of the Northern campaign.

The reception of the rival leaders, by their respective governments, was as different as had been their fortune in battle. Gates was enrolled among the most celebrated heroes of the world, by Congress, country, and army; while Burgoyne was not permitted to present himself to his sovereign, but, by the injustice of the very

---

* The expedition of Sir Henry Clinton up the North River no doubt induced General Gates to admit, in the convention, the article which stipulated that the captive army should not serve against the United States until exchanged, and should be permitted in the mean time to return to England. Nevertheless the army of Burgoyne never did return to England, Congress having for the first time stifled the fair claims of its enemy, under color of pretenses as frivolous as was the detention of the army unjustifiable. There was a very great disproportion of force. Gates' army consisted of 9,000 Continental troops, and 4,060 militia; while that under Burgoyne amounted to 5,700 by the official statement of the number surrendered, which of course includes persons of every description. The British general rated his fighting force at 3,500, and that of Gates may be fairly estimated, including militia, at 8,500.

cabinet to whose former preference he owed his elevation, was deprived of all the rewards of his long service, and died in disgrace, *at court*, adored by his gallant troops—the companions, the witnesses of his toil and peril, and esteemed by those of his countrymen who could sensibly discriminate between incidental misfortune and deserved infamy.

Where is the general who ever more prodigally risked his life in his country's cause than did the unfortunate Burgoyne? where the army which more bravely executed its leader's will, than did that which he conducted? what danger was avoided? what effort unessayed? what privation not submitted to? what difficulties not encountered? But all terminated in disaster; and the army, from whose prowess so much was expected, yielded to its equal in courage, to its superior in number.

To be unfortunate is to be disgraced: imperfect man! infatuated government! The Roman senate did not thus think; that illustrious body of sages examined the intention; the exertion, in conjunction with the issue, and made up their decision accordingly. Vanquished generals have been reanimated by their unvanquished senate, who, ever true to itself, was just to others. See Varro thanked after the loss of the battle of Cannæ, for not having despaired of the commonwealth. See the great Fabius, although for a time obscured by the machinations of detractors, hailed in a long succession of the highest confidence, "the shield of his country." But a Roman senate is too rarely to be found in the annals of power.

CHAPTER III.

Sir Wm. Howe sails from New York to the Chesapeake.—Washington marches to the same neighborhood.—Battle of Brandywine.

WHILE this severe and eventful contest occupied the armies of the North, Washington patiently waited the development of Sir William Howe's intention. This officer, commanding in chief the British forces, had left New York with 18,000 men, completely appointed and equipped, under convoy of a powerful fleet directed by his brother Lord Howe.

Weighing from Sandy-Hook, in July, the fleet steered for the South, which General Washington supposed to be the intended course; but, lest it might have been a feint to draw the American army frn from the Hudson, with a view of returning with the first fair wiad and seizing West Point, the American Thermopylæ,* washed by that river; Washington proceeded no farther south than to Bucks County, in Pennsylvania, sufficiently near, for his timely interposition, should Sir William Howe suddenly change his direction. There, after a lapse of five weeks, he received information that the fleet had entered the Chesapeake, and was standing up that bay. He instantly decamped, and took a position on White-Clay Creek, in the county of New Castle, State of Delaware, while his light troops extended to the vicinity of Elkton, in the State of Maryland; below which, at Cecil Old Court-House, the enemy disembarked

---

* Properly so termed, whether we regard its natural difficulties, or its military importance. The highlands begin their ascent a little above King's Ferry on the Hudson, forty miles up the river from New York, communicating between Stony and Verplanck's Point. In Pennsylvania and Maryland the same ridge of mountains is known by the name of the North Mountain, being the only one which passes through all the Northern States. Continuing south, the Alleghany, misnamed the back-bone of Anglican America, absolutely sinks, before it reaches the southern limits of Virginia, into the North Mountain, or *Blue Ridge*. This spot, of precipice linked to precipice, now and then separated by a fissure admitting the pass of men in single file, rugged, sharp, and steep, was selected by Washington to hold safe the possession of the upper Hudson, indispensable to the free egress and regress between the North and the South; without which military resistance could not be upheld. This mountainous region is computed to be twenty miles in breadth, alike rugged and impenetrable on both sides of the river near its margin. About midway, on its eastern bank, is Anthony's Nose, 363 yards perpendicularly high; and opposite to it, 123 feet above the level of the river, is a spur of the mountain, with table-land on its summit sufficient for the erection of works, separated from another spur by Preploap's Kill or Creek (kill is the Dutch word for creek), presenting the same facility. Both these tops were fortified: the first called Fort Clinton, after the respectable and zealous governor of the State of New York; and the last named Montgomery, after the hero of Quebec.

Anthony's Nose, in its first step of ascent, is washed by Peekskill, which falls into the Hudson, on the northern banks of which was erected Fort Independence; and six or seven miles above the Nose, toward the declivity of the highlands, is Fort Constitution. These were our land defences.

In the river, between the water projection of the spur on whose summit stood Fort Clinton, and the base of Anthony's Nose, here perpendicular, was sunk a boom of mountain timber fastened together by all the ligaments of art, ponderous and durable. In front of which was affixed to the rocky base of the mountain, on each side of the river, an iron chain sixty tons in weight, whose every link was two inches and a half square, and which in its sweep across the river presented its point to the enemy, in the channel. Behind the boom rode two frigates, two galleys, and a sloop of war, commensurate with the theatre of action. Thus were we prepared by water.

All the defiles, narrow and difficult as they were by nature, were made more difficult by the rolling of rocks into them, and by felling trees across them, over and through which the assailant must clamber and creep for many miles before he could present himself against our works.

This assemblage of defences is known among us by the designation of West Point, and constituted the primary object of Washington's care during the war.

on the 28th of August. With very little delay, Sir William advanced to Elkton, whence he moved to his left, preferring the upper route, where the water-courses were fordable; where, from the presumed security of the farmers, provisions were more readily procurable; and where he avoided those artificial impediments known to be prepared for him on the lower route. As soon as this movement was ascertained by Washington, he broke up from White Clay Creek, and, turning to his right, took post on the eastern side of the Brandywine, fronting Chadsford, where he waited the approach of his foe. Sir William continued to advance by steady marches, holding up the strength of his troops, whose valor, he foresaw with pleasure, would be tested in a few days.

Having reached Kennet's Square on the 11th of September, not more than six or seven miles from Chadsford, Howe advanced in two columns;* the right inferior in force, and charged with the care of the baggage, provisions, &c., under the direction of Lieutenant-General Knyphausen, took the road to Chadsford, with orders to delay passing the Brandywine until the commencement of the battle by the left should announce itself. This other column, made up of the best corps, and consisting of nearly two-thirds of the whole force, commanded by Sir William Howe in person, having under him Lord Cornwallis, diverged to the left, and making an extensive circuit, crossed the two branches of the Brandywine; when turning down the river it approached the American right. The battle

---

* Washington was quickly informed of the separation of the enemy's columns, as he was subsequently informed not only of its continuance, but that the left column was making a very circuitous sweep. Persuaded of the fact, he wisely determined to pass the Brandywine with his whole force and strike at Knyphausen. In the very act of giving his orders to this effect, Colonel Bland, of the Virginia horse, brought him intelligence which very much obscured, if it did not contradict, the previous information; and the original judicious decision was abandoned. Colonel Bland was noble, sensible, honorable, and amiable; but never intended for the department of military intelligence. The third regiment of Virginia, first Mercer's, who fell covered with glory at Princeton; next Weedon's, at this time Marshall's, exhibited an example worthy of itself, its country, and its leader. Already high in reputation from the gallant stand made by one battalion under Major Leitch on York Island, when supporting the brave Colonel Knowlton, in the first check given to the enemy, flushed with his victory of Long Island, in which check Knowlton was killed and Leitch mortally wounded, having received three balls successively through his body, at the head of his victorious battalion; from its firmness on our retreat through New Jersey: from its intrepidity at Trenton, and its valor at Princeton, it now surpassed its pristine fame. Our loss amounted to 300 killed, 600 wounded, and 400 prisoners, chiefly wounded. Major-General de la Fayette and Brigadier Woodward were wounded. Sir William Howe stated in his official report the British loss to be only 100 killed and 400 wounded. The vanquished army will always suffer most.

soon began in this quarter; and quickly afterward Knyphausen forcing Brigadier Maxwell, who commanded the light infantry stationed on the western side of the Brandywine, advanced upon our left. Three small detachments, commanded by the Lieutenant-Colonels Parker, Heth, and Simms, of the Virginia line, were early in the morning separately and advantageously posted by the brigadier contiguous to the road, some distance in his front; and Captain Porterfield, with a company of infantry, preceded these parties with orders to deliver his fire as soon as he should meet the van of the enemy, and then to fall back. This service was handsomely performed by Porterfield, and produced the desired effect. The British van pressed forward rapidly and incautiously, until it lined the front of the detachment commanded by Lieutenant-Colonel Simms, who poured in a close and destructive fire, and then retreated to the light corps. The leading officer of the enemy was killed; and the detachment suffered severely. The contest which began on our right spread to our left, and was warm in some parts of the American line; and many of the corps distinguished themselves. The most conspicuous were the brigades of Wayne and Weedon, and the third regiment of Virginia, commanded by Colonel Marshall;* to which, with the artillery directed by Colonel Proctor of Pennsylvania, much praise was given. Of these the third regiment stood pre-eminent, part of Woodford's brigade: it occupied the right of the American line, and being advanced to a small eminence some little distance in front, for the purpose of holding safe that flank, it received the first shock of the foe. One column moved upon it in front, while a second struck at its left. Cut off from co-operation by the latter movement, it bravely sustained itself against superior numbers, never yielding one inch of ground, and expending thirty rounds a man, in forty-five minutes. It was now ordered to fall back upon Woodford's right, which was handsomely accomplished by Colonel Marshall, although deprived of half his officers, where he renewed the sanguinary contest. The regiment, having been much reduced by previous service, did not amount to more than a battalion; but one field officer, the colonel, and four captains were with it. Marshall escaped unhurt, although his horse received two balls. Of the captains, two only, Blackwell and Peyton, remained fit for duty. Chilton was killed, and Lee mortally wounded. The subalterns suffered in proportion. Lieutenants White, Cooper, and Ensign Peyton were killed; Lieutenants Mercer, Blackwell, and

---

* Father of Chief-Justice Marshall.

Peyton, wounded. Thirteen non-commissioned officers and sixty privates fell.

The opposing enemy was severely handled; and the leading officer of one of the columns, with several others, was killed. The action closed with the day, in our defeat.

CHAPTER IV.

Washington advances to meet the enemy.—The armies separated by a tempest.—Sir Wm. Howe moves toward Philadelphia.—Narrow escape of Hamilton and Lee.

WASHINGTON retired during the night to Chester ; * whence he decamped the next morning. Taking the route to Philadelphia and crossing the Schuylkill, he moved up that river, halted one day at Germantown, then recrossed it near Swedesford, and gained the Lancaster road. On the 15th he advanced to meet the enemy, who, after three days' repose on the field of battle, quitted the Brandywine, pointing his march to the upper fords of the Schuylkill. A violent storm, accompanied by a deluge of rain, stopped the renewal of battle on the following day, near the Warren tavern on the road from Philadelphia to Lancaster; for which the two armies were arrayed, and in which the van troops were engaged. Separated by the tempest, the American general exerted himself to replenish his ammunition, destroyed by the fall of water, from the insecurity of our cartouch boxes and artillery tumbrels;† while the British general pursued his route across the Schuylkill, directing his course to the American metropolis. Contiguous to the enemy's route lay some mills stored with flour, for the use of the American army.

---

* It is worthy of remark that Howe was but eighteen miles ‡ from Philadelphia ; and Washington, who reached Chester on the night of the battle was sixteen miles distant, the Delaware on his right, the Schuylkill in his front, and his enemy on his left. Was it not surprising that the British general did not perceive and seize the advantage so plainly before him, by a forced march as soon as his troops had snatched food and rest ?

† Among the many and afflicting disadvantages imposed on the American general, the insufficiency of the implements covering our powder, was not the least. There existed another ground of disparity, which continued nearly to the end of the war—inferiority of arms. Some of our musketry were without bayonets, and not a single brigade had muskets of the same calibre ; by which means, a corps expending its ammunition, could not use that of an adjoining corps. The latter deficiency is imputable to our poverty, as arms in that stage of the war could only be procured by purchase from abroad ; but the former is justly to be ascribed to the criminal supineness of our contractors, as we abounded in leather and good workmen.

‡ More probably twenty-five miles.—NOTE BY THE ED.

Their destruction was deemed necessary by the commander-in-chief; and his aid-de-camp, Lieutenant-Colonel Hamilton,* attended by Captain Lee,† with a small party of his troop of horse, were dispatched in front of the enemy, with the order of execution. The mill, or mills, stood on the bank of the Schuylkill. Approaching, you descend a long hill leading to a bridge over the mill-race. On the summit of this hill two vedettes were posted; and soon after the party reached the mills, Lieutenant-Colonel Hamilton took possession of a flat-bottomed boat for the purpose of transporting himself and his comrades across the river, should the sudden approach of the enemy render such retreat necessary. In a little time this precaution manifested his sagacity: the fire of the vedettes announced the enemy's appearance. The dragoons were ordered instantly to embark. Of the small party, four with the lieutenant-colonel jumped into the boat, the van of the enemy's horse in full view, pressing down the hill in pursuit of the two vedettes. Captain Lee, with the remaining two, took the decision to regain the bridge, rather than detain the boat.

Hamilton was committed to the flood, struggling against a violent current, increased by the recent rains; while Lee put his safety on the speed and soundness of his horse.

The attention of the enemy being engaged by Lee's push for the bridge, delayed the attack upon the boat for a few minutes, and thus afforded to Hamilton a better chance of escape. The two vedettes preceded Lee as he reached the bridge; and himself with the two dragoons safely passed it, although the enemy's front section emptied their carbines and pistols ‡ at the distance of ten or twelve paces. Lee's apprehension for the safety of Hamilton continued to increase, as he heard volleys of carbines discharged upon the boat, which were returned by guns singly and occasionally. He trembled for the probable issue; and as soon as the pursuit ended, which did not long continue, he dispatched a dragoon to the commander-in-chief, describing, with feelings of anxiety, what had passed, and his sad presage. His letter was scarcely perused by Washington before Hamilton himself appeared; and ignorant of the contents of the

---

* The celebrated Alexander Hamilton.
† Henry Lee, afterward Lieutenant-Colonel Lee, of the Legion cavalry.
‡ The fire of cavalry is at best innocent, especially in quick motion, as was then the case. The strength and activity of the horse, the precision and celerity of evolution, the adroitness of the rider, boot-top to boot-top, and the keen edge of the sabre, with fitness of ground and skill in the leader, constitute their vast power so often decisive in the day of battle.

paper in the general's hand, renewed his attention to the ill-boding separation, with the probability that his friend Lee had been cut off, inasmuch as instantly after he turned for the bridge, the British horse reached the mill, and commenced their operations upon the boat.

Washington with joy relieved his fears, by giving to his aid-de camp the captain's letter.

Thus did fortune smile upon these two young soldiers, already united in friendship, which ceased only with life. Lieutenant-Colonel Hamilton escaped unhurt; but two of his four dragoons, with one of the boatmen, were wounded.

CHAPTER V.

Sir Wm. Howe marches to Philadelphia.—Cornwallis at Germantown.—Washington moves to Skippack Creek.—Battle of Germantown.

SIR WILLIAM HOWE, having passed the Schuylkill on the 23d, pursued by easy marches his route to Philadelphia.

On the 26th he took a position in the village of Germantown, seven or eight miles distant from the city, which was on the follow ing day possessed by Lord Cornwallis with one division of the army The position of Germantown has some advantages, mingled with many disadvantages. Its right is accessible with ease; and its centre presents no obstruction from superiority of ground to the assailant. Its chief, if not sole advantage, consisted in the safety of the left, and its proximity to Philadelphia, which city it was necessary to secure. A few miles more remote is Chestnut Hill, which Sir William might have occupied, and where he might have defied annoyance. This ground probably did not escape his observation; but it was not so near to Philadelphia, and, what was more to be regarded, too remote to permit him to give his undivided exertions toward the opening of the Delaware to his fleet, on whose propinquity depended the safety of his army.

The possession of Philadelphia, however anxiously desired, and highly rated by the British ministry, did not produce any of those advantageous results so confidently expected: nor indeed could the discriminating statesman have justly calculated upon extensive benefit from the achievement. The American nation is spread over a vast region; the great body of whose population live upon their farms, pursuing exclusively the occupations of agriculture. The loss of a town, though the first, is not felt by a people thus situated as it is in Europe, where whole countries resemble a continued village; and where the commercial and manufacturing interests have spread and ramified themselves to a considerable extent. However the loss of Philadelphia may have advanced the hopes of the British nation and government, it was slightly regarded by the States and Congress. This body of virtuous sages had discerned, by deep examination of the resources of the United States, that the nation's safety was not endangered by such fleeting occurrences; they placed, under God, their confidence in the fidelity of their fellow-citizens, in the courage of their armies, in the purity and wisdom of their general-in-chief, and in the fiscal ability of the nation:* on all of which they had a right to count with certainty, dreadfully as the last failed from the imbecility of the government.

Experience too had not withheld its chastening admonition. New York had before fallen, after having been held too long, from the influence which, in a free country, the public wish will ever possess even over the stern soldier. By obedience to the impulse flowing from this cause, the main body of the American army had been risked improvidently in the bold attempt to hold that city; and with much difficulty and much loss did the commander-in-chief extricate his army from the perils in which it had been consequently involved.†

Washington, following Sir William Howe with a view to place himself in a strong position at a convenient distance, ready to seize the first fit opportunity to measure swords with his antagonist, encamped on the western side of Skippack Creek, about sixteen miles from Germantown.

Both generals now turned their attention to the river impediments; the one, to open a passage for his fleet, which, after disembarking the army, had returned to sea, destined for the Delaware;

---

* The Congress was composed of deputies from the several States, and resembled more a diplomatic corps executing the will of the sovereign, than the sovereign commanding the execution of its will. It cannot excite surprise to the reflecting reader that our finances, under such auspices soon sunk.

† It is natural for the inhabitants of the same country to feel for the losses and injuries of any portion of their countrymen from the operations of a common enemy. This influence is accompanied by a disposition to criminate him who may be intrusted with the direction of the means of protection, sharpened by an indisposition to retribute those who lose by not receiving that protection however strongly called for by equity. To save New York, our second, if not first town, was the wish of all; and Washington, sharing in this feeling with his fellow-citizens, seems to have indulged his inclination too far upon this occasion. After various marches and manœuvres, and some loss, the erroneous plan was concluded by the fall of Fort Washington, with a numerous garrison, whose aid in the field could ill be spared.

the other, to impede, as long as was practicable, this much-desired junction. The American general had neglected no means within his power to stop the advance of the fleet, by preparing to maintain the defence of the various obstructions fixed in the channel of the river. With this view, two fortresses had been erected: one on Mud Island, denominated Fort Mifflin, after General Mifflin, since governor of Pennsylvania; and the other at Billingsport, on a point of land opposite to the lower line of chevaux-de-frise, of which three rows, formed of the heaviest timber, strengthened and pointed with iron, had been sunk across the channel. Billingsport was abandoned on the approach of a detachment under Colonel Stirling, sent to dislodge the American garrison; and a high bluff on the same side of the river, opposite to Mud Island, called Red Bank, was fortified, which with Fort Mifflin protected the two upper lines of chevaux-de-frise. Above, and near to these, was stationed our maritime force, consisting of row-galleys, floating batteries, fire ships, and rafts. The fortification of Red Bank consisted of an intrenchment and redoubt, called Fort Mercer, in commemoration of Brigadier-General Mercer, of Virginia, who died of his wounds received at the battle of Princeton, nobly sustaining his beloved commander in consummating the masterly movement made by him from his position in front of Lord Cornwallis at Trenton; by which single stroke was liberated nearly the whole State of New Jersey.

Officers were selected to command at these particular posts, high in the confidence of the commander-in-chief; and the naval force was committed to Commodore Hazelwood.

Great were the exertions of Sir William Howe to restore the navigation; and equally great were the efforts of Washington to hold it closed. Aware that the necessary operations to reduce the forts, Mercer and Mifflin, would call for considerable detachments from the British army, the American general continued in his position at Skippack Creek, within reach of his enemy, still encamped in the village of Germantown, patiently watching for the opportune moment to strike his meditated blow.

Cautious as Washington undoubtedly was, his caution was exceeded by his spirit of enterprise. He resembled Marcellus rather than Fabius, notwithstanding his rigid adherence to the Fabian policy during our war. Ardent and impetuous by nature, he had, nevertheless, subjected his passions to his reason; and could with facility, by his habitual self-control, repress his inclinations whenever his judgment forbade their indulgence; the whole tenor of his military life evinces uniform and complete self-command.

Province Island, close to the Pennsylvania shore, and contiguous to Mud Island, had been possessed by General Howe, with a view to hasten the fall of Fort Mifflin. This service, with other accompanying claims on his force, compelled him to draw rather improvidently from his main body, already weakened by his occupation of Philadelphia with a considerable detachment under Lord Cornwallis.

Understanding the condition of his foe, Washington decamped on the evening of the third of October, and, moving with secrecy and circumspection, attacked the enemy in his camp at Germantown, early in the morning of the fourth. The commencement was favorable; but, by the failure of punctual co-operation, and the brave stand of Colonel Musgrave with six companies of the fortieth regiment at Chew's house on the discomfiture of the British van, the flattering dawn was soon and sadly changed.

Washington was compelled to retire; which he effected with ease, the enemy showing no disposition to risk serious pursuit. Our loss was considerable, and unhappily augmented by the capture of the ninth Virginia regiment and its brave colonel, Matthews, who had, with a part of the sixth, led by Colonel Towles, victoriously pierced into the midst of the British army, where, gallantly contending unsupported, he was compelled to surrender.

Here, as at Brandywine, some of our corps greatly distinguished themselves. Major-General Sullivan's division, made up chiefly of the Maryland line, did honor to its general and its State; especially the brigade commanded by Conway, who led into battle on the right. Such partial efforts, however honorable to the particular troops, never can terminate in victory; this precious fruit is only to be plucked by the co-operating skill and courage of the whole body. The loss of the British in killed and wounded was nearly equal to that sustained by us, which did not exceed six hundred.*

The sudden change which we experienced, was attributed to the delay of the left column's entrance into action,† to the fog of the

---

* Besides the ninth regiment, but few prisoners were taken. The whole amounted to 400, which, added to our killed and wounded, gave a total of 1,000.

† The left column was under the order of Major-General Greene. Some attempts at that time were made to censure that officer; but they were too feeble to attract notice, when levelled at a general whose uniform conduct had already placed him high in the confidence of his chief and of the army.

morning which was uncommonly dense, and to the halt at Chew's
house. These certainly were the ostensible causes of the defeat;
and some of them lightly contributed to our disaster. A critical
examination of the operations of that day, however, will lead all
impartial inquirers to one conclusion; namely, that although the
fog withheld from us the important advantage resulting to assailing
troops from a clear view of the enemy's incipient measures to repel
the assault; and although the halt at Chew's house had cooled the
ardor which, at the beginning, success had infused into our soldiers;
yet these incidents could not have produced the disastrous change
in the fortune of the day.

But this turn must be ascribed to deeper causes: to the yet
imperfect discipline of the American army; to the broken spirit of
the troops, who, from day to day, and from month to month, had
been subjected to the most trying and strength-wasting privations,
through the improvidence or inability of government; to the inex-
perience of the tribe of generals; and to the complication of the
plan of assault—a complication said to have been unavoidable.

The halt at * Chew's house was taken after some deliberation,
as the writer well recollects; being for that day in the suite of the
commander-in-chief, with a troop of dragoons charged with duty
near his person.

Many junior officers, at the head of whom were Colonel Pickering and Lieutenant Colonel Hamilton, urged with zeal the propriety
of passing the house. Brigadier Knox opposed the measure with
earnestness, denouncing the idea of leaving an armed force in the
rear; and, being always high in the general's confidence, his opinion prevailed. A flag of truce was instantly dispatched to summon
the British colonel, while appropriate bodies of troops were prepared to compel his submission. As had been suggested, the summons was disregarded by Musgrave, who persevered in his judicious
defence; and Captain Smith, of the first Virginia regiment, deputy
adjutant-general, bearing the flag, fell with it waving in his hands.
Thirsting after military fame, and devoted to his country, he obeyed
with joy the perilous order; advanced through the deadly fire
pouring from the house, presuming that the sanctity of his flag

---

* Colonel Musgrave and the fortieth regiment received the cordial thanks of
Sir William Howe, and were held up to the army as an example for imitation.
Nor was the applause which was lavishly bestowed upon Musgrave, restricted
to America. It resounded in Great Britain; and the successful colonel received
a letter from the British monarch, expressing his sense of his meritorious conduct.

would at length be respected; vain expectation! he fell before his admiring comrades, a victim to this generous presumption.

Unfortunate * as was the issue of the battle at Germantown, it manifested the unsubdued, though broken spirit, of the American army; and taught the enemy to expect renewal of combat whenever adequacy of force or fitness of opportunity should authorize repetition of battle; it gave, too, animation to the country at large, exciting in Congress and in the people invigorated zeal in the great cause in which they were engaged.

CHAPTER VI.

Howe directs his attention to opening the Delaware.—Count Donop moves on Fort Mercer.—Lieutenant-Colonel Simms reaches the fort at Red Bank and proceeds to Mud Island.—Hessians repulsed at Red Bank.—Donop killed.—Colonel Smith of the Maryland line, succeeds to the command at Mud Island.

BOTH armies having resumed their former positions, the respective leaders, with renovated vigor, directed their views to the cardinal point of all their movements and all their conflicts.

Howe felt and understood the late bold attempt of his adversary; and, withdrawing from his position in Germantown, concentrated his force in the vicinity of Philadelphia, strengthening his camp by field-works, which in effect increased his disposable force.

He soon became convinced that the dislodgment of the American garrisons from the forts, Mifflin and Mercer, was an indispensable prerequisite to the opening of the passage of the river, where the admiral and fleet had arrived from the Chesapeake, prepared to co-operate in removing those obstructions; and immediate measures were taken toward the accomplishment of this object.

A detachment of Hessians, led by Colonel Count Donop, crossed the Delaware from Philadelphia, and took the route for Fort Mercer. A few miles only in its van was a re-enforcement for the post of Mud Island, sent by Washington, under Lieutenant-Colonel Simms, of the sixth Virginia regiment.†

---

* Congress voted their thanks to the general and army, expressing without reserve their approbation of the plan of battle, and of the courage exhibited on the occasion.

† Lieutenant-Colonel Simms, after passing the Delaware below Bristol, arrived, with the detachment under his command, at Moore's Town, eight miles from Cooper's Ferry, opposite Philadelphia, about ten o'clock at night. He was informed that a detachment of the enemy were crossing at that ferry; the safety of his detachment required that he should ascertain whether the enemy were

7

Simms continued to precede Donop, and reached the fort at Red Bank the evening before the enemy appeared. No doubt existed but that Donop would make his assault the next day. Simms entreated Colonel Greene, of the Rhode Island line, commandant in Fort Mercer, to avail himself of the accidental aid under his command. To this proposal Greene readily assented; and a disposition was accordingly made of the united force, to receive the assailant. Matured reflection in the course of the night, induced Colonel Greene to renounce the welcome and seasonable aid before accepted. He considered that the detachment under Lieutenant-Colonel Simms was destined for Mud Island, a place of the highest importance; and which, for aught he knew, might be attacked by the fleet and army at the moment of the intended assault upon himself. He revolved in his mind the weighty responsibility he should assume by changing the disposition of the commander-in-chief, increased tenfold should an attack be made upon Fort Mifflin, destitute of the aid sent to contribute to its defence.

These soldier-like reflections determined this gallant officer to rely solely upon his inferior force, which he directed to resume its original disposition, assigning his entire corps to that part of the works heretofore contracted to fit his strength; nor could the persevering solicitations of Lieutenant-Colonel Simms, seconded by the anxious wishes of his troops, shake the fixed resolve of Greene.

Disappointed in his sought participation of the terrible conflict impending, this zealous officer hastened to his destined post, to share with the commandant of Mud Island the dangers of his arduous and momentous struggle.

Filing off through the postern gate of the fort, he embarked in boats prepared to transport his detachment to the island. This movement was quickly discerned by Count Donop, who, having some hours before arrived, was engaged in the necessary preparations for attack.

Not doubting, from what he saw, that the garrison was attempting to escape, Donop relinquished his preparations, though abso-

actually crossing the Delaware or not; and he immediately, with a small escort of dragoons, proceeded with great circumspection to the ferry, and found that the information he had received was not true; nor could he discover any movement of troops in the city. A party of militia were posted at the ferry, whom Lieutenant-Colonel Simms found asleep; being roused and informed of their danger from such negligence, they providentially escaped certain destruction; for before the dawn of day the van of Donop's corps had landed with hope of striking them.

lutely requisite, and arrayed his troops for assault. Rushing on to our works, he entered that part of them designedly abandoned in consequence of the contraction made by Greene : and, finding these evacuated, his temerity increased, of which the American commandant took full advantage. Having approached, tumultuously, close to the muzzles of our guns, a severe fire from the garrison ensued, which was so fatal in its effects as to destroy instantly every hope of success. The gallant Donop fell, mortally wounded ; and the carnage was so dreadful as to render immediate flight on the part of the survivors indispensable. Nor was the naval diversion in favor of the assault by land, free from disaster. The Augusta, a ship of the line, and Merlin sloop of war, part of the squadron employed on this occasion, were both lost : the first by fire accidentally communicated ; the last, having grounded, was purposely destroyed.

Thus was requited scrupulous adherence to military obedience. The hero of Fort Mercer received with universal acclamation the honor conferred on him by Congress, so nobly earned ; * which through the eventful vicissitudes of after service, he sustained with unfading lustre.

* IN CONGRESS, November 4, 1777.

Resolved, That Congress have a high sense of the merit of Colonel Greene and the officers and men under his command, in their late gallant defence of the fort at Red Bank, on Delaware River, and that an elegant sword be provided by the Board of War, and presented to Colonel Greene.

Extract from the Minutes.

CHARLES THOMPSON, *Sec'y.*

WAR OFFICE OF THE UNITED STATES, New York, June 7, 1786.

SIR,—I have the honor to transmit to you, the son and legal representative of the late memorable and gallant Colonel Greene, the sword directed to be presented to him by the resolve of Congress of the 4th November, 1777.

The repulse and defeat of the Germans, at the foot of Red Bank on the Delaware, is justly considered as one of the most brilliant actions of the late war. The glory of that event is inseparably attached to the memory of your late father and his brave garrison. The manner in which the supreme authority of the United States are pleased to express their high sense of his military merit, and the honorable instrument which they annex in testimony thereof, must be peculiarly precious to a son emulative of his father's virtues.

The circumstances of the war prevented the obtaining and delivery of the sword previous to your father's being killed at Croton River, in the year 1780. On that catastrophe his country mourned the sacrifice of a patriot and soldier, and mingled its tears with those of his family.

That the patriotic and military virtues of your honorable father may influence your conduct in every case in which your country may require your services, is the sincere wish of

Your most obedient and very humble servant,

JOB GREENE, Esq.   H. KNOX.

This successful resistance on the part of the Americans, was soon followed by the exhilarating intelligence from the North, placing out of doubt the surrender of Burgoyne and his army.

To protract as long as possible the defence of the obstructions to the river navigation, became more and more dear to Washington ; for, with the re-enforcements to be derived from the Northern army, he flattered himself to be at length able to act with that vigor his own temper had invariably courted ; but which his impotent condition had prevented. Could he have left a sufficient force in his camp at White Marsh, to which position he had advanced on the enemy's retreat to Philadelphia, to protect his hospitals and stores in Bethlehem, Reading, and their vicinity, he would have placed himself on the western heights of the Schuylkill, whence he could with facility have driven the enemy from Province Island,* by which establishment Fort Mifflin was essentially endangered. This movement on the part of Washington, must have compelled Sir William Howe to venture the perilous operation of fighting his enemy on his own ground, passing a river into battle, or passing it above or below him. The latter was the most ready approach ; but very disadvantageous was the access, through the intermediate marshes of the Delaware and the Schuylkill ; nor was it easy to convey artillery, baggage, and the ammunitions of war, through those humid grounds ; and delay in the operation would endanger the health of his troops.

To pass above Washington comported better with a due regard to the health, the comfort, and the labor of his army ; but to this course were annexed weighty objections. The route would be extensive ; it would place Howe, when he reached the western banks of the Schuylkill, too remote from Philadelphia ; a weak garrison, if left there, must fall if struck at ; an adequate garrison he could not spare, in his then effective strength.

Whatever choice he might adopt in the difficult condition to which the transfer of the American head-quarters to the western heights of the Schuylkill, opposite to the city, must have reduced

---

* A small detachment was landed on Province Island with a view to expel the enemy engaged in erecting this battery. Major Vatap, who commanded the British covering party, abandoned most shamefully the artillery, which was however retaken by a subaltern officer. The above is stated by Mr. Stedman, whose history of the American war is marked by an invariable disposition to record the truth. I believe it is the single instance of dastardly conduct among the British officers during the war. Vatap belonged to the tenth regiment, and was obliged to quit the service, and sell out below the regulated price.

him ; it is very certain his decision, when taken, would be replete with hazard. Our army being re-enforced from the North with the faithful battalions of New England, flushed with victory, and surpassing, if possible, their comrades in devotion to the American chief, even upon equal ground the battle would have been keenly contested, and must have been profusely bloody.

Victory, on the side of America, presented the richest rewards, peace and independence. Exhortations, drawn from such sources, could not have been applied without effect. But suppose Sir William Howe to have readily surmounted the presumed obstacles to his advance, and to have approached the American army, he would have found Washington in a position selected by himself, ready for battle. Bloody must have been the conflict, and uncertain the event. Yet it may be fairly suggested, had fortune continued to cling to Sir William Howe, such would have been the obstinacy of the contest, that, situated as he was, it was highly probable all the advantages resulting from the battle would have been gathered by his adversary. Nothing short of a complete victory, followed by the destruction of his enemy, could have relieved the British general, which, in existing circumstances, was scarcely possible ; whereas a well-fought day, crippling both armies, would in its consequences have produced decisive benefits to his antagonist. Fort Mifflin, still sustaining itself against the persevering exertions of the enemy, could never have been reduced by the debilitated foe ; and the junction of the fleet, on which depended the safety of the army, never could have been effected.

Delighted as was Washington with a prospect so magnificent, he had, on the first intimation of the probable issue to the Northern campaign, given orders to General Gates to hasten to his succor a portion of that army, as soon as the state of things would warrant a separation of his force. Meanwhile, restricted as he was to inferior numbers, he continued to exert every means in his power to support Mud Island, whose commandant, Count d'Arenat, having been disabled by indisposition to execute the duties of his station, Lieutenant-Colonel Smith,* of the Maryland line, second in command, supplied his place. On this active and determined officer and his brave garrison the attention of both armies was turned ; each being justly impressed with the momentous result of successful resistance.

---

* Now General Samuel Smith of Maryland and Senator of the United States.

Smith felt the high responsibility devolved upon him, and was well apprised of the vast odds against which he had to contend. Unhappily the commodore and himself soon disagreed; an event, no doubt, productive of injurious effects to the service. Nevertheless, Lieutenant-Colonel Smith and his gallant garrison preserved the most imposing countenance, submitting to every privation, surmounting every difficulty, and braving every danger.

CHAPTER VII.

Operations against Mud Island.—Colonel Smith wounded.—Gallant resistance under Major Hayes.—Forts Mifflin and Mercer abandoned.—Sir Wm. Howe moves against Washington.—Skirmish with the light troops.—Major Moses killed.—Sir Wm. Howe returns to Philadelphia.

THE enemy increased his works on Province Island, mounting them with thirty-two pounders; which being completed on the 9th of November, a demolishing cannonade took place without delay, and continued without intermission. Being erected within four or five hundred yards of the nearest defences on Mud Island, the blockhouses were soon battered down; and the breach in that quarter encouraged immediate resort to the ultimate operations, which would most likely have been attempted, had not the heroic stand made by Colonel Greene at Fort Mercer presented an admonition too impressive to be disregarded by an officer of Sir William Howe's prudence. This attempt was considered by Lieutenant-Colonel Smith not only practicable but probable; and he advised the withdrawal of the troops. Nor was his counsel unsupported by the actual condition of the fort and garrison: the first dismantled in various points; and the second always greatly inadequate in strength, and now extremely incapacitated, by fighting, watching, and working, for close and stubborn action. Indeed so desperate was the prospect, and so probable the last appeal, that Colonel Smith assembled his officers, for the purpose of deciding on the course to be pursued; when, with one voice, it was determined that, should the expected event take place, and the enemy succeed in forcing the outer works, the garrison should retreat to an inclosed intrenchment in the center of the fort, and there demand quarters; which, if refused, a match should be instantly applied to the magazine, and themselves, with their enemy, buried in one common ruin.

Washington, still sanguine in his expectation of being soon formidably re-enforced from the army under Gates, frowned upon every suggestion of evacuation. He established a small camp in New Jersey under Brigadier Varnum, contiguous to Fort Mercer, for the purpose of affording daily relief to the garrison of Mud Island, whose commandant received orders to defend it to the last extremity.

The enemy, from his ships below, and from his batteries on Province Island, and the heights above Schuylkill, continued to press his attack with renewed vigor and increased effect. In the course of the fierce contest, Lieutenant-Colonel Smith received a contusion from the shattered walls of the fort, which, obliging him to retire, the command devolved on his second, Lieutenant-Colonel Simms, who continued to sustain the defence with unyielding firmness, until he was relieved by Colonel Russell, of Massachusetts, who preserved the undaunted resistance uniformly exhibited. Russell and his officers, being unacquainted with the condition of the works, and some movement indicating a determination to storm the fort being discovered, Lieutenant-Colonel Simms proposed to the retiring garrison to remain until the next day. This proposition was generously assented to; and the united force repaired to their post, determined to defend, at every hazard, our dilapidated works. In the course of the night a floating battery was descried falling down the river, the precursor, as was supposed, of the long-expected assault. But whatever may have been the enemy's design, it proved abortive; as only that single battery reached us, which was soon silenced by our guns, and abandoned by its crew.

Russell was succeeded by Major Thayer, of the Rhode Island line, an officer singularly qualified for the arduous condition in which he was placed. Resistance could not slacken, under such a leader. Entering with ardor into the wishes of his general, he labored with diligence, during the night, to repair the destruction of the day; he revived the hopes of his brave soldiers, by encouraging them to count on ultimate success; and retrieved their impaired strength, by presenting to their view the rich harvest of reward and glory sure to follow in the train of victory. The terrible conflict became more and more desperate. Not the tremendous fire from Province Island and the heights of Schuylkill; not the thunder from the hostile fleet, nor the probable sudden co-operation of the army down the river, could damp the keen and

Novem. 10th.

Novem. 11th.

Novem. 12th.

Novem. 13th.

Novem. 14th.

soaring courage of Thayer. Cool and discriminating amidst surrounding dangers, he held safe the great stake committed to his
skill and valor.

A new assailant now presented itself. Between Province and
Mud Islands water and time had worked a ship channel, on high
tide, through a mere gut, which had never been observed by those
on whose examination and information the defenses in the river
and on the island had been planned and executed. A succession of high tides for several preceding days, it is supposed, had
at this period added considerably to the width and depth of this
channel. However this may be, it is certain that this pass was
first shown by the enemy, prepared to apply the advantage it bestowed.

An East Indiaman, cut down to its depth of water, was, by the
skill and perseverance common to British seamen, readily brought
to the desired station, close to the fort. Thayer saw himself gone,
unless the commodore could crush this unexpected and decisive
operation. He lost not a moment in reporting his changed condition, and claiming immediate relief. Hazelwood felt with the same
heart the altered and menaced state to which Fort Mifflin was reduced; but all his efforts to repel this new enemy were ineffectual.
Nothing now remained for the valiant Thayer but to abandon the
high-prized station. He retired in the second night of his
command, admired by the brave garrison who had experienced the value of his able predecessors, and honored by the
commander-in-chief, though compelled to a measure fatal to his
wisely-projected and well-supported system.

Novem.
15th

Notwithstanding the loss of Fort Mifflin, Washington was very
unwilling to abandon Fort Mercer, knowing that the Northern re-
enforcement must soon arrive; to accelerate whose progress, he had
some time before dispatched Lieutenant-Colonel Hamilton. He
consequently determined to counteract Lord Cornwallis's operations,
who, after Donop's repulse, had been detached across the Delaware
with a respectable force, and was now moving upon Fort Mercer.
To this end, Major-General Greene, by his order, entered New
Jersey with a considerable detachment, to be strengthened by the
first division of the troops expected from the North. Disappointed
in the promised aid,* and very inferior to his enemy in number, who

---

* Glover's brigade, the van of the Northern re-enforcement, did not, as was
expected, reach Major-General Greene; whereas Lord Cornwallis united to
his corps a re-enforcement lately arrived in the river from New York.

had been re-enforced in his march by troops just arrived from New York, Greene could not act offensively: the fort of Red Bank was consequently evacuated; and the two generals rejoined without delay their respective leaders.

Novem. 18th.

Washington soon after Sir William Howe retired from Germantown, had advanced, as before mentioned, to White Marsh, within reach of the enemy; a strong position, rendered stronger by the application of art and labor wherever requisite. On the return of Lord Cornwallis from New Jersey, the British general resolved to bring the American army to battle; with which view he moved from Philadelphia on the 4th of December, and took post on Chestnut Hill, distant three miles from White Marsh. Here he passed two days, making many demonstrations of a general assault. On the third he changed his ground and encamped in front of our left, the most vulnerable part of Washington's position, as it might have been turned by pursuing the old York road; which measure would infallibly have produced battle or have forced retreat. Here the British general renewed his demonstrations of assault; and Lord Cornwallis engaged the light troops on our left flank, who were driven in after a sharp rencontre, in which Major Morris, of New Jersey, was mortally wounded. This officer's distinguished merit had pointed him out to the commander-in-chief as peculiarly calculated for the rifle regiment, made up with a view to the most perilous and severe service, and which had, under its celebrated colonel (Morgan), eminently maintained its renown in the late trying scenes of the memorable campaign in the North; in all of which Morris bore a conspicuous part. His loss was deeply felt, and universally regretted, being admired for his exemplary courage, and beloved for his kindness and benevolence.

This skirmish concluded the manifestations of battle exhibited by Howe. He returned to Philadelphia, unequivocally acknowledging by his retreat, that his adversary had at length attained a size which forbade the risk of battle on ground chosen by himself.*

Truth, spoken in terms so imperative, would have conveyed to the British minister salutary admonition, had his mind been open to its reception. This was the period for the restoration of the blessings of peace; and the loss of one army, with the late un-

---

* Washington, on receiving intelligence of Howe's retreat, said, "Better would it have been for Sir William Howe to have fought without victory, than thus to declare his inability."

equivocal declaration * of the British commander-in-chief, ought to have led to the acknowledgment of our independence, and to the renewal of amity, with preferential commercial intercourse; thus saving the useless waste of blood and treasure which followed, stopping the increase of irritation which twenty years of peace have not eradicated, and preventing the alliance soon after effected, between their ancient enemy and these States—the prolific parent of great and growing ills to Great Britain and to America.

CHAPTER VIII.

Washington goes into winter quarters at Valley Forge.—Inoculates his army.—Sir Wm. Howe recalled.—Sir Henry Clinton in command.—Conduct of Sir Wm. Howe.—His check at Bunker's Hill.

HOWE's abandonment of the field, and the rigor of the season, induced the American general to prepare for winter quarters. Comparing the various plans suggested by his own comprehensive mind, and by the assisting care of those around him, he adopted a novel experiment, the issue of which gave increase of fame to his already highly-honored name. He determined to hold his main force in one compact body, and to place some light troops, horse and foot, with corps of militia, in his front, contiguous to the enemy, for the double purpose of defending the farmer from the outrages of marauders, and of securing to himself quick information of any material movement in the enemy's camp. He selected for his winter position Valley Forge, which lies on the western side of the Schuylkill, convenient to the rich country of Lancaster and Reading, and in the first step of the ascent of hills which reach to the North Mountain or Blue Ridge. It possessed every advantage which strength of ground or salubrity of climate could bestow. Here, by the hands of his soldiers, he erected a town of huts, which afforded a comfortable shelter from the inclemency of the season, and strengthened his position by all the help of art and industry. This work, of his selection, soon evinced its preference to the common mode of cantonment in contiguous towns and villages.

* There are two sorts of victory,—that, generally understood, when two armies meet and fight, and one yields to the other; or, when the object of contest is given up without battle, by voluntary relinquishment, as was now the case, rather than risk battle.

Close under the eye of the officer, and far from the scenes of delight, the hardy character of the troops did not degenerate by effeminate indulgences, but was rather confirmed by unremitting attention to the acquirement of military knowledge, and the manly exercises proper for a camp. Intent upon bringing his army to a thorough knowledge of the most approved system of tactics, the American general adopted the means most likely to produce this essential effect, watching and encouraging with care and indulgence his beloved troops in their progress, always tenderly mindful of the preservation of their health; as on their fidelity, skill, and courage his oppressed country rested for relief and safety. He not only enforced rigid attention to all those regulations and usages generally adopted to keep off disease, but determined to risk the critical and effectual measure of extinguishing the small-pox in his army; whose pestilential rage had already too often thinned its ranks, and defeated the most important enterprises. Preparations to accomplish this wise resolution having been made with all possible secrecy, the period of the winter most opposed to military operations was selected for its introduction in succession to the several divisions of the army; and what is really surprising, nearly one-half of the troops had gone through the disease before the enemy became apprised of its commencement.

While Washington was engaged, without cessation, to perfect his army in the art of war, and to place it out of the reach of that contagious malady so fatal to man, Sir William was indulging, with his brave troops, in all the sweets of luxury and pleasure to be drawn from the wealthy and populous city of Philadelphia; nor did he once attempt to disturb that repose, now so essential to the American general. Thus passed the winter; and the approaching spring brought with it the recall of the commander of the British army, who was succeeded by Sir Henry Clinton, heretofore his second.*

It is impossible to pass over this period of the American war without giving vent to some of those reflections which it necessarily excites. Sir William Howe was considered one of the best soldiers in England, when charged with the important trust of subduing the revolted colonies. Never did a British general, in any period

---

* After Sir William Howe returned home, a parliamentary inquiry was made into his conduct upon a motion of his brother, Admiral Lord Howe, which was in a little while dropped. It plainly appears, from the documents exhibited, that Sir William Howe's plans were cordially adopted by the minister, and that he was as cordially supported by government in whatever he desired.—See parliamentary debates for 1779.

of that nation, command an army better fitted to insure success than the one submitted to his direction, whether we regard its comparative strength with that opposed to it, the skill of the officers, the discipline and courage of the soldiers, the adequacy of all the implements and munitions of war, or the abundance of the best supplies of every sort. In addition, his brother Lord Howe commanded a powerful fleet on our coast, for the purpose of subserving the views, and supporting the measures, of the commander-in-chief. Passing over the criminal supineness which marked his conduct after the battle of Long Island, and the fatal mistake of the plan of the campaign in 1777 (the first and leading feature of which ought to have been junction with Burgoyne and the undisturbed possession of the North River), we must be permitted to look at him with scrutinous though impartial eyes, when pursuing his own object and directed by his own judgment, after his disembarkation at the head of the Chesapeake.

We find him continuing to omit pressing the various advantages he dearly gained from time to time. He was ever ready to appeal to the sword, and but once retired from his enemy. But he does not seem to have known, that to win a victory was but the first step in the actions of a great captain. To improve it is as essential; and unless the first is followed by the second, the conqueror ill requites those brave companions of his toils and perils, to whose disregard of difficulties and contempt of death, he is so much indebted for the laurel which entwines his brow; and basely neglects his duty to his country, whose confidence in his zeal for her good, had induced her to commit to his keeping her fame and interest.

After his victory at Brandywine, he was, by his own official statement, less injured than his adversary; yet with many of his corps entire and fresh, we find him wasting three precious days, with the sole ostensible object of sending his wounded to Wilmington. Surely the detachment charged with this service, was as adequate to their protection on the field of battle, as afterward on the march; and certainly it required no great exertion of mind to have made this arrangement in the course of one hour, and to have pursued his beaten foe, after the refreshments and repose enjoyed in one night. This was omitted. He adhered to the same course of conduct after the battle of Germantown, when the ill-boding tidings from the Northern warfare, emphatically called upon him to press his victory, in order to compensate for the heavy loss likely to be sustained by the captivity of Burgoyne and his army. But what is surprising, still more, after the Delaware was restored to his use, and the communication with the fleet completely enjoyed, he relinquished his resolution of fighting Washington at White Marsh, having ascertained, by his personal observations, that no material difficulty presented itself on the old York road, by which route he could, with facility, have turned Washington's left, and have compelled him to a change of position with battle, or to a perilous retreat.   And last, though not least in magnitude, knowing as Sir William ought to have known, the sufferings and wants of every kind to which Washington was exposed at Valley Forge, as well as that his army was under inoculation for the small-pox, while he himself was so abundantly supplied with every article requisite to give warmth and comfort to his troops, it is wonderful how he could omit venturing a winter campaign, to him promising every advantage, and to his antagonist menacing every ill—this too, when the fate of Burgoyne was no longer doubtful, and its adverse influence on foreign powers unquestionable, unless balanced by some grand and daring stroke on his part.   The only plan practicable was that above suggested; an experiment urged by all the considerations which ever can command high-spirited enterprise.

These are undeniable truths; and they involve an inquisitive mind in a perplexity not easy to be untangled.   It would be absurd to impute this conduct to a want of courage in Sir William Howe; for all acknowledge that he eminently possessed that quality.   Nor can it be justly ascribed to either indolence of disposition, or a habit of sacrificing his duties to ease; for he possessed a robust body, with an active mind, and although a man of pleasure, subdued, when necessary, its captivating allurements with facility.   To explain it, as some have done by supposing him friendly to the revolution, and therefore to connive at its success, would be equally stupid and unjust; for no part of Sir William's life is stained with a single departure from the line of honor.   Moreover, traitors are not to be found among British generals; whose fidelity is secured by education, by their grade and importance in society, and by the magnificent rewards of government sure to follow distinguished efforts.   The severe admonition which Sir William had received from the disastrous battle of Bunker's, or rather Breed's, Hill, furnishes the most probable explanation of this mysterious inertness. On that occasion, he commanded a body of chosen troops inured to discipline, and nearly double in number to his foe; possessing artillery in abundance, prepared in the best manner; with an army at hand ready to re-enforce him, and led by officers, many of whom had seen service, all of whom had been bred to arms. His enemy was a corps of peasants, who, for the first time, were unsheathing their swords; without artillery; defectively armed with fowling pieces, and muskets without bayonets; destitute of that cheerful comfort, with which experience animates the soldier; with no other works than a slight redoubt, and a slighter trench, terminating in a yet slighter breastwork.

Sir William found this feeble enemy posted on the margin, and along the acclivity of the hill, commanded by Colonel Prescott,[*] then unknown to fame: yet Sir William beheld these brave yeomen—while the conflagration of a town was blazing in their faces, while their flanks were exposed to maritime annoyance, and their front was assailed by regulars in proud array under the protection of cannon in full discharge—receive the terrible shock with firmness, coolly await his near approach, and then resolutely pour in a charge, which disciplined courage could not sustain. He saw his gallant troops fly—afterward brought to rally with their colors, and, indignant at the repulse, return with redoubled fury. Sir William again saw these daring countrymen, unappalled in heart, unbroken in line, true to their generous leader and their inbred valor, calmly reserving themselves for the fatal moment, when his close advance presented an opportunity of winging every ball with death. Again the British soldiers, with the pupil of the immortal Wolfe at their head, sought safety in flight. Restoring his troops to order, Sir William Howe advanced the third time, supported by naval co-operation, and a large battery on the side of Boston, which had now nearly demolished our slender defences. Notwithstanding this tremendous combination, Sir William saw his gallant enemy maintain their ground, without prospect of succor, until their ammunition was nearly expended: then, abandoning their works as

---

* The honor conferred upon Colonel Prescott was only a promotion in the army soon after established; and this, the writer was informed by a gentleman residing in Boston who was well acquainted with Colonel Prescott, consisted only in the grade of lieutenant-colonel, in a regiment of infantry. Considering himself entitled to a regiment, the hero of Breed's Hill would not accept a second station. Warren, who fell nobly supporting the action, was the favorite of the day, and has engrossed the fame due to Prescott. Bunker's Hill too had been considered as the field of battle, when it is well known that it was fought upon Breed's Hill, the nearest of the two hills to Boston. No man reveres the character of Warren more than the writer; and he considers himself not only, by his obedience to truth, doing justice to Colonel Prescott, but performing an acceptable service to the memory of the illustrious Warren, who, being a really great man, would disdain to wear laurels not his own.

the British entered them, they took the only route open to their escape with decision and celerity.

The sad and impressive experience of this murderous day sank deep into the mind of Sir William Howe; and it seems to have had its influence, on all his subsequent operations, with decisive control. In one instance only did he ever after depart from the most pointed circumspection; and that was in the assault on Red Bank, from his solicitude to restore the navigation of the Delaware, deemed essential to the safety of his army. The doleful issue of this single departure renewed the solemn advice inculcated at Breed's Hill, and extinguished his spirit of enterprise. This is the only way in which, it seems to me, the mysterious inertness which marked the conduct of the British general, so fatal in its effect to the British cause, can be intelligibly solved.

The military annals of the world rarely furnish an achievment which equals the firmness and courage displayed on that proud day by the gallant band of Americans; and it certainly stands first in the brilliant events of our war.

When future generations shall inquire, Where are the men who gained the highest prize of glory in the arduous contest which ushered in our nation's birth? upon Prescott and his companions in arms will the eye of history beam.

CHAPTER IX.

Sir H. Clinton evacuates Philadelphia and moves toward Monmouth.—Washington follows —Battle of Monmouth.—British continue their retreat.—Washington moves to the Hudson.—Arrest of General Charles Lee.—His suspension from command. —Arrival of the French fleet.—Alliance with France.

SIR HENRY CLINTON * had no sooner assumed the command in chief than he began to prepare for the evacuation of Philadelphia, which was readily effected with his maritime assistance. Having put on board his ships every thing too heavy and cumbrous for land transportation, with the superfluous baggage of his army, he passed the river from the city, on the 18th of June, completely prepared for the difficult retreat it became his duty to undertake.

Washington early apprised of the intended movement, gradually drew near to the Delaware, in the vicinity of Corryell's Ferry, wait-

* Sir Henry Clinton had served in the war of 1755 under Prince Ferdinand, into whose family he was introduced, and continued as aid-de-camp to the prince throughout the war, highly respected and esteemed.

ing for the unequivocal demonstration of the enemy's intention, before he ventured to leave Pennsylvania. In the mean time, he collected his scanty means of water transportation to the points on the river most convenient for his passage, and prepared himself for quick movement. The restoration of the metropolis of the Union to its rightful possessors, was as unimpressive in its general effect on the American mind, as had been its relinquishment to Sir William Howe some months before. Congress, who had left it with some precipitation, on the approach of the enemy, assembled at York-town, one hundred miles west of the city, where, having continued to hold its session, that body now returned to Philadelphia.

The loss of towns began to be properly understood in America: experience more and more illustrated the difference between the same events in our thinly-settled country, and the populous regions of Europe.

Clinton pursued his retreat slowly, betraying no symptoms of precipitation, but rather indicating a disposition for battle. Such conduct on his part was wise, and worthy of the pupil of Prince Ferdinand. Having reached Mount Holly, he pointed his march to Brunswick: whether this was the route preferred by him, or such demonstration was made only to throw Washington more to his left, and further distant from the route he ultimately took, and which perhaps was that of his original choice, remains unascertained. It appears evidently from the movements of the American general, that he accredited the demonstrations made by his enemy toward Brunswick, never, however, putting himself too far to the left, should Clinton suddenly turn toward South Amboy or the heights of Middletown—the only lines of retreat left, should that to Brunswick be relinquished. Washington passed the Delaware three or four days after Clinton had crossed that river, and was nearer to either point of retreat, than was the British general. The Fabius of America, made up, as has been before observed, of great caution with superior enterprise, indulged the most anxious desire to close with his antagonist in general action. Opposed to his wishes was the advice of his general officers: to this, he for a time yielded; but as soon as he discovered that the enemy had reached Monmouth Court-House, not more than twelve miles from the heights of Middletown, he determined that he should not escape without a blow. He therefore selected a body of troops, and placing them under the order of the Marquis de la Fayette (a French nobleman, whose zeal to acquire renown in arms had brought him to the tented fields of America), directing that officer to approach close to the foe, and to seize any advantageous occurrence for his annoyance, himself following with the main body in supporting distance. The marquis was young, generous, and brave, and, like most of his brother generals, yet little versed in the art of war. It was certainly a high trust to be confided to the young and captivating foreigner, though afterward well justified by his conduct throughout the war. Nothing is more dangerous than to hang with an inferior force upon a gallant enemy, never disinclined to draw his sword, and watchful to seize every advantage within his reach. Soon after La Fayette moved, a second corps was ordered to join him; and the united body was placed under the command of Major-General Lee,* for the express purpose of bringing on battle, should the enemy still continue in his position at Monmouth Court-House. In this officer was combined long and varied experience, with a profound military genius. He held too, not only the peculiar confidence of the commander-in-chief, but that of Congress, the nation, and the army. On approaching Englishtown, a small village seven miles from the Court-House, where Sir Henry continued in his camp, he learned that the enemy, having held back the *élite* of his army, was determined to cover Kniphausen, who, charged with the care of the baggage, was on his march to the heights of Middletown. Here he received orders from Washington to strike at the British rear, unless "strong reasons" forbade it; at the same time advising him of his approach to support him. Continuing to advance, he discovered the enemy in motion. Clinton having perceived various bodies of troops moving on his flanks, and apprehending that the column with his baggage might be grossly insulted, if not seriously injured, wisely resolved, by a forward movement, to check further pursuit. Cornwallis, who led the van troops, advanced upon Lee. This officer, concluding that he should most effectually answer the object of Washington by drawing the enemy to him, thus inducing the foe to expend his bodily strength, while he saved that of the American army, in a day of uncommon heat, instantly began to retrograde; to take which step he was additionally induced by discerning that the corps on his flank, under Brigadier Scott, had repassed the ravine in his rear. This country abounds with defiles of a peculiar sort: the valleys are cut by small rivulets with marshy grounds, difficult to man and horse, and impracticable to artillery, except in particular spots.

1773.
June 28th.

* Charles Lee, second in command of the army. See Appendix.

Such was the one in Lee's rear, which Scott had passed. Persevering in his decision to join, rather than recall Scott, he continued to retire, making good his retreat without injury, and exposing his person to every danger. At this moment Washington came up, and finding his orders disobeyed, required explanation from General Lee with warmth. Unhappily Lee took offence at the manner in which he had been accosted, and replied unbecomingly, instead of entering into that full explanation, which his own honor, duty to his superior, and the good of his country, demanded. Such conduct in an inferior officer could not be brooked; and met, as it merited, marked disapprobation. As soon as Lee perceived it proper to deviate from his instructions, he certainly ought to have advised the commander-in-chief of such deviation, with the reasons which produced it. Thus acting he would probably have received commendation; and a combined attack, founded upon the full representation of the relative state of himself and the enemy, might have led to the happiest result.

This communication was neglected; and Lee was ordered into the rear, while the army moved on to battle. The action shortly after commenced; the day was remarkably sultry; and the American army considerably fatigued by its previous march.

The battle was, nevertheless, contested with peculiar keenness, and ceased in the evening as if by mutual consent. The American general determined to renew it in the morning, while Sir Henry Clinton was as determined to avoid it.*

* The enemy having united his columns on the heights of Middletown, an attempt to dislodge him would have been blind temerity. Had Sir Henry Clinton not possessed this vast advantage, the victory would have been improved; and in any other period of the retreat might have been made decisive in all probability.

General Lee, in a letter dated Englishtown, June 28th, gives the following account of the battle of Monmouth :—

"What the devil brought us into this level country (the very element of the enemy), or what interest we can have (in our present circumstances) to hazard an action, somebody else must tell you, for I cannot. I was yesterday ordered (for it was against my opinion and inclination) to engage. I did, with my division, which consisted of about four thousand men. The troops, both men and officers, showed the greatest valor; the artillery did wonders; but we were outnumbered; particularly in cavalry, which was at twenty different times, on the point of turning completely our flanks. This consideration naturally obliged us to retreat; but the retreat did us, I will venture to say, great honor. It was performed with all the order and coolness which can be seen on a common field-day. Not a man or officer hastened his step, but one regiment regularly filed off from the front to the rear of the other. The thanks I received from his excellency were of a singular nature. I can demonstrate that had I not acted as I did, this army, and perhaps America, would have been ruined."

Judging from the official statements, which were published, the loss was trifling and not very unequal ; but the " stubborn fact " of burying the dead, manifests a great error in the report made by Sir Henry Clinton to his government. He rated his dead and missing at one hundred and eighty-eight ; whereas, we buried on the field of battle two hundred and forty-nine. Both sides claimed the victory, as is commonly the case when the issue is not decisive. Without doubt, Sir Henry Clinton obtained his object, security from further molestation, and the completion of his retreat. This, however, was effected not in the usual style of conquerors, but by decamping in the night, and hastily joining Kniphausen, who had reached the heights of Middletown, near to the place of embarkation, and secure from assault. It must be admitted, on a full view of the action, that the palm of victory clearly belonged to Washington, although it was not decisive, nor susceptible of improvement.

Having rested his army a few days in the position of Middletown, the British general embarked in the transports waiting his arrival, and soon reached New York. Washington, after paying his last respects to the dead, and tenderly providing for the wounded, moved by easy marches to the Hudson, comforting, by every means in his power, his faithful troops, and once more took his favorite position near the western shore of that river, which was always considered by him as the point of connection to the two extremes of the Union.

Major-General Lee was arrested upon sundry charges, tried, found guilty, and sentenced to be suspended from his command in the army for one year. The effect of which was, that the veteran soldier who had relinquished his native country, to support a cause dear to his heart, became lost to that of his adoption, and soon after lost to himself ; as the few years he survived seemed to have been passed in devotion to the sway of those human tormentors, envy and hate. The records of the court-martial manifest on their face the error of the sentence ; and it is wonderful how men of honor and of sense could thus commit themselves to the censures of the independent and impartial. If General Lee had been guilty of all the charges as affirmed by their decision, his life was forfeited ; and its sacrifice only could have atoned for his criminality. He ought to have been cashiered and shot : instead of which the mild sentence of suspension, for a short time, was the punishment inflicted. The truth is, the unfortunate general was only guilty of neglect in not making timely communication of his departure from orders, subject to his discretion, to the commander-in-chief, which constituted no part of the charges against him. This was certainly a very culpable omission ; to which was afterward added personal disrespect, where the utmost respect was not only due, but enjoined by martial law, and enforced by the state of things ; two armies upon the very brink of battle, himself intrusted with the direction of an important portion of one of them, for the very purpose of leading into action, to withhold the necessary explanations from his chief, and to set the example of insubordination by his mode of reply to an interrogatory, indispensably, though warmly, put to him, merited punishment. But this offence was different, far different from " disobedience to orders," or " a shameful retreat ; " neither of which charges were supported by testimony ; and both of which were contradicted by fact.

Soon after Sir Henry Clinton's return to New York, the first result of the alliance concluded during the preceding winter at Paris, between the United States and his most Christian majesty, announced itself in decisive operations on the part of the French monarch.

Admiral d'Estaing sailed from France in the beginning of the summer for the American coast, to co-operate with the American army ; and would have arrived in time to stop Lord Howe in the Delaware, as was intended, had not his voyage been greatly retarded by the unusual continuance of contrary winds. The arrival of the fleet of our ally, though unproductive of the immediate effects expected, the destruction of the enemy's fleet in the Delaware, gave birth to new and interesting enterprises ; the relation of which, not coming within the scope of this work, must necessarily be omitted. In the cursory survey taken, my single object has been, to present to the reader a lucid and connected statement of those transactions which bear in any degree upon the Southern war, either by their own relation, or by their introduction of characters, destined to act principal parts upon that theatre.

CHAPTER X.

Attempt at negotiation.—Lord North.—Lord Chatham.—The enemy's attention directed toward the South.

ALTHOUGH the surrender of Burgoyne, and Howe's declining to execute his menaced attack upon his adversary at White Marsh, did not convince the British minister of the futility of his attempt to subjugate these States, it produced a change in the temper of the cabinet. An idle and fruitless essay was made to reconcile the revolted colonies : idle, because too late; and fruitless, because founded on the revocation of their independence. Little minds always, in difficulty, resort to cunning, miscalling it wisdom ; this quality seems to have been predominant in the cabinet of Great Britain, and was alike conspicuous in its efforts to coerce, and in its proffers to conciliate.

Lord North was premier and first lord of the treasury. Heavy in mind as in body, dexterous in the management of the House of Commons, dead to all those feelings whose infusion into the mass of the people, gives comfort to the ruled and strength to the ruler; cherishing with ardor the prerogative of the king, restricting with stubbornness the rights of the people; he seems never to have discerned that the only way to make the monarch great, is to make the subject happy—in finance rather systematic, plodding, and adroit, than original, deep, and comprehensive—in Parliament decent, sensible, and laborious, with some of the glitter of wit, but with none of the effulgence and majesty of eloquence—in private life amiable and exemplary, better qualified for the enjoyments of its tranquil scenes, than to direct, in the storm of war, the helm of a brave, intelligent, powerful nation. The minister, in addition to the difficulties growing out of his own inadequacy, had to contend with obstacles inherent in the nature of the conflict, and powerful in their effect. Slavery, however dressed, is loathsome to the British palate ; and the attempt to deprive America of her birthright, never could be cordially relished, although ostensibly supported. This innate abhorrence formed a current against the administration, constant though slow, puissant though calm. Nor were statesmen wanting who proclaimed, with resistless force, the danger to British liberty from American slavery. At the head of this patriot band, stood the mighty Chatham. Towering in genius, superb in elo- quence, decisive in council, bold in action, loving England first and England always, adored by the mass of the people, and dreaded by the enemies of English liberty, he unceasingly cherished the good old cause, for which Hampden fought, and Sydney bled. The premier, driven from his original purpose by events resulting from his liberticide system, had not that sublimity of mind which can renounce error with dignity and turn calamity to account, or he would ere now have closed his vain and wasting war by the acknowledgment of our independence, restoring and riveting our commercial intercourse.

Despairing of the subjugation of all the States, he determined to apply his disposable force to the reduction of the weakest portion of the Union. With this view Sir Henry Clinton, on his return to New York, began to make arrangements for a plan of operation to be executed as soon as the French fleet should quit the American coast.

The Count d'Estaing sailed from Boston, for the West Indies, on the 3d of November; soon after which Lieutenant-Colonel Campbell was detached with three thousand men for the reduction of Georgia; orders having been dispatched to Brigadier-General Prevost, commanding the British troops in East Florida, which adjoins the State of Georgia on the southwest, to invade it from that quarter, and to assume the direction of the united detachments.

CHAPTER XI.

Colonel Campbell embarks for Savannah.—Lands and defeats General Howe.—General Prevost enters Georgia.—Colonel Pickens at Kettle Creek.—General Lincoln supersedes Howe in command of the South; repairs to Charleston; moves thence to Purysburg.—Gardner dislodged by General Moultrie.

SINCE the expedition under Sir Henry Clinton, in 1776, against Charleston, which had been completely baffled by the judicious arrangements of Major-General Lee, seconded by the gallant defence of Fort Moultrie, by the excellent officer whose name it bears, then a colonel in the South Carolina line, the Southern States had remained safe from hostile interruption, with the exception of some light predatory incursions from East Florida.

The squadron conveying Lieutenant-Colonel Campbell appeared off the Tybee River in the latter part of December; and no time was lost by that active officer in effecting his debarkation, which took place on the 29th at Gerridge's plantation, twelve miles up the river, and three miles below Savannah, the capital of the State, situated on the south side of the river Savannah.

1778.
Dec. 29.

Major-General Robert Howe commanded the American force in Georgia, consisting of some regulars, and such portion of the militia as he might be able to collect. At this period it is supposed he had under him one thousand five hundred men, having considerably reduced his effective strength by an unsuccessful expedition to East Florida, from which he had just returned, and was now encamped in a position which seems to have been judiciously selected, one half mile from the town of Savannah, across the main road leading to it.

The ground was well adapted to his force, and was secured by advantages of art and nature. At a small distance in his front, extending parallel to it, was a lagoon, through which the road passed. The bridge over the rivulet, running through the lagoon, was destroyed to retard the enemy's advance. His right was covered by a morass, thick set with woods, and interspersed with some houses occupied by riflemen; his left rested on the swamps of the river; and his rear was sustained by the town and old works of Savannah. To give additional strength to his position, he dug a trench from one morass to the other, a small distance in his front.

Thus posted, the American general coolly waited the approaching attack with his inferior force.

A small skirmish ensued as the British van emerged out of the low grounds; in which Captain Campbell, of the seventeenth regiment, fell, much regretted.

The lieutenant-colonel, having landed with the first division, occupied himself with preparations for action. While reconnoitring our position, he accidentally learned, that a by-path within his view led through the swamp to our rear. Intelligence so acceptable was instantly applied to his plan of battle.

Having arrayed his troops in our front, Sir James Baird* was detached with the light infantry and the New York volunteers to gain our rear by moving occultly along the accidentally discovered path.

Waiting the effect of this operation, the British continued quiet in line of battle. Very soon Sir James reached his destined point; when issuing out of the swamp, he charged a body of militia stationed in our rear. This was the signal for general assault. The British line advanced with promptitude, driving our troops, broken and embarrassed by this unexpected attack in the rear, from their ground. The defeat was instantaneous and decisive. Howe was pursued through Savannah, and with a small part of his army escaped into South Carolina, losing before night five hundred and fifty men, killed and taken, with his artillery and baggage.

---

* This officer has since been extensively employed, and much distinguished.

Never was a victory of such magnitude so completely gained, with so little loss, amounting only to seven killed and nineteen wounded. The town, fort, cannon, shipping, and stores of every kind, fell into the hands of the victor: whose conduct to the inhabitants was peculiarly kind and amiable.

General Howe was, after a considerable lapse of time, brought before a court of inquiry, and acquitted.

However we must applaud the judgment displayed by the American general in selecting and improving his position; however we must honor his gallant determination to receive the enemy's attack, with an inferior force; yet, as his resolution, in prudence, must have been formed in the advantages of his ground, we cannot excuse the negligence betrayed by his ignorance of the avenues leading to his camp.

How happens it that he, who had been in command in that country for many months, should not have discovered the by-way passing to his rear, when Lieutenant-Colonel Campbell contrived to discover it in a few hours? The faithful historian cannot withhold his condemnation of such supineness. Thus it is that the lives of brave men are exposed, and the public interest sacrificed. Yet notwithstanding such severe admonitions, rarely does government honor with its confidence the man whose merit is his sole title to preference: the weight of powerful connections, or the arts of intriguing courtiers, too often bear down unsupported though transcendent worth.

Brigadier-General Prevost, having entered Georgia in conformity with his orders, invested Sunbury, which he soon compelled to surrender. Having placed a garrison in the fort, the brigadier continued his march to Savannah, and took upon himself the command of the united forces. He detached Lieutenant-Colonel Campbell to 1779. Augusta, then a frontier town, and, like Savannah, situated on the southern bank of the same river. Meeting with no resistance, Campbell readily effected his object by possessing himself of the town. Thus in the short period of one month, Feb. 1. was the State of Georgia restored to the British crown.

General Prevost persevered in the lenient course adopted by Lieutenant-Colonel Campbell, sparing the property, and protecting the persons of the vanquished. Nor was he disappointed in the reward due to policy so virtuous and wise.

The affections of the people were enlisted on the side of the conqueror, and our youth flocked to the British standard.

From Augusta Lieutenant-Colonel Hamilton, of the North Carolina regiment, advanced, with a suitable detachment, further west, to crush all remaining resistance, and to encourage the loyalists to step forward and give their active aid in confirming the establishment of royal authority. Every attempt to interrupt the progress of this officer was ineffectual; and seven hundred loyalists embodied with the determination to force their way to the British camp.

Colonel Pickens, of the South Carolina militia, true to his country, and correctly interpreting the movement under Hamilton, assembled his regiment and drew near to him for the purpose of counteracting his operations.

Finding this officer invulnerable, he suddenly turned from him to strike at the loyalists advancing toward Augusta. He fell in with them at Kettle Creek, and instantly attacked them. The action was contested with zeal and firmness; when Colonel Boyd, the commander of the loyalists, fell; and his death was soon followed by the rout of his associates. Nevertheless, three hundred of the body contrived to effect their union with the British army.

This single, though partial check, was the only interruption of the British success from the commencement of the invasion.

The delegates in Congress from the States of South Carolina and Georgia, had some time before urged the substitution of a more experienced commander of the Southern Department* in the place of General Howe.

This solemn application did not fail to engage the serious attention of that respectable body. Not only was the desired substitution made, but the States of Virginia and North Carolina 1778. were pressed, in the most forcible terms, to hasten succor Sept. 25. to their afflicted sisters.

North Carolina obeyed with promptitude the demand of Congress; and two thousand of her militia, under Generals Ashe and Rutherford, reached Charleston before the expedition under Lieutenant-Colonel Campbell was announced on the Southern coast. But this auxiliary force was unarmed; North Carolina being very destitute of that primary article of defence. South Carolina, more provident, because more attractive from the wealth concentred in its capital, had in due time furnished herself with arms, but was indisposed to place them out of her control, especially as it was then uncertain whether she might not be the point of invasion.

---

* The Southern Department comprehended Virginia, the two Carolinas, and Georgia; lately Maryland and Delaware were added.

The zeal displayed by North Carolina, while it entitled her to commendation, was thus unproductive of the expected effect. Nor until after the defeat of Howe was this force in readiness to repair to the theatre of action.

Major-General Lincoln, of Massachusetts, had been selected by Congress in the place of Howe.* This officer was a soldier of the Revolution ; his stock of experimental knowledge, of course, could not have been very considerable, although he had seen more service than most of our officers of the same standing. He had uniformly possessed the confidence of Washington, who had often intrusted him with important commands; and he was second to Gates at Saratoga, greatly contributing by his judicious and spirited conduct, to the happy issue of that momentous campaign. Upright, mild, and amiable, he was universally respected and beloved ; a truly good man, and a brave and prudent, but not consummate soldier. Lincoln hastened toward his post, and having reached Charleston, bestowed his unremitted attention to the timely completion of the requisite arrangements for the defence of the South.

Here he heard of the descent of Lieutenant-Colonel Campbell, and the disastrous overthrow of Howe. Hurried by this event he quick-
1779. ly reached the confines of Georgia, and having united the
Jan. 7. remains of the defeated army, with the troops of the two Carolinas, he established himself in Purysburg, a small village on the northern side of the Savannah, about fifteen miles above the capital of Georgia.

The British force under Prevost at this period is stated to have been nearly four thousand; while that under Lincoln did not exceed three thousand and six hundred ; of which, only eleven hundred were Continentals.† The superiority of Prevost, especially in the quality of his troops, was in a great degree lost by their distribution, in different stations, from Savannah to Augusta, a distance of one hundred and forty miles. Nor would it have been a safe operation, had his force been concentred, to pass the difficult river of Savannah, with its broad and deep swamps, in the face of Lincoln. The

---

* General Howe joined the main army under the commander-in-chief, where he served to the end of the war. A court of inquiry was held to investigate the cause of his defeat before Savannah, who reported favorably to the major-general.

† " Continentals " mean regular soldiers, enlisted and paid under the authority of Congress. The Continental troops had not seen service, being composed of the line of the Carolinas and Georgia, with the exception of the gallant defenders of Fort Moultrie in 1776.

British general, satisfied for the present with the possession of Georgia, devoted his mind and force to the preservation and confirmation of the fruits of his success. With this view, and to this end, he persevered in sustaining his long line of defence, although his enemy, separated only by the river, kept his force compact.

About this time Prevost, availing himself of his naval aid, and of the interior navigation, made an establishment on the island of Port Royal, under Major Gardner, with two hundred men. The object of this inexplicable movement could not then be ascertained ; nor has it since been developed. Colonel, now General, Moultrie, soon dislodged Gardner, with considerable loss, and would have annihilated the detachment, had not the want of ammunition prevented the victor from improving his advantage. The Charleston militia behaved admirably in this affair. The Captains Barnwell, Heyward, Rutledge, and Lieutenant Wilkins, eminently distinguished themselves : the latter officer was killed.

CHAPTER XII

Gen. Ashe moves against Augusta, then crosses the Savannah.—Is routed by Prevost.—John Rutledge dictator in South Carolina.—Lincoln moves upon Augusta.—Prevost threatens Charleston.—Charleston saved.—Proposition that South Carolina should remain neutral.—Rejected by Prevost.

GENERAL LINCOLN, at length strengthened by considerable re-enforcements of the militia, came to the resolution of acting offensively. _{February.}

A considerable detachment (nearly one thousand and five hundred, all militia, except one hundred regulars) was placed under the orders of General Ashe, who was directed to take post opposite to Augusta. Before Ashe reached the place of his destination, the British troops fell back from Augusta, and crossing Brier Creek, encamped at Hudson's Ferry, twenty-four miles above Ebenezer, then the head-quarters of the royal army.

The abandonment of Augusta very much gratified Lincoln, who was extremely anxious to cover the upper parts of the State, for the double purpose of reducing the enemy to narrower limits, and uniting to his arms the hardy sons of the West. He therefore ordered Ashe to pass the river, and to place himself behind Brier Creek, where it falls into the Savannah ; secured in _{Feb. 28th.} his front by the creek, on his left by the river, he could only be assailed on his right. To enable him to explore accurately this quarter, a squadron of dragoons was annexed to his corps, and to give to his condition the utmost activity, the baggage of the detachment was ordered to be removed to the north side of the Savannah.

General Prevost was not at a loss for the motives of this operation, nor insensible to its consequences.

He determined without delay to dislodge Ashe from the position he had taken. To conceal his real object, he made some demonstrations of crossing the Savannah with his main body, when the detachment prepared to strike at General Ashe, advanced upon Brier Creek. Major Macpherson openly moved along the main road, and attracted, as was intended, the undeviating attention of the American brigadier, while Lieutenant-Colonel Prevost, by an occult march of fifty miles, forded the creek fifteen miles above our position, and fell suddenly in its rear. Colonel Elbert with the band of Continentals made a brave but ineffectual stand. They were made prisoners, and the whole body put to the rout, with the loss of only five privates killed, and one officer and ten privates wounded. Great was the loss on the side of America; and, of those who did escape, only four hundred and fifty rejoined our army.

Lieutenant-Colonel Prevost did honor to himself by the handsome manner in which he accomplished the enterprise committed to his conduct. While commendation is justly bestowed upon the British officer, censure cannot be withheld from the American commandant. The flattering prospect of recovering a lost State was dashed to pieces in an instant, by the culpable inattention of an officer high in rank, highly intrusted, and imperatively summoned to take care that his country should not be injured by his negligence; yet it was injured, and that too, while the late terrible blow, sustained from the same cause by General Howe, was fresh in recollection, and while the wounds there received were still bleeding.

Relieved, by this decisive victory, of all apprehension heretofore entertained of the stability of the change effected in Georgia, the British general re-established by proclamation the royal government, as it existed at the commencement of the Revolution, and renewed his endeavors to rekindle the spirit of loyalty, which had been very much damped by the victory of Pickens, the evacuation of Augusta, and the menacing movement of General Lincoln.

Disaster upon disaster called for increased vigor in our coun-

March 4.

sels. This manly disposition happily ensued. John Rutledge, who had taken an early and distinguished part in the Revolution, was called to the chair of government in South Carolina, and invested with dictatorial power. An accomplished gentleman, a profound statesman, a captivating orator, decisive in his measures, and inflexibly firm, he infused his own lofty spirit into the general mass. The militia rallied around the American standard; and General Lincoln soon found himself in strength to resume the judicious plan of holding Augusta and the upper country of Georgia.

About this time the legislature of Georgia was to convene in Augusta. To protect it was a weighty consideration with the American general, whose force had increased to five thousand men. Leaving, therefore, one thousand under General Moultrie, for the defence of the posts of Purysburg and the Black Swamp, Lincoln decamped on the 23d of April for Augusta. The British general observed this movement with those emotions it was cal- April 25. culated to excite; nor did he pause a moment in taking the resolution to counteract it. To advance upon Augusta was the plan which caution suggested and which policy dictated, for, although inferior in numbers, he far excelled in the character of his troops, in the quality of his arms, and in the abundance of every thing requisite to preserve the health, strength, and spirit of his soldiers. Battle, without delay, was the true system for a general thus situated, more especially as conquest, not defence, was his object. Believing that he could compel Lincoln to relinquish his plan without the hazard of engaging him, remote from a place of safety, and with inferior numbers, he determined to cross the Savannah, and to threaten Charleston. In a few days after Lincoln's decampment, the British general passed this river, and pressed with vigor upon our posts of Purysburg and the Black Swamp, which were successively evacuated. Driving General Moultrie before him, Prevost continued to advance with rapidity. Moultrie sat down at Tulifinny bridge, leaving Lieutenant-Colonel Laurens with a small party of Continentals and a body of the militia at Coosawhatchie bridge to defend that pass. Laurens executed his orders with zeal and gallantry, but at length was obliged to fall back upon Moultrie, his troops having suffered considerably, and himself having been wounded. Captain Shubrick conducted our retreat much to his honor. Communication of Prevost's passage across the river, and of his subsequent operations, was, from day to day, transmitted to the

American commander, who, penetrating his enemy's design, sternly
held his original course, detaching three hundred light infantry under Colonel Harris, to General Moultrie. The unexpected facility
with which the British general moved, the slight resistance opposed to him, the favorable intelligence received, and the fame of
the signal success which had heretofore crowned his exertions, from
the first moment of the invasion, combined, produced a conclusion
in his favor too flattering to be resisted.

He converted a feint into a fixed operation, and henceforward
marched on with the avowed purpose of seizing the metropolis of
South Carolina.   Nor was this avowal unsupported by appearances.
For Lincoln, by steady adherence to his original purpose, founded
on his just conviction, that the enemy's entrance into South Carolina meant nothing more than to draw him from Augusta, had now
gone too far to return and afford timely interposition.

Governor Rutledge, with the reserve militia had established himself at Orangeburg, a central position, perfectly adapted to the convenient reception and distribution of this species of force, which is
ever in a state of undulation.

He was far on Prevost's left, and, like Lincoln, was *hors de combat.* Moultrie only could gain the town; and Moultrie's self was
a host; but his force was not of that patient and stubborn sort,
who would dig and fight, and fight and dig, systematically. Charleston, too, was unprepared for an attack by land, heretofore providing
defence on the water side only ; and as to this mode of protection,
through the blunder of Sir Henry Clinton, and the gallantry of
General Moultrie in 1776, the reputation of adequacy had been
attached, the inhabitants reposed with confidence in their security
until the unequivocal demonstration of General Prevost's intention
with his rapid approach expelled their groundless belief. Here
mark the fallibility of man; observe the difference between the
mediocre and the consummate soldier. The British general had
been led, as before explained, to change stratagem into a fixed invasion. The boldness of the design, and the rapidity of its execution, produced the state of things which occasioned this change
of plan. Ought not the same boldness and the same rapidity to
have been continued to the completion of the enterprise ? Common sense forbids a negative to the interrogation ; and yet this
general, this conqueror, stops about half-way for two days.

On the third he advances; but forty-eight hours lost, in his sit
uation, gave a finishing blow to his grand project.

The father of the State had removed from Orangeburg with the reserve, to throw himself into Charleston, if possible. What was before impossible, had become possible by ^{May 10th.} the forty-eight hours' delay of Prevost. Rutledge joined Moultrie; and Charleston became safe.*

Pulaski, a name dear to the writer, from a belief in his worth and a knowledge of the difficulties he always had to encounter, entered also; and on the same day which brought the British army before the town. All that was wanted for its ^{May 11th.} defence was now done. Persuaded that the means in possession were adequate, if faithfully applied, and feeling the noble ardor which men, defending their houses in which the precious treasures of wives and children are deposited, always feel, the spirit resulting from such emotions spread through every rank, and formed a phalanx of courage impenetrable to the fiercest assaults. Such was now the condition of the besieged town; and such had been the error of the victorious general.

The time gained by the Americans had been most advantageously used. Defences on the land side had been pushed with unceasing exertion, and though not complete were formidable. Masters and servants, boys and girls, mixed in the honorable work of self-defence. The beloved governor and the heroic defender of Fort Moultrie, by their dictation and their example, reinspired effort, even when drooping nature begged repose. On the day subsequent to investiture, the town was summoned, and favorable ^{May 12th.} terms of surrender were proffered. These were rejected, and our works permitted to advance during the discussion. The rejection surely ought to have been followed by immediate storm or retreat.

Neither took place: the whole day was intentionally, on the part of the besieged, and erroneously on the part of the besieger, spent in the adjustment of terms. Thus twelve precious hours more were

---

* Military history abounds with examples illustrating the preciousness of a few hours. It seems unaccountable that, nevertheless, the salutary counsel to be drawn from its instructive page is seldom regarded. General Prevost consumed the time in deliberating upon his measures which, properly used, would have secured his success. The moment he began to doubt, he was lost. Hannibal, the prince of war, is charged with having lost Rome by his waste of a few days after the battle of Cannæ. Whether his failure before Rome resulted from his delay remains uncertain. His great name forbids the credence of any imputation lessening his fame without full proof. No man can doubt but that the British general lost Charleston by his waste of forty-eight hours; and yet, for aught the writer knows, the delay might have proceeded from necessity, not from choice.

gained.   The correspondence closed with the proposal on our part, of neutrality to the town and State during the war, the peace to fix its ultimate condition.   This offer was rejected by the British general ; and he followed its rejection, by retiring from before the town during the night.   What train of reason- May 13th. ing could have produced the rejection of the proposition to surren- der the town on condition of neutrality by a general situated as was Prevost, I confess myself incapable of discerning.

The moment he found that the works could not be carried, he ought to have exerted himself to procure possession by negotiation ; and certainly the condition of neutrality was in itself eligible.   It disarmed South Carolina for the war ; the effect of which upon her infant sister, already nearly strangled, would have been conclusive ; and Congress would have soon found, that their army, unaided by South Carolina, could not be maintained in Georgia.

No British force would have been retained from the field, to preserve the neutral State ; and the sweets of peace, with the al- lurements of British commerce, would probably have woven a con- nection with Great Britain fatal in its consequences to the inde- pendence of the Southern States.

At all events, by the rejection of the proposal, when about to withdraw with his army, the expedition became abortive.   Where- as acceptance of the proffered condition would have obviated the disgrace attached to such a result, and deprived General Lincoln of a great portion of his force, and of all the arms, stores, &c., deposit- ed in Charleston.   General Prevost had scarcely crossed the Ashley River, before the American general, returning from Augusta by forced marches, reached Dorchester, the thresh- May 14th. old of the isthmus, leading to Charleston, made by the Ashley and Cooper rivers, which uniting below the town pass to the sea.

Reposing a few days in his camp, on the south of Ashley River, Prevost commenced his retreat along the sea-coast, which, with his maritime means, was readily and safely effected.

He first entered James' Island, then John's Island, where he es- tablished himself, waiting for a supply of stores, daily expected from New York.

CHAPTER XIII.

Lincoln approaches John's Island.—Battle of Stono.—Prevost returns to Georgia.

GENERAL LINCOLN, having called in his different corps, broke up from his position in Dorchester, and sat down close to John's Island, which the Stono Inlet separates from the main.

On the main at the ferry, upon this inlet or river, the van of the British was posted, consisting of one thousand five hundred men under Lieutenant-Colonel Prevost, who had erected three redoubts in his front for the security of his position. The numerous small craft, being fastened together, formed a communication between the van and the main body on the island.

Notwithstanding the British expedition had resulted in disappointments, to which in military transactions more or less ignominy is always attached, Lincoln was not satisfied, but was very desirous to wind up with *éclat* the toilsome and passive operations, into which he had been reluctantly drawn by his enterprising adversary. The van of the enemy only was within his reach; and as the bridge of boats afforded the sole conveyance to troops detached to its support, the supporting force was necessarily limited. Relying upon the advantage this circumstance afforded, Lincoln moved toward Stono on the 4th of June, with the resolution of ^{June 4th} striking at the van post; but after examining the enemy's condition, he thought proper to decline risking an assault.

In the course of ten or twelve days, Lieutenant-Colonel Prevost, with a portion of the army, was detached to the Savannah. The vessels forming the temporary bridge being taken by this officer (in consequence of the intention then entertained of retiring from the main) for the purpose of conveying his troops, the communication across the Stono, reverted to ferry transportation. General Prevost afterward relinquished his design of drawing his van into the island, and sent Lieutenant-Colonel Maitland to take charge of it.

This officer possessed a growing reputation which he well deserved. Not only was the boat bridge broken up, rendering the communication more inconvenient, but the garrison had been reduced to five hundred men. Maitland hastened to improve his condition by separating from it every encumbrance. His sick, his spare baggage, his horses, with every other appurtenance, not necessary to defence, were conveyed across the Stono; and he added to the security of his post all those aids from labor which genius and industry beget.

Lincoln was soon advised of the departure of Lieutenant-Colonel Prevost, with the simultaneous occurrences. Resuming his original design, he did not hesitate to seize the present inviting opportunity to execute it. On the 19th he moved with his army, determined to attack Maitland on the next morning. In accordance with this decision, General Moultrie was directed to take possession of James' Island with a detachment from Charleston, for the purpose of passing thence into John's Island, in order to draw upon himself the attention of the British general, and thus divert him from the attack upon his van. The ground in front of the enemy was level, and covered, at a small distance from his works, with a grove of large pine-trees.

On the 20th, Lincoln advanced to the assault. The North Carolina militia composed his right,* under Brigadier Butler, and his regulars his left, under General Sumner. The flanks were covered by light troops, Lieutenant-Colonel Henderson at the head of one, and Colonel Malmedy at the head of the other corps; and the reserve consisted of the cavalry, with a small brigade of Virginia militia under General Mason. The Highlanders, called the best troops of the enemy, being known to take post on his right, became by this order of battle opposed to the Continental soldiers. Maitland's pickets announced the American approach; and the British detachments formed for action. The seventy-first regiment was posted on the right, and a regiment of Hessians on the left. Lieutenant-Colonel Hamilton, with the North Carolina regiment, composed the centre. The British flanks seemed to be secure; as the one rested upon a morass, and the other upon a deep ravine. Notwithstanding appearances, both were, in fact, assailable; for the first was firm enough to bear infantry, and the other was not intersected by water. The retiring pickets were supported by two companies of the seventy-first regiment, who, with their usual intrepidity, rushed into close action, and, fighting bravely, were mostly destroyed. This advantage encouraged the assailants, who

June 20th.

---

* General Lincoln set an example, in his order of battle, worthy of imitation by all commanders at the head of unequal troops, as was invariably the case with American commandants.

Knowing that the Highlanders would take the enemy's right, he placed his Continentals on his left, whereas, agreeably to usage, they should have composed our right. Form ought ever to yield to substance, especially in the arrangements for battle.

were now ordered to reserve their fire and to put the issue of the battle on the bayonet.

Our troops advanced with alacrity ; and the enemy waited their approach until they got within sixty yards of the abatis, when a full fire from the artillery and small-arms was delivered. Disobeying orders, our line returned the fire, which was continued on both sides without intermission for half an hour. The action became keen and general ; the Americans continuing their fire with ardor. The enemy's left was driven back ; and Maitland seeing his danger made a quick movement with the seventy-first regiment, from the right to the left supplying its vacancy with his reserve. The Highlanders revived the contest on the left. The Hessians, being rallied, were brought again into line: and the action raged with increased fury. Lincoln, foreseeing the consequences, was chagrined to find his plan of battle interrupted ; and exerted himself to stop the fire. At length he succeeded : a pause ensued ; and the order for charge was renewed. Vain attempt ! the moment was passed ; and instantly the firing recommenced and continued for more than one hour, when the army of General Prevost was seen hastening to the ferry ; Moultrie having failed in making the intended diversion for want of boats. The British lieutenant-colonel manifested by the past conflict the probable issue of the future, strengthened, as he soon would be, by the support fast approaching ; which consideration induced Lincoln to order a retreat. This movement produced now, as it generally does, some disorder ; which being perceived by Maitland, he advanced upon Lincoln with his whole force. The cavalry (Pulaski was not present) were ordered up by the American general to charge the enemy, whose zeal in pursuit had thrown them into loose order. This was gallantly executed ; but Maitland closed his ranks as the horse bore upon him, and giving them a full fire from his rear rank, the front, holding its ground with charged bayonets, brought this corps (brave but undisciplined) to the right about. Mason, with his Virginia brigade, now advanced, delivering a heavy fire. The enemy drew back ; and our retreat was effected in tolerable order.

Thus terminated the battle of Stono. It was evidently lost, first, by the failure in the diversion from Charleston ; secondly, by the erroneous plan of attack ; and, lastly, by the deviation from orders in its execution. It seems surprising that if, as we must presume, a sufficiency of boats had been ascertained to be at our command before the assault was determined upon, how it could

happen that any deficiency should occur in the moment of execution, unless from want of due attention in the department charged
with their collection, which evinces culpable negligence.   Our
force of battle was pointed against the enemy's front, in which lay
his strength, as he had improved that part of his position by three
redoubts, and other defences; whereas our chief effort ought to
have been on his flanks, which invited primary attention, as they
were unfortified, and would, upon due examination, have been
found only to present an opposition easily to be surmounted.   The
morass was considered as impassable, whereas it was a firm marsh,
Lieutenant-Colonel Henderson having passed it in the course of the
action with a part of his corps.   The halt of the line, returning the
enemy's fire instead of pressing on with the bayonet, baffled our
last hope of victory ; nor is it improbable, had the appeal to the
bayonet been uninterrupted, but that our courage would have
surmounted all difficulties ; and that we should have obtained the
desired prize with heavy loss, which was attainable by a small sacrifice of lives, had we directed our attack against the enemy's vulnerable points.   There was throughout our war, a lamentable ignorance of the topography of the country in which we fought, imposing upon our generals serious disadvantages.   They had to ascer
tain the nature of the ground by reconnoitring, or by inquiry among
the inhabitants.   The first was not always practicable ; and the result of the last was generally defective.   Government ought to provide, in time of peace, maps on a large scale of the various districts
of the country, designating particularly the rivers, their tributary
streams, the bridges, morasses, and defiles, and hold them ready
for use when wanting, or we shall have to encounter the same difficulties in any future, that we experienced in this, war.

   The loss was nearly equal, amounting to one hundred and sixty-
five killed and wounded on the side of America.   Among our killed
was Colonel Robert, of the Charleston artillery, a much-respected
officer.   The American troops conducted themselves in this affair
very much like genuine soldiers, except in the deranging breach of
orders.

   Lieutenant-Colonel Hamilton, with the Majors M'Arthur and
Moncrieff, supported Maitland throughout the action, with zeal and
firmness.

   In the course of a few days, the British general retired from
John's Island and the adjacent main, unperceived, pursuing his
route along the interior navigation to Georgia, leaving Lieutenant-

Colonel Maitland at Beaufort, in the island of Port Royal, while General Lincoln, reduced by the return of the militia to the Continentals (about eight hundred), established himself at Sheldon, conveniently situated to attend to the enemy at Beaufort. The sultry season had set in; which, in this climate, like the frost of the North, gives repose to the soldier.* Preparations for the next campaign, and the preservation of the health of the troops, now engrossed the chief attention of the hostile generals.

Prevost, having reached Savannah, took up his quarters for the season, detaching Lieutenant-Colonel Cruger with one of the Provincial regiments to Sunbury.† This division of his force very well corresponded with the resumption of offensive operations, athough it subjected the British to great hazard, should a superior French fleet visit our coast, as had happened the previous year.

CHAPTER XIV.

Bland and Baylor's regiments sent to the South by Washington.—Gen. Matthews detached to Virginia by Sir H. Clinton.—Destroys all the stores at Portsmouth and Gosport and returns to New York.—French fleet under Count d'Estaing arrives on the coast of Georgia.—Lincoln and the French unite before Savannah.—Allied armies besiege the town.—Repulsed in an attempt to carry it by storm.—Pulaski killed.—D'Estaing returns to the West Indies.—Lincoln to Charleston.

THE contest for the Southern section of the United States had been regarded, by the respective commanders-in-chief, with watchful attention; and each took measures to strengthen and invigorate the operations in that quarter. Washington, enfeebled as he was, detached to the south Bland and Baylor's regiments of horse, and the new levies recruited for the Virginia line ;‡ while Sir Henry

* The heat in the months of July and August forbade the toils of war. In 1781 we found the heat of September and October very oppressive.

† By retaining the post at Beaufort, the British general could readily penetrate by means of the inland navigation into South Carolina, unmolested by the Americans, destitute as we were of naval force.

‡ *Copy of a letter to General Washington on Southern affairs.*

PHILADELPHIA, *April 28th*, 1779.

SIR :—The inclosed letter from the lieutenant-governor of South Carolina, committed to the consideration of a committee of three, and which, in the name of the committee, I have now the honor to inclose your excellency, will show you the extremity to which our affairs in that quarter are driving. The committee find a choice of difficulties in this business, because the reliance on militia from Virginia having in a great degree failed, there appears no remedy but such as will lessen the force you had a right to expect from Virginia for re-enforcing the main army. We have no reason to suppose that a greater force than fourteen

Clinton, viewing the destruction of the resources of the commonwealth of Virginia, as cutting up by the roots resistance in the
South, planned an enterprise against that State, no sooner conceived
than executed.*

A body of troops amounting to two thousand men was, early in
May, placed under the command of Brigadier-General Matthews.
Having immediately embarked on board the British squadron, conducted by Sir George Collier, the fleet stood out to sea on the 5th,
and on the 9th anchored in Hampton Roads. No country presents
more easy access by water than Virginia, the object of his invasion.
Deep navigable rivers everywhere intersect it, presenting to the
maritime invader advantages too obvious to be overlooked, and
trammelling the measures of defence with those difficulties which
the severance of the inhabitants, by the enemy's possession of the
rivers, and the toils and delays of circuitous marches, inevitably
produce.

Aware of the disadvantages to which the State is exposed in war
by these bountiful gifts of heaven, government had erected in the
most vulnerable points slight fortifications to protect the inhabitants
from predatory incursions, and raised a regiment of artillery at
State expense, and for State purposes, particularly with the view of
furnishing garrisons to their dispersed forts.

hundred militia, perhaps not more than one thousand, will go from North Carolina; and of the one thousand ordered by the government of Virginia, we learn
that not more than three hundred and fifty have been obtained. In this state
of things, the committee submit to your excellency's wisdom and better knowledge of the general state of military affairs and intended operations, the following measures. That the two thousand new recruits now in Virginia be forthwith regimented and ordered to join the Southern army; that a sum of money
be sent to Colonel Bland, with orders to re-enlist the men of his regiment, and
proceed without delay to the same destination, with his battalions of light
horse. If, sir, this plan should meet your approbation, the committee are of
opinion, that the sooner it were carried into execution the better.
Your excellency will be pleased to return the inclosed letter; and the committee wish to be favored with your opinion of the eligibility of this measure,
and if there is a probability of its being soon executed; or what additional or
other method may occur to your excellency for the relief of the Southern States,
which we find by conversing with General Howe (who has just arrived here),
demands speedy and powerful assistance.
I have the honor to be, with the highest sentiments of esteem and regard, sir,
Your excellency's most obedient and very humble servant,
RICHARD HENRY LEE.

* This opinion of Sir Henry Clinton was well founded: the destruction of the
resources of Virginia must have led to the annihilation of Southern opposition.
She may be truly styled the matrix of resistance in the South. The other States
were too remote to furnish many supplies, indispensable to the prosecution of
the war in that extremity of the Union.

Norfolk, the great seat of Virginia commerce, is situated on the east side of Elizabeth River; opposite lies Portsmouth; and to the south, in the fork of the two branches of the Elizabeth, which unite immediately above Norfolk, is Gosport; where had been established a navy yard for the use of the State. To this river, and to these towns, the British armament advanced. No difficulty interposed but the annoyance to be expected from one of those slight forts heretofore mentioned, and like all others erected in the State, exposed on the land side, being designed exclusively to defend the channel of the rivers on which they stood. Fort Nelson,* the principal of these defences, was situated on the west side of the Elizabeth, a little below the town of Norfolk, and in full command of the channel of the river.

Major Matthews,† with a garrison not exceeding one hundred and fifty men, was charged with the care of this post. On the 10th the fleet entered Elizabeth River, the army debarking three miles below Fort Nelson: preparations were made to gain its rear the next morning, and to carry the works by storm.

Open in this quarter, resistance would have been temerity. The major, foreseeing the enemy's intention, evacuated the fort during the night, and retired to the margin of the Great Dismal Swamp, where he could, when necessary, secure his corps from insult or injury. The British general having thus possessed himself of the sole obstruction to his views, established his head-quarters in Portsmouth, detaching troops to Norfolk, Gosport, and the circumjacent depots of naval and military stores. Finding in these places abundant magazines, he destroyed all not shipped for New York, confounding private with public property.

The loss sustained was great, and the injury resulting from it greater, as our stores were much wanted, and could not be quickly replaced.

The invasion was as short as it had been effectual; for before the close of the month the fleet and army reached New York.

Louis XVI., true to his plighted faith, had given instructions to his admirals in the West Indies to be always ready, in the intermission of active operations in that quarter, to extend assistance to

---

* So named in commemoration of the patriotic and virtuous General Nelson, afterward governor of the State, not more distinguished for his estimable qualities as a man, than he was by his pure and gallant exertions in the cabinet and in the field.

† Thomas Matthews, since speaker of the house of delegates of Virginia.

his allies.   Count d'Estaing, the same admiral who, in the past year, had been disappointed in his various efforts to contribute to our relief, still commanded on that station.

Governor Rutledge and General Lincoln, convinced from the impotent condition of the enemy in the South, that he must soon fall, could the force of France in the West Indies be brought to bear upon him in conjunction with the Southern American army, described, in concert with Mons. Plombard, French consul at Charleston, the feeble and divided condition of the army, under General Prevost, urging the count, by the many weighty considerations involved in the project, to devote himself to the proposed enterprise during the hurricane months, when, in the West India seas, naval operations cease.   No mind was more obedient to the calls of duty, connected with the prospect of increasing his personal fame, than that of the French admiral ; and he must have felt some anxiety to make amends in a second, for the disappointments experienced in his first, visit to our coast.   He acceded instantly to the proposition ; and, as soon as the season and his state of preparation permitted, he set sail from Cape François for Tybee with forty-one sail, mostly of the line, having on board ten regiments amounting to six thousand men.

On drawing near the American coast, the count dispatched two ships of the line and three frigates to Charleston, with Major-General Fontanges, to announce his approach, and to concert, with the governor and general, a plan of operations.   Pursuing his course, with the remainder of the fleet, he arrived on the coast of Georgia early in September.   Unapprehensive of danger from a French fleet, knowing, as did General Prevost, the British power upon the sea, the appearance of the Count d'Estaing was as unexpected as it was alarming.

Several of the British ships of war on the Georgia station fell a prey to this sudden invasion ; and the rest were saved by running them up the Savannah River.

Lincoln* immediately put his force in motion, and passed into Georgia at Zubly's Ferry on the 9th; while Governor Rutledge, with his usual activity, embodied the militia, hurrying them on by regiments to join the American general.   At the same time he col-

---

* General Lincoln passed the Savannah River at Zubly's Ferry.   On the south the swamps are very extensive, pierced by three creeks, over which bridges had been erected.   These had been broken down by the British general, and thus our progress was much retarded.

lected a number of shallops, and dispatched them to the French admiral for the purpose of facilitating the debarkation of his army.

On the 13th, D'Estaing landed three thousand men at Beaulieu; on the 15th he was joined by Pulaski and his Legion; and on the next day the union of the allied army took place in front of the town of Savannah, General Lincoln having been delayed longer than he expected by the various obstacles opposed to his progress.

The British general was no sooner apprised of the appearance of the French fleet than he devoted himself to vigorous preparations to meet the unequal contest. Orders were hastened to the Lieutenant-Colonels Maitland and Cruger, to join him by forced marches; and Captain Henry, of the navy, laying up the remnant of his small and useless squadron, the marines, sailors, and cannon were landed, and the first united to the garrison, the last mounted on the batteries. Two hundred negroes were associated with the troops in labor; old works were strengthened and new works erected. These were designed and executed by Major Moncrieff, of the engineers, an officer of superior merit. Lieutenant-Colonel Cruger, with the garrison of Sunbury, had reached Savannah before the French army sat down before it. Maitland, with that of Beaufort, consisting of veteran troops, was yet absent.

Before the union of the two armies, the Count d'Estaing summoned the British general in the name of his most Christian majesty only. This offensive style violated the respect due from one sovereign to another, and could not have been relished by the American general, although policy may have forbidden his noticing it at the moment.*

General Prevost, recollecting the late transactions before Charleston, determined to imitate the example furnished by his enemy on that occasion. He answered so as to protract negotiation, which terminated in his proposition of a truce for twenty-four hours, for the purpose of enabling him, as he suggested, to adjust terms of surrender, should he thus conclude. This was granted; so confident was Count d'Estaing of ultimate success. Unfortunate respite! it gave not only time for the completion of much of the unfinished work; but what was infinitely more important, it enabled Lieutenant-Colonel Maitland to assume his part in the defence before a

---

* Whether General Lincoln remonstrated to the count for this folly, if unmeant, and for this impertinence, if meant, the writer cannot decide: but it has been often and confidently asserted, that the French commander explained the matter to General Lincoln's satisfaction.

single offensive step was taken by the assailant. Cut off by the French fleet from the customary route to Savannah, the lieutenant-colonel took the only one left which offered a prospect of arrival.

Great were the obstacles he had to encounter, sometimes on water, sometimes on land, in deep swamps and marshes, through which his soldiers had to drag the boats, himself ill with a bilious fever, and in every step of his progress subject to interception. Braving all these difficulties, this undaunted and accomplished officer made his way good to the river Savannah; where, embarking in boats above the anchorage ground of the French fleet, he entered the town before the expiration of the truce. Every benefit expected from the delay being derived, Prevost now answered, "that he should defend himself to the last extremity." This resolution accorded with the wish of all; such had been the change effected during the truce in the state of the besieged. Maitland's junction diffused universal joy, not only because he added one-third to the number of the garrison, and that too in troops of the best quality, but because he added himself, always the source of comfort where danger reigned.

The allied army having brought up their ordnance intended for the siege, broke ground on the 23d; and with such diligence were their approaches pushed that, in the course of twelve days, fifty-three pieces of battering cannon and fourteen mortars were mounted. All of these opened on the 4th of October, threatening speedy destruction to the enemy's defences. This dreadful display induced General Prevost to solicit the removal of the aged, the women and children, to a place of safety; a request sustained by the claims of humanity, and in no way injurious to the besieged (the expectation of gaining the town being unconnected with the state of provisions), was unaccountably rejected by the confederate generals.

On the approach of the French, few guns were mounted in the works of the enemy; but such had been the vast exertions of General Prevost that now nearly one hundred of different calibres were in full array.

Savannah lying on the river, is on that side safe. A deep morass stretches from the river above, and gives security to that quarter.

Fields environ it on the other two sides. Here the allies were approaching; and here were found the enemy's defences. Throughout had been erected redoubts and batteries, secured wherever necessary in the rear, with impalements and traverses, and the whole surrounded with a ditch and abatis. So well prepared for defence, the change from regular approaches to storm was the wish of the besieged, their fate being otherwise sealed unless relieved by a British fleet. Prevost did not waste his force in attempts to impede our advances, only two sorties being made during the siege; from neither of which did any material consequence ensue. He calculated on a storm, knowing the danger to the French fleet and army, separated as they were, from the active and daring operations of the British navy, as well as from those agitations of nature usual in the autumn, and so often destructive to ships on the coast. He also counted upon the impatient temper of the French identified in the character of their commander, not doubting from his being our voluntary assistant, he would take his measures from and for himself. Lincoln's wisdom, Lincoln's patience, Lincoln's counsel would be very limited in its effect.

Thus judging, Prevost was right in preserving his full strength for the decisive hour. It soon came; already Count d'Estaing had spent one month in the completion of an enterprise, which from the information he had received in Cape François, he calculated would have detained him ten days.* His naval officers felt for the safety of the fleet, and daily growing anxious for change of station, now became more pressing in their remonstrances; and the affairs in the West Indies (to which aid to us was always secondary) began to demand his attention. The count's own character gave pungency to the conclusion growing out of these considerations. He accordingly made known to Lincoln that the siege must be raised forthwith, or a storm attempted. Situated as the American general and the country in his care were, no alternative remained. However sincerely he must have wished for the continuance of the adopted system, safe and sure, he could not hesitate in renouncing it, and putting every thing to hazard, sooner than to abandon so important an enterprise.

It was, of course, determined to carry the enemy by storm, and the 9th of October, close at hand, was fixed for the assault. The plan of attack was judicious; the morass stretching from the river, and covering one quarter of the town, gave a concealed approach from a sink in the ground, along its margin leading to the British

* The information derived by the communication from the governor-general, and French consul, before mentioned, and which led to the enterprise, was correct. D'Estaing found the enemy subdivided, the best officer and the best troops did not join until the truce was nearly expired. Any four hours before the junction of Lieutenant-Colonel Maitland was sufficient to have taken Savannah.

right, believed by the assailants to be the most vulnerable.* This advantage was seized by D'Estaing and Lincoln; they drew into it two columns, the *élite* of the confederate force, determined to confide the issue to their prowess; while the American militia, threatening the centre and left, should thus distract the enemy's resistance. Prevost, anticipating with delight the chance of safety which could only be realized by a change in system on the part of the assailants, or by the approach of the British fleet, was always prepared. To the care of Lieutenant-Colonel Maitland he assigned his right, his weakest part. The centre he confided to Lieutenant-Colonel Hamilton, of the North Carolina regiment, and the left to Lieutenant-Colonel Cruger.

General Prevost having lined the intrenchments with appropriate troops, held disposable to succeeding incidents the seventy-first regiment, two Hessian regiments, one battalion of the New Jersey brigade, one of the New York brigade, and the light infantry in a second line, safe from the injury of our fire.

The 9th of October dawned; the allied troops moved to the assault. The serious stroke having been committed to two columns, one was led by D'Estaing and Lincoln united, the other by Count Dillon; the third column moved upon the enemy's centre and left, first to attract attention, and lastly to press any advantage which might be derived from the assault by our left.

The troops acted well their parts; and the issue hung for some time suspended. Dillon's column, mistaking its route in the darkness of the morning, failed in co-operation, and very much reduced the force of the attack; while that of D'Estaing and Lincoln, concealed by the same darkness, drew with advantage near to the enemy's line undiscovered. Notwithstanding this loss of concert in assault by the two columns destined to carry the enemy, gallant and determined was their advance. The front of the first was greatly thinned by the foe, sheltered in his strong and safe defences, and aided by batteries operating not only in front but in flank.

Regardless of the fatal fire from the covered enemy, this unappalled column, with Lincoln and D'Estaing at its head, forced the

---

* The hollow way which led to the enemy's right gave great advantage to the assailant. It brought him close, unperceived and uninjured. The small distance to pass over when discovered, and when exposed to the enemy's fire, diminished greatly the loss to be sustained before he reached the ditch. So persuaded was the British general that his right was the part to be especially guarded, that there he posted his best troops, and there commanded Lieutenant-Colonel Maitland.

abatis, and planted their standards on the parapet. All was gone, could this lodgment have been sustained. Maitland's comprehensive eye saw the menacing blow; and his vigorous mind seized the means of warding it off. He drew from the disposable force the grenadiers and marines nearest to the point gained. This united corps under Lieutenant-Colonel Glazier assumed with joy the arduous task to recover the lost ground. With unimpaired strength it fell upon the worried head of the victorious column; who, though piercing the enemy in one point, had not spread along the parapet; and the besieged bringing up superior force, victory was suppressed in its birth. The triumphant standards were torn down; and the gallant soldiers who had gone so far toward the goal of conquest, were tumbled into the ditch and driven through the abatis. About the time that Maitland was preparing this critical movement, Count Pulaski, at the head of two hundred horse, threw himself upon the works to force his way into the enemy's rear. Receiving a mortal wound, this brave officer fell; and his fate arrested an effort which might have changed the issue of the day.* Repulsed in every point of attack, the allied generals drew off their troops. The retreat was effected in good order; no attempt to convert it into rout being made by the British general; who having gained his object, wisely refrained from hazarding by this measure the safety of the town and garrison. From the enemy's artillery only, the retiring army received injury, which was considerable. Count D'Estaing, who,

---

* This gallant soldier was a native of Poland, whose disastrous history is well known. Vainly struggling to restore the lost independence of his country, he was forced to seek personal safety by its abandonment. Hearing of the noble struggle in which we were engaged, he hastened to the wilds of America, and associated himself with our perils and our fortune. Congress honored him with the commission of brigadier-general, with a view, as was rumored, of placing him at the head of the American cavalry, the line of service in which he had been bred. But his ignorance of our language, and the distaste of our officers to foreign superiority, stifled this project. He was then authorized to raise a legionary corps, apnointing his own officers.

Indefatigable and persevering, the count collected about two hundred infantry and two hundred horse, made up of all sorts, chiefly of German deserters. His officers were generally foreign, with some Americans. With this assemblage the count took the field; and after serving some time in the Northern army, he was sent to the South, and fell as has been described. He was sober, diligent, and intrepid, gentlemanly in his manners, and amiable in heart. He was very reserved, and, when alone, betrayed strong evidence of deep melancholy. Those who knew him intimately spoke highly of the sublimity of his virtue, and the constancy of his friendship. Commanding his heterogeneous corps, badly equipped and worse mounted, this brave Pole encountered difficulty and sought danger. Nor have I the smallest doubt if he had been conversant in our language, and better acquainted with our customs and country, but that he would have become one of our most conspicuous and useful officers.

with General Lincoln, had courted danger to give effect to the assault, was wounded, as was Major-General Fontange, with several other officers. The French killed and wounded, were rated at seven hundred men. The American regulars suffered in proportion; two hundred and forty being killed and wounded, while the militia from Charleston, their companions in danger, lost one captain killed, and six privates wounded. The enemy, fighting under cover of their skilfully constructed works, suffered but little, only one hundred and twenty of the garrison being killed and wounded. The British general gained, as he merited, distinguished applause for the wisdom, vigilance, and courage displayed throughout the siege. He was supported with zeal by every man under him, each in his station contributing his full share to the desired end. Captain Tawes, of the provincial troops, signalized himself by his intrepidity in defend-ing the redoubts committed to his charge, the leading point of our assault. He fell dead at the gate, with his sword plunged into t¹ body of the third enemy whom he had slain.

Lieutenant-Colonel Maitland, always great, surpassed upon thi. occasion his former glory; but to the deep regret of his admiring comrades, in a few days after our repulse, fell a victim to the fever which he had brought with him from Beaufort. Major Moncrieff, chief engineer, Captain Charlton, commanding the artillery, and Captain Henry, of the navy, acting with the garrison, received the general's marked acknowledgments for their exemplary exertions. Nor was the allied army behind their successful foe in the race of glory. Every thing was done which brave men could do. The darkness of the morning produced the loss of punctual combination between the columns charged with the assault; which unfortunate occurrence probably led to our repulse. The daring effort of the intrepid Pulaski to retrieve the fortune of the day, failing with his much regretted fall, presents additional proof of the high spirit which actuated the besiegers, demonstrating that every difficulty was encountered, every danger braved, to crown the enterprise with success. While with pleasure we offer the praise due to con-federates in the hour of assault, we cannot pass from this disastrous day without examining the preceding conduct of the leaders of the allied army.

First, we ask why the route between Beaufort and Savannah had not attracted primary attention. It must have been known that Lieutenant-Colonel Maitland would level all obstacles sooner than fail to unite himself with General Prevost; and it ought to have been known that, Maitland being stopped, Savannah would fall. Yet it appears that this first object was entirely neglected ; and it also appears that Maitland's junction, though unobstructed, was replete with difficulty.

Secondly, we cannot but express surprise (it being clearly understood that the French co-operation must be very limited in time) at the long delay of the assault. Had Count d'Estaing, when his summons was answered by proposing a truce, penetrated the design of the enemy, rejected the proposal, and commenced the attack, the British general would have surrendered, as Maitland had not arrived, and the works were still incomplete. The rash decision, of defending himself thus circumstanced, could not have been adopted ; and had it been adopted with the same gallantry which was displayed at a future day, the French must then have succeeded. The American general had not come up, and is of course exempt from his share in this animadversion : a delay unexpected and unfortunate, for probably had Lincoln been in place, the truce might have been rejected, and an assault adopted.

Our repulse was followed by raising the siege. The allied armies separated in good humor, although so lamentably foiled in their sanguine expectations.*

Without delay the Count d'Estaing re-embarked his troops, and, resuming his naval station in the West Indies, went himself to France, while General Lincoln returned to South Carolina.

The abandonment of the siege of Savannah closed the campaign, which had been active, daring, and novel, ever presenting, sometimes to one side, sometimes to the other, splendid prospects, and turning the moment of expected success into bitter disappointment : Charleston and Savannah alternately struck at by the opposite armies, both within the grasp of the assailant, and neither taken ; the American army under Howe defeated ; an imposing detachment under Ashe cut to pieces ; Lincoln baffled at Stono Ferry ; the united forces of America and France repulsed before Savannah ; yet notwithstanding these heavy disasters, the upper country of Georgia, the object of the contending generals, rested in possession of the United States.

---

* The thorough good will, exemplified by the general's troops when separating, induces the belief that the offensive style in which the summons had been couched, had either been satisfactorily explained, or was understood by the American general to have been an accidental slip on the part of the Count d'Estaing in the hurry of the moment.

CHAPTER XV.

Extraordinary enterprise and success of Col. White.—Sir H. Clinton sails for the South.—
    Siege of Charleston.—Fall of Charleston and surrender of Lincoln's army.—Spain
    joins in the war against Great Britain.—Don Galvez, Governor of New Orleans,
    subdues the British settlements on the Mississippi and Bay of Mobile.

WHILE the allied army was engaged before Savannah, Colonel
John White, of the Georgia line, conceived and executed an extraordinary enterprise. Captain French, with a small party of the
British regulars, was stationed on the Ogeechee River, about twenty-five miles from Savannah. At the same place lay five British
vessels, of which four were armed, the largest mounting fourteen
guns. White, having with him only Captain Etholm and three soldiers, kindled many fires, the illumination of which was discernible
at the British station, exhibiting, by the manner of ranging them,
the plan of a camp. To this stratagem he added another: he and
his four comrades, imitating the manner of the staff, rode with
haste in various directions, giving orders in a loud voice. French
became satisfied that a large body of the enemy were upon him;
and, on being summoned by White, he surrendered (1st of October) his detachment, the crews of the five vessels, forty in number,
with the vessels, and one hundred and thirty stand of arms.

Colonel White having succeeded, pretended that he must keep
back his troops, lest their animosity, already stifled by his great
exertions, should break out, and indiscriminate slaughter take place
in defiance of his authority; and that, therefore, he would commit
his prisoners to three guides who would conduct them safely to
good quarters. This humane intention on the part of White was
thankfully received. He immediately ordered three of his attendants to proceed with the prisoners, who moved off with celerity,
anxious to get away lest the fury of White's corps, believed to be
near at hand, might break out, much disposed though he himself
was to restrain it.

White, with the soldier retained by him, repaired, as he announced to his guides and prisoners, to his troops for the purpose
of proceeding in their rear.

He now employed himself in collecting the neighborhood militia,
with whom he overtook his guides, their charge safe and happy in
the good treatment experienced.

The extraordinary address of White was contrasted by the extraordinary folly of French; and both were necessary to produce this

wonderful issue. The affair approaches too near the marvellous to have been admitted into these Memoirs had it not been uniformly asserted, as uniformly accredited, and never contradicted.

Congress, undismayed by the gloom which the unexpected issue to the siege of Savannah had spread over the South, took immediate measures to re-enforce Lincoln; and Sir Henry Clinton, encouraged by his success, determined to press to completion its subjugation.

In pursuance of a resolution of Congress, the North Carolina line was ordered to South Carolina; and solemn assurances were given of effectual support to the languishing resistance in the South.

Sir Henry Clinton having withdrawn the British garrison from Newport, thereby restoring the elastic patriotism of the State of Rhode Island to its wonted energy and freedom, and being re-enforced from England, prepared a respectable detachment of chosen troops to be led by himself for the reduction of South Carolina. Waiting for the departure from the American coast of the French fleet, he was no sooner apprised of this event than he began the embarkation of his army; which being completed, Admiral Arbuthnot, the British naval commander on the American station, took upon himself the direction of the escorting fleet, and sailed from Sandy Hook on the 26th of December.

The voyage was tempestuous and tardy; some of the transports were lost, and others taken; all the horses for the cavalry and artillery perished: and the fleet, being much crippled in its stormy passage, never reached Tybee, its destined point, until the end of January. Here the damaged ships were repaired with all practicable haste; and the admiral put to sea, steering his course for North Edisto Sound, in South Carolina. The armament arrived there on the 10th of February; and the next day was employed in disembarking the army on John's Island.

Sir Henry Clinton was now on terra firma, within thirty miles of Charleston. He took immediate measures for advancing, but with the utmost circumspection, sacrificing much time in fortifying intermediate posts to hold safe his communication with the fleet. There are occasions and situations when such conduct is entitled to commendation, indeed when the omission would be highly reprehensible. But this was not the case now; no possible interruption was practicable on the part of Lincoln, whose regular force consisted of about two thousand men, including the North Carolina regulars, and four hundred Virginians, who had lately joined him under Lieutenant-Colonel Heth. To these the militia of 1780.

the town only is to be added; for that of the country was much indisposed to shut themselves up in a besieged fortress. The recollection of the repulse which himself and Admiral Parker had sustained at this spot, in 1776, must have inspired Sir Henry Clinton with more respectful considerations of the power of his enemy, and the strength of his defences, than accurate information would warrant. Determined to avoid a second rebuff, the general pursued with unvarying pertinacity, the most cautious system.* The necessary boats for the transportation of the army, passing along the interior navigation to Waapoocut, entered into Ashley River under the command of Captain Elphinston. On the 29th of March the van of the British reached the banks of the river, having marched thirty miles since the 11th of February, and never meeting, during the whole period, with the smallest resistance, except in the solitary instance of a rencontre between Lieutenant-Colonel Washington, commanding Baylor's diminished regiment of cavalry, and Lieutenant-Colonel Tarleton, whose dragoons, having been remounted, or horses procured by Sir Henry Clinton since his landing, covered the left flank of a division advancing from Savannah. This first meeting terminated favorably for Lieutenant-Colonel Washington, who in the sequel took a few prisoners; among whom was Lieutenant-Colonel Hamilton, of the royal regiment of North Carolina.

On the 30th Sir Henry Clinton passed Ashley River above Charleston, and on the following day sat down in front of our works. On his march the van of the leading column was gallantly attacked by Lieutenant-Colonel Laurens with a corps of light infantry; in which skirmish the Earl of Caithness, aid-de-camp to Sir Henry Clinton, was wounded. It is possible that the extraordinary delay, with which the movements of the British general were made, might have been intended with the double view of excluding the possibility of failure, and of seducing his enemy to continue in Charleston. If so, he succeeded completely in both objects. He certainly secured himself from insult; and his delay as certainly fixed the fate of the

---

* In the whole course of the American war, there seems to have been a systematic sacrifice of time by the British generals. Excepting where Lord Cornwallis commanded, I do not recollect any operations wherein the British resorted to forced marches. Washington, in 1776, was hurried through the Jerseys. Upon this occasion Lord Cornwallis was the operating general; and we all remember how he pushed Morgan, and afterward Greene, in the Carolinas. The delay of Sir Henry Clinton in this short march of thirty miles is inexplicable, unless from habit, or from a wish to induce the American general to shut himself up in Charleston.

SULLIVAN ISLAND

Ft Sullivan, now Ft Moultrie

CHARLESTOWN HARBOUR

Estill

Mount Pleasant

Haddrells Point

Hog Island Channel

Shutes Folly

British Fleet

Fort JOHNSTON

JAMES ISLAND

Lempries

COOPERS RIVER

Hobcaw

Fort Town

PLAN OF
the Siege of
CHARLESTOWN,
IN
SOUTH CAROLINA,

Engraved for Lees' Memoirs of the War.

½

One English Mile.

Union

Beaucau

Starling

Lightwood

Ditt

Shubrick

Distillery

Izards Bridge

Fitzgerald

Hadrell

Filbin Landing

Gibbes Landing

Williams

Wappoo

Hampstead

Fenwick

R Green

Preneau

Harry

ASHLEY RIVER

STONO RIVER

U.P. Co. No. 4 Bond. St.

Southern army, which never could have been inclosed in the untenable town, had not the sound mind of Major-General Lincoln been bent from its own resolve by the wishes of all the influential characters of the State, and by the confident expectation of adequate support; neither of which considerations would have influenced him but for the long lapse of time which intervened between the day of disembarkation, 11th of February, and the 30th of March, the day of beginning investiture.

At the bottom of the short and narrow isthmus, as has been observed, made by the rivers Ashley and Cooper, stands Charleston, the metropolis of South Carolina, and the emporium of the Southern commerce. The rivers uniting south of the town make a convenient bay which glides by a slight current into the sea, assisting to form some handsome islands in its flow, and creating, by its resistance to the overbearing surge of the ocean, a bank of sand, emphatically called the Charleston Bar. On two of these islands, Sullivan's and James's, defences had been erected in the beginning of the war: on the first, Fort Moultrie, on the last, Fort Johnston. In 1776 Colonel Moultrie, by his intrepid resistance on Sullivan's Island, repulsed a formidable fleet and army, as has been before recited.

Estimating the defence of the approach from sea as momentous to the safety of South Carolina, Congress had prepared a small squadron, under Commodore Whipple, to co-operate with the insular fortifications. United to those of the State, our naval force, then in Charleston harbor, consisted of nine sail, the largest mounting forty-four guns. From the successful resistance made by Colonel Moultrie, in 1776, it was confidently, and with much reason, presumed that the difficulty of passing the bar, the co-operation of the squadron with the Forts Moultrie and Johnston, and the numerous batteries erected to protect the harbor, the British fleet would meet obstacles not easily to be surmounted. Fort Moultrie, with its appendages, was committed to Colonel Pinckney,* fitted in heart and head to uphold its splendid fame.

Confiding in his defences by water, the American general bestowed his unremitted attention to strengthen and enlarge those on land. The two rivers which form Charleston neck, like all the rivers in that country, are lined on both shores with extensive swamps, deep in water and in mud, and impervious to the passage of troops. Profiting by these natural impediments, a canal at a

---

* Charles Cotesworth Pinckney.

proper distance in front was cut from swamp to swamp. Beyond the canal, strong deeply laid abatis in two rows presented themselves, and were rendered more formidable by a double picketed ditch. Between this line of defence and the main works, holes dug in the ground were interspersed to break the order of advancing columns; strong redoubts and batteries skilfully constructed were erected to enfilade the flanks; and in the centre was an inclosed hornwork of masonry. The slow approach of the enemy, the active exertions of Governor Rutledge, invested by the general assembly with every power * but that of life and death, and the indefatigable efforts of Major-General Lincoln, had rendered our land defences respectable and imposing, when the enemy appeared in our front. On the 1st of April Sir Henry Clinton began his first parallel at the distance of eight hundred yards; previous to which the fleet had taken its station off Charleston Bar.

1780.

This natural obstacle had been uniformly regarded as presenting decided advantage to the besieged; and Commodore Whipple, with his squadron, was therefore detached to Charleston, presuming that with his force he could successfully stop the enemy from passing the bar, inasmuch as their ships must be lightened, taking out their guns and other encumbrances, to enable them to float its water. Strange to tell, this uniformly accredited opinion was on the moment of trial found fallacious.†

It was discovered that our frigates could not approach near enough to oppose the passage of the bar with any kind of success; and we necessarily abandoned without a struggle this point of de-

* The legislature passed an act "delegating to Governor Rutledge, and such of his council as he could conveniently consult, a power to do every thing necessary for the public good, except taking away the life of a citizen without legal trial." This is dealing out power with a profuse hand.

† A critical research into the various proceedings of Congress and of the States, in making preparations of defence, evince a negligence in the ascertainment of facts essential to the accurate execution of measures which excites surprise and regret. We have before seen that a British admiral first discovered that a small inlet between Mud Island and the Pennsylvania shore would admit ships with cannon, and that, availing himself of this discovery, he forced us to abandon Mud Island, and thus probably saved the British army. We now see that it was reserved for the moment of trial to learn that the bar of Charleston was not defensible by our squadron, because the water within the bar was too shallow for our frigates. Would not due inquiry have ascertained these truths in due time, when the inlet so destructive to Mud Island might have been readily shut up by immovable obstructions, close as it was under the command of our fort, and when a naval force, fitted for the depth of water within the bar, might have been as readily prepared and sent to Charleston as was the useless squadron which, by the surrender of the town, became the property of the enemy.

fence so much relied on.   Commodore Whipple took a second station with his squadron in range with Fort Moultrie, where it was confidently expected effectual opposition to the progress of the enemy's fleet could be made.

The British ships selected for this operation lay two weeks without the bar, deprived of their guns, waiting for wind and tide.

These being favorable on the 20th of March, a sixty-four, with some frigates, passed without injury of any sort.   No sooner had this been effected but it was discerned that the obstructions in the channel were not of magnitude, and that no probability of successful resistance offered itself in our new station.   The squadron was a second time ordered to retire; and having sunk most of our armed ships in the mouth of Cooper River to prevent the British admiral's holding that important pass, the crews and guns were landed and applied in the defence of the town, now relying for its safety solely upon the strength of its fortifications and the valor of its garrison.

With a fair wind, on the 9th of April, the British admiral weighed, with the determination to pass Fort Moultrie.

This he readily accomplished, notwithstanding all the opposition which it was possible for Colonel Pinckney to make.   Not a ship was disabled; and only twenty-seven men killed and wounded.   A convincing proof that unless the hostile fleet is stopped by obstructions in the channel difficult and tedious to remove, the fire of forts and batteries never can avail.*   Having passed this our only remaining point of resistance, the British fleet anchored within the harbor out of reach of further offence.   On the same day Sir Henry Clinton finished his first parallel, when the British commanders demanded the surrender of the town.   To this summons General Lincoln replied: "Sixty days have been past, since it has been known that your intentions against this town were hostile, in which time has been afforded to abandon it; but duty and inclination point to the propriety of supporting it to the last extremity." This answer was no sooner received than the British batteries commenced the dire assault, which continued without intermission.

As the British were possessed of the harbor and of Charleston

---

* Was this the solitary instance within our own experience of the accuracy of this observation, the result so confidently relied upon might be doubted; but every attempt made by the naval force of the enemy during the war succeeded in like manner; and many such operations took place.

Experience everywhere proves the truth of the remark; and it ought to influence government in their preparation of water defences whenever they may be resorted to.

neck, only the pass across Cooper River, and up to its eastern bank remained open to General Lincoln. A retreat was effectible, and ought in prudence to have been attempted as soon as the defence of the bar was discovered to be impracticable; being then omitted it ought now to have been attempted. For although it certainly had been rendered more hazardous than it was, before the enemy's fleet passed the bar, yet it was still practicable.* Only one difficulty of force was attached to the attempt—discovery before the garrison had crossed the river and begun its march. This certainly, might have been prevented by lining all the avenues to the enemy's posts with troops of approved fidelity. But this salutary plan was not adopted.

It does not seem *then* to have been even contemplated; for shortly before, Brigadier-General Woodford, with seven hundred of the Virginia line, detached from the main army by General Washington entered the town. This would not have taken place had retreat been in view. Woodford would have been halted at Monk's Corner, where Brigadier Huger, of the South Carolina line, was posted with the cavalry, to preserve communication between the town and country. Indeed the loss of Charleston was a sad deranging blow to the South; the force of which was aggravated by the injudicious, though faithful, effort to preserve it. Not only the metropolis of the State, and the depot of its commerce, with a portion of that of its Northern neighbor, but the unrivalled seat of Southern beauty, taste, art, science, and wealth, Charleston, from its foundation, had been the pride, the boast, and delight of the high-spirited gentry and gallant yeomanry of that country. And as if nature had stepped out of its ordinary course to give superiority to its advantages, it is the region of salubrity, and draws within its pale, in the season of summer, the sick to be cured, and the well to enjoy health, reversing the common order in Europe and America.†

---

* Our cavalry was now safe; and we had a small force of militia. All the horses in Charleston might have been conveyed across the river with saddles, bridles, and swords, which would have enabled Lincoln to mount some of his infantry, to act as dragoons, and thus given to the retreating army a decided superiority in that important force. At the same time it would have deprived the enemy of the means of transportation of stores, baggage, and munitions, without which, in adequate quantities, he would not have pursued any great distance. Gaining one march in this situation of things, Lincoln was safe; and this advantage was certain, if his caution and secrecy prevented discovery.

† In the sickly season (the summer and autumn) Charleston is resorted to, as with us, and everywhere else on the two continents, are the upper country

Such a combination of influence was not to be resisted by the brave and amiable Lincoln,* especially when supported by the co-incident wish of the brave fathers of the State, and encouraged by his reliance on assurances of adequate succor. It is to be regretted that the general's thorough knowledge of his own situation, of the enemy's strength and object, and of the imbecility of government, had not induced him to adopt that plan of operations which would have upheld the commonweal should disappointments, which too often happened, follow the assurances received from Congress. It was very certain that the possession of Charleston only, was not the sole object of the hostile armament, but the conquest of that State, in the first place, and then of as many others as could be added to it. It was equally certain that the preservation of the country would soon regain the town, whereas the loss of the country would irretrievably fix the doom of the town. Nor could it be doubted that the salvation of the country depended on the timely evacuation of the town, as thus only the army would be preserved to arrest the enemy's advance. After this had been done, if the assurances made General Lincoln should be realized, the subjugation of the State became visionary, and the invader would abandon Charleston, which would have probably stopped the prosecution of the war. If the assurances should turn out illusory, as they did, the army safe, would have given a rallying point to our militia, and drawn together such a force as might have resisted the enemy effectually, whenever Sir Henry Clinton returned to New York.†

Those afflicting disasters which followed never could have taken place, heightened by the intestine divisions in the two Carolinas. The leading characters of the country never could have been shut up in Charleston, to be thence transported in captivity; and the people under the direction of their accustomed lights and guides, linked together by sameness of birth, of habit, of religion, and of law, never could have been thrown into those deadly feuds, engen-

and its waters. This used to be the case; and I believe it still continues, with the exception of some who visit the Northern States in the sultry season.

* The American general partakes in character more of Æneas than of Hector.

† Sir Henry Clinton had left New York with a reduced force, and under a German general; admitting that he was safe from the intrusion of a French navy, as was probable, still he was not safe from General Washington, whose army never received its full annual strength sooner than July. Such was the dilatory progress, under our weak government. It therefore could not be doubted but that Sir Henry Clinton would return, and that as soon as was practicable, after the fall of Charleston.

dering that sanguinary warfare, in some sections of the country, which, with the fury of pestilence, destroyed without discrimination.

Let this sad though faithful record of our own experience admonish the rulers of the nation, if, in future vicissitudes of the everchanging scenes of human affairs, they should be called upon to act in a similar conjuncture; and let it impress on future generals, situated as was Major-General Lincoln, that the wiser course is that which promises to promote the common good, when the known impotence of the government renders the failure of its promises probable. Although this opportunity for retreat* was neglected, yet the

---

* In proof of the sad expectations which prevailed in Charleston about this time, I subjoin an intercepted letter, published by Mr. Stedman, whose history of the American war I have perused with great satisfaction, "from Mr. B. Smith to Mrs. Smith, dated, Charleston, April 30."

"Having never had an opportunity of writing to her since the enemy began to act with vigor, and knowing that a thousand evil reports will prevail to increase her, uneasiness—mine I have supported pretty well until last night, when I really almost sunk under the load. Nothing remains around to comfort me but a probability of saving my life, after going through many difficulties. Our affairs are daily declining; and not a ray of hope remains to assure us of our success. The enemy have turned the siege into a blockade, which in a short time must have the desired effect; and the most sanguine do not now entertain the smallest hope of the town being saved. The enemy have continued their approaches with vigor continually, since I wrote the inclosed, and are now completing batteries about two hundred yards distance from our lines. They but seldom fire from their cannon; but their popping off rifles and small guns do frequent mischief, and every night throw an amazing number of shells among our people, which at the lines, though not attended with the damages that might be reasonably expected, do some mischief. Our communication is entirely cut off from the country (excepting by a small pass at great risk) by Lord Cornwallis, who occupies every landing-place from Hadrell's Point, a considerable way up the river, with two thousand and five hundred men. When I wrote last, it was the general opinion that we could evacuate the town at pleasure; but a considerable re-enforcement having arrived to the enemy, has enabled them to strengthen their posts so effectually as to prevent that measure. The same cause prevents our receiving further supplies of provisions or re enforcements; and a short time will plant the British standard on our ramparts. You will see by the inclosed summons that the persons and properties of the inhabitants will be saved; and consequently I expect to have the liberty of soon returning to you; but the army must be made prisoners of war. This will give a rude shock to the independence of America: and a Lincolnade will be as common a term as a Burgoynade. But I hope in time we shall recover this severe blow. However, before this happens, I hope I shall be permitted to return home, where I must stay, as my situation will not permit me to take any further an active part; and therefore my abandoning my property will subject me to many inconveniences and losses, without being any way serviceable to the country. This letter will run great risk, as it will be surrounded on all sides ; but as I know the person to whose care it is committed, and feel for your uneasy situation, I could not but trust it. Assure yourself that I shall shortly see you; as nothing prevents Lincoln's surrender but a point of honor of holding out to the last extremity. This is nearly at hand, as our provisions

governor and general concerted measures well calculated to maintain the communication between the town and country.   The
governor, with a moiety of the executive counsel, left the town for
the purpose of encouraging the collection of the militia, and of
establishing a succession of posts, with supplies of provision, in case,
at any future day, a retreat might be deemed proper; while the
lieutenant-governor, the aged and respectable Mr. Gadsden, with
the other moiety, continued in the town to encourage, by their presence, their fellow-citizens, and to assist, by their authority, the military operations.   Governor Rutledge formed two camps, one between the rivers Cooper and Santee, and the other on the Santee.
But although clothed with dictatorial powers, and exerting these
powers with unabating zeal, he was never able to collect a force in
any degree respectable.

To be the principal, or to be the auxiliary, is very differently
relished by man.

The militia, feeling their imperfections, can rarely be brought to
act the first character, though willing, as they proved themselves, to
assume the second.

To encourage the efforts of the governor, General Lincoln, inadequate as his garrison was, detached three hundred regulars, who,
with the cavalry and the militia, it was confidently hoped might have
held open the communication yet remaining, especially as portions
of the promised re-enforcements were daily expected; all of which
would probably have been annexed to this incipient army.

Sir Henry Clinton, soon after the establishment upon John's
Island, had drawn from Savannah one thousand two hundred men,
and sent orders to Lieutenant-General Knyphausen to re-enforce him
with three thousand more from New York. This succor was daily
expected.

Proceeding without disturbance in his second parallel, and anxious to close the investiture of the town by extending his operations
on the north of Cooper River, he placed under Lieutenant-Colonel
Webster a corps of one thousand five hundred for the execution of
this object.   Webster found that the American cavalry still lay at

---

will soon fail; and my plan is to walk off as soon as I can obtain permission.
Should your father be at home, make him acquainted with the purport of this
letter, and remember me to him, also to your mother; but do not let the intelligence go out of the house.   But a mortifying scene must first be encountered;
the thirteen stripes will be levelled in the dust, and I owe my life to the clemency of the conqueror.

(Signed)   "B. SMITH."

Monk's Corner. To this point he devoted his attention ; soon informed, as well of their strength and position as of their precautions to guard against surprise, he determined to break up the post, and selected the night of the 14th of April for his enterprise. Taking some neglected by-paths, his van composed of Tarleton's Legion, and Ferguson's riflemen, by avoiding the patrols, approached our vedettes unperceived. Lieutenant-Colonel Tarleton drove at them with his habitual promptitude, and entered the camp with the vedettes.

Although accoutred for action, yet so instantaneous was the assault, that the American cavalry were routed without resistance. Lieutenant-Colonel Washington and most of the corps saved themselves by their knowledge of the country, while the inhabitants suffered outrages shocking to relate.* All the extra horses, wagons, baggage, &c., fell into the hands of the enemy. The British and American statements differ as to our loss widely. By our account we lost only thirty dragoons besides the baggage of the corps. Mr. Stedman, to whom I have before recurred, places it much higher ; and I have never been able to satisfy myself as to the real loss.†

---

* "Some dragoons of the British Legion attempted to ravish several ladies in the house of Dr. John Collington, in the neighborhood of Monk's Corner, where they were protected. A carriage being provided, they were escorted to the house of M——. The dragoons were apprehended and brought to Monk's Corner, where by this time Colonel Webster had arrived and taken the command. The late Colonel Patrick Ferguson, of whom we shall have to speak more hereafter, was for putting the dragoons to death. But Colonel Webster did not conceive that his power extended to holding a general court-martial. The prisoners were, however, sent to head-quarters; and, I believe, were afterward tried and whipped."—Stedman.

† "Forty-two wagons, one hundred and two wagon horses, and eighty-two dragoon horses, and several officers' horses ; a quantity of ammunition, flour, butter, clothing, camp and horse equipage, harness for all the wagons, all the officers' clothing and baggage, together with five puncheons of rum, six hogsheads muscovado sugar, four barrels indigo, a quantity of tea, coffee, spices, nails in casks, some French cloth, three barrels of gunpowder, swords, &c., found in a store, which was set on fire and blown up by the carelessness of a sentinel. The loss of the Americans in men was Major Bernie, of Pulaski's Legion of dragoons, and three captains, one lieutenant and two privates, killed ; fifteen privates, one captain, and two lieutenants, taken prisoners, including the wounded. Major Bernie was mangled in the most shocking manner : he had several wounds, a severe one behind his ear. This unfortunate officer lived several hours, reprobating the Americans for their conduct on this occasion ; and even in his last moments cursing the British for their barbarity, in having refused quarter after he had surrendered. The writer of this, who was ordered on the expedition, afforded every assistance in his power, and had the major put upon a table in a public-house in the village, and a blanket thrown over him. The major, in his last moments, was frequently insulted by the privates of the Legion."—Stedman.

This successful exploit enabled Lieutenant-Colonel Webster to establish a position on the Wando, thus securing all the country between that river and the Cooper. Lincoln learned with deep regret the disaster of our cavalry, and its direct consequence, the enemy's establishment on the Wando. He came to the resolution of striking at this post; but so weak was his garrison, that, by the advice of a council of war called upon the occasion, he relinquished his intention; and the post, fatal to his communication with the country, was left undisturbed, although held by only six hundred infantry and some cavalry. The re-enforcement from New York arriving about this time, Lord Cornwallis was appointed to undertake the investiture of the town on the north side of Cooper River, with considerable augmentation to the corps operating under Webster. Sir Henry Clinton had now completed his second parallel without interruption, Lincoln wisely determining to preserve his force undiminished by offensive efforts on his part, that he might be more able to meet a storm, or to make good his retreat.

But seeing that a third parallel must bring the enemy upon his canal, and render further resistance chimerical, he determined to interrupt its prosecution. Lieutenant-Colonel Henderson, of the South Carolina line, commanded a night sortie: it was executed with honor to the commandant and his detachment; but so thoroughly stable were the enemy's advances, that it was ineffectual, and a repetition was never attempted.

Lord Cornwallis having, with his detachment, joined Lieutenant-Colonel Webster, the retreat of the garrison became scarcely practicable, nevertheless such was the solicitude of the American general to save his army for the defence of the country, that he called a council of war to ascertain, through their advice, the course to be pursued. No longer doubting of the fall of the town, the council recommended that an offer of surrender should be made on two conditions, viz.: Safety to the persons and property of the inhabitants; and permission to the garrison to continue in arms. The first condition was that which every conqueror ought to grant with pleasure; the second, that which no conqueror can grant, unless situated very differently from the British commander. The proposition was rejected; and the besiegers pressed forward on their road to victory. The admiral prepared a detachment from his fleet under Captain Hudson to attack Fort Moultrie, from which Colonel Pinckney, and a greater part of the garrison, had been withdrawn soon after the fleet passed the fort. Why a single man should have

been left, much as the lines before Charleston required additional
force, seems inexplicable, especially after the evacuation of our
small posts at Lempriere's Point, and on the Wando.*

The menace against Fort Moultrie produced surrender; the flag
of that renowned post was now lowered; and the remnant garrison, about two hundred men, were made prisoners.

The American cavalry, after the surprise at Monk's Corner,
withdrew to the north of the Santee for security, where Lieutenant-
Colonel White, of Moylan's regiment, took the command. This
officer, discovering that Lord Cornwallis extended his foraging parties to the southern banks of the river on which he was encamped,
determined to interrupt the collection of his supplies. Prepared
to execute this proper decision, upon the first notice of the enemy's
approach, he passed the Santee, struck at the foe, broke up the
forage excursion, captured most of the party, with which he retired
to Lenew's Ferry upon the Santee, where he had ordered boats to
meet him; and at the same time communicating his success to
Lieutenant-Colonel Buford, who commanded a regiment of Virginia
levies, stationed near the ferry, on the north side of the river, requiring his aid in the transportation of himself and prisoners to the
opposite shore.

How it happened is not ascertained; but it did happen, that
Buford's co-operation, nor the boats ordered by White were felt or
seen; and the successful lieutenant-colonel, expecting instantly the
means of conveyance, incautiously waited on the southern bank of
the river instead of moving to some secret and strong position.

Lieutenant-Colonel Tarleton was on his march to Lenew's Ferry
with his cavalry; sent thither by the British general to procure
intelligence; falling in with a royalist, he was informed of White's
success, and instantly pressed forward to strike him. He came up
with our cavalry on the banks of the Santee, and repeated the catastrophe at Monk's Corner. The knowledge of the country was a
second time beneficial to the fugitives; the swamps saved some,
while others swam the river. Between thirty and forty only were
killed and taken.

The evacuation of our small posts on Wando and Lempriere's
Point, with the surrender of Fort Moultrie, and the second discom-

* Lord Cornwallis had taken possession of Mount Pleasant, which produced
the evacuation of Lempriere and Wando posts.

It applied as precisely to the withdrawing of the garrison from Fort Moultrie; as that post had never been fortified in this quarter, and was, of course,
subject to approach without difficulty.

fiture of our cavalry, gave to the enemy uncontrolled possession of all the country between the Cooper and Santee rivers, and extinguished the glimmering hopes that had been still entertained of the practicability of a retreat from the town.

Soon followed the completion of the third parallel, which placed the garrison at the mercy of the besiegers. Unwilling, from motives of humanity, to increase the hardships of the unfortunate, the British admiral and general a second time demanded surrender.

Lincoln now, from necessity, yielded up his army ; but still, anxious to save the militia and inhabitants from captivity, he excepted them in his assenting answer, which exception being declared inadmissible, the negotiation ceased.

Reluctantly Sir Henry Clinton renewed the contest by opening the batteries of the third parallel, and pushed his works under their fire to the brink of the canal, which by a sap to the dam was drained. This first barrier was now possessed by the enemy, and a double sap carried thence under the abatis, within thirty steps of our work. For two days, the fire from the third parallel continued without intermission, and with great execution : and the sharpshooters were planted so close to our lines as to single out every man who exposed himself to view.

The enemy being prepared to strike the last blow, the orders for assault only remained to be given, when the inhabitants became assured that the concluding scene could not long be deferred, and though heretofore devoted to the defence of the town, now with one accord supplicated General Lincoln to relinquish the exception made in their favor, and to accept the terms proffered.*

The amiable Lincoln could no longer hesitate in stopping the effusion of blood. He communicated to Sir Henry Clinton his readiness to lay down his arms upon the conditions before offered.

Highly honorable was the conduct of the British commanders. They did not press the unfortunate, but agreed that the terms before rejected should form the basis of capitulation, which being

---

* This change in temper and feelings of the people of Charleston belongs to man similarly situated all over the world ; and therefore military commandants, in taking military measures, while they hear with patience and decorum, the desires of the inhabitants, ought never to regard them in the adoption of their plans or measures. General Lincoln no more ought to have been influenced by the remonstrances of the citizens of Charleston, when weighing in his mind the propriety of evacuation, than ought a tender father to regard the crying of his child on his administering a dose of physic to save its life.

soon prepared, signed, and ratified, Charleston was surrendered on
the 12th, six days after the third parallel was finished.*

* CHARLESTON, *May* 11, 1780.

SIR: The same motives of humanity which inclined you to propose articles of
capitulation to this garrison, induced me to offer those I had the honor of sending you on the 8th instant. They then appeared to me such as I might proffer,
and you receive with honor to both parties. Your exceptions to them, as they
principally concerned the militia and citizens, I then conceived were such as
could not be concurred with; but a recent application from those people,
wherein they express a willingness to comply with them, and a wish on my
part to lessen, as much as may be, the distresses of war to individuals, lead me
now to offer you my acceptance of them.

I have the honor to be, &c.,

(Signed)   B. LINCOLN.

His Excellency Sir H. CLINTON.

CAMP BEFORE CHARLESTON, *May* 11, 1780.

SIR: When you rejected the favorable terms which were dictated by an earnest
desire to prevent the effusion of blood, and interposed articles that were wholly
inadmissible, both the admiral and myself were of opinion, that the surrender
of the town at discretion was the only condition that should afterward be
attended to; but as the motives which then induced them are still prevalent,
I now inform you that the terms then offered will still be granted.

A copy of the articles shall be sent for your ratification as soon as they can
be prepared; and immediately after they are exchanged, a detachment of grenadiers will be sent to take possession of the hornwork opposite your main gate.
Every arrangement which may conduce to good order in occupying the town,
shall be settled before noon to-morrow; and at that time your garrison will
march out.

I have the honor to be, &c.,

H. CLINTON.

Major-General LINCOLN.

ARTICLES OF CAPITULATION BETWEEN THEIR EXCELLENCIES SIR HENRY CLIN-
TON, MARIOT ARBUTHNOT, ESQ., AND MAJOR-GENERAL BENJAMIN LINCOLN.

ART. 1ST.—That all acts of hostility and work shall cease between the besiegers and the besieged, until the articles of capitulation shall be agreed on,
signed, and executed, or collectively rejected.

Answer.—All acts of hostility and work shall cease, until the articles of capitulation are finally agreed to or rejected.

ART. 2D.—The town and fortifications shall be surrendered to the commander-
in-chief of the British forces, such as they now stand.

Answer.—The town and fortifications, with the shipping at the wharves,
artillery, and all other public stores whatsoever, shall be surrendered in their
present state to the commanders of the investing forces; proper officers shall
attend from the respective departments to receive them.

ART. 3D.—The Continental troops and sailors, with their baggage, shall be
conducted to a place to be agreed on, where they shall remain prisoners of war
until exchanged. While prisoners, they shall be supplied with good and wholesome provisions in such quantity as is served out to the troops of his Britannic
majesty.

Answer.—Granted.

ART. 4TH.—The militia now in garrison shall be permitted to return to their
respective homes, and be secured in their persons and property.

Answer.—The militia now in garrison shall be permitted to return to their

The adverse generals, in their official dispatches, speak in very approving terms of the zeal and gallantry with which they were

respective homes as prisoners on parole; which parole, as long as they observe, shall secure them from being molested in their property by the British troops.

ART. 5TH.—The sick and wounded shall be continued under the care of their own surgeons, and be supplied with medicine and such necessaries as are allowed to the British hospitals.

Answer.—Granted.

ART. 6TH.—The officers of the army and navy shall keep their horses, swords, pistols, and baggage, which shall not be searched, and retain their servants.

Answer.—Granted, except with respect to the horses, which will not be allowed to go out of the town; but may be disposed of by a person left from each corps for that purpose.

ART. 7TH.—The garrison shall at an hour appointed, march out with shouldered arms, drums beating, and colors flying, to a place to be agreed on, where they wi'l pile their arms.

Answer.—The whole garrison shall, at an hour to be appointed, march out of the town to the ground between the works of the place and the canal, where they will deposit their arms. The drums are not to beat a British march, or colors to be uncased.

ART. 8TH.—That the French consul, his house, papers, and other movable property shall be protected and untouched, and a proper time granted to him for retiring to any place that may afterward be agreed upon between him and the commander-in-chief of the British forces.

Answer.—Agreed, with this restriction, that he is to consider himself as a prisoner on parole.

ART. 9TH.—That the citizens shall be protected in their persons and properties.

Answer.—All civil officers, and the citizens who have borne arms during the siege, must be prisoners on parole; and with respect to their property in the city, shall have the same terms as are granted to the militia: and all other persons now in the town, not to be described in this or other article, are, notwithstanding, understood to be prisoners on parole.

ART. 10TH.—That a twelvemonth's time be allowed all such as do not choose to continue under the British government to dispose of their effects real and personal in the State, without any molestation whatever; or to remove such parts thereof as they choose, as well as themselves and families; and that during that time, they or any of them may have it at their option to reside occasionally in town or country.

Answer.—The discussion of this article of course cannot possibly be entered into at present.

ART. 11TH.—That the same protection to their persons and properties, and the same time for the removal of their effects, be given to the subjects of France and Spain, as are required for the citizens in the preceding article.

Answer.—The subjects of France and Spain shall have the same terms as are granted to the French consul.

ART. 12TH.—That a vessel be permitted to go to Philadelphia with the general's dispatches, which are not to be opened.

Answer.—Granted; and a proper vessel with a flag will be provided for that purpose.

All public papers and records must be carefully preserved and faithfully delivered to such persons as shall be appointed to receive them.

Done in Charleston, May 12, 1780.   B. LINCOLN.

Done in camp before Charleston, May 12, 1780.

(Signed)   H. CLINTON,
                            M. ARBUTHNOT.

respectively supported.   The loss was by no means correspondent to the length and obstinacy of the conflict, because of the safe and judicious system adopted by the besieger in his advances, and from the inadequacy of the garrison, which induced the besieged to husband with care his force, in the hope that some propitious event might occur on the part of our ally, and force Sir Henry Clinton to change his plan of operations, as had taken place with Lincoln himself before Savannah ; and relying also upon the reiterated assurance of ample support from Congress and the governments of North and South Carolina.

The enemy lost seventy killed, and one hundred and eighty-nine wounded : our loss, including militia and inhabitants, amounted to one hundred and two killed, and one hundred and fifty-seven wounded.   Among the former was Lieutenant-Colonel Richard Parker, of the first Virginia regiment.   He was one of that illustrious band of youths who first flew to their country's standard when she was driven to unsheath the sword.   Stout and intelligent, brave and enterprising, he had been advanced from the command of a company in the course of the war to the command of a regiment.   Always beloved and respected, late in the siege he received a ball in the forehead, and fell dead in the trenches, embalmed in the tears of his faithful soldiers, and honored by the regret of the whole army.

The British official statement gave a total of prisoners exceeding five thousand, including, no doubt, all the inhabitants capable of bearing arms, it being certain that Lincoln's Continental force did not reach two thousand, exclusive of officers, when he surrendered. His effective militia, by his official return, amounted at the same time to five hundred men.   In addition we lost, by the British account, one thousand seamen, American and French, with four hundred pieces of ordnance, abundant magazines of military and naval stores, and all the shipping in the harbor.*   The loss of men,

---

* Return of the ships and vessels taken and destroyed in the siege of Charleston.   The Bricole, pierced for sixty, mounting forty-four guns, twenty-four and eighteen pounders, her captain, officers, and company, prisoners.   Queen of France, twenty-eight nine-pounders, sunk, her captain and company prisoners. Notre Dame, brig, sixteen guns, sunk, captain and company prisoners.   Providence, thirty-two eighteen and twelve pounders, taken, captain and company prisoners.—Ranger, twenty six-pounders, taken, crew prisoners.

French ships.—L'Aventure, twenty-six nine and six pounders, captain and crew prisoners.   Polacre, sixteen six-pounders, captain and crew prisoners. Some empty brigs, and other smaller vessels, lying at the wharves, taken, with four row-galleys.

stores, &c., though somewhat exaggerated, was a severe blow upon the United States, and excited very gloomy sensations throughout America. The error of risking a country to save a town which only can be retained by the reduction of the country, was now perceived with all its pernicious consequences.

Nevertheless, so well established was the spotless reputation of the vanquished general that he continued to enjoy the undiminished respect and confidence of Congress, of the army, and of the commander-in-chief.

During the winter the king of Spain had been accepted as mediator by the king of England and his most Christian majesty, with the ostensible and laudable view of putting a stop to the ravages and waste of war.

The negotiations terminated unsuccessfully; and the mediating power united with France in the contest. Timely communication of the resolution of the Spanish court was sent to Don Galvez, the governor of New Orleans. Availing himself of the information, he collected a military force, and falling upon the unprepared British settlements on the Mississippi, annexed them to the government of Spain. Soon after his return to New Orleans, Don Galvez made arrangements for the reduction of West Florida. In the month of January he embarked two thousand men on board of transports under convoy of a small squadron, and sailed for the bay of Mobile.

Unluckily he encountered a storm in his voyage, and suffered severely. Several of the vessels foundered; many of the troops perished; and most of his stores were lost. With the remainder he at length entered the bay of Mobile. Here he established himself, and waited for a supply of men and stores from New Orleans. These having reached him, he stood up the bay, and on the 25th of February landed in the vicinity of the town of Mobile, where the English had erected a stockade fort, then garrisoned by one company of regulars. Don Galvez pursuing the cautious system exemplified by Sir Henry Clinton before Charleston, beset this little stockade with regular approaches, laboring at them incessantly until the middle of March, when opening a battery of heavy cannon he demolished it in twelve hours. The garrison surrendered by capitulation. Had the dilatoriness of the Spanish operations consumed a few days more, Don Galvez would have been compelled to relinquish his enterprise, as General Campbell, pressing forward by forced marches with a body of troops from St. Augustine, approached the neighborhood of Mobile soon after it surrendered.

This incursion gratified the feelings of the defenders of the Southern States, as it cherished the expectation that the invasion of the two Floridas already begun, would be prosecuted, and consequently would employ some of the enemy's troops, thus diminishing the force against which they had to contend.

CHAPTER XVI.

Proclamation of Sir H. Clinton.—Augusta, Ninety-Six, and Camden taken possession of, fortified, and garrisoned by Col. Brown.—Col. Balfour and Cornwallis.—Retreat of Col. Buford.—Loyalists under Moore, dispersed by Col. Locke.—Sir H. Clinton embarks for New York.—Cornwallis left in command.—Major McArthur advanced to Cheraw Hill.—Cornwallis returns to Charleston, leaving Lord Rawdon in command of the army.—Major Davie surprises a British convoy near Hanging Rock.

We have seen that, for the two years subsequent to the conclusion of our treaty with France, in pursuance of the plan adopted by Louis XVI., a French fleet had annually visited our coast. Although heretofore disappointed in the expected benefits of extending naval co-operation to our army, it could not be doubted, but that the same wise course would be pursued this summer, especially as now the fleet of Spain was added to that of France. Sir Henry Clinton, aware of this probable event, hastened the completion of his measures for the security of his conquests. Solicitous to avoid that interruption to his return to New York, which delay might interpose, he wisely determined to pursue in his arrangements the dictates of clemency and of justice, the only possible way to secure the submission of freemen. In this spirit he published a manifesto calling to the recollection of the inhabitants, his avoidance heretofore of urging their interference in the contest, because he was unwilling to involve them in hazard so long as the issue was in suspense. That the state of things being completely changed, not only by the surrender of Charleston, but by the destruction or capture of the various armed corps in the country, it was time that the friends of peace and of the royal government should boldly come forth and contribute by their assistance to the restoration of order and tranquillity. He proposed that the militia with families should arm for the security of the province, while the youth should embody to serve six months with the army, enjoying the privilege of acting only in the Carolinas and Georgia, assuring to them the same treatment and compensation as was allowed to the regulars, and permitting them to elect their own officers, with an immunity from all further military duty after the expiration of six months, excepting the ordinary militia duty at home. To men disposed to continue upon their farms, and to obey the existing powers, the proffered conditions could not be unacceptable. But to those in whose generous breasts were deeply planted the love of country, and the love of liberty, accordance with the proposition was not to be expected: they would abandon their homes, and unite with the defenders of their country whenever called upon. These of course fled the State, determined never to arm against a cause which they believed to be the cause of right.

On the 22d of May the general issued his proclamation, cherishing, by assurances of protection and support, the king's peaceful subjects, and menacing all who should hereafter be found in arms, or detected in any resistance or combination to resist the lawful authority, with the confiscation of property and condign corporal punishment. In nine days after, another proclamation appeared from the general and admiral as joint commissioners for restoring peace, promising a full and free pardon to all who should forthwith return to their allegiance, excepting those who in the mock forms of justice had shed the blood of their fellow-citizens for their loyalty to their king; and pledging the restoration of the blessings of legal government as soon as the state of things would permit, with exemption from the payment of taxes not imposed by their own assembly. The consequence of these measures was favorable to British views: the greater part of the inhabitants manifested a disposition to comply with the requisites enjoined; some armed in support of the royal government, while a few abandoned the country, determined, if they fought on either side, it should be on that of America.

While Sir Henry Clinton was engaged in these arrangements, Lord Cornwallis had advanced toward the frontiers with a part of the force which was to remain under his command for 1780. May. the security and extension of the recent conquest. Formed into three divisions after reaching Dorchester, each division took the route to the destined object: the first under Lieutenant-Colonel Brown, moved up the Savannah to Augusta; while the second, led by Lieutenant-Colonel Balfour, passed along the southern banks of the Wateree to Ninety-six; and the third, directed by his lordship, advanced toward Camden, to which place it was understood Lieutenant-Colonel Buford, commanding the remnant of the Continental force in the South, had retired after hearing of the fall of Charleston. Neither of these divisions experienced the slightest resistance.

Augusta, Ninety-six, and Camden, were possessed, fortified, and garrisoned; all the intermediate country was submissive; and protestations of loyalty resounded in every quarter. Cornwallis had no sooner passed the Santee than he became informed of Lieutenant-Colonel Buford's relinquishment of Camden and precipitate march to North Carolina. Despairing himself to overtake this detachment, he determined on a pursuit with his cavalry, strengthened by one hundred mounted infantry. This detachment was intrusted to Lieutenant-Colonel Tarleton, an officer rising fast in military reputation. More distinguished for courage and activity than for management and address, his mode of operation was to overtake and fight. Entering without delay upon his expedition, he pressed forward with his usual zeal and celerity, though not so expeditiously as his anxious mind suggested to be necessary. Leaving his mounted infantry to follow, he advanced at the head of his cavalry with quickened pace, and marching one hundred and five miles in fifty-four hours, a rapid movement for his inferior horse, he approached Buford on his march in the friendly settlement of the Waxhaws on the 29th.* This officer immediately offered to surrender upon the

---

* This account, although countenanced by other American narratives of Buford's disaster, is probably incorrect. Tarleton declares he summoned Buford, and offered him the same terms that had been granted to the garrison of Charleston—and gives Buford's reply in these words:—

"WAXHAWS, *May 29th*, 1780.

"SIR:—I reject your proposal, and shall defend myself to the last extremity.   "I have the honor to be, &c.,
"Lt.-Col. TARLETON,   "ABM. BUFORD.
     Comm'g British Legion."

Marshal, who was well acquainted with Buford, confirms the statement of Tarleton, and has probably given the best account of the affair which exists. It is as follows:—

"A surrender was immediately demanded on the terms which had been granted to the garrison of Charleston. These were refused. While the flags were passing, Tarleton continued to make his dispositions for the assault. The instant the truce was over, his cavalry made a furious charge on the Americans, who had received no order to engage, and who seem to have been uncertain whether to defend themselves or not. In this state of dismay and confusion, some threw down their arms and begged for quarter, while others fired on the assailants. No quarter was given. Colonel Buford with a few cavalry, escaped; and about one hundred infantry, who were somewhat advanced, saved themselves by flight; but the regiment was almost demolished. The official account given by Colonel Tarleton, the exactness of which is not questioned, states one hundred and thirteen to have been killed on the spot, one hundred and fifty to have been so badly wounded as to be paroled because they were incapable of being moved; and the remaining fifty-three to have been brought away as prisoners. The loss of the British amounted only to twelve killed, and five wounded.

"An attempt was made to justify this carnage, by alleging that the Americans,

terms granted to the garrison of Charleston; and why the British commandant rejected the proffered submission is inexplicable. The detachment would have been prisoners of war; and the barbarous scene which ensued to the disgrace of the victor, dimming the splendor of all his exploits, would not have taken place. The moment the negotiation ceased, Tarleton charged the still unprepared foe. Wounds and death, with some partial resistance, followed; and many of our soldiers fell under the British sabre requesting quarters.

The unrelenting conqueror shut his ears to the voice of supplication, as he had steeled his heart against the claims of mercy. By the official report, one hundred and thirteen were killed, one hundred and fifty so badly wounded as to be paroled on the ground, most of whom died; and fifty-three prisoners being capable of moving, graced the entrance of the sanguinary corps into Camden; at which place Lord Cornwallis had arrived.* Lieutenant-Colonel Tarleton excused this butchery by asserting that, after their submission, some of the Americans re-seized their arms and fired upon his troops. Admit the fact, though it is denied, some correction ought to have been inflicted on the guilty; but the dreadful sacrifice which took place was unjustifiable. In the annals of our Indian war nothing is to be found more shocking; and this bloody day only wanted the war dance, and the roasting fire, to have placed it first in the records of torture and of death in the West.

This tragic expedition sunk deep in the American breast, and produced the unanimous decision among the troops to revenge their murdered comrades whenever the blood-stained corps should give an opportunity. This happened soon after at the Cowpens; but Lieutenant-Colonel Washington, who commanded the horse on that

---

after affecting to yield, had again taken up their arms, and fired on the assailants. The American officers who escaped the massacre of the day, aver the contrary; and when their situation comes to be considered, there is much reason to believe that the fact conforms to their statement of it."

I do not know from what source the author of the memoirs derived his statements—probably from his remembrance of oral remarks made, near the time of this transaction.   ED.

* How Lord Cornwallis could encourage such barbarity, by omitting to punish the perpetrator, has never been satisfactorily explained. It tended to diminish the respect entertained for his lordship's character in the camp of his enemy, which had been invariably admired for that happy mixture of goodness as a man, with greatness as a soldier, heretofore strongly exemplified by his conduct. For my own part I am persuaded that the commanding officer is as much bound by the obligations of his station to punish the cruel, as the deserting, soldier; and it is to be lamented, whenever he intentionally fails to do it, that he is not himself punished by his sovereign.

day with so much glory, while he pushed the just claims of vengeance, preserved his laurels pure and spotless.

Turning from this ire-exciting occurrence, let us search for the causes of our calamity. A small party of the saved American cavalry was with Buford; and had it been properly marched in his rear by half-sections, in sight of each other, admitting the enemy's horse to have been the swifter, which is not probable, still the nearest sections would have been safe, should those in the rear have been overtaken; and the American commandant, thus advised of the enemy's approach, he could have prepared for his de fence. This, it seems, never occurred to the retreating officer; or, if it did occur, was neglected. To this want of precaution Lieutenant-Colonel Buford added evidently much indecision, always fatal in the hour of danger. His soldiers were levies, mostly new troops; but his officers were generally experienced, and many of them equal to any in our army. If Buford had prepared for battle instead of sending in a flag, or even had so done while the negotiation was going on, Tarleton must have been foiled. The road was lined on both sides with woods; and the wagons, if placed in front and rear, filled in the body, under the body, and along the wheels, with as many men as could conveniently use their arms, would have afforded an obstruction sufficient to check effectually any charge made in the road. The main body disposed in the woods on each side the road, with an adequate interval for its movements, between the front and the rear obstruction of wagons, would have given to the infantry an advantage which must have secured victory. There was, too, a considerable disparity of force in our favor. Tarleton had but one hundred and seventy dragoons, his mounted infantry far in the rear, while our force exceeded four hundred, including our small party of dragoons. Had Buford, thus posted, deemed it dangerous to continue in his position until night, lest his antagonist should be re-enforced, he might safely have moved in the order suggested; and the moment night had overspread the earth, his retreat would have been secured; for light is indispensable to the effectual operation of cavalry. Before the break of day he might have reached Charlotte, where he was sure of affectionate and gallant assistance from its patriotic inhabitants; and where, too, he had reason to expect to find Lieutenant-Colonel Porterfield, an officer of zeal and talents, who had marched from Virginia in the latter end of April, with a corps of horse, foot, and artillery, amounting to four hundred men. But nothing of this sort was essayed, and our countrymen were wantonly slaughtered by an inferior foe. Lieutenant-Colonel Buford, with the horse, escaped, as did about eighty or ninety of our infantry, who fortunately being advanced, saved themselves by flight.

The calm which succeeded the sweeping success of the enemy from his debarkation continued uninterrupted; and Cornwallis, shortly after Buford's defeat, advanced a corps of light infantry to the Waxhaw settlement, inhabited by citizens whose love of country remained unshaken even by these shocks.

This settlement is so called from the Waxhaw Creek, which passes through it, and empties itself into the Catawba. Brigadier Rutherford, of North Carolina, hearing of the advance of this corps, assembled eight hundred of the militia with a determination to protect the country. His troops can scarcely be said to have been armed; they generally had fowling-pieces instead of muskets and bayonets, pewter instead of lead, with a very trifling supply of powder. Information of this assemblage being sent to Camden, the British detachment was recalled, and this valued settlement, rich in soil, and abounding in produce, was for this time happily released. The repose which the district enjoyed, in consequence of the abandonment of the station at the Waxhaws, was of short duration. So ardent was the zeal of the disaffected, and so persuaded were they that rebellion in the South was crushed, that their desire to manifest their loyalty could not be repressed.

A large body of loyalists collected under Colonel Moore at Armsaour's mill on the 22d of June; among whom were many who had not only taken the oath of allegiance to the State, but had served in arms against the British army. Rutherford lost no time in taking his measures to bring Moore to submission. But so destitute was he of ammunition that only three hundred men could be prepared for the field. This detachment was intrusted to Colonel Locke, who was ordered to approach the enemy and watch his motions, while Rutherford continued to exert himself in procuring arms for the main body to follow under his own direction.

Moore, finding an inferior force near him, determined to attack it, in which decision he was gallantly anticipated by Locke, who perceiving the enemy's purpose, and knowing the hazard of retreat, fell upon Moore in his camp. Captain Falls, with the horse, led, and rushing suddenly, sword in hand, into the midst of the insurgents, threw them into confusion, which advantage Locke pressed forward to improve, when he suspended the falling blow in consequence of Colonel Moore proposing a truce for an hour, with the view of amicable adjustment. During the negotiation, Moore and his associates dispersed, which appears to have been their sole object in proposing the suspension of hostilities.

The cheering intelligence of the unmolested advance of the three detachments to Augusta, Ninety-six, and Camden, the establishment of submission and professions of loyalty which were everywhere proffered by the inhabitants, crowned by the destruction of Buford, extirpating all Continental resistance, confirmed the long-indulged persuasion in the breast of Sir Henry Clinton, that he had reannexed Georgia and South Carolina to the British empire. He now determined, as his final act, to bolt doubly his conquest. On the 3d of June he issued his last proclamation, undoing of his own accord a very important condition established in his first, without consulting, much less receiving, the assent of the party who had accepted the terms proffered therein. He declared to the inhabitants who had in pursuance of his pledged faith, taken parole, that, with the exception of the militia surrendered at Charleston, such paroles were not binding after the 20th of the month, and that persons so situated should be considered as liege subjects, and thenceforward be entitled to all the rights, and subjected to all the duties of this new state; not forgetting to denounce the pains and penalties of rebellion against those who should withhold due allegiance to the royal government. This arbitrary change of an understood contract affected deeply, and afflicted sorely, all to whom it applied; and it was in the consequence, as its injustice merited, fatal to the bright prospect so gratifying to the British general. It demonstrated unequivocally that the hoped-for state of neutrality was illusory, and that every man capable of bearing arms must use them in aid or in opposition to the country of his birth. In the choice to be made, no hesitation existed in the great mass of the people: "for our country" was the general acclaim. The power of the enemy smothered for a while this kindling spirit; but the mine was prepared; the train was laid; and nothing remained but to apply the match. Sir Henry Clinton, having secured the conquered State, as he fondly believed, embarked on the 6th with the greater part of his army for New York, leaving Lord Cornwallis with four thousand regulars to prosecute the reduction of the Southern States.[*] Succeeding Clinton in his civil as well as military powers, his lordship was called

* The garrisons added to the field army amounted to 5,400 in South Carolina, and 1,100 in Georgia.

from the field for the purpose of establishing the many arrangements which the altered condition of the State required. Commercial regulations became necessary, and a system of police for the government of the interior was indispensable.

Previous to his departure from Camden, he had advanced a body of Highlanders under Major McArthur to Cheraw Hill, on the Pedee, for the purpose of preserving in submission the country between that river and the Santee, and for communicating readily with his friends in North Carolina, especially with the Highland settlement at Cross Creek. Through the agency of Major McArthur a regular correspondence was established with the loyalists: they were advised of his lordship's determination, as soon as the approaching harvest furnished the means of subsistence, to advance with his army into North Carolina, when he should count upon their active assistance; and in the mean while they were exhorted to continue passive under the evils to which they were exposed. At the same time recruiting officers were employed in South Carolina and Georgia, by whose exertions the provincial regiments were considerably augmented. These preliminary measures for the invasion of North Carolina being in execution, his lordship repaired to Charleston, leaving Lord Rawdon in command of the army. Meanwhile Major Davie returned to the county of Mecklenburg as soon as he recovered from the wounds received in the attack of Stono, and assembling some of his faithful associates of that district, took the field.

Hovering near the British posts, he became acquainted with the intended movement of a convoy, with various supplies, from Camden to the enemy's post of Hanging Rock, which, amounting only to a small company of infantry, was within the power of Davie's force. He made a rapid and long march in the night, and having eluded the hostile patrols, gained the route of the convoy five miles below Hanging Rock before the break of day Here he halted in a concealed position. In a few hours the convoy appeared, and Davie, falling vigorously upon it, instantly overpowered its escort. The wagons and stores were destroyed; the prisoners, forty in number, were mounted on the wagon horses, and escorted by the major, were safely brought within our lines.

About the same time, Captain Huck, of Tarleton's Legion, had been detached by Lieutenant-Colonel Turnbull, commanding at Hanging Rock, to disperse some of the exiles of South Carolina, who had lately returned to the State, and were collecting in the neighborhood of that place to assist in protecting their country. The captain, with forty dragoons, twenty mounted infantry, and sixty militia, ventured thirty miles up the country, where the very exiles he was ordered to disperse, attacked and destroyed his detachment. The captain, notorious for his cruelties and violence, was killed, as were several others, and the rest dispersed.

These breezes of fortune fanned the dying embers of opposition.

CHAPTER XVII.

The Maryland and Delaware lines ordered to the South under Baron de Kalb.—Gates appointed to the command af the Southern Department.—The patriotic energies of South Carolina aroused at the apprcach of Gates, Marion, Sumter, Pickens.—Concerted movement of Sumter and Davie against Rocky Mount and Hanging Rock.—Gates and Rawdon arrive at opposite sides of Lynch's Creek.—Battle of Camden.—Death of Baron de Kalb.—Sumter's success against the British convoy.—Is warned by Davie of the defeat at Camden.—Escapes Turnbull.—Is surprised by Tarleton at Fishing Creek.—Gates retires to Hillsborough to collect the fragments of his army.—Reflections on Gates' disaster.—Activity of Davidson, Davie, and Sumter.—Cornwallis vigorously enforces Sir H. Clinton's proclamation.

THE Southern war, from its commencement, had been peculiarly disastrous to the United States. Army after army had been defeated, detachments cut off, posts carried; and at length two States were reannexed to the mother country, and the conquering army ready to invade a third. This alarming conjuncture necessarily engaged the ardent attention of Congress and the commander-in-chief. Virginia and North Carolina were again called upon to hasten re-enforcements from their respective militia to the South; the Maryland and Delaware lines, under the orders of Major-General Baron de Kalb, were put in motion for North Carolina; and the conqueror at Saratoga was called from his retreat in Virginia, and charged to display the stars of America in the South.

The annunciation of these preparations reanimated the patriots of Carolina and Georgia; and the smothered discontents growing out of the despotic change, dictated by Sir Henry Clinton's last proclamation, with the visitations daily experienced from an insolent, licentious soldiery, began to burst forth. Lord Rawdon drew in McArthur from the Cheraw Hill, and broke up most of his small posts, dispersed throughout the country, concentrating the British force in the positions of Augusta, Ninety-six, and Camden. Previous to this measure, the disaffected of North Carolina, forgetting the salutary caution of Lord Cornwallis, and sore under the necessary vigilance of the State government, had embodied with the determination to force their way to the British camp. This ill-advised insurrection was speedily crushed, as we have seen in the case of Colonel Moore; but Colonel Bryan had the address to keep together eight hundred of his followers, and to conduct them safely to the post at Cheraw Hill, although actively pursued by General Rutherford. Faithful adherents to the royal cause, they were formed into a military corps under their leader, and incorporated with the British troops. Meanwhile, the progress of Baron de Kalb was much retarded by the necessity he was under of procuring subsistence by his own exertions. He at length reached Hillsborough, in North Carolina, where he halted until the preparations for his further advance were consummated. The militia of this State, being embodied under General Caswell, were prepared to join the baron on his route; while Brigadier-General Stevens, with some militia from Virginia, was hastening to the appointed rendezvous. Caswell and Stevens were selected in consequence of past services. The first had, early in the war, given unquestionable proofs of his decision, zeal, and activity, by the gallant stand he made, in 1776, at Moore's Bridge against a superior force, which terminated in the complete discomfiture of the royalists, and the consequent suppression of a formidable insurrection. The second had commanded a Continental regiment, during the campaigns of 1777 and 1778: he fought under Washington in all the battles of those years, very much respected as a brave, vigorous, and judicious officer. The Baron de Kalb, leaving Hillsborough, had reached Deep River, where he was overtaken on the 25th of July by General Gates, who was hailed to the command of the army with universal gratulations. The Continental force did not exceed one thousand five hundred men, including Armand's dragoons and three companies of Harrison's regiment of artillery. The militia of Virginia and North Carolina had not yet reached head-quarters; and Lieutenant-Colonel Porterfield continued on the confines of South Carolina with a detachment of four hundred men. White and Washington, after the fall of Charleston, had retired to North Carolina with a view of recruiting their regiments of cavalry (Moylan's and Baylor's originally) which had so severely suffered at Monk's Corner, and at Lenew's Ferry; and they solicited General Gates to invigorate their efforts by the aid of his authority, so as to enable them to advance with him to the theatre of action. Gates paid no attention to this proper request, and thus deprived himself of the most operative corps belonging to the Southern army. Although unfortunate, these regiments had displayed undaunted courage, and had been taught in the school of adversity that knowledge which actual service only can bestow. It is probable that this injurious indifference on the part of the American commander resulted from his recurrence to the campaign of 1777, when a British army surrendered to him unaided by cavalry; leading him to conclude, that Armand's corps, already with him, gave an adequate portion of this species of force. Fatal mistake! It is not improbable that the closeness and ruggedness of the country in which he had been so triumphant, did render the aid of horse less material; but the moment he threw his eyes upon the plains of the Carolinas, the moment he saw their dispersed settlements, adding difficulty to difficulty in the procurement of intelligence and provisions; knowing too, as he did, that the enemy had not only a respectable body of dragoons, but that it had been used without intermission, and with much effect; it would seem that a discriminating mind must have been led to acquiesce in the wish suggested by the two officers of horse.

To the neglect of this salutary proposition, may with reason be attributed the heavy disaster soon after experienced. In no country in the world are the services of cavalry more to be desired than in that which was then committed to the care of Major-General Gates; and how it was possible for an officer of his experience to be regardless of this powerful auxiliary, remains inexplicable. Calculating proudly on the weight of his name, he appears to have slighted the prerequisites to victory, and to have hurried on to the field of battle with the impetuosity of youth; a memorable instance of the certain destruction which awaits the soldier who does not know how to estimate prosperity. If good fortune begets presumption, instead of increasing circumspection and diligence, it is the sure precursor of deep and bitter adversity.

General Gates, leaving behind the broken and gallant remains of our cavalry, quickly put his army in motion, taking the direct road to the enemy, which led through a sterile and thinly settled country. The Baron de Kalb had prudently fixed upon a route more to the right, which, though longer, passed through well-improved settlements, yielding in abundance wholesome provisions for the troops. The extreme want to which the army was exposed by this singular decision of General Gates, was productive of serious ills. The troops substituting green corn and unripe fruit for bread, disease ensued, which in its effect reduced considerably our force.

The horses, destitute of forage, were unable to support those sudden persevering marches so often necessary in war. The strength and spirits of the army became enfeebled and low, when true policy required they should have been braced to the highest pitch, inasmuch as not many days could intervene before it would approach the enemy, always ready for battle, and now urged to seek it by the most cogent considerations.

The advance of Gates to South Carolina roused into action all the latent energies of the State. The most resolute of the militia, indignant at the treatment they had received, and convinced by Sir Henry Clinton's proclamation, which had been faithfully acted upon by Lord Cornwallis, that repose during the war was a chimerical expectation, determined to become open from concealed enemies. In the country between the Pedee and Santee the spirit of revolt manifested itself by an overt act. Major McArthur, when retiring from Cheraw Hill, had availed himself of the river to transport his sick to Georgetown; at which place had been established a small British post. Colonel Mills, with a party of militia, formed the escort for the sick. As soon as the boats had reached a proper distance from McArthur, the militia rose upon their colonel, who with difficulty escaped, made prisoners of the sick, and conveyed them safely into North Carolina.

In the district lying between Camden and Ninety-six, the like determination of the inhabitants to turn upon their invader was exhibited. A Lieutenant-Colonel Lyle, who, in pursuance of Sir Henry Clinton's proclamation, had exchanged his parole for a certificate of his being a liege subject, led a great portion of the regiment to which he belonged, with their arms and accoutrements, to the frontiers, where they joined their countrymen now assembling to unite their efforts in support of the American army advancing under Gates. These unexpected symptoms of a general rising of the people did not a little embarrass the British general, who wisely determined to seek battle without delay; not doubting but that the most effectual remedy for the growing disorders would be the destruction of that force on whose prowess these bold adventurers grounded their hope of ultimate success.

Upon the fall of Charleston, many of the leading men of the State of South Carolina sought personal safety with their adherents in the adjoining States. Delighted at the present prospect, these faithful and brave citizens hastened back to their country to share in the perils and toils of war.

Among them were Francis Marion and Thomas Sumter; both colonels in the South Carolina line, and both promoted by Governor Rutledge to the rank of brigadier in the militia of the State. Marion was about forty-eight years of age, small in stature, hard in visage, healthy, abstemious, and taciturn. Enthusiastically wedded to the cause of liberty, he deeply deplored the condition of his beloved country. The commonweal was his sole object; nothing selfish, nothing mercenary, soiled his ermine character. Fertile in stratagem, he struck unperceived; and retiring to those hidden retreats selected by himself in the morasses of the Pedee and Black River, he placed his corps not only out of the reach of his foe, but often out of the discovery of his friends.* A rigid disciplinarian, he reduced to practice the justice of his heart; and during the difficult course of warfare through which he passed, calumny itself never charged him with violating the rights of person, property, or humanity. Never avoiding danger, he never rashly sought it; and acting for all around him as he did for himself, he risked the lives of his troops only when it was necessary. Neither elated with prosperity, nor depressed by adversity, he preserved an equanimity which won the admiration of his friends, and exacted the respect of his enemies. The country from Camden to the seacoast, between the Pedee and Santee rivers, was the theatre of his exertions.

Sumter was younger than Marion, larger in frame, better fitted in strength of body to the toils of war, and, like his compeer, devoted to the freedom of his country. His aspect was manly and stern, denoting insuperable firmness and lofty courage. He was not over scrupulous as a soldier in his use of means, and was apt to make considerable allowances for a state of war. Believing it warranted by the necessity of the case, he did not occupy his mind with critical examinations of the equity of his measures, or of their bearings on individuals; but indiscriminately pressed forward to

---

* Lieutenant-Colonel Lee was ordered to join Marion after Greene determined to turn the war back to South Carolina in 1781. An officer with a small party, preceded Lee a few days' march to find out Marion, who was known to vary his position in the swamps of Pedee; sometimes in South Carolina, sometimes in North Carolina, and sometimes on the Black River. With the greatest difficulty did this officer learn how to communicate with the brigadier; and that by the accident of hearing among our friends on the north side of the Pedee, of a small provision party of Marion's being on the same side of the river. Making himself known to this party, he was conveyed to the general, who had changed his ground since his party left him, which occasioned many hours' search even before his own men could find him.

his end—the destruction of his enemy, and liberation of his country. In his military character he resembled Ajax; relying more upon the fierceness of his courage than upon the results of unrelaxing vigilance and nicely adjusted combination. Determined to deserve success, he risked his own life and the lives of his associates without reserve. Enchanted with the splendor of victory, he would wade through torrents of blood to attain it. This general drew about him the hardy sons of the upper and middle grounds; brave and determined like himself, familiar with difficulty, and fearless of danger. He traversed the region between Camden and Ninety-six.

A third gentleman quickly followed their great example. Andrew Pickens, younger than either, inexperienced in war, with a sound head, a virtuous heart, and a daring spirit, joined in the noble resolve to burst the chains of bondage riveted upon the two Southern States, and soon proved himself worthy of being ranked with his illustrious precursors. This gentleman was also promoted by the governor to the station of brigadier-general; and having assembled his associates of the same bold and hardy cast, distinguished himself and corps in the progress of the war by the patience and cheerfulness with which every privation was borne, and the gallantry with which every danger was confronted. The country between Ninety-six and Augusta received his chief attention.

These leaders were always engaged in breaking up the smaller posts and the intermediate communications, or in repairing losses sustained by action. The troops which followed their fortunes, on their own or their friends' horses, were armed with rifles, in the use of which they had become expert; a small portion only, who acted as cavalry, being provided with sabres. When they approached the enemy they dismounted, leaving their horses in some hidden spot to the care of a few of their comrades. Victorious or vanquished, they flew to their horses, and thus improved victory or secured retreat.

Their marches were long and toilsome, seldom feeding more than once a day. Their combats were like those of the Parthians, sudden and fierce; their decisions speedy, and all subsequent measures equally prompt. With alternate fortunes they persevered to the last, and greatly contributed to that success which was the first object of their hearts.

With Marion on his right and Sumter on his left, and General

Gates approaching in front, Rawdon, discerning the critical event at hand, took his measures accordingly.

He not only called in his outposts, but drew from the garrison of Ninety-six four companies of light infantry, and made known to Lord Cornwallis the menacing attitude of his enemy.

Sumter commenced his inroads upon the British territory by assaulting, on the first of August, the post of Rocky Mount, in the charge of Lieutenant-Colonel Turnbull, with a small garrison of one hundred and fifty of the New York volunteers and some South. Carolina militia. The brigadier, attended by the colonels, Lacy, Irvine, and Neale, having each collected some of their militia, repaired on the 30th of July to Major Davie, who still continued near the enemy, and was now encamped on the north of Waxhaw Creek, for the purpose of concerting a joint assault upon some of the British outposts. They were led to hasten the execution of this step, fearing that, by delay, their associates might disperse without having effected any good. After due deliberation they came to the resolution of carrying the posts of Rocky Mount and Hanging Rock in succession. The first of these is situated on the west side of the Catawba, thirty miles from Camden, and the last was established on the east side of the same river, twenty-four miles from Camden. They are distant from each other twelve miles.

Sumter, having under him the three colonels, advanced with the main body upon Rocky Mount; while Major Davie, with his corps and a part of the Mecklenburg militia, under Colonel Heaggins, marched to Hanging Rock to watch the motions of the garrison, to procure exact intelligence of the condition of the post, and to be ready to unite with Sumter in the intended blow.

Rocky Mount station is fixed on the comb of a lofty eminence, encircled by open wood. This summit was surrounded by a small ditch and abatis; in the centre whereof were erected three log buildings, constructed to protect the garrison in battle, and perforated with loop-holes for the annoyance of the assailants.

As Davie got near to Hanging Rock he learned that three companies of Bryan's loyalists, part of the garrison, were just returning from an excursion, and had halted at a neighboring farm-house. He drew off, determined to fall upon this party. This was handsomely executed, and completely succeeded. Eluding the sentinels in one quarter with his infantry, and gaining the other point of attack with his horse undiscovered, by marching through some adjoining woods, he placed the enemy between these two divisions, each of which pressed gallantly into action.

The loyalists, finding their front and rear occupied, attempted to escape in a direction believed to be open, but were disappointed; the major having detached thither a party of his dragoons in time to meet them. They were all, except a few, killed and wounded; and the spoils of victory were safely brought off, consisting of sixty horses with their trappings, and one hundred muskets and rifles.

The brigadier approached Rocky Mount with his characteristic impetuosity; but the British officer was found on his guard, and defended himself ably. Three times did Sumter attempt to carry it; but being always foiled, having no artillery to batter down the houses, he drew off undisturbed by the garrison, having lost a few of his detachment, with Colonel Neale, an active, determined, influential officer, and retired to his frontier position on the Catawba. Here he rested no longer than was necessary to recruit his corps, refresh his horses, and provide a part of the provisions necessary to support him on his next excursion. Quitting his retreat with his brave associates, Davie, Irvine, Hill, and Lacy, he darted on the British line of communication, and fell on the post at Hanging Rock (6th of August), which was held by Major Carden with five hundred men, consisting of one hundred and sixty of the infantry of Tarleton's Legion, a part of Colonel Brown's regiment, and Bryan's North Carolina corps, a portion of which had, a few days before, been cut to pieces by Major Davie. His attack was, through the error of his guides, pointed at the corps of Bryan, which being surprised, soon yielded and took to flight. Sumter pressed with ardor the advantage he had gained, and bore down upon the Legion infantry, which was forced. He then fell upon Brown's detachment. Here he was received upon the point of the bayonet. The contest grew fierce, and the issue doubtful; but at length the corps of Brown fell back, having lost nearly all its officers and a great proportion of its soldiers.

Hamilton's regiment, with the remains of Brown's and the Legion infantry, now formed in the centre of their position, a hollow square.

Sumter advanced with the determination to strike this last point of resistance; but the ranks of the militia had become disordered; and the men scattered from success, and from the plunder of part of the British camp, so that only two hundred infantry, and Davie's dragoons, could be brought into array. The musketry opened;

but their fire was ineffectual; nor could Sumter, by all his exertions, again bring his troops to risk close action with his well-posted enemy, supported by two pieces of artillery. The cavalry under Davie fell upon a body of the loyalists, who, having rallied, had formed in the opposite quarter, and menaced our right flank. They were driven from their ground, and took shelter under the British infantry still in hollow square.

The spoils of the camp, and the free use of spirits in which the enemy abounded, had for some time attracted and incapacitated many of our soldiers. It was therefore determined to retreat with the prisoners and booty. This was done about twelve o'clock very leisurely in face of the enemy; who did not attempt interruption, so severely had he suffered. A party was now for the first time seen drawn up on the Camden road, with the appearance of renewal of the contest; but on the approach of Davie it fell back. Our loss was not ascertained, from the usual inattention to returns prevalent with militia officers; and many of our wounded were immediately carried home from the field of battle. The corps of Davie suffered most. Captain McClure of South Carolina, and Captain Reed of North Carolina, were killed; Colonel Hill, Major Winn, and Lieutenant Crawford, were wounded, as were Captain Craighead, Lieutenant Flenchau, and Ensign McClure of North Carolina. The British loss exceeded ours. Captain McCullock, who commanded the Legion infantry with much personal honor, two other officers, and twenty men of the same corps, were killed, and nearly forty wounded. Many officers and men of Brown's regiment were also killed and wounded, and some taken.

Bryan's loyalists were less hurt, having dispersed as soon as pressed. The error of the guides which deranged the plan of attack, the allurement of the spoils found in the enemy's camp, and the indulgence in the use of liquor, deprived Sumter of the victory once within his grasp, and due to the zeal, gallantry, and perseverance of himself and his officers.

Checked but not dismayed, disappointed but not discouraged, Sumter sought his remote asylum to recruit and repair. About this period Gates was advancing near to the scene of action. The American general soon after he entered South Carolina, directed his march toward Lynch's Creek, the southern branch of the Pedee, keeping on his right the friendly and fertile country about Charlotte, the principal town of Mecklenburg County. Lord Rawdon, unwilling that Gates should find him in Camden, where were deposited his stores, ammunitions, and sick, advanced to a strong position, fifteen miles in front, on the southern bank of Lynch's Creek.

This being ascertained by General Gates, he moved to Lynch's opposite to Lord Rawdon; and the two armies remained for four days, separated only by the creek. Gates broke up from this ground inclining to his right, which putting in danger the British advanced post at Rudgely's mill, Lord Rawdon directed its evacuation, and fell back to Logtown, in the vicinity of Camden. Here, he became acquainted with the insurrection of the inhabitants on Black River, headed by Brigadier Marion, which, although suspected, it was presumed would have been delayed until the American army should obtain some decisive advantage. Gates, desirous of opening his communication with Sumter, continued to advance upon the north side of Lynch's Creek, and took post at Rudgely's mill, where he was joined by Brigadier Stevens with seven hundred of the Virginia militia. At the same time he received information from General Sumter that a detachment of the enemy from Ninety-six, with stores for the main body at Camden, was on its march, which he could conveniently intercept as it passed the ferry on the Wateree, one mile below Camden, if supplied with artillery to batter down a redoubt which covered the ferry. Gates weakened his army, though in striking distance of his foe, by detaching to Sumter four hundred men under the command of Lieutenant-Colonel Woolford, of the Maryland line, with two light pieces. As soon as this detachment was put in motion, preparations were made to advance still nearer to Camden.

The evacuation of Rudgely's mill and the falling back of Lord Rawdon from Lynch's Creek, seem to have inspired General Gates with the presumption that his approach would drive the enemy from Camden. No conclusion more erroneous could have been drawn from a fair view of the objects and situation of the respective armies.

The British general was under the necessity of maintaining his position; for retreat yielded up that country which he was bound to retain, and encouraged that spirit of revolt which he was bound to repress. All the disposable force under his orders had been concentrated at Camden; delay would not thicken his ranks, while it was sure to add to those of his adversary. Every consideration urged the British general to battle; and no commander was ever more disposed than Lord Cornwallis to cut out relief from em-

barrassment by the sword. The foundation of the policy pursued
by General Gates, was laid in error; and we ought not to be surprised at its disastrous termination. Had Gates not confidently
presumed that a retrograde movement on the part of the enemy
would have been the effect of his advance, he certainly would have
detained Woolford's detachment, and ordered Sumter to join him:
it being unquestionable that victory in the plains of Camden would
give to him the British army, and with it all the posts in South
Carolina except Charleston. To this end his means ought to have
been solely directed; or, if he preferred the wiser course, to spin
out the campaign, condensing his main body, and beating the enemy
in detail, he should have continued in his strong position behind
Lynch's Creek, ready upon Cornwallis's advance to have fallen
back upon its head-waters, in the powerful and faithful counties of
Cabarrus, Rowan, and Mecklenburg.*

No doubt General Gates was unfortunately persuaded that he had
nothing to do but to advance upon his enemy, never supposing that
so far from retiring, the British general would seize the proffered
opportunity of battle.

Unhappily for America, unhappily for himself, he acted under
this influence, nor did he awake from his reverie until the proximity of the enemy was announced by his fire in the night, preceding
the fatal morning.

Lord Cornwallis having been regularly informed of the passing
occurrences, hastened to Camden, which he reached on the 13th;
spending the subsequent day in review and examination, he found
his army very much enfeebled; eight hundred being sick, his effective strength was reduced to somewhat less than two thousand
three hundred men, including militia and Bryan's corps, which,
together, amounted to seven hundred and fifty men. Judging
from the exertions of Congress and the States of Virginia and North
Carolina, by their publications, he rated his enemy at six thousand;
in which estimation his lordship was much mistaken, as from official returns on the evening preceding the battle, it appears that

---

* The inhabitants of these three counties, among the most populous in the
State, were true and zealous in their maintenance of the Revolution; and they
were always ready to encounter any and every peril to support the cause
of their hearts. Contiguous to the western border over the mountains lived
that hardy race of mountaineers, equally attached to the cause of our common
country, and who rolled occasionally like a torrent on the hostile territory.
The ground was strong, and the soil rich and cultivated. In every respect,
therefore, it was adapted to the American general until he had rendered himself completely ready for offence.

our force did not exceed four thousand, including the corps detached under Lieutenant-Colonel Woolford; yet there was a great disparity of numbers in our favor, but we fell short in quality, our Continental horse, foot, and artillery, being under one thousand, whereas the British regulars amounted to nearly one thousand six hundred.

Notwithstanding his diminished force, notwithstanding the vast expected superiority of his enemy, the discriminating mind of the British general paused not an instant in deciding upon his course.

No idea of a retrograde movement was entertained by him. Victory only could extricate him from the surrounding dangers; and the quicker the decision, the better his chance of success. He therefore gave orders to prepare for battle, and in the evening of the 15th put his army in motion to attack his enemy next morning in his position at Rudgely's mill.

Having placed Camden in the care of Major McArthur, with the convalescents, some of the militia, and a detachment of regulars expected in the course of the day, he moved, at the hour of ten at night, in two divisions. The front division, composed of four companies of light infantry, with the twenty-third and thirty-third regiments, was commanded by Lieutenant-Colonel Webster.

The rear division, consisting of the Legion infantry, Hamilton's regiment of North Carolinians, the volunteers of Ireland, and Bryan's corps of loyalists, was under the orders of Lord Rawdon. Two battalions of the seventy-first, with the Legion cavalry, formed the reserve.

After Gates had detached Woolford to Sumter, and prepared his army to move, it was resolved in a council of war to march on the night of the 15th, and to sit down behind Saunder's Creek, within seven miles of Camden. Thus it happened that both the generals were in motion at the same hour, and for the same purpose: with this material distinction, that the American general grounded his conduct in his mistaken confidence of his adversary's disposition to retreat; whereas the British commander sought for battle with anxiety, regarding the evasion of it by his antagonist as the highest misfortune.

Our baggage, stores, and sick having been sent off to the friendly settlement of the Waxhaws, the army marched at ten o'clock at night. Armand's* Legion, in horse and foot, not exceeding one

---

* Armand was one of the many French gentlemen who joined our army, and was one of the few who were honored with important commands. His officers

hundred, moved as a van-guard, flanked by Lieutenant-Colonel Porterfield's corps on the right, and by Major Armstrong's light infantry, of the North Carolina militia, on the left.   The Maryland and Delaware lines composed the front division, under Baron de Kalb ; the militia of North Carolina, under General Caswell, the centre; and the Virginia militia, under Brigadier Stevens, the rear.   Some volunteer cavalry were placed to guard the baggage. Midway between Camden and Rudgely's mill, the two armies met, about one in the morning.   They instantly felt each other; when the corps of Armand shamefully turned its back, carrying confusion and dismay into our ranks.   The leading regiment of Maryland was disordered by this ignominious flight; but the gallant Porterfield, taking his part with decision on the right, seconded by Armstrong on the left, soon brought the enemy's van to a pause.   Prisoners being taken on both sides, the adverse generals became informed of their unexpected proximity.*   The two armies halted, each throbbing with the emotions which the van rencounter had excited. The British army displayed in one line, which completely occupied the ground, each flank resting on impervious swamps.   The infantry of the reserve took post in a second line, one half opposite the centre of each wing; and the cavalry held the road, where the left of the right wing united with the volunteers of Ireland, which corps formed the right of the left wing.   Lieutenant-Colonel Webster commanded on the right, and Colonel Lord Rawdon on the left With the front line were two six and two three pounders, under Lieutenant McLeod of the artillery ; with the reserve were two six pounders.   Thus arranged, confiding in discipline and experience, the British general waited anxiously for light.

were generally foreign, and his soldiers chiefly deserters.   It was the last corps in the army which ought to have been intrusted with the van post; because, however unexceptionable the officers may have been, the materials of which the corps was composed did not warrant such distinction.

* Mr. Marshall, in his "Life of Washington," gives a summary of the principal events in the Southern war.   This faithful historian tells us, that in the night, as soon as the skirmish terminated, some prisoners were brought to Gates ; from whom he learnt that the British army was in front.   The general officers were immediately assembled.   The intelligence received from the prisoners was communicated to them, and their opinions asked on the measures to be adopted.

General Stevens, of the Virginia militia, answered, that "It was now too late to retreat."   A silence of some moments ensued ; and General Gates, who seems himself to have been disposed to try the chance of a battle, understanding silence to be an approbation of the sentiments delivered by Stevens, broke up the council by saying, "Then we must fight: gentlemen, please to take your posts."

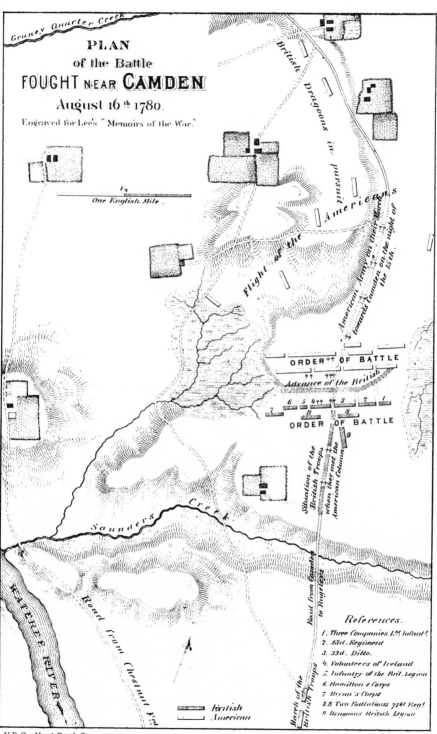

PLAN
of the Battle
FOUGHT NEAR CAMDEN
August 16ᵗʰ 1780.

Engraved for Lee's "Memoirs of the War."

Graney Quarter Creek

One English Mile.

British Dragoons in

Flight of the Americans

American Army on their March towards Camden on the night of the 15th.

ORDER ++ OF BATTLE

Advance of the British

6 5 4 ++ 3 2 1
8   8
ORDER OF BATTLE
9

Situation of the British Troops when they met the American Column

Saunders Creek

Road from Camden to Rugeley.

KATERE E RIVER

Road from Chestnut Ford

March of the British Troops

British
American

References.
1. Three Companies Lᵗ Infantᵗ
2. 23ᵈ Regiment
3. 33ᵈ Ditto.
4. Volunteers of Ireland
5. Infantry of the Brit. Legion
6. Hamilton's Corps
7. Bryan's Corps
8.8 Two Battalions 71st Regᵗ
9. Dragons British Legion

U.P. Co. No. 4 Bond. St.

The Maryland leading regiment was soon recovered from the confusion produced by the panic of Armand's cavalry. Battle, although unexpected, was now inevitable; and General Gates arrayed his army with promptitude. The second brigade of Maryland, with the regiment of Delaware, under General Gist, took the right; the brigade of North Carolina militia, led by Brigadier Caswell, the centre; and that of Virginia, under Brigadier Stevens, the left. The first brigade of Maryland was formed in reserve, under the command of General Smallwood, who had on York Island, in the beginning of the war, when colonel of the first regiment of Maryland, deeply planted in the hearts of his country the remembrance of his zeal and valor, conspicuously displayed in that the first of his fields. To each brigade a due proportion of artillery was allotted; but we had no cavalry, as those who led in the night were still flying. Major-General Baron de Kalb, charged with the line of battle, took post on the right; while the general-in-chief, superintending the whole, placed himself on the road between the line and the reserve. The light of day dawned,—the signal for battle. Instantly our centre opened its artillery, and the left of our line, under Stevens, was ordered to advance. The veterans of the enemy, composing its right, were of course opposed to the Virginia militia; whereas they ought to have been faced by the Continental brigade.* Stevens, however, exhorting his soldiers to rely on the bayonet, advanced with his accustomed intrepidity. Lieutenant-Colonel Otho Williams, adjutant-general, preceded him with a band of volunteers, in order to invite the fire of the enemy before they were in reach of the militia, that experience of its inefficacy might encourage the latter to do their duty. The British general, closely watching our motions, discovered this movement on the left, and gave orders to Webster to lead into battle with the right. The command was executed with the characteristic courage and intelligence of that officer. Our left was instantly overpowered by the assault; and the brave Stevens had to endure the mortifying spectacle exhibited by his flying brigade. Without exchanging more than one fire with the enemy, they threw away

---

* General Gates did not, in his disposition, conform to the judicious principle which we find observed by General Lincoln; or our Continentals would have been posted on the left to oppose the British right. Indeed such seems to have been Gates' hurry, from the moment he was called to the command in the South, as to forbid that full inquiry into his enemy's and his own situation, as well as intimate acquaintance with the character of his own and his enemy's troops, so necessary to the pursuit of right measures in war.

their arms; and sought that safety in flight, which generally can be
obtained only by courageous resistance. The North Carolina brigade, imitating that on the left, followed the shameful example.
Stevens, Caswell, and Gates himself, struggled to stop the fugitives,
and rally them for battle; but every noble feeling of the heart was
sunk in base solicitude to preserve life; and having no cavalry to
assist their exertions, the attempted reclamation failed entirely.
The Continental troops, with Dixon's regiment of North Carolinians, were left to oppose the enemy; every corps of whose army
was acting with the most determined resolution. De Kalb and Gist
yet held the battle on our right in suspense. Lieutenant-Colonel
Howard, at the head of Williams's regiment, drove the corps in
front out of line. Rawdon could not bring the brigade of Gist to
recede:—bold was the pressure of the foe; firm as a rock the
resistance of Gist. Now the Marylanders were gaining ground;
but the deplorable desertion of the militia having left Webster un-
employed, that discerning soldier detached some light troops with
Tarleton's cavalry in pursuit, and opposed himself to the reserve
brought up by Smallwood to replace the fugitives. Here the battle was renewed with fierceness and obstinacy. The Marylanders,
with Dixon's regiment, although greatly outnumbered, firmly maintained the desperate conflict; and De Kalb, now finding his once
exposed flank completely shielded, resorted to the bayonet. Dreadful was the charge! In one point of the line the enemy were
driven before us with the loss of many prisoners. But while
Smallwood covered the flank of the second brigade, his left became
exposed; and Webster, never omitting to seize every advantage,
turned the light infantry and twenty-third regiment on his open
flank. Smallwood, however, sustained himself with undiminished
vigor; but borne down at last by superiority of force, the first
brigade receded. Soon it returned to the line of battle;—again
it gave ground, and again rallied. Meantime De Kalb, with our
right, preserved a conspicuous superiority. Lord Cornwallis, sensible of the advantages gained, and aware of the difficulty to which
we were subjected by the shameful flight of our left, concentrated
his force, and made a decisive charge. Our brave troops were
broken; and his lordship, following up the blow, compelled the
intrepid Marylanders to abandon the unequal contest. To the
woods and swamps, after performing their duty valiantly, these
gallant soldiers were compelled to fly. The pursuit was continued
with keenness, and none were saved but those who penetrated

swamps which had been deemed impassable. The road was heaped
with the dead and wounded. Arms, artillery, horses, and baggage,
were strewed in every direction; and the whole adjacent country
presented evidences of the signal defeat.

Our loss was very heavy. More than a third of the Continental
troops were killed and wounded; and of the wounded one hundred
and seventy were made prisoners. The regiment of Delaware
was nearly annihilated; and Lieutenant-Colonel Vaughn and Major
Patton being taken, its remnant, less than two companies, was afterward placed under the orders of Kirkwood, senior captain.* The
North Carolina militia also suffered greatly; more than three hundred were taken, and nearly one hundred killed and wounded.
Contrary to the usual course of events and the general wish, the
Virginia militia, who set the infamous example which produced the
destruction of our army, escaped entirely.

De Kalb, sustaining by his splendid example the courageous
efforts of our inferior force, in his last resolute attempt to seize victory, received eleven wounds, and was made prisoner. His yet
lingering life was rescued from immediate death by the brave interposition of Lieutenant-Colonel Du Buysson, one of his aids-de-camp;
who embracing the prostrate general, received into his own body
the bayonets pointed at his friend. The heroic veteran, though
treated with every attention, survived but a few days. Never were
the last moments of a soldier better employed. He dictated a letter
to General Smallwood, who succeeded to the command of his division, breathing in every word his sincere and ardent affection for
his officers and soldiers; expressing his admiration of their late
noble though unsuccessful stand; reciting the eulogy which their
bravery had extorted from the enemy; together with the lively
delight such testimony of their valor had excited in his own mind,

* The State of Delaware furnished one regiment only; and certainly no
regiment in the army surpassed it in soldiership. The remnant of that corps,
less than two companies, from the battle of Camden, was commanded by Captain Kirkwood, who passed through the war with high reputation; and yet as
the line of Delaware consisted but of one regiment, and that regiment was reduced to a captain's command, Kirkwood never could be promoted in regular
routine,—a very glaring defect in the organization of the army, as it gave advantages to parts of the same army denied to other portions of it. The sequel
is singularly hard. Kirkwood retired, upon peace, a captain; and when the
army under St. Clair was raised to defend the West from the Indian enemy,
this veteran resumed his sword as the eldest captain of the oldest regiment.
In the decisive defeat of the 4th November, the gallant Kirkwood fell, bravely
sustaining his point of the action. It was the thirty-third time he had risked
his life for his country; and he died as he had lived, the brave, meritorious,
unrewarded, Kirkwood.

then hovering on the shadowy confines of death. In this endearing
adieu he comprehended Lieutenant-Colonel Vaughn, with the Delaware regiment and the artillery attached to his division; both of
which corps had shared in the glory of that disastrous day. Feeling the pressure of death, he stretched out his quivering hand to his
friend Du Buysson, proud of his generous wounds; and breathed his
last in benedictions on his faithful, brave division.* We lost, besides
Major-General Baron de Kalb, many excellent officers; and among
them Lieutenant-Colonel Porterfield, whose promise of future greatness had endeared him to the whole army. Wounded in his brave
stand in the morning, when our dragoons basely fled, he was taken
off the field, never more to draw his sword! Brigadier Rutherford,
of the North Carolina militia, and Major Thomas Pinckney, of the
South Carolina line, aid-de-camp to General Gates, were both
wounded and taken.

The British loss is stated to have amounted to eighty killed, and
two hundred and forty-five wounded.

In the dreadful gloom which now overspread the United States,
the reflecting mind drew consolation from the undismayed gallantry
displayed by a portion of the army, throughout the desperate conflict; and from the zeal, courage, and intelligence exhibited by
many of our officers. Smallwood and Gist had conducted themselves with exemplary skill and bravery. Stevens and Caswell both
deserved distinguished applause, although both were the mortified
leaders of spiritless troops. Colonel Williams, adjutant-general,
was conspicuous throughout the action; cheerfully risking his valuable life out of his station, performing his assumed duties with precision and effect, and volunteering his person wherever danger
called. Lieutenant-Colonel Howard demonstrated a solidity of
character which, on every future occasion, he displayed honorably
to himself and advantageously to his country. The general-in-
chief, although deeply unfortunate, is entitled to respect and regard.
He took decisive measures to restore the action, by unceasing efforts
to rally the fugitive militia; and had he succeeded, would have led
them to the vortex of battle. By seconding the Continental troops
with this rallied corps, he would probably have turned the fortune
of the day, or have died the hero of Saratoga.

None, without violence to the claims of honor and justice, can
withhold applause from Colonel Dixon and his North Carolina regi-

* See Appendix D.

ment of militia. Having their flank exposed by the flight of the other militia, they turned with disdain from the ignoble example; and fixing their eyes on the Marylanders, whose left they became, determined to vie in deeds of courage with their veteran comrades. Nor did they shrink from this daring resolve. In every vicissitude of the battle, this regiment maintained its ground, and when the reserve under Smallwood, covering our left, relieved its naked flank, forced the enemy to fall back. Colonel Dixon had seen service, having commanded a Continental regiment under Washington. By his precepts and example he infused his own spirit into the breasts of his troops; who, emulating the noble ardor of their leader, demonstrated the wisdom of selecting experienced officers to command raw soldiers.*

In the midst of this heart-rending defeat, General Gates received advice of the success of Sumter against the British convoy. Some consolation † was thus administered to his wounded spirit. The corps under Sumter, added to those who had escaped this day of destruction, would have formed a force, which could preserve the

---

* The American war presents examples of first-rate courage occasionally exhibited by corps of militia, and often with the highest success.

Here was a splendid instance of self-possession by a single regiment, out of two brigades. Dixon had commanded a Continental regiment; and, of course, to his example and knowledge much is to be ascribed; yet praise is nevertheless due to the troops. While I record, with delight, facts which maintain our native and national courage, I feel a horror lest demagogues, who flourish in a representative system of government (the best, when virtue rules, the wit of man can devise) shall avail themselves of the occasional testimony to produce a general result.

Convinced as I am, that a government is the murderer of its citizens, which sends them to the field uninformed and untaught, where they are to meet men of the same age and strength, mechanized by education and disciplined for battle, I cannot withhold my denunciation of its wickedness and folly; much as I applaud, and must ever applaud, those instances, like the one before us, of armed citizens vying with our best soldiers in the first duty of man to his country.

† This consolation was necessarily mingled with acute remorse. It must have reminded the general of the advantages once at his command, by pursuing the prudent system of striking his adversary in detail; and if victory with him was only pleasant by being immediate, it would bring to his recollection the propriety of having brought Sumter to him, instead of detaching Woolford from him.

Lord Cornwallis, hearing from his commandant at Camden of the success of Sumter, in the midst of his prosperity turned his mind to the recovery of the loss he had sustained,—an example meriting imitation from all who may command in war. Small as was the advantage gained, had it been enjoyed, great would have been the good derived in its consequences. The British general foreseeing this, did not indulge even in the proud moments of victory, but gave his mind and time to prepare Sumter's destruction.

appearance of resistance, and give time for the arrival of succor. Major McArthur, about the same time, communicated the occurrence to Lord Cornwallis ; who occupied his first moments after our defeat in dispatching orders to Lieutenant-Colonel Turnbull, then stationed on Little River with the New York volunteers, and Major Ferguson's corps of loyalists, to intercept General Sumter and bring him to action.

Major Davie's corps, part of the force under Sumter, in his preceding operations, had suffered severely on the 6th of August, in the unsuccessful attempt on the post of Hanging Rock ; and was subsequently engaged in escorting our wounded to Charlotte, where Davie had previously established a hospital. The moment this service was performed, Major Davie hastened to the general rendezvous at Rudgley's mill. On the fifteenth, arriving after Gates had moved, he followed the army ; and marching all night, met the first part of our flying troops about four miles from the field of battle. With an expectation of being useful in saving soldiers, baggage, and stores, he continued to advance ; and meeting with Brigadier-General Huger, of the South Carolina line, driving his tired horse before him, he learned the probability of Sumter's ignorance of the defeat of our army, and of the consequent danger to which he would be exposed. Major Davie, therefore, instantly dispatched Captain Martin, attended by two dragoons, to inform Sumter of this afflicting event ; to urge him to take care of his corps by immediate retreat, and to request him to repair to Charlotte, whither himself meant to proceed, and assemble, as he returned, all the force which could be induced to take the field. On the night following, Captain Martin reached Sumter, who immediately decamped with his prisoners and booty. Turnbull's attempt failed, from the celerity with which Sumter had moved. Apprehensive that Sumter might escape Turnbull, and anxious to break up this corps, the British general was not satisfied with a single effort to destroy him ; and on the same evening directed Lieutenant-Colonel Tarleton, with his Legion and some light infantry, to proceed in the morning from the field of battle across the Wateree in pursuit of that enterprising officer.

Having avoided Turnbull, Sumter seems to have indulged a belief that he was safe ; and accordingly encamped on the night of the 17th at Rocky Mount, about thirty miles from Camden, and much nearer Cornwallis. To halt for the night within striking distance of the British army was evidently improvident. After a few hours' rest, he ought certainly to have renewed his march. At day-light he did, indeed, resume it; but having passed Fishing Creek, eight miles distant, he again halted. His troops occupied, in line of march, a ridge contiguous to the north side of the creek, at which place his rear-guard was stationed; and two vedettes were posted at a small distance in its front. Confiding in this hazardous situation to these slender precautions, his arms were stacked, the men were permitted to indulge at pleasure, some in strolling, some bathing, and others reposing. Our troops, no doubt, were extremely wearied; but bodily debility does not warrant inattention in a commander: it should redouble his caution and exertion. If the halt at Fishing Creek was unavoidable, the troops least fatigued and best armed should have been selected and posted for combat, while those most fatigued, snatched rest and food. With this alternate relief the retreat ought to have been continued; and the corps would have been saved.

Lieutenant-Colonel Tarleton moved with his accustomed velocity; and after a rapid march on the 17th, approached Sumter's line of retreat. Finding many of his men and his horses too much exhausted to proceed with the requisite dispatch, he left behind more than half his force, and pressed forward with about one hundred and sixty. Passing the Catawba at Rocky Mount Ford, he got into Sumter's rear, whose precautions for security were readily eluded. The enemy reached him unperceived, when consternation at the unlooked for assault became general. Partial resistance was attempted, but soon terminated in universal flight. Sumter's force, with the detachment under Lieutenant-Colonel Woolford, was estimated at eight hundred: some were killed, others wounded, and the rest dispersed. Sumter himself fortunately escaped, as did about three hundred and fifty of his men; leaving two brass pieces of artillery, arms, and baggage, in possession of the enemy, who recovered their wagons, stores, and prisoners.*

---

* The officer adventuring, as did General Sumter, must never be satisfied with common precautions: they will not do.

It is difficult to prescribe rules upon the subject, because every single case is to be regarded, and must suggest its own regulations to a meditating mind. One fixed principle, however, we may venture to lay down, viz.: that the captured, with a portion of the victorious corps, ought to be immediately dispatched, with orders to move night and day until out of reach; while the commander, with the least fatigued troops, should hold himself some hours in the rear, sweeping with the best of his cavalry all the country between him and his enemy, thus procuring correct information, which will always secure a retiring corps.

In this enterprise, although fortunate in its issue, Lieutenant-Colonel Tarleton evinced a temerity, which could not, if pursued, long escape exemplary chastisement. Had Sumter discovered his approach, that day would at least have arrested his career, if it had not closed his existence. But unhappily for America, her soldiers were slaughtered, sometimes from the improvidence of their leaders, more often from their own fatal neglect of duty, and disobedience of orders. Vain is it to place guards around your camp, and vedettes in their front, if unmindful of the responsibility of their stations, they indulge in repose, or relinquish their posts. The severe consequences of such criminal neglect, we may suppose, would prevent the repetition of the evil; but soldiers are not to be corrected by their own observations or deductions. Rewards and punishments must be added ; and execution on the spot, of a faithless or negligent sentinel, is humanity in the end. Militia will not endure this rigor, and are therefore improperly intrusted with the sword of the nation in war. The pursuance of that system must weaken the best resources of the state, by throwing away the lives of its citizens ; and those rulers must provoke the vengeance of Heaven, who invite such destruction by adhering to this impotent policy.

The tragedy of the 16th, closing with the catastrophe of the 18th, the army of the South became a second time nearly annihilated. General Gates halted at Charlotte, where some of his defeated army had arrived. Soon after he retired to Salisbury, and afterward to Hillsborough, one hundred and eighty miles from Camden, where he determined to collect his scattered forces, and to draw re-enforcements, with a resolution of again facing his successful adversary.* Smallwood and Gist continued at Salisbury, until all the dispersed Continentals were assembled. The militia of both States passed on toward their respective homes, selecting their own route, and obtaining subsistence from the charity of the farmers on the road.

We shall here break the thread of our narrative, and go into those inquiries which our misfortunes require; it being the object of these Memoirs, by a faithful and plain elucidation of the occur-

* This rapid retreat of General Gates has been generally supposed to diminish his reputation. Not so in truth. It does him honor ; as it evinced a mind capable, amidst confusion and distress, of discerning the point most promising to renew with expedition his strength ; at the same time incapable of being withheld from doing his duty, by regarding the calumny with which he was sure to be assailed.

rences of our war, connecting events with their causes, to enlighten the future defenders and rulers of our country. The character of a military chief contributes not a little to give character to his army; provided the pressure of circumstances does not urge him to the field before he has time and opportunity to know and be known. Major-General Gates assumed the command under the happiest circumstances. He was hailed as the conqueror of Saratoga ; and our gallant troops, anticipating the future from reflecting on the past, proudly presumed that his skill, directing their valor, would liberate the South, and diffuse over his evening an effulgence more brilliant than his meridian glory.

Considering the condition of the respective armies, this fond expectation will not appear chimerical. But, unhappily for us, the inviting opportunity was neglected ; and General Gates, buoyed up by his campaign in the North, seems to have acted under a conviction that it was only necessary to meet the foe to conquer. What heavy misfortunes spring from our own fatuity! The day after the Virginia militia* joined at Rudgely's mill, he rashly advanced toward the enemy; and persevered in the same precipitancy, until stopped by his adversary, moving to strike him in his camp. Let us suppose that he had conducted his operations on different principles ; what would have been the probable result? Had he wisely taken with him the old regiment of dragoons under White and Washington, as those brave officers in vain solicited, instead of a dastardly flight, an example of heroism would have been exhibited. The enemy would have been driven in ; prisoners would have been made by, but none from, us ; intelligence would have been shut to the enemy, but open to ourselves ; and the dawn of day would have found our troops, emboldened by the example of the calvary, panting for battle. He would, moreover, have been provided with a body of horse, more numerous and capable than that of his enemy ; and would have carried his army, full of bodily strength and high in spirits, into the neighborhood of his foes. By falling back from Lynch's Creek, when Lord Rawdon retired to Logtown, he would have placed himself in a friendly, strong, and plentiful country ; where, out of striking distance, he might have employed a week or ten days in training his militia, and infusing into them that self-

* " In justice to these troops it ought to be stated that the heat was so oppressive they could not march in the day, and therefore they had for several nights made forced marches to come up with us, which broke the spirits of the men."—*Note from Colonel Howard.*

confidence which doubly arms the soldier in the day of battle.[*]
While improving the condition of his army, he might, by dispatching influential characters to the west of the Alleghany, have brought
down one or two thousand of those hardy warriors to Charlotte, to
be used as an army of reserve, should events require it. What was
of the highest importance, he must, by this delay, have ascertained
with precision the intention of the enemy in time to elude or resist
it; and would have drawn Cornwallis further from his point of
safety; thus more and more exposing him to the harassing attacks
of Marion and Sumter on his flanks and in his rear. All these advantages were within the general's grasp. The partial, though sure,
game of destruction had commenced. Sumter had seized the stores
and convoy from Ninety-six, with which he could have regained his
asylum, had not General Gates's impatience to approach the enemy
refused even one day's rest to the Virginia brigade. Tarleton could
not have been spared from the main body in face of our army;
which, although inactive, would be in the fit attitude for striking
whenever the opportune moment should arrive; and consequently
he would not have been detached in pursuit of Sumter. Obvious
as was this mode of operation, General Gates, with the " Veni, vidi,
vici " of Cæsar in his imagination, rushed on to the fatal field, where
he met correction, not more severe than merited.

Hillsborough having been selected as head-quarters, thither the
fragments of our beaten army repaired; so that the best affected
and most powerful district of North Carolina, situated between the
Catawba and Yadkin rivers, became exposed to the depredations of
the enemy. Brigadier Davidson and Colonel Davie, now promoted
by the governor, and appointed to the command of the cavalry of
the State, remained true to the obligations which honor and duty
alike imposed. Encouraging all around them, they drew together
their faithful comrades, and took measures for the collection of
requisite supplies; resolved to desist from resistance only with the
loss of life. In this manly resolution they were cordially joined
by Brigadier Sumner. The two generals returned to assemble their
militia; while Colonel Davie, with eighty dragoons and Major

---

* Lord Rawdon's retrograde movement from Lynch's Creek was certainly a
favorable movement for General Gates's correction of his erroneous system,
and might have enabled the general to work his own troops into the best spirits.
Had he so done, and fallen back himself, holding his main body safe, and supporting, by fit and occasional succor, Marion and Sumter in their sudden inroads into the enemy's territory, and upon his flanks, we must then have recovered South Carolina, with the exception of Charleston.

Davidson's two mounted companies of riflemen, established himself in the Waxhaw settlement, about thirty-five miles from Charlotte. Here he continued actively employed in watching the movements of the enemy, and repressing their predatory excursions, which, in consequence of the devastation of the country between Camden and the Waxhaws, were extended to the latter district.

Lord Cornwallis, necessarily delayed from the want of stores which he expected from New York, devoted his leisure to the civil duties of his station. Persevering in the policy adopted by Sir Henry Clinton, he enforced the penalty of this general's proclamation with rigor. A commissioner was named to take possession of the estates of all who adhered to the enemies of the king, with directions first to support the wives and children of such offenders, and next to pay the residue of the proceeds of the estates to the paymaster-general of the royal forces.

Death was again denounced against all persons, who, having received protections, should be found in arms against the king's troops. Some of the militia, taken in the late defeat, being charged with that offence, were actually hung. This sanguinary conduct, in the amiable, humane Cornwallis, evinces the proneness of military men, however virtuous, to abuse power. The injustice of breaking a contract, and the criminality of Sir Henry Clinton in that respect, have been already mentioned. Confiding in the plighted faith of the British general, many of our countrymen had taken protection which never would have been accepted, had it been understood they converted those who received them into liege subjects. When Sir Henry Clinton deemed it eligible, by an arbitrary fiat, to annul those protections, justice demanded that he should have left it optional with the holder to take the oath of allegiance, or abandon the State. A severe alternative, but justifiable in war. To break solemn compacts; to transmute the party from the state in which he stood, to a mere dependence on human will, and to hang him for not conforming to that will, is crying injustice. Instead of demanding reparation, and proclaiming the "lex talionis," we submitted, with folded arms, to the criminal outrage. We must look back, with feelings of degradation, to this disgraceful period of our history. Although no advocate for the law of retaliation on slight occasions, it often happens that the unjust can only be taught the value of justice by feeling the severity of retort: and those in power should never hesitate to apply its rigor, when so imperatively demanded.

The severity of the British commander was not restricted to the deluded class who had taken protections; it was extended to the most respectable characters of the State, who had been made prisoners at the fall of Charleston. Letters were found from some of these gentlemen to their friends, killed or taken on the 16th, making communications, as was alleged, but never proved, incompatible with their paroles. The venerable Mr. Gadsden, lieutenant-governor, with several other gentlemen, were first confined on board prison-ships in Charleston harbor; and afterward sent to St. Augustine, in East Florida, where they were again admitted to very limited indulgences.

We shall soon find how the injustice and severity now practised, recoiled upon their authors.

CHAPTER XVIII.

Cornwallis invades North Carolina.—Gallant defence of Charlotte by Davie.—Cornwallis advances toward Salisbury.—Battle of King's Mountain.—Death of Col. Williams of South Carolina.

The British general, having received his supplies, moved from Camden on the 8th of September, to accomplish the great object which he had with much regret deferred. The conquest of North Carolina, before Congress could bring another army into the field, was deemed certain, and would enable the victorious general to approach Virginia, the devoted victim of the ensuing spring's operations. During the winter he expected to restore the royal authority, to lay up magazines, to provide all the necessary horses for the next campaign, and what was very desirable, to fill up his ranks with young Americans. Elated with these flattering expectations, Cornwallis took his route through those parts of the State distinguished for their firm adherence to their country. The main body moved first to the Waxhaws settlement, and next to Charlotte, with an intention to proceed to Salisbury.

Corresponding with the main body on its left, Lieutenant-Colonel Tarleton traversed the country, west of the Wateree, at the head of his Legion and the light infantry. Still nearer to the frontiers, Lieutenant-Colonel Ferguson marched with his corps of provincials. The route of the army lay intermediate to the two settlements of Cross Creek and Tryon County; with both of which, favoring his views, his lordship wished to open safe and direct intercourse. Lieutenant-Colonel Tarleton united with the main body, in its camp at the Waxhaws, where Cornwallis had halted.

The approach of Cornwallis compelled Colonel Davie to fall back upon Charlotte, and his abandoned position was comprehended in the British camp. Davie took post at Providence, on the Charlotte road, twenty-five miles from the Waxhaws. So exhausted was the country, that in this well-improved settlement, the British general was straitened for provisions, and obliged to send his light party in every direction; for whose safety he entertained no apprehension, knowing the humble condition to which his successes had reduced us. Colonel Davie was not unapprised of his lordship's wants, and mode of supplying them; and having ascertained that, while the main body of the enemy was encamped on the north of the Catawba, some of the light troops and the loyalists occupied the southern banks of that river, some distance on the right of the British position, he determined to beat up their quarters in the night. With this view he decamped on the evening of the 20th of September; and taking an extensive circuit, turned the left of Cornwallis, and gained, unperceived, the camp of the loyalists. They had changed their ground, falling nearer to the light troops, and now were stationed at Wahab's plantation. Davie, nevertheless, persevered in his enterprise. Being among his friends, he was sure to receive accurate intelligence; and he had with him the best guides, as many of his corps were inhabitants of this very settlement; and their property, wives, and children were now in the possession of the enemy. He came in sight of Wahab's early the next morning, where he discovered a part of the loyalists and British Legion, mounted, and arrayed near the house, which, in this quarter, was in some degree concealed by a cornfield, cultivated quite to the yard. Detaching Major Davidson through the cornfield with the greater part of the riflemen, with orders to seize the house, he himself gained the lane leading to it. The enemy were completely surprised; and being keenly pushed, betook themselves to flight. Sixty killed and wounded were left on the ground; and as little or no resistance was made, only one of Davie's corps was wounded. The colonel, having collected ninety-six horses with their equipments, and one hundred and twenty stand of arms, retired with expedition; the British drums beating to arms in the contiguous quarters. Captain Wahab, the owner of the farm, spent the few minutes, halt in delicious converse with his wife and children, who ran out as soon as the fire ceased, to embrace their long-lost and beloved protector.

Sweetly passed these moments; but they were succeeded by the
most bitter. The British troops reaching the house, the commanding officer, yielding to diabolical fury, ordered it to be burnt. A
torch was instantly applied, and Wahab saw the only shelter of his
helpless, unprotected family wrapped in flames, without the
power of affording any relief to his forlorn wife and children.
"These were times which tried men's souls." Davie made good
his retreat, and returned to his camp at Providence, having marched
sixty miles in twenty-four hours. On the evening of his return,
General Sumner and Davidson arrived with their militia, amounting to one thousand men, enlisted for a short period. This body,
with the small corps under Colonel Davie, not two hundred, constituted all our force opposed to the advancing enemy.

Four days after the affair at Wahab's, the British general put his
army in motion, taking the Steel Creek road to Charlotte. This
being announced to General Sumner by his light parties, he decamped from Providence and retired on the nearest road to Salisbury, leaving Colonel Davie with his corps, strengthened by a
few volunteers under Major Graham, to observe the movements
of the enemy. Hovering round the British army, Colonel Davie
took several prisoners during the evening, and reached Charlotte
about midnight. This village, standing on elevated ground, contained about twenty houses, built on two streets crossing each
other at right angles. The court-house, constructed of stone, stood
at the intersection of the two streets. The common, on the right
of the street leading through the town, in the direction of the
enemy's advance, was covered with a growth of underwood, and
bounded by the gardens and other inclosures of the village; on the left
was an open field. Colonel Davie, being informed of the approach
of the enemy, and relying on the firmness of his troops, determined
to give them an earnest of the spirit of the country into which they
had entered. Dismounting his cavalry, who, in addition to the
sword and pistol, were armed with muskets, he posted them in
front of the court-house, under cover of a strong stone wall, breast
high. His infantry, also dismounted, with Graham's volunteers,
were advanced eighty yards in front, on each side of the street,
covered by the inclosures of the village. While this disposition
was making, the Legion of Tarleton, led by Major Hanger, Tarleton
being sick, appeared on the common, and formed in column,
widened in front to correspond with the street, and flanked by
parties of light infantry. The charge being sounded, the column

of horse moved slowly, giving time for the light infantry to clear its flanks by dislodging their advanced adversaries. The moment these parties engaged, Hanger rushed along the street to the court-house, where Davie poured in his fire, and compelled him to recede. The dragoons fell back hastily, and were rallied on the common, Meanwhile our infantry, on the right of the street, were driven in. although bravely resisting; upon which Colonel Davie recalled those on our left, who still maintained their ground. The British light infantry continued to advance, and the action was vigorously renewed on our flanks. The centre reserved its fire for the cavalry, who, now returning to the charge, met with a repetition of their first reception, and retired in confusion to their former ground. The British infantry persevered; and having gained Davie's right flank, he drew off from the court-house, and arrayed his gallant band on the eastern side of the town. Cornwallis now came up to the Legion cavalry, and upbraided them by contrasting their present conduct with their past fame. Advancing a third time, they pressed down the street, and ranged with the light infantry, who were still urging forward on our flank; when meeting with our brave corps, now mounted, they received as usual a well-aimed fire, and were again repulsed. The flank companies of the seventy-first and thirty-third regiments advanced to support the light infantry; and Davie receded from the unequal contest, for a long time well supported, and retreated on the great Salisbury road. An attempt was made by the cavalry to disturb our retreat, which succeeded, so far as to drive in our rear-guard; but stopped the moment the supporting company opened its fire. Lieutenant Locke and five privates were killed, and Major Graham and twelve were wounded. The enemy lost twelve non-commissioned officers and privates killed; Major Hanger, Captains Campbell and McDonald, and many privates, were wounded.

Lord Cornwallis established a post at Blair's mill, which he confided to Major McArthur, in order to preserve his communication with Camden, and advanced toward Salisbury. Thus the farther he advanced the more his field force was necessarily reduced. This inconvenience an invading army must feel, and a judicious opponent will turn it to his advantage.

Lieutenant-Colonel Ferguson, still pursuing his course, reached Gilbert-town, and was there informed by his friends that a large force of Western militia was in motion. The British general had selected this excellent officer to command the only detachment from

his army which could be exposed to serious resistance. The principal object of the expedition was to excite the loyalists, in that
quarter, to rebel openly and unite with the British army. While
Ferguson was endeavoring to effect this purpose, he was advised
by Lord Cornwallis of an assault on Augusta, with directions to
intercept, if practicable, the assailants on their return. Augusta
was commanded by Lieutenant-Colonel Thomas Browne; who had
been in the British service, previous to the war, and resided in
Georgia. Pleasing and sensible, he was popular; and possessing
influence with the Indian tribes bordering on that State, from
official connection, he was dangerous. With a view to preserve
control over the affections and conduct of the Indians, the British
government not only continued the established custom of bestowing annual presents in arms, ammunition, blankets, salt, liquor,
and other like articles, precious to the forester, but in consequence
of the war had much increased the annual gift.*

When Georgia fell, many of the most virtuous and distinguished
citizens of that State (as did afterward those of South Carolina) fled
to their brethren in the West. The most prominent among these
voluntary exiles was, Colonel Clarke, who employed his time and
mind in preparing a sufficient force to enable him, on the first
opportunity, to return and renew the contest. Vigilantly watching
every occurrence, he was soon informed of the arrival at Augusta
of the annual Indian presents. The desire to recover Augusta, always ascendant in Clarke's breast, now became irresistible. He
called forth his comrades, and expatiated on the rich harvest of reward and glory within their reach, and the facility of obtaining it at
that moment. His arguments were successful, and the warriors
of the hills shouted for battle. No time was lost by their active
leader in preparing for the enterprise. The wallets were filled with
provisions, the guns cleaned, bullets moulded, and a scanty supply
of powder was distributed out of their scanty magazine.

These were the simple preparations of our hardy mountaineers
for battle; a lesson, pregnant with instruction, to all military
commanders. The nearer an army can be brought to this un-
encumbered and alert condition, the more is its effective capacity
increased, the better are the public resources husbanded, and the

---

* I never could see the justice of denominating our Indian borderers savage.
They appear to me to merit a very different appellation, as we well know they
are not behind their civilized neighbors in the practice of many of the virtues
most dear to human nature.

quicker will the war be terminated. Two hours only were occupied in getting ready to move, which followed as soon as the horses could be brought from pasture and accoutred. The grass of nature gave subsistence to the horse, while the soldier feasted on the homely contents of his wallet, made and filled by his wife or mother.

Marching through friendly settlements, intelligence was gained, guides were procured, and accessions of strength acquired. Having reached the confines of the enemy, the leader halted, made his last arrangements, and issued his final orders. Then with the velocity of an eagle, he pounced on his prey; but missing it, recurred to the slow and systematic operations which require patient vigilance and prevent hazard. The watchful Browne, informed of the gathering storm, was not surprised by its approach. Augusta being untenable with his weak force, he retired toward Garden Hill with his garrison of one hundred and fifty men, a few Indians, and two small brass pieces. In front of the latter position, he was vigorously attacked by Clarke, at the head of seven hundred men; but under cover of his artillery, he at length dislodged his enemy, and forced his way to the hill at the point of the bayonet. So soon as he had gained the hill, Colonel Browne began to fortify himself in the best possible manner, being determined to hold out to the last moment, in order to give time to Colonel Cruger, who commanded at Ninety-six, and was informed of Browne's situation and views, to relieve him. Among other expedients to form suitable defences, Colonel Browne put in requisition all the bales of cloth, osnaburgs, blankets, &c., found in the store at Garden Hill, and converted them, with the assistance of rails and paling, into a breastwork, proof against musketry. Clarke, nevertheless, persevered in his attempt to bring the enemy to submission; which he would have certainly accomplished, by availing himself of the two pieces of artillery gained in the first conflict, had not the ammunition belonging to them been nearly exhausted. Deprived of this aid, he resorted to other expedients, and at length succeeded in depriving the garrison of water. But, unluckily, his adversary was no less fertile in mental resource than intrepid in battle. To remedy this menacing evil, Colonel Browne ordered all the earthen vessels in the store to be taken, in which the urine was preserved; and when cold, it was served out with much economy to the troops, himself taking the first draught. Disregarding the torture of a wound in his leg, which had become much swollen from exertion, he continued booted at the head of his small gallant band, directing his defence, and animating his troops by his presence and example. Thus Browne courageously supported himself until the fourth day, when Colonel Cruger appeared on the opposite banks. Colonel Clarke immediately withdrew, leaving his artillery behind, and disappointed, by the invincible prowess of his enemy, of a reward which, with less perseverance and gallantry, he might justly have expected to obtain.

Ferguson no sooner received the order of Cornwallis to attack the assailants of Augusta on their return, than he drew nearer to the mountain, prepared to fall upon Clarke as soon as he reached his vicinity. While waiting to execute this object, he heard that a new enemy was approaching him, for the very purpose of proceeding on the same enterprise, in which Clarke had just been foiled. A numerous assemblage of rifle militia had been drawn together from Kentucky, the western country of Virginia, and North Carolina, and were in motion under Colonels Campbell, Cleveland, Williams, Sevier, and Shelby, toward Augusta ; when, hearing of Clarke's repulse and Ferguson's expedition, they relinquished their enterprise on Browne, and turned against Ferguson. Reaching Gilbert-town, from which place Ferguson had lately retired, they selected one thousand five hundred of their warriors, who followed the British partisan, bent upon his destruction. Ferguson, apprised of their pursuit, took post on the summit of King's Mountain, a position thickly set with trees, and more assailable by the rifle than defensible with the bayonet. Here he was overtaken by our mountaineers, who quickly dismounted, and arrayed themselves for battle. Our brave countrymen were formed into three divisions under their respective leaders, and coolly ascended the mountain in different directions. Colonel Cleveland first reached the enemy, and opened a destructive fire from behind the trees. Ferguson resorted to the bayonet ; Cleveland necessarily gave way. At that instant, from another quarter, Colonel Shelby poured in his fire, alike sheltered and alike effectual. Upon him Ferguson furiously turned, and advanced with the bayonet, gaining the only, though immaterial, advantage in his power, of forcing Shelby to recede. This was scarcely effected, before Colonel Campbell had gained the summit of the mountain ; when he too commenced a deadly fire. The British bayonet was again applied ; and produced its former effect. All the divisions now returned in co-operation, and resistance became temerity. Nevertheless, Ferguson, confiding in the bayonet, sustained the attack with undismayed gallantry. The battle raged for fifty minutes, when the British commander received a ball, and fell dead. Deprived of their leader, the fire of the enemy slackened, and the second in command wisely beat a parley, which was followed by his surrender. Three hundred were killed and wounded; one hundred regulars and seven hundred loyalists were taken, with one thousand five hundred stand of arms; Lieutenant-Colonel Ferguson being provided with supernumerary muskets, to arm such of the inhabitants as might repair to the royal standard. Our loss was trifling in numbers; but among the killed was Colonel Williams, of South Carolina, who had joined these gallant patriots, with his adherents, from the district of Ninety-six, and was among the most active and resolute of this daring assemblage.

Although Clarke failed in the reduction of Augusta, his attempt led to the destruction of Ferguson; and with it, to the present relief of North Carolina.

CHAPTER XIX

Cornwallis retreats to Camden.—Leslie detached to Virginia by Sir Henry Clinton.—Is ordered to Charleston.—Cornwallis establishes himself at Winnsborough.—Activity of Marion.—Sumter threatens Ninety-six.—Tarleton detached against him.—Is defeated at Blackstock Hill.—Activity of Pickens, Harden, and Clarke.

WHEN prepared to advance to Salisbury, the British general received the unwelcome news of the battle of King's Mountain. Disappointed in his expectation of important benefit from the exertions of Colonel Ferguson among the loyalists of Tryon County; deprived of that officer and his corps, which constituted more than a fourth of the army, Lord Cornwallis abandoned his project of advancing, and began a retreat to Camden. The security of South Carolina, then threatened by the sudden incursions of the mountain warriors, and endangered by the activity of Sumter, Marion, and Pickens, and the necessity of procuring additional force before his preconcerted conquest could be pursued, required his lordship's return. On the 14th of October, the British army commenced its retreat from a country which it had entered a few weeks before with a confident expectation of reannexing it to the British empire.

As soon as Sir Henry Clinton was informed of the defeat of Gates and dispersion of the force under Sumter, in order to promote the operations of his general in the South, he detached three thousand men from New York to Virginia under the orders of Major-General Leslie. About the time Cornwallis retired from Charlotte, Leslie arrived in the Chesapeake, and commenced his operations on the

south side of James River, making Portsmouth his principal position. The annihilation of Ferguson's force, having changed Lord
Cornwallis's plan, Leslie's continuance in Virginia became unnecessary; and he was directed by his lordship to embark without
delay, and proceed to Charleston.

The preparations for resisting this officer were hardly begun, when
the commonwealth was relieved from an invasion which it had
deemed fixed, inasmuch as no doubt could exist that Leslie was
intended to co-operate with Lord Cornwallis, who, after the reduction of North Carolina, would advance upon Virginia. Soon after
his lordship left Charlotte, the rainy season set in, which rendered
his march very inconvenient and harassing. The ground being
saturated with incessant rain, the troops were exposed to its chill ex-
halations, and became sickly. The general himself was seized with
a bilious fever, and was so much indisposed as to resign the army
to the direction of Lord Rawdon.

This young nobleman had difficulties to encounter, in addition to
those springing from the humidity of the air and ground. The
swell of water-courses presented new obstacles, not only to his progress, but to the procurement of forage and provisions for daily
subsistence, which were before very difficult to obtain. The royal
militia became now peculiarly useful. Inured to the climate, they
escaped the prevailing sickness; and being mounted, were employed
unceasingly in hunting, collecting, and driving cattle from the woods
to the army. * This meagre supply was the only meat procurable;

---

* In reviewing the military correspondence and statements of our war, the
activity and usefulness of the Americans who joined the British, forces itself
upon our attention. Not more than one-tenth of our population is rated as
attached to Great Britain in the late contest, of which not more than a hun-
dredth is supposed to have taken an active part with the enemy. Yet great and
effective were the services derived from them; not only in the field, where they
fought with acknowledged valor, but in procuring intelligence, and providing
provision. Mr. Stedman, a British officer, and in the commissariat under Lord
Cornwallis, tells us that the army would have been often destitute of provisions,
but for the capacity and activity of the inhabitants who repaired to the royal
standard. In our war, no liberal mind will deny, that every man had a right to
take his side, as it grew out of a domestic difference; whereas, in a foreign war
every citizen is bound to support his country. While, therefore, we lament the
opposition of this part of our fellow-citizens, we cannot condemn them for
taking the part believed by them to be right.

It is to be hoped, that should we be brought (which in the course of things
too often occurs) to make the last appeal again, that we shall be exempted from
the ills which inevitably follow the want of unanimity. That government best
deserves applause which is administered with a view to preserve union at home
as its first object, it being the cheapest and surest defence against injustice
from abroad.

and young corn, gathered from the field, and boiled, or grated into meal, was the substitute for bread.* The British troops complained grievously of their sufferings on this march, which, in comparison with those endured by our army, were nothing. They were comfortably supplied with clothes, shoes, and blankets; and a short interruption of regular meals, although not agreeable, was certainly not oppressive. Had they been in rags, without shoes, with one blanket only for three men, and pursued by a superior foe, patience and alacrity under the hardships of retreat would have entitled them to the praise which was lavished on their loyalty and fortitude.

After a fatiguing march of two weeks, through deep wet roads, and full water-courses, all of which were necessarily forded, the enemy reached the country lying between Camden and Ninety-six, on the 29th of October. To support these two stations, and to shield the intermediate space from American incursions, Cornwallis established himself at Winnsborough, a position very convenient for the purposes contemplated. Here he desired to repose until the junction of the detachment from Virginia, under Leslie, should enable him to resume his operations in North Carolina. But Marion and Sumter, continuing unchanged amid the despondency which the disasters of August had produced, boldly pushed their disturbing inroads into the enemy's territory. With a force fluctuating from fifty to two hundred and fifty men, Marion held himself in his recesses on the Pedee and Black rivers, whence he darted upon the enemy whenever an opportunity presented itself. He not only kept in check all the small parties of the enemy, whom the want of forage and provisions, or the desire of plunder, occasionally urged into the region east and south of Camden, but he often passed the Santee, interrupting the communication with Charleston, and sometimes alarming the small posts in its vicinity. To such a height had his interruption reached, that Cornwallis turned his attention to the subject. Lieutenant-Colonel Tarleton was dispatched with his Legion and the light infantry, with orders to find out Marion's haunts, and to destroy him. Having passed the Santee, and approached the Black River, this officer exerted himself to bring Marion to action; but the American partisan, having ascertained the very superior force of his adversary, eluded all the attempts made to entrap him.

* During this retreat the British rasped the young corn into a coarse meal, which was considered a better mode of preparing the corn than roasting or parching, common with us. Biscuit made of flour, from which only the bran has been taken, is the best and cheapest for winter quarters, when the soldier may conveniently bake his bread.

At length Tarleton contrived, by his manœuvres, to circulate an opinion that, by detachments from his corps, he had very much reduced its force. This rumor, as was intended, soon reached Marion, who was always willing to seize every opportunity of striking at his antagonist. Presuming that Tarleton was reduced to an equality with himself, he cheerfully relinquished his asylum, wishing to give battle to his adversary. His caution and vigilance were not intermitted; and discovering that he was proceeding upon erroneous intelligence, he skilfully withdrew to his unassailable position, leaving Tarleton to deplore the inefficacy of his wiles and toils.

While Marion engaged the attention of Cornwallis, whose cavalry and artillery were drawn to the east of the Santee, Sumter hovered on the west of that river, searching for some vulnerable point to assail. This officer, equally enterprising and indefatigable with his compeer, had the mountainous country of the Carolinas to draw upon for assistance. He had, therefore, the advantage of Marion in numbers; sometimes commanding five hundred, and at others eight hundred men. When Lord Cornwallis became acquainted with the approach of Sumter, Major Wemyss was detached in pursuit of him, with the sixty-third regiment, and the remains, about forty in number, of the Legion cavalry. The American general having displayed, on past occasions, a character of more boldness than vigilance, the British officer was inspired with a hope of surprising him; and directed his march, with great secrecy, to Broad River, where Sumter was encamped. The celerity with which Wemyss advanced, brought him, sooner than he intended, to the vicinity of his enemy; and, apprehending that Sumter might be apprised, before morning, of his proximity, he determined on a nocturnal attack. His corps was immediately formed for battle, and advanced on Sumter's camp. Anxious to observe the condition of his foe, Major Wemyss placed himself with the van officer, who soon fell on our picket, and threw them back on the main body, after a feeble resistance. Only five muskets were discharged; and, happily for us, two balls pierced the major, and disabled him from further exertion. The command devolved upon a subaltern, who, although unacquainted with the ground, and uninformed as to the plan, determined to press the attack. He found Sumter prepared to receive him; and very soon the contest terminated in the repulse of the British, who retired, leaving their commandant and twenty men on the ground.[*]

---

[*] Major Wemyss was very remiss in not having opened his plan and views to his second in command; for it often happens that the first is stopped from ser-

The American officer, satisfied with his success, did not pursue it, but crossed the Broad River, for the purpose of proceeding to the chief object of his expedition. He had concerted with Colonels Clarke and Banner, who commanded bands of mountaineers, measures for surprising Ninety-six. To cover that enterprise, he menaced Camden; intending, by a forced march, to join Clarke and Banner on the west side of the Broad River. On the day following, a junction was effected, and Sumter, at the head of the combined forces, proceeded to the execution of his design. These occurrences excited in Lord Cornwallis apprehensions for the safety of Ninety-six. Orders were instantly dispatched, recalling Tarleton from his expedition against Marion, and directing him to proceed without delay against Sumter. The sixty-third regiment, which had not yet returned from its unsuccessful enterprise, was ordered to join Tarleton as he advanced. As soon as that officer received the order of Cornwallis, he left his position in the vicinity of Black River, and hastened toward Ninety-six. Accustomed to quick movements, he arrived in the neighborhood of Sumter before the latter had even heard of his advance. Pushing up the Ennoree River, Tarleton hoped to place himself in his enemy's rear; but, very luckily, a deserter from the British infantry had apprised the American general of his adversary's movement. Sumter immediately drew off and passed the Ennoree, where the British van overtook a part of our rear-guard, and handled it roughly. Sumter continued to retreat, having the Tyger, one of the most rapid and obstructive rivers of that country, in his front. Tarleton, foreseeing that, should his adversary pass the Tyger, there would be little prospect of bringing him to action, redoubled his exertions to overtake him. Well knowing the character of his foe, he had preserved his force in a compact order; but his apprehension that Sumter might escape, his ardor in pursuit, and desire to continue the success with which his zeal had been generally crowned, impelled him to deviate from that prudent course. In the evening of the 20th of November, at the head of his cavalry, about one hundred and seventy in number, and eighty mounted infantry of the sixty-third regiment, he dashed forward to bring Sumter to battle, before the latter had passed the Tyger, and soon came in

vice during the action. What might have been the issue of this enterprise, had the British major properly informed his next in command of his plan, resources, and expectations, cannot be determined; but no doubt can exist that the effect of the assailing troops must have been diminished considerably by this culpable omission in the commandant.

sight of his enemy, who had selected a strong position on Black-stock Hill, on the eastern banks of the river. Here prudence would have dictated to Colonel Tarleton a pause. The residue of the sixty-third regiment, the Legion and light infantry, were follow-ing with all possible dispatch, and in one hour might have joined him. There was no possibility of his enemy's escape without battle; and the co-operation of his infantry was indispensable to secure victory. But delay did not comport with the ardent zeal or the experience of Tarleton, and he bodly advanced to the assault. "That part of the hill," says McKenzie, in his strictures on the campaigns of Tarleton, "to which the attack was directed, was nearly perpendicular, with a small rivulet, brushwood, and a rail fence in front. The rear of the Americans, and part of their right flank, was secured by the river Tyger; and their left was covered by a large log-barn, into which a considerable division of their force had been thrown, and from which, as the apertures between the logs served them for loop-holes, they fired with security. British valor was conspicuous in this action, but no valor could surmount the obstacles that here stood in its way. Of the sixty-third regiment, the commanding officer, two others, and one-third of the privates fell.* Lieutenant-Colonel Tarleton, ob-serving their situation, charged with his cavalry; but unable to dislodge the enemy, either from the log barn on his right, or the height on his left, he was obliged to fall back. Lieutenant Skin-ner, with a presence of mind useful to such emergencies, covered the retreat of the sixty-third; and in this manner did the whole party continue to retire, till they formed a junction with their infantry, who were advancing to support them, leaving Sumter in quiet possession of the field. This officer occupied the ground for several hours; but having received a severe wound, and knowing that the British would be re-enforced before the next morning, he thought it hazardous to wait. He accordingly retired, and taking his wounded men along with him, crossed the rapid river Tyger. The wounded of the British detachment were left to the mercy of their enemy; and it is doing but bare justice to General Sumter

---

* Major Money, Lieutenant Gibson, Lieutenant Cope; the infantry amounted only to eighty. What presumption! to expect to dislodge an officer acknowl-edged to be the most brave, posted on ground chosen by himself, at the head of five or six hundred troops, whose valor had been often before tested, with one hundred and sixty, mostly dragoons. The British cavalry could not act with effect from the nature of the ground, as was evinced by the nugatory attempt made by Lieutenant-Colonel Tarleton at their head.

to declare that the strictest humanity took place upon the present occasion: they were supplied with every comfort in his power." This faithful and plain relation was made from the representations of officers in the action. Lieutenant-Colonel Tarleton, however, viewed his own conduct in the most favorable light; and not only considered the assault warrantable, but even claimed the victory. If the principle, on which his pretension is founded, be correct, nothing short of exterminating success can give title to victory. What more could the assailed party have done than to fight, to retain his ground, bury the dead, and take care of the enemy's wounded? Of his own wounded, General Sumter had but four to take care of, and of his own dead, but three to bury. But he did not wait until Colonel Tarleton might return with a superior force, and as Tarleton *did* return and occupy the field of battle on the day following, therefore Tarleton was the victor. Such logic does not merit refutation. But however interested military disputants may contest the point, impartial posterity will concur in the conclusion of common sense, that Sumter gained a decisive victory. A grievous wound suspended his personal exertions, and probably prevented him from improving his success. After performing the funeral rites of the dead, and placing the wounded of the enemy in the most comfortable condition in his power, he continued his' retreat. His faithful associates, agreeably to usage, separated as soon as they reached their point of safety.

Sumter's wound, unfortunately for his country, long detained him from the field; but useful consequences continued to result from the deep impression of his example, from the spirit he had infused, and the experience gained under his guidance. Pickens, Harden, Clarke, and others, persevered in their arduous exertions. Frequently interrupting the communication between the different posts of the enemy, they obliged the British general to strengthen his stations, spread throughout the country, and thereby weaken his operative force.

Tarleton was no sooner recalled from the east of the Santee, than Marion emerged from his concealed retreat, traversed the country, from Georgetown to Camden, and endangered the communication between them. Frequently crossing the Santee, he interrupted the intercourse between Charleston and Camden; to secure which, an intermediate post had been established at Motte's Hill, on the south side of the Congaree.

Thus, in this gloomy period, was resistance in the South continued, as embarrassing to the enemy, as exhilarating to the scattered refugees from South Carolina and Georgia. It produced, too, in Congress and the nation, a solacing conviction that the spirit of the people was unsubdued ; and promised, if seconded with vigor, and directed with wisdom, to restore the two lost States to the Union.

CHAPTER XX.

Gates reorganizes his army.—Is recalled.—Gen. Greene appointed to fill his place.—
Letter of General Washington to George Mason, on that event.—Delaware and
Maryland added to the Southern Department.—Lieut.-Col. Lee, with his Legion,
consisting of three troops of horse and three companies of infantry, ordered to the
South.

CORNWALLIS still held his position at Winnsborough, waiting for the expected re-enforcement under Leslie, and devoting his attention to the repression of the daring enterprises devised and executed by Marion, Sumter, and their gallant associates.

In the mean while Gates was laboring with unceasing zeal and diligence to prepare a force capable of meeting his successful adversary. Having collected the shattered remains of his army at Hillsborough, in pursuance of a regulation established by the commander-in-chief, the broken lines of Maryland and Delaware were compressed into one regiment, and placed under Colonel Williams, of Maryland. The officers of cavalry had not been very successful in their efforts, for but four complete troops could be formed from the relics of Bland's, Moylan's, and Baylor's regiments, when united with the new recruits. These were embodied, and placed under the command of Lieutenant-Colonel Washington, of Virginia.* The supernumerary officers of Maryland and Delaware, and of the cavalry, were dispatched to their respective States, for the purpose of recruiting. Brigadier Gist, who had so nobly seconded De Kalb on the fatal 16th of August, was charged with the direction of this service, there being no command for him with the army, in consequence of its reduced state. General Smallwood was retained as second to Gates. Morgan, the distinguished leader of the rifle corps, was promoted to the rank of brigadier by brevet, and repaired to the Southern army. About the same time, the recruits of the

---

* Lieutenant-Colonel Washington found among his difficulties that of acquiring proper swords not the least considerable ; and hearing that the arsenal of his native State in Richmond abounded with dragoon swords, he dispatched an officer to Governor Jefferson, stating his wants, and soliciting relief.

Virginia line reached Hillsborough; and the remaining companies of Harrison's artillery also joined our army.

The union of these several corps gave to General Gates about one thousand four hundred Continentals. The deliverance of North Carolina from the late invasion, by the fortunate victory of King's Mountain, afforded time for the government of the State to understand its real condition, and to prepare for the impending danger. A division of its militia had been called into the field under the command of the Generals Sumner and Davidson, to which was united a volunteer corps under Colonel Davie.

While Gates remained at Hillsborough, Sumner had taken post, with the militia, in the country washed by the Yadkin, the main branch of the Pedee. Smallwood was dispatched to take charge of the troops in that quarter, while General Gates moved, with the Continentals, to Charlotte. As soon as the head-quarters of the American army were transferred to this place, Smallwood was advanced from the Yadkin to the Catawba, having Brigadier Morgan, at the head of a corps of light troops, in his front.

The Pedee flows near the northern boundary of South Carolina; the Savannah is its limit on the southwest; and the Santee, whose main branch is the Catawba, is the intermediate of the three large rivers of that State. Just below Motte's, where the British had erected a small fortification, the Santee is formed by the confluence of the Wateree and the Congaree. The former of these rivers, descending from the north, runs through the hilly country, where it is called Catawba; and, passing Camden, rolls on to its junction with the Congaree. The Congaree, after the union of its head branches, the Broad River and the Saluda, takes a southern direction.

The position now taken by Gates, and the arrangement of his force, presented a strong contrast to his former conduct, and afforded a consoling presumption that he had discovered his past error, and had profited by the correction of adversity.* Neither Congress nor the nation were reconciled, however, to the severe blow which our arms had sustained under his guidance. The annihilation, in a few hours, of an army from which much had been expected, was a sufficient cause of investigation and inquietude; and when that mis-

---

* When General Gates was about to set out from Virginia for the South, his old acquaintance and fellow-soldier, General Charles Lee, waited on him to take leave; and, pressing him by the hand, bade him to bear in mind that the laurels of the North must not be exchanged for the willow of the South.

fortune, in the exhausted and worried condition of the people, was
followed by a necessity of replacing the lost force, or of submitting
to the subjugation of an important portion of the Union, the most
awful and afflicting sensations were unavoidably excited. Congress
entertained, indeed, a high respect for the unfortunate general, and
a grateful recollection of his past services; but that homage, however merited, could not, and ought not, to suppress those inquiries
which always follow miscarriage or misfortune, where the sovereign
power is careful of the public good. It was, moreover, necessary
to check the conqueror, and two lost States were to be recovered.
To effect such important objects, a general, obscured by adversity,
was, though of respectable talents, inadequate. It required the fire
of superior genius, aided by an untarnished reputation, to reanimate
despondency, restore confidence, and turn the current of adversity.

Such reflections daily gained strength; and Congress, at length,
resolved that a court of inquiry should examine into the conduct of
Major-General Gates, commanding in the Southern department, and
that the commander-in-chief should, in the interim, appoint a successor. This unpleasant resolution was immediately transmitted
to General Gates at Charlotte, and he prepared to obey the summons of the court, as soon as his successor should arrive and assume
the duties of command. In the mean while, he continued, with
unremitting exertion, his preparations for resisting the enemy, by
endeavoring to discover their force and plans, by collecting magazines of provisions, and stimulating the governments of North
Carolina and Virginia to a timely contribution of their aids. Happy,
if his efforts should smooth the way for a more prosperous course to
his successor, he acted, throughout this disagreeable period, with
intelligence, assiduity, and zeal.

Washington did not long deliberate on the appointment which he
was directed to make. Major-General Greene* had served under

----

* HEAD-QUARTERS, PASSAIC FALLS, *October* 22d, 1780.

DEAR SIR:—In consequence of a resolve of Congress, directing an inquiry
into the conduct of Major-General Gates, and authorizing me to appoint some
other officer in his place during this inquiry, I have made choice of Major-
General Greene, who will, I expect, have the honor of presenting you with this
letter.

I shall, without scruple, introduce this gentleman to you as a man of abilities, bravery, and coolness. He has a comprehensive knowledge of our affairs,
and is a man of fortitude and resources. I have not the smallest doubt, therefore, of his employing all the means which may be put into his hands to the
best advantage, nor of his assisting in pointing out the most likely ones to answer
the purposes of his command. With this character I take the liberty of recom-

him from the commencement of the war, and from that period had enjoyed his unvarying confidence and esteem. In a time of extreme derangement and difficulty, he had been called to the station of quartermaster-general, in which he acquitted himself with consummate ability. He commanded the division of the army opposed to Lieutenant-General Knyphausen, at Springfield, in 1780, and acquired, as he merited, distinguished applause.

We have before seen, that he checked the advance of the British with Weedon's brigade in the close of the battle of Brandywine; that he was opposed to Lord Cornwallis in New Jersey, when the maintenance of the obstruction to the navigation of the Delaware was ardently pursued by the commander-in-chief; and that he commanded the left wing of the army at the action of Germantown. He was honored at the battle of Monmouth with the direction of the right wing, which was conducted much to his credit, and to the annoyance of the enemy. He was under Sullivan in the invasion

mending him to your civilities and support; for I have no doubt, from the embarrassed situation of Southern affairs, of his standing much in need of the latter from every gentleman of influence in the assemblies of those States.

As General Greene can give you the most perfect information in detail of our present distresses and future prospects, I shall content myself with the aggregate account of them; and, with respect to the first, they are so great and complicated, that it is scarcely within the powers of description to give an adequate idea of them. With regard to the second, unless there is a material change both in our civil and military policy, it will be in vain to contend much longer.

We are without money, and have been so for a long time; without provision and forage, except what is taken by impress; without clothing, and shortly shall be (in a manner) without men. In a word, we have lived upon expedients till we can live no longer; and it may truly be said, that the history of this war is a history of false hopes and temporary devices, instead of system—and economy, which results from it.

If we mean to continue our struggles (and it is to be hoped we shall not relinquish our claims), we must do it upon an entire new plan. We must have a permanent force; not a force that is constantly fluctuating, and sliding from under us, as a pedestal of ice would leave a statue in a summer's day; involving us in expense that baffles all calculation, an expense which no funds are equal to. We must at the same time contrive ways and means to aid our taxes by loans, and put our finances upon a more certain and stable footing than they are at present. Our civil government must likewise undergo a reform; ample powers must be lodged in Congress as the head of the Federal Union, adequate to all the purposes of war. Unless these things are done, our efforts will be in vain, and only serve to accumulate expense, add to our perplexities, and dissatisfy the people, without a prospect of obtaining the prize in view. But these sentiments do not appear well in a hasty letter, without digestion or order. I have not time to give them otherwise, and shall only assure you that they are well meant, however crude they may appear. With sincere affection,

I am, dear sir,
Your most obedient servant,

GEORGE MASON, Esq.   GEORGE WASHINGTON.

of Rhode Island, and contributed very much to the excellent retreat which became necessary. Indeed, so manifold and important were his services, that he became a very highly trusted counsellor of the commander-in-chief; respected for his sincerity, prized for his disinterestedness, and valued for his wisdom. It followed, of course, when calamity thickened, and the means of resistance grew thin, that Greene should be summoned to break the force of the one, and to nerve the imbecility of the other.

He was accordingly nominated by Washington to the command of the Southern army.

Congress passed a resolution incorporating the States of Delaware and Maryland with the Southern department, and the commander-in-chief detached from his army Lieutenant-Colonel Lee, with his Legion, to the South. This corps consisted of three troops of horse, and three companies of infantry, giving a total of three hundred and fifty effectives. But it was not complete; and after its arrival in the South, gradually diminished. Such was the debilitated condition of our military force, that only this trifling re-enforcement could be spared to a general charged with the arduous task of saving Virginia and North Carolina, and of reannexing to the Union the States south of them.

What better testimony could be furnished of our fitness at that time for the repose of peace? But it was necessary to prosecute the war with zeal and vigor, or the great prize for which the confederate States were struggling would be lost, or but partially gained. The enemy's strength had also very much dwindled, and his replenishment of the waste of war was not exempt from difficulty. He had to contend by sea and by land with potent nations, and to spread his force in every quarter of the globe. Such was the effect of our alliance with the house of Bourbon, and the result of Gates's victory at Saratoga.

CHAPTER XXI.

GENERAL GREENE, after employing a few days in preparing for his journey, relinquished, with reluctance, his inferior station, to take upon himself the honorable though weighty command to which he had been called. He passed through the States of Delaware and Maryland, for the purpose of ascertaining the extent of the assistance to be obtained from that quarter.

Here he was informed that Brigadier Gist had been indefatigably engaged in executing the trust reposed in him; but such was the difficulty at this period of procuring recruits, as to forbid the expectation of filling up the regiments, without the substitution of some new mode. On this, and all other subjects connected with his duty, he held full and free conferences with the State governments; and having made his final arrangements, pursued his journey to Richmond, the capital of Virginia.

This State was properly considered the fountain of Southern resistance. Her relative antiquity, the stock of loyalty for which she had been always distinguished, her well-known obedience to law and hatred of change, had convinced the wavering and the doubting that our resistance was just, and consistent with the great charter of British liberty. Thus, by the sanction of her authority, she had stripped resistance of its imaginary horrors. The extent of her domain, the value of her products, the vigor of her councils, and the political fame she had acquired in the first Congress by a happy selection of delegates, placed her high in the respect and confidence of her sister States.* The uniform sample of wisdom exhibited by her deputies in that body, inspired the nation with exalted sentiments of the place of their nativity. To the hand of one of her sons had been committed the sword of defence; from the lips of another, in obedience to the commands of his constituents, came the proposal of our independence; and by the pen of a third that independence was declared. Although the most ancient and loyal of the colonies, she had, in our just war, been uniformly decisive and active; and though not particularly injured by the first hostile acts of parliament, she nevertheless kept pace with Massachusetts, the devoted object of ministerial vengeance, in the incipient steps of resistance. Thus distinguished, she was marked as a peculiar victim by the common enemy. Happily for herself, as well as for the Union, few

---

* The selection of our first deputies establishes an important truth, that the people in danger, and free from the distraction of feuds and factions, will always act wisely. When distracted by feud and severed by faction, they will rarely do so. The Virginia Assembly made its first election of delegates exempt from the art and rage of faction. They were Peyton Randolph, George Washington, Richard H. Lee, Patrick Henry, Edmund Pendleton, Richard Bland, and Benjamin Harrison.

of her inhabitants had taken side with the mother country ; and most of those few in the first stage of the revolution had left the State. Thus her undivided ability was employed in the firm maintenance of the war.

As soon as Sir Henry Clinton took command of the British army, the humbling of Virginia became a leading object of his plans. For, by maiming her strength, he lessened her ability to give support and countenance to that division of the States which he had then selected as the principal theatre of the war. A devastating expedition had been successfully prosecuted under General Matthews, and as soon as the defeat of General Gates was known at New York, Leslie, as had been mentioned, was detached with three thousand men to the Chesapeake, for the purpose of co-operating with Lord Cornwallis, then expected to have been considerably advanced in completing the conquest of North Carolina.

When Greene reached Richmond, he found the government engaged in preparing means of defence against Leslie, who had established himself at Portsmouth. Relying upon this State for his principal support in men and stores, he was sensibly affected by the difficulties in which he found her. But, active and intelligent, penetrating and laborious, he persevered in his exertions. Having brought his arrangments to a satisfactory conclusion, he proceeded to the South, leaving Major-General Baron Steuben* to direct the defence of Virginia, and to superintend the re-enforcements preparing for the Southern army. From Richmond he hastened to Hillsborough, the seat of government of North Carolina. Here he found the executive, apprised of the dangers by which the State was threatened, well disposed to exert their authority in preparing means to resist the advancing enemy. This State very much resembles Virginia in the manners and habits of the people, so much so, as to induce the conclusion of its being settled principally by

---

* This officer was a Prussian by birth, and had passed his youth in arms, during the war of 1754, chiefly under the orders of Prince Henry, brother to the Great Frederick, and his rival in military celebrity. Toward the close of that war, Steuben had been introduced into the family of the prince, whose confidence and esteem he enjoyed forever after. On his arrival in America he attracted the consideration of Congress, and was soon promoted to the station of inspector-general of the army, with the rank of major-general. To him we are indebted for the great proficiency in tactics acquired by the troops in 1777, 1778, at Valley Forge. He was singularly useful in this line, and much respected for his military experience. Faithful and honorable, he supported the cause of his adopted country with the ardor of youth, gained high confidence with the commander-in-chief, and was honored, on many occasions, with important trusts.

emigrants from that State. Its population, though double that of South Carolina, was very disproportionate to the extent of its territory.

North Carolina is watered by many rivers, few of which are navigable for ships. Cape Fear is the most considerable, and that only navigable to Wilmington, situated not very distant from the sea. In a state of war, when naval superiority is conclusively in favor of the enemy, as was the case in our contest, this privation of nature was replete with advantage to us, though extremely incommodious in peace. It is only to be assailed with effect through Virginia or South Carolina, through each of which her foreign commerce passes. At this time it was threatened on both sides, as Leslie still continued in Virginia, waiting, as was presumed, for the advance of Lord Cornwallis. Although, in this State, horses, bacon, Indian corn, and beef, which constitute the most essential supplies of an army, could be found in abundance, yet, from the thinness of population, the collection of them was inconvenient.

The mountainous region of North Carolina was inhabited by a race of hardy men, who were familiar with the use of the horse and rifle, were stout, active, patient under privation, and brave. Irregular in their movements, and unaccustomed to restraint, they delighted in the fury of action, but pined under the servitude and inactivity of camp. True to the American cause, they displayed an impetuous zeal, whenever their wild and ardent temper prompted the contribution of their aid. In the middle and Atlantic sections lived a race, less capable of labor, and less willing to endure it ; who were much divided in political opinions, and encumbered with that dreadful evil,* which the cruel policy of preceding times had introduced.† The prospect of efficient aid from a State so situated, was not encouraging. But the fertile genius of Greene deriving new influence from his conciliating manners, soon laid the

---

* Negro slavery.

† The Constitution of the United States, adopted lately with so much difficulty, has effectually provided against the increase of this evil (by importation), after a few years. This single benevolent and judicious trait ought to have recommended that instrument strongly to the pious and amiable throughout the Union, and to the slaveholder of every description. Yet, in most of the States, it was pertinaciously opposed.

It is much to be lamented, that having done so much good in this way, a provision' had not been made for the gradual abolition of slavery. In a state of war, what can be more dreadful than the conviction, that we have in our bosoms an inveterate enemy ready to turn upon us in our beds, whenever opportunity and instigation shall prompt to the execution of the bloody tragedy ; yet this is the state of the Union south of Susquehanna.

foundation of a support which would have been completely ade
quate to his purpose, had the quality of the troops corresponded
with their number. Having finished his preparatory measures, he
hastened to Charlotte, pleased with the hope of rescuing the State
from the impending calamities. On the 2d of December he reached
the army, and was received by General Gates with the most cordial
respect. The translation of the command was announced in
general orders on the ensuing day. After devoting a short time to
to those communications which were essential to the information
of his successor, Gates took leave of the army, and proceeded to
meet the inquiry into his conduct which had been ordered by Congress. His progress was slow, his manners were grave, his demeanor was condescending, his conversation reserved. On his lone
road, no countenance shed the balm of condolence; all were
gloomy, all scowling. The fatal loss of the 16th of August was
acutely remembered; but the important victory of Saratoga was
forgotten. The unfortunate general at length reached Richmond,
where the General Assembly of Virginia was in session. Great
and good men then governed the State. Instructed by history,
guided by the dictates of virtue, and grateful for eminent services,
they saw a wide difference between misfortune and criminality,
and weighed the exploits in the North against the disasters in the
South. These fathers of the commonwealth appointed a committee
of their body to wait on the vanquished general, and " to assure
him of their high regard and esteem ; that their remembrance of
his former glorious services was never to be obliterated by any reverse of fortune; but, ever mindful of his great merit, they would
omit no opportunity of testifying to the world the gratitude which
Virginia, as a member of the American Union, owed to him in his
military character." *

---

* Extract from the minutes of the House of Delegates.

Thursday, 28th December, 1780.

" *Resolved,* That a committee of four be appointed to wait on Major-General
Gates, and to assure him of the high regard and esteem of this house; that the
remembrance of his former glorious services cannot be obliterated by any reverse of fortune, but that this House, ever mindful of his great merit, will omit
no opportunity of testifying to the world the gratitude which, as a member of
the American Union, this country owes him in his military character."

And the said resolution being read a second time, was, on the question put
thereupon, agreed to by the House, *nemine contradicente.*

Ordered, That Mr. Henry, Mr. R. H. Lee, Mr. Yane, and General Nelson, be
appointed of the said committee.

General Gates had supported his fall from splendid elevation to obscurity with apparent fortitude and complacency. He was sensibly affected and comforted by this kind reception, and retired to his farm in the county of Berkeley, where the keen regrets of disappointment and misfortune were softened by the soothing occupations of agriculture, and the condolence of the State in which he resided.

The dignified and wise policy of the Virginia legislature was highly honorable to that body, and furnishes an instructive lesson to sovereigns. Amiable and enlightened as is such conduct, it is, nevertheless, uncommon; and our revolutionary records furnish no similar instance. Washington, indeed, uniformly experienced the gratitude of Congress, and of the State Assemblies; and their resolves of approbation sometimes followed his defeats. But the judgment and circumspection displayed by the commander-in-chief, even in his most severe disasters, manifested the propriety of his conduct, and the necessity of the risk he incurred. Never did this general precipitately seek action; but when it became unavoidable, he prepared himself, in the best practicable manner, for the conflict. Limiting, by his foresight, the extent of his loss; guarding, by his disposition, security of retreat; and repairing with celerity the injury sustained,* his relative condition was often me-

Friday, 29th December, 1780.

Mr. Henry reported from the committee appointed to communicate the resolution of the house of yesterday to Major-General Gates, that the committee had, according to orders, communicated the same to that gentleman, and that he had been pleased to return the following answer.

RICHMOND, 28th *December*, 1780.

I shall remember, with the utmost gratitude, the honor this day done me by the honorable House of Delegates of Virginia. When I engaged in the cause of freedom, and of the United States, I devoted myself entirely to the service of obtaining the great end of this Union. The having been once unfortunate is my great mortification; but let the event of my future services be what it may, they will, as they always have been, be directed by the most faithful integrity, and animated by the purest zeal for the honor and interest of the United States.   HORATIO GATES.

This conduct comes nearest to that of the Roman Senate, who thanked Varro, the author of the defeat at Cannæ, for returning to Rome, and for not having despaired of the commonwealth. A magnanimity unequalled in the history of nations.

* This fact was eminently illustrated by the battle of Germantown. Sir William Howe gained the day, but the advantages which resulted from the action were evidently on the side of Washington. The British general gave up the small district of the country he held, and submitted to the inconveniences of a position around Philadelphia. Exchanging an open country for the suburbs

liorated, although victory adorned the brow of his adversary. Very
different had been the conduct of General Gates in Carolina, and
very different was the result on the 16th of August.

Washington rivalled the magnanimity which the General Assembly
of Virginia had displayed. Although he remembered the dilatory
advance of a portion of the Northern army to his succor, when that
succor was indispensable and expected; although he remembered
that its commander had dared to trifle with his mandate; and was
not insensible that this conduct had proceeded from a settled design
to supplant him in his high station ; yet he repressed the feelings
which such recollections would naturally have excited in most
breasts, and with all the delicacy of superior virtue, extended his
condolence, to assuage the asperity which clings to misfortune.
With a hope that the speedy termination of the war might preclude
the necessity of an investigation, so mortifying to a soldier still
proud of his former fame, though fallen in public estimation, General Washington compassionately deferred the assembling of the
court. The war soon afterward closed, and the prosecution of the
inquiry necessarily ceased.*

of the city, salubrity for insalubrity, and drawing upon his troops the additional
labor of field-works, to put himself safe, while pursuing his measures for the
restoration of the river navigation.

* Mr. Marshall, in his "Life of Washington," has treated this interesting transaction with peculiar attention. The correspondence between the two generals,
with which this writer has favored the public, is so characteristic, that I cannot refrain from transcribing it.

ALBANY, *December 18th*, 1777.

SIR :—I shall not attempt to describe, what, as a private gentleman, I cannot help feeling, on representing to my mind the disagreeable situation which
confidential letters, when exposed to public inspection, may place an unsus-
pecting correspondent in ; but as a public officer, I conjure your Excellency to
give me all the assistance you can, in tracing out the author of the infidelity
which put extracts from General Conway's letters to me into your hands.
These letters have been stealingly copied; but which of them, when, or by
whom, is to me, as yet, an unfathomable secret. There is not one officer in my
suite, or among those who have free access to me, upon whom I could, with
the least justification to myself, fix the suspicion; and yet my uneasiness may
deprive me of the usefulness of the worthiest men. It is, I believe, in your
Excellency's power to do me and the United States a very important service,
in detecting a wretch who may betray me, and capitally injure the very operations under your immediate direction. For this reason, sir, I beg your Excellency will favor me with the proofs you can procure to that effect. But the
crime being eventually so important, that the least loss of time may be
attended with the worst consequences, and it being unknown to me, whether
the letter came to you from a member of Congress, or from an officer, I shall
have the honor of transmitting a copy of this to the President, that Congress
may, in concert with your Excellency, obtain, as soon as possible, a discovery

CHAPTER XXII.

State of the army when Greene took command.—Greene moves down the Pedee.—
Tarleton detached against Morgan.—Col. Lee joins the army and is sent to support
Marion.—Their expedition against Georgetown.

GENERAL GREENE directed his whole attention to the high duties
of his command. On reviewing his army, he found its total not

which deeply affects the safety of these States. Crimes of that magnitude
ought not to remain unpunished.

I have the honor to be, sir, with the greatest respect,

Your Excellency's most humble and most obedient servant,

HORATIO GATES.

His Excellency General WASHINGTON.

VALLEY FORGE, *January 14th*, 1778.

SIR:—Your letter of the 18th ultimo came to my hands a few days ago, and
to my great surprise informed me, that a copy of it had been sent to Congress;
for what reason I find myself unable to account; but as some end doubtless
was intended to be answered by it, I am laid under the disagreeable necessity
of returning my answer through the same channel, lest any member of that
body should harbor some unfavorable suspicion of my having practised some
indirect means to come at the contents of the confidential letters between you
and General Conway.

I am to inform you then, that * * * * on his way to Congress, in the
month of October last, fell in with Lord Stirling at Reading; and not in confidence that I ever understood, informed his aid-de-camp, Major McWilliams,
that General Conway had written thus to you : "Heaven has been determined
to save your country ; or a weak general and bad counsellors would have ruined
it." Lord Stirling, from motives of friendship, transmitted the account, with
this remark: "The inclosed was communicated by * * * * to Major
McWilliams; such wicked duplicity of conduct I shall always think it my duty
to detect."

In consequence of this information, and without having any thing more in
view, than merely to show that gentleman that I was not unapprised of his intriguing disposition, I wrote him a letter in these words: " Sir, a letter which
I received last night contained the following paragraph : ' In a letter from General Conway to General Gates, he says, Heaven has determined to save your
country ; or a weak general and bad counsellors would have ruined it.' I am,
sir, &c."

Neither the letter nor the information which occasioned it was ever, directly
or indirectly, communicated by me to a single officer in the army (out of my
own family), excepting the Marquis de la Fayette, who, having been spoken to
on the subject by General Conway applied for and saw, under injunctions of
secrecy, the letter which contained this. So desirous was I of concealing every
matter that could, in its consequences, give the smallest interruption to the
tranquillity of this army, or afford a gleam of hope to the enemy by dissensions
therein.

I trust, sir, with that openness and candor which I hope will ever character-
ize and mark my conduct, I have complied with your request. The only concern I feel upon the occasion, finding how matters stand, is, that in doing this
I have been necessarily obligated to name a gentleman, who, I am persuaded
(although I never exchanged a word with him upon the subject) thought he was
rather doing an act of justice than committing an act of infidelity ; and sure I

more than two thousand, of which the major part was militia. Notwithstanding the exertions of his predecessor to establish magazines, he found three days' provision only on hand, and the country around him exhausted. His supply of ammunition was very scanty, and Virginia was the nearest point from which a replenishment could be obtained.

Such means and resources badly comported with the grand design of arresting the progress of the conqueror, and restoring the two lost States to the Union. Capable of doing much with little, Greene was not discouraged by this unfavorable prospect. His vivid plastic genius soon operated on the latent elements of martial capacity in his army, invigorated its weakness, turned its confusion into order, and its despondency into ardor. A wide sphere of intellectual resource enabled him to inspire confidence, to rekindle courage, to

am, that until Lord Stirling's letter came to my hands, I never knew that General Conway (whom I viewed in the light of a stranger to you) was a correspondent of yours; much less did I suspect that I was the subject of your confidential letters. Pardon me then for adding, that so far from conceiving that the safety of these States can be affected, or in the smallest degree injured, by a discovery of this kind, or that I should be called upon in such solemn terms to point out the author, that I considered the information as coming from yourself, and given with a friendly view to forewarn, and consequently to forearm, me against a secret enemy; or, in other words, a dangerous incendiary: in which character, sooner or later, this country will know General Conway. But in this, as well as other matters of late, I have found myself mistaken.

I am, sir,
Your most obedient servant,
To Major-General GATES.   GEORGE WASHINGTON.

Whatever part General Conway may have taken in this flagitious attempt, whether principal or secondary, is not ascertained; but he had gone far enough to warrant the commander-in-chief in denouncing him a "dangerous incendiary."

Nevertheless, justice requires that I should add, that this officer was among the most respectable and the most experienced of the many French gentlemen who joined the American army; and that he afterward made, to his much injured commander, the best amends in his power, as is manifested by the following letter, written after resignation of his commission, and when he expected to die in consequence of a wound received in a duel with General Cadwallader, produced by his animadversion on the commander-in-chief.

PHILADELPHIA, *February 23d,* 1778.

SIR,—I find myself just able to hold my pen during a few minutes, and take this opportunity of expressing my sincere grief for having done, written, or said, any thing disagreeable to your Excellency. My career will soon be over; therefore, justice and truth prompt me to declare my last sentiments. You are in my eyes, the great and good man. May you long enjoy the love, esteem, and veneration of these States, whose liberties you have asserted by your virtues.

I am, with the greatest respect,
Your Excellency's most obedient humble servant,
PH. CONWAY.

decide hesitation, and infuse a spirit of exalted patriotism in the citizens of the State. By his own example, he showed the incalculable value of obedience, of patience, of vigilance, and temperance. Dispensing justice, with an even hand, to the citizen and soldier; benign in heart, and happy in manners; he acquired the durable attachment and esteem of all. He collected around his person able and respectable officers; and selected, for the several departments, those who were best qualified to fill them. His operations were then commenced with a boldness of design, well calculated to raise the drooping hopes of his country, and to excite the respect of his enemy.

This illustrious man had now reached his thirty-eighth year. In person he was rather corpulent, and above the common size. His complexion was fair and florid; his countenance serene and mild, indicating a goodness which seemed to shade and soften the fire and greatness of its expression. His health was delicate, but preserved by temperance and exercise.

The British army still remained at Winnsborough. General Greene determined to draw in the detachment under Smallwood, which was advanced some distance in his front, and to risk the division of his force by taking two distant positions on each flank of the British army.

Previous to this movement, Brigadier Morgan, who commanded the van of Smallwood's detachment, attempted to strike a foraging party of the enemy, which had penetrated the country between the two armies. But the vigilant adversary eluded the blow, and returned in safety to Camden. Lieutenant-Colonel Washington, at the head of the cavalry, having taken a more extensive range than the infantry, discovered that a party of loyalists were stationed at Rudgley's farm, about twelve miles from Camden. He moved instantly toward them, in expectation of carrying the post by surprise; but in this he was disappointed, as they occupied a barn, surrounded by abatis, and secure from any attempt of cavalry. Rudgley and his friends were delighted with the safety their precaution had produced, and viewed the approach of horse with indifference. Short was their repose. Washington, well informed of the character of his enemy, shaped the trunk of a tree in imitation of a field-piece; and, bringing it up in a military style, affected to prepare to cannonade the barn. To give solemnity to the device, he sent in a flag, warning the garrison of the impending destruction, which could be only avoided by immediate submission.

Not prepared to resist artillery, Colonel Rudgley seized with promptitude the auspicious opportunity, and, with his garrison, one hundred men, surrendered at discretion ! No circumstance can more strongly demonstrate the propriety of using every effort in war. A soldier should intimately know the character of his enemy, and mould his measures accordingly. This stratagem of Washington, although conceived and executed with little hope of success, was completely successful ; and enabled him to effect an object, which, at first view, most would have abandoned as clearly unattainable.

The return of Smallwood's detachment to camp was followed by the immediate departure of the army from Charlotte. The division intended for operations in the western quarter was composed of four hundred Continental infantry, under Lieutenant-Colonel Howard, of the Maryland line ; two companies of the Virginia militia, under Captains Triplett and Taite ; and the remnants of the first and third regiments of dragoons, one hundred in number, under Lieutenant-Colonel Washington. It was placed under the care of Brigadier-General Morgan, who was to be strengthened on his march by bodies of mountain militia from Carolina and Georgia. He was ordered to pass the Catawba, and take post in the country between the Broad and Pacolet rivers. Greene, with the main body, moved down the Pedee, and took a position on its eastern bank, nearly opposite Cheraw Hill. By this disposition, General Greene secured an abundance of wholesome provisions for his troops ; afforded safe rendezvous for the militia in the East and West, on whose aid he necessarily relied ; re-excited by his proximity the spirit of revolt, which preceding events had repressed ; menaced the various posts of the enemy, and their intermediate communications ; and compelled Lord Cornwallis to postpone his advance into North Carolina, until he should have cleared the country to the west of his enemy. During Brigadier Morgan's march, he received a part of the expected succor, amounting nearly to five hundred militia under General Pickens ;* and passing the Broad River, he established himself near the point of its confluence with the Pacolet.

About the 13th of December, prior to Greene's departure from Charlotte, Major-General Leslie arrived with his detachment at Charleston, where he found orders to repair with one thousand five hundred of his troops to Camden. As Leslie was approaching this place, Lord Cornwallis learned the disposition of the hostile army,

---

* "Some militia joined us in the march, but Pickens, with its principal force, did not join us until the evening before the battle of the Cowpens."—COL. H.

and about the end of December became acquainted with the progress of Morgan. Greene was seventy miles to his right, and Morgan fifty on his left. Lord Cornwallis began to apprehend a design
on Ninety-six, and determined to direct his first steps against Morgan, lest the junction of numerous bodies of mountain militia with
that enterprising officer, should enable him to destroy all communication with Augusta, and finally to carry that post, if not Ninety-
six. The Legion, horse and foot, the light infantry attached to it,
the seventh regiment, and first battalion of the seventy-first, with
two field-pieces, were put in motion under Lieutenant-Colonel Tarleton. The first object was to protect Ninety-six ; and the next to
bring Morgan to battle, or repel him into North Carolina.

Soon after General Greene had taken his position opposite to
Cheraw Hill, Lieutenant-Colonel Lee, with his Legion, making about
two hundred and eighty, in horse and foot, joined the army. This
corps, being in excellent condition, was on the next day ordered to
cross the Pedee, in order to support BrigadierMarion, who continued to intercept and harass the enemy's posts between the
Pedee and the Santee. In a few days after Lee's junction with
Marion, they projected an enterprise against the garrison of Georgetown, a small village in South Carolina, situated on the bay into
which the Pedee empties. Colonel Campbell commanded in this
town, with a garrison of two hundred men. In his front he had
prepared some slight defences, better calculated to repel a sudden,
than resist a determined assault. Between these defences and the
town, and contiguous to each, was an inclosed work with a fraise
and palisade, which constituted his chief protection. A subaltern
guard held it. The rest of the troops were dispersed in light parties
in and near the town, looking toward the country. The plan of
assault was founded on the facility with which the assailant might
convey down the Pedee a part of his force undiscovered, and land
in the water suburb of the town, which, being always deemed secure,
was consequently unguarded. After this body should have reached
the wharves, it was to move in two divisions. The first was to force
the commandant's quarters, known to be the place of parade, then
to secure him, and all who might flock thither on the alarm. The
second was to be charged with the interception of such of the garrison as might attempt to gain the fort, their chief point of safety or
annoyance. The militia and cavalry of the Legion, under Marion
and Lee, were to approach near the town in the night; and
when the entrance of the infantry, passed down by water, should

be announced, they were to rush into it for co-operation and support.

The plan being approved by General Greene, preparations were immediately made for its execution. The infantry of the Legion were embarked in boats, under the command of Captain Carnes, with orders to fall down the Pedee to a designated island, during the first night; to land, and lie concealed there the ensuing day; to re-embark at an early hour of the night following, and reach George-town between one and two in the morning. Marion and Lee proceeded to their destination, having taken all the requisite precautions to prevent any intimation to the enemy of their approach. At twelve o'clock in the second night, they occupied, unperceived, a position in the vicinity of the town, and waited anxiously for the annunciation of Carnes' arrival. This officer met with no difficulty in descending the river, and reached the appointed island before dawn of light. He remained there the ensuing day; and so un-usual is inland navigation in South Carolina, so impervious are the deep swamps which line its rivers, that he might have sojourned for weeks on the island without discovery. Gaining his place of desti-nation with precision in point of time, he landed unperceived, and instantly advanced to the quarters of Lieutenant-Colonel Campbell. The commandant was secured; and Carnes judiciously posted his division for seizing such parties of the garrison as might flock to the parade-ground. Captain Rudolph, who led the second division, with equal good fortune, gained the vicinity of the fort; and arranged his troops on the route of communication, in order to arrest the fugitives. On the first fire which took place at the com-mandant's quarters, the militia of Marion and the dragoons of Lee rushed into the town, prepared to bear down all resistance. To the astonishment of these officers, every thing was quiet; the Legion infantry holding its assigned stations, and Lieutenant-Colonel Camp-bell a prisoner. Not a British soldier appeared; not one attempted either to gain the fort, or repair to the commandant. Having dis-covered their enemy, the troops of the garrison kept close to their respective quarters, barricaded the doors, and determined there to defend themselves. The assailants were unprovided with the requi-site implements for battering doors and scaling windows. The fort was in the possession of the enemy, and daylight approaching. Marion and Lee were, therefore, compelled to retire with a partial accomplishment of their object. Colonel Campbell was suffered to remain on parole, and the troops withdrew from Georgetown, un-

Ranney

MARION CROSSING THE PEDEE

University Publishing Company

J. A. O'Neill

hurt and unannoyed. The plan of this enterprise, although conceived with ingenuity, and executed with precision, was too refined
and complicated for success. Marion and Lee were singularly tender
of the lives of their soldiers ; and preferred moderate success, with
little loss, to the most brilliant enterprise, with the destruction of
many of their troops. This principle is wise and commendable;
but when carried too far it is sure to produce disappointment.
If, instead of placing Rudolph's division to intercept the fugitives,
it had been ordered to carry the fort by the bayonet, our success
would have been complete. The fort taken, and the commandant
a prisoner, we might have availed ourselves of the cannon, and have
readily demolished every obstacle and shelter.

CHAPTER XXIII.*

Movements of Cornwallis and of Morgan.—Battle of the Cowpens.—Reflections
thereon.

SOON after Tarleton had been detached in pursuit of Morgan,
the British general put his army in motion. Having in view the
interception of Morgan, should he elude Tarleton, and preferring
to advance into North Carolina on the upper route, to avoid as much
as possible the obstructions, usual at that season, from the rising of
water-courses, Cornwallis directed his march between the Catawba
and Broad River. To keep in doubt his plan of operations, General Leslie had been continued at Camden ; but he was now directed
to move on the eastern side of the Wateree and Catawba, parallel
to his lordship's route.

Lieutenant-Colonel Tarleton lost no time in approaching his
enemy. Morgan was duly apprised of his advance, and of the
movement of the British army. At the head of troops, able and
willing to fight, he was rather disposed to meet than to avoid his
foe ; and would probably have resolved on immediate action, had he
not felt the danger of delay in consequence of Cornwallis's advance
up the Catawba. Nevertheless, he indicated a desire to dispute the
passage of the Pacolet, to which Tarleton was fast approaching ; but
he relinquished this plan, in consequence of the enemy's having

* The judicious reader will perceive that the personal narrative which the
author had entered upon is here discontinued, and is not resumed until the
junction of the American forces at Guilford C. H., is mentioned.

These interchanges of memoirs and history recur subsequently, and agreeably
diversify the style of the work.—ED.

passed the river on his right or above him, and retired with a degree of precipitation which proved how judiciously the British commandant had taken his first steps. Tarleton passed through the ground on which Morgan had been encamped, a few hours after the latter had abandoned it; and, leaving his baggage under a guard, with orders to follow with convenient expedition, he pressed forward throughout the night in pursuit of the retiring foe. After a severe march through a rugged country, he came in sight of his enemy about eight o'clock in the morning (January 17, 1781), and having taken two of our vedettes, he learned that Morgan had halted at the Cowpens, not far in front, and some distance from Broad River. Presuming that Morgan would not risk action unless driven to it, Tarleton determined, fatigued as his troops were, instantly to advance on his enemy, lest he might throw his corps safe over Broad River.

Morgan having been accustomed to fight and to conquer, did not relish the eager and interrupting pursuit of his adversary; and sat down at the Cowpens to give refreshment to his troops, with a resolution no longer to avoid action, should his enemy persist in pressing it. Being apprised at the dawn of day of Tarleton's advance, he instantly prepared for battle. This decision grew out of irritation of temper, which appears to have overruled the suggestions of his sound and discriminating judgment.* The ground about the Cowpens is covered with open wood, admitting the operation of cavalry with facility, in which the enemy trebled Morgan. His flanks had no resting-place, but were exposed to be readily turned; and Broad River ran parallel to his rear, forbidding the hope of a safe retreat in the event of disaster. Had Morgan crossed this river, and approached the mountain, he would have gained a position disadvantageous to cavalry, but convenient for riflemen, and would have secured a less dangerous retreat. But these cogent reasons, rendered more forcible by his inferiority in numbers, could not prevail. Confiding in his long-tried fortune, conscious of his personal superiority in soldiership, and relying on the skill and courage of his troops, he adhered to his resolution. Erroneous as

1781.

---

* On this passage Colonel Howard remarks—that Morgan did not decide on action until he was joined in the night by Pickens and his followers—and adds: "I well remember that parties were coming in the most of the night, and calling on Morgan for ammunition, and to know the state of affairs. They were all in good spirits, related circumstances of Tarleton's cruelty, and expressed the strongest desire to check his progress." The probability is, that these circumstances confirmed the decision Morgan had already formed.—Ed.

was the decision to fight in this position, when a better might have been easily gained, the disposition for battle was masterly.

Two light parties of militia, under Major McDowel, of North Carolina, and Major Cunningham, of Georgia, were advanced in front, with orders to feel the enemy as he approached; and, preserving a desultory well-aimed fire as they fell back to the front line, to range with it and renew the conflict. The main body of the militia composed this line, with General Pickens at its head. At a suitable distance in the rear of the first line a second was stationed, composed of the Continental infantry and two companies of Virginia militia, under Captains Triplett and Taite,* commanded by Lieutenant-Colonel Howard. Washington's cavalry, re-enforced with a company of mounted militia armed with sabres, was held in reserve, convenient to support the infantry, and protect the horses of the rifle militia, which were tied, agreeably to usage, in the rear. On the verge of battle, Morgan availed himself of the short and awful interim to exhort his troops. First addressing himself, with his characteristic pith, to the line of militia, he extolled the zeal and bravery so often displayed by them, when unsupported by the bayonet or sword; and declared his confidence that they could not fail in maintaining their reputation, when supported by chosen bodies of horse and foot, and conducted by himself. Nor did he forget to glance at his unvarying fortune, and superior experience ; or to mention how often, with his corps of riflemen, he had brought British troops, equal to those before him, to submission. He described the deep regret he had already experienced in being obliged, from prudential considerations, to retire before an enemy always in his power; exhorted the line to be firm and steady ; to fire with good aim; and if they would pour in but two volleys at killing distance, he would take upon himself to secure victory. To the Continentals he was very brief. He reminded them of the confidence he had always reposed in their skill and courage; assured them that victory was certain if they acted well their part; and desired them not to be discouraged by the sudden retreat of the militia,

---

* These two companies of militia were generally Continental soldiers, who, having served the time of their enlistment, had returned home regularly discharged.

A custom for some time past prevailed, which gave to us the aid of such soldiers. Voluntary proffer of service being no longer fashionable, the militia were drafted conformably to a system established by law ; and whenever the lot fell upon the timid or wealthy, he procured, by a douceur, a substitute, who, for the most part, was one of those heretofore discharged.

that being part of his plan and orders. Then taking post with this line, he waited in stern silence for the enemy.

The British lieutenant-colonel, urging forward, was at length gratified with the certainty of battle; and being prone to presume on victory, he hurried the formation of his troops. The light and Legion infantry, with the seventh regiment, composed the line of battle; in the centre of which was posted the artillery, consisting of two grasshoppers; and a troop of dragoons was placed on each flank. The battalion of the seventy-first regiment, under Major McArthur, with the remainder of the cavalry, formed the reserve. Tarleton placed himself with the line, having under him Major Newmarsh, who commanded the seventh regiment. The disposition was not completed, when he directed the line to advance, and the reserve to wait further orders.* The American light parties quickly yielded, fell back, and arrayed with Pickens. The enemy shouting, rushed forward upon the front line, which retained its station, and poured in a close fire; but, continuing to advance with the bayonet on our militia, they retired, and gained with haste the second line. Here, with part of the corps, Pickens took post on Howard's right, and the rest fled to their horses; probably with orders to remove them to a further distance. Tarleton pushed forward, and was received by his adversary with unshaken firmness. The contest became obstinate; and each party, animated by the example of its leader, nobly contended for victory. Our line maintained itself so firmly, as to oblige the enemy to order up his reserve. The advance of McArthur re-animated the British line, which again moved forward; and, outstretching our front, endangered Howard's right. This officer instantly took measures to defend his flank, by directing his right company to change its front; but mistaking this order, the company fell back; upon which the line began to retire, and General Morgan directed it to retreat to the cavalry. This manœuvre being performed with precision, our flank became relieved, and the new position was assumed with promptitude. Considering this retrograde movement the precursor of flight, the British line rushed on with impetuosity and disorder; but, as it drew near, Howard faced about, and gave it a close and murderous fire. Stun-

---

* Tarleton's cavalry are stated at three hundred and fifty, while that under Morgan did not exceed eighty.

Morgan's militia used rifles, and were expert marksmen; this corps composed nearly one half of his infantry.

Tarleton's detachment is put down as one thousand. Morgan, in a letter to General Greene, after his victory, gives his total as eight hundred.

ned by this unexpected shock, the most advanced of the enemy recoiled in confusion. Howard seized the happy moment, and followed his advantage with the bayonet.* This decisive step gave us the day. The reserve having been brought near the line, shared in the destruction of our fire, and presented no rallying point to the fugitives. A part of the enemy's cavalry, having gained our rear, fell on that portion of the militia who had retired to their horses. Washington struck at them with his dragoons, and drove them before him. Thus, by simultaneous efforts, the infantry and cavalry of the enemy were routed. Morgan pressed home his success, and the pursuit became vigorous and general. The British cavalry having taken no part in the action, except the two troops attached to the line, were in force to cover the retreat. This, however, was not done. The zeal of Lieutenant-Colonel Washington in pursuit having carried him far before his squadron, Tarleton turned upon him with the troop of the seventeenth regiment of dragoons, seconded by many of his officers. The American lieutenant-colonel was first rescued from this critical contest by one of his sergeants, and afterward by a fortunate shot from his bugler's pistol.† This check concluded resistance on the part of the British officer, who drew off with the remains of his cavalry, collected his stragglers, and hastened to Lord Cornwallis. The baggage guard, learning the issue of battle, moved instantly toward the British army. A part of the horse, who had shamefully avoided action, and refused to charge when Tarleton wheeled on the impetuous Washington, reached the camp of Cornwallis at Fisher's Creek, about twenty-five miles from the Cowpens, in the evening. The remainder arrived with Lieutenant-Colonel Tarleton on the morning following. In this decisive battle we lost about seventy men, of whom twelve only were killed. The British infantry, with the exception of the baggage guard, were nearly all killed or taken. One hundred, in-

---

* In this charge the brave Kirkwood, of the Delawares, was conspicuous.—See "Garden's Anecdotes," p. 397.

† "In the eagerness of pursuit, Washington advanced nearly thirty yards in front of his regiment. Observing this, three British officers wheeled about, and made a charge upon him. The officer on his right was aiming to cut him down, when a sergeant came up and intercepted the blow by disabling his sword arm. At the same instant the officer on his left was also about to make a stroke at him, when a waiter, too small to wield a sword, saved him by wounding the officer with a ball, discharged from a pistol. At this moment the officer in the centre, who was believed to be Tarleton, made a thrust at him, which he parried; upon which the officer retreated a few paces, and then discharged a pistol at him, which wounded his knee."—MARSHALL's *Life of Washington*.

cluding ten officers, were killed ; twenty-three officers and five hundred privates were taken. The artillery, eight hundred muskets,
two standards, thirty-five baggage wagons, and one hundred dragoon
horses, fell into our possession.*

The victory of the Cowpens was to the South what that of Bennington had been to the North. General Morgan, whose former
services had placed him high in public estimation, was now deservedly ranked among the most illustrious defenders of his country.
Starke fought an inferior, Morgan a superior, foe. The former
contended with a German † corps ; the latter, with the *élite* of the
Southern army, composed of British troops. In military reputation
the conqueror at the Cowpens must stand before the hero of Bennington. Starke was nobly seconded by Colonel Warner and his
Continental regiment ; Morgan derived very great aid from Pickens
and his militia, and was effectually supported by Howard and Washington. The weight of the battle fell on Howard ; who sustained
himself admirably in trying circumstances, and seized with decision
the critical moment to complete with the bayonet the advantage
gained by his fire.

Congress manifested their sense of this important victory by a
resolve, approving the conduct of the principal officers, and com-
memorative of their distinguished exertions. To General Morgan
they presented a gold medal, to Brigadier Pickens a sword, and to
Lieutenant-Colonels Howard and Washington a silver medal, and to
Captain Triplett a sword.

While all must acknowledge the splendor of this achievement,
it must be admitted, that the errors of the British commandant contributed not a little to our signal success. The moment he came in
sight of the American detachment, he must have been sure of his
first wish and object—battle. Where then was the necessity for
that hurry with which he took his measures ? It was but little
after sunrise ; and consequently, after giving rest to his fatigued
troops, there would have been time enough for the full accomplish-

---

* Cornwallis's letter to Sir H. Clinton.

† This remark is not made to disparage the German troops serving with the
British army in America. They were excellent soldiers ; but, for light services,
they were inferior to the British. Ignorant of our language, unaccustomed to
woods, with their very heavy dress, they were less capable of active and quick
operations.

The splendid issue of the subsequent campaign, and the triumph of Gates
has been noticed, as well as the instrumentality of Morgan in producing the
auspicious event. Great and effectual as were his exertions, General Gates did
not even mention him in his official dispatches.

ment of his views. That interval he might have advantageously employed in a personal examination of his enemy's position, and in a disclosure of his plans to his principal officers. He knew well the composition of Morgan's corps, and the American mode of fighting. The front line, being composed of militia, he was well apprised would yield; and that the struggle for victory must take place after he reached our regulars. He ought not to have run upon the retiring militia with his infantry, but should have brought them up in full bodily capacity for the contest. A portion of dragoons might and ought to have borne down on Pickens, when retiring. But instead of that, Tarleton himself, with the first line, pressed forward and fell on our main body with exhausted breath. The fatigued, panting, disappointed British, as might have been expected, paused. Tarleton instantly called up his reserve, which approached near the line, suffered with it from our fire, and became useless. Here he violated the fundamental rules of battle. The reserve, as the term indicates, ought not to be endangered by the fire levelled at the preceding body; but, being safe from musketry by its distance, should be ready to interpose in case of disaster, and to increase advantage in the event of victory. In his "Campaigns," he acknowledges that the ground was disadvantageous to his adversary, and favorable to himself; speaks of the alacrity with which his troops advanced into action; and admits the leading facts, on which these observations are founded. He could not deny that he had two field-pieces, and Morgan none; that he was vastly superior in cavalry; that his troops were among the best of the British army; and that he rather exceeded his enemy in numbers, whose regulars, horse and foot, were less than five hundred.

These facts admitted, how can the issue of the battle be satisfactorily explained without acknowledging that the British leader did not avail himself of the advantage he possessed; that his improvidence and precipitancy influenced the result, and that General Morgan exhibited a personal superiority in the art of war? This conclusion, however contested by Lieutenant-Colonel Tarleton and his particular friends, will be approved by the enlightened and impartial of both armies; and posterity will confirm the decision.

CHAPTER XXIV.

Cornwallis converts his army into light troops.—His keen pursuit of Morgan.—Greene retreats, and joins the main army at Guilford Court-House.—The command offered to Morgan.

LORD CORNWALLIS received the unexpected, doleful tidings of Tarleton's defeat with serenity, but deep regret. He had been baffled in his first expedition into North Carolina by the fall of Ferguson; and this late disaster seemed to forbid perseverance in his second. With a view to retrieve, by the celerity of his movements, the severe loss he had sustained, he formed the wise resolution of converting his army into light troops by the destruction of his baggage. Commanding this sacrifice without respect to persons, he set the example himself, by committing to the flames the baggage of head-quarters. With zeal and alacrity his faithful army obeyed the mandate. Every thing was destroyed, save a small supply of clothing, and a sufficient number of wagons for the conveyance of hospital stores, of salt, of ammunition, and for the accommodation of the sick and wounded. We are at a loss whether to admire more the wisdom of the chief, or the self-denial of his followers; a memorable instance, among many others in this unnatural war, of the immutable disposition of the British soldiers to endure every privation in support of their king and country. This arrangement being finished, Lord Cornwallis moved from Fisher's Creek, determined on unceasing efforts to destroy Morgan, and recover his captured troops; to keep separate the two divisions of Greene's army; and, should he fail in these attempts, to bring Greene to action before he could reach Virginia.

Morgan, always attentive to his duty, took measures for retreat the moment victory had declared in his favor. In the evening of the same day he crossed the Broad River, and moved by forced marches to the Catawba, before Lord Cornwallis could reach its banks.

General Greene was quickly advised of the advance of the British army from Winnsborough and Camden, through the upper country; and accordingly issued his preparatory orders for movement. On the subsequent day he received the gratifying intelligence of the victory at the Cowpens. Foreseeing the enemy's object, he hastened his march in conformity with his previous disposition, and dispatched a courier to Marion and Lee, apprising them of his decampment, and ordering the latter to rejoin with all possible celerity. Escorted by a few dragoons, General Greene hastened to reach Morgan, which he happily accomplished on the last day of January, after that officer had passed the Catawba. Aware of the rapidity with which the British general would advance to strike him before he could gain that point, Morgan redoubled his exertions to reach it; but with all his activity, so keen and persevering had been Cornwallis's pursuit, that he had just crossed the river on the evening of the 29th of January, when the British van appeared on the opposite banks. A heavy fall of rain during the night rendered the Catawba unfordable. Morgan availed himself of this fortunate occurrence; and continuing in his position during the swell of the river, sent off his prisoners, with the arms, stores, &c., taken at the Cowpens, under the protection of a part of his militia, on a route nearer to the mountain than that intended to be taken by himself. The waters continued high for two days, and gave the brigadier time to place his prisoners in safety. His light troops, joined by some of the neighboring militia, were disposed, by order of General Greene, to dispute the passage of the river. This was attempted with the hope of retarding the British general in his advance so long as to allow time for Brigadier Huger, of South Carolina, who had succeeded Smallwood, after the retirement of that officer from Charlotte, to reach Salisbury, the first point assigned for the junction of the two divisions of the American army.

As soon as the fall of the water admitted the passage of troops, Lord Cornwallis resumed his march. Lieutenant-Colonel Webster, at the head of one division, was directed to follow the main road to Beattie's Ford, indicating an intention to pass there; while the British general, with the remainder of his army, decamping about midnight, moved down the river to McCowan's, a distant and private ford, which he presumed would be neglected by his adversary. On his approach, at the dawn of day, on the first of February, the light of fires on the opposite banks announced his lordship's miscalculation. Private as was this ford, it had not escape t the vigilance of Greene, who had detached, on the preceding evening, General Davidson, with three hundred of the North Carolina militia, to defend it. A disposition was immediately made to dislodge Davidson, which Brigadier O'Hara, with the guards, effected. Lieutenant-Colonel Hall led with the light company, followed by the grenadiers. The current was rapid, the stream waist deep, and five hundred yards in width. The soldiers crossed in platoons, supporting each other's steps. When Lieutenant-Colonel Hall reached the middle of the river, he was descried by the American sentinels, whose challenge and fire brought Davidson's corps into array. Deserted by his guide, Hall passed directly across, not knowing the landing place which lay below him. This deviation from the common course rendered it necessary for Davidson to incline to the right;[*] but this manœuvre, although promptly performed, was not effected until the light infantry had gained the shore. A fierce conflict ensued, which was well supported by Davidson and his inferior force. The militia at length yielded, and Davidson, while mounting his horse to direct the retreat, was killed. The corps dispersed, and sought safety in the woods.[†] Our loss was small, excepting the brigadier, an active, zealous, and influential officer. Lieutenant-Colonel Hall was also killed, with three of the light infantry, and thirty-six were wounded. Lord Cornwallis followed the guards; and, as soon as his division had passed, detached Lieutenant-Colonel Tarleton with the cavalry, supported by the twenty-third regiment, in pursuit of the militia. Terrant's tavern, ten miles in front, had been assigned as the place of rendezvous for the different corps of militia, assembled and assembling. Tarleton, approaching this place, discovered a body of troops in his front, and fell upon them with vigor. The militia made little or no resistance, and fled. A few of them were killed, but none taken.[‡]

Feb. 1st.

The inhabitants of this region of the State were well affected to the American cause, and General Greene had flattered himself with an expectation of here drawing around him re-enforcements, which, with the light troops under Morgan, would enable him to hold Lord Cornwallis back for some days. But the fall of David-

---

* The movement to the right was prompt for militia, and did credit to Davidson and his corps, but not so prompt as the occasion required. Had Brigadier Davidson's troops been regulars, the change would have been effected before the British gained the shore. With such advantage on our part, the resistance would have been more effectual, and the injury to the enemy greatly augmented. Davidson, too, would probably have been saved.

Lord Cornwallis's horse was shot under him, and fell as soon as he got upon the shore. Leslie's horse was carried down the stream, and with difficulty saved; and O'Hara's tumbled over with him in the water. This evinces the zeal of the pursuit; for in other circumstances, the British general would have waited for the further fall of the waters.

† Lieutenant-Colonel Tarleton, in his campaigns, speaks of forty being killed; but other officers, who examined the ground, asserted they found but ten.

‡ A heavy rain had come on, so that their rifles could not be fired, which gave every advantage to Tarleton's horse.—Col. H.

son, and the rencounter at Terrant's Tavern, disappointed, in their effect, this fond calculation. He dispatched orders to Brigadier Huger to relinquish the route to Salisbury, and to take the direct course to Guilford Court-House, to which point he pressed forward with the light corps under Morgan. Passing through Salisbury, he proceeded to the trading ford on the Yadkin, where he arrived on the night of the second of February.

General Greene having withdrawn his troops from Beattie's Ford, on his lordship's passage below, Lieutenant-Colonel Webster and his division crossed the Catawba without opposition, and in the course of the day joined the British general. Cornwallis had now gained one of the great roads leading to Salisbury, and the pursuit of our light troops was renewed with activity.

General Greene passed the Yadkin during the night of, and day following, his arrival at that river. The horse forded the stream, the infantry and most of the baggage were transported in flats. A few wagons fell into the hands of the enemy ;* for, notwithstanding the unfavorable condition of the roads and weather, Brigadier

Feb. 3d. O'Hara pressed forward with the British van, and overtook our rear guard. The retreating corps was again placed in a critical situation, and heaven was again propitious. The rain continued during the night; the Yadkin became unfordable; and Greene had secured all the flats on its northern bank. †

The British general was a second time delayed by an unforeseen event. Relinquishing his anxious wish to bring the light troops to action before their junction with the main body, he recurred to his last expedient, that of cutting Greene off from the upper fords of the Dan, and compelling his united force to battle, before he could

---

* The wagons of the army escaped, but a few belonging to the country people who were following the army to avoid the enemy, were taken.—Col. H.

† To an attentive observer of the events during our war, very many strong exemplifications of Providential succor occur, besides the two just noticed.

Brigadier-General Weedon served under Washington, and was with him when he made the brilliant manœuvre from before Cornwallis in Trenton; leaving his position in the night, and falling suddenly the next morning on the enemy at Princeton.

General Weedon was one of the council of war, called by the commander-in-chief, to advise in his perilous situation. When the members met, the ground was so deep and soft, that it was presumed the artillery would necessarily be left on the road. Before the council broke up, so immediate had been the change of the weather, that the ground became hard, and all apprehensions on the score of the artillery vanished. This information the writer received from General Weedon, who remarked, that so evidently advantageous was this, sudden change, that it was universally understood by the troops, and as universally ascribed to a protecting Providence.

either reach Virginia, or derive any aid from that State. With this view, he moved up the Yadkin to fords which were still passable. There his lordship crossed; and, directing his course to the Dan, held Greene on his right, with a determination to throw the American general on the lower Dan, which the great fall of rain had rendered impassable without the assistance of boats, which he supposed unattainable. This object, his last hope, the British general pursued with his accustomed rapidity.

Greene was neither less active, nor less diligent. Continuing on the direct road to Guilford Court-House, he reached that place on the 7th of February. Brigadier Huger, who had been overtaken by the Legion of Lee, arrived on the same day. The united force of Greene, including five hundred militia, exceeded two thousand three hundred; of which, two hundred and seventy were cavalry of the best quality. The army of Cornwallis was estimated at two thousand five hundred; but his cavalry, although more numerous than that of his adversary, was far inferior in regard to the size, condition, and activity of the horses. Taking into view his comparative weakness, General Greene determined to continue his retreat to Virginia. The British general was twenty-five miles from Guilford Court-House; equally near with Greene to Dix's Ferry on the Dan, and nearer to the upper shallows or points of that river, which were supposed to be fordable, notwithstanding the late swell of water. Lieutenant-Colonel Carrington, quartermaster-general, suggested the propriety of passing at Irwin's Ferry, seventy miles from Guilford Court-House, and twenty below Dix's. Boyd's Ferry was four miles below Irwin's; and the boats might be easily brought down from Dix's to assist in transporting the army at these near and lower ferries. The plan of Lieutenant-Colonel Carrington was adopted, and that officer was charged with the requisite preparations. The route of retreat being determined, the place of crossing designated, and measures taken for the collection of boats, General Greene formed a light corps, consisting of some of his best infantry under Lieutenant-Colonel Howard, of Washington's cavalry, the Legion of Lee, and a few militia riflemen, making in all seven hundred. These troops were to take post between the retreating and the advancing army, to hover round the skirts of the latter, to seize every opportunity of striking in detail, and to retard the enemy by vigilance and judicious positions: while Greene, with the main body, hastened toward the Dan, the boundary of his present toils and dangers.

The command of the light corps was offered to Brigadier Morgan, whose fitness for such service was universally acknowledged, and whose splendid success had commanded the high confidence of the general and army. Morgan declined the arduous task; and being at that time afflicted, as he occasionally was, with rheumatism, intimated a resolution of retiring from the army. Greene listened with reluctance to the excuse, and endeavored to prevail on him to recede from his determination. Lieutenant-Colonel Lee, being in habits of intimacy with Morgan, was individually deputed to persuade him to obey the universal wish. Many commonplace arguments were urged in conversation without success. Lee then represented that the brigadier's retirement at that crisis might induce an opinion unfavorable to his patriotism, and prejudicial to his future fame; that the resignation of a successful soldier at a critical moment was often attributed, and sometimes justly, to an apprehension that the contest would ultimately be unfortunate to his country, or to a conviction that his reputation had been accidentally acquired, and could not survive the vicissitudes of war. These observations appeared to touch the feelings of Morgan : for a moment he paused; then discovered a faint inclination to go through the impending conflict; but finally returned to his original decision. His refusal of the proferred command was followed by a request to retire, which was granted.

CHAPTER XXV.

Col. O. Williams appointed to the command of the Light Corps.—Greene retreats toward the Lower Dan.—Williams moves in front of Cornwallis.—Skirmish between Lee's and Tarleton's cavalry.

COLONEL WILLIAMS, of Maryland, an accomplished gentleman and experienced soldier, being called to the station, so anxiously, but vainly pressed on Morgan, accepted it with cheerfulness, and diffidence. This last arrangement being finished, Greene put his army in motion, leaving Williams on the ground. The greater the distance between the main body and the light troops, the surer would be Greene's retreat. Williams, therefore, soon after breaking up from Guilford Court-House, on the 10th, inclined to the left, for the purpose of throwing himself in front of Lord Cornwallis. This movement was judicious, and had an immediate effect. His lordship, finding a corps of horse and foot close in front, whose strength and object were not immediately ascertainable, checked the rapidity of his march to give time for his long extended line to condense.

Could Williams have withdrawn himself from between Greene and Cornwallis, he might, probably, by occultly reaching the British rear, have performed material service. Although his sagacity discovered the prospect, yet his sound judgment could not adopt a move:nent which might endanger the retreat of an army, whose safety was the object of his duty, and indispensable to the common cause. He adhered, therefore, to the less dazzling, but more useful system; and fastened his attention, first on the safety of the main body, next on that of the corps under his command; risking the latter only (and then without hesitation) when the security of Greene's retreat demanded it. Pursuing his course obliquely to the left, he reached an intermediate road; the British army being on his left and in his rear, the American in front and on his right. This was exactly the proper position for the light corps, and Williams judiciously retained it.*

The enemy persevering in his rapid advance, our rear-guard, (composed of the Legion of Lee) and the British van under Brigadier O'Hara, were in sight during the day. Throughout the night, the corps of Williams held a respectable distance, to thwart, as far as was practicable, the nocturnal assault.

The duty, severe in the day, became more so at night; for numerous patrols and strong pickets were necessarily furnished by the light troops, not only for their own safety, but to prevent the enemy from placing himself, by a circuitous march, between Williams and Greene. Such a manœuvre would have been fatal 1781. to the American army; and, to render it impossible, half of the troops were alternately appropriated every night to duty: so that each man, during the retreat, was entitled to but six hours' repose in forty-eight. Notwithstanding this privation, the troops were in fine spirits and good health; delighted with their task, and determined to prove themselves worthy the distinction with which they had

---

* The reader will take notice, whenever he meets with the term *right* or *left*, he is to ask himself in what direction the armies are moving, which will explain the import of the term. At present we are moving north, and Lord Cornwallis being on the upper route, was relatively to our left.

The route we had marched being deemed safe, as it was known that his lordship was on a parallel road to our left, the lesser precautions were applied to it; nevertheless, the enemy's advance would have been notified in due time from the horse patrol, or from the infantry picket, should he have avoided or intercepted the patrol—not a probable occurrence.

been honored. At the hour of three, their toils were renewed; for Williams always pressed forward with the utmost dispatch in the morning, to gain such a distance in front as would secure breakfast to his soldiers, their only meal during this rapid and hazardous retreat. So fatigued was officer and soldier, and so much more operative is weariness than hunger, that each man not placed on duty surrendered himself to repose as soon as the night position was taken. Situated as was Williams, no arrangement could have been devised better calculated to effect the great object of his trust, and to secure food once a day to his troops.

The moment Lord Cornwallis found it necessary to change his course and to push for Dix's Ferry, he ordered his van to proceed slowly; and separating from it at the head of the main body, which had now arrived at a causeway leading to the desired route, he quickly gained the great road to Dix's Ferry, the course of the American light corps.

In pursuance of his system, Williams made a rapid morning's march; and leaving small patrols of cavalry near the enemy, sent forward the staff to select ground and prepare fires.

Feb. 13th.

The officers and dragoons, who had been necessarily kept in sight of the British, upon joining, were hastened in front to a farm-house near the road, where they enjoyed, although a few hours later, a more comfortable meal. Lieutenant Carrington, who commanded the dragoons near the enemy's van, reported from time to time, in conformity to custom, by which it appeared that Cornwallis was moving as usual. The morning was cold and drizzly; our fires, which had been slow in kindling, were now lively; the meat was on the coals, and the corn-cake in the ashes. At this moment, a friendly countryman appeared, riding in haste to our camp, whither he had been directed by the sergeant of one of the horse patrols, with which he fell in on his way. The hurry of his approach, and the tired condition of his meagre pony, evinced sincerity of heart; while the joy of his countenance declared his participation of interest. Asking for "the general," he was conducted to Colonel Williams, whom he bluntly informed that Lord Cornwallis, leaving his former route, had got into our road; that one half hour past he left the British army advancing, then only four miles behind; that accidentally discovering it from his field, where he was burning brushwood, he ran home, took the first horse he could find, and hastened to give his friends intelligence, which he deemed important. To attach doubt to the information of an honest-looking farmer would have violated all the rules of physiognomy. Williams always delighted to indulge and comfort his brave troops; and although he credited the countryman, was unwilling to interrupt their hasty repast. He therefore ordered Lieutenant-Colonel Lee to detach from his cavalry, in order to ascertain the correctness of the intelligence. Captain Armstrong, with one section of the horse, was dispatched accordingly, with the countryman for his guide. Soon after their departure, Carrington, still near the enemy, communicated the unusually slow progress of the van-guard. Combining this intelligence with that just received, Williams ordered Lieutenant-Colonel Lee to strengthen Armstrong, and to take upon himself the command intrusted to that officer. Lieutenant Lewis, with the required addition, attended Lee, who dispatched one of the dragoons to overtake Armstrong, with orders directing him to move slowly until he should join. Quickly reaching Armstrong, who had not advanced more than a mile, Lee proceeded, in conformity with the advice of the countryman, two miles further; but seeing no enemy, he began to believe that his guide, however well affected, was certainly in a mistake. He determined, therefore, to return to breakfast, and leave Armstrong with three dragoons and the guide to proceed on to the spot, where the countryman's information had placed the enemy one hour before. Armstrong selected the dragoons mounted on the swiftest horses, and was in the act of moving, when the amicable countryman protested against accompanying him, unless furnished with a better horse. While with the whole detachment, he had thought himself safe, and never manifested any unwillingness to proceed; but now, being associated with the most alert of alert dragoons, whose only duty was to look and fly, he considered his danger extreme. This remonstrance, the justice of which could not be resisted, added another reason for crediting the information. Lee dismounted his bugler, whose horse was given to the countryman; and the bugler was sent back to camp to inform Williams how far the lieutenant-colonel had proceeded without seeing any portion of the enemy, and of his intention to return after advancing Armstrong still further in front. Not doubting that the countryman had seen the British army, but supposing him to be mistaken in the distance, Lee led his detachment into the woods, and retired slowly, in sight of the road. He presumed, that should Armstrong be followed, the enemy would discover the trail of advancing horse in the road, and be deterred from a keen pursuit, which he did not wish to encourage, as it might

deprive the light troops of their meal; although he was disposed
in that event to seize any advantage which might offer. Not many
minutes elapsed before a discharge of musketry announced that
Armstrong had met the enemy; and shortly after the clangor of
horses in swift speed declared the fast approach of cavalry. Armstrong soon appeared, closely followed by a troop of Tarleton's
dragoons. Lee saw his captain and small party well in front, and
hard in hand. For them he felt no apprehension; but for the
safety of his bugler, on the countryman's pony, every feeling of
his heart became interested. Being passed unperceived by the
pursued and pursuers, Lee continued in the woods, determined
to interpose in time to rescue his bugler, yet wishing to let the
enemy take the utmost allowable distance, that they might be
deprived of support. Directing one of his lieutenants to halt with
the rear file and ascertain whether additional cavalry was following,
he hastened his progress, and soon saw the enemy's near approach
to his defenceless bugler, who was immediately unhorsed, and sa-
bred several times while prostrate on the ground. Lee was pressing forward to the road in the enemy's rear, when the officer who
had been left behind rejoined with the acceptable information that
no re-enforcement was approaching. Gaining the road, the lieutenant-colonel rushed forward in quick charge, and fell upon the troop
of Tarleton soon after it had reached his bugler. Captain Miller
instantly formed, and fronted his approaching adversary; but his
worn-down ponies were as ill calculated to withstand the stout, high-
conditioned, active horses opposed to them, as were the intoxicated,
inexpert riders unfit to contend with dragoons always sober, and
excelling in horsemanship. The enemy was crushed on the first
charge: most of them were killed or prostrated; and the residue,
with their captain, attempted to escape. They were pursued by
Lieutenant Lewis, who was commanded by Lee to give no quarters.
This sanguinary mandate, so contrary to the American character,
proceeded from a view of the bugler—a beardless, unarmed youth,
who had vainly implored quarter, and in the agonies of death presented a spectacle resistless in its appeal for vengeance.* Having
placed the much wounded, hapless boy in the arms of the stoutest

---

* This ill-fated boy was one of the band of music, and exclusively devoted
in the field to his bugle, used in conveying orders. Too small to wield a sword,
he was armed only with one pistol, as was the custom in the Legion; that sort
of weapon being considered of little import in action: now, he had not even
his pistol, it being with the countryman mounted on his horse.

of his dragoons, and directed another soldier to attend them to camp, the lieutenant-colonel proceeded in support of Lewis. Soon this officer was met, returning with Captain Miller, and all, save two, of the fugitives. The British captain was unhurt; but his dragoons were severely cut in the face, neck, and shoulders. Lewis was reprimanded on the spot for disobedience of orders; and Miller, being peremptorily charged with the atrocity perpetrated in his view, was told to prepare for death. The captain, with some show of reason, asserted that intelligence being his object, it was his wish and interest to save the soldier; that he had tried to do so; but his dragoons being intoxicated, all his efforts were ineffectual. He added, that in the terrible slaughter under Lieutenant-Colonel Buford, his humanity was experienced, and had been acknowledged by some of the Americans who escaped death on that bloody day. Lee was somewhat mollified by this rational apology, and was disposed to substitute one of the prisoners; but soon overtaking the speechless, dying youth, whose relation to his supporting comrade of the tragical particulars of his fate, when able to speak, confirmed his former impressions, he returned with unrelenting sternness to his first decision. Descending a long hill, he repeated his determination to sacrifice Miller in the vale through which they were about to pass; and handing him a pencil, desired him to note on paper whatever he might wish to make known to his friends, with an assurance that it should be transmitted to the British general. At this moment, the rear-guard communicated, by pistol discharge, the approach of the British van. Miller and his fellow-prisoners were hurried on to Colonel Williams, who was at the same time informed of the enemy's advance. Williams put his corps in motion, and forwarded the captured officers and soldiers to head-quarters, ignorant of the murder of the bugler, and the determination of Lieutenant-Colonel Lee. Thus Miller escaped the fate to which he had been doomed, in order to convince the British cavalry under Lieutenant-Colonel Tarleton, that American blood should no longer be wantonly shed with impunity. Believing himself indebted for his life to the accident just recited, Captain Miller took care to represent, by letter, to his friends in the British army, what had happened, and his conviction of what would have followed; and never afterward were such cruelties repeated by the British cavalry acting against the army of Greene.

The dead, eighteen in number, being left on the road where they fell, were buried by order of Lord Cornwallis as he passed. On the part of the American officer no life was lost, except that of the beardless bugler, who died soon after the advance of the enemy was announced. His corpse was necessarily deposited in the woods adjoining the road, with the hope that some humane citizen might find it.*

The pursuit was continued with unceasing activity. Williams retiring in compact order, with the Legion of Lee in his rear, held himself ready to strike, whenever an opportunity presented. The skilful enemy never permitted any risk in detail, but preserved his whole force for one decisive struggle.

CHAPTER XXVI.

Unexpected meeting of Lee's Legion and the van under O'Hara.—The main army crosses the Dan.—The light corps pass the river.—Reflections on this retreat.—Carrington's services in its accomplishment.

HAVING continued on the route to Dix's Ferry as far as he deemed advisable, and presuming that General Greene would on the next day reach the vicinity of the Dan, Colonel Williams determined to pass to the road on his right, leading to Irwin's Ferry, the route of the main body. He communicated this intention to the rear officer; and moved forward with increased celerity, for the purpose of gaining a distant night position, that he might be able to diminish the guards necessary for the security of his corps when close to the enterprising enemy.

Lieutenant-Colonel Lee, having discovered, from conversation with his guides, that a by-way in front would lead him into Williams's rear before the close of the evening, and save a considerable distance, determined to avail himself of the accommodation. A subaltern's command of dragoons was left to proceed on the route taken by Colonel Williams, with orders to communicate any extraordinary occurrence to the commandant and to Lieutenant-Colonel Lee. The cavalry, who met Miller in the morning, had lost their breakfast; and Lee's chief object in taking the short course was to avail himself of an abundant farm for the refreshment of his party. As soon as he reached the proposed route, the infantry were hastened forward, with directions to halt at the farm, and prepare for the accommodation of the corps; while the cavalry

---

* His name was Gillies—see an interesting anecdote connected with his burial, in "Garden's Anecdotes," second series, p. 119.—ED.

continued close to the enemy. In due time afterward, they were drawn off and passed through the woods, leaving in front of the British van the detachment which had been selected to follow the route of the light troops. The obscurity of the narrow road taken by Lee lulled every suspicion with respect to the enemy; and a few vedettes only were placed at intermediate points, rather to give notice when the British should pass along, than to guard the Legion from surprise. This precaution was most fortunate; for it so happened that Lord Cornwallis, having ascertained that Greene had directed his course to Irwin's Ferry, determined to avail himself of the nearest route to gain the road of his enemy, and took the path which Lee had selected. Our horses were unbridled, with abundance of provender before them; the hospitable farmer had liberally bestowed his meal and bacon, and had given the aid of his domestics in hastening the much-wished repast. To the surprise and grief of all, the pleasant prospect was instantly marred by the fire of the advanced vedettes—certain signal of the enemy's approach. Before the farm was a creek, which, in consequence of the late incessant rains, could be passed only by a bridge, not more distant from the enemy than from our party. The cavalry being speedily arrayed, moved to support the vedettes; while the infantry were ordered, in full run, to seize and hold the bridge.

The enemy was equally surprised with ourselves at this unexpected meeting; and the light party in front halted, to report and be directed. This pause was sufficient. The bridge was gained, and soon passed by the corps of Lee. The British followed. The road over the bridge leading through cultivated fields for a mile, the British army was in full view of the troops of Lee as the latter ascended the eminence, on whose summit they entered the great road to Irwin's Ferry.

Thus escaped a corps, which had been hitherto guarded with unvarying vigilance, whose loss would have been severely felt by the American general, and which had been just exposed to imminent peril from the presumption of certain security. Criminal improvidence! A soldier is always in danger, when his conviction of security leads him to dispense with the most vigilant precautions.

Cornwallis, at length in Greene's rear, urged his march with redoubled zeal, confident of overtaking his adversary before he could reach the Dan. Adverse efforts to accelerate and to retard were unceasingly exhibited during the evening; the enemy's van being sometimes so close as to indicate a determination to force the light troops to prepare for defence. Avoiding a measure replete with peril, Williams persevered in his desultory retreat. More than once were the Legion of Lee and the van of O'Hara within musket-shot; which presented so acceptable an invitation to the marksmen flanking the Legion, that they were restrained with difficulty from delivering their fire. This disposition being effectually checked, the demeanor of the hostile troops became so pacific in appearance, that a spectator would have been led to consider them members of the same army. Only when a defile or a water-course crossed our route did the enemy exhibit any indication to cut off our rear; in which essays, being always disappointed, their useless efforts were gradually discontinued.

The fall of night excited pleasure, as it promised respite from toil. But illusory was the expectation; for the British general was so eager to fall on Greene, whom he believed within his grasp, that the pursuit was not intermitted. The night was dark, the roads deep, the weather cold, and the air humid. Williams throwing his horse in front, and the infantry of the Legion in the rear, continued his retreat.

About eight in the evening, numerous fires discovered an encampment before us. No pen can describe the heart-rending feelings of our brave and wearied troops. Not a doubt was entertained that the descried camp was Greene's; and our dauntless corps were convinced that the crisis had now arrived when its self sacrifice could alone give a chance of escape to the main body. With one voice was announced the noble resolution to turn on the foe, and by dint of desperate courage, so to cripple him as to force a discontinuance of pursuit. This heroic spirit, first breathed in whispers, soon gained the ear of Williams; who, alike daring and alike willing to offer up his life for the safety of an army on which the hopes of the South rested, would have been foremost in the bold conflict. But his first impressions soon yielded to conclusions drawn from a reference to the date of General Greene's last letter, which demonstrated the mistaken apprehension of the troops. Enjoying the delight inspired by their manly ardor, and commending their devotion to their country, he calmed their disquietude. They shortly reached the camp of fires, and discovered that it was the ground where Greene had halted on the evening of the 11th. Relieved from the dire foreboding, the light corps continued its march until the rear officer made known to the commandant that the enemy had halted. The first convenient spot was occupied for the night; the fires were instantly kindled; the cold and wet, the cares and toils of the day, were soon forgotten in the enjoyment of repose.

About midnight our troops were put in motion, in consequence of the enemy's advance on our pickets, which the British general had been induced to order, from knowing that he was within forty miles of the Dan, and that all his hope depended on the exertions of the following day. Animated with the prospect of soon terminating their present labors, the light troops resumed their march with alacrity. The roads continued deep and broken, and were rendered worse by being incrusted with frost: nevertheless, the march was pushed with great expedition. In the forenoon, one hour was applied by both commanders to the refreshment of their troops.

About noon Colonel Williams received a letter from General Greene, communicating the delightful tidings of his pas-

Feb. 13th. sage over the Dan on the preceding day. The whole corps became renovated in strength and agility; so powerful is the influence of the mind over the body. The great object of their long and faithful labor being so nearly accomplished, a general emulation pervaded all ranks to hasten to the boundary of their cares and perils. The hopes of the enemy were still high, and he rivalled our increased celerity, the van of O'Hara following close on the rear of Lee. About three in the evening we arrived within fourteen miles of the river; and Colonel Williams, leaving the Legion of Lee to wait on the enemy, took the nearest course to Boyd's Ferry. Before sunset he gained the river, and was soon transported to the opposite shore.

Lee, at the assigned period, directed his infantry to follow on the route of Williams; and about dark withdrew with his cavalry, the enemy being still in motion. Between the hours of eight and nine, the cavalry reached the river, just as the boats had returned from landing the Legion infantry. In obedience to the disposition of Lieutenant-Colonel Carrington, quartermaster-general, who superintended, in person, his arrangements for the transportation of the army, the horses were turned into the stream, while the dragoons, with their arms and equipments, embarked in the boats. Unluckily, some of the horses turned back, and gaining the shore, fled into the woods; and for a time some apprehensions were entertained that they might be lost. They were, however, recovered; and being forced into the river, followed their fellows. In the last boat, the quartermaster-general, attended by Lieutenant-Colonel Lee and the rear troop, reached the friendly shore.

In the evening Lord Cornwallis had received the unwelcome news of Greene's safe passage over the Dan ; and now, relinquishing his expectation of annihilating a second army, and despairing of striking the light corps, so long in his view and always safe, he gave repose to his vainly wearied troops.

Thus ended, on the night of the 14th of February, this long, arduous, and eventful retreat.

No operation during the war more attracted the public attention than this did : not only the toils and dangers encountered by a brave general and his brave army interested the sympathy of the nation, but the safety of the South, hanging on its issue, excited universal concern. The danger of this contingency alarmed the hearts of all, especially the more reflecting, who deemed the integrity of the Union essential to American liberty and happiness, and indispensable to our future safety and strength.

Destroy the army of Greene, and the Carolinas with Georgia inevitably became members of the British empire. Virginia, the bulwark of the South, would be converted first into a frontier, then into the theatre of war. Already drained nearly to the bottom, she would be committed in a contest for life with reduced means and broken spirits. All the country south of James River, so convenient to predatory incursions from the Southern States, would soon be ground to dust and ashes. Such misery, without hope, could not be long endured : and re-annexation to the mother country, presenting the only cure within reach, would be solicited and obtained. That part of the State north of James River, and west of the Blue Ridge, might continue united ; and so far as its ability permitted, would be found a daring and destructive foe. But in this desperate condition of affairs, with the enemy's uncontrolled maritime superiority, and the facile admission into the bosom of the country presented by its fine rivers, its resistance could not be of long duration. The stoutest heart trembles lest the Potomac should become the boundary of British dominion on the east of the Blue Ridge.

Happily for these States, a soldier of consummate talents guided the destiny of the South.

Cordially supported and truly beloved by the august personage at the head of the American armies, the bosom of Greene, gratefully reciprocating feelings so honorable to his character, never was assailed by those degraded passions, envy and malevolence—which too often disturb the harmony of associated leaders, and generate deep disasters to the common cause.

The glory of Washington, next to the safety of his country, was the prime object of his wishes. Pure and tranquil from the consciousness of just intentions, the undisturbed energy of his mind was wholly devoted to the effectual accomplishment of the high trust reposed in him.

The difficulty of retreat from South Carolina with an inferior army, and that army acting necessarily in two divisions at a great distance from each other—the State of North Carolina, stored with faithful abettors of the royal cause, who waited with solicitude for a fit opportunity to demonstrate their unshaken loyalty—presented in themselves impediments great and difficult. When we add the comfortless condition of our troops in point of clothing,* the rigor of the season, the inclemency of the weather, our short stock of ammunition, and shorter stock of provisions—and contrast it with the comfortable raiment and ample equipment of the enemy, inured to service, habituated to daring enterprises, the very troops which had taken Lincoln and destroyed Gates, rendered capable of the most rapid movements by their voluntary sacrifice of baggage, provisions, and liquor, and conducted by a general always to be dreaded—we have abundant cause to honor the soldier whose mental resources smoothed every difficulty, and ultimately made good a retreat of two hundred and thirty miles (unaided, except occasionally by small corps of friendly militia) without the loss of either troops or stores. Nor can we hesitate in acknowledging, that the scene just closed, presented satisfactory displays of that masterly genius, which, in the sequel, unfolded itself with such utility and splendor.

The British army have also a clear title to praise. More comfortably clad, the soldier was better able to bear the extremes of the season : in every other respect he equalled his enemy—bearing in-

---

* The shoes were generally worn out, the body clothes much tattered, and not more than a blanket for four men. The light corps was rather better off; but among its officers there was not a blanket for every three : so that among those whose hour admitted rest, it was an established rule, that at every fire, one should, in routine, keep upon his legs to preserve the fire in vigor. The tents were never used by the corps under Williams during the retreat. The heat of the fires was the only protection from rain, and sometimes snow : it kept the circumjacent ground and air dry, while imparting warmth to the body.

Provisions were not to be found in abundance, so swift was our progress. The single meal allowed us was always scanty, though good in quality and very nutritious, being bacon and corn meal.

cessant toil, courting danger, and submitting to privation of necessary food with alacrity; exhibiting, upon all occasions, unquestionable evidence of fidelity, zeal, and courage, in seconding the hardy enterprise of his admired leader.

General Greene, reviewing his army, at length safely enjoying wholesome and abundant supplies of food in the rich and friendly county of Halifax, bestowed upon all his commendation; distinguishing, by his marked approbation, Colonel Williams, and Lieutenant-Colonel Carrington, quartermaster-general; the first for his complete execution of the very difficult task assigned to him—exposed with his very inferior force to the daily and nightly assault of a sagacious and intrepid foe, he was never foiled himself, and seized the only opportunity presented of impressing the enemy with due respect for the corps under his orders; the last, for his multifarious services during the retreat. Lieutenant-Colonel Carrington had been detached with that portion of the Virginia regiment of artillery retained with the main army, when some of its companies had attended the Virginia line to the South, and had been taken with it at the surrender of Charleston, which loss was now supplied by some companies formerly attached to the Maryland line. On reaching North Carolina with De Kalb, Colonel Harrison, commandant of the Virginia artillery, unexpectedly arrived, and assumed command. In consequence of a misunderstanding with his colonel, Carrington retired, and was dispatched, upon Gates's arrival, to superintend the examination of the Roanoke River, to ascertain the readiest points of communication across it—not only for the purpose of expedition and celerity to his supplies coming from Virginia, but also with the view of insuring a safe retreat from North Carolina, should such a measure, then probable, become necessary. In this service Carrington was found by Greene, who pressed upon him the untried station of chief of the quartermaster's department, and dispatched him to hasten the execution of the various arrangements which he had formed as he passed through Richmond. Among those which, under this order, claimed the lieutenant-colonel's attention, was the examination of the Dan (the southern branch of the Roanoke), for the same purposes for which he had, by order of General Gates, explored the last-mentioned river; and with the further object of discovering whether the water of the Dan would admit of an inland navigation to be connected by a portage with the Yadkin; which mode of intercourse, in case of protracted war in the Carolinas, would be attended by the most beneficial conse-

quences. Captain Smith, of the Maryland line, was appointed to
this service by Lieutenant-Colonel Carrington, and performed the
duty with much intelligence.

So engaged was Carrington in accomplishing the orders of the
general, that he only joined the army two days before its concentration at Guilford Court-House, where he assumed the direction of
the trust assigned to him. We have before mentioned the judicious
plan which he submitted to Greene for the passage of the river Dan,
founded on the report made by Captain Smith of his examination.*

In this most difficult crisis Carrington commenced his official
duties; his subordinate officers habituated to expedients and
strangers to system, his implements of every sort in a wretched
condition, and without a single dollar in the military chest. Nevertheless, he contrived, by his method, his zeal, and his indefatigable
industry, to give promptitude to our movements, as well as accuracy and punctuality to the supplies of subsistence, and to collect
in due time all the boats upon the Dan, above Boyd's Ferry, at the
two points designated for the passage of that river.

CHAPTER XXVII.

Cornwallis's head-quarters at Hillsborough.—Issues a proclamation.—Greene's army
    reposes in Halifax.—Volunteers tender their services.—Pickens and Lee recross
    the Dan and move toward Haw River.—Find they have been preceded by
    Tarleton; go in pursuit of him.—Tarleton retreats in the night.—Greene recrosses
    the Dan and moves to the head-waters of Haw River.—Cornwallis advances in the
    same direction.—Affair at Wetzell's Mill.—Cornwallis moves suddenly to New
    Garden.—Attempt of Lee to intercept his baggage and stores.—Battle of Guilford
    Court-House.—Greene retreats to his old position on Troublesome Creek.—Corn-
    wallis retires to New Garden.—Lee and Campbell detached to follow him.—Greene
    pursues.—A cartel established.—Death and character of Colonel Webster.—Corn-
    wallis arrives at Wilmington.—Endeavors to rouse the loyalists.—Examination (per
    note) of charge of cruelty toward them.

CORNWALLIS, baffled in every expectation, much as he deserved
success (for certainly no man could have done more than he did),
now turned his attention to produce solid advantage out of the *éclat*
he had acquired in forcing Greene to abandon the State. Selecting
Hillsborough as head-quarters, one of the principal towns of North

---

* As soon as Greene adopted the plan prepared by the quartermaster-general
for crossing the Dan, Carrington detached the same Captain Smith, of the Maryland line, heretofore employed by him in the examination of the Roanoke
River. The service was performed highly to the satisfaction of the general, and
much to Captain Smith's credit.

Carolina,* he, after one day's repose of his army, proceeded thither by easy marches. Here he erected the king's standard, and invited by his proclamation, judiciously prepared and opportunely promulgated, all liege subjects to prove their fidelity by contributing their aid in restoring the blessings of peace and order in their convulsed country. He reiterated his orders prohibiting the disorderly of his army from indulging their licentious passions, commanding the protection of the persons and property of the inhabitants, with threats of severe and prompt punishment upon all and every offender.

In the camp of Greene, joy beamed in every face; and as if every man was conscious of having done his duty, the subsequent days to the reunion of the army on the north of the Dan were spent in mutual gratulations; with the rehearsal of the hopes and fears which agitated every breast during the retreat; interspersed with the many simple but interesting anecdotes with which every tongue was strung.

Meanwhile, the indefatigable Greene gave his mind and time to the hastening of his long pressed, and much wanted re-enforcements: devising within himself, in the same moment, plans to augment his force through his personal weight, and the influence of those ready to co-operate with him. Brigadier Stevens, whom we have seen overwhelmed with distress and mortification, in consequence of the shameful conduct of his brigade at the battle of Camden, as soon as he had conducted his militia to Pittsylvania Court-House, for the purpose of laying up their arms, returned to the army, in the expectation of such accession of force as would enable the general to replace him in the line of service. He had shared with the army in all the toils and perils of the retreat until he was ordered to Pittsylvania Court-House; and he was now anxious to participate with it in the honors and dangers of advance.

The people of Halifax County received us with the affection of brethren, mingled with admiration of the brave devotion to coun-

---

* Newbern and Hillsborough were the alternate seats of royal government in North Carolina; as were Burlington and Perth Amboy in the province of New Jersey. To the west of Newbern lies Wilmington, on the Cape Fear River, convenient to the Scotch emigrants' settlement on the waters of that river, whose inhabitants had for some years past, in the character of regulators, resisted the royal authority, but were now firm abettors of kingly government. It is one of the few towns convenient to ship navigation: consequently necessarily occupied by the British general. Here all his supplies of every sort were brought from New York and Charleston, and deposited till further orders, in care of the garrison.

try just exhibited. Volunteers began to tender their services, of which laudable enthusiasm Greene availed himself; and naming Stevens* as their leader, referred them to him for organization. Encouraging the spread of this honorable spirit, which Stevens took care to cherish with incessant diligence, very soon the foundation of a partial force was laid, which, gradually increasing, constituted that brigade which covered itself and general with glory in the sequel.

Grateful as was this display of zeal in the people of Halifax, and anxious as was the general to give to the efforts of Stevens full effect, he could not long enjoy the agreeable scene, nor indulge his faithful army in its novel state of ease and abundance. On North Carolina his mind was fixed. Its subjugation was inadmissible; and ill-brooking his forced abandonment of it, he was restless in safety; because that safety, in his estimation, was inglorious and injurious. Urging the governor of Virginia to press forward the long-expected aid, patronizing the exertions of Stevens to bring to him succor, derived from community of feelings and of interest, he now turned himself to the recovery of North Carolina, determined to contend upon its own soil for its independence.

Well acquainted with the high character of his able adversary, he knew that every hour of submission, growing out of our acknowledged inferiority of force, proved by long evasion of battle, would be turned by him to solid advantage in support of the royal cause. Also knowing the divided condition of the inhabitants of the State, he dreaded the effects of victory, when used by a sagacious soldier, and applied to a people almost equally balanced in their political feelings. Under the influence of such calculations, on the 17th he issued preparatory orders for movement.

The American general was not mistaken in his deductions. Availing himself of Greene's abandonment of North Carolina, of his undisturbed occupation of Hillsborough, and of his quiet possession of Wilmington upon the Cape Fear River by a detachment

---

* This officer, as has been mentioned, had proceeded with his militia to Pittsylvania Court-House to discharge his men, whose time of service had expired, and for the purpose of placing the public arms in the magazines allotted for their reception. He was well apprised of Greene's difficulties; and hearing, on his way home, by some reports that had overtaken him, that these difficulties were increased, and that it was very likely that his army might be crippled before he crossed the Dan, Stevens, instead of going home, returned to camp, taking with him some of the militia of Pittsylvania, collected by the exertions of the county lieutenant, determined to share the fate of Greene and of his army.

from Charleston under the orders of Major Craig, Lord Cornwallis began to realize the expectations he had so long and so sanguinely indulged. The royalists everywhere were preparing to rise, while the well affected to the cause of America, despairing of protection, began to look for safety in submission.

Greene persevering in his determination to risk his army again in North Carolina—to rouse the drooping spirits of his friends, and to check the audacity of his foes—the Legion of Lee, strengthened by two companies of the veterans of Maryland, under Captain Oldham, with the corps of South Carolina militia, under Brigadier Pickens, was ordered, in the morning of the 18th, to pass the Dan. This was readily performed; all the boats heretofore collected being still held together by Carrington for the use of the army.

Pickens and Lee were commanded to gain the front of Cornwallis, to place themselves as close to him as safety would permit, in order to interrupt his communication with the country, to repress the meditated rising of the loyalists, and, at all events, to intercept any party of them which might attempt to join the enemy.

These officers lost no time in advancing to the theatre of operations; and having in the course of the march provided capable guides, sat down that evening in a covert position, short of the great road leading from the Haw River to Hillsborough, and detached exploring parties of cavalry on the roads toward Hillsborough and toward the Haw. In the course of the evening, Greene, never avoiding toil or danger, with a small escort of Washington's cavalry, left his army, and overtook the advanced corps in its secret position. He continued with it during the night, and renewed to the two commandants explanations of his plan and object. He communicated his intention of repassing the Dan with the army in a few days, directing his route toward the upper country; too remote, as he remarked, from the advanced corps to afford the smallest protection; urged cordial concert, pressed in fervid terms the necessity of unceasing vigilance, and the most cautious circumspection. Before dawn, the officer who had been dispatched toward the Haw returned with intelligence that on the preceding day Lieutenant-Colonel Tarleton had passed up that route from Hillsborough with horse, foot, and artillery; their number unascertained; destined, as was presumed, to pass the Haw River, with the view of hastening the embodying of the loyalists, and of protecting them on their march to Hillsborough. The wisdom of the measure adopted by Greene was now shown, as already an important object presented itself to the detached corps. Greene having set out on his return to camp, Pickens and Lee advanced; first sending recon- noitring parties in their front, with orders to conceal themselves in sight of the road to watch passing occurrences, and to report from time to time the result of their observations. The main body moving obliquely to their right through an unsettled region, they encamped within three miles of the great road, with the Haw on their right, about seven miles distant. Here they were joined by the light parties sent out in the morning, and by the officer who had the day before been detached toward Hillsborough. The first reported that every thing was still on the road, and that they had not seen a single person, except a well-grown boy, during the day, whom they had brought along with them agreeable to orders. From this lad we discovered that Tarleton had not passed the river yester- day, but would do it on the next morning.

The officer who had approached Hillsborough found all quiet in that quarter, and neither saw nor heard any thing indicating a move- ment on the part of the enemy. Resting for the night, the corps proceeded after breakfast the next day, waiting until then to give time for the exploring parties to renew their efforts in obtaining more precise intelligence.

Approaching the road, it was met by a dragoon bringing informa- tion that the British detachment had passed the Haw. This being ascertained, Pickens and Lee gained the great road, and followed on the enemy's route. Guides became unnecessary now; for the British detachment had plundered all the houses on the road, known, as they were, to be the property of patriots, and symbols of devasta- tion marked their steps. The men having all fled, none but wom- en could be seen. From them the American commandants learned that the loyalists between the Haw and Deep rivers were certainly embodying, and that the British detachment would not advance far on the other side of the river, it being commonly said among the soldiers, that they should return in a few days. By what could be gathered from report, and judging by the time of passing any one house, it appeared that most of the cavalry, two light brass pieces, and four hundred infantry, composed the detachment. Sending again a small party of dragoons down the road, to discover whether any second body of troops were moving from Hillsborough, Pickens and Lee continued on to the Haw, which they passed without delay, hearing that Lieutenant-Colonel Tarleton was encamped four miles in front. At this moment the officer sent down the road rejoined, communicating that there was no prospect of interruption from that quarter.

Soon after we had crossed the river, which was fordable, a countryman was discovered by the cavalry in front; and being overtaken, was sent to the commandants. From him it was ascertained that Lieutenant-Colonel Tarleton, as had been reported, commanded the party, and that he was encamped within three miles of us about noon; that his horses were unsaddled, and that appearances indicated his confidence of security. With respect to his strength, the countryman's information rated it the same as it was before understood to be. This being correct, Tarleton had the advantage in number of cavalry, but was inferior in quality; he had two light pieces, the Americans none; he was numerically inferior in infantry, but his troops were all tried regulars, while half of our infantry were militia, though of the best sort. A disposition for attack was immediately made. The infantry of the Legion led by Lieutenant-Colonel Lee, forming the centre, moved directly toward the enemy, with the cavalry in column, under Major Rudolph, upon its right; and the militia riflemen, conducted by Brigadier Pickens, on its left. Oldham, with the two Maryland companies, composed the reserve. Presuming a surprise probable, the march was concealed by keeping through woods, having faithful guides with each division. In this event, Major Rudolph had orders to charge in full gallop, supported by Oldham with the reserve; while the Legion infantry, covered on its left by the riflemen, in whatever state the enemy might be found, was destined to carry the field-pieces with fixed bayonets. Should he be apprised of our advance, and consequently prepared for our reception, Oldham, with his Marylanders, was ordered to take the place of the cavalry on the right of the Legion infantry, and Rudolph, with the dragoons, to stand in reserve.

Thus arrayed, the divisions proceeded to their designated points, every precaution having been adopted to prevent discovery. The movement was conducted with the utmost precision and correspondency. When arriving within a few hundred yards of the expected theatre of glory, the farm and house were seen, but no enemy. The van of the horse galloping to the house brought off two of the enemy's staff, who had been delayed in settling for the subsistence of the detachment; and hearing from the family that Lieutenant-Colonel Tarleton would not advance above six miles further, Pickens and Lee instantly proceeded toward him, hoping that fortune would be more propitious upon the next occasion.

Thus did the bright prospects of the morning vanish, exciting of itself deep chagrin; rendered more galling, by finding that Tarleton, believing himself perfectly secure, had been unusually remiss, and would have been caught in a condition out of which neither skill nor courage could have extricated him.

To give success, if possible, to this second attempt, it was determined to pass as a re-enforcement sent from Hillsborough to Lieutenant-Colonel Tarleton; and the two prisoners being placed in the centre of the cavalry, were charged to conduct themselves so as to give currency to the deception: in default of which, the sergeant having the care of them was directed to put them to death instantly. The Legion taking the lead, with the horse in front, Lieutenant-Colonel Lee put himself at its head, to direct operations both delicate and important. This stratagem could not fail of imposing on the country people, however well acquainted they might be with the appearance of British troops, so far as respected the Legion, inasmuch as both cavalry and infantry were dressed in short, green coats, with other distinctions exactly resembling some of the enemy's light corps.

Lee's van officer preceding him a few hundred yards only, was met by two well-mounted young countrymen, who being accosted in the assumed character, promptly answered, that they were rejoiced in meeting us, having been sent forward by Colonel Pyle for the purpose of ascertaining Tarleton's camp, to whom the colonel was repairing with four hundred loyalists. These youths were instantly sent to Lieutenant-Colonel Lee, preceded by a dragoon, with the information imparted. Immediately after the arrival of the dragoon, Lee dispatched his adjutant with the intelligence to Brigadier Pickens, requesting him to place his riflemen (easily to be distinguished by the green twigs in their hats, the customary emblem of our militia in the South) on the left flank, out of sight; which was readily to be done, as we were then in a thick wood; at the same time to assure him that Lee was determined, in conformity with the concerted plan, to make an attempt with the Legion, of turning the occurrence to advantage. The prisoners were also reminded, as was the sergeant having them in care, of the past order. This communication was scarcely finished, before the two dragoons rode up with the two countrymen, who were received with much apparent cordiality by Lieutenant-Colonel Lee, who listened with seeming satisfaction to their annunciation of the laudable spirit which had actuated

Colonel Pyle and his associates, and which they asserted was rapidly spreading through the country. Finding them completely deceived (for they not only believed the troops they saw to be British, but overlooking what had been told them, took them to be Tarleton's, addressing the commandant as that officer), Lee sent one of them back with two dragoons to his van, thence to proceed to Colonel Pyle with Lieutenant-Colonel Tarleton's gratulations, and his request that he would be so good as to draw out on the margin of the road, so as to give convenient room for his much fatigued troops to pass without delay to their night position, while the other was detained to accompany the supposed Tarleton. Orders were at the same time dispatched to the van officer to halt as soon as he got in sight of the loyalists.

As Lee approached, his officer, who had halted, highly gratified with the propitious prospect, and listening to the overflowings of respect and devotion falling incessantly from the lips of his young attendant, his comrade, who had been sent to Colonel Pyle, returned with his expected compliance, announced in most respectful terms.

The column of horse now became complete by union with the van, and Colonel Pyle was in sight of the right of the road, drawn up as suggested, with his left to the advancing column.* This last circumstance was fortunate, as Lieutenant-Colonel Lee had concluded to make known to the colonel his real character as soon as he should confront him, with a solemn assurance of his and his associates perfect exemption from injury, and with the choice of returning to their homes, or of taking a more generous part, by uniting with the defenders of their common country against the common foe. By Pyle's lucky occupation of the right side of the road, it became necessary for Lee to pass along the whole line of the loyalists before he could reach their colonel; and thus to place his column of horse in the most eligible situation for any vicissitude.

They were mounted like our militia, fitted like them to move on horseback, and to fight dismounted. Their guns (rifles and fowling-pieces) were on their shoulders, the muzzles consequently in an opposite direction to the cavalry. In the event of discovery, they

---

* Had Pyle accidentally arrayed upon the left of the road, he would have been found on the right of his regiment, the flank first reached by the column of the horse. Some pretext must have been adopted to have moved on to the other flank, so as to place the horse in the requisite posture, before Lieutenant-Colonel Lee could make the desired communication; therefore it was fortunate that he should have chosen the side of the road on which he was found posted.

must have changed the direction before they could fire—a motion not to be performed, with a body of dragoons close in with their horses' heads and their swords drawn.

The danger of this rare expedient was by no means so great as it appears to be on first view.

Lee passed along the line at the head of the column with a smiling countenance, dropping, occasionally, expressions complimentary to the good looks and commendable conduct of his loyal friends. At length he reached Colonel Pyle, when the customary civilities were promptly interchanged. Grasping Pyle by the hand, Lee was in the act of consummating his plan, when the enemy's left, discovering Pickens's militia, not sufficiently concealed, began to fire upon the rear of the cavalry commanded by Captain Eggleston. This officer instantly turned upon the foe, as did immediately after the whole column. The conflict was quickly decided, and bloody on one side only. Ninety of the royalists were killed, and most of the survivors wounded. Dispersing in every direction, not being pursued, they escaped. During this sudden rencounter, in some parts of the line the cry of mercy was heard, coupled with assurance of being our best friends; but no expostulation could be admitted in a conjuncture so critical. Humanity even forbade it, as its first injunction is. to take care of your own safety, and our safety was not compatible with that of the supplicants, until disabled to offend. Pyle, falling under many wounds, was left on the field as dying, and yet he survived. We lost not a man, and only one horse. The object so sedulously pressed was thus a second time baffled. Tarleton, within a mile, more fatally secure, if possible, than before, escaped the impending blow; when to get at him a measure had been hazarded, not warranted on ordinary occasions, but now enforced by the double motive of sparing the lives of deluded fellow-citizens, and humbling effectually the British partisan and his active corps, whose destruction in the relative condition of the two armies would have probably led to the termination of the war in the South. Lord Cornwallis was at the head of a brave enterprising force, but small in number; too small, when reduced by the loss of Tarleton's corps, to have made head against Greene, when assisted, as the American general must have been, by the surrounding country, animated to their best exertions by such signal success.*

* This transaction is thus circumstantially given to repel the unfounded stigma attached to the officer and corps engaged with Colonel Pyle. Mr.

The discomfiture of Pyle being soon effected, Lee ordered the cavalry to resume its march, and to take post so as to arrest any sudden interference on the part of Lieutenant-Colonel Tarleton, who must have heard the enemy's fire, and might probably interpose with the expectation of controlling the event of the conflict.

Brigadier Pickens, following quickly, soon reached the van of the Legion, whose cavalry had approached in view of Tarleton's camp. Then were seen incontestable evidences of the embarrassing confusion which an unexpected enemy never fails to produce, even among the best disciplined troops—demonstrating, without shadow of doubt, our certain success, had Pyle and his party been, as they ought to have been, at their own firesides. The sun was· setting; and for some moments Pickens and Lee hesitated whether immediate action was not, even at that hour, the eligible course. The troops were fatigued by their long march, increased by preparation for two combats and the rencounter with Pyle. This consideration, combined with the close approach of night, determined them to postpone battle until the morning. Moving to their left, they placed themselves between the British and the upper country, on the great road leading through Tarleton's camp to Hillsborough. The advanced sentinels and the patrols were stationed everywhere in sight of each other.

Here they heard from some countrymen, who, abandoning their houses on the enemy's advance, had fallen in with Pickens, that a small party of militia had collected for mutual safety a few miles in

Stedman (of whose impartiality and respect for truth I have acknowledged my conviction) has from misinformation been led upon this occasion into a palpable mistake, or he would have refrained from the following observation : "When at last it became manifest, they called out for quarter, but no quarter was granted : and between two and three hundred of them were inhumanly butchered while in the act of begging for mercy. Humanity shudders at the recital of so foul a massacre; but cold and unfeeling policy avows it as the most effectual means of intimidating the friends of royal government." So far from its being a "foul massacre," growing out of cold and unfeeling policy, it was not foul, and was unintentional; and one of the two corps of cavalry, belonging to the army of Greene, was hazarded for the express purpose of preventing the necessity of imbruing our hands in the blood of our fellow-citizens. The fire commenced upon us, and self-preservation commanded the limited destruction which ensued. Only ninety of the loyalists were killed; not between two and three hundred, as Mr. Stedman states: and less than ninety could not have been spared from the close condition of the dragoons, and the necessity of crushing resistance instantly. Had the officer or corps been capable of massacre, it was only necessary to have ordered pursuit, and not a man of the enemy would have escaped. So far from doing so, Lee resumed his march, leaving all that had dispersed to secure themselves without interruption.

the rear. A dragoon, attended by one of the informants, was immediately dispatched with a letter to the officer, requesting him to hasten to camp; more for the purpose of procuring accurate information of the ground expected soon to be the theatre of action, and of furnishing faithful intelligent guides, than from any expectation of aid in battle. It so happened, that with the militia company was found Colonel Preston, of Montgomery County in Virginia, just arrived at the head of three hundred hardy mountaineers, who, hearing of Greene's retreat, had voluntarily hastened to his assistance—alike ignorant until that hour of the general's having re-crossed the Dan, and of Tarleton's corps being but a few miles in front.

The wisdom of the measure so speedily adopted by the commander in the South, after securing his retreat, was again now happily illustrated. It not only produced the annihilation of the first body of loyalists which had embodied and armed, but probably saved from destruction a detachment of brave men, induced by love of country to seek and to succor their hard-pressed friends. Colonel Preston accompanied the dragoon to the camp, followed by his battalion of riflemen. Although Pickens and Lee were before determined to engage, such an opportune, unlooked-for auxiliary force, could not but excite new spirits in their troops, always proudly conscious of ability. Preston, his officers and soldiers, spent their first hour in gazing at the corps. They were much gratified with the orderly appearance it universally exhibited, and particularly delighted with the cheering looks of the dragoons, and the high condition of their stout horses.

Our upper militia were never alarmed in meeting with equal numbers of British infantry. Selecting their own ground (which, being mounted, they could readily do) before they would engage, they considered themselves their equal; but they entertained dreadful apprehensions of the sabre of the cavalry, particularly when associated with the name of Tarleton, who had, upon many occasions, used it with destructive effect. From this source was derived the satisfaction expressed on reviewing the Legion horse. They became convinced that no equal number of dragoons ought to excite the smallest apprehensions on their part, and they were assured that the British cavalry were not only inferior in their horses, but very much so in horsemanship. Thoroughly satisfied, these welcome auxiliaries retired to their post, responding with ardor the general wish to be led to battle with the dawn of day. Every arrangement being made to meet the approaching conflict, the troops assumed the disposition in which they were to fight, and lay down to rest.

From the intelligence procured, it was ascertained that the field in which the British were encamped had three or four wood dwelling-houses on the road near its centre, and was sufficiently capacious to admit conveniently the major part of the respective combatants to close action. The Legion infantry, led by Lieutenant-Colonel Lee, marched along the road, for the purpose, as before, of attending specially to the enemy's artillery, of which it has been mentioned we were destitute. Oldham, with his Marylanders, advanced on the right, parallel with Lee; and on his right, in a wood skirting the field, Brigadier Pickens moved, having under him some of the same soldiers who had so nobly supported Howard's right at the Cowpens. Colonel Preston covered Lee's left; having also the advantage of a copse of wood bordering the field in that direction, and being completely secured on his flank by a very extensive millpond. The cavalry were formed in reserve, the head of the column pointing to the interval between Oldham and Pickens, where the field could be entered out of fire from the houses, should Tarleton, as was apprehended, occupy them with musketry. Rudolph, who commanded the horse, was directed to fly to the aid of any portion of the troops hard pressed, as well as to be ready to improve our, and to limit their, victory. Between the hours of two and three in the morning, concurring intelligence was received from the pickets and patrols, announcing that the enemy was in motion, and, soon afterward, that he was retiring.

The pickets being assembled by the officer of the day, were ordered to advance; while the main body, hastening to arms, followed with celerity. Anxious to know the cause of this sudden and unexpected movement, an officer was directed to call at the houses lately occupied by the enemy for the purpose of inquiry. He reported that Lord Cornwallis, having been apprised of the advance of Pickens and Lee, hastened his orders to Lieutenant-Colonel Tarleton, communicating the information he had received, and requiring him to repass the Haw instantly; which order the lieutenant-colonel very reluctantly obeyed. He further learned that Tarleton and his officers were in high spirits, had enjoyed an abundant supper together, and were anxiously wishing for the return of light, determined to take complete revenge for the loss of Pyle; and assured of victory, delighted themselves with the prospect of mounting, in the course of the day, the chosen horses of the Legion. So solicitous

Lord Cornwallis appears to have been, that he dispatched three successive couriers, all of whom arrived ; the two last, just as the British corps was ready to move.   There were three contiguous passages of the Haw.   The nearest within four miles, to be passed in a boat, which, from the size of the flat kept at the ferry, and the narrowness of the river, would not have been very inconvenient : the infantry and artillery might have been thrown over before day-light, and the cavalry would have readily swam across.   One mile below was another ferry, alike commodious ; and seven miles lower down was a ford, the same which both corps had used the day be-fore.   The Legion, accustomed to night expeditions, had been in the habit of using pine-torch for flambeaux.   Supplied with this, though the morning was dark, the enemy's trail was distinctly discovered whenever a divergency took place in his route.   He first took the road leading to the upper ferry, the direct route to Hillsborough ; but it being always presumed that he would avail himself of the ford, though out of his way, the van officer took care occasionally to examine, by the help of his pine-knots, and soon ascertained that after passing some small distance on that road, he crossed to the second route.   Here repeating his feint, he at length turned to the road leading to the ford.

The diligence of the leading officer saved to the main body loss of ground ; as the enemy's stratagem was detected before we reached the points of their separation from each road.   As the day broke, the American troops, pursuing with zeal, had reached within two miles of the ford.   The cavalry now taking the front, supported by the riflemen (all mounted) were ordered to press upon the enemy, and hold him back until the infantry could get up.   Before sunrise they gained the enemy's rear, descending the hill to the river, over which the main body having just passed, was placed on a height commanding the ford for the protection of the rear-guard.   Too near to be struck at without rashly exposing the troops, it was omitted ; much as it was desired to gain some evidence of our triumphant pursuit.   At first Pickens and Lee determined, by a quick retrograde, to pass at the ferry above, and to throw them-selves in Tarleton's rear.   This was effectible, in case he loitered only one hour on the banks of the Haw, a very probable event.   But there was cause to apprehend, from the solicitude displayed by the British general to bring him safely back, that he would send a re-enforcement to meet him.   In this incertitude, desire to give rest to the troops prevailed ; and keeping up the western margin of the

Haw, the corps halted in the first settlement capable of supplying the necessary subsistence. Thus closed twenty-four hours of very active service; its chief object uneffected, and a secondary one completely executed, which produced a very favorable result, by repressing thoroughly the loyal spirit just beginning to burst forth. Fortune, which sways so imperiously the affairs of war, demonstrated throughout the operation its supreme control. Nothing was omitted on the part of the Americans to give the expedition the desired termination ; but the very bright prospects which for a time presented themselves were suddenly overcast—the capricious goddess gave us Pyle and saved Tarleton.

General Greene, in pursuance of his plan, passed the Dan on the 23d, strengthened in a small degree by the corps of militia under Stevens, and took a direction toward the head-waters of the Haw River. He was highly gratified by the success of his advanced troops officially communicated to him after he had entered North Carolina; and was pleased to estimate the destruction of Pyle and his loyalists as more advantageous in its effects than would have been a victory over Lieutenant-Colonel Tarleton.

Soon after Tarleton returned to Hillsborough, the British general quitted his position—moving with his whole force to the country from which Tarleton had been just chased, for the purpose of giving complete protection to his numerous friends inhabiting the district between the Haw and Deep rivers, whose danger in attempting to join him while so distantly situated, had lately been fatally exemplified. As soon as this movement on the part of his lordship was known to General Greene, he again resorted to his former expedient of placing a strong light corps between him and the enemy. Colonel Williams was of course intrusted with its direction, who, moving toward his lordship, directed Pickens and Lee, a part of his establishment, to join him. Colonel Preston, still continuing with Pickens, now made a part of Williams's force. The return of Greene to North Carolina, and the destruction of Colonel Pyle's loyalists, baffled the hopes so long entertained by the British general, and fast realizing after his possession of Hillsborough; where, in the course of one day, seven independent companies of loyalists were raised. Lord Cornwallis's project of filling up his ranks with the youth of North Carolina, which he pressed by every means in his power, although suspended by the late event, was not abandoned. Determined to effect it, he had, as we have seen, left Hillsborough, and placed himself among his friends, whose

Feb., 1781.

spirits he wished to revive by some decisive success. Encamped
upon the Almance, he held himself ready to seize any opportunity
which might be presented, and heard with pleasure of the approach
of our light corps under Colonel Williams. This officer was his first
object; the next was to force Greene to battle, which he believed
would be risked by the American general to save his light troops.
In the opinion of many, General Greene committed himself to much
hazard in his newly adopted system. It was asked, why not continue in his safe position on the north of the Dan, until, receiving
all his expected succor, he could pass into North Carolina, seeking,
instead of avoiding, his enemy? This safe and agreeable course
was relinquished from necessity. Greene, penetrating Cornwallis's
views, foresaw their certain success, if he had remained long out of
the State, waiting for re-enforcements himself. He discerned the
probability that his enemy would acquire a greater proportionate
strength : with the essential difference, that what we obtained would
be mostly militia, a fluctuating force ; whereas, that gained by the
enemy would stand to him throughout the contest.

To arrest the progress of this scheme, pursued with pertinacity
by the British general, it was necessary again to risk himself, his
army, and the South. He therefore passed the Dan as soon as it
was in his power; depending on the resources of his fertile mind,
and the tried skill and courage of his faithful, though inferior army.
Crossing the Haw near its source, the American general established
himself between Troublesome Creek and Reedy Fork. And changing his position every day, sometimes approaching Colonel Williams, and then falling back upon the Troublesome, he held Cornwallis in perfect ignorance of his position, and stopped the possibility of sudden interruption. Showing himself in so many
different quarters, he considerably augmented the fears of the
loyalists, who had not yet recovered from the consternation produced by the slaughter of their associates. Williams pursued the
same desultory game, preserving correspondency in his movements
with those of Greene.* As yet Lord Cornwallis had not been able
to find any opportunity to execute his purpose. Williams, more
and more satisfied of his safety from his superiority in the quality

---

* On the 2d of March the Legion and Preston's riflemen had a rencounter
with Tarleton, which General Greene, in a dispatch to General Washington,
thus notices : " On the second, Lieutenant-Colonel Lee, with a detachment of
riflemen, attacked the advance of the British army under Tarleton, and killed
and wounded, by report, about thirty of them."—See *Tarleton's Campaigns*,
p. 235.—Ed.

of his cavalry, and wishing to take a distance whence he could conveniently interrupt the British parties while collecting provisions and forage, placed himself a few miles on the east side of Reedy Fork, having the Almance Creek between him and the enemy. Lord Cornwallis well knew the superiority of our horse; feeling it daily in the counteraction of his efforts to obtain intelligence so important in military operations. Indisposed to such a near neighborhood with us, he moved from his camp at three o'clock on the 6th of March, and passing the Almance, pushed forward under the cover of a heavy fog, with the expectation of beating up Williams's quarters. The left of the light troops was composed of militia, who had lately joined under Colonel Campbell, one of the heroes of King's Mountain, relieving Brigadier Pickens and the corps who had so faithfully adhered to General Greene during the trying scenes just passed. Campbell's militia were part of the conquerors of Ferguson; better suited, as has been before observed, for the field of battle than for the security of camp. In this quarter, through some remissness in the guards, and concealed by the fog, Lieutenant-Colonel Webster, commanding the British van, approached close before he was discovered.

The alertness of the light troops soon recovered the momentary disadvantage; and the Legion of Lee advancing to support Campbell, the enemy's van was held back, until Colonel Williams, undisturbed, commenced his retreat, directing the two corps above mentioned to cover his rear. Having crossed the Reedy Fork, Williams made a disposition, with a view of opposing the enemy's passage. Campbell following Williams, joined on the opposite banks—the infantry of the Legion proceeding in the rear of Campbell, followed by the cavalry, which corps continued close to the enemy's advancing van. During this movement, Webster made several efforts to bring the rear-guard to action, having under him the British cavalry. All his endeavors were successively counteracted by the celerity and precision with which the Legion horse manœuvred: establishing evidently in the face of the enemy their decided superiority.* As soon as Lieutenant-Colonel Lee was

---

* No country in the world affords better riders than the United States, especially the States south of Pennsylvania. The boys from seven years of age begin to mount horses; riding without saddle, and often in the fields, when sent for a horse, without bridle. They go to mill on horseback, and perform all the other small domestic services mounted. Thus they become so completely versed in the art of riding by the time they reach puberty, as to equal the most expert horsemen anywhere.

apprised of the rear infantry's passage over the river, he retired by troops from before Webster in full gallop; and reaching Reedy Fork, soon united with Colonel Williams, unmolested. There being convenient fords over the creek, above and below, after Williams had safely brought over his corps, he determined no longer to continue in his position. Resuming retreat, he left the Legion supported by Colonel Campbell, with orders to retard the enemy as long as it was practicable, without hazarding serious injury. Lieutenant-Colonel Lee, having detached a company of Preston's militia to guard the pass at Wetzell's Mill, a little distance upon his left, drew up his infantry in one line, with its right on the road, and its front parallel with the creek; while the riflemen under Colonels Campbell and Preston occupied a copse of heavy woods on the right of the road, with their left resting upon the right of the Legion infantry.

The horse formed a second line in a field well situated to curb the progress of the British cavalry, should it press upon the first line when retiring, and to protect the horses of the militia, tied at some distance back, agreeably to usage. On the first appearance of the enemy Colonel Williams dispatched a courier to Greene, communicating what had passed, and advising him of the course he should pursue after crossing the Reedy Fork. Unwilling to approximate Greene, this officer moved slowly, waiting the disclosure of the enemy's intention. Should he halt on the opposite side of the creek, Colonel Williams would take his night position within a few miles of Wetzell's Mill, giving time to the troops to prepare food before dark; but should the enemy advance to the hither side, he would necessarily continue his retreat, however much opposed to his wishes. This state of suspense lasted but a little while. The British van appeared; and after a halt for a few minutes on the opposite bank, descended the hill approaching the water, where, receiving a heavy fire of musketry and rifles, it fell back, and quickly reascending, was rallied on the margin of the bank. Here a field-officer rode up, and in a loud voice addressed his soldiers, then rushed down the hill at their head, and plunged into the water, our fire pouring upon him. In the woods occupied by the riflemen stood an old log school-house, a little to the right of the ford. The mud stuffed between the logs had mostly fallen out, and the apertures admitted the use of the rifles with ease. In this house twenty-five select marksmen, of King's Mountain militia, were posted by Lee, with orders to forego taking any part in the general resistance, but to hold themselves in reserve for particular objects. The leading officer, plunging into the water, attracted general notice ; and the school-house party, recollecting its order, singled him out as their mark. The stream being deep, and the bottom rugged, he advanced slowly; his soldiers on each side of him, and apparently some of them holding his stirrup leathers. This select party discharged their rifles at him, one by one, each man sure of knocking him over ; and having reloaded, eight or nine of them emptied their guns a second time at the same object.* Strange to tell, though in a condition so perilous, himself and horse were untouched ; and having crossed the creek, he soon formed his troops, and advanced upon us. The moment that the head of his column got under cover of our banks, Lieutenant-Colonel Lee directed the line to retire from its flanks, and gain the rear of the cavalry. In the skirmish which ensued in our centre, after some of the enemy ascended the bank, three or four prisoners fell into our hands. The enemy's column being now formed, soon dislodged our centre; and pushing Lee, came in front of the cavalry. Here it paused, until the British horse, which followed the infantry, passed the creek, and took post on the enemy's right—the nearest point to the road, which we must necessarily take. This attitude indicated a decision to interrupt our retreat ; at all events, to cut off our rear.

Lee ordered Rudolph to incline in an oblique direction to his left ; and, gaining the road, to wait the expected charge. Tarleton advanced with his cavalry, followed by Webster. The Legion infantry, close in the rear of the riflemen, had now entered the road, considerably advanced toward Colonel Williams, still waiting in his position first taken for night quarters, and afterward held to protect the rear-guard. Rudolph, with the cavalry, was drawn off, moving slowly, with orders to turn upon the British horse if they should risk a charge.

It was now late in the evening, and nothing more was attempted. The British halted on the ground selected by Williams for our use,

---

* The twenty-five riflemen were selected from their superior excellence as marksmen. It was no uncommon amusement among them to put an apple on the point of a ramrod, and holding it in the hand with the arm extended, to permit their comrades, known to be expert, to fire at it, when many balls would pass through the apple ; and yet Lieutenant-Colonel Webster, mounted upon a stout horse, in point-blank shot, slowly moving through a deep water-course, was singled out by this party, who fired, *seriatim*, thirty-two or thirty-three times at him, and neither struck him nor his horse.

which he had abandoned. Having proceeded some miles further, he encamped on the northeast side of a range of hills covered with wood, some distance from the road; thus our fires were concealed from view, while the margin of the road and every avenue to our camp was vigilantly guarded.

General Greene, as soon as he was advised in the morning of the enemy's advance, retired and passed the Haw; repeating in his answer, his order to Colonel Williams to avoid action, which he well knew was very practicable, unless our cavalry should meet with disaster. As soon as all appearances of further contest ceased, the prisoners, as was customary, were brought to the commandant; who, among other inquiries, asked what officer led the enemy into the creek, and crossed with the leading section of the column? He was told that it was Lieutenant-Colonel Webster; and that he had passed unhurt.

Inscrutable are the ways of Providence. That superior soldier, whose life was in such imminent danger, was now safely shielded, though doomed to fall in a very few days.

Lord Cornwallis, finding that his attempt to bring Greene to action issued only in wearing down his brave army, and convinced that Williams was unassailable so long as he preserved his superiority in cavalry, withdrew toward Bell's Mill, on Deep River, with the resolution of restoring, by rest, the strength of his troops, and of holding it up for that decisive day, which, from his knowledge of the character of his adversary, he was assured would arrive as soon as he had acquired his expected re-enforcements. The last ten days presented a very interesting and edifying scene. Two generals of high talents, ardently supported by their respective armies, contending by a series of daring manœuvres, for a vast prize, which either might have lost by one false step. Had Cornwallis risked any partial operations against Williams, the destruction of the assailing corps would have led to the capture of the British army; whereas, had Greene, by incorrect intelligence or mistaken calculations, placed himself within reach of the British general, our army would have been cut to pieces. The loyalists looked on with anxious solicitude; and finding that all the efforts of the royal leader were unavailing—the American army retaining its ground, and its active cavalry penetrating in every direction—they recurred to past admonition, and determined to repress their zeal, and to wait in quietude until the British superiority should be manifested by signal success.

Thus the American general completely succeeded in his object, adding a new claim to the high confidence already acquired, and leaving it doubtful which most to admire—his sagacity in counsel, his promptitude in decision, or his boldness and skill in execution.

In this position, at the iron-works on Troublesome Creek, General Greene received the pleasing intelligence, that his re-enforcements and supplies were approaching; and hearing at the same time from Colonel Williams, that Lord Cornwallis had retired from the contest of skill, he determined to give repose to his troops and wait for his long-expected succor. In a few days the new levies under Colonel Green, and the militia from Virginia under Brigadier-General Lawson, with a part of the supplies and stores so much wanted, reached camp. The levies were distributed in the regiments of Virginia, commanded by Colonel Green and Lieutenant-Colonel Hawes. The militia being united to those collected by Stevens while at Halifax Court-House, were divided into two brigades, under the direction of that general and Brigadier Lawson, who, like Stevens, had commanded a Continental regiment, and with many other brave and active officers, had been left without troops by the compression of our regular corps; yet being unwilling to abandon the service of their country, still in jeopardy, they both had offered to take command of the militia.

Soon afterward came in the North Carolina force, led by the Brigadiers Butler and Eaton. Previously Colonels Campbell and Preston and Lynch* had joined, whose united corps did not exceed six hundred rank and file. Our force now was estimated at four thousand five hundred, horse, foot, and artillery; of which, the Continental portion did not amount to quite one thousand six hundred. To acquaint himself with the character of his late accession of troops, and to make ready the many requisite preparations for service, the general continued in his position at the iron-works, having drawn in most of the light corps. The Legion of Lee, and the Virginia militia attached to it under the Colonels Preston and Campbell, still hovered around the enemy under the direction of Lieutenant-Colonel Lee.

The American dragoons, far superior in the ability of their horses, stuck so close to the British camp as to render their intercourse

---

* Colonels Campbell and Preston had been with the light troops for some days; succeeding the corps under Brigadier Pickens, now returned home. Colonel Lynch had lately joined, commanding one of the battalions of the Virginia militia, which arrived under Brigadier Lawson.

with the country very difficult, and subjected the British general to many inconveniences, besides interrupting his acquirement of intelligence.

No equal party of the enemy's horse would dare to encounter them; and if a superior force approached, the fleetness of their horses mocked pursuit. Feeling his privations daily, Lord Cornwallis, leaving his baggage to follow, made a sudden movement late in the evening from Bell's mill toward New Garden, a Quaker settlement, abounding with forage and provisions. Some of the small parties of the Legion horse, traversing in every quarter, one of them approached Bell's mill, and found it abandoned. When informed by the inhabitants that the baggage had but lately proceeded under a very small escort, the officer commanding the horse determined to trace secretly the progress of its march. It so happened, that early in the night the escort with the whole baggage mistook the road; proceeding directly on, instead of turning toward New Garden. Fortunately, the vigilant officer discovered this error; and having ascertained the fact beyond doubt, he dispatched a courier to Lieutenant-Colonel Lee with the information, attended by two guides well acquainted with the route taken by the British army, that taken by the escort, and the intermediate cross-roads.

The intelligence reached Lee about eleven o'clock (later than was expected), as he had, from the advance of the enemy, taken a more distant position. Instantly the Legion horse, with two companies of infantry mounted behind two of the troops, were put in motion: Lieutenant-Colonel Lee, taking the guides sent to him, advanced with the certain expectation of falling in with the lost escort. The night was extremely dark, and the country covered with woods; but the guides were faithful, intelligent, and intimately versed in all the roads, by-roads, and even paths. Estimating the distance to march by their computation, it did not exceed nine miles, which we reckoned, dark as was the night, to make in two hours. Pushing on with all practicable dispatch, the first hour brought us to a large road: this the guide passed, leading the detachment again into a thick wood. Here we continued another hour; when, finding no road, doubts began to be entertained by the guides, which issued at last in attempting to return to the very road they had passed, it being concluded to be the one desired. Unhappily, they became bewildered, after changing their course, sometimes to the right, sometimes to the left; ever believing every change would surely bring us to our desired route, and yet always disappointed.

At length, with great anxiety, they proposed a halt, while themselves, accompanied by a few dragoons, should take different directions on our flanks in search of a house. This was readily acceded to, and the detachment dismounted, having not before halted. In the space of an hour one of them returned, and shortly after the other, both without success. It was now three o'clock, as well as we could make out the time by feeling the hour and minute-hands of our watches. Again we mounted, and again moved as our guides directed; more and more bewildered, and more and more distressed; persevering, and yet in vain. Lieutenant-Colonel Lee, apprehensive that the detachment might be carried too remote from the place assigned for junction in the morning with the militia under Campbell, again halted and dismounted, determining to wait for the light of day. It at last, to our great joy, appeared; and even then our guides were so completely out of their reckoning, as to detain us a long time in the woods before they were satisfied of the course to be taken.

By examining the bark of the trees, they ascertained the north, and thus recovered their knowledge of our locality. We were within a mile of the road we had crossed, and which turned out to be the very road desired. When we passed it the enemy were, as was afterward ascertained, two miles only on our right, as much bewildered as ourselves. For finding that they had not reached camp within the period expected, calculating time from distance; and knowing that New Garden must be upon their left; they took a cross-road which offered, and soon found themselves encompassed with new difficulties—fallen trees, and cross-ways as large as the road they had pursued—when the officer determined to halt and wait for day.

Lord Cornwallis became extremely alarmed for the safety of his baggage; dispatching parties of horse and foot in various directions to fall in with it, and detaching in the rear of these parties a strong corps to re-enforce the escort. Not one of the various detachments either met with the escort or with Lee. As soon as it was light, the officer having charge of the baggage retraced his steps; and shortly after gaining the road he had left in the night fell in with the last detachment sent by Lord Cornwallis, and with it safely reached the British camp; while Lieutenant-Colonel Lee and his harassed Legion, with his afflicted guides, much mortified, joined

Campbell.* Here he found orders from General Greene, now nearly prepared for forward movement, to return to camp. The March 14, British general remained in his new position; enjoying, 1781. without interruption, the wholesome supplies with which this fertile settlement abounded. Lee having proceeded toward the iron-works, found the American army on the 14th at Guilford Court-House, distant about twelve miles from the enemy, and was immediately advanced on the road toward the Quaker meeting-house, with orders to post himself within two or three miles of the court-house, and to resume his accustomed duties. Lieutenant Heard, of the Legion cavalry, was detached in the evening with a party of dragoons to place himself near the British camp, and to report from time to time such occurrences as might happen. About two in the morning, this officer communicated that a large body of horse were approaching the meeting-house, which was not more than six miles from our head-quarters, and near the point where the road from Deep River intersects the great road leading from Salisbury to Virginia. The intelligence received was instantly forwarded to the general, and Heard was directed to proceed with a few of his dragoons down the flank of the enemy to discover whether the British army was in motion, leaving his second to hold their front. Hear-

* Upon Lee's junction with Campbell, he found a packet from General Greene to Lord Cornwallis. which he sent off the ensuing morning by Cornet Middleton, of South Carolina, with a flag. The cornet reached the British picket just after the captain had breakfasted, and was politely invited to take breakfast, while the packet for his lordship should be sent to head-quarters, from whence a reply would be forwarded, if requisite, which Middleton could convey. Cornwallis was on his rounds, agreeably to his custom; and soon after Middleton had finished his breakfast, called at the picket, when he was informed by the captain, of the packet from General Greene, with his detention of the officer for the answer, if any was requisite. His lordship dismounting, entered the captain's quarters, where Cornet Middleton was introduced to him. Presuming from his dress that he belonged to Lee's Legion, he asked if he did not belong to that corps; and being answered in the affirmative, with a smile he significantly inquired where it had þeen the preceding night. The amiable Middleton, somewhat surprised and confounded at a query so unexpected, with evident confusion replied, that it had not been far off. Upon which Lord Cornwallis familiarly said, the object of his inquiry was unimportant, the matter to which it related being past, and that he asked the information to gratify his curiosity. Middleton, blushing, then told him that Lieutenant-Colonel Lee had received intelligence of his lordship's escort, with the baggage and stores, being lost in the night, and instantly proceeded in the expectation of putting them in the right course. This idea tickling the British general, he laughingly asked, "Well, why did he not do it?" "Because," says Middleton, "we got lost ourselves; traversing the roads all night. and, as it appeared afterward, within two miles of our much desired prize." Turning to his aids, Cornwallis said, "You see, I was not mistaken."

ing from Heard, agreeably to rule, every half hour, it was known that the enemy continued, though slowly, to approach; and at length he communicated that his various attempts to pass down the flank, as directed, had proved abortive, having been uniformly interrupted by patrols ranging far from the line of march; yet that he was persuaded that he heard the rumbling of wheels, which indicated a general movement. This being made known to General Greene, Lee was directed to advance with his cavalry, to bear down these interruptions, and to ascertain the truth. Expecting battle as soon as Heard's last information was received, the van was called to arms at four in the morning, and to take breakfast with all practicable haste. This had just been finished, when the last-mentioned order from the general was communicated. Lieutenant-Colonel Lee instantly mounted, and took the road to the enemy, at the head of the horse, having directed the infantry and rifle militia to follow, the first on his right, and the second on his left. The cavalry had not proceeded above two miles, when Lee was met by Lieutenant Heard and his party, who were retiring, followed leisurely by the enemy's horse. Wishing to approach nearer to Greene, and at all events to gain the proximity of the rifle militia and Legion infantry, lest the British army might be up, as was, suspected, Lee ordered the column to retire by troops, taking the proper distance for open evolution. The rear troop, under Rudolph, going off in full gallop, and followed in like manner by the centre troop under Eggleston, the British commandant flattered himself with converting this retrograde movement into rout, and pressed upon the front under Armstrong, still in a walk, it being necessary, to gain the open order required, that this officer should not change his pace. With him was Lieutenant-Colonel Lee, attentively watching the British progress. Finding that the charge did not affect Armstrong's troop, now the rear, the enemy emptied their pistols, and then raising a shout, pushed a second time upon Armstrong; who, remaining sullen as before, the leading section having nearly closed with us, drew up.

At this moment, Lee ordering a charge, the dragoons came instantly to the right about, and, in close column, rushed upon the foe. This meeting happened in a long lane, with very high curved fences on each side of the road, which admitted but one section in front. The charge was ordered by Lee, from conviction that he should trample his enemy under foot, if he dared to meet the shock; and thus gain an easy and complete victory. But only the front section of each corps closed, Tarleton sounding a retreat, the moment he discovered the column in charge. The whole of the enemy's section was dismounted, and many of the horses prostrated; * some of the dragoons killed, the rest made prisoners: not a single American soldier or horse injured. Tarleton retired with celerity ; and getting out of the lane, took an obscure way leading directly across the Salisbury road toward the British camp—while Lee, well acquainted with the country, followed the common route by the Quaker meeting-house, with a view to sever the British lieutenant-colonel from his army, by holding him well upon his left, and with the determination to gain his front, and then to press directly upon him with his condensed force, and thus place his horse between Tarleton and Cornwallis, presumed to be some distance behind. By endeavoring to take the whole detachment, he permitted the whole to escape ; whereas, had he continued to press on the rear, he must have taken many. As Lee, with his column in full speed, got up to the meeting-house, the British guards had just reached it ; and, displaying in a moment, gave the American cavalry a close and general fire.† The sun had just risen above the trees, and shining bright, the refulgence from the British muskets, as the soldiers presented, frightened Lee's horse so as to compel him to throw himself off. Instantly remounting another, he ordered a retreat. This manœuvre was speedily executed ; and, while the cavalry were retiring, the Legion infantry came running up with trailed arms, and opened a well-aimed fire upon the guards, which was

March 15, 1781.

* This is not stated with a view to extol one, or disparage the other corps ; but merely to state the fact. Lieutenant-Colonel Tarleton was obliged to use such horses as he could get ; whereas his opponent had the whole South to select out of. The consequence was, the British dragoons were mounted upon small, weak horses : those of the Legion on stout, active horses, and kept in the highest condition. When they met, the momentum of the one must crush the other ; and if the latter fled, he could not escape from his enemy, so excellently mounted. There was very little credit, with such superior means, due to the Americans upon victory ; whereas, the disgrace of defeat would have been extreme, and Lee's corps ought to have been decimated.

† This was not at *New Garden meeting-house*, which was twelve miles from Guilford, and from which Cornwallis had moved at the dawn of day. It was now about one hour after sunrise—"the sun had just risen above the trees;" and Cornwallis in his report, says this affair happened about four miles from Guilford ; that is, about eight miles from New Garden meeting-house. Colonel Howard confirms this estimate of distance, for he says the firing was distinctly heard at Guilford. It was probably, therefore, a meeting-house of less notoriety than that at New Garden.

Captain Tate, who commanded a company of Virginia militia at the battle of the Cowpens, and shared in the memorable charge of Howard, was attached to Lee's party on this occasion, and had his thigh broken.—ED.

followed in a few minutes by a volley from the riflemen under Colonel Campbell, who had taken post on the left of the infantry. The action became very sharp, and was bravely maintained on both sides.* The cavalry having formed again in column, and Lee being convinced, from the appearance of the guards, that Cornwallis was not far in the rear, drew off his infantry ; and, covering them from any attempt of the British horse, retired toward the American army. General Greene, being immediately advised of what had passed, prepared for battle ; not doubting, that the long avoided, now wished-for, hour was at hand.

Guilford Court-House, erected near the great State road, is situated on the brow of a declivity, which descends gradually with an undulating slope for about a half mile. It terminates in a small vale, intersected by a rivulet. On the right of the road is open ground with some few copses of wood until you gain the last step of the descent, where you see thick glades of brushy wood reaching across the rivulet ; on the left of the road from the court-house a deep forest of lofty trees, which terminates nearly in a line with the termination of the field on the opposite side of the road. Below this forest is a small piece of open ground, which appeared to have been cultivated in corn the preceding summer. This small field was long, but narrow, reaching close to the swamp bordering upon the rivulet.

In the road Captain Singleton was posted, in a line with the termination of the large field and the commencement of the small one, with two six-pounders within close shot of the rivulet, where the enemy, keeping the road, would pass. Across the road on his left, some few yards in his rear, the North Carolina militia were ranged, under Generals Butler and Eaton. At some distance behind this

* The British sustained a much heavier loss in killed and wounded than we did. His fire was innocent, overshooting the cavalry entirely ; whose caps and accoutrements were all struck with green twigs, cut by the British ball out of the large oaks in the meeting-house yard, under which the cavalry received the volley from the guards. Some of the infantry and riflemen were killed, and more wounded ; among them was Lieutenant Snowden, of the Legion infantry, who, with most of the wounded, was necessarily left on the field.
Lee, after the battle of Guilford, wrote to Lieutenant-Colonel Tarleton, asking his care of the wounded of the Legion and rifle corps ; it being common for officers, in the habit of meeting in the course of service, mutually to solicit such favors. Tarleton very politely answered by an amanuensis, that he would, with pleasure, execute the request ; and apologized for not writing himself ; saying that he had received a ball in his right hand in our morning rencounter. Captain Schutz, of the guards, was badly wounded, with other officers and soldiers of that corps.

line, the Virginia militia, led by the Generals Stevens and Lawson, were formed in a deep wood; the right flank of Stevens and the left flank of Lawson resting on the great road. The Continental infantry, consisting of four regiments, were drawn up in the rear of the Virginia militia, in the field to the right of the road; the two regiments of Virginia, conducted by Colonel Green and Lieutenant-Colonel Hawes, under the order of Brigadier Huger, composing the right; and the two of Maryland, led by Colonel Gunby, and Lieutenant-Colonel Ford, under the orders of Colonel Williams, composing the left. Of these, only the regiment of Gunby was veteran; the three others were composed of new soldiers, among whom were mingled a few who had served from the beginning of the war; but all the officers were experienced and approved. Greene, well informed of his enemy's inferiority in number, knew he could present but one line, and had therefore no reserve; considering it injudicious to weaken either of his lines by forming one. On the right, Lieutenant-Colonel Washington, with his cavalry, the old Delaware company, under the brave Captain Kirkwood, and Colonel Lynch, with a battalion of Virginia militia, was posted, with orders to hold safe that flank. For the same purpose, and with the same orders, Lieutenant-Colonel Lee was stationed on the left flank with his Legion and the Virginia riflemen commanded by Colonel Campbell.

In the rear line our small park was placed, with the exception of two sixes with Captain Singleton, who was now with the front line, but directed to repair to the rear as soon as the enemy should enter into close battle, and there take his assigned station.

As soon as the British van appeared, Singleton opened a cannonade upon it, convincing Lord Cornwallis of his proximity to the American army. Lieutenant McCleod, commanding the royal artillery, hastened up with two pieces, and stationing himself in the road near the rivulet, returned our fire. Thus the action commenced: the British general in the mean time arranging his army in order of battle. Although he could form but one full line, he took the resolution of attacking an able general advantageously posted, with a force more than double, a portion whereof he knew to be excellent, supported by cavalry of the first character. Yet such was his condition, that Lord Cornwallis was highly gratified with having it in his power, even on such terms, to appeal to the sword. The seventy-first, with the regiment of Bose, formed his right, under the order of Major-General Leslie; his left was composed of the twenty-

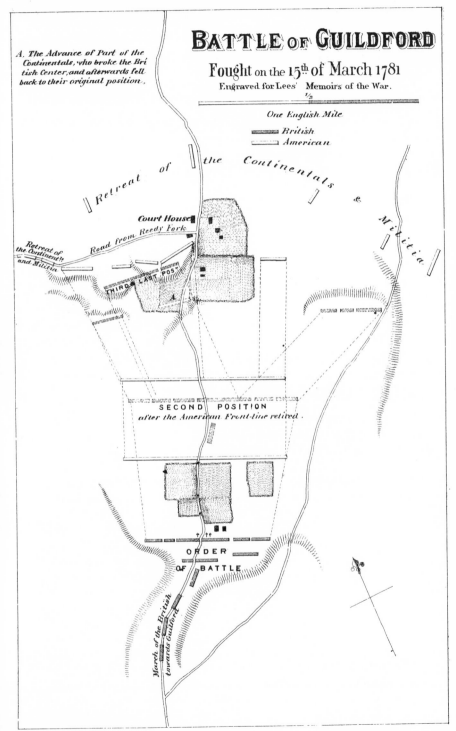

A. The Advance of Part of the Continentals, who broke the British Center, and afterwards fell back to their original position.

BATTLE of GUILDFORD

Fought on the 15th of March 1781

Engraved for Lees' Memoirs of the War.

One English Mile

British
American

Retreat of the Continentals & Militia

Court House

Road from Reedy Fork

Retreat of the Continentls. and Militia

THIRD & LAST POST

SECOND POSITION
after the American Front-line retired.

ORDER

OF BATTLE

March of the British towards Guilford

U.P. Co. No. 4 Bond. St.

third and thirty-third regiments, led by Lieutenant-Colonel Webster.

The royal artillery, directed by Lieutenant McCleod, and supported by the light infantry of the guards and the yagers, moved along the road in the centre. The first battalion of guards, under Lieutenant-Colonel Norton, gave support to the right; while Brigadier O'Hara, with the grenadiers and second battalion of guards, maintained the left. Lieutenant-Colonel Tarleton, with the cavalry in column, formed the reserve on the road, in the rear of the artillery.

The moment the head of the British column passed the rivulet, the different corps, in quick step, deployed to the right and left, and soon were ranged in line of battle.

Leslie instantly advanced upon the North Carolina militia. These troops were most advantageously posted under cover of a rail fence, along the margin of the woods; and Campbell's riflemen and the Legion infantry connected in line with the North Carolina militia, turning with the fence as it approached the rivulet, raked by their fire the right of the British wing, entirely uncovered; the Legion cavalry, in the woods, in a column pointing to the angular corner of the fence ready to support the militia on its right, or the infantry of the Legion to its left. The appearance in this quarter was so favorable, that sanguine hopes were entertained by many of the officers, from the manifest advantage possessed, of breaking down the enemy's right before he approached the fence; and the troops exhibited the appearance of great zeal and alacrity.

Lieutenant-Colonel Webster took his part with his usual ability, moving upon the Virginia militia, who were not so advantageously posted as their comrades of North Carolina, yet gave every indication of maintaining their ground with obstinacy. Stevens, to give efficacy to this temper, and stung with the recollection of their inglorious flight in the battle of Camden, had placed a line of sentinels in his rear, with orders to shoot every man that flinched. When the enemy came within long shot, the American line, by order, began to fire. Undismayed, the British continued to advance; and having reached a proper distance, discharged their pieces and rent the air with shouts. To our infinite distress and mortification, the North Carolina militia took to flight, a few only of Eaton's brigade excepted, who clung to the militia under Campbell; which, with the Legion, manfully maintained their ground. Every effort was made by the Generals Butler and Eaton, assisted by Colo-

nel Davie, commissary general, with many of the officers of every
grade, to stop this unaccountable panic ; for not a man of the corps
had been killed, or even wounded. Lieutenant-Colonel Lee joined
in the attempt to rally the fugitives, threatening to fall upon them
with his cavalry. All was vain; so thoroughly confounded were
these unhappy men, that, throwing away arms, knapsacks, and even
canteens, they rushed like a torrent headlong through the woods.
In the mean time the British right became so injured by the keen
and advantageous contest still upheld by Campbell and the Legion,
as to render it necessary for Leslie to order into line the support
under Lieutenant-Colonel Norton, a decided proof of the difficult
condition to which he must have been soon reduced, had the North
Carolina militia done their duty. The chasm in our order of battle,
produced by this base desertion, was extremely detrimental in its
consequences ; for, being seized by Leslie, it threw the corps of
Lee out of combination with the army, and also exposed it to destruction. General Leslie, turning the regiment of Bose, with the
battalion of guards, upon Lee, pressed forward himself with the
seventy-first to cover the right of Webster, now keenly engaged
with the Virginia militia ; and seized the most advantageous position, which he preserved throughout the battle. Noble was the
stand of the Virginia militia ; Stevens and Lawson, with their faithful brigades, contending for victory against the best officer in the
British army, at the head of two regiments distinguished for intrepidity and discipline ; and so firmly did they maintain the battle
(secured on their flank by the position taken by Washington, who,
anxious to contribute to the aid of his brave countrymen, introduced
Lynch's battalion of riflemen upon the flank of Webster, already
fully engaged in front), that Brigadier O'Hara, with the grenadiers
and second battalion of the guards, were brought into the line in
support of Webster. As soon as this assistance was felt, Lieutenant-
Colonel Webster, turning the thirty-third upon Lynch, relieved
his flank of all annoyance ; and instantly O'Hara, advancing with
the remainder of the left wing with fixed bayonets, aided by the
seventy-first under Leslie, compelled, first Lawson's brigade, and
then Stevens's, to abandon the contest. Unhappily, the latter general received a ball through his thigh, which accelerated not a little the retreat of his brigade. The militia no longer presented
even the show of resistance ; nevertheless, such had been the
resolution with which the corps under Lee, sustaining itself on the
left against the first battalion of guards and the regiment of Bose,

and so bravely did the Virginia militia support the action on the right, that, notwithstanding the injurious desertion of the first line without exchanging a shot, every corps of the British army, except the cavalry, had been necessarily brought into battle, and many of them had suffered severely. It cannot be doubted, had the North Carolina militia rivalled that of Virginia upon this occasion, that Lord Cornwallis must have been defeated ; and even now, the Continental troops being in full vigor, and our cavalry unhurt, there was good ground to expect victory.

Persevering in his determination to die or conquer, the British general did not stop to concentrate his force, but pressed forward to break our third line. The action, never intermitting on his right, was still sternly maintained by Colonel Norton's battalion of guards and the regiment of Bose, with the rifle militia and the Legion infantry ; so that this portion of the British force could not be brought to bear upon the third line, supported by Colonel Washington at the head of the horse, and Kirkwood's Delaware company. General Greene was well pleased with the present prospect, and flattering himself with a happy conclusion, passed along the line, exhorting his troops to give the finishing blow. Webster, hastening over the ground occupied by the Virginia militia, sought with zeal the Continental line, and presently approached its right wing. Here was posted the first regiment of Maryland, commanded by Colonel Gunby, having under him Lieutenant-Colonel Howard. The enemy rushed into close fire ; but so firmly was he received by this body of veterans, supported by Hawes's regiment of Virginia and Kirkwood's company of Delawares (being weakened in his contest with 'Stevens's brigade, and, as yet unsupported, the troops to his right not having advanced, from inequality of ground or other impediments), that with equal rapidity he was compelled to recoil from the shock.

Recrossing a ravine in his rear, Webster occupied an advantageous height, waiting for the approach of the rest of the line. Very soon Lieutenant-Colonel Stuart, with the first battalion of guards, appeared in the open field, followed successively by the remaining corps, all anxious to unite in the last effort. Stuart, discovering Ford's regiment of Maryland on the left of the first regiment, and a small copse of wood concealing Gunby, pushed forward upon Ford, who was strengthened by Captain Finley with two six-pounders. Colonel Williams, commanding the Maryland line, charmed with the late demeanor of the first regiment, hastened toward the second, expecting a similar display, and prepared to combine his whole force with all practicable celerity ; when, unaccountably, the second regiment gave way, abandoning to the enemy the two field-pieces.

Gunby being left free by Webster's recession, wheeled to his left upon Stuart, who was pursuing the flying second regiment. Here the action was well fought ; each corps manfully struggling for victory ; when Lieutenant-Colonel Washington, who had, upon the discomfiture of the Virginia militia, placed himself upon the flank of the Continentals, agreeably to the order of battle, pressed forward with his cavalry.

Stuart beginning to give ground, Washington fell upon him sword in hand, followed by Howard with fixed bayonets, now commanding the regiment in consequence of Gunby being dismounted. This combined operation was irresistible. Stuart fell by the sword of Captain Smith, of the first regiment ; the two field-pieces were recovered ; his battalion driven back with slaughter, its remains being saved by the British artillery, which, to stop the ardent pursuit of Washington * and Howard, opened upon friends as well as foes ; for Cornwallis, seeing the vigorous advance of these two officers, determined to arrest their progress, though every ball levelled at them must pass through the flying guards. Checked by this cannonade, and discovering one regiment passing from the woods on the enemy's right, across the road, and another advancing in front, Howard believing himself to be out of support, retired, followed by Washington.

To these two regiments (which were the seventy-first, which General Leslie had so judiciously conducted after the ignominious flight of the North Carolina militia, and the twenty-third, the right of Webster) Brigadier O'Hara, though grievously wounded, brought the remnant of the first battalion of guards, whom he in person rallied ; and, with the grenadiers, filled up the interval between the left and right wing.

Webster, the moment Stuart appeared in the field, putting Ford to flight, recrossed the ravine and attacked Hawes's regiment of

---

* " After passing through the guards into the open ground, Washington, who always led the van, perceived an officer surrounded by several persons, appearing to be aids-de-camp. Believing this to be Lord Cornwallis, he rushed on with the hope of making him prisoner, when he was arrested by an accident. His cap fell from his head, and as he leaped to the ground to recover it, the officer leading his column was shot through the body and rendered incapable of managing his horse. The horse wheeled round with his rider, and galloped off the field : he was followed by all the cavalry, who supposed this movement had been directed."—MARSHALL's *Life of Washington.*

Virginia, supported by Kirkwood's company. The action was renewed in this quarter with vigor; the seventy-first and twenty-third, connected in their centre by the first battalion and grenadiers of the guards, having at the same time moved upon Howard. Meanwhile the long-impending contest upon the enemy's right continued without intermission; each of the combatants getting gradually nearer to the flanks of their respective armies, to close with which was the desired object of both. At length Lieutenant-Colonel Norton, with his battalion of guards, believing the regiment of Bose adequate to the contest, and close to the great road to which he had been constantly inclining, pressed forward to join the seventy-first. Relieved from this portion of the enemy, Lieutenant-Colonel Lee dispensed with his cavalry, heretofore held in the rear to cover retreat in case of disaster, ordering it to close with the left of the Continental line, and there to act until it should receive further orders. Upon Bose the rifle and the Legion infantry now turned with increased animation, and with confidence of success. Major De Buy, of the regiment of Bose, continued to defend himself with obstinacy; but pressed as he was by superior force, he at length gave ground, and fell back into the rear of Norton. Still annoying him with the rifle corps under Campbell, Lee hastened with his infantry to rejoin his cavalry upon the flank of the Continentals, the point so long and vainly contended for. In his route, he found the battalion of guards under Norton in possession of the height first occupied by Lawson's brigade of Virginia militia. With this corps, again the Legion infantry renewed action; and supported by the van company of the riflemen, its rear still waiting upon Major De Buy, drove it back upon the regiment of Bose. Every obstacle now removed, Lee pressed forward, followed by Campbell, and joined his horse close by Guilford Court-House.

Having seen the flight of the second regiment of Maryland, preceded by that of the North Carolina militia, the corps of Lee severed from the army, and considering it, if not destroyed, at least thrown out of battle by Leslie's judicious seizure of the interval produced by the panic of the North Carolina militia, and in all probability not able to regain its station in the line—Greene, immutable in the resolution never to risk annihilation of his force, and adverting to his scanty supply of ammunition, determined, when he found all his personal efforts, seconded by Colonels Williams and Carrington, to rally the second regiment of Maryland nugatory, to provide for retreat. Colonel Green, one of the bravest of brave soldiers, with his regiment of Virginia, was drawn off without having tasted of battle, and ordered to a given point in the rear for the security of this movement.*   Had General Greene known how severely his enemy was crippled, and that the corps under Lee had fought their way to his Continental line, he would certainly have continued the conflict ; and in all probability would have made it a drawn day, if not have secured to himself the victory. Ignorant of these facts, and finding Webster returned to battle—O'Hara, with his rallied guards in line—and General Leslie, with the seventy-first connected with them on the right, and followed, as he well knew, by the remnant of his wing—he persevered in his resolution, and directed a retreat, which was performed deliberately under cover of Colonel Green.   General Huger, who had, throughout the action, given his chief attention to the regiment of Hawes, the only one of the two constituting his brigade ever engaged, and which, with Kirkwood's company, was still contending with Lieutenant-Colonel Webster, now drew it off by order of the general ; while Colonel Williams effected the same object in his quarter ; both abandoning our artillery, as their horses had been mostly killed ; and General Greene preferred leaving his artillery, to risking the loss of lives in drawing them off by hand. Just after this had taken place, Lieutenant-Colonel Lee joined his cavalry at the court-house ; and, unpursued, retired down the great Salisbury road, until a cross-road enabled him to pass over to the line of retreat. The seventy-first and twenty-third regiments, supported by the cavalry of Tarleton, followed our army with the show of falling upon it ; but the British general soon recalled them, and General Greene, undisturbed, was left to pursue his retreat. He halted first

---

* Colonel Green was much dissatisfied with the general's selection of his regiment for this service, though esteemed among the most honorable—so anxious was the veteran officer to be led at once into keen conflict.

When it was announced upon the first of the retreat, that the British were close advancing, he became better humored ; but soon the pursuit was discontinued, and his sourness returned. His friends would often console him by stating his selection as an evidence of the confidence reposed in him as a soldier. This would not satisfy the colonel, who never failed to reply that he did not like such sort of distinction ; and he hoped the general would, upon the next occasion, attach to some other regiment the honor of covering his retreat. Getting to the general's ear, he took the first opportunity of telling the colonel, whom he much esteemed and respected, that he had heard he did not relish the post assigned to his regiment the other day. "No, that I did not," replied the old colonel. "Well," rejoined Greene, "be patient : you shall have the first blow the next time." This delighted him, and he always reckoned upon the promised boon with pleasure.

three miles from the field of battle, to collect stragglers and fugitives, and afterward retired leisurely to his former position at the iron-works.

The pertinacity with which the rifle corps of Campbell and the Legion infantry had maintained the battle on the enemy's right induced Lord Cornwallis to detach the British horse to that quarter. The contest had long been ebbing before this corps arrived; and Lieutenant-Colonel Tarleton found only a few resolute marksmen in the rear of Campbell, who continued firing from tree to tree. The appearance of cavalry determined these brave fellows to retire and overtake their corps.

Thus the battle terminated. It was fought on the 15th of March, a day never to be forgotten by the southern section of the United States. The atmosphere calm, and illumined with a cloudless sun; the season rather cold than cool; the body braced and the mind high toned by the state of the weather. Great was the stake, willing were the generals* to put it to hazard, and their armies seemed to support with ardor the decision of their respective leaders.

The British general fought against two to one;† but he had

---

* Never did two generals exert themselves more than did these rival leaders upon this occasion. Long withheld from each other by the sagacious conduct of Greene, until he acquired sufficient strength to risk battle, they seized with ardor the opportunity at length presented of an appeal to the sword. This decision was wise in both; and every step taken by the one and by the other, as well in preparation for battle as in the battle, demonstrated superior abilities.

Greene's position was masterly, as was the ground selected for the combat peculiarly adapted to his views and troops. Cornwallis saw the difficulties thrown in his way by the skill of his antagonist, and diminished their weight by the disposition of his force, as far as it was practicable. Having done all that was possible to accomplish their purpose, no attention was omitted, no peril avoided in the course of the action, to produce the desired issue. They exposed their persons, unconscious of danger, and self-devoted to national triumph. Upon one occasion Greene was nearly passed by a body of the enemy within thirty paces of him, when Major Pendleton, one of his aids, discovered them. Luckily a copse of woods intervened, which covered Greene's return to our line.

Soon afterward, Cornwallis, seeing the discomfiture of one battalion of the guards, repaired in person to direct the measures for the recovery of the lost ground; when, by the dauntless exposure of himself, he was placed in extreme danger. It was upon this occasion he ordered his artillery to open through his flying guards, to stop Washington and Howard. Brigadier O'Hara remonstrated, by exclaiming, that the fire would destroy themselves. "True," replied Cornwallis; "but this is a necessary evil which we must endure, to arrest impending destruction."

† Our field return, a few days before the action, rates Greene's army at four thousand four hundred and forty-nine, horse, foot, and artillery; of which, one thousand six hundred and seventy were Continentals; the residue militia. The enemy rate us at upward of five thousand. He is mistaken: we did not reach that number, though some call us seven thousand.

greatly the advantage in the quality of his soldiers. General Greene's veteran infantry being only the first regiment of Maryland, the company of Delaware, under Kirkwood (to whom none could be superior), and the Legion infantry; altogether making on that day not more than five hundred rank and file. The second regiment of Maryland and the two regiments of Virginia were composed of raw troops; but their officers were veteran, and the soldier is soon made fit for battle by experienced commanders. Uniting these corps to those recited, and the total (as per official return) amounted to one thousand four hundred and ninety; so that even estimating our old and new troops in one class, still our infantry was considerably less than his lordship's. The North Carolina militia, as has been seen, abandoned us; and we had only the Virginia militia and the rifle corps under Colonel Campbell and Colonel Lynch to balance the enemy's superiority over our regular infantry. In artillery, the two armies were nearly equal, as they may be also considered in cavalry; the superiority in number, on the part of the British, being counterbalanced by our excellence in quality.

The slaughter was prodigious on the side of the enemy, making, in killed and wounded, nearly one-third of his army. The official report states the loss to amount to five hundred and thirty-two men, of whom ninety-three were found dead on the field of battle.

Lieutenant-Colonel Stuart, of the guards, and Lieutenant O'Hara, of the royal artillery, brother to the general, with many other officers, were killed.

The Brigadiers O'Hara and Howard, Lieutenant-Colonels Webster and Tarleton, the Captains Stuart and Maynard,* Goodryche, Mait-

---

Lord Cornwallis's army engaged is put down at one thousand four hundred and forty-nine infantry; the cavalry has generally been estimated at three hundred. Allowing the artillery to make two hundred, it will bring the British force nearly to two thousand, probably the real number at Guilford Court-House. Lieutenant-Colonel Hamilton, with his own regiment, one hundred infantry of the line, and twenty dragoons, was left with the baggage sent off on the evening of the 14th to Bell's mill. The British force *in toto* may be put down at two thousand four hundred: one hundred less than it was when Lord Cornwallis destroyed his baggage at Ramsour's mill, notwithstanding the companies of infantry raised while he lay at Hillsborough, and other small accessions.—See Appendix, S and S.

* We shall here relate an anecdote of the late Captain Maynard, of the guards. He was naturally of a cheerful disposition and great hilarity, and in several actions during the course of the war, he had shown great gallantry; but a certain presentiment of his fate on the day of the action at Guilford possessed his mind, which presentiment was too fatally realized. While the troops were marching to form the line of battle, he became gloomy, and gave way to despondency. Not less than two or three times did he tell Colonel Norton, who

land, Schutz, Peter, and Lord Dunglas, with several subalterns, were wounded; as were Captains Wilmonsky and Eichenbrodt, of the regiment of Bose, with five subalterns.

Our loss was very disproportionate;* only fourteen officers and three hundred and twelve rank and file of the Continental troops killed, wounded, and missing. As few prisoners were made, it is probable that those returned as missing were killed. Among the first was Major Anderson, of the regiment of Maryland, much esteemed and highly regretted; with Captain ―――― and three subalterns. Among the last was General Huger, commanding the Virginia brigade. Our loss of militia was still less. The four captains

＊　　＊　　＊　　＊　　＊　　＊　　＊

and seventeen privates killed; Brigadier Stevens, Major ――――, three captains, eight subalterns, and sixty privates wounded. Many were missing, as is always the case with militia after battle; but they generally are to be found safe at their own firesides. General Greene, after reaching Troublesome Creek, arrayed himself again for battle; so persuaded was he that the British general would follow up his blow, and so well satisfied with his own condition,

commanded the battalion, that he felt himself very uncomfortable, and did not like the business at all. Colonel, now the honorable Major-General Norton, endeavored to laugh him out of his melancholy ideas, but in vain; for even after the cannonade began, he reiterated the forebodings of what he conceived was to happen. Early in the action he received a wound in his leg. Unable to proceed, he requested Mr. Wilson, the adjutant of the guards, to lend him his horse, that he might ride on with the battalion; and when in the act of mounting, another shot went through his lungs, and incapacitated him from proceeding. After being conveyed in a litter to Wilmington, and there lingering a few days, he died of his wound, greatly regretted.—Stedman.

Similar instances of fatal presentiment are on record; among them that of General La Harpe, which is thus mentioned by Bonaparte in his Memoirs (vol. 3, Montholon, pp. 209 and 210): "C'était un officier d'une bravoure distingué. On a remarqué que, pendant le combat de Fombo, tout le soir qui a précédé sa mort, il avait été fort préoccupé, très abattu, ne donnant point d'ordres, privé, en quelque sort, de ses facultés ordinaires, tout à fait dominé par un présentiment funeste." He was killed by a mistaken fire from his own pickets, while in command of an advanced division of the French army, just previous to the battle of Lodi, in May, 1796. A similar anecdote is related of Sir Thomas Picton, at the battle of Waterloo.—Ed.

* The disproportion in loss on this day is readily to be accounted for. We had great advantage in the ground, and were sheltered in various points until the enemy approached very near; while he was uncovered, and exposed from his first step to his last. We had spent the previous day in ease, and the night in rest; he had been preparing during the day, and marching part of the night. We were acquainted with wood and tree fighting; he ignorant of both. And lastly, we were trained to take aim and fire low, he was not so trained; and from this cause, or from the composition of his cartridge (too much powder for the lead), he always overshot.

though considerably reduced by the flight of the North Carolina militia, and by the voluntary and customary return of portions of that from Virginia. But the enemy was in no condition to advance. The name of victory was the sole enjoyment of the conqueror, the substance belonged to the vanquished. Truly did the eloquent Fox exclaim in the British House of Commons, " Another such victory would destroy the British army."

On no occasion, in any part of the world, was British valor more heroically displayed. The officers of every grade did their duty; and each corps surpassed its past, though arduous exertions, in this terrible conflict. But the advantage of ground, the weight of numbers, the skill of the general, and the determined courage of such portions of the American army as fought, presented obstacles not to be surmounted by inferior force. So maimed was the British army, that notwithstanding the flight of the North Carolina militia, had the second regiment of Maryland acted like the first, little doubt can exist but that Lord Cornwallis must have shared the fate on this day which he experienced afterward. Afflicting were the sensations of the British general, when he looked into his own situation after the battle. Nearly a third of his force slaughtered ; many of his best officers killed or wounded ; and that victory for which he had so long toiled, and at length gained, bringing in its train not one solitary benefit. No body of loyalists crowding around his standards ; no friendly convoys pouring in supplies; his wants pressing, and his resources distant. The night succeeding this day of blood was rainy, dark, and cold ; the dead unburied, the wounded unsheltered, the groans of the dying and the shrieks of the living, cast a deeper shade over the gloom of nature. The victorious troops, without tents and without food, participated in sufferings which they could not relieve.* The ensuing morning was spent in performing the last offices to the dead, and in providing comfort for the wounded. In executing these sad duties, the British general regarded with equal attention friends and foes. As soon as this service was over, he put his army in motion for New Garden, where his rear-guard, with his baggage, met him. All his wounded, incapable of moving (about seventy in number), he left to the humanity of General Greene.

---

* Fatigued as the British troops were, by a night march, and the late action, after a small rest they were employed in collecting the wounded of both armies, which were indiscriminately taken the best care of the situation would admit; but having no tents, and the houses being few, many of both armies were necessarily exposed to the deluge of rain, which fell during the night; and it was said that not less than fifty died before morning.

Here he issued a proclamation, depicting in strong colors the splendid victory obtained by the British army on the 15th; and calling upon the liege subjects of his Britannic majesty to come forward at this important juncture, to contribute their aid in completing the restoration of that happy government, not less the object of their hearts, than the guard of their lives and property. This done, his lordship proceeded, on the 18th, by easy marches to Cross Creek, the centre of the Highland settlement, and convenient to Wilmington, then in possession of Major Craig, as before mentioned, and the depot of supplies for the royal army.

The retreat of the British general evinced, unequivocally, his crippled condition. No consideration, but conviction of his inability to improve the victory he had gained, would have deterred a general less enterprising than Lord Cornwallis from giving full effect to the advantage his skill and courage had procured. Confident, as was General Greene, that his antagonist had suffered severely, he had not conceived his situation to be so impotent as it now appeared to be. Prepared to renew the combat, had the enemy sought it, he now determined to pursue the retiring foe, and bring him to action before he could gain his point of safety;* but this resolution was unhappily for several days delayed through the want of ammunition, with which it was necessary first to supply himself. In the mean time he detached Lieutenant-Colonel Lee with his Legion, and the militia rifle corps under Campbell, to hang upon the rear of the retreating general, lest the inhabitants of the region through which he passed might presume that our army had been rendered incapable of further resistance, and might flock to the royal standard.

The advanced corps soon came up with the British army, which had proceeded very slowly, with a view of cherishing its numerous wounded by the collection of every comfort which the country

---

Nine o'clock P. M., March 18th, 1781.

Lieutenant-Colonel Lee :—

Dear Sir,—I have this moment got your note. I am perfectly agreed with you in opinion, that to attack the enemy on their march will be best. I have written to Colonel Williams to that purpose.

It will be next to impossible to get the militia to send away their horses. They are so attached to this mode of carrying on the war, that they will not listen to any other. Frequent attempts have been made without effect. However, we can try the experiment. Sound some of the more sensible on the subject. My letter must be short, as I write in pain,

Your affectionate, &c.,

N. Greene.

afforded, as well as to avoid fatigue, which the debilitated state of the troops could not bear. Upon the appearance of the light troops this system was in a degree abandoned; Lord Cornwallis, conceiving it probable that the American army was not far in the rear, seeking battle, which his situation now made him anxious to avoid. At length he reached Ramsay's mill, on Deep River, where he halted a few days to renew his humane exertions for the comfort of his wounded, and to collect, if possible, provisions; the country between this place and Cross Creek being sterile and sparsely settled. During this delay his lordship threw a bridge over the river, by which he might readily pass as he moved down on its northern bank. Nothing material occurred between the adverse van and rear corps; nor did the British general even make any serious attempt to drive from his neighborhood the corps of Lee; so sorely did he continue to feel the effects of his dear-bought victory.

General Greene lost not a moment in moving from his camp on the Troublesome, after the arrival of his military stores ; and notwithstanding the inclemency of the weather and the deepness of the roads, he pressed forward from day to day by forced marches ;* but interruptions, unavoidable, occasionally delayed his progress. When the quartermaster-general assumed the duties of his station at Guilford Court-House, as has been before remarked, all that department of the army was entirely deranged; and such had been the rapid succession of keen and active service, that with all his laborious application, he had not been able to introduce into full operation his own system, although he had contrived to afford the means of prompt motion to the army. New duties became, from the necessity of the case, connected with his department. Without

---

* HEAD-QUARTERS, 11 *o'clock*, *March* 21*st*, 1781.

LIEUTENANT-COLONEL LEE :—

DEAR SIR,—Your letter dated at New Garden, yesterday, has this moment come to hand. Our army marched yesterday in the direct route, for Magee's Ordinary, near the head-waters of Rocky River, which will be twelve miles from Bell's mill. We expect to get about two or three miles beyond Passley to-night. We have got provisions to draw, cartridges to make, and several other matters to attend to, which will oblige us to halt a little earlier than common.

I beg you will try to forward me the best intelligence you can get of the enemy's situation this morning, and whether they move or not.

I mean to fight the enemy again, and wish you to have your Legion and riflemen ready for action on the shortest notice. If in the mean time you can attempt any thing which promises an advantage, put it in execution. Lord Cornwallis must be soundly beaten before he will relinquish his hold.

I am, dear sir, &c.,

NATHANIEL GREENE.

money to purchase, the subsistence of the troops depended upon compulsory collection from the country through which the army marched; and Colonel Davie could with difficulty procure within one day enough for that day; so that the general would be often obliged to extend or contract his march to correspond with the fluctuating supply of provisions. Our difficulties in this line were considerably increased, as the British army had preceded us; and nothing but the gleanings of an exhausted country were left for our subsistence. To settlements which had from their distance escaped the British foraging parties, it became necessary for our commissary general to resort; and the conveyance to camp of supply, when collected, devolved upon the quartermaster-general.

Lieutenant-Colonel Carrington shrunk not from this new duty; and by his zeal and perseverance contributed greatly to remove an obstacle which had not only retarded the advance of Greene, but sometimes menaced the necessity of a temporary separation of his troops, by detaching them to different districts for the procurement of food. The usual method of providing magazines had been necessarily avoided, inasmuch as the enemy, heretofore our superior, would alone have received the benefit of such arangement. Surmounting all impediments, Greene at length approached Ramsay's mill; but not until Lord Cornwallis had completed his bridge. The American general, having informed Lieutenant-Colonel Lee of the delays to which he was subjected, with directions to obstruct the completion of the bridge, if practicable—that officer moved from the rear of the enemy in the night, and, taking a circuitous route, passed the river ten miles above the British position, with a determination to dislodge the party stationed on its western side for the protection of that head of the bridge. This enterprise was deemed of easy execution, as both the celerity of the movement and the darkness of the night prevented his lordship penetrating the design, and as only two hundred men under a major constituted the guard. Defeating this body by a sudden blow, we might have, in a little time, by axes and fire, so far damaged the work, as to have produced one day's further halt, which would have afforded General Greene sufficient time to come up. But well timed as the march of the light corps was, which with much alacrity moved upon the detachment, the major having been re-enforced in the course of the night, produced the abandonment of the enterprise. On the subsequent day the British general decamped; and, passing the river, took the route toward Cross Creek. The Legion of Lee, with the rifle corps of Campbell, entering into his late camp as the rear-guard drew off, prevented the destruction of the bridge. On the subsequent day, the 28th, General Greene reached Ramsay's mill; having failed in his anxious wish to bring the British general to action, in consequence of waiting for ammunition, and the difficulty with which subsistence was obtained.

It was in vain to persevere in pursuit, as the country through which the British general marched, until he reached Cross Creek settlement, was so barren and thinly settled as to forbid every hope of obtaining the requisite supplies. Dismissing all his militia except a small corps from North Carolina, Greene took the decision of reposing his wearied troops in this position, and preparing for the renewal of active service by arrangements tending to secure adequate subsistence.

The campaign so far presents the undulation common to war. It opened with the victory of the Cowpens,—an event very propitious to the United States, which was followed by our perilous retreat through North Carolina, when for many days the fate of Greene and his army hung in mournful suspense; and after a grand display of military science in marches, countermarches, and positions, in consequence of the bold return of the American army into North Carolina, concluded with our defeat at Guilford Court-House. Replenished in military stores, grown stronger by defeat, and bolder from disaster, the American general is now seen seeking with keener appetite a renewal of the conflict, while the British conqueror sedulously and succesfully avoids it.

During this trying period, which closely occupied the respective generals, the claims of humanity were not unattended to. The establishment of a cartel, to operate as occasion might require, had long engaged the heart of Greene, and was not unacceptable to Cornwallis. The first was actuated, not only by his disposition to restore to their country our many prisoners, but to cancel obligations, which the inhabitants of the Southern States deemed binding, though subversive of the duty which every citizen owes to his country. In the course of British success in South Carolina, a usage prevailed of taking the paroles of the inhabitants in the manner practised often with commissioned officers when prisoners. In consequence of this custom, the whole population in the conquered States continuing at home, because incapacitated from serving against the enemy : a condition so agreeable to the harassed, the wavering, and the timid, as to be sought with solicitude, and preserved with zeal. Greene determined in his negotiations for the exchange of prisoners to abrogate obligations resulting from a practice entirely inadmissible. He consequently instructed his commissioner, Lieutenant-Colonel Carrington, to repel the recognition of this pernicious and unwarrantable usage, by urging the incapability of an individual to renounce his social obligations by contract with the enemy, unless sanctioned by a public officer. The honorable Captain Broderick, aid-de-camp to Earl Cornwallis, being appointed on the part of his lordship, met Carrington on the 12th of March; when, after comparing their credentials, the object of the meeting was taken up. It was soon discerned, that the article respecting private paroles, enjoined on his commissioner by General Greene, had introduced an unexpected principle; and being not contemplated by the British commander, his commissioner was not prepared to decide upon it.

Carrington and Broderick agreed therefore to separate for the present, and to meet again as soon as Lord Cornwallis should make up his decision upon the proposition submitted.

The battle of Guilford following three days after, the negotiation became postponed; nor was it resumed until the latter end of April; when Lieutenant-Colonel Carrington, and Captain Cornwallis, of the thirty-third (substituted for Broderick), entered upon it with a disposition, by mutual concessions, to conclude the long-spun discussion. It was, after some time, happily accomplished; Carrington having ingrafted in the cartel the following clause: " That no non-commissioned officer, or private, admitted to parole, shall be considered as a prisoner of war, but finally liberated, unless admitted to such parole on the faith of some commissioned officer." The proceedings of the commissioners were ratified by the respective generals, and a general exchange of prisoners soon after took place.

Lord Cornwallis halted at Cross Creek, where, staying a few days, the friendly Highland settlement zealously contributed from its small stock, every thing necessary for his army which the district afforded. Decamping, he proceeded to Wilmington; to which place he was obliged to go, contrary to his original plan, because he found the country about Cross Creek too poor to subsist him; and because his troops were suffering for many necessaries to be obtained only in his abundant magazines at Wilmington.

During the march from Cross Creek, several of the British officers died of their wounds received at Guilford Court-House. Among them were Lieutenant-Colonel Webster, of the thirty-third, and Captain Maynard * of the guards. The first escaped, as we have before seen, unhurt, when crossing the Reedy Fork on horseback, in face of a chosen party of marksmen, devoting their undivided attention to his destruction ; and the last was that officer, who, by his conversation with his commandant, Lieutenant-Colonel Norton, on the eve of the battle, so strongly manifested a presentiment of his fate.

To be first among the officers in the army under Lord Cornwallis, must be admitted to be no slight distinction ; and this station had been long assigned with one voice to the gallant Webster. To this superiority in arms was combined the winning amiability which virtue in heart and virtue in habit never fail to produce, especially when united to the embellishment of literature and the manners of polished life. Such a loss was deeply and sincerely deplored. His body was committed to the grave with every honor and attention, accompanied with tears of admiration and affection, in the small village of Elizabethtown, where he died.

Lieutenant-Colonel Tarleton, in his " Campaigns," very handsomely depicts his worth, when he declares, that he " united all the virtues of civil life to the gallantry and professional knowledge of a soldier ; " and Lord Cornwallis has left an imperishable monument, in his letter to the father of the deceased (so long as the tenderest feeling of sorrow, expressed in language which can only flow from the heart, shall be admired), of his unrivalled respect for the departed hero :—" It gives me great concern to undertake a task, which is not only a bitter renewal of my own grief, but must be a violent shock to an affectionate parent.

" You have for your support, the assistance of religion, good sense, and the experience of the uncertainty of human happiness. You have for your satisfaction, that your son fell nobly in the cause of his country, honored and lamented by all his fellow-soldiers ; that he led a life of honor and virtue, which must secure to him everlasting happiness.

" When the keen sensibility of the passions begins to subside, these considerations will give you real comfort. That the Almighty may give you fortitude to bear this severest of strokes, is the earnest wish of your companion in affliction."

All who know the value of friendship will feel in their own breasts

---

* Stedman says Captain M. died at Wilmington. See note, p. 356, ante.—ED.

how much Lord Cornwallis must have been affected by the loss of Webster. Bred up under him, the lieutenant-colonel commandant of the thirty-third (Cornwallis's regiment), every opportunity, with full time, had been afforded for thorough mutual understanding of character. Alike virtuous, amiable, and intrepid, mutual affection had reared upon the foundation of their hearts a temple sacred to honor and to friendship.

Throughout six campaigns the public service derived from Lieutenant-Colonel Webster those signal benefits which never fail to result from the friendship of men high in station and in genius. Introduced by his illustrious friend to posts of difficulty and consequence, he drew upon himself, by his exemplary discharge of duty, universal admiration. At Quibbletown, in New Jersey, during the eventful winter of 1776-7, he commanded on the line of communication between Brunswick and New York, and preserved it safe in spite of the many attempts to break up his defences. In 1779 he had charge of the post at Verplank's Point: which was comprehended in General Washington's plan of operations, when Stony Point was carried. On the ensuing morning the batteries from this eminence, overlooking Webster, were turned upon him, and afforded an unexpected and weighty assistance to the assailant. Nevertheless, such was the circumspection and sagacity with which he had taken his measures, that, after a close examination of his situation, it was deemed advisable to withdraw our force, though ready for assault.

In the yet bleeding disaster of Camden, Webster commanded the right wing of the enemy's army; exhibiting with splendid success the presence of mind and the discriminating judgment for which he was conspicuous. And in the late, his last field, he commanded the left wing, and upheld, in full lustre, his eminent fame.

Lord Cornwallis arrived at Wilmington on the 7th of April, where he found Major Craig with his small garrison—perfectly secure, by his judicious defences, from injury or insult, and holding in his care abundant magazines, yielding not only every implement necessary for the further prosecution of the campaign, but affording in profusion all the comforts of food, raiment, and liquor, to his worn and faithful troops. Indulging himself yet with the hope that his expulsion of Greene out of that State, followed by his victory at Guilford Court-House, would rouse into action his numerous friends, he continued to urge, by every inducement, the consummation of his wishes. But, taught by the correction of experience, deliberation, and caution, the loyalists could not be induced to unite in the British construction of the events of the campaign. They knew that, though driven out of the State, General Greene had speedily returned; they knew that, though vanquished at Guilford Court-House, he had shortly turned upon his enemy; and they were not strangers to the eager pursuit arrested but a few days past by the impracticability of procuring subsistence.

With these truths before them, self-love forced the repression of their zeal; and the unceasing vigilance of government* confirmed

* The British writers speak in very severe terms of the cruelties inflicted by the State authorities and individuals, unchecked by government, on the loyalists. The State government was not cruel, although extremely vigilant; and this stigma being unfounded, ought to be repelled. I select two of the many presumed illustrations, which might be produced, of this erroneous, though accredited, accusation. Mr. Stedman tells us, that in the course of his duty he fell in with a very sensible Quaker in North Carolina, "who, being interrogated about the state of the country, replied, that it was the general wish of the people to be united to Britain; but as they had been so often deceived in promises of support, and the British had so frequently relinquished posts, the people were now afraid to join the British army, lest they should leave the province; in which case the resentment of the revolutioners would be exercised with more cruelty :—that although they might escape or go with the army, yet such was the diabolical conduct of the people, that they would inflict the severest punishment upon their families. 'Perhaps,' said the Quaker, 'thou art not acquainted with the conduct of thy enemies toward those who wish well to the cause thou art engaged in. There are some who have lived for two and even three years in the woods without daring to go to their houses, but have been secretly supported by their families. Others, having walked out of their houses on a promise of their being safe, have proceeded but a few yards before they have been shot. Others have been tied to a tree and severely whipped. I will tell thee of one instance of cruelty. A party surrounded the house of a loyalist; a few entered; the man and his wife were in bed: the husband was shot dead by the side of his wife.' The writer of this replied, that those circumstances were horrid; but under what government could they be so happy as by enjoying the privileges of Englishmen. 'True,' said the Quaker; 'but the people have experienced such distress, that I believe they would submit to any government in the world to obtain peace.'" Mr. Stedman assures us that his friend, the Quaker, was a man of irreproachable manners, and well known as such to some gentlemen,of the British army. But to confirm this tale, he adds another, which he states as known to the whole army. "A gentleman, still residing in North Carolina, and therefore his name is concealed, reported that the day before the British army reached Cross Creek, a man bent with age joined it. He had scarcely the appearance of being human. He wore the skin of a racoon for his hat, his beard was some inches long, and he was so thin that he looked as if he had made his escape from Surgeon's Hall. He wore no shirt; his whole dress being skins of different animals. On the morning after, when this distressed man came to draw his provisions, Mr. Price, the deputy muster-master-general of the provincial forces, and the commissary, asked him several questions. He said that he had lived for three years in the woods, under ground; that he had been frequently sought after by the Americans, and was certain of instant death whenever he should be taken. That he supported himself by what he got in the woods; that acorns served him for bread; that they had from long use become agreeable to him. That he had a

the salutary decision.   The British general found himself completely disappointed, after all his toil and all his danger.
They would occasionally visit his camp, and renew their   April, 1801.
protestations of attachment; but no additional regiment could be

family, some of whom, once or twice in the year, came to him in the woods.
That his only crime was being a loyalist, and having given offence to one of the
republican leaders in that part of the country where he used to reside."
    It excites in my mind all the surprise which Mr. Stedman must have felt
when he heard these tales, on reading them from his pen. He believed in their
truth, I am sure, or he would not have recorded them; yet it seems to me, to
require a stock of credulity not common to soldiers to have seriously regarded
either the Quaker or the escaped tenant from Surgeons' Hall. Suppose Mr.
Stedman had doubted for a moment, and the odd tale warranted at least a
pause before belief; suppose in this moment of doubt he had asked the Quaker,
"How came it, that when for two years we have had a post at Camden, and
for months another at Cheraw Hill (both convenient to the district in which
Mr. Stedman held this conversation); that last year the British head-quarters
were at Charlotte, and this year Lord Cornwallis had traversed the State; how
came it that the out-lying, maltreated loyalists did not resort to one of the
points of safety so near to them? The same patience and caution which secured them from discovery, lying out in the woods for years, could not have
failed to secure safe passage to some one of our posts, which required but a
few days."
    To this query the Quaker would have replied, "Why really, friend, I cannot
say; but I assure thee, that I have told thee precisely what was currently reported." If further pressed, the sensible Quaker would have added, "I never
believed it myself; and I wonder how thou canst take it so seriously."
    There is a feature in the Quaker's tale, which Lieutenant-Colonel Webster
would not have misunderstood, had the conversation been addressed to him. It
is his bitter sarcasm on British operations, when accounting for the cautious
conduct of the loyalists.   He speaks of "deception in promise," and "relinquishment of posts."   Mr. Stedman seems to have given no attention to this
just admonition; but is entirely engrossed with the accusation levelled against
the American people, which was nothing more than a report; as the Quaker
does not say (the interrogation being omitted by Mr. Stedman), that he knew
any of the particulars stated by him, from his own knowledge. It appears
evident to me, that the defamation was only meant as a pleasing supplement to
the philippic he had ventured to pronounce against the conduct of the war.
The Quaker goes on to add, that a husband was shot in bed with his wife. Such
a thing is possible, but very improbable, and entirely repugnant to the American
character, which is tender and respectful to the fair sex. It would not have
been difficult for the party to have taken the individual off to a fit place for
their purpose, and thus to have spared their own as well as the feelings of an
innocent woman. But here again we find the Quaker does not assert it from his
own knowledge; and yet it is ushered to the world as a truth.   To a Briton,
who should accredit this fable, I answer, that we are descended with his countrymen from one stock; that he would not believe such stuff told upon an
Englishman, and that he ought not to believe it when applied to an American.
We have not degenerated by transplantation, notwithstanding Mr. Buffon's
reveries, as our short history testifies.
    The second anecdote fits so exactly the first, that I should treat it as a fabri-
cation, made to aid the Quaker, but for my just respect for the character of
Mr. Stedman.   Considering it as a real occurrence, I have no doubt but that
the unhappy being was deranged. Recollect that he joined the army the day

formed; nor could even Hamilton's North Carolina corps, with all his address and influence, be restored to its complement; so unpropitious in the opinion of the loyalists had been the result of the late active and sanguinary operations.

While the British army was enjoying the stores which the providence of their leader had prepared for its use, General Greene continued in his camp at Ramsay's mill. Equally affectionate and equally provident, he could not present to his much-loved troops refitments and refreshments so much wanted. No magazines were opened for our accommodation; rest to our wearied limbs was the only boon within his gift. Our tattered garments could not be exchanged; nor could our worn-out shoes be replaced. The exhilarating cordial was not within his reach, nor wholesome provision in abundance within his grasp. The meagre beef of the pine barrens, with corn-ash cake, was our food, and water our drink; yet we were content; we were more than content—we were happy. The improved condition of the South, effected by our efforts, had bestowed the solace of inward satisfaction on our review of the past; and experience of the lofty genius of our beloved leader, encouraged proud anticipations of the future.

before it reached Cross Creek, the centre of an extensive settlement of Highlanders, by Mr. Stedman's own authority, devoted to the royal cause. His weak state of body forbade long travel; and his singular dress exposed him to notice and detection if his journey to camp had been from a distance. It clearly results that the Surgeon's Hall tenant had been in the vicinity or in the midst of the Highland settlement; and yet from lunacy, I presume, he preferred the solitude of a cavern and the food of acorns to the hospitable fare which distressed loyalists were sure to receive from the Highland emigrants.

Who can believe that a being thus acting possessed his senses? No rational unprejudiced man can so believe. But why did not Mr. Stedman give us the name and place of residence of this miserable? Secrecy in this case was unnecessary; and the fallacy of the accusation might readily have been confronted with legal testimony. The fact is, that the constitution of the Southern people is warmer than that of their Northern brethren, or of their late enemy; consequently the war in some parts of Georgia and the Carolinas was conducted with great bitterness among the inhabitants, and some tragical scenes took place on both sides. These were, however, confined to a few neighborhoods, and to a few instances. But the demeanor of the mass of the people was kind and forgiving, the policy of Congress and of the State governments humane, and the conduct of the army amiable. Seldom, during the war, was even retaliation resorted to, though often menaced; and surely it cannot be pretended that we had not ample opportunity to gratify such menace if it had comported with our disposition. This discussion proceeds from a desire to vindicate the national character from unjust detraction.

CHAPTER XXVIII.

Arnold's invasion of Virginia.—Unprepared condition of the State.—Debarks at Westover.—Marches to Richmond.—Simcoe destroys the public stores and cannon-
foundry at Westham.—Arnold returns to Westover and descends the river.—Baron
Steuben and Gen. Nelson follow.—Reflections on these operations.—Their effect
upon Greene and Cornwallis.—Abortive attempt to relieve Virginia.—Drawn battle
of a French and English squadron at sea.—Arnold re-enforced by Phillips, who
takes command in Virginia.—La Fayette detached there.—Continued repineness of
Virginia.—Phillips carries on the work of destruction.—Our squadron sunk and
burned.—Prevented from crossing to Richmond.—Phillips moves to Petersburg.—
La Fayette establishes himself on the north side of James River.

It has been before observed, that the British cabinet, despairing
of the subjugation of the United States, had changed its plan of
operations, in the expectation of wresting from the Union its richest though weakest division.

In pursuance of this system, the breaking-up of Virginia was
deemed of primary importance, and to this object Sir Henry Clinton devoted all his disposable force. It will be remembered, that
General Mathews, with a small detachment, in 1779, laid waste the
sea-board of the State; destroying, or transporting to New York, a
large quantity of naval and military stores, besides private property; and that a subsequent expedition under Major-General Leslie
had taken place, which was soon abandoned, in consequence of the
derangement which occurred in the plans of Lord Cornwallis by the
defeat and death of Lieutenant-Colonel Ferguson.

The British commander-in-chief, pursuing steadily this favorite
object, prepared as soon as it was practicable, a third expedition for
that devoted country. It consisted only of one thousand six hundred men, and was placed under the direction of Brigadier-General
Arnold; who, preferring wealth with ignominy, to poverty with
honor, had lately deserted from the service of his country, having
been detected in the infamous attempt to betray West Point, with
the care of which fortress he was then intrusted. The object
being devastation and plunder, Sir Henry Clinton could not have
made a more appropriate selection; but when we consider the nice
feelings inherent in soldiership, he ran no inconsiderable risk of
alienating the affections of his army, by honoring a traitor with the
command of British troops. Mortifying as was this appointment
to many, it seems that the British officers determined to submit in
silence, lest their opposition might delay, if not prevent, an expedition deemed necessary by their commander-in-chief. Arnold, foul
with treason to his country and with treachery to his friend,

escaped from the probable consequence of a well-digested plan laid
by Washington for his seizure, which had advanced almost to the
point of consummation, when he removed from his quarters to prepare for the expedition to Virginia. He was accidentally withdrawn from surrounding conspirators, ready, on the night of that
very day, to seize his person, and convey him across the North
River to Hoboken, where they would have been met by a detachment of dragoons, for the purpose of conveying the traitor to head-
quarters. Thomas Jefferson still continued at the head of the
government; a gentlemen who had taken an early and distinguished part in the revolution, highly respected for his literary
accomplishments, and as highly esteemed for his amiability and
modesty. General Greene, when passing to the South through
Richmond, had left, as has been mentioned, Major-General Baron
Steuben in command in Virginia.

Early in December the governor was informed, by letter from
the commander-in-chief, of the preparations in New York for an expedition to the South; but neither the governor nor the baron seems
to have acted under this communication, presuming, probably, that
the detachment making ready in New York was destined for
South Carolina, to re-enforce the British force under Lord Cornwallis. It would appear that a due recollection of the preceding
attempts upon Virginia, with the knowledge that as long as that
State could hold safe its resources, so long would resistance in the
South be maintained, ought to have admonished the governor and
the general to prepare, at once, means to meet the invasion, should
it be directed against that quarter. General Arnold's preparations
were slow; for the British had not yet relinquished their apprehensions that the Count de Terney, commanding the French
squadron at Rhode Island, would receive from the West Indies
a re-enforcement that would give him such a naval superiority as to
endanger any maritime expedition of theirs. In November this
apprehension ceased, and about the middle of the next month the
convoy with the expedition left the Hook. After a tedious passage, it reached the Chesapeake on the thirtieth, when was felt the
fatal effect of omitting timely preparations to defend the country.
The governor detached General Nelson to the coast, as soon as he
was informed of the entrance of the enemy into the bay, for the
purpose of bringing the militia into the field; while Baron Steuben, believing Petersburg, the depot for the Southern army, to be
the object, hastened his Continental force, about two hundred

recruits, to that town. Arnold, embarking his troops in the lighter vessels, proceeded up James River, and on the fourth of January approached City Point, situated at the confluence of the Appomattox with James River. It was now evident, and, indeed, a little reflection would have before demonstrated that the lower country was not the primary object with the enemy. Mathews, in his incursion, had deprived the State of the contents of her arsenals in that quarter; and had our ability permitted their renewal, prudence would have forbidden the collection of articles of value in spots so accessible. As soon, therefore, as the governor and general learned that the squadron had cast anchor in Hampton Roads (however hope may heretofore have prevailed over vigilance), due reflection would have shown, that Richmond or Petersburg, or both, were the probable destination of this small armament, more formidable from the suddenness of its approach, than its force. It is true that the honorable and continued efforts to support the Southern States, had exhausted much of the resources of Virginia; yet she possessed enough, more than enough, to have sustained the struggle for their restoration, and to have crushed any predatory adventure like that conducted by Arnold. But unfortunately we were unprepared, and efforts to make ready commenced after the enemy was knocking at our doors. The government which does not prepare in time, doubles the power of its adversary, and sports with the lives of its citizens; for to recover lost ground, when the required force becomes ready, compels resort to hazardous enterprise, sometimes ruinous by disappointment, always debilitating by the prodigal expense of blood and treasure.

Upon this occasion, the celerity of the enemy's advance, however unequivocally it exemplified the first, furnished no illustration of the last part of the remark.

On the 4th of January, Arnold debarked at Westover, the seat of Mrs. Byrd, relict of Colonel Byrd, the honorable associate of Washington in defence of the frontiers of Virginia against the Indian enemy, then guided and aided by France. This step, though indecisive, from the facility with which the conveyance derived from naval co-operation admitted him to withdraw to the southern banks of the river, in case Petersburg had been his principal object, gave serious alarm to the governor and general. Now, for the first time, they discovered that the seat of government was to receive a visit from Arnold; and now they ascertained, that although General Nelson had been sent below, and the militia commandants had been summoned to furnish aid from above, yet the postponement of commencing preparations on the receipt of the letter of advice from General Washington, to the hour of the enemy's arrival in Chesapeake Bay, had left them, the archives of the State, its reputation, and all the military stores deposited in the magazines of the metropolis, at the mercy of a small corps conducted by a traitor, who, feeling the rope about his neck tightening in every step he advanced, would have hastened to his naval asylum the moment he saw the probability of adequate resistance. Yet for the want of due preparation on the part of the invaded State, nine hundred British troops, with Arnold at their head, dared to leave their ships, and advance to Richmond, twenty-five miles distant from their place of safety. It will scarcely be credited by posterity, that the governor of the oldest State in the Union, and the most populous (taking for our calculation the ratio established by the present Constitution of the United States to designate the number of representatives allowed to each State), was driven out of its metropolis, and forced to secure personal safety by flight, and that its archives, with all its munitions and stores, were yielded to the will of the invader, with the exception of a few, which accident, more than precaution, saved from the common lot. Incredible as the narrative will appear, it is nevertheless true.

On the 5th of January, Arnold entered Richmond untouched by the small collection of militia detached to interrupt his advance ; and on the following day Lieutenant-Colonel Simcoe, one of the best officers in the British army, proceeded at the head of his corps of rangers, horse and foot, supported by a detachment from the line, to Westham, and there destroyed the only cannon foundry in the State. Here, unluckily, the public stores, removed from Richmond in the perturbation excited by the novel appearance of British battalions, had been deposited ; the last spot which ought to have been selected ; as the most common reflection ought to have suggested the probability that the enemy in Richmond, safe as he was, would never retire until he had destroyed an important military establishment so near as Westham. Making it a place of additional deposit, was therefore increasing the inducement for its destruction.

Simcoe, having fully executed his mission, undisturbed by even a single shot, returned to Richmond, where devastation had been extended under Arnold's direction, until even his greedy appetite was cloyed, and his revengeful heart sated. Having spread desolation all around, the brigadier decamped, and on the 7th returned to Westover, without meeting even the semblance of resistance. Our militia were now assembling ; brave men, always willing to do their duty, never brought to understand how best to execute it, never properly equipped, or judiciously conducted.

Some few unfortunately assembled at Charles City Court-House, in conformity to orders from government, not more than eight or nine miles from Westover. Simcoe hearing of it, put his corps in motion and soon dispersed them, happily with very little loss, in consequence of the impatience of the enemy, who omitted some of those precautions necessary to secure complete success. The object was trivial, or this superior soldier would have conducted his enterprise with the proper forecast and circumspection.* Nothing re-

* This officer commanded a legionary corps called the Queen's Rangers, and had during the war signalized himself upon various occasions. He was a man of letters, and, like the Romans and Grecians, cultivated science amid the turmoil of camp. He was enterprising, resolute, and persevering ; weighing well his project ere entered upon, and promptly seizing every advantage which offered in the course of execution. General Washington expecting a French fleet upon our coast in 1779-80, and desirous of being thoroughly prepared for moving upon New York, in case the combined force should warrant it, had made ready a number of boats, which were placed at Middlebrook, a small village up the Raritan River, above Brunswick. Sir Henry Clinton, being informed of this preparation, determined to destroy the boats. The enterprise was committed to Lieutenant-Colonel Simcoe. He crossed from New York to Elizabethtown Point with his cavalry, and setting out after night, he reached Middlebrook undiscovered and unexpected. Having executed his object he baffled all our efforts to intercept him on his return, by taking a circuitous route. Instead of turning toward Perth Amboy, which was supposed to be the most probable course, keeping the Raritan on his right, he passed that river, taking the direction toward Monmouth County, leaving Brunswick some miles to his left. Here was stationed a body of militia, who being apprised (it being now day) of the enemy's proximity, made a daring effort to stop him, but failed in the attempt. Simcoe, bringing up the rear, had his horse killed, by which accident he was made prisoner. The cavalry deprived of their leader, continued to press forward under the second in command, still holding the route to Elizabethtown. As soon as the militia at Brunswick moved upon the enemy, an express was dispatched to Lieutenant-Colonel Lee then posted in the neighborhood of Englishtown, waiting for the expected arrival of the French fleet, advising him of this extraordinary adventure.

The Legion cavalry instantly advanced toward the British horse ; but notwithstanding the utmost diligence was used to gain the road leading to South Amboy (which was now plainly the object) before the enemy could reach it, the American cavalry did not effect it. Nevertheless the pursuit was continued, and the Legion horse came up with the rear soon after a body of infantry sent over to South Amboy from Staten Island by Sir Henry Clinton to meet Simcoe had joined, and given safety to, the harassed and successful foe.

This enterprise was considered, by both armies, among the handsomest exploits of the war. Simcoe executed completely his object, then deemed very important ; and traversed the country from Elizabethtown Point to South Amboy, fifty-five miles, in the course of the night and morning; passing through a most hostile region of armed citizens ; necessarily skirting Brunswick, a military

maining to be done, Arnold re-embarked on the 10th, and descending the river, landed detachments occasionally, for the purpose of destroying whatever could be discovered worthy of his attention. At Smithfield, and at Mackay's mill, were found some public stores; these shared the fate of those in Richmond and at Westham. On the 20th, the British detachment reached Portsmouth, where General Arnold commenced defences indicating the intention of rendering it a permanent station.

Major-General Steuben, having under him the indefatigable patriot and soldier General Nelson, had by this time drawn together a considerable body of militia, in consequence of the exertion of the governor. With all who were armed * the baron followed Arnold; and at Hood's, Lieutenant-Colonel Clarke, † by a well-concerted stratagem, allured Simcoe to pursue a small party exposed to view, with the expectation of drawing him into an ambuscade, prepared for his reception. Judiciously as the scheme was contrived, it was marred in the execution, by the precipitation with which the militia abandoned their post, after discharging one fire. Simcoe lost a few men, and deeming pursuit useless, retired to the squadron.

Recurring to the past scene, we find that the British general entered the Chesapeake on the 30th of December; that he took possession of Richmond on the 5th of January, ninety miles from Hampton Roads, destroying all the public stores there and at Westham, with such private property as was useful in war; that he reached Portsmouth on the 20th, spreading devastation as he descended the river, wherever any object invited his attention; and

station; proceeding not more than eight or nine miles from the Legion of Lee, his last point of danger, and which became increased from the debilitated condition to which his troops were reduced by previous fatigue. What is very extraordinary, Lieutenant-Colonel Simcoe being obliged to feed once in the course of the night, stopped at a depot of forage collected for the Continental army, assumed the character of Lee's cavalry, waked up the commissary about midnight, drew the customary allowance of forage, and gave the usual vouchers, signing the name of the Legion quartermaster, without being discovered by the American forage commissary or his assistants. The dress of both corps was the same, green coatees and leather breeches; yet the success of the stratagem is astonishing.

* Arnold was practically acquainted with the dilatoriness attendant on militia movements; and finding, on his arrival in the State, that no preparations for defence had been made, or even ordered, he determined to avail himself of the supineness of the government, and by taking the first fair wind to approach within one day's march of Richmond, possess himself of it, and destroy the arms; which were then useless for want of men, as now men had become useless for want of arms. A well-conceived and well-executed project.

† George Rogers Clarke, the Hannibal of the West.—ED.

that during this daring and destructive expedition, he never was seriously opposed at any one point.

What must posterity think of their ancestors, when they read these truths! Had not the war demonstrated beyond doubt that the present generation possessed its share of courage and love of country, we should have been pronounced destitute of these distinguished characteristics. There was, in fact, no deficiency of inclination or zeal (unequal as was the contest) in our militia to advance upon the foe; but there was a fatal want of preparation, of military apparatus, and of system.

Abounding in the finest horses, and our citizens among the best riders in the world, no regular corps of horse had been provided for State defence; although the face of our country, intersected in every quarter by navigable rivers unprotected by floating batteries and undefended by forts, manifested the propriety of resorting to this species of defence, as better calculated than any other within our command, to curb the desultory incursions, under which we had so often and severely suffered.

One single legionary corps of three hundred horse and three hundred musketry, with a battalion of mounted riflemen, accompanied by a battalion of infantry, under a soldier of genius, would have been amply sufficient to preserve the State from insults and injuries; and as this body might have been conveyed with the dispatch of horse, by double mounting, it would in some degree have diminished the disadvantage we labored under from the facility and ubiquity of our navigation. Such a force might readily have been made up by drafts from the militia, and being devoted to local defence, many would have enlisted to avoid more distant service.

Throughout the State were interspersed officers, bred under Washington, compelled to turn away from the field of battle, because our diminished number of rank and file rendered a proportionate diminution in officers incumbent: they were devoted to the great cause for which they had fought, and with alacrity would have rallied round the standard of their country, whenever summoned by government. In the manner suggested, the commonwealth might have been held untouched, and our military stores, so much wanted, and so hard to obtain, would have been secured.

Indeed, when known in New York that such means of defence were provided, no attempt like that intrusted to Arnold would have been projected; and Sir Henry Clinton, not having it in his power to spare large divisions of his force, these injurious and debasing incursions would not have taken place. Never in the course of the war was a more alluring opportunity presented for honorable enterprise, with so fair a prospect of success.

Had the governor fortunately prepared, on receipt of General Washington's letter early in December, six or seven hundred militia from the neighborhood of Richmond and Petersburg, being the only two places within the State possessing objects which could attract the British armament, well-directed efforts against Arnold, as soon as he approached Rockets's, would have saved Richmond and Westham; and might have terminated in the capture of the traitor and the destruction of his detachment.

The position at Rockets's is strong, and peculiarly adapted for militia: the enemy's right flank being exposed, as soon as his front crossed the creek, to a sudden assault from the main force posted along the rivulet and upon the heights, while the houses in front gave defences from which it would not be very easy to dislodge an inferior force determined to do its duty. Opposition in this quarter would have stopped the invader. The country through which he must retreat presents three points where he might have been advantageously assailed. The first at Four Mile Creek, where the ground not only affords powerful aid to the assailant, but is exactly suitable to the Americans, who understand passing with facility through mud, water, and thick brush, fighting from covert to covert; whereas the enemy would never feel himself safe, unless in close order and unison of action, neither of which could long be preserved when attacked in such a position.

The next is, as you pass from Richmond, at Pleasant's mills, and the last, more advantageous than either, is close under Malvern Hills, the north margin of the creek which intersects the road.

A discriminating officer, with inferior force, availing himself with dexterity of the advantages which in many places the country affords between Richmond and Westover, against a retreating foe, could hardly fail to bring him to submission.

But we were unprepared for resistance; and this inviting opportunity for service was lost. Our people in the lower country, finding the metropolis gone, and the enemy unresisted, followed the example of the government, abandoned their habitations, exposed their families to the miseries of flight, and left their property at the mercy of the invader. What ills spring from the timidity and impotence of rulers! In them attachment to the common cause is vain and illusory, unless guided in times of difficulty by courage, wisdom, and concert.

This scene of dismay, confusion, and destruction took place much about the time Lord Cornwallis again opened the campaign in the South; and during the difficult retreat which soon after ensued, the intelligence of Arnold's success soon reached the two armies, deeply afflicting to the one, and highly encouraging to the other. Greene saw the State, on whose resources and ability he relied for supplies and re-enforcements, prostrated at the feet of a handful of men, led by a traitor and deserter, while Lord Cornwallis anticipated with delight his ultimate success, from comparing Arnold and his detachment with himself and his army.

Baron Steuben, not being in a condition to force intrenchments, wisely distributed his militia in the vicinity of the enemy, for the purpose of protecting the country from light incursions, made with a view to collect provisions or to seize plunder. No event occurred in this quarter worthy of notice, General Arnold continuing to adhere to his position in Portsmouth, and Baron Steuben never having force sufficient to drive him from it.

Congress and the commander-in-chief, not less surprised than mortified at the tidings from Virginia, bestowed their immediate attention upon that quarter. The Virginia delegation, deploring the situation of the country, pressed the Chevalier la Luzurne, minister plenipotentiary from his most Christian majesty, to interpose his good offices with the commander of the French fleet at Rhode Island, for the purpose of inducing him to detach an adequate naval force to the Chesapeake, conceiving that such co-operation was alone wanting to restore the tarnished fame of the State, and to punish the base invader. Washington, participating in the feelings of the delegation, and urged by the duty of his station, took measures forthwith to assist the invaded State. He addressed himself to Count Rochambeau, commanding the land forces of his most Christian majesty, and to Monsieur Destouches, admiral of his squadron in the American seas, urging them to seize the present moment for inflicting a severe blow on the common enemy. He represented the condition and situation of the British armament in Virginia; and expatiated in fervid terms on the signal good which a prompt movement with the fleet, having on board a small auxiliary force from the army, to the Chesapeake, would certainly produce. He deprecated a naval operation unaided by an adequate detachment from the army, as incapable with the militia of the country to effect the desired object; and pressing co-operating exertions from the general and admiral, he announced his intention, arising from the confidence he felt that they would adopt his proposal, of drawing a corps of twelve hundred men from his army, and detaching it with orders to reach by forced marches the position of the enemy. Providentially, the French possessed at this moment naval superiority; the British having just before suffered severely in a storm off Long Island. The loss of one ship of the line, and the subtraction of two additional ships rendered unfit for service until repaired, gave this advantage. Had the admiral and general adopted at once the plan proposed by Washington, the object might have been effected before the disabled British ships could have been refitted for sea: but for reasons not explained, Monsieur Destouches did not move with his squadron, but dispatched a part of it only to the Chesapeake, without a single regiment from the army. The commodore had no sooner reached his place of destination than, discovering his inability to execute the expected service, he hastened back to his admiral. Falling in with a British frigate on his return, he captured her; thus obtaining some little compensation for the otherwise useless expedition. In the mean time, General Washington's detachment, under the Marquis de la Fayette, proceeded to the head of Elk, where embarking in bay craft collected for the purpose, the marquis soon reached Annapolis; from which place, in pursuance of the proposed plan, he was to have been taken down the bay, under convoy of Monsieur Destouches.

In all military operations there is a crisis, which, once passed, can never be recalled. So it was now. We had failed to seize the favorable moment, when in our grasp; it went by, and was irrecoverably lost. Had the suggestion of Washington been adopted in the first instance, the British armament must have fallen, and the American traitor would have expiated upon a gibbet his atrocious crime. So persuaded was Washington that such was now to be the termination of his infamous life, that he instructed the marquis not to admit any stipulation in his surrender for his safety, and forbade, as he had done on a former occasion, the smallest injury to the person of Arnold; his object being to bring him to public punishment, agreeably to the rules and regulations established by Congress for the government of the army. The commander-in-chief was much mortified when he learned that his proposition to the general and admiral had not been executed, as he was well convinced the propitious opportunity was irretrievably past. His chagrin arose not only from failure in striking his enemy, from failure in vindicating the reputation of Virginia, but also from this second escape of Arnold, whose safe delivery at head-quarters engaged his attention from the moment of his desertion. Nevertheless, he concurred with zeal in the tardy adoption of his plan by the French commanders, and continued the marquis at Annapolis for co-operation. Monsieur Destouches finding, by the return of his commodore, that the contemplated object had not been effected, sailed from Rhode Island with his squadron on the 8th of March, with a suitable detachment from the army, under the Count de Viominil. Time had been afforded for refitting the two disabled ships belonging to the British fleet, which being accomplished, Admiral Arbuthnot put to sea on the 10th, in pursuit of the French fleet, and came up with it on the 16th, off the capes of Virginia.

The hostile fleets were not long in view before they engaged. The action was not general, and, like most sea-battles, indecisive.* After one hour's combat the fleets separated, each claiming the victory. However well supported might be the title of the French admiral, it cannot be doubted that he entirely failed in the object of the expedition; nor is it less certain that his disappointment resulted from the rencounter that had just taken place, which was followed by the British admiral's possession of the entrance into the Chesapeake, and by the return of the French fleet to Rhode Island.

Nevertheless, Congress, the States, and the commander-in-chief, were considerably elated by the issue of the naval combat; for although the fleet of our ally had not gained any decisive advantage, and had been obliged to abandon its enterprise, still, without superiority of force, it had sustained an equal combat against an enemy whose predominance on the ocean had been long established. Congress complimented Monsieur Destouches with a vote of thanks, expressing their approbation and confidence; while General Washington, with much cordiality and satisfaction, tendered to the admiral his sincere congratulations. So sensible had been Sir Henry Clinton of the vulnerable condition of Arnold, that he hastened the embarkation of a considerable body of troops, under Major-General Phillips (lately exchanged), intended ultimately to co-operate with Lord Cornwallis, but now to re-enforce the detachment in Virginia, as soon as the British fleet should be enabled to put to sea.

Arbuthnot had not long sailed when he was followed by the

---

* Before those of Howe, St. Vincent, Duncan, and, above all, of Nelson.

transports with the armament under Phillips, which, steering directly for the Chesapeake, safely arrived, after a short passage ; and, proceeding up Elizabeth River, the troops debarked at Portsmouth, to the great joy of Brigadier Arnold, whose apprehensions during the preceding three weeks had been excruciating.

The Marquis de la Fayette was recalled from Annapolis to the head of Elk, whence he was directed to proceed to Virginia, and take upon himself the command of the troops collected and collecting for its protection.   The British force, united at Portsmouth, amounted to three thousand five hundred; and, to the great satisfaction of the officers heretofore serving under Arnold, was now placed under the direction of General Phillips.   This officer occupied himself in completing the fortifications begun by Arnold, and in making such additional defences as the security of the post required.   As soon as this was effected, he prepared for offensive operations.

Leaving one thousand men in Portsmouth, he embarked with the residue in vessels selected for the purpose, and proceeded up James River, with a view of consummating the system of destruction so successfully pursued by Arnold during his short expedition.

Although the heavy hand of the enemy had been stretched twice before across this defenceless country, withering every thing it touched ; although the difficulty with which our infant nation, without money and without credit, gathered together small quantities of supplies, without which resistance must terminate ; and although the state of our interior forbade the hope of effectual opposition, not from the want of means, but from the want of wisely husbanding and wisely applying our resources, proved again and again by severe experience ; yet the interval since Arnold's unopposed visit to the metropolis was passed in inactivity, as all preceding periods of quietude had passed.   What little remained of the vitals of resistance was still left in the exposed region of the State, instead of being collected and transported over the Blue Ridge, our nearest security. Instead of admonishing our planters of the dangers to which their tobacco was exposed in the public warehouses on the navigable rivers, and urging them to keep this valuable resource safe at home for better times, our towns were filled with our staple commodity, ready to be burned, or to be exported, as might best comport with the enemy's views.

Indeed, we left undone those things which we ought to have done, and did those things which we ought not to have done, and well might follow the disgraces and distresses which ensued.

At Yorktown were deposited some naval stores, and in its harbor were a few public and private vessels. This little assemblage seems first to have engaged the notice of the British general. Having advanced up the river opposite to Williamsburg, the former seat of government, Phillips landed with his troops at Burwell's Ferry, and took possession of this deserted city without opposition; hence he detached to Yorktown, where, destroying our small magazine, he returned to his fleet, and proceeded up the river. Reaching City Point, which is situated on the south side of James River, where it receives the Appomattox, the British general again embarked his army.

Petersburg, the great mart of that section of the State which lies south of Appomattox, and of the northern part of North Carolina, stands upon its banks, about twelve miles from City Point; and, after the destruction of Norfolk, ranked first among the commercial towns of the State. Its chief export was tobacco, considered our best product, and at this time its warehouses were filled. In addition were some public stores; as this town, being most convenient to the army of Greene, had become a place of depot for all imported supplies required for Southern operations.

Phillips directed his march to Petersburg, which he soon reached, without opposition, as appeared then to be the habit of Virginia.

All the regular force of this State being under Greene in South Carolina, its defence depended entirely upon the exertions of its executive government, and its militia. Two thousand of this force were now in the field, directed by the Baron Steuben, seconded by General Nelson; half of which was stationed on each side of James River. Steuben, not doubting Phillips's object, put himself at the head of the southern division in the vicinity of Petersburg, the safety of which he endeavored to effect; but as he was incapable of doing more than merely to preserve appearances, this effort was abortive. Advancing into the town, the British troops fell upon Steuben's division, well posted, and, as usual, willing, but incapable, to resist effectually. A distant rencounter ensued; adroitly managed by the baron, and sharply upheld by his troops. It terminated, as was foreseen, in the retreat of Steuben over the Appomattox, breaking down the bridge after passing it, to prevent pursuit. Phillips, now in quiet possession of the town, pursued the British policy of crushing Southern resistance, by destroying the resources of

Virginia. The warehouses, stored with tobacco, our best substitute
for money, were consumed. Every thing valuable was destroyed;
and the wealth of this flourishing town in a few hours disappeared.
Pursuing this war of devastation, he crossed the Appomattox, having
repaired the bridge; and dividing his superior force, he detached
Arnold to Osborne's, another place of tobacco storage, while he
proceeded himself to the court-house of Chesterfield County, which
lies opposite to Richmond, between the James and Appomattox
rivers. At this latter place was no tobacco, then the chief object
of British conquerors; but barracks had been erected, and stores
collected there, for the accommodation of our recruits, when assembled at this place to join the Southern army. Arnold destroyed tobacco and every thing he found at Osborne's, as did Phillips the
barracks and stores at the court-house. These exploits being performed, the two divisions of the army rejoined on the route to Manchester, a small village south of James River, in view of the metropolis, one of them passing through Warwick, another small village:
here was more tobacco,—of course more devastation followed.

The tobacco war being thus far finished, our small squadron of
armed vessels lying in the river, here very narrow, became the next
object of the British detachment. This naval force had been collected for the purpose of co-operating with the French expedition
from Newport against Portsmouth, which proved abortive and,
among other ills flowing from the abortion, was the loss of this
little squadron. The commodore was very politely summoned to
surrender, to which summons he bid defiance, declaring " his determination to defend himself to the last extremity." Quickly two
sixes and two grasshoppers were brought to bear upon him; when
he as quickly scuttled and set fire to his vessels, escaping with his
crew to the northern banks of the river : one way of " holding out
to the last extremity," but not that commonly understood by the
term. Reaching Manchester, General Phillips renewed hostility
upon tobacco, of which great quantities were found in the warehouses; this village, although in sight of Richmond, having been
saved by the intervening river from sharing with the metropolis in
Arnold's ravages. Nothing now remained on the south side of
James River, below the falls, for British fire; all the tobacco, with
all our valuables within reach, were burnt, or conveyed on board
ship. It was necessary to cross to Richmond, or to lay aside the
torch. The former measure was the one desired, and would have
been executed, had not the opportune arrival, on the preceding

evening, of the Marquis de la Fayette, with his New England regulars put an insuperable bar to the object. No bridge then united the two shores, and no maritime aid was at hand to accelerate a passage, now to be effected only by the bayonet, covered by adequate and commanding batteries. The British force under Phillips was between three and four thousand, fully adequate of itself to prepare a bridge of boats, and to force its way across; but nature had bestowed upon the north side of the river heights commanding effectually both shores. The marquis, strengthened* by two thousand militia,† presented a respectable force, better appropriated to marches and countermarches, waiting for the assistance which time and opportunity never fail to present, than for the close and stubborn conflicts which defences of posts and resistance to river passage are sure to produce. Had Phillips been in Richmond, and the marquis in Manchester, the river would have been passed with ease. Such is the value of what is called the advantage of ground in war.‡ Relinquishing his design, General Phillips quitted Manchester, marching down the south side of the river to Bermuda Hundred; the only spot in the State which retained the old Anglican term brought over by the first settlers; situated on the south shore of the James, at its confluence with the Appomattox River. Although no

---

* Whenever the commitment of our militia in battle with regulars occurs, the heart of the writer is rent with painful emotions, knowing, as he does, the waste of life resulting from the stupid cruel policy. Can there be any system devised by the wit of man, more the compound of inhumanity, of murder, and of waste? Ought any government to be respected, which, when peace permits substitution of a better system, neglects to avail itself of the opportunity? was a father to put his son, with his small-sword drawn for the first time, against an experienced swordsman, would not his neighbors exclaim, Murderer! vile murderer! Just so acts the government; and yet our parents are all satisfied, although, whenever war takes place, their sons are to be led to the altar of blood. Dreadful apathy! shocking coldness to our progeny!

† And sixty dragoons, see Marshall, v. 4, p. 428, and infra, p. 29.—ED.

‡ These observations appear to be just and instructive, in reference to that most beautiful and important military operation, the passage of rivers in the face of an enemy. They will serve to illustrate many recollections of the military reader, particularly Bonaparte's passage of the Beresina, where, by seizing on a commanding bank of that river, his artillery secured the passage in spite of the army of Tchitchakoff, posted on the opposite side, in spite of the hasty and imperfect structure of the bridges, of the inclement weather, and the exhausted condition of his troops. Surrounded by danger, disappointment, and despair, his genius lost none of its resources, and extricated him by an operation which would have done honor to his most brilliant and successful campaigns. The most celebrated examples of the military passage of rivers are, probably, that of the Rhine by Cæsar; that of the Po by Prince Eugene; that of the Rhine, by Prince Charles of Lorraine; and of the Danube by Bonaparte at Inder Lobau.—ED.

tobacco warehouses, with their contents, remained to attract the exertion of British valor, yet various articles presented themselves in this ill-fated district, which, exciting cupidity, could not fail in being taken into safe-keeping by this formidable army.

When governments adopt the policy of plunder and conflagration, they owe to the world, as well as to their nation, the justification of such departure from the liberal usage of war. In every condition of things such justification is difficult; in this state of affairs it was impracticable. The subjugation of the weakest portion of the Union, to which alone all the disposable force of Great Britain had been and was devoted, began to be viewed as chimerical even by the British officers. The battle of Guilford had fixed an impression on the condition of the war, which audibly declared the futility even of victory itself. To burn and to destroy, where no hope of effecting the object could exist but with the infatuated, was not less cruel than disgraceful. That the only people in the world, understanding and enjoying political liberty, powerful and enlightened, the brethren of Locke, of Newton, and of Hampden, should encourage, by their example, a return to barbarism, affords a melancholy proof of the inefficacy of the arts and the sciences, the sweets of civilization,—nay, even of liberty itself, over passion supported by power. The British nation guided by ministers without talents, disappointment could not but ensue to many of their enterprises; which, imbittering the heart instead of correcting the head, produced this baneful system, so destructive to the comfort first of the farmers of Connecticut, now of the planters of Virginia; heaping up a stock of irritation and hate, to be dissipated only by the force of time.

Opposite to Bermuda Hundred is City Point, where Phillips had disembarked when proceeding to Petersburg; the fleet continuing in this harbor, the British general re-embarked his army and fell down the river.

The Marquis de la Fayette, informed by his light parties of the movement of the enemy, followed cautiously on the north side of the river, until he reached the head-waters of the Chickahominy, one of the branches of James River, behind which he took post. Here he learned, by his exploring parties, that the British fleet was re-ascending the river; when, breaking up from Chickahominy, the marquis hastened back to Richmond.

On his route he was informed that Phillips was again disembarking his army on the south side of the river; one division at Brandon, the seat of Benjamin Harrison, Esq., and the second division at City Point. Persuaded that the enemy's present object was the possession of Petersburg, for the purpose of meeting Lord Cornwallis, whose approach to Halifax was known, La Fayette determined to move by forced marches in that direction. The British general advancing with equal rapidity, and being nearer to Petersburg, reached it first. Phillips had flattered himself, that the powerful advantage derived from the celerity and ease with which his army might be conveyed by water, would enable him to strike decisively the American general, whom he hoped to allure low down the neck formed by the James and Chickahominy. While occupied in the incipient step to this end, he received Lord Cornwallis's dispatch, forwarded, as has been before mentioned, when that general commenced his march from Wilmington; and therefore hurried to Petersburg, the designated point of junction. Though young and enterprising, La Fayette was too sagacious to have risked the bold measure of occupying Petersburg, even had he been free to act as his own judgment might direct; but acting as he did in a subordinate character, he never could have been induced to violate orders. Major-General Greene, commanding in the Southern Department, directed the operations in Virginia as well as in Carolina; and apprehending loss from temerity, he enjoined, first on Baron Steuben, and afterward upon his successor, the preservation of the army, by avoiding general action, and confining his operation to the " petit guerre;" convinced that a steady adherence to this system only could save the South. It is not to be presumed, that, with such instructions from his superior, at the head of a force inferior to that under Phillips, with a few lately raised cavalry, the American general would have hazarded placing himself between Cornwallis and the army under Phillips. But in his difficult situation, it was necessary to preserve appearances, to keep the country in good spirits, as well as to render his soldiers strict in attention to duty, never so susceptible of discipline as when impressed with the conviction that battle is at hand. Finding the British general in occupation of Petersburg, La Fayette fell back; and recrossing James River, took a position upon its northern margin, some miles below Richmond. Here he exerted himself to increase the ability of his army, by diminishing his baggage, establishing system and punctuality in its several departments, and introducing throughout rigid discipline. Nor was he unmindful of the peril which awaited the public stores again collected in Richmond; notwithstanding the

severe admonition lately received from Brigadier Arnold.   To their
removal he applied all the aid in his power, which was effected in
due time, though unhappily not to a proper place.*

* Upon this and similar observations in the text, the following correspondence
was held with Mr. Jefferson a short time before his death.   His eloquent justification appears to be directed against severer strictures than those to be found
in the memoirs which apply rather to the inefficiency of the government of
Virginia at the time, than to the particular executive magistrate.   It is certain
that, during the excitement of the revolutionary contest, and subsequent political
contentions, injurious accusations were levelled at this illustrious patriot; and
it would seem that, not having a copy of this work before him, he wrote under
the impression that it repeated them.   The fact is otherwise, and the reader
will perceive that the tone of the author is moderate, and the character of his
observations for the most part general.—ED.

" WASHINGTON, 3d May, 1826.

" SIR,—At the request of some military friends, and in compliance with a desire which I have for several years entertained, I am preparing a second edition
of my father's Memoirs of the Southern War—with his own MS. corrections,
with the advantage of various suggestions from Colonel Howard, and with such
additions and explanations, as my own acquaintance with the subject will enable me to furnish.

" In this undertaking I have reached the second volume, and find that the
account given of Arnold's invasion is not favorable to your foresight or energy.
Between the 1st and 19th pages, the narrative and reflections will be found to
which I allude, and I think it my duty as an impartial understrapper in historic
labors to notify you of the task I am now engaged in, and to offer either to
incorporate such explanations, as you may choose to furnish me with, and as
may appear satisfactory to my judgment, in my own notes to the work; or to
subjoin your own statements, under your own name, with a proper reference to
the text, and every advantage that may secure you *fair play*.

" Reserving at the same time, if you prefer the latter course, the right of
accompanying your statements with such observations as my sense of truth and
justice may dictate, if it should dictate any.   I make this reservation with a
view of holding the independence of my own mind clear and undoubted, as
every man who writes of his contemporaries ought to do.   In this sentiment I
hope you will agree with me, and see that it is compatible with perfect respect
for yourself.   With the highest esteem, your ob't servant,
                                                     " H. LEE."

" 9th May, 1826.

" SIR,—Since my last letter, it has occurred to me that it should have contained an idea which it did not express.   It is this,—that under the circumstances in which the governors of States, and the Continental officers were placed,
it is reasonable to suppose that, however correct the conduct of the former may
have been, the opinions of the latter would be unfavorable to them.   Indeed,
the more accurate, the more limited by law, and those considerations which
have now ripened into *State rights*—the more tender of individual liberty and
private property the governor may have been, the more censorious and dissatisfied would the Continental officer become, whose views were solely and ardently
fixed on rescuing the country from subjection to Britain, and who was ready to
risk even liberty itself for independence.   It is therefore really a proof of your
respective merits that my father and General Greene should have supposed you
were not quite as military and energetic—not quite as prompt and grasping in'
preparing and applying the means of the State—' our lives, our fortunes, and
our sacred honor,' to public use and warlike purposes, as you ought to have
been ; and I have little doubt if Jefferson had been the ' military chieftain,'

CHAPTER XXIX.

Greene carries the war into South Carolina.—Lee detached to join Marion.—Cornwallis invades Virginia.—Singular occurrence to Lee's Legion.—Lee and Marion move against Fort Watson and advance against Col. Watson.—Operations around Camden and battle of Hobkirk's Hill.—Marion and Lee move against Col. Watson.—Greene crosses the Wateree.—Rawdon evacuates Camden.—Fort Motte taken by Marion and Lee.—Orangeburg taken by Sumter.—Lee takes Fort Granby.—Greene joins the Light Corps.—Rawdon retires to Monk's Corner.—Lee takes Fort Galphin.—Joins Pickens and Clarke before Augusta.—They take Fort Grierson.—Death of Major Eaton.—Greene besieges Ninety-six.—Fall of Augusta.—Various operations resulting in the evacuation of Ninety-six.—Skirmishes and manœuvres.—Greene retires to the high hills of Santee.—Col. Hampton disperses and captures a body of mounted refugees.—Affair at Quimby Bridge.—The Light Corps join the main army at the High Hills.—Reflections on the campaign.

THE hostile army being separated, General Greene turned his attention to the improvement of his unresisted possession of the field.

and Greene the regulated statesman—the *élève* of Montesquieu and Locke—that Greene would have occasioned the same strictures, which were actually applied to Jefferson. Hence, from these distinct forces, arose our federal and democratic parties—'*ex illo fonte derivata clades.*' The men of the sword who defended the country necessarily for the most part became federalists—the men of the pen who taught the nature and value of liberty, and 'snuffed the approach of tyranny in every tainted breeze,' became democrats, adhered more literally to the true grounds of the revolution, and had to protect liberty from her most devoted friends. I cannot pursue this interesting subject at present any further, but it is my intention in a work which I propose commencing as soon as I get out this second edition of my father's, to unfold from this foundation the history and character of our political parties—their relation to the events of the revolution, and their operations on the structure and administration of our government. I have ventured to trouble you with this reference to the subject, in hopes of obtaining in addition to such matter as may relate to your own history, lights that may lead and quicken me in developing this branch of our annals. I will add, that I think the effect of this division has on the whole been useful, and that I hope to explain in what manner, and in what degree. Of course I use the word *clades* in the quotation, not as Horace intended it. With veneration and esteem, your ob't serv't,

" MR. JEFFERSON, *Monticello.*" " H. LEE.

" MONTICELLO, *May* 15, 1826.

" DEAR SIR,—The sentiments of justice which have dictated your letters of the third and ninth instant, are worthy of all praise, and merit and meet my thankful acknowledgments. Were your father now living, and proposing as you are, to publish a second edition of his memoirs, I am satisfied, he would give a very different aspect to the pages of that work, which respect Arnold's invasion and surprise of Richmond, in the winter of 1780-1. He was then, I believe, in South Carolina, too distant from the scene of these transactions, to relate them on his own knowledge, or even to sift them from the chaff of rumors, then afloat, rumors which vanished soon before the real truth, as vapors before the sun obliterated, by their notoriety, from every candid mind, and by the voice of the many, who, as actors or spectators, knew what had truly passed. The facts shall speak for themselves.

" General Washington had just given notice to all the governors on the sea-

Whether to approach Wilmington, with a view of opposing Cornwallis's operations at the threshold ; or to take a more salubrious

board, north and south, that an embarkation was taking place at New York,
destined for *the southward, as was given out there,* and on Sunday, the 31st of
December, 1780, we received information that a fleet had entered our Capes;
it happened fortunately, that our legislature was at that moment in session,
and within two days of their rising. So that, during these two days, we had
the benefit of their presence, and of the counsel and information of the members,
individually. On Monday, the 1st of January, we were in suspense, as to the
destination of this fleet, whether up the bay or up our river. On Tuesday, at
10 o'clock, however, we received information that they had entered the James
River ; and, on general advice, we instantly prepared orders for calling in the
militia, one half from the nearer counties, and a fourth from the more remote,
which would constitute a force of between four and five thousand men ; of which
orders the members of the legislature, which adjourned that day, took charge,
each to his respective county, and we began the removal of every thing from
Richmond. The wind being fair and strong, the enemy ascended the river as
rapidly as the expresses could ride, who were dispatched to us from time to
time to notify their progress. At 5 P. M. on Thursday, we learnt that they had
then been three hours landed at Westover. The whole militia of the adjacent
counties were now called for, and to come on individually, without waiting any
regular array. At 1 P. M. the next day (Friday), they entered Richmond, and on
Saturday, after twenty-four hours' possession, burning some houses, destroying
property, &c., they retreated, encamped that evening ten miles below, and
reached their shipping at Westover, the next day (Sunday).

" By this time had assembled three hundred militia under Colonel Nicholas,
six miles above Westover, and two hundred under General Nelson, at Charles
City Court-House, eight miles below ; two or three hundred at Petersburg had
put themselves under General Smallwood, of Maryland, accidentally there on his
passage through the State ; and Baron Steuben with eight hundred, and Colonel
Gibson with one thousand, were also on the south side of James River, aiming
to reach Hood's before the enemy should have passed it ; where they hoped they
could arrest them. But the wind having shifted, carried them down as prosperously as it had brought them up the river. Within the first five days, therefore, about twenty-five hundred men had collected at three or four different
points ready for junction.

" I was absent myself from Richmond, but always within observing distance
of the enemy, three days only ; during which I was never off my horse but to
take food or rest ; and was everywhere, where my presence could be of any
service ; and I may, with confidence, challenge any one to put his finger on the
point of time when I was in a state of remissness from any duty of my station.
But I was not with the army!—True: for, 1st. Where was it? 2d. I was engaged in the more important functions of taking measures to collect an army
and, without military education myself, instead of jeopardizing the public safety
by pretending to take its command, of which I knew nothing, I had committed
that to persons of the art—men who knew how to make the best use of it; to
Steuben, for instance, to Nelson and others, possessing that military skill and
experience of which I had none.

" Let our condition, too, at that time, be duly considered ; without arms, without money of effect, without a regular soldier in the State, or a regular officer,
except Steuben ; a militia scattered over the country and called at a moment's
warning to leave their families and friends, in the dead of winter, to meet an
enemy ready marshalled and prepared at all points to receive them ! Yet had
time been given them by the tardy retreat of that enemy, I have no doubt but
the rush to arms, and to the protection of their country, would have been as

and distant position, with Virginia in his rear, and there to wait his lordship's advance toward his long-meditated victim, became at first

rapid and universal as in their invasion during our late war; when at the first moment of notice our citizens rose in mass, from every part of the State, and, without waiting to be marshalled by their officers, armed themselves, and marched off by ones and by twos, as quickly as they could equip themselves. Of the individuals of the same house, one would start in the morning, a second at noon, a third in the evening; no one waiting an hour for the company of another. This I saw myself on the late occasion, and should have seen on the former, had wind and tide, and a Howe, instead of an Arnold, slackened their pace ever so little.

" And is the surprise of an open and unarmed place, although called a city and even a capital, so unprecedented as to be matter of indelible reproach ?—Which of our capitals during the same war, was not in possession of the same enemy, not merely by surprise and for a day only, but permanently ? That of Georgia? of South Carolina? North Carolina? Pennsylvania? New York? Connecticut? Rhode Island? Massachusetts? And, if others were not, it was because the enemy saw no object in taking possession of them—add to the list in the late war, Washington also, the metropolis of the Union, covered by a fort, with troops, and a dense population; and, what capital on the continent of Europe (St. Petersburg and its regions of ice excepted) did not Bonaparte take and hold at his pleasure ? Is it then just that Richmond and its authorities alone should be placed under the reproach of history, because, in a moment of peculiar denudation of resources, by the *coup de main* of an enemy, led on by the hand of fortune, directing the winds and weather to their wishes, it was surprised and held for twenty-four hours? Or, strange that that enemy, with such advantages should be enabled then to get off without risking the honors he had achieved by burnings and destructions of property, peculiar to his principles of warfare ? We at least may leave these glories to their own trumpet.

" During this crisis of trial I was left alone, unassisted by the co-operation of a single public functionary; for, with the legislature, every member of the council had departed, to take care of his own family, unaided even in my bodily labors, but by my horse, and he, exhausted at length by fatigue, sank under me in the public road, where I had to leave him, and, with my saddle and bridle on my shoulders, to walk a-foot to the nearest farm, where I borrowed an unbroken colt, and proceeded to Manchester, opposite Richmond, which the enemy had evacuated a few hours before.

" Without pursuing these minute details, I will here ask the favor of you to turn to Girardin's History of Virginia, where such of them as are worthy the notice of history are related in that scale of extension, which its objects admit. That work was written at Milton, within two or three miles of Monticello ; and at the request of the author, I communicated to him every paper I possessed on the subject, of which he made the use he thought proper for his work (see his pages 453, 460, and the Appendix xi.-xv.). I can assure you of the truth of every fact he has drawn from these papers, and of the genuineness of such as he has taken the trouble of copying. It happened that during these eight days of incessant labor, for the benefit of my own memory, I carefully noted every circumstance worth it. These memorandums were often written on horseback, and on scraps of paper taken out of my pocket at the moment, fortunately preserved to this day, and now lying before me. I wish you could see them. ᵗBut my papers of that period are stitched together in large masses, and ᵴo tattered and tender, as not to admit removal farther than from their shelves to a reading table. They bear an internal evidence of fidelity which must carry conviction to every one who sees them. We have nothing in our neighborhood which could compensate the trouble of a visit to it, unless perhaps our University,

the subject of deliberation. Very soon a plan of action was submitted to the general, radically repugnant to those which had risen

which I believe you have not seen, and I can assure you is worth seeing. Should
you think so, I would ask as much of your time at Monticello, as would enable
you to examine these papers at your ease. Many others, too, are interspersed
among them, which have relation to your object, many letters from General
Gates, Greene, Stevens, and others engaged in the Southern war; and in the
North also. All should be laid open to you without reserve—for there is not a
truth existing which I fear, or would wish unknown to the whole world. During the invasion of Arnold, Phillips, and Cornwallis, until my time of office expired, I made it a point, once a week, by letters to the President of Congress
and to General Washington, to give them an exact narrative of the transactions
of the week. These letters should still be in the Office of State, in Washington,
and in the presses of Mount Vernon. Or, if the former were destroyed by the
conflagrations of the British, the latter are surely safe, and may be appealed to in
corroboration of what I have now written.

" There is another transaction very erroneously stated in the same work, which,
although not concerning myself, is within my own knowledge, and I think it a
duty to communicate it to you. I am sorry that, not being in possession of a
copy of the Memoirs, I am not able to quote the passage, and still less the facts
themselves, verbatim, from the text; but of the substance recollected, I am
certain. It is said there, that about the time of Tarleton's expedition up the
North branch of James River to Charlottesville and Monticello, Simcoe was
detached up the Southern branch, and penetrated as far as New London, in
Bedford, where he destroyed a depot of arms, &c., &c., I was with my family
at the time at a possession I have within three miles of New London, and I can
assure you of my knowledge, that he did not advance to within fifty miles of
New London. Having reached the lower end of Buckingham, as I have understood, he heard of a depot of arms and a party of new recruits under Baron
Steuben, somewhere in Prince Edward. He left the Buckingham road, immediately at or near Francisco's, pushed directly south at this new object, was
disappointed and returned to and down James River to head-quarters. I had
then returned to Monticello myself, and from thence saw the smoke of his conflagration, of houses and property on that river, as they successively arose in the
horizon at a distance of twenty-five or thirty miles. I must repeat that his excursion from Francisco's is not within my own knowledge, but as I have heard
it from the inhabitants on the Buckingham road, which for many years I trav-
elled six or eight times a year. The particulars of that therefore may need inquiry and correction.

" These are all the recollections within the scope of your request, which I can
state with precision and certainty, and of these you are free to make what use
you think proper in the new edition of your father's work; and with them I
pray you to accept assurances of my great esteem and respect.

" TH. JEFFERSON.

" H. LEE, Esq."

" MONTICELLO, *May* 30, 1826.

" DEAR SIR,— Your favor of the 25th came to hand yesterday, and I shall
be happy to receive you at the time you mention, or at any other if any other
shall be more convenient to you.

" Not being now possessed of a copy of General Lee's Memoirs, as I before
observed to you, I may have mis-remembered the passage respecting Simcoe's
expedition, and very willingly stand corrected. The only facts relative to it,
which I can state from personal knowledge are, that being at Monticello on the
9th, 10th, and 11th of June, '81, on one of those days (I cannot now ascertain
which) I distinctly saw the smokes of houses successively arising in the horizon

into notice, and which, combating both in principle, reduced the discussion to a single point : " Shall the army wait upon the enemy, or shall it instantly advance upon Camden." *

a little beyond James River, and which I learned from indubitable testimony were kindled by his corps ; and that being within three or four miles of New London, from that time to the 25th of July, he did not, within that space of time, reach New London ; but all this may be better explained *viva voce ;* and in the mean time I repeat assurances of my great esteem and respect.

"TH. JEFFERSON.

"H. LEE, Esq."

In further justification of Mr. Jefferson, it may be proper to add, that although a motion to impeach him was made in the Assembly, by Mr. George Nicholas, and a day appointed for commencing the trial—on which day Mr. Jefferson attended, prepared to meet the prosecution—the mover abandoned the impeachment and both houses unanimously adopted the following resolution :—"*Resolved,* That the sincere thanks of the General Assembly be given to our former governor, Thomas Jefferson, Esq., for his impartial, upright, and attentive administration whilst in office. The assembly wish, in the strongest manner, to declare the high opinion which they entertain of Mr. Jefferson's ability, rectitude, and integrity, as chief magistrate of this Commonwealth ; and mean, by thus publicly avowing their opinion, to obviate and to remove all unmerited censure."

It is obvious that, if Mr. Jefferson had been in fault, the General Assembly would have been equally to blame, for the unprepared and defenceless state in which Arnold found the seat of government of Virginia ; and that the exhausted state of the Commonwealth, both as to men and money, the disinclination of the people to any thing like the maintenance of a standing force, with the uncertainty of Arnold's destination, and the fortuitous rapidity of his progress, were sufficient causes for his success and our disasters.   In so far as the observations in the text are applicable to these causes, they are perfectly just.—ED.

* The natural inference from the language of this passage is, that Lee himself suggested the plan of operations which is here about to be detailed ; and as it eventuated so happily for the fame of General Greene and the independence of America, it appears proper to furnish the reader with a summary of such facts as substantiate the intrinsic probability of the intimation.   First among these is the positive affirmation of competent and unimpeachable witnesses. The honorable Peter Johnston of Virginia, who was a lieutenant in Lee's Legion, and Doctor Matthew Irvine of Charleston, who was his cavalry surgeon, and the confidential friend of himself and of General Greene ; both testifying to the same point, and the latter declaring that he was himself the organ confided in by Lee for communicating this counsel to Greene.   (See the letters of these gentlemen, in the Campaign of 1781, p. 399, and seq.)   Next in order are the expressions of Greene himself in his letter written (p. 297) three days after his defeat at Camden, and under the mortifying reflections it produced.   "I have run every hazard to promote *your plan of operations.*" Showing clearly, that Greene well knew it belonged to Lee.   Indeed it is impossible to believe that at this moment of depression and anxiety he would be so weak and ungenerous as to impute to the counsels of a friend and fellow-soldier, the origin of a disastrous measure, which he was conscious had proceeded from the uninfluenced conceptions in his own mind.   The evidence of these circumstances appears to be conclusive, that the suggestion was made by Lee ; and the only doubt which can remain is, whether Greene might not have conceived the plan simultaneously with Lee, or independently of him.   At best, this is merely possible, and I know not, that history has any thing to do with *possibilities.* That Lee conceived it, is an historical fact, as well attested as that he conceived the eloquent

The proposer suggested, that, leaving Cornwallis to act as he might choose, the army should be led back into South Carolina. That the main body should move upon Camden, while the light corps, taking a lower direction, and joining Brigadier Marion, should break down all intermediate posts, completely demolishing communication between Camden and Ninety-Six with Charleston; and thus placing the British force in South Carolina in a triangle, Camden and Ninety-Six forming the base, insulated as to co-operation, and destitute of supplies, even of provision, for any length of time.

From the first moment the substitute was presented to the mind of Greene, it received his decided preference. There was a splendor in the plan which will always attract a hero. Yet the stake was great, the subject difficult, and powerful arguments, pressed by deservedly influential soldiers, maintained the propriety of adhering to the first contemplated system.

They contended, that the battle of Guilford had given a superiority to the American arms which might be preserved; and if preserved, the liberation of the South must follow. They admitted the in-

expressions which Marshall pronounced on the death and character of General Washington, viz: "First in war, first in peace, and first in the hearts of his fellow-citizens." Marshall himself says (vol. 5, p. 765), Lee was the author of the resolutions containing these memorable words: and Greene, in his letter of the 28th of April, 1781, says he was the author of this military plan, which General Hamilton, in an oration delivered before the Society of Cincinnati in honor of Greene's memory, affirmed, was not surpassed in boldness and wisdom by Scipio's famous determination to invade Africa. And, while it would be as reasonable to disbelieve Marshall in the first case, as Greene in the second, it appears as probable that the eloquence of Lee was anticipated by the historian, as that his invention was forestalled by the general.

Although the supposition that Greene did also conceive this plan, is a mere metaphysical hypothesis, having no connection whatever with facts, or with testimony, these are circumstances which have a tendency to render it highly improbable. One is, that his letters to Lee, particularly that of the 19th of March, prove that, from the moment he resolved to advance from the position to which he retreated after the battle of Guilford, until the British army got beyond his reach by crossing the main branch of the Cape Fear at Ramsay's mills, his views were solely bent upon the pursuit of Cornwallis—upon the *obvious* course of warfare; from which the plan suggested by Lee was a signal departure. Another is, that throughout his operations he had made it a point to keep between Virginia and his adversary, and that under the influence of these habits and views, and the numerous considerations which prompted and impressed them, his mind would not be likely, suddenly, to conceive a plan perfectly at variance with them. It may be added, that his inclination to recur to the *obvious* from the *indirect* mode of warfare; that is, to proceed to Virginia and face Cornwallis before the evacuation of Camden, is further evidence that this plan was not the offspring of his own mind. His great and just fame is not at all affected by this conclusion. When the plan was proposed, his judgment embraced and acknowledged its utility, and his enterprising spirit immediately entered on its execution.—Ed.

salubrity of the lower country, but denied the necessity of placing the army in it; as the healthy region was sufficiently near to the enemy for all the purposes of offence, whenever he should advance. They laid it down as a cardinal principle, never to be relinquished or even slighted, that the safety of the South hung upon the safety of Virginia; and the sure way to yield to that State full protection, was to face Cornwallis. They re-enforced this argument by dwelling, with much emphasis, upon the singular fitness of Greene to cope with his lordship, as well as the superior capacity of his army to contend with that under Cornwallis; that the British general and the British soldier had been taught, through the keen and trying struggles just concluded, the value of their enemy—a consideration entitled to weight; and that this value of character would be thrown away by abandoning that army on which it would always most bear; that the British dragoons, so dreadful heretofore, had been rendered comparatively innocent by the superior ability of the American horse; and that withdrawing the curb now imposed upon their prowess, would be sure to restore them to their pristine sway and effect. They contended, by observing that our Continental force exceeded in number the army of Cornwallis, that should his lordship even abandon Wilmington, which was not probable, because injudicious, he would only bring himself to an equality; and the State of North Carolina, already in high spirits from what had passed, would exert itself to give to us the weight of numbers, so long as it found the contest directed by a general deep in its confidence: whereas, the relinquishment of the State, with the enemy in its bosom, as proposed, would be sure to excite gloom and apprehension, which would infallibly lead to the ancient state of apathy, the fatal effects of which had been severely experienced.

In opposition it was admitted, that the primary object in all the measures to be adopted was the safety of Virginia, as it could not be denied that on its preservation depended the restoration of the subjugated States; and the various arguments adduced were acknowledged to be correct and cogent, but not entitled to that preponderance which was so strenuously pressed. It was urged, as the surest mode of reaching right conclusions, to lay down the probable conduct of the enemy, and to compare the effects of the northern or southern movement upon that conduct. The British general would either return to South Carolina, to hold the ground already gained; or, leaving his conquest to the force left for its protection, he would advance upon Virginia. Should he return to South Carolina—ignorant as for days he must be of our movement, and incapable, from his crippled condition, of immediate operation, should he even be so fortunate as to learn with celerity the design of his foe—very probably we should in the interval obtain an advantage which the British general would not be able soon to retrieve, even with his united force. But, granting that we should fail in this expectation ; and that Cornwallis should, by crossing the Pedee at the Cheraw Hills, force the light corps and Marion to fall back upon Greene, relieve Camden, and unite to his army its garrison, still we should be safe, and greatly the gainer. For, re-enforced as General Greene would be by the corps of Marion, of Sumter, and of Pickens, he would preserve a numerical superiority over the enemy, although strengthened by all the disposable troops under Lord Rawdon. The quality of these corps, and the well-known ability of their leaders, placed them far above any force to be derived from North Carolina, should General Greene renew his contest in that State. We should, therefore, be in better condition to risk battle by going to the South than by continuing here ; and we should enjoy the immense advantage of rendering a campaign from which so much was expected by the enemy, entirely abortive ; inasmuch as we brought our opponent back to the very ground which he had left months before, when menacing the subjugation of North Carolina instantly, and that of Virginia remotely. This single good would be of itself adequate compensation ; as it would confirm the superiority of our arms, and demonstrate, even to a British cabinet, the folly of persevering in the hopeless, destructive conflict.

But supposing Lord Cornwallis should not return to take care of his conquest—inasmuch as it would unequivocally declare the mastership of his opponent, and when we reflect how often the best and wisest men prefer any course to that which is coupled with admission of their own inferiority, we might presume that his lordship would follow in the beaten track—what will be the consequences? The States of Georgia and South Carolina restored to the Union ; the disaffected in North Carolina restored to their senses, by feeling unequivocally the frivolity of British conquest ; North Carolina in a capacity to contribute its portion of annual force ; and Virginia saved from that devastating flight of human vultures which follow in the train of conquering armies, whose appetite for plunder is insatiate so long as objects of prey are attainable. How can you so effectually save Virginia, it was asked, as by withholding from her territory a visitation so dreadful, the precursor of famine and of plague? This was completely effected by moving to the South, as the contest for the Carolinas continuing, that state of quiet submission could not take place—and that condition must ensue before these destroyers of property would adventure to approach a new theatre of plunder.

This reasoning, however respectfully regarded, did not persuade the advocates for the original plan to concur. They had felt the degradation of one retreat through North Carolina, and they could not be readily induced to advise the risk of its repetition, which was deemed the infallible consequence of a return to South Carolina, should Lord Cornwallis act the part which his finished military reputation induced them to expect. They persevered in maintaining the propriety of holding Virginia as our primary object; and contended that the proposed substitute did effectually reduce her to a secondary station, however sincerely its author shared in the general policy of giving to her, in all our measures, a decided preference. They rejected the idea of the British general's leaving General Greene in the undisturbed pursuit of his object; and although, at first, his return would convey the acknowledgment presumed, yet the effect of this acknowledgment would be short-lived, as the superior force of the enemy would enable him to push Greene a second time into Virginia; and the sole benefit we should derive from this perilous movement, would be entering Virginia a few weeks later, greatly overweighed by the loss of that superiority in arms, now possessed, and to be sacrificed by a second retreat.

That highly as Marion, Sumter, and Pickens, were respected, and much as was prized the tried courage of their associates, yet the effect of their co-operation was overrated; but, even admitting it to the presumed extent, a movement of such magnitude never could be warranted by a reliance on means so precarious.

The discussions being now extremely narrowed, by presuming on the British general's return into South Carolina, it was only necessary to demonstrate, that the same perilous retreat would not necessarily ensue, to secure the adoption of the substituted plan of operations.

The fact of equality in force was reasserted, and proved by recurrence to official data. The precariousness of militia succor could not be denied; but it was urged that the South Carolina corps, above designated, formed an exception to the general rule. What rendered our retreat in the course of the past winter so difficult and dangerous was, not only a numerical inferiority, but an inferiority

in quality also, and a separation of the two divisions of the army.*
Now the army was united; the untried battalions had now gone
through severe service, and had confessedly improved in soldiership; its numerical strength was now at least equal, and would be
sure to be increased by the adoption of timely measures to secure
re-enforcements; whereas that of the enemy could not increase,
and must insensibly diminish without battle.

That the strong and faithful country west of Charlotte gave a
safe retreat; that a powerful corps of the King's Mountain militia
could be readily brought to meet us in that neighborhood, or upon
the Yadkin, if deemed advisable farther to retire. With this re-enforcement, the corps of South Carolina, and our superior cavalry,
General Greene would be much better prepared to appeal to the
sword than he was when he fought at Guilford Court-House, where
all admitted that he gained an advantage. That Lord Cornwallis
must either sit down in the vicinity of Camden, to guard South
Carolina—an inert condition, as foreign to his disposition as it was
incompatible with his duty—or he would, in conformity to his temper and his duty, advance upon General Greene. That, should he
presume upon a repetition of retreat, he would not only be disappointed, but would probably be destroyed; for the moment he passed
Lynch's Creek, his danger commenced, and increased every step he
took toward the Yadkin. He would, therefore, be compelled to be
satisfied with protecting his line of posts from Camden to Augusta,
or he would again encounter the peril of a Guilford Court-House
victory, out of which he would not so happily escape as he had done.
By taking the first course, he lost a year; by taking the second, he
lost himself.

That, from the Yadkin, Greene could readily reach Virginia, if
necessary, should the British general forbear to approach him, and
in a few weeks drive all the force collected there to the ocean—the
asylum of Englishmen—and return to South Carolina in time for a
winter campaign.

These, with other arguments equally forcible, were offered in
maintenance of the proposed substitute; and the effect upon Vir-

---

* Two of our Continental regiments, the second of Maryland, and the first of
Virginia, were composed of raw troops, although the officers were experienced.
These regiments had, in course of the preceding service, been much improved.
The two divisions of our army being at a great distance from each other, Greene
was necessarily compelled to fall back; and we find that, with all his exertions,
he could not reunite them until he reached Guilford Court-House.

ginia, which would probably ensue, should the British general proceed thither instead of returning to South Carolina as presumed by its author, was examined in all its bearings.*

General Greene gave to the subject that full and critical investigation which it merited, and which, by long habit, had become familiar to his mind. He perceived advantages and disadvantages attendant upon either course, and felt for the evils to which Virginia must be exposed, whichever plan he might adopt. Doubting whether her sufferings would not be increased, rather than mitigated, by rendering her the seat of the Southern war; and convinced that he had much to hope, and little to apprehend, from returning into South Carolina, he determined to carry the war into that State.

No sooner had he decided, than he commenced operations. The Legion of Lee, with Captain Oldham's detachment was ordered to move on the subsequent morning (6th of April), and the army was put in motion the following day. Previous to the general's departure from Deep River, he communicated his intentions to the Brigadiers Sumter and Pickens, and required those generals to assemble all the force they could collect for the purpose of co-operation.

To the first he signified his desire that he would be prepared to join him when he should reach the vicinity of Camden: to the last he expressed his wishes that he would invest Ninety-Six; or, at all events, counteract any attempt to re-enforce Camden from that post. To the commander-in-chief he made known at large his plans, with his hopes and his doubts, assuring him that he should take every measure to avoid a misfortune; "but necessity obliges me to commit myself to chance, and, if any accident should attend me, I trust my friends will do justice to my reputation."

Lieutenant Colonel Lee being instructed to join Marion, was directed to deliver to that officer the general's dispatch, and to assure him of the entire confidence reposed in his faithful efforts to maintain his share in the expected co-operation.

Lord Cornwallis had not long indulged in the enjoyment of repose and abundance, before his active mind turned to the probable

---

* No man was more familiarized to dispassionate and minute research than General Greene. He was patient in hearing every thing offered, never interrupting or slighting what was said; and, having possessed himself of the subject fully, he would enter into a critical comparison of the opposite arguments, convincing his hearers, as he proceeded, of the propriety of the decision he was about to pronounce.

measures of his antagonist, and, shortly after he reached Wilmington, he advised Lord Rawdon, commanding in South Carolina, of his apprehensions, lest General Greene might direct his attention to the recovery of the lost States.

If, as I believe, a general is sure to act wisely when he takes the course most dreaded by his adversary, the late decision of General Greene was indubitably correct. For never was a leader more affected than Cornwallis was, by the disclosure of his enemy's object. Day after day did his lordship revolve in his mind the difficulties of his situation, seeking the most eligible course to diminish or to surmount them.*

Sometimes he determined to follow Greene into South Carolina, and to punish him for his temerity; at other times he would proceed to Virginia, and, by the rapidity of his success in that quarter, compel Greene to abandon his object, and hasten to its relief. At length he decided in favor of the latter measure; persuaded that Greene had gained so much time as would probably enable him to strike his first blow, in which, if he failed, his presence would not be requisite, and if he succeeded, his lordship's approach might place his own army in extreme danger.†

This reasoning was plausible, but not solid; for, by taking the route by Cheraw Hill to Nelson's Ferry, he held himself safe, even had Greene succeeded against Rawdon—an event which, however practicable, was not to be effected under many weeks, unless fortune should indeed be extremely propitious to the American general.

Lee, in obedience to his orders, took the route toward Cross Creek, which, it was inferred, would very much conceal his real object, by inducing the British general to believe that Greene proposed to place himself in his neighborhood.

After advancing in this course, as long as was compatible with a speedy union with Marion, the light corps turned to the right,

---

* Lord Cornwallis was exceedingly perplexed in making up his decision, and at length took the course which risked all to gain all, and, as generally happens, he lost all. Thus it often occurs in war. The great Frederic of Prussia committed the same error before Prague, when he attempted to force the intrenched camp of Marshal Daun, and afterward at Cunnersdorf against the Russians and Marshal Laudohn. Once the resolution to follow Greene was not only adopted but in execution, a portion of the British army having passed to the southern banks of Cape Fear. This decision being soon after changed, the troops were recalled.

† Lord Cornwallis to Sir H. Clinton, April 24th, and to Lord G. Germain and General Phillips, 23d.—Ed.

and, by a very expeditious march, gained Drowning Creek, a branch of Little Pedee. In a large field, on the southern side of this stream, Lee encamped for the night, when a very extraordinary occurrence took place, worthy, from its singularity, of relation.

Between two and three in the morning, the officer of the day was informed that a strange noise had been heard in front of the picket, stationed on the great road near the creek, resembling that occasioned by men moving through a swamp.

Presently, and toward that quarter, a sentinel fired, which was followed by a sound of the bugle calling in the horse patrols, as was the custom on the approach of the enemy. The troops were immediately summoned to arms, and arrayed for defence. The officer of the day reported very particularly every thing which had passed, adding that several of the sentinels and one patrol concurred in asserting, that they heard plainly the progress of horsemen, concealing with the utmost care their advance. Never was a more perplexing moment: yet, knowing as Lieutenant-Colonel Lee did, that no enemy could be near him, unless Lord Cornwallis, divining Greene's plan and Lee's route, had pushed a body from Wilmington, with orders to proceed until it reached Drowning Creek, where Lee would probably pass it, for the purpose of intercepting him, he was induced to consider the intelligence as the fabrication of imagination, which sometimes leads the most serene and circumspect into error.

In a few moments, in a different quarter of our position, another sentinel fired, and soon afterward the same report, from that point, was made, as had just been received from the other. Appearances were now so strong as to dissipate the first conclusion, and what was deemed imaginary, was felt to be real.

A change in the formation of the troops was made to correspond with this last annunciation of the enemy's approach.

This was not completed before, in a different direction, we heard the discharge of a third sentinel. Now the most excruciating sensations were experienced; it appeared as if these different feelings of our position were wisely and dexterously made, preparatory to a general assault, to take effect as soon as the approach of light should warrant its commencement. All that could be done, was done. The pickets and sentinels held their stations; the horse patrols had been called in; and the corps changed its position in silence and with precision upon every new annunciation, having in view the conjoint object of keeping the fires between us and the enemy, and holding the horse in the rear of the infantry. During our last evolution to this end, we were again interrupted by the discharge of the line of sentinels in our rear, along the great road. Thus the enemy had traversed the major segment of our position, and had at length fixed himself upon the road of our march.

No doubt now remained, not only of the enemy being upon us, but that he was in force, and well understood his object. He had reconnoitred with penetration and perseverance, and had ultimately placed himself in the very spot most certainly promising success.

To attempt to regain Deep River was idle, if practicable ; for Greene must now be two or three days' march toward Camden, the intermediate country hostile, and the British army within striking distance of some points of our route. Marion only could afford safety ; and he was on the south of the Pedee, at least two days' march from us. The review of our situation admitted but one conclusion—that hope of aid could not be indulged, and that we must rely upon ourselves only. Brave soldiers can always be safely trusted with their situation. Lee, passing along the line of infantry, made known our condition : reminding them of their high reputation ; enjoining profound silence throughout the approaching contest ; and assuring them, with their customary support, he had no doubt but that he should force his way to the Pedee, where we should find all that was desirable. To the cavalry he briefly communicated the dangers which surrounded us, mingled with expressions of his thorough confidence that every man would do his duty, and concluded by pressing upon the officers not to permit any partial success to tempt pursuit, without orders, or to relax circumspection, but to bear in mind, that the contest before us was not the affair of an hour, but might last for days.

This address was answered by whispers of applause ; and having formed in columns, one of horse, and the other of foot, Lee waited anxiously for the break of day, the presumed signal for action.

It soon appeared, and the columns advanced to the great road, infantry in front, baggage in the centre, and the cavalry in the rear. As soon as the head of the column reached the road, it turned to the left, pursuing the route to the Pedee. The van officer, proceeding a few hundred yards, now got up to the sentinel who had fired last, and received from him the same account so often given. before. The enigma still remained unexplained, and the corps continued its march, in slow motion, expecting every moment the enemy's fire. In this state of suspense we might have continued long, had not the van officer directed his attention to the road, for the purpose of examining the trail of our active foe, when to his astonishment, he found the tracks of a large pack of wolves. It was now evident, that the presumed enemy was a troop of wild beasts, collected together, and anxious to pass along their usual route, when finding it obstructed, they turned from point to point to pass through the field : everywhere fired upon, they continued widening their circuit until they reached the great road from which they had been originally turned. Our agitation vanished, and was succeeded by facetious glee. Nowhere do wit and humor abound more than in camps ; and no occurrence was more apt to elicit it than that which we had just experienced. Never was a day's march more pleasant, being one continued scene of good humor, interspersed with innocent flashes of wit. For a time the restraint of discipline ceased. Every character, not excepting the commandant's, was hit ; and very salutary counsel was often imparted under cover of a joke. Each considered himself a dupe, all laughing at a credulity, any attempt to remove which, during the scene, would have been treated as insulting temerity. The pickets, the patrols, the sentinels, and the officer of the day, were marked as the peculiar objects of derision. Wonderful that not one of the many could distinguish between the movement of wolves and soldiers ! They were charged with disgraceful ignorance, shameful stupor, bordering close upon rank cowardice. Vain was the attempt of the abused individuals to defend their character and conduct : it was the interest of the many to fix the supposed stigma on the few, and the general verdict was against them. Reaching a settlement, the corps halted, and for a while the remembrance of the ludicrous occurrence of the night yielded to the solicitude of every one to provide his breakfast.

Here what had passed was imparted to the inhabitants, and the unintelligible adventure was very satisfactorily solved. We were informed that there had been in the field, where the corps had encamped, a store of provisions collected for the army ; but that it never had been conveyed to camp, being too distant from the line of march. Being neglected, its contents became putrid : the wild beasts soon profited by the neglect, and enjoyed nightly the food intended for the soldier. Having comprehended within our range of sentinels this abandoned store, we had interrupted their usual visits, and the circle which they nearly completed was from solicitude to find access to their nightly repast.

This was what had been termed "acute reconnoitring," and "an enemy in force, well understanding his own views."

Such is frail man, in war as well as in peace, subject to be imposed upon by his own conceits, notwithstanding the remonstrances of reason, and his experience of the delusions of credulity. Yet, when we consider that the night was very dark, that the troops were waked from sleep to prepare for defence, and that it was possible, though improbable, for the British general to have been advised of the march of Lee, in time to strike him, our surprise at the alarm excited will vanish.

Having finished our repast we resumed our march; and, after getting within a day's distance of the Pedee, Lieutenant-Colonel Lee dispatched an officer, with a small body of dragoons, to discover in what part of his extensive range Brigadier Marion then was. The officer, on reaching the river, learned that the brigadier, when heard from, not many days before, was in the swamps of Black River. This was his general quarters when he found it necessary to retire from active service. It not only afforded safety, but there being several fertile plantations in one settlement, he was well supplied with provisions and forage. Marion received with joy Lee's officer, and furnished boats, which he kept concealed on the Pedee, for the transportation of the corps across that river. On the 14th of April, Lee joined the general.

These military friends had not before met since their wire-drawn expedition against Georgetown, and very cordially rejoiced at being again united in the great attempt of wresting South Carolina from the enemy. The letter from the general inclosing his plan of operations, was delivered to the brigadier, and the references to Lieutenant-Colonel Lee fully explained. The evening was devoted to repose, and on the next day the two corps quitted the dark and favorite recess, for the execution of the trust confided to them. During their separation, many had been the vicissitudes produced by the fickleness of fortune; now blazoning with glory, then shading with disaster, the American standard. From the battle of Guilford, the long-wished reannexation of South Carolina and Georgia to the Union became the avowed, as it had before been the meditated object of the American general. Emboldened by the effect of that well-fought day, he no longer veiled in the mysteries of war his object, but openly disclosed the end to which all his toils and perils pointed. North Carolina became encouraged, by finding that her safety was not now considered precarious, and that the contest turned, not upon *her* defence, but upon the expulsion of the common enemy from her Southern neighbors.   The ethereal spirit which had animated Marion, Sumter, and Pickens, and year after year had sustained, through their example and efforts, the unequal conflict, had been long subsiding.   Enthusiasm is short-lived; and is soon succeeded by apathy, which deadens vigorous exertion as fully as the former promotes it.

In this state of dejection was the country when Greene entered South Carolina.   Lord Rawdon, well apprised of the feelings of the people, adopted measures to give a finishing blow to further resistance.   Beginning with the eastern quarter of the State, where opposition was still sustained by Marion, Rawdon detached Lieutenant-Colonel Watson, with five hundred infantry, toward Nelson's Ferry, for the purpose of forcing Marion to submission, or to flight into North Carolina.   Watson was sent from Camden soon after Cornwallis had communicated to the commandant there the victory obtained at Guilford Court-House; and having established a post on the Santee, some miles above Nelson's Ferry, which he fortified, and where he deposited the baggage of his corps, he continued his march toward Georgetown; vainly endeavoring to induce Marion, with his inferior force, to advance from his impenetrable recess, in order to defend the country; and was, as Marion believed, taking measures with a view of entering into the swamps and driving him across the Pedee,—an enterprise much desired by him, and to meet which he was fully prepared,—when the approach of the corps of Lee was announced.

Active operations now became practicable, and, on the evening of the 15th, Marion and Lee took a position in the open country, with Watson to their left, considerably below them, and on the route for the fort called by his name, which he had erected.

Determined to carry this post without delay, Marion and Lee sat down before it early in the evening; not doubting from the information received, that the garrison must soon be compelled to surrender for want of water, with which it was supplied from an adjacent lake, and from which the garrison might be readily and effectually excluded.   In a very few hours the customary mode of supplying the post with water was completely stopped; and had the information received been correct, a surrender of the garrison could not have been long delayed.   The ground selected by Colonel Watson for his small stockade, was an Indian mount, generally conceived to be the cemetery of the tribe inhabiting the circumjacent region : it was at least thirty feet high, and surrounded by table land. Captain McKoy, the commandant, saw at once his inevitable fate, unless he could devise some other mode of procuring water, for which purpose he immediately cut a trench secured by abatis, from his fosse to the river, which passed close to the Indian mount. Baffled in their expectation, and destitute both of artillery and intrenching tools, Marion and Lee despaired of success ; when Major Maham, of South Carolina, accompanying the brigadier, suggested a plan, which was no sooner communicated than adopted. He proposed to cut down a number of suitable trees in the nearest wood, and with them to erect a large strong oblong pen, to be covered on the top with a floor of logs, and protected on the side opposite to the fort with a breastwork of light timber. To the adjacent farms dragoons were dispatched for axes, the only necessary tool, of which a sufficient number being soon collected, relays of working parties were allotted for the labor ; some to cut, some to convey, and some to erect. Major Maham undertook the execution of his plan, which was completely finished before the morning of the 23d, effective as to the object, and honorable to the genius of the inventor. The besieged was, like the besieger, unprovided with artillery, and could not interrupt the progress of a work, the completion of which must produce immediate submission.

A party of riflemen, being ready, took post in the Maham tower the moment it was completed; and a detachment of musketry, under cover of the riflemen, moved to make a lodgment in the enemy's ditch, supported by the Legion infantry with fixed bayonets. Such was the effect of the fire from the riflemen, having thorough command of every part of the fort, from the relative supereminence of the tower, that every attempt to resist the lodgment was crushed. The commandant, finding every resource cut off, hung out the white flag. It was followed by a proposal to surrender, which issued in a capitulation. This incipient operation having been happily effected by the novel and effectual device of Major Maham, to whom the commandants very gratefully expressed their acknowledgment, Marion and Lee, preceded by the Legion cavalry under Major Rudolph, who had been detached on the day subsequent to the investiture of the fort, turned their attention to Lieutenant-Colonel Watson, now advancing from below to relieve his garrison. Knowing that the fall of Camden was closely connected with the destruction of Watson, the American commandants viewed with delight his approach ; and having disposed of the prisoners, moved to join the cavalry, now retiring in front of the enemy.

General Greene broke up from Ramsay's mills on the seventh of April, the day after he had detached Lee to join Marion; and determined to approach Camden with a celerity which would preclude the British general from being apprised of his movement until the appearance of his army announced it. In this expectation, notwithstanding his pressing endeavors, he was disappointed. The country through which he marched was barren, its settlements few, the produce of the soil scanty, and the inhabitants disaffected.

Being obliged to depend upon himself for subsistence, always difficult to be procured from the inadequacy of the annual products, and rendered more so by the concealment of part of the little made (from hostility to the American cause, or from the natural and powerful claim of securing sustenance at home), General Greene did not reach the neighborhood of Camden until the nineteenth. _{April 19th.}

By the last return made before the American army decamped from Ramsay's mills, the regular force of every sort under Greene, may be put down at one thousand eight hundred effectives.

Deducting the corps under Lee, about three hundred horse and foot, the army when arrived before Camden, exclusive of a small body of North Carolina militia, cannot be estimated at more than one thousand five hundred. Here the American general confidently expected to be joined by Brigadier Sumter, in consequence of his instructions to that officer previous to his movement from Deep River; with whose aid, and the co-operation of Marion and Lee below, Greene very justly concluded that the evacuation of Camden was certain, and the destruction of Rawdon and his army probable. Brigadier Sumter held off, much to the surprise, regret, and dissatisfaction of the American general, and very much to the detriment of his plans and measures. Happily this disappointment was balanced by the accidental absence of a large portion of the garrison of Camden, under Lieutenant-Colonel Watson; who, as before mentioned, was low down the eastern quarter of the State.

General Greene, not having adequate force to invest Camden, placed himself before it; not doubting that, by depriving the garrison of its usual supplies from the country, he should compel the British general to withdraw; when he flattered himself opportunities would occur for striking him in detail, until re-enforced by the junction of Marion, Lee, and Sumter; after which he might fall upon his retreating enemy, with well-grounded expectation of decisive success.

Severed as Watson was from Camden, Rawdon's effective force was not more than nine hundred men; nor was there any possibility of adding to this force but by the safe return of Lieutenant-Colonel Watson, to whom Lord Rawdon dispatched a courier as soon as he was informed of General Greene's approach, communicating that event, and requiring his immediate junction. Informed of the union of the corps under Marion and Lee, and of their advance upon Fort Watson, with the situation of Watson, then returning toward Camden on the north side of the Santee, Greene determined to change his position from the north to the east side of Camden; by which movement he could readily bring 'to him Marion and Lee, if circumstances should demand it, and more effectually oppose the junction of Watson, should he force or elude the corps below.

This change of position could not be effected without passing Sandhill Creek, with its deep and difficult swamps, impracticable with artillery and baggage, or making an extensive circuit alike forbidden by the posture of affairs and the want of time. To surmount the obstacles opposed to his plan, the American general determined to relieve himself of every incumbrance, and, by a rapid movement on the direct route through the swamps, to gain his desired position on the road leading from Camden to Nelson's Ferry. With this view he placed in charge of the quartermaster-general, Lieutenant-Colonel Carrington, his baggage and artillery; directing that officer to retire to the strong country north of Lynch's Creek, putting himself with his small detachment safe from any practicable attempt to break him up. This being done, General Greene assumed his desired position on the east of Camden; where his communication with Marion and Lee being direct, he soon was informed of their condition, and the situation of Watson.

With pleasure he heard that the operations against Fort Watson were advancing to a close, with the prospects of certain success; and that not only the Legion cavalry had been detached to attend the movements of Lieutenant-Colonel Watson, but that a strong pass on the route of the British officer had been occupied with a detachment of infantry, to which place the whole corps would hasten, the moment the garrison of Fort Watson submitted, an event which was soon expected.   Finding that the approach of Watson could not speedily take place, if at all; and not doubting but that by this time Brigadier Sumter must be in the vicinity of Camden; Greene relinquished his position lately taken, and returned to the north side of the town.   The moment this resolution was adopted, the general dispatched orders to Lieutenant-Colonel Carrington, to rejoin him with celerity.   Within a small distance of Camden, on the Waxhaw's road, is Hobkirk's Hill, the position selected by General Greene after repassing Sandhill Creek, not only from its being on the route prescribed for the rejunction of Carrington, and most convenient to the union with Sumter, but because the ground gave advantages in case of battle; which, though not presumed upon, was nevertheless always to be kept in view.   Regarding this consideration, the American army encamped in order of battle.

The regulars composed one line, with their centre on the road; the militia, amounting to two hundred and fifty, with the cavalry, formed the reserve, in a suitable distance in the rear.   Strong pickets were posted in front, aided by the customary patrols ranging in front and on the flanks.   Thus prepared for whatever might happen, the American army lay waiting for the expected return of Carrington, and the much desired junction of Sumter.

On the 24th, Greene was officially informed of the surrender of Fort Watson; and, in the course of the day, the prisoners reached head quarters.   Among them were a few American soldiers, who had been taken, as they represented, and who had enlisted with the enemy, as affording the best chance in their judgment for escape to their friends.   These men were cheerfully received into the regiments to which they belonged.   One of them, a drummer in the Maryland line, availed himself of the confidence with which the whole had been treated, and in the course of the night deserted. Being intelligent, he communicated to Lord Rawdon the position of Greene with accuracy; and informed his lordship, that as yet the detachment under Lieutenant-Colonel Carrington, with the artillery, &c., had not joined, nor had Greene been re-enforced by Sumter, or any other corps.

Already straitened for provisions, and despairing of succor, this enterprising young soldier resolved to risk battle at once; confident that every day would strengthen his adversary, and consequently diminish his chance of victory (without which not only the evacuation of Camden must ensue, but with it might follow the destruction of his army), and hoping that he would find Greene destitute of artillery, conformably to the information just derived from the drummer. Giving orders for his troops to make ready, and placing Camden in charge of the convalescents, he advanced at nine in the morning of the 25th, with nine hundred men only, of every description. Avoiding the direct approach to his enemy, he took a circuitous course to his right, along the margin of the swamp which lines Pine-Tree Creek, and winds with its meanders.

The position of Greene was on a ridge covered with uninterrupted wood, the Waxhaw's Road running directly through it; his army resting with its left upon the swamp of Pine-Tree Creek, where the ridge or eminence was easiest of ascent, and extending on the right to woods uncovered by water-courses or any other obstructions. In this quarter the American position was easiest assailed, but the probability of an undiscovered approach was not so encouraging. Therefore Lord Rawdon preferred the route to our left; inasmuch as an unexpected assault upon our camp was a leading feature in his plan.

In the morning Carrington joined, with a comfortable supply of provisions, which had been rather scarce during the late hurried changes of position. These were issued, and of course engaged a portion of the troops; while the residue were employed along the rivulets in washing their clothes, an occupation which had been for some days past impracticable.

Absorbed in these employments, the period was very propitious to the enemy's object. His advance was never discovered until his van fell upon our pickets. The two in front commanded by Captain Benson, of Maryland, and Captain Morgan, of Virginia, received him handsomely; and, retiring in order, disputed bravely every inch of ground, supported by Kirkwood with the remains of the Delaware regiment. This rencounter gave the first announcement of the contest at hand. Disposed for battle by the order of encampment, the American army, notwithstanding its short notice, was quickly ranged for action—an event, although unexpected, of all others the most desirable; because, in all probability, the readiest for the production of that issue so anxiously coveted by the American general.

During the contest with the pickets, Greene formed his army. The Virginia brigade with General Huger at its head, having under him the Lieutenant-Colonels Campbell and Hawes, took the right; the Maryland brigade, led by Colonel Williams, seconded by Colonel Gunby, and the Lieutenant-Colonels Ford and Howard, occupied the

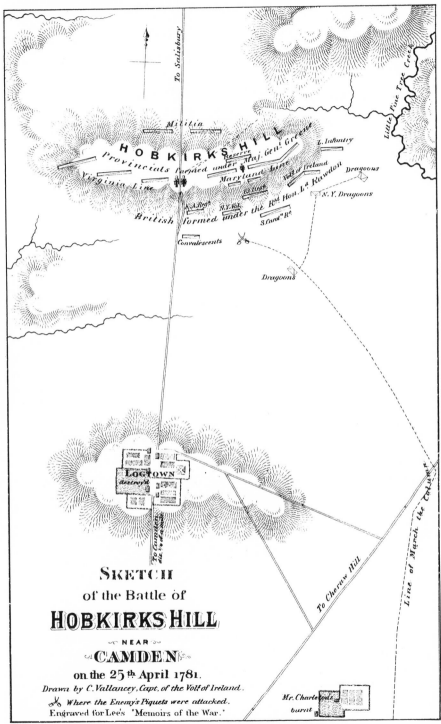

To Salisbury

Little Pine Tree Creek

Militia

HOBKIRKS HILL

Provincials formed under Maj. Gen.ˡ Greene

Reserve

L. Infantry

Virginia Line

Maryland Line

Vol.ˢ of Ireland

Dragoons

K.⁵ A. Reg.ᵗ

N.Y. Vol.ˢ

63 Reg.ᵗ

British formed under the R.ᵗ Hon.ᵇ L.ᵈ Rawdon

N. Y. Dragoons

S. Carol.ⁿ R.ᵗ

Convalescents

Dragoons

LOGTOWN
destroy'd

To Camden the ¼ of a mile

Line of March the Column

To Cheraw Hill

SKETCH
of the Battle of
HOBKIRKS HILL
NEAR
CAMDEN
on the 25ᵗʰ April 1781.

Drawn by C. Vallancey, Capt. of the Vol.ᵗ of Ireland.

Where the Enemy's Piquets were attacked.

Engraved for Lee's "Memoirs of the War."

Mr. Charleton's burnt

U.P. Co. No. 4 Bond. St.

left. Thus all the Continentals, consisting of four regiments, much reduced in strength, were disposed in one line, with the artillery, conducted by Colonel Harrison, in the centre. The reserve consisted of the cavalry, under Lieutenant-Colonel Washington, with a corps of North Carolina militia, about two hundred and fifty, commanded by Colonel Reade.

The British general, pushing before him the pickets and Kirkwood, pressed forward to battle. The king's American regiment on the right, the New York volunteers in the centre, and the sixty-third on the left, formed the line of battle. His right wing was supported by Robertson's corps, and his left by the volunteers of Ireland. The reserve consisted of the South Carolina regiment, with a few dragoons, all the cavalry then at Camden.

Greene, examining attentively the British disposition, discovered the very narrow front which it presented; and gratified as he was with the opportunity, so unexpectedly offered, of completing, by one blow, his first object, he determined to avail himself of the advantage given by the mode of attack.

He directed Lieutenant-Colonels Campbell and Ford to turn the enemy's flanks; he ordered the centre regiments to advance with fixed bayonets upon him ascending the height; and detached Lieutenant-Colonel Washington with his cavalry to gain his rear. Rawdon no sooner cast his eyes on our disposition than he perceived the danger to which his unequal front exposed him, and, bringing up the volunteers of Ireland into line, he remedied the defect seized by Greene in time to avert the expected consequence.

The battle opened from right to left with a vigor which promised a keen and sanguinary contest; but the superiority of our fire, augmented by that from our well-served artillery, must have borne down all opposition, had the American line maintained itself with becoming firmness. On the right Huger evidently gained ground; Washington was carrying every thing before him in the rear; and Lieutenant-Colonel Hawes, with fixed bayonets, conformable to order, was descending the hill ready to fall upon the New York volunteers.

In this flattering moment the veteran regiment of Gunby, having first joined in the fire, in violation of orders, paused, its right falling back. Gunby unfortunately directed the disordered battalion to rally by retiring to its right company.* Retrograde being the con-

---

* Although the army of Greene was not surprised, yet it was very suddenly assailed; no notice of the attack having been given until our pickets fired. The

sequence of this order, the British line, giving a shout, pressed forward with redoubled ardor; and the regiment of Gunby, considered as the bulwark of the army, never recovered from the panic with which it was at this moment unaccountably seized. The Virginia brigade, and the second regiment of Maryland, with the artillery, notwithstanding the shameful abandonment by the first Maryland, maintained the contest bravely. Williams with Gunby, assisted by Lieutenant-Colonel Howard, who had so often and so gloriously borne down with this very regiment all opposition, vainly exerted themselves to bring it to order. Not the menaces of the one, not the expostulations of the other, and the exhortations of the third, not the recollection of its pristine fame, could arouse its cowering spirit.

The second Maryland, which had from the commencement of the action acted with gallantry, feeling severely the effect produced by the recession of the first, became somewhat deranged; and Lieutenant-Colonel Ford being unluckily wounded, while endeavoring to repress the beginning disorder, this corps also fell back. Rawdon's right now gained the summit of the eminence, flanking Hawes' regiment, which had undeviatingly held its prescribed course, although early in the action abandoned on its left by the first Maryland, and now but feebly sustained on the right by the first Virginia—for this corps had now begun to recede, notwithstanding its preceding success. Greene recalled Hawes, our only unbroken regiment; and finding every effort to reinstate the battle illusory, conscious that his reserve was not calculated to face the veteran foe, wisely determined to diminish the ills of the sad and unaccountable reverse by retiring from the field. Orders were given to this effect, and Lieutenant-Colonel Hawes was commanded to cover the broken line.

The retreat was performed without loss, although the enemy continued to pursue for a few miles. Washington with his cavalry retiring from the rear the moment he discovered that our infantry

troops, in the hurry of forming, had not got settled before they advanced. Gunby was anxious to lead his regiment into battle thoroughly compacted; and, therefore, ordered Lieutenant-Colonel Howard to call back Captain Armstrong, who, with two sections, was moving upon the enemy. This Howard did, and Armstrong very reluctantly obeyed. The enemy was not yet in strength in this point; and it is probable had Gunby, instead of recalling Armstrong, made him the point of view in forming, that the fate of the day would have been favorable to our arms. This Greene always declared as his opinion, and Gunby as uniformly denied. The latter officer was called before a court of inquiry, at his own request; whose statement of the facts, as before recited, was followed by the general's order announcing the spirit and activity displayed by Colonel Gunby as unexceptionable; but his order for the regiment to fall back improper, and the probable cause of the loss of a complete victory.

had been forced, came in time to contribute greatly to the safety of the army, having necessarily relinquished most of the fruits of his success. Checking the enemy's efforts to disturb our rear,* he at length, by a rapid charge, effectually discomfited the British van, and put a stop to further pursuit. General Greene having passed Saunders' Creek, about four miles from the field of battle, encamped for the night, and on the next day proceeded to Rudgely's mill.

The loss sustained by the respective armies was nearly equal. On the side of America two hundred and sixty-eight were killed, wounded, and missing; on the side of the enemy two hundred and fifty-eight, including the prisoners brought off by Lieutenant-Colonel Washington, and those paroled by him on the ground. The British lost no officer of distinction, which was not the case with us. The wound of Lieutenant-Colonel Ford proved mortal, and Captain Beatty, of the first Maryland, was killed, than whom the army did not possess an officer of more promise.

No military event had occurred in the course of the war, whose issue was so inexplicable as that of the late engagement. The daring attempt of the enemy was readily accounted for, and exhibits in the most convincing manner the wisdom of the movement into South Carolina. Without risk or loss, the American general, although disappointed in the aid of Brigadier Sumter, had in six days placed his adversary in a situation so dangerous as to compel him to resort to the measure of all others the most desired by his enemy. Greatly inferior in infantry, more so in cavalry, and destitute of artillery, the British general, aware of the inevitable consequence of holding himself shut up in Camden, took the bold resolution of attacking his antagonist, notwithstanding his many advantages, considerably augmented by the convenience of a position selected with the view and from the hope that the critical condition of Rawdon would force him to hazard an action. Lord Rawdon certainly chose the most propitious moment for his gallant attempt, and as certainly conducted it in the most martial manner. Yet he would have been destroyed, had the troops of Greene exe-

---

* After Greene halted at Saunders' Creek, Washington returned with his cavalry to examine the situation of the enemy. His advanced patrol was pursued by Major Coffin with his cavalry. Washington, hearing their approach, placed himself in ambush, covered by some thick bushes, near the road, and pressed upon his adversary. Coffin attempted to bring his men to face Washington; but they put spurs to their horses to regain their camp. Some were killled, some taken, and the rest dispersing reached Lord Rawdon. Coffin himself escaped.

cuted his orders with common resolution. The satisfaction enjoyed by the American general, on discerning the enemy advancing upon him, was not confined to himself, but prevailed throughout the army, and afforded no inconsiderable pledge that, upon this occasion, every man would do his duty. So decisive was the confidence which actuated the general, that he held all his Continental infantry in one body, never doubting their sufficiency to insure success; and, with the same impression, on his first view of his enemy, he gave orders for striking him in front, in rear, and on both flanks: thus conveying to his troops his conviction that victory was certain, as well as his determination that it should be complete.

Sad and immediate was Greene's disappointment. The first regiment of Maryland, as has been mentioned, deservedly held up to the army as its model, and which upon all preceding occasions behaved well,* now shrank from the conflict, abandoning their general, their country, and their comrades: this, too, in defiance of the efforts and example of Williams, Gunby, and Howard, all dear to the troops, and when the British line, so far from having gained any advantage, was beginning to stagger under the combined operation fast bearing upon it. It is true that Captain Beatty, commanding the company on the right, fell at this moment; and it is also true that Colonel Gunby, with a view of bringing the regiment to range with its colors, ordered it to fall back to the right company; but Morgan had given the same order, at the Cowpens, to the corps of Howard, which was not only executed with promptitude, but was followed by its decisive advance, and consequent signal success.

Relinquishing an investigation which does not promise a satisfactory solution, I cannot but observe that the battle of Hobkirk's adds to the many evidences with which military history abounds of the deranging effects of unlimited confidence. It is the only instance in Greene's command, where this general implicity yielded to its delusive counsel, and he suffered deeply in consequence of it; for had he for a moment doubted the certainty of success, the cavalry would not have been detached in the rear until the issue of the battle had begun to unfold itself.

Nor is it risking too much to suggest the probability that, had the horse been still in reserve, not only would the forward move-

---

* It was this regiment which forced the guards at the battle of Guilford Court-House, killing their commandant, and driving them back, seeking shelter under cover of the British artillery; and a portion of the same regiment constituted a part of the infantry, which, under Howard, gave us the victory at the Cowpens, by the free use of the bayonet.

ment of the enemy, which followed the recession of the first regiment of Maryland, been delayed, but that regiment would have been restored to order, and the battle renewed with every reason still to conclude that its event would have been auspicious to America. The maxim in war, that your enemy is ever to be dreaded until at your feet, ought to be held inviolate; nor should a commander permit the gratifying seductions of brilliant prospects to turn him from the course which this maxim enjoins.

Honorable as this victory was to the British general and to the British arms, it yielded not one solitary benefit. The loss sustained being proportionate, the relative strength of the combatants was unchanged; and Lord Rawdon,. experiencing his inadequacy to improve success after gaining it, reluctantly relinquished his offensive plan of operations, and returned to Camden, in the expectation of Lieutenant-Colonel Watson's arrival before the American general would feel himself in strength and spirits to renew his investment.

General Greene, heretofore soured by the failure of his expected succor from Sumter, now deeply chagrined by the inglorious behavior of a favorite regiment—converting his splendid prospects into the renewal of toil and difficulty, of doubt and disgrace—became for awhile discontented with his advance to the South. He sent orders to Lieutenant-Colonel Lee, requiring him to join the army forthwith; and indicated by other measures a disposition to depart from his adopted system.

As soon as the capitulation for the surrender of Fort Watson was signed, Lee followed by his infantry hastened to the cavalry, still in front of Watson; and on the subsequent morning was joined by Brigadier Marion, who had been necessarily delayed until the prisoners and stores were disposed of. The British lieutenant-colonel, seeing that the passes on his route were occupied, and knowing that the advantages possessed by his enemy would be strenuously maintained, relinquished his project of gaining Camden on the direct route, and determined, by passing the Santee, to interpose it between himself and the corps opposed to him; presuming that he might with facility make his way good to Camden, by recrossing the Santee above; or, by taking the route by Fort Motte, pass first the Congaree, and then the Wateree, which unite some small distance below the post at Motte's.

Drawing off in the night, he placed himself at a considerable distance from his enemy before his change of plan was discovered. Nevertheless he would have been pursued, with the expectation of falling upon him before he could make good his passage of the river, had not the general's orders directing the junction of the corps under Lee arrived, which necessarily arrested the proposed attempt upon Watson. With all possible dispatch Lieutenant-Colonel Lee set out for the army; and, in the course of the day and a small part of the night, marched thirty-two miles.

Sorely as Greene felt the disappointment lately experienced, he did not long permit his accustomed equanimity to be disturbed; nor could his strong mind long entertain suggestions growing out of adverse fortune. Persuaded that his movement upon South Carolina was, under all the circumstances of his situation, the most promising of good to his country, he determined to adhere to his plan of operations with firmness, and to obliterate his late repulse by subsequent success. Fixed in this resolution, he dispatched an officer to meet Lee, countermanding his orders, followed by Captain Finley, of the artillery, with a six-pounder, detached by General Greene to Marion and Lee; in consequence of representations from those officers soliciting this aid.

As soon as Finley joined, Lee returned to Marion, who had approached the vicinity of the confluence of the Congaree and Wateree, waiting for Watson's advance. The dispatch from General Greene contained directions to proceed in the execution of his original orders, taking care by every practicable exertion to repel Watson's attempt to throw himself into Camden; and communicated the general's decision to pass the Wateree with the army, for the purpose of intercepting Lieutenant-Colonel Watson, should he select that route to Camden. In conformity with this decision, Greene broke up from Rudgely's mill, and, passing the Wateree above Camden, sat down in a strong position, which deprived the British garrison of its usual supplies in this quarter as effectually as it debarred Watson's approach to Camden on the southern route.

Rawdon now demonstrated by his conduct that his late victory, though brilliant, produced no support or benefit to him; as he was compelled to a painful inactivity in the face of his enemy, who but a few days before had retired before him. The accession of the corps under Watson only could save him; and this accession he saw completely prevented, on the most eligible route, by his adversary, —he saw it without being able to take a single step in furtherance of the desired aid.

Marion and Lee lost not a moment after their union in taking measures to execute the command of their general, well apprised of the vast importance attached to the interception of Watson. The militia general, being perfectly acquainted with the country, guided the measures adopted.   He well knew that, although General Greene's position would stop the lieutenant-colonel on the usual route from Motte's post to Camden, it would not stop him from passing the Wateree at or below the high hills of Santee; and that Lieutenant-Colonel Watson, to avoid the corps destined to strike him, would probably, notwithstanding the judicious position taken by Greene, pass the Congaree at Motte's, and afterward pass the Wateree below the high hills.   If Watson should not deem it eligible to pass the Congaree, but one way was left for him, and that was to recross the Santee at the confluence of the two rivers just mentioned.   Whether to sit down on the north side of the Santee prepared to fall upon the British lieutenant-colonel in the act of passing the river, or to cross it and strike at him on the southern banks, was the alternative presented to the American commandants.   Well informed of every step taken by Watson after he reached the southern side of the Santee, no doubt remained but that he would pass either the Congaree or the Santee on the ensuing morning.   It was now decided to cross to his side of the river, from a conviction that we should reach him on its southern banks, whichever course of the two before him he might select.   The indefatigable Marion, seconded by his zealous associates, foreseeing the probable necessity of a quick passage over the Santee, had provided the means of transportation, which was effected in the course of the night, and, with the dawn of day, the troops moved with celerity up the Santee. It was then ascertained that Lieutenant-Colonel Watson had taken the route leading over that river where its two branches unite—the very spot which had so forcibly attracted the attention of Marion and Lee, and would have been selected by them, had it not been apprehended that the British lieutenant-colonel might prefer the route across the Congaree.

Had these two officers confined their attention entirely to the north side of the river, the much-desired interception would have been effected: for with horse, foot, and artillery, it was not to be expected that a corps of infantry only could make good its landing in the face of an equal foe, and secure its arrival into Camden.

Mortified with the result of their unceasing exertions, the deranging information was immediately forwarded to General Greene, and the disappointed commandants moved upon Fort Motte.

Persuaded that Lord Rawdon would resume offensive operations, the moment Watson joined him, Greene withdrew from the vicinity of Camden, and took a more distant position in the high grounds behind Sawney's Creek. On the seventh of May the long-expected succor reached Camden; and on the next day the British general put his army in motion, passed the Watcree at the ferry below Camden, and advanced to attack Greene. On his way he was informed of the American general's decampment, and proceeded toward Sawney's Creek, still determined to execute his object.

The two armies were nearly equal, about twelve hundred each. The advantage in number and quality of infantry was on the side of Rawdon, while Greene continued to hold his superiority in cavalry. Convinced that the British general would press battle, and anxious to restore the humbled spirits of his troops, General Greene broke up from his position and retired to Colonel's Creek, leaving Washington with his cavalry and some infantry on the ground to cover his retreat. Rawdon, examining critically his adversary's situation, and perceiving his well-prepared condition, did not deem it advisable to carry into effect his projected enterprise, but withdrew about the time that Greene commenced his retreat, and returned to Camden. Thus it happened that both armies retired at the same moment from each other. Convinced that he could not force the American general from his neighborhood, and persuaded that the breaking up of the intermediate posts between him and Charleston would not only endanger his army, but must complete that spirit of revolt which had begun to manifest itself on the entrance of the American army into the State, his lordship wisely decided to give up Camden, and, with it, all the country north of the Congaree. Preparing for retreat, he sent orders to Lieutenant-Colonel Cruger to abandon Ninety-six and to join Browne at Augusta, and directed Major Maxwell, commanding at Fort Granby, to fall back upon Orangeburgh.

This arrangement was indubitably the best practicable; and, duly maintained, would have preserved all the country south of the Congaree, and west of the Santee. But so completely had the American general taken his measures to prevent all communication with Lord Rawdon, that none of his dispatches reached their destination.

On the 10th, the evacuation of Camden took place, and the British general proceeded to Nelson's Ferry, with the expectation of crossing the Santee in time to dislodge Marion and Lee, still prosecuting the siege of Fort Motte. Previous to his lordship's departure he burned the jail, the mills, and some private houses,

May.

May 10th.

and destroyed all the stores which he could not take with him. He carried off four or five hundred negroes, and all the most obnoxious loyalists accompanied him.

As soon as Greene was informed of the retreat of the enemy, persuaded that Rawdon's first effort would be directed to relieve Fort Motte, he advanced toward the Congaree, determined to pass that river, if necessary, and to cover the operations of the besieging corps.

This post was the principal depot of the convoys from Charleston to Camden, and sometimes of those destined for Fort Granby and Ninety-six. A large, new mansion-house, belonging to Mrs. Motte, situated on a high and commanding hill, had been selected for this establishment. · It was surrounded with a deep trench, along the interior margin of which was raised a strong and lofty parapet. To this post had been regularly assigned an adequate garrison of about one hundred and fifty men, which was now accidentally increased by a small detachment of dragoons, which had arrived from Charleston a few hours before the appearance of the American troops, on its way to Camden, with dispatches for Lord Rawdon. Captain McPherson commanded, an officer highly and deservedly respected.

Opposite to Fort Motte, to the north, stood another hill, where Mrs. Motte, having been dismissed from her mansion, resided, in the old farm-house. On this height Lieutenant-Colonel Lee with his corps took post, while Brigadier Marion occupied the eastern declivity of the ridge on which the fort stood.

Very soon the fort was completely invested; and the six-pounder was mounted on a battery erected in Marion's quarter for the purpose of raking the northern face of the enemy's parapet, against which Lee was preparing to advance. McPherson was unprovided with artillery, and depended for safety upon timely relief, not doubting its arrival before the assailant could push the preparations to maturity.

The vale which runs between the two hills admitted our safe approach within four hundred yards of the fort. This place was selected by Lee to break ground. Relays of working parties being provided for every four hours, and some of the negroes from the neighboring plantations being brought, by the influence of Marion, to our assistance, the works advanced with rapidity. Such was their forwardness on the 10th, that it was determined to summon the commandant.

A flag was accordingly dispatched to Captain McPherson, stating to him with truth our relative situation, and admonishing him to avoid the disagreeable consequences of an arrogant temerity. To this the captain replied, that, disregarding consequences, he should continue to resist to the last moment. The retreat of Rawdon was known in the evening to the besiegers; and in the course of the night a courier arrived from General Greene confirming that event, urging redoubled activity, and communicating his determination to hasten to their support. Urged by these strong considerations, Marion and Lee persevered throughout the night in pressing the completion of their works. On the next day, Rawdon reached the country opposite to Fort Motte; and in the succeeding night encamping on the highest ground in his route, the illumination of his fires gave the joyful annunciation of his approach to the despairing garrison. But the hour was close at hand when this joy was to be converted into sadness.

The large mansion in the centre of the encircling trench, left but a few yards of the ground within the enemy's works uncovered; burning the house must force their surrender.

Persuaded that our ditch would be within arrow-shot before noon of the next day, Marion and Lee determined to adopt this speedy mode of effecting their object. Orders were instantly issued to prepare bows and arrows, with missive combustible matter. This measure was reluctantly adopted; for the destruction of private property was repugnant to the principles which swayed the two commandants, and upon this occasion was peculiarly distressing. The devoted house was a large, pleasant edifice, intended for the summer residence of the respectable owner, whose deceased husband had been a firm patriot, and whose only marriageable daughter was the wife of Major Pinckney, an officer in the South Carolina line, who had fought and bled in his country's cause, and was now a prisoner with the enemy. These considerations powerfully forbade the execution of the proposed measure; but there were others of much cogency, which applied personally to Lieutenant-Colonel Lee, and gave a new edge to the bitterness of the scene.

Encamping contiguous to Mrs. Motte's dwelling, this officer had, upon his arrival, been requested in the most pressing terms to make her house his quarters. The invitation was accordingly accepted; and not only the lieutenant-colonel, but every officer of his corps, off duty, daily experienced her liberal hospitality, politely proffered, and as politely administered. Nor was the attention of this amiable lady confined to that class of war which never fail to attract attention. While her richly-spread table presented with taste and fashion all the luxuries of her opulent country, and her sideboard offered without reserve the best wines of Europe—antiquated relics of happier days—her active benevolence found its way to the sick and to the wounded ; cherishing with softest kindness infirmity and misfortune, converting despair into hope, and nursing debility into strength.

Nevertheless the obligations of duty were imperative; the house must burn ; and a respectful communication to the lady of her destined loss must be made. Taking the first opportunity which offered, the next morning, Lieutenant-Colonel Lee imparted to Mrs. Motte the intended measure ; lamenting the sad necessity, and assuring her of the deep regret which the unavoidable act excited in his and every breast.

With a smile of complacency this exemplary lady listened to the embarrassed officer, and gave instant relief to his agitated feelings, by declaring, that she was gratified with the opportunity of contributing to the good of her country, and that she should view the approaching scene with delight. Shortly after, seeing accidentally the bow and arrows which had been prepared, she sent for the lieutenant-colonel, and presenting him with a bow and its apparatus imported from India, she requested his substitution of these, as probably better adapted for the object than those we had provided.

Receiving with silent delight this opportune present, the lieu-tenant-colonel rejoined his troops, now making ready for the concluding scene. The lines were manned, and an additional force stationed at the battery, lest the enemy, perceiving his fate, might determine to risk a desperate assault, as offering the only chance of relief. As soon as the troops reached their several points, a flag was again sent to McPherson, for the purpose of inducing him to prevent the conflagration and the slaughter which might ensue, by a second representation of his actual condition.

Doctor Irvine, of the Legion cavalry, was charged with the flag, and instructed to communicate faithfully the inevitable destruction impending, and the impracticability of relief, as Lord Rawdon had not yet passed the Santee; with an assurance that longer perse-verance in vain resistance, would place the garrison at the mercy of the conqueror, who was not regardless of the policy of preventing waste of time by inflicting exemplary punishment, where resistance was maintained only to produce such waste. The British captain received the flag with his usual politeness, and heard patiently Irvine's explanations; but he remained immovable; repeating his determination of holding out to the last.

It was now about noon, and the rays of the scorching sun had prepared the shingle roof for the projected conflagration. The return of Irvine was immediately followed by the application of the bow and arrows. The first arrow struck, and communicated its fire; a second was shot at another quarter of the roof, and a third at a third quarter; this last also took effect; and like the first, soon kindled a blaze. McPherson ordered a party to repair to the loft of the house, and by knocking off the shingles to stop the flames. This was soon perceived, and Captain Finley was directed to open his battery, raking the loft from end to end.

The fire of our six-pounder, posted close to one of the gable-ends of the house, soon drove the soldiers down; and no other effort to stop the flames being practicable, McPherson hung out the white flag. Mercy was extended, although policy commanded death, and the obstinacy of McPherson warranted it. The commandant, with the regulars, of which the garrison was chiefly composed, were taken possession of by Lee; while the loyalists were delivered to Marion. Among the latter was a Mr. Smith, who had been charged with burning the houses of his neighbors friendly to their country. This man consequently became very obnoxious, and his punishment was loudly demanded by many of the militia serving under the brigadier; but the humanity of Marion could not be overcome. Smith was secured from his surrounding enemies, ready to devote him, and taken under the general's protection.

McPherson was charged with having subjected himself to punishment, by his idle waste of his antagonist's time; and reminded as well of the opportunities which had been presented to him of saving himself and garrison from unconditional submission, as of the cogent considerations, growing out of the posture of affairs, which urged the prevention of useless resistance by exemplary punishment. The British officer frankly acknowledged his dependent situation, and declared his readiness to meet any consequence which the discharge of his duty, conformably to his own conviction of right, might produce. Powerfully as the present occasion called for punishment, and rightfully as it might have been inflicted, not a drop of blood was shed, nor any part of the enemy's baggage taken. McPherson and his officers accompanied their captors to Mrs. Motte's, and partook with them of a sumptuous dinner; soothing in the sweets of social intercourse the ire which the preceding conflict had engendered.* Requesting to be permitted to return to Charleston, on parole, they were accordingly paroled, and sent off in the evening to Lord Rawdon, now engaged in passing the Santee at Nelson's Ferry. Soon after, General Greene, anxious for the success of his detachment against Fort Motte, attended by an escort of cavalry, reached us, for the purpose of knowing precisely our situation, and the progress of the British general, who he expected would hasten to the relief of McPherson, as soon as he should gain the southern banks of the Santee; to counteract which the American general had resolved, and was then engaged in preparing boats, to transport his army over the Congaree. Finding the siege prosperously concluded, he returned to camp, having directed Marion, after placing the prisoners in security, to proceed against Georgetown, and ordering Lee to advance without delay upon Fort Granby, to which place the American army would also move. As soon as the troops had finished their repast, Lee set out with his detachment, composed of horse, foot, and artillery, and marching without intermission, he approached the neighborhood of Fort Granby before the dawn of the second day. Brigadier Sumter, having recovered of his wound, as soon as he received Greene's dispatch from Ramsay's mill, assembled his corps of militia. For reasons not understood by the author, the brigadier, instead of joining Greene before Camden, directed his attention to the fort of Ninety-six, and its upper communication with Charleston, Fort Granby, and Orangeburgh. He had moved from before Fort Granby, but a few days before Lee's arrival, for May 14. the purpose of forcing the small post at Orangeburgh, which he accomplished on the 14th.

Fort Granby was erected on a plain, which extended to the southern banks of the Congaree, near Friday's Ferry. Protected on one side by that river, it was accessible in every other quarter with facility; but being completely finished, with parapet encircled by fosse and abatis, and being well garrisoned, it could not have been carried without considerable loss, except by regular approaches; and in this way would have employed the whole force

* The deportment and demeanor of Mrs. Motte gave a zest to the pleasures of the table. She did its honors with that unaffected politeness which ever excites esteem mingled with admiration. Conversing with ease, vivacity, and good sense, she obliterated our recollection of the injury she had received; and though warmly attached to the defenders of her country, the engaging amiability of her manners, left it doubtful which set of officers constituted these defenders.

of Greene for a week at least, in which period Lord Rawdon's interposition was practicable. Lieutenant-Colonel Lee, apprised of the readiness with which the British general might attempt its relief, determined to press to conclusion his operations with all possible celerity, having detached, before he left Motte's, Captain Armstrong, with one troop of cavalry, to attend to the movements of Lord Rawdon.

As soon, therefore, as he reached the neighborhood of the fort, relying upon the information of his guides, he began to erect a battery in the margin of the woods, to the west of the fort. The morning was uncommonly foggy, which fortunate circumstance gave time to finish the battery before it was perceived by the enemy. Captain Finley, with his six-pounder mounted in the battery, was directed, as soon as the fog should disperse, to open upon the fort; when the infantry, ready for action, would advance to gain the ground selected for the commencement of our approaches. The garrison consisted of three hundred and fifty men, chiefly loyal militia, commanded by Major Maxwell, of the Prince of Wales's regiment (a refugee from the Eastern Shore of Maryland), represented to Lee as neither experienced in his profession, nor fitted by cast of character to meet the impending crisis. He was the exact counterpart of McPherson; disposed to avoid, rather than to court, the daring scenes of war. Zealous to fill his purse, rather than to gather military laurels, he had, during his command, pursued his favorite object with considerable success, and held with him in the fort his gathered spoil. Solicitous to hasten the surrender of the post, Lieutenant-Colonel Lee determined to try the effect of negotiation with his pliable antagonist; and prepared a summons, couched in pompous terms, calculated to operate upon such an officer as Maxwell was represented to be. The summons was intrusted to Captain Eggleston, of the Legion horse, who was authorized to conclude finally upon the terms of capitulation, if he found the enemy disposed to surrender.

The fog ceasing, Finley announced our unexpected proximity, which excited much alarm and some confusion, evidently discerned from our position. The Legion infantry advancing at the same time, took possession of the desired ground without opposition; severing the enemy's pickets in this quarter from the fort. Eggleston now setting out with his flag, produced a suspension of our fire, which induced the pickets and patrols, cut off by our disposition, to attempt to gain the fort. This effort was partially checked by the rapid movement of the cavalry; and an officer was dispatched to Captain Eggleston, requiring him to remonstrate with Major Maxwell upon the impropriety of the conduct of his pickets and patrols, and to demand that he would order them to resume their station; it being never intended, by presenting him with an opportunity of avoiding the useless effusion of blood, to permit the improvement of his capacity to resist. Eggleston's remonstrance was duly respected; and Maxwell dispatched his adjutant with the required orders, replacing the portion of his force on duty out of the fort in its original station. The negotiation was begun, and the British major testified a favorable disposition to the proposition submitted to him. After consulting with some of his officers, he agreed to deliver up the fort, upon condition that the private property of every sort, without investigation of title, should be confirmed to its possessors; that the garrison should be permitted to return to Charleston prisoners of war, until exchanged; that the militia should be held in the same manner as the regulars; and that an escort, charged with the protection of persons and of property should attend the prisoners to the British army.

The first condition being diametrically repugnant to the course contemplated by Lee, as it prevented restoration of plundered property, Captain Eggleston did not think proper to act under the full discretion with which he had been so properly invested, but submitted by letter the enemy's demands to the lieutenant-colonel, accompanied with one from Major Maxwell, requiring two covered wagons for the conveyance of his own baggage, free from search. In reply, Eggleston received directions to accede to the proposed terms with the single exception of all horses fit for public service, and to expedite the conclusion of the business. This exception was ill relished by many of the officers, although not resisted by the commandant. Finding that the capitulation would be thus arranged, the Hessian officers came in a body to Eggleston, protesting against proceeding, unless they were permitted to retain their horses; a protest not to be overruled by the authority of Maxwell. The capitulation was suspended, and a second time Eggleston found it necessary to refer to Lee. About this moment a dragoon arrived from Captain Armstrong, commanding the detachment of horse near Lord Rawdon, communicating his lordship's passage across the Santee, and his advance toward Fort Motte. Had Lieutenant-Colonel Lee determined to resist the requisition of the Hessian officers, this intelligence would have induced a change in his decision. He directed Captain Eggleston to make known to the officers, that he took pleasure in gratifying them, by considering all horses belonging to individuals in the fort as private property, and claiming only such, if any, belonging to the public.

This obstacle being removed, the capitulation was signed; and the principal bastion was immediately occupied by Captain Rudolph with a detachment from the Legion infantry. Before noon, Maxwell with his garrison, consisting of three hundred and forty men (sixty regulars, the rest loyalists), the baggage of every sort, two pieces of artillery, and two covered wagons, moved from the fort; and the major with the garrison, protected by the stipulated escort, proceeded on their route to Lord Rawdon. The public stores of every sort, consisting chiefly of ammunition, salt, and liquor, were faithfully delivered, and presented a very convenient as well as agreeable supply to our army. The moment Maxwell surrendered, Lee dispatched an officer with the information to General Greene, who had passed on with much expedition, and was within a few miles of Friday's Ferry when he received Lee's dispatch. The army continued its march to Ancram's plantation, near the ferry; and the general crossing the river, joined his light corps. Delighted with the happy event, his satisfaction was considerably increased when he saw the strength of the fort, connected with that of the garrison. He testified with much cordiality, and in most gratifying terms, his obligations to the light corps; applauding as well the rapidity of its advance as the vigor of its operations.

Lord Rawdon made but one day's march toward Fort Motte; yielding up with much reluctance his anxious desire to defend his line of posts, already broken through in its weakest points, and about to be assailed throughout. Retiring to Monk's Corner, he there encamped; impatiently waiting for an accession of force to enable him to resume offensive operations.

Fort Watson, Fort Motte, Fort Granby, and the fort at Orangeburgh, had successively yielded; Marion was now before Georgetown, which was sure soon to fall. Thus in less than one month since General Greene appeared before Camden, he had compelled the British general to evacuate that important post, forced the submission of all the intermediate posts, and was now upon the banks of the Congaree, in the heart of South Carolina, ready to advance upon Ninety-six (the only remaining fortress in the State, besides Charleston, in the enemy's possession), and to detach against Augusta, in Georgia; comprehending in this decisive effort, the completion of the deliverance of the two lost States, except the fortified towns of Charleston and Savannah—safe, because the enemy ruled at sea.

The American general, reposing his army for the day, and strengthening the light corps with a battalion of North Carolina levies under Major Eaton, directed Lieutenant-Colonel Lee to move upon Augusta; to which post Brigadier Pickens, with his corps of militia had been commanded to repair. Lee commenced his march in the course of a few hours, marching thirteen miles in the evening of the day on which Maxwell had surrendered. Resuming motion at a very early hour in the morning, he pressed forward with the utmost expedition; relieving the fatigued infantry by occasionally dismounting his dragoons and mounting his infantry. Not only the claim for celerity, arising out of the general state of affairs, enforced this exertion; but there was cause to apprehend that Lieutenant-Colonel Cruger, apprised of Lord Rawdon's abandonment, first of Camden and lastly of the field, would, in consequence of these untoward events, hasten to Augusta; giving up South Carolina to save Georgia. To reach Pickens before Cruger could join Browne became in this view of events, a duty of the first importance. Pickens and Lee united could readily strike Cruger on his march, with the prospect of bringing him to submission. This done, the destruction of Browne only remained to be effected for the complete re-annexation (except the sea-coast) of these States to the Union.

Approaching in the course of his march the point nearest Ninety-six, Lieutenant-Colonel Lee detached a squadron of horse, under Major Rudolph, toward that post, for the purpose of ascertaining whether the enemy exhibited the appearance of breaking up, and with the hope by this sudden dash of seizing some of the garrison; a very acceptable present to the American general, then on his march for that place, and in want of that accurate information to be derived only from residents in the place. Rudolph concealing his approach, appeared suddenly near the town; but was not so fortu-nate as to find a single individual of the garrison without the lines. He seized one or two countrymen returning home, who accompanied him to camp. From these we learned that Lieutenant-Colonel Cruger was informed of the events that had lately taken place; but hearing of Greene's advance upon Camden, he had been industriously engaged in strengthening his fortifications, and was determined not to abandon his post. Lee dispatched a friendly countryman to General Greene with the intelligence procured, which banished all those apprehensions heretofore entertained lest Cruger might unite himself to Browne. Persevering in his march, Lieutenant-Colonel Lee reached, on the third day, the vicinity of Augusta, which is seventy-five miles from Fort Granby, preceded by Captain O'Neale, with a light party of horse, charged with the collection of provisions and intelligence. From this active and discerning officer the pleasing information was received of the recent arrival of the annual royal present to the Indians, which was deposited at Fort Galphin, about twelve miles below Augusta on the north side of the river, consisting of articles extremely wanted in the American camp.* To relieve the wants of the army was in itself grateful, but this intelligence was important in a military view; because it showed that Colonel Browne's force in Augusta was reduced by detachments from it to secure his deposit at Fort Galphin. Two companies of infantry now made the garrison of this latter post, which was a small stockade. Persuaded that his approach was alike unknown to Browne and to the officer commanding here, from the precautions which, by his superior cavalry, he had been enabled to adopt, Lee determined by a forced march, with a detachment of infantry mounted behind his dragoons, to seize the Indian present. Leaving Eaton behind with his battalion, the artillery, and the tired of the corps, to follow, he accordingly pushed on to Fort Galphin.

On the ensuing morning (21st of May), sultry beyond measure, the fatigued detachment gained the desired point; and halting in the pine barrens which skirted the field surrounding the fort, waited for the moment of assault. For many miles not a drop of water had been procurable; and the extreme heat of the scorching sun, rendered more oppressive by the necessary halt under the pines, without any liquid whatsoever to revive sinking nature, produced a debility forbidding exertion. Having with him some mounted militia, Lee directed them to dismount and to advance upon the fort in the opposite direction—not doubting that the garrison, as was the custom, would eagerly pursue them, when an opportunity would be presented of obtaining the contemplated prize without loss. The major part of the garrison, as had been expected, ran to arms on sight of the militia, and, leaving the fort,

May 21st.

* Powder, ball, small-arms, liquor, salt, blankets, with sundry small articles, were gained, one of the many useful and valuable acquisitions occasionally procured by the Legion: for which, of the promised remuneration, not a cent has been ever paid to officer or soldiers.

pursued them. A selection having been made of all the infantry whose strength was fitted for action, a portion of them under Captain Rudolph was ordered to rush upon the fort, while the residue, supported by a troop of dragoons, took a direction which shielded the militia from the menaced blow. Rudolph had no difficulty in possessing himself of the fort, little opposition being attempted, and that opposition being instantly crushed. We lost one man from the heat of the weather; the enemy only three or four in the skirmish. The garrison, with the valuable deposit in its keeping, gave a rich reward for our toils and sufferings. Never was a beginning more auspicious. This success not only deprived Browne of a very important portion of his force, but yielded to his enemy an abundance of supplies much wanted by the army of Greene—among which were the essentials of war—powder and ball—which articles had become scarce in the American camp, notwithstanding the occasional contributions of the several posts wrested from the enemy.

Lieutenant-Colonel Lee, reposing his infantry for a few hours, detached Major Eggleston, at the head of his horse, to pass the Savannah below Augusta ; and taking a western direction, to join a corps of militia, known to be in the neighborhood, under Colonel Clarke, in case Brigadier Pickens should not yet have arrived. Eggleston was also ordered to make himself thoroughly acquainted with the enemy's situation for the information of his commandant, who wished to begin his operations the moment of his arrival ; and was further enjoined to send in a flag with a summons from himself, stating the near approach of part of Greene's army, with the investiture of Ninety-six by the main body under the general himself; and urging the propriety of sparing the useless waste of life— the certain consequence of resistance—cruel, because vain. The substitution of a second officer for his superior in summoning the fort arose from the course taken by Browne. He had refused to receive flags, forbidding all intercourse with the militia officers ; and Lee, having profited by the negotiation at Fort Granby, was desirous of removing the obstacles which prevented resort to the like course here. To effect this, he thought it advisable to authorize Eggleston, then the senior Continental officer on the south of the Savannah, to attempt negotiation. Browne, either discredited the information contained in the summons, or, immutable in the decision he had taken, would not answer the letter addressed to him, and forbade the renewal of such communication.

In the evening Lieutenant-Colonel Lee, with the artillery and infantry, joined Eggleston, then united to the militia under Pickens and Clarke, and encamped in the woods to the west of Augusta. This town is situated on the southern bank of the Savannah, in an oblong plain, washed by the river on the east and covered by deep woods in the opposite direction. In its centre stood Fort Cornwallis, judiciously constructed, well finished, and secure from storm. A half mile in its front up the river, the plain is interrupted by a lagoon or swamp with a rivulet passing through it; and on the northwestern border of this lagoon was erected another, but inferior, fortress called Grierson from the militia colonel who commanded its garrison. Browne commanded the British forces in upper Georgia, and resided in Fort Cornwallis. Lieutenant-Colonel Lee, hearing from Eggleston the affrontive rejection of his proffered negotiation, was considerably ruffled at the contemptuous treatment received, and determined never to enter into any communication with the British commandant until solicited by himself. Thus decided, he was gratified in discovering the divided condition of the enemy—its regulars in Fort Cornwallis, and its militia in Fort Grierson; not doubting, if the moment was duly improved, that a tender of negotiation, on the part of Browne, would follow.

While the troops, still concealed, were engaged in taking refreshments, Lieutenant-Colonel Lee employed himself in examining the ground. He did not hesitate in his decision, which was instantly to drive Grierson out of his fort, and to destroy or intercept him in his retreat to Fort Cornwallis.

Communicating his plan to Pickens and Clarke, it was adopted; and the troops were soon after arrayed for executing it.

Brigadier Pickens, with the militia, was to attack the fort on its north and west; Major Eaton, with his battalion, by passing down the north side of the lagoon, was to approach it on the south, co-operating with the militia; while Lieutenant-Colonel Lee, with his infantry and artillery, was to move down the lagoon on its southern margin, parallel with Eaton, ready to support his attack if required, or to attend to the movements of Browne, should he venture to leave his defences and interpose with a view to save Grierson. The cavalry, under Eggleston, were ordered to draw near to Fort Cornwallis, keeping in the wood and ready to fall upon the rear of Browne, should he advance upon Lee. These arrangements being finished, the several commandants proceeded to their respective points. Lee's movement, open to view, was soon discerned by

Browne, who, drawing his garrison out of his lines, accompanied by two field-pieces, advanced with the appearance of risking battle to save Grierson, now assailed by Pickens and Eaton. This forward movement soon ceased. Browne, not deeming it prudent, under existing circumstances, to persevere in its attempt, confined his interposition to a cannonade, which was returned by Lee, with very little effect on either side.* Grierson's resistance was quickly overpowered; the fort was evacuated; himself with his major and many of his garrison killed; the lieutenant-colonel with others taken; and the few remaining, by reaching the river, escaped under cover and concealment of its banks to Fort Cornwallis. Lieutenant-Colonel Browne, perceiving the fall of this post, withdrew into his fort; and apprehending, from what he had seen, that he had to deal with troops fitted for war, applied himself to strengthening his situation. Whatever was attainable in the town, and necessary to his defence, was now procured; and every part of the works requiring amendment was repaired with industry. These exertions on the part of the enemy could not be counteracted; all now to be done was to assume proper stations for close investiture, and, by regular approaches, to compel his surrender.

In the late contest our loss was trivial—a few wounded, and fewer killed. But unhappily among the latter was Major Eaton, of North Carolina, who had served only a few weeks with the light corps, and in that short period had endeared himself to his commandant and fellow-soldiers by the amiability of his manners. He fell gallantly at the head of his battalion in the moment of victory.

On the banks of the Savannah, south of the lagoon near its flow into the river, was situated a large brick building, the mansion-house of a gentleman who had joined the enemy. Here Lieutenant-Colonel Lee with his corps took post, while Brigadier Pickens with the militia occupied the woods on the enemy's left. The morning was spent in ascertaining the most eligible mode of approach; to execute which all the requisite tools found at Fort Galphin, with many collected from the neighboring farms, had been brought to camp.

---

* The militia of Georgia, under Colonel Clarke, were so exasperated by the cruelties mutually inflicted in the course of the war in this State, that they were disposed to sacrifice every man taken, and with great difficulty was this disposition now suppressed. Poor Grierson and several others had been killed after surrender; and, although the American commandants used every exertion, and offered a large reward to detect the murderers, no discovery could be made. In no part of the South was the war conducted with such asperity as in this quarter. It often sank into barbarity.

Fort Cornwallis was not far from the Savannah River, the shelter of whose banks afforded a safe route to the troops. It was determined to break ground in this quarter, and to extend our works toward the enemy's left and rear.

General Greene did not continue in his camp at Friday's Ferry longer than to give time to Lieutenant-Colonel Carrington to procure means for the transportation of the stores gained by the fall of Fort Granby, all of which were necessary to the army in the proposed operations. Taking the direct road for Ninety-six, he sat down before it on the 22d; his effective force, exclusive of militia, not exceeding one thousand: Marion, after taking Georgetown, having continued in that quarter for the protection of the country; and Sumter, who had joined Greene while at Friday's Ferry, being sent to apply his attention to the care of the region south and west of the Congaree.

May 22.

Ninety-six derives its name from the circumstance of its being ninety-six miles distant from the principal town of the Cherokee Indians, called Keeowee; and is the chief village in the district of country lying between the Saluda (the southern branch of the Congaree) and the river Savannah, the southwestern boundary of the State, to which district it gives its name.

The country is strong, the climate salubrious, and the soil fertile; and Ninety-six exceeded in its white population any of the nine districts into which South Carolina is divided. When the British recovered the State, here, as has been before observed, was fixed a post—forming, with Camden to its right and Augusta to its left, the frontier barrier established for the security of the country. The village of Ninety-six, previous to the war, had been slightly fortified for defence against the neighboring Indians. These works were considerably strengthened after the arrival of the British troops; and additional fortifications, to secure the post from assault, were erected, under the superintendance of Lieutenant Haldane, of the corps of engineers, aid-de-camp to Lord Cornwallis.

Lieutenant-Colonel Cruger, the present commandant, was a native of New York, of respectable connections, who had taken part from the first with the British army, and commanded one of the provincial regiments raised in that State. His garrison amounted to five hundred and fifty men; three hundred and fifty of whom were regulars, and, like himself, Americans; the residue were loyal militia of South Carolina, conducted by Colonel King. On the left of the village, in a valley, ran a small rivulet which furnished water to the town and troops. Passing this rivulet westwardly, you ascend an eminence, on which was erected a stockade fort, which, with the fortified prison contiguous to the valley, constituted the chief defence of the water. On the right of the village stood the principal work, called the star, from its form. It consisted of sixteen salient and re-entering angles, with a ditch, fraise, and abatis: and was judiciously designed, and well executed. We have before mentioned that Lord Rawdon, previous to his retreat from Camden, had informed Lieutenant-Colonel Cruger of the changed and changing condition of affairs, with orders to him to evacuate Ninety-six; and to join Browne in Augusta; but that all his attempts to communicate with Cruger had been frustrated. Entirely ignorant of these events, Lieutenant-Colonel Cruger, nevertheless, guided by his own reflections, wisely employed his time in making all the necessary repairs to his works and some additional defenses. A mound of earth, parapet high, was thrown up around the stockade, and secured by abatis; block-houses were erected, traverses made, and covered communications between the different works established. Throughout the preparations directed by Cruger, the garrison, regulars, and militia, officers and soldiers, vied with each other in the execution of their commandant's orders. The appearance of Greene's army increased the vigorous exertions of Cruger and his garrison, in completing their defensive measures; and very soon the works became strong, affording additional confidence to the besieged.

Colonel Kosciusko, a Polish officer, at the head of the engineers in the Southern army, was considered skilful in his profession, and much esteemed for his mildness of disposition and urbanity of manners. To this officer General Greene committed the designation of the course and mode of approach. Never regarding the importance which was attached to depriving the enemy of water, for which he depended on the rivulet to his left, Kosciusko applied his undivided attention to the demolition of the star, the strongest point of the enemy's defence. Breaking ground close to this fortress, he labored during the first night with diligence, but had not been able to place in great forwardness his incipient works. No sooner was this attempt of the besieger perceived, than Lieutenant-Colonel Cruger determined to prepare a platform in one of the salient angles of the star, opposite to our works, for the reception of three pieces of artillery, all he possessed, with intention to cover a detachment charged with the expulsion of our working parties, to be followed

by a second for the demolition of the works.   Before noon the platform was finished, and the artillery mounted in it.   The parapet
was manned with infantry ; and the sallying party under Lieutenant
Roney, supported by Major Greene, ready in the enemy's ditch,
rushed upon our works, covered by the artillery and musketry.
Roney drove before him our guards and working parties, putting
to the bayonet all whom he found ; and was followed by a detachment of loyalists, who quickly demolished the works, carrying off
the intrenching tools.   The enemy sustained no loss in this first
exhibition of his decision and courage, but that of Lieutenant Roney,
who died of a wound he received while gallantly leading on his
men.

So judiciously was this sally planned, and so rapidly conducted,
that, although Greene instantly sent a detachment to support Kosciusko, the object was accomplished before the support could arrive.
Taught by this essay that his enemy was of a cast not to be rashly
approached, Kosciusko was directed to resume his labors under
cover of a ravine, and at a more respectful distance.   He broke
ground again in the night of the 23d, still directing his approaches
against the star redoubt.

Pickens and Lee pressed forward their measures against Fort
Cornwallis with zeal and diligence ; but not with the wished-for
celerity, so vigilant and resolute was the active and sagacious officer
opposed to them.   The condition of several of the wounded taken
in the attack on Fort Grierson called for various comforts not to be
found in the American camp, and the principal officer who had
been taken asked permission to procure the requisite supply from
Colonel Browne, whom he knew to be well provided, and whose
disposition to cherish his soldiers he had often experienced.   To this
application Pickens and Lee answered, that, after the ungracious
determination to stop all intercourse, announced by the commandant of Fort Cornwallis, disposed as they were to obey the dictates
of humanity, it could not be expected that any consideration could
prevail with them again to expose the American flag to contumely.
If, however, he thought proper to wait upon Colonel Browne, they
would permit him to proceed whenever he pleased, on the faith of
his parole, returning immediately after receiving Browne's reply.

This offer was cheerfully accepted, and a letter was prepared on
the part of the American commandants, expressing the regret with
which they permitted a flag to pass from their camp, though borne
by a British officer after the treatment experienced upon a late

occasion, and assuring the commandant of Fort Cornwallis, that no consideration affecting themselves or their troops would ever have led to such a condescension.

To this letter Browne returned a very polite answer by the prisoner (whose application was instantly complied with), excusing what had passed by a reference to some previous altercations, which had rendered such a decision necessary on the part of the British commandant, so long as the individual to whom he alluded continued to command,* and who he really did believe had sent in the flag refused to be received, not knowing or suspecting the extraordinary change of force opposed to him which had taken place. Pickens and Lee were very much gratified that, while obeying the claims of humanity, they should have produced a renewal of intercourse, without which the contest drawing to a close could not be terminated but by a painful waste of human life.

The works contiguous to the river had advanced nearly to the desired state, and those which had been subsequently commenced in the rear of the fort began to assume a formidable appearance; yet extreme difficulty occurred in the consummation of the plan adopted by the besiegers, as the surrounding ground presented no swell or hill which would enable them to bring their six-pounder to bear upon the enemy. It was determined to resort to the Maham tower, the effect of which Lee had so happily witnessed at Fort Watson; and orders were accordingly issued to prepare and bring in timber of such a size as would sustain our only piece of artillery.

Browne heretofore had patiently looked on at our approach, diligently working within his fort, as we discovered by the heaps of fresh-dug earth in various directions, but with what view remained unascertained. Seeing that his enemy's works were rapidly advancing, he now determined to interrupt our progress by sallies, however hazardous, which he foresaw could alone retard his approaching fate—hoping that in the delay he might find safety. On the 28th he fell upon our works in the river quarter at midnight, and, by the suddenness and vigor of his onset, drove the guard be-

---

* The individual meant was Colonel Clarke. Browne and this officer had before (as will be recollected) a very severe conflict. Clarke was often beating up the British quarters, and striking at the light parties of the enemy, chiefly loyalists; with whom and the militia a spirit of hate and revenge had succeeded to those noble feelings of humanity and forgiveness which ought ever to actuate the soldier. At length all intercourse between the troops was broken off, and the vanquished lay at the mercy of the victor.

fore him; but the support under Captain Handy[*] coming up, after an obstinate conflict, regained the trenches, and forced the enemy to take shelter in the fort. The determined spirit manifested by the foe in this attempt to destroy our approaches, induced Lieutenant-Colonel Lee to appropriate his infantry exclusively for their defence at night, relieving them from any further share in labor and from every other duty. It was divided into two divisions, to one of which was alternately committed the protection of our works. On the succeeding night, Browne renewed his attempt in the same quarter; and for a long time the struggle was continued with mutual pertinacity, till at length Captain Rudolph, by a combined charge with the bayonet, cleared the trenches, driving the enemy with loss to his stronghold. On the 30th, the timber required to build the Maham tower was prepared and conveyed to the intended site. In the evening we commenced its erection, under cover of an old house to conceal our object from the enemy. In the course of the night and ensuing day we had brought our tower nearly on a level with the enemy's parapet, and began to fill its body with fascines, earth, stone, brick, and every other convenient rubbish, to give solidity and strength to the structure. At the same time the adjacent works, in the rear of the fort, were vigorously pushed to the enemy's left to connect them with the tower, the point of termination.

May 30th.

Browne's attention was soon drawn to this quarter; and, penetrating the use to which the log building would be applied, he determined to demolish it without delay.

Pickens and Lee, well assured from what had passed that their judicious opponent would leave nothing unessayed within his power

---

* In the progress of this work under the hands of its author, reference was frequently had to the authority and reminiscences of Colonel Howard, and he suggested, on one of those occasions, that Captain Oldham should be mentioned during the siege of Augusta, instead of Captain Handy. He repeated the same suggestion recently to me. The author however adhered to his own impression, and the result of my inquiries having justified me that Captain Handy was distinguished in the affair, I have not felt myself at liberty, highly as I respect the authority of Colonel Howard, and the memory of Captain Oldham, to vary the reading so deliberately insisted on by the author. To the name of Captain Oldham, too much praise cannot be given. He was engaged in almost every action in the South, and was uniformly distinguished for gallantry and good conduct. With the exception of Kirkwood of Delaware, and Rudolph of the Legion infantry, he was probably entitled to more credit than any officer of his rank in Greene's army. A distinction which must place him high on the rolls of fame. In the celebrated charge on the British at Eutaw, of thirty-six men, which he led, all but eight were killed or wounded; yet he forced the enemy.—ED.

to destroy their tower, on the completion of which their expectation of immediate success chiefly depended, determined to prepare
before night for the counteraction of any attempt which might be
made. The lines in that quarter, intrusted to the militia, were
doubly manned; and Handy's division of the infantry, though on
duty every other night, was drawn from the river quarter to maintain the militia. The North Carolina battalion supplied its place;
and to Captain Handy on one side, and to Captain Rudolph on the
other (approved officers), were committed henceforward the protection of our lines. The tower was designated as the peculiar object
of attention, and to its defence one company of musketry was exclusively applied. Not more than one-third of the night had passed
when the enemy began to move; concealing his real object by re-
newing his attempt upon the river quarter, where Rudolph, with his
accustomed gallantry, gave him a warm reception. While the contest here was bravely urged, and as bravely sustained, Lieutenant-
Colonel Browne, with the *élite* of his garrison, fell upon our works
in his rear. Here for awhile the militia of Pickens contended with
vigor, but at length were forced by the bayonet out of the trenches. Handy leaving one company at the tower, with his main body
hastened to support the militia, who very gallantly united with the
regulars, and turned upon the successful foe. The conflict became
furious; but at length the Marylanders under Handy carried the
victory by the point of the bayonet. Upon this occasion the loss
on both sides exceeded all which had occurred during the siege.
Browne, finding that every effort to destroy our works by open war
proved ineffectual, now resorted to stratagem. Lee had omitted to
pull down,* as was originally intended, the old wooden house, under cover of which the tower had been commenced, and which by
accidentally taking fire would have probably consumed it. This
house attracted Browne's notice, and he determined, by burning it,
to rid himself of the tower. He had by this time erected a platform in one of the angles of the fort opposite to our Maham tower,
and which, being mounted with two of his heaviest pieces of
ordnance, opened upon it before it was finished.

Nevertheless the exertions of the builders did not slacken, and
June 1st. on the first of June the tower was completed, and was found
to overlook the enemy's parapet. The upper logs having

* This omission resulted from that spirit of procrastination common to man,
and was certainly highly reprehensible. Luckily no injury resulted, whereas
very great might have ensued.

been sawed to let in an embrasure for our six-pounder, it only remained to make an apron upon which the matrosses could draw up their piece to the floor of the tower.

This was done in the course of the day, and at dawn on the second our six-pounder was mounted, completely commanding the enemy's fort. Finley instantly announced his readiness to act by returning the enemy's cannonade, which had been continued without intermission. Before noon the enemy's two pieces were dismounted from the platform, and all the interior of the fort was racked, excepting the segment nearest to the tower, and some other spots sheltered by traverses. It was now that Lieutenant-Colonel Browne determined to put in execution his concerted stratagem. In the course of the night, a deserter from the fort was sent to Lieutenant-Colonel Lee. He was a Scot, with all the wily sagacity of his country, and a sergeant of the artillery. Upon being questioned upon the effect of our cannonade, and the situation of the enemy—he answered, that the strange log-house lately erected, gave an advantage, which, duly improved, could not fail to force surrender ; but that the garrison had not suffered so much as might be presumed ; that it was amply supplied with provisions, and was in high spirits. In the course of the conversation which followed, Lee inquired, in what way could the effect of the cannonade be increased ? Very readily, replied the crafty sergeant, adding : that knowing the spot where all the powder in the fort was deposited, with red-hot balls from the six-pounder, the magazine might be blown up. This intelligence was received with delight, and the suggestion of the sergeant received with avidity, although it would be very difficult to prepare our balls, as we were unprovided with a furnace. It was proposed to the sergeant, that he should be sent to the officer commanding our battery, and give his aid to the execution of his suggestion, with assurance of liberal reward in case of success. This proposition was heard with much apparent reluctance, although every disposition to bring the garrison to submission was exhibited by the sergeant, who pretended that Browne had done him many personal injuries in the course of service. But he added, it was impossible for him to put himself in danger of capture, as he well knew a gibbet would be his fate, if taken. A good supper was now presented to him, with his grog ; which being finished, and being convinced by the arguments of Lee, that his personal safety could not be endangered, as it was not desired or meant that he should take any part in the siege, but merely attend at the tower to

June 2d.

direct the pointing of the piece, he assented ; declaring that he entered upon his task with dire apprehensions, and reminding the lieutenant-colonel of his promised reward. Lee instantly put him in care of his adjutant, to be delivered to Captain Finley, with the information communicated, for the purpose of blowing up the enemy's magazine. It was midnight, and Lieutenant-Colonel Lee, expecting on the next to be much engaged, our preparations being nearly completed retired to rest. Reflecting upon what had passed, and recurring to the character of his adversary, he became much disquieted by the step he had taken, and soon concluded to withdraw the sergeant from the tower. He had not been many minutes with Captain Finley, before an order remanding him was delivered, committing him to the quarter-guard. In the morning we were saluted with a new exhibition, unexpected though not injurious. Between the quarters of Lee and the fort stood four or five deserted houses ; some of them near enough to the fort to be used with effect by riflemen from their upper stories. They had often engaged the attention of Pickens and Lee, with a view of applying them, whenever the enemy should be assaulted, to aid in covering their attack. Browne, sallying out before break of day, set fire to all but two of the houses. No attempt was made to disturb the operation, or to extinguish the flames after the enemy had returned ; it being deemed improper to hazard our troops in effecting any object not material in its consequence. Of the two left, one was more commodious for the purpose originally contemplated by Pickens and Lee in the hour of assault.

The besiegers being incapable of discovering any reason for the omission to burn the two houses, and especially that nearest the fort, various were their conjectures as to the cause of sparing them ; some leading to the conclusion that they were left purposely, and consequently with the view of injuring the assailant. The fire from the tower continued, and being chiefly directed against the parapet fronting the river, in which quarter the proposed attack would be directed, demonstrated satisfactorily that the hour had arrived to make the decisive appeal. Orders were accordingly issued to prepare for the assault, to take place on the next day at the hour of nine in the forenoon. In the course of the night, a party of the best marksmen were selected from Pickens's militia, and sent to the house spared by Browne, and nearest to the fort.

The officer commanding this detachment, was ordered to arrange his men in the upper story, for the purpose of ascertaining the number which could with ease use their rifles out of the windows, or any other convenient aperture; then to withdraw, and report to the brigadier. It was intended, before daylight, to have directed the occupation of the house by the same officer, with such a force of riflemen as he should report to be sufficient. Handy was ordered to return to the river quarter at the dawn of day, as to his detachment and the Legion infantry the main assault would be committed. These, with all the other preparations, being made, the troops continued in their usual stations—pleased that the time was near which would close with success their severe toils.

About three in the morning of the fourth of June, we were aroused by a violent explosion, which was soon discovered to have shattered the very house intended to be occupied by the rifle party before daybreak. It was severed and thrown into the air thirty or forty feet high, its fragments falling all over the field. This explained, at once, not only the cause of Browne's omitting its destruction, but also communicated the object of the constant digging which had until lately employed the besieged.

June 4th.

Browne pushed a sap to this house, which he presumed would be certainly possessed by the besieger, when ready to strike his last blow; and he concluded from the evident maturity of our works, and from the noise made by the militia, when sent to the house in the first part of the night, for the purpose of ascertaining the number competent to its capacity, that the approaching morning was fixed for the general assault. Not doubting but the house was occupied with the body destined to hold it, he determined to. deprive his adversary of every aid from this quarter: hoping, too, by the consternation which the manner of destruction could not fail to excite, to damp the ardor of the troops charged with storming.

Happily he executed his plan too early for its success, or our gallant band would certainly have shared the fate of the house. This fortunate escape excited grateful sensations in the breasts of the two commandants, for the gracious interposition of Providence; and added further evidence of the penetration and decision which marked the character of their opponent. The hour of nine approached, and the columns for assault were in array, waiting the signal to advance. Pickens and Lee having determined, as intercourse with the fort was now open, to present to the enemy another opportunity of avoiding the impending blow by capitulation, had dispatched a flag, with a joint letter, adapted to the occasion. Lieutenant-Colonel Browne, in reply, repeated his determination to

defend the post.   This resolution could not be maintained ; and on
June 5th. the next day an officer with a flag, proceeded from the fort.
The bearer was received at the margin of our trenches,
and presented a letter addressed to the two commandants, offering
to surrender upon conditions detailed in the communication.   Some
of these being inadmissible, the offer was rejected, and other prop-
ositions made, which would be ratified by them, if acceded to by
Browne.   This discussion produced the delay of one day, which was
gratifying to Browne; it being unpleasant to surrender on the birth-
day of his king.*   The terms, as altered, were accepted; and eight

* Brigadier Pickens and Lieutenant-Col. Lee to Lieutenant-Col. Browne.

Augusta, *May 31st,* 1781.

Sir,—The usage of war renders it necessary that we present you with an opportunity of avoiding the destruction which impends your garrison.

We have deferred our summons to this late date, to preclude the necessity of
much correspondence on the occasion. You see the strength of the investing
forces; the progress of our works; and you may inform yourself of the situation of the two armies, by inquiries from Captain Armstrong, of the Legion,
who has the honor to bear this.

Lieutenant-Colonel Browne, in answer, to Pickens and Lee.

Gentlemen,—What progress you have made in your works I am no stranger
to.   It is my duty and inclination to defend this place to the last extremity.

Pickens and Lee to Lieutenant-Colonel Browne.

Augusta, *June 3d,* 1781.

Sir,—It is not our disposition to press the unfortunate. To prevent the
effusion of blood, which must follow perseverance in your fruitless resistance,
we inform you, that we are willing, though in the grasp of victory, to grant
such terms as a comparative view of our respective situations can warrant.

Your determination will be considered as conclusive, and will regulate our
conduct.

Lieutenant-Colonel Browne to Pickens and Lee.

Fort Cornwallis, *June 3d,* 1781.

Gentlemen,—I have the honor to acknowledge the receipt of your summons
of this day, and to assure you, that as it is my duty, it is likewise my inclination, to defend the post to the last extremity.

Pickens and Lee to Lieutenant-Colonel Browne.

Head-quarters, *June 4th,* 1781.

Sir,—We beg leave to propose, that the prisoners in your possession may be
sent out of the fort; and that they may be considered yours or ours, as the
siege may terminate.

Confident that you cannot oppose the dictate of humanity and custom of
war, we have only to say, that any request from you of a similar nature, will
meet our assent.

Lieutenant-Colonel Browne to Pickens and Lee.

Gentlemen,—Though motives of humanity, and a feeling for the distresses of
individuals, incline me to accede to what you have proposed concerning the

o'clock in the morning of the 5th was designated for the delivery of the fort, &c., to Captain Rudolph, appointed on the part of the

prisoners with us; yet many reasons, to which you cannot be strangers, forbid my complying with this requisition. Such attention as I can show, consistently with good policy and my duty, shall be shown to them.

LIEUTENANT-COLONEL BROWNE TO PICKENS AND LEE.

GENTLEMEN,—In your summons of the 3d instant, no particular conditions were specified; I postponed the consideration of it to this day.

From a desire to lessen the distresses of war to individuals, I am inclined to propose to you my acceptance of the inclosed terms; which being pretty similar to those granted to the commanding officers of the American troops and garrison in Charleston, I imagine will be honorable to both parties.

PICKENS AND LEE TO LIEUTENANT-COLONEL BROWNE.

June 5th, 1781.

SIR,—There was a time when your proposals of this day ought to have been accepted. That period is now passed. You had every notice from us, and must have known the futility of your further opposition.

Although we should be justified by the military law of both armies to demand unconditional submission, our sympathy for the unfortunate and gallant of our profession, has induced us to grant the honorable terms which we herewith transmit.

LIEUTENANT-COLONEL BROWNE TO PICKENS AND LEE.

June 5th, 1781

GENTLEMEN,—Your proposition relative to the officers of the king's troops and militia being admitted to their paroles, and the exclusion of the men, is a matter I cannot accede to.

The conditions I have to propose to you are, that such of the different classes of men who compose this garrison be permitted to march to Savannah, or continue in the country, as to them may be most eligible, until exchanged.

PICKENS AND LEE TO LIEUTENANT-COLONEL BROWNE.

June 5th, 1781.

SIR,—In our answer of this morning, we granted the most generous terms in our power to give, which we beg leave to refer to as final on our part.

LIEUTENANT-COLONEL BROWNE TO PICKENS AND LEE.

GENTLEMEN,—As some of the articles proposed by you are generally expressed, I have taken the liberty of deputing three gentlemen to wait upon you, for a particular explanation of the respective articles.

ARTICLES OF CAPITULATION PROPOSED BY LIEUTENANT-COLONEL THOMAS BROWNE, AND ANSWERED BY GENERAL PICKENS AND LIEUTENANT-COLONEL LEE.

ARTICLE 1ST.—That all acts of hostilities and works shall cease between the besiegers and the besieged, until the articles of capitulation shall be agreed on, signed, and executed, or collectively rejected.

Answer.—Hostilities shall cease for one hour; other operations to continue.

ART. 2D.—That the fort shall be surrendered to the commanding officer of the American troops, such as it now stands. That the king's troops, three days after signing the articles of capitulation, shall be conducted to Savannah, with their baggage; where they will remain prisoners of war until they are ex-

victors to take possession of it with its appurtenances. At the appointed hour the British garrison marched out, Lieutenant-Colonel Browne, having been taken into the care of Captain Armstrong,

changed. That proper conveyances shall be provided by the commanding officer of the American troops for that purpose, together with a sufficient quantity of good and wholesome provisions till their arrival at Savannah.

Ans.—Inadmissible. The prisoners to surrender field prisoners of war; the officers to be indulged with their paroles; the soldiers to be conducted to such places as the commander-in-chief shall direct.

ART. 3D.—The militia now in garrison shall be permitted to return to their respective homes, and be secured in their persons and properties.

Ans.—Answered by the second article, the militia making part of the garrison.

ART. 4TH.—The sick and wounded shall be under the care of their own surgeons, and be supplied with such medicines and necessaries as are allowed to the British hospitals.

Ans.—Agreed.

ART. 5TH.—The officers of the garrison, and citizens who have borne arms during the siege, shall keep their side-arms, pistols, and baggage, which shall not be searched, and retain their servants.

Ans.—The officers and citizens who have borne arms during the siege, shall be permitted their side-arms, private baggage, and servants; their side-arms not to be worn, and the baggage to be searched by a person appointed for that purpose.

ART. 6TH.—The garrison, at an hour appointed, shall march out with shouldered arms and drums beating, to a place agreed on, where they will pile their arms.

Ans.—Agreed. The judicious and gallant defence made by the garrison, entitles them to every mark of military respect. The fort to be delivered up to Captain Rudolph at twelve o'clock, who will take possession with a detachment of the Legion infantry.

ART. 7TH.—That the citizens shall be protected in their persons and properties.

Ans.—Inadmissible.

ART. 8TH.—That twelve months shall be allowed to all such as do not choose to reside in this country to dispose of their effects, real and personal, in this province, without any molestation whatever; or to remove to any part thereof as they may choose, as well themselves as families.

Ans.—Inadmissible.

ART. 9TH.—That the Indian families, now in garrison, shall accompany the king's troops to Savannah, where they will remain prisoners of war, until exchanged for an equal number of prisoners in the Creek or Cherokee nations.

Ans.—Answered in the second article.

ART. 10TH.—That an express be permitted to go to Savannah with the commanding officer's dispatches, which are not to be opened.

Ans.—Agreed.

ART. 11TH. (Additional.)—The particular attention of Colonel Browne is expected toward the just delivery of all public stores, moneys, &c.; and that no loans be permitted to defeat the spirit of this article.

Signed at Head-quarters, Augusta, June 5th, 1781, by
ANDREW PICKENS, Brig. Militia.
HENRY LEE, Jr., Lt.-Col. Commandant, V. L.
THOMAS BROWNE, Lt.-Col. commanding the king's troops at Augusta.

of the dragoons, with a safeguard to protect his person from threatened violence.* This precaution, suggested by our knowl edge of the inveteracy with which the operations in this quarter had been conducted on both sides, turned out to be extremely fortunate; as otherwise in all probability, the laurels acquired by the arms of America would have been stained by the murder of a gallant soldier, who had committed himself to his enemy on their plighted faith. Browne was conveyed to Lee's quarters, where he continued until the next day, when himself and a few of his officers were paroled, and sent down the river to Savannah, under the care of Captain Armstrong, with a party of infantry, who had orders to continue with Lieutenant-Colonel Browne until he should be placed out of danger. During the few hours' residence in Lee's quarters, the British colonel inquired after his artillery sergeant, who had, a few nights before, deserted from the fort. Upon being told that he was in the quarter-guard, he took the first opportunity of soliciting from Lee his restitution; frankly declaring that he was no deserter, but was purposely sent out by him in that character, to destroy by fire the newly-erected log-house, which he plainly dis-cerned to be destructive to his safety, and which his sergeant un-dertook to do, while pretending to direct our fire with the view of blowing up the magazine of the fort.

This communication showed the danger to which the besiegers were exposed for a few minutes, by the readiness with which Lieu-tenant-Colonel Lee entered into the plan of the deserter, but which, upon further reflection, he fortunately changed; and demonstrates the great caution with which the offer of aid·from deserters ought to be received; especially when coming from a besieged fortress on the point of surrender, and in the care of an experienced and sagacious soldier. The request of Browne was granted, and the sergeant with joy rejoined his commander. As soon as the capitu-lation was signed, preparations for decamping were begun, and

---

* This precaution was indispensable. Already had the humanity of the besieging corps been dreadfully outraged by the slaughter of Colonel Grierson and some of his associates. To risk a repetition of the same barbarity, would have justly exposed the commandants to reproach and censure. It was deter-mined to take measures in time to prevent such an issue. Lieutenant-Colonel Browne's life was, we knew, sought with avidity; consequently it became our duty to secure his person before the garrison marched out. Browne had him-self suffered very cruel and injurious personal treatment in the beginning of the revolution; and succeeding events more and more imbittered both himself and the Georgia militia, heretofore his only opponents, till at length in this quarter a war of extermination became the order of the day.

early the next morning, the baggage of the corps under Lee was transported across the Savannah ; about noon, the infantry followed ; June 6th. and in the evening of the sixth, Lee joined with his cavalry ; proceeding with expedition to Ninety-six, in obedience to orders from General Greene. Brigadier Pickens remained at Augusta until conveyance for the stores taken there and at Fort Galphin could be provided; which being accomplished in a few days, he also marched for head-quarters. Without delay, after the British garrison had laid down their arms, Pickens and Lee dis- patched intelligence of the event to Greene; who announcing the success in general orders, was pleased to express to the two commandants, and their respective corps, the high sense he entertained of their merit and service, with his thanks for the zeal and vigor exhibited in the execution of the duty assigned to them. Lee pressing forward with dispatch, reached Ninety-six on the forenoon of the eighth. Two routes led south of the enemy to the American June 8th. head-quarters, which had been established on the enemy's right. The officer dispatched with the garrison of Fort Cornwallis in his charge, mistaking the intended course, took the road nearest to the town, which brought his troops under command of the enemy's batteries for a small distance. Believing that the exhibition was designed with a view to insult the feelings of the garrison, Lieutenant-Colonel Cruger gave orders for the contiguous batteries to open upon this corps, notwithstanding it enveloped his fellow-soldiers taken at Augusta, and was very near chastising the supposed bravado, which in fact was only the error of the conducting officer. Luckily no injury was sustained ; but the officer was very severely reprimanded by Lieutenant-Colonel Lee, for the danger to which his inadvertance had exposed the corps.

General Greene had exerted himself, with unremitting industry, to complete the works against the star redoubt; to which single object Colonel Kosciusko directed all his efforts. The enemy's left had been entirely neglected, although in that quarter was procured the chief supply of water.* As soon as the corps of Lee entered camp, that officer was directed to take post opposite to the enemy's

---

* Kosciusko was extremely amiable, and, I believe, a truly good man, nor was he deficient in his professional knowledge; but he was very moderate in talent,—not a spark of the ethereal in his composition. His blunders lost us Ninety-six; and General Greene, much as he was beloved and respected, did not escape criticism, for permitting his engineer to direct the manner of approach. It was said, and with some justice too, that the general ought certainly to have listened to his opinion, but never ought to have permitted the pursuit of error, although supported by professional authority.

left, and to commence regular approaches against the stockade.
Very soon Lee pushed his ditch to the ground designated for the
erection of the battery, under the cover of which the subsequent
approaches would be made.   In the course of the next day this
battery was erected, and Lieutenant Finn, with a six-pounder, took
possession of it.   The besiegers advancing closer and closer, with
caution and safety, both on the right and left, Lieutenant-Colonel
Cruger foresaw his inevitable destruction, unless averted by the
approach of Lord Rawdon.   To give time for the desired event, he
determined, by nocturnal sallies, to attempt to carry our trenches ;
and to destroy with the spade whatever he might gain by the bayonet. These rencounters were fierce and frequent, directed sometimes
upon one quarter and sometimes upon another ; but so judicious
had been the arrangements of the American general to counteract
these expected attempts, that in no one instance did the British
commandant succeed.   The mode adopted was nevertheless pursued
without intermission ; and although failing to effect the chief object
contemplated, became extremely harassing to the American army,
whose repose during the night was incessantly disturbed, and
whose labor in the day was as incessantly pressed.   Ignorant of
the situation and prospects of the British general as Lieutenant-
Colonel Cruger continued to be, he nevertheless indulged the confidence, that every effort would be made for his relief, and persevered with firmness and vigor in his defence.   As soon as the
second parallel was finished, General Greene directed Colonel Williams, Adjutant-General, to summon the British commandant ;
stating to him his relative situation, and assuring him that perseverance in resistance would be vain, and might produce disagreeable consequences to himself and garrison.   Cruger returned by his
adjutant, a verbal answer ; declaring his determination to hold out
to the last extremity, and his perfect disregard of General Greene's
promises or threats.   Failing in this attempt, our batteries opened
from the second parallel, under cover of which Kosciusko pressed
forward his approach with indefatigable labor.

Lord Rawdon heard, with deep regret, the loss of Augusta, and
was not insensible to the danger which threatened Ninety-six ; but
destitute of the means to furnish immediate relief, he was obliged
to arm himself with patience, anxiously hoping that every southern
gale would waft to him the long-expected re-enforcement.

On the 3d of June this event took place, and his lordship instantly
prepared to take the field.   On the 7th he set out from Charleston

for the relief of Ninety-six, with a portion of the three regiments just arrived from Ireland, and was joined on his route by the troops from Monk's Corner, giving him a total of two thousand men. All his endeavors to transmit information to Cruger having failed, his lordship apprehended, that, pressed by the difficulties to which that officer must be reducéd, and despairing of succor, he might be induced to surrender, with a view to obtaiñ favorable conditions for his garrison; to stop which, he renewed his efforts to advise him of the propitious change of his condition, and his consequent advance for his relief.

Greene was informed by Sumter, on the 11th, of the arrival from Ireland, and of the measures immediately taken by Rawdon to resume offensive operations. Directing Sumter to keep in his lordship's front, he re-enforced him with all his cavalry, conducted by Lieutenant-Colonel Washington; urging the brigadier to exert every means in his power to delay the advance of the British army. Marion was also ordered to hasten from the lower country, as soon as he should discover the intention of Rawdon to move upon Greene; and Brigadier Pickens, just joined from Augusta, was detached to Sumter.

Our approaches continued to be pushed with unabated diligence, in the hope that they might be brought to maturity in time to enforce the submission of the garrison, before the British general could make good his long march.

We now began to deplore the early inattention of the chief engineer to the enemy's left; persuaded that had he been deprived of the use of the rivulet in the beginning of the siege, he must have been forced to surrender before the present hour. It was deemed practicable to set fire to the stockade fort, and thus to demolish the water defence on the left of the rivulet. In the succeeding day, a dark, violent storm came on from the west, without rain. Lieutenant-Colonel Lee proposed to General Greene to permit him to make the attempt. This being granted, a sergeant with nine privates of the Legion infantry, furnished with combustible matter, was directed to approach the stockade in the most concealed direction, under cover of the storm, while the batteries in every quarter opened upon the enemy, and demonstrations of striking at the star redoubt were made, with the expectation of diverting his attention from the intrepid party, which, with alacrity, undertook the hazardous enterprise. The sergeant conducted his gallant band in the best manner; concealing it whenever the ground permitted, and when exposed to view crawling along upon the belly. At length he reached the ditch with three others; the whole close behind. Here unluckily he was discovered, while in the act of applying his fire. Himself and five were killed; the remaining four escaped unhurt, although many muskets were discharged at them running through the field, before they got beyond the nearest rise of ground which could cover them from danger. After this disappointment, nothing remained but to force our works to maturity, and to retard the advance of the British army. In the evening a countryman was seen riding along our lines south of the town, conversing familiarly with the officers and soldiers on duty. He was not regarded, as from the beginning of the siege our friends in the country were in the habit of visiting camp, and were permitted to go wherever their curiosity led them, one of whom this man was presumed to be. At length he reached the great road leading directly to the town, in which quarter were only some batteries thrown up for the protection of the guards. Putting spur to his horse, he rushed with full speed into town, receiving the ineffectual fire of our sentinels and guards nearest to him, and holding up a letter in his hand as soon as he cleared himself of our fire. The propitious signal gave joy to the garrison, who running to meet their friend, opened the gate, welcoming his arrival with loud expressions of joy. He was the bearer of a dispatch from Rawdon to Cruger, communicating his arrival at Orangeburgh in adequate force, and informing him that he was hastening to his relief. This intelligence infused new vigor into the garrison.

It also inspired the besieger with additional motives to push to conclusion his preparations, as he now yielded up every hope heretofore derived from Cruger's ignorance of the movement of the British general, and the forwardness of our works. Major Green, who commanded in the star with great ability, finding that our third parallel was nearly finished, and that a Maham tower was erecting which would overlook his parapet, very judiciously covered it with sand-bags, to lessen the capacity derived from superior height, leaving between each bag an aperture for the use of his riflemen. Nor were the approaches on the left less forward than those on the right; they not only were directed against the stockade, but also were carried so near the rivulet, as to render supplies of water difficult and precarious. The fire during the 17th was so effectual, as to induce the enemy to withdraw his guards established between the rivulet and the stockade; and parties of the troops on the left were posted in various points, to annoy the communication with the rivulet. These arrangements succeeded throughout the day completely, and the enemy suffered greatly from this privation, though accomplished too late to produce material advantage. Rawdon continued to advance by forced marches, and inclining to his right, made a vigorous push to throw himself between Sumter and Greene.

In this effort he completely succeeded, and thus baffled all the measures adopted by Greene to delay his approach. It now became necessary to hazard an assault, to meet Rawdon, or to retire. The American general was disposed to imitate Cæsar at Alesia; first to beat the relieving army, and then to take the besieged town. But his regular force did but little exceed the half of that under Rawdon, which, added to his militia, consisting of the corps of Sumter, Marion, and Pickens, still left him numerically inferior to the British general. Nevertheless, confiding in his known superiority of cavalry, he would have given battle to his lordship, could he have left an adequate corps to attend to the garrison. Compelled to relinquish this plan, he determined to storm the fort, although his works were yet unfinished. On our left, our third parallel was completed, two trenches and a mine were nearly let into the enemy's ditch, and the Maham tower was finished.

On our right, the trenches were within twenty yards of his ditch; and the battery directed by Lieutenant Finn gave to the assailant in this quarter advantages which, well supported, insured success. Greene, anxiously as he desired to conclude his severe toils in triumph, was averse to the unequal contest to which he must necessarily expose his faithful troops, and would probably have decided on the safe course, had not his soldiers, with one voice, entreated to be led against the fort. The American army having witnessed the unconquerable spirit which actuated their general, as well as the unexpected results of former battles, could not brook the idea of abandoning the siege without one bold attempt to force a surrender. They recollected, with pain and remorse, that by the misbehavior of one regiment at the battle of Guilford, and of another at Hobkirk's Hill, their beloved general had been deprived of his merited laurels; and they supplicated their officers to entreat their commander to give them now an opportunity of obliterating their former disgrace. This generous ardor could not be resisted by Greene. Orders were issued to prepare for storming; and the June 18th. hour of twelve, on the next day (18th of June), was appointed for the assailing columns to advance by signal from the centre battery.

Lieutenant-Colonel Campbell, of the first Virginia regiment, with a detachment from the Maryland and Virginia brigades, was charged with the attack on the left; and Lieutenant-Colonel Lee, with the Legion infantry and Kirkwood's Delawares, with that on the right. Lieutenants Duval, of Maryland, and Seldon, of Virginia, commanded the forlorn hope of Campbell, and Captain Rudolph, of the Legion, that of Lee. Fascines were prepared to fill up the enemy's ditch; long poles with iron hooks were furnished to pull down the sand-bags, with every other requisite to facilitate the progress of the assailant. At eleven the third parallel was manned, and our sharp-shooters took their station in the tower. The first signal was announced from the centre battery, upon which the assailing columns entered the trenches, manifesting delight in the expectation of carrying by their courage the great prize in view.

At the second cannon, which was discharged at the hour of twelve, Campbell and Lee rushed to the assault. Cruger, always prepared, received them with his accustomed firmness. The parapets were manned with spike and bayonet, and the riflemen, fixed at the sand-bag apertures, maintained a steady and destructive fire. Duval and Seldon entered the enemy's ditch at different points, and Campbell stood prepared to support them, in the rear of the party furnished with hooks to pull down the sand-bags. This party had also entered the enemy's ditch, and began to apply the hook. Uncovering the parapet now would have given us victory; and such was the vigorous support afforded by the musketry from the third parallel, from the riflemen in the tower, and from the artillery mounted in battery, that sanguine expectations of this happy issue were universally indulged. The moment the bags in front were pulled down, Campbell would have mounted the parapet, where the struggle could not have been long maintained. Cruger had prepared an intermediate battery with his three pieces, which he occasionally applied to right and left. At first it was directed against Lee's left, but very soon every piece was applied upon Campbell's right, which was very injurious to his column.

Major Green, commanding in the star redoubt, sensible of the danger to which he was exposed if the attempted lodgment upon his front curtain succeeded, determined to try the bayonet in his ditch as well as on his parapet. To Captains Campbell and French was committed this bold effort. Entering into the ditch through a sally-port in the rear of the star, they took opposite directions, and soon came in contact, the one with Duval, the other with Seldon. Here ensued a desperate conflict. The Americans, not only fighting with the enemy in front, but with the enemy overhead, sustained gallantly the unequal contest, until Duval and Seldon became disabled by wounds, when they yielded, and were driven back, with great loss, to the point of entry. The few surviving escaped with the hookmen to our trenches, where yet remained Campbell, the sand-bags not being removed. On the left the issue was very different. Rudolph gained the enemy's ditch, and, followed by the column, soon opened his way into the fort, from which the enemy, giving their last fire, precipitately retreated. Measures were in train on the part of Lee to follow up his blow, by passing the rivulet, entering the town, and forcing the fortified prison, whence the left might have yielded substantial aid to the attack upon the star, by compelling Cruger to struggle for the town, or forcing him, with all his troops, to take refuge in the star, a situation not long to be held, crowded as he must have been, and destitute of water. The adverse fortune experienced by our left column made the mind of Greene return to his cardinal policy, the preservation of adequate force to keep the field.

Charmed with the courage displayed in his view, and regretting its disadvantageous application, he sent orders to Campbell to draw off, and to Lee to desist from farther advance, but to hold the stockade abandoned by the enemy.

Our loss amounted, during the siege, to one hundred and eighty-five, killed and wounded; that of the garrison to eighty-five. Captain Armstrong, of the Maryland line, was the only officer killed on our side, as was Lieutenant Roney the only one on theirs. After our repulse Greene sent a flag to Lieutenant-Colonel Cruger, proposing a cessation of hostilities for the purpose of burying the dead; but as to the burial of the dead, the proposition was rejected, Cruger not choosing to admit our participation in a ceremonial which custom had appropriated to the victor.

As soon as it was dark the detachment was withdrawn from the stockade, and preparations were begun for retreat.

On the nineteenth, Greene communicated to Sumter the event of the preceding day, advised him of the route of retreat, and ordered the corps in his front, with the cavalry under Washington, to join him with celerity. Taking leave of Mrs. Cruger and Mrs. Green, and leaving for the protection of the ladies the usual guard,*

---

* When General Greene approached Ninety-six, he found the ladies of Lieutenant-Colonel Cruger and Major Green in a farm-house in the neighborhood.

until Colonel Cruger should be advised of his retreat, and take his measures for their security, the American general withdrew, having two days before sent forward his sick and wounded. During the preceding night, gloom and silence pervaded the American camp: every one disappointed—every one mortified. Three days more, and Ninety-six must have fallen ; but this short space was unattainable. Rawdon had approached our vicinity with a force not to be resisted, and it only remained to hold the army safe, by resuming that system which adverse fortune had rendered familiar to us. Greene alone preserved his equanimity ; and, highly pleased by the unshaken courage displayed in the assault, announced his grateful sense of the conduct of the troops, as well during the siege as in the attack ; presaging from the past, the happiest result whenever an opportunity should be presented of contending with the enemy upon equal terms—to the attainment of which his best exertions would be invariably directed, relying, as he did, upon the same dauntless spirit recently exhibited. Conscious as the army was of having done its duty, it derived consolation from this exhilarating address, and burying in oblivion the grating repulse, looked forward with the anticipation of soon displaying their courage in a decisive battle.

General Greene, moving with celerity, gained the Saluda, where he was joined by his cavalry. Forming a rear-guard of his horse, the Legion infantry and Kirkwood's Delawares, he continued his retreat toward Charlotte in North Carolina, and passed successively the Enoree, the Tiger, and Broad rivers, his sick and wounded continuing to precede him.

In the morning of the twenty-first, the British army reached Ninety-six, having for fourteen days been incessantly pressing forward by forced marches ; exposed not only to the privations inseparable from rapid movement through an exhausted country, but also to the Southern sun, in the sultry season debilitating and destructive.

Here followed a delightful scene, and one which soldiers only can enjoy. The relieving army was welcomed with the fulness of

---

The American general tranquillized the fears of the ladies, and, as they preferred continuing where they were, he not only indulged them, but placed a guard at the house for their protection. The guard was left until Lieutenant-Colonel Cruger was apprised of our departure, when he sent the guard with his passport to rejoin our army. Some hours after Greene had withdrawn, one of our light parties, absent some days, returned, and passing by the farm-house, was going directly to our late camp before Ninety-six, when Mrs. Cruger sending for the officer, communicated what had happened, and instructed him to overtake the retiring general.

gratitude due to its exertions and their effect. Responsive to this was the hearty applause bestowed on the garrison, equally merited by the courage and firmness displayed throughout the late trying period. Officer embracing officer, and soldiers mingling with soldiers, gave themselves up to those gratulations resulting from the happy conclusion of their mutual toils and mutual perils. This pleasing scene lasted only a few hours; for Rawdon, not satisfied with the relief of Ninety-six, flattered himself with adding to the triumph already gained, by destroying or dispersing the army of Greene. Having replaced his fatigued and sick with a part of the force under Cruger, notwithstanding his long march, notwithstanding the sultry season, he moved in the evening in pursuit of Greene.

Passing the Saluda he pressed forward to the Enoree, on the south side of which his van came up with the American rear under Washington and Lee. Although his lordship had, during his repose in the lower country, contrived to strengthen himself by a newly-raised corps of horse under Major Coffin,* he did not derive, in this excursion, any material good from this accession of force. No attempt was hazarded against the American rear, which, conscious of its superior cavalry, retired slowly, always keeping the British van in view. While at the Enoree, Lord Rawdon acquired information which convinced him of the impracticability of accomplishing his enterprise, and induced him to spare his harassed troops unnecessary increase of fatigue. Halting here for the night, the British general retraced his steps next morning to Ninety-six. This being made known to Greene, he directed Lieutenant-Colonel Lee with his corps to follow the enemy, for the purpose of obtaining and communicating intelligence. After reaching Ninety-six, Rawdon prepared to evacuate the post; and having entered into arrangements with the loyalists of that district for the removal of themselves and families into the lines intended to be retained, he adopted a plan of retreat calculated to secure the undisturbed execution of his views. Dispatching orders to Lieutenant-Colonel Stewart to advance with his regiment from Charleston (and to take in his charge a convoy destined for the army) to Friday's Ferry, on the Congaree, his lordship, leaving at Ninety-six the major part of his force, took with the residue the direct road for the concerted point of junction.

---

* The corps was badly mounted—small meagre horses being the only sort procurable. The best officers and the best riders, thus mounted, cannot stand tolerable cavalry, much less such as then composed our rear.

Cruger was ordered to hasten the preparations necessary for the removal of the loyalists, then to abandon the theatre of his glory, and, by taking a route considerably to his lordship's right, to interpose the river Edisto between himself and his enemy, moving down its southern banks to Orangeburgh, where the road from Friday's Ferry to Charleston crossed that river. This disposition was advantageous to the column of Cruger, which was the most vulnerable, being heavily encumbered with property of the loyalists, as well as with public stores. But it would not have availed, had not the distance from Cruger been too great for Greene to overtake him, without much good fortune, before he should place himself behind the Edisto; after which, the course of Cruger's route would expose Greene to the sudden and co-operative attack of Rawdon and Lieutenant-Colonel Stewart. When the determination of the British general to abandon Ninety-six, and with it all the upper country yet held by him, was communicated to Greene, he immediately drew near to the enemy, in order to seize any advantage which might present itself; previously directing his hospital and heavy baggage at Winnsborough to be removed to Camden. As soon as the preparations for the evacuation of Ninety-six and the removal of the loyalists had advanced to their desired maturity, Rawdon separated himself from Cruger, and marched to Friday's Ferry; inviting, in appearance, the American general to strike Cruger.

For the reasons before assigned, this course of operations was avoided, and General Greene determined to pursue Rawdon; and in this decision he was confirmed by the information derived from an intercepted letter from Lieutenant-Colonel Balfour, the commandant of Charleston, to Lord Rawdon, stating the reasons which produced the recall of Stewart, with his corps, after he had commenced his march toward Friday's Ferry, in pursuance of orders from Cornwallis. Lee was accordingly directed to continue close to the British army, and to gain its front upon reaching Friday's Ferry, where he would find Sumter and Marion, ordered to take the same position, with the confident expectation that by their united exertions the advance of Lord Rawdon (uninformed of Stewart's recall), should he quit his position on the Congaree, might be retarded until Greene could come up with him. Obeying this order, Lieutenant-Colonel Lee continued on the left flank and rear of the retiring army; when, finding that his lordship had halted at Friday's Ferry, he prepared in the course of the night to pass from the left to the right flank of the enemy, the Congaree River rendering this change in direction indispensable ; as otherwise the enemy's front could not be gained, who was on the south of that river, and Lee's position to the rear of the British being on its north. Well apprised, from his knowledge of the adjacent country, acquired when before Fort Granby, that only the rich settlement south of Friday's Ferry could afford sufficient forage for the British army, Lee determined to avail himself of the probable chance to strike the enemy, which would be presented the ensuing morning by the British foragers.   In the evening he directed Captain Eggleston, of the cavalry, to proceed with thirty dragoons along the enemy's right, and taking with him Armstrong, previously dispatched in that quarter with a reconnoitring party, to make in the course of the night a proper disposition of his force for the contemplated purpose. Eggleston immediately joined Armstrong and repaired to the expected theatre of action, placing himself in a secret and convenient position. Soon after daylight the next morning, a foraging party, consisting of fifty or sixty dragoons and some wagons, were discovered approaching the very farm to which Eggleston had directed his attention. As soon as the wagons and escort had advanced within reach of Eggleston, he rushed upon the enemy, broke up the foragers, routed the party, and brought off forty-five dragoons prisoners. This handsomely-executed stroke was the more agreeable, as Eggleston, by his judicious position and rapid charge, contrived to accomplish his object without any loss. General Greene complimented the captain and party in general orders ; and the Legion horse derived credit with the enemy very flattering to its reputation, from the brilliant success of this detachment.

July 8th.

The prisoners being dispatched to head-quarters, Lee pursued his route to the enemy's front, which passed over a difficult defile in a line with the British camp. The infantry, preceding the cavalry, was directed to pass the defile, and to occupy the heights on the left to cover the horse, whose passage was tedious, they being compelled to move in single file. The course taken by Lee was too near the enemy, and his cavalry must have suffered considerably had Rawdon been apprised of his movement, and of the difficulty of the defile in his route. When the troops in the centre had entered the defile, we were alarmed by beating to arms in the camp of the infantry, which was soon followed by their forming in line of battle.

This unexpected event was felt by all ; but most by the amiable surgeon of the infantry, who was at that moment leading his horse through the defile.* Not doubting but that battle must instantly take place, and believing the wiser course was to avoid it, the surgeon turned his horse with a view of getting (as he believed) out of danger; never reflecting in his panic that the passage did not admit the turning of a horse. Ductile to the force of the bridle, the horse attempted to turn about, but was brought upon his head athwart the narrow passage, from which position he could not possibly extricate himself. The troop, which had passed the defile, instantly galloped up the hill and arrayed with the infantry, while the remaining two troops were arrested by the panic of an individual.

Eggleston, who commanded the troop so unhappily situated, dismounting several of his strongest dragoons, pulled the horse back again lengthways of the defile. He had then space to use his limbs, and soon stood upon his feet, and our deranged and distressed cavalry were enabled to pass the defile. This accident interrupted the progress of the horse for ten minutes—ample time for their destruction had the enemy been at hand. It turned out that Captain Handy, the officer of the day, deviating a little from his course in visiting the sentinels, was seized by a small patrol of the enemy, and carried off out of musket fire. There he was stripped of his watch and money, and left upon condition of not stirring until his captors should reach a designated point in view, when he was permitted to return to his corps. It was his return which produced that sudden change upon the hill, which as suddenly alarmed our surgeon, and led to the described occurrence in the defile. The remainder of the cavalry hurried, as they passed, to join their friends; and Lieutenant-Colonel Lee, with the last troop, at

---

* Alexander Skinner was a native of Maryland. He was virtuous and sensible; full of original humor of a peculiar cast, and eccentric in mind and manners. In person and in love of good cheer, as well as in dire objection to the field of battle, he resembled with wonderful similitude Shakespeare's Falstaff. Yet Skinner had no hesitation in fighting duels, and had killed his man. Therefore, when urged by his friends why *he*, who would when called upon by feelings of honor to risk his life in single combat, advance to the arena with alacrity, should abhor so dreadfully the field of battle, he uniformly in substance answered, that he considered it very arrogant in a surgeon (whose province it was to take care of the sick and wounded) to be aping the demeanor and duty of a commissioned officer, whose business was to fight—an arrogance which he cordially contemned, and which he should never commit. Moreover, he would add that he was not more indisposed to die than other gentlemen, but that he had an utter aversion to the noise and turmoil of battle; it stunned and stupefied him. However, when Congress should think proper to honor him with a commission, he would convince all doubters that he was not afraid to push the bayonet.

length got over. Finding no enemy, as, from what had passed, was strongly apprehended, the agitating scene concluded with continuance of the march, after some humorous animadversions on the surprised captain and the American Falstaff. Moving in silence, and with much caution, at length the Legion reached undisturbed the enemy's front. Here it turned toward the British camp, and Rudolph, with the infantry, drove in the pickets at the bridge over the water-course which had just been passed.

Having destroyed the bridge, and posting guards along the water-course to the river, Lee encamped one mile in the enemy's front, expecting hourly to hear of the advance of the corps under Sumter and Marion.

Lord Rawdon was not inattentive to the changing condition of affairs. The daring measure executed in his view was truly interpreted. Not joined by Stewart, and unacquainted with the cause of his delay, he determined not to risk the approach of Greene. He accordingly put his army in motion, and dispatched his light troops to the river shore, where the creek in his front emptied into the river, and where the meeting of the waters formed a bar. As soon as the light troops made good their passage, the American guards were driven in and the bridge replaced, over which the main body and baggage of the enemy proceeded, forcing Lee before them.

The whole evening was spent in rapid movement; the corps of Lee falling back upon Beaver Creek, in the confident expectation of being immediately joined by Sumter, Marion, and Washington, when a serious combined effort would have been made to stop the progress of the enemy. In this expectation, founded on Greene's dispatch, Lee was disappointed: neither Sumter, Marion, nor Washington appeared, nor was any communication received from either. Lieutenant-Colonel Lee, not doubting that the wished-for junction would be effected the next morning, determined, if practicable, to establish his night quarters near Beaver Creek, on the south side of which the road by the Eutaws and Motte's Post from Charleston intersected that from Charleston by the way of Orangeburgh. This spot, too, gave advantages favorable to that effort which it was presumed would follow the union of the three corps.

Rawdon, still uninformed as to Stewart, and feeling his own inferiority, persevered in his determination to avoid any exposure; not doubting that the American general was pressing forward to bring him to action before he could be re-enforced. He continued to ad-

vance until nine P. M., when he halted for the night: Lee, moving
a few miles in his front, took up also his night position. With the
dawn of day the British van appeared, and the corps of Lee retired.
Repeating their rapid movement this day, this day passed like the
preceding, till at length the American corps reached Beaver Creek,
and took post behind it.

Not yet had any intelligence been received of or from the militia
corps; and here was the last point where the junction was practicable, as Sumter and Marion were in the eastern country, to Lee's
left, and would advance on the road from Motte's Post, which here
fell into that going to Orangeburgh. Lord Rawdon upon reaching
the creek hastened over; and Lieutenant-Colonel Lee, finding his
expectation illusive, turned to his left, proceeding down the Congaree; yielding up any further struggle to hold the enemy's front.

The British general advanced along the Orangeburgh road, and
halted at this small village, where he was joined on the next day by
Lieutenant-Colonel Stewart with the regiment of Buffs and convoy.
Informed of the march of Stewart from Charleston with the convoy,
Greene ordered Marion and Washington to make an attempt upon
this officer, encumbered as he was; not doubting that this service
could be performed in time to unite with Lee. Stewart's march was
very slow, which, consuming more time than was expected, prevented Marion and Washington from reaching Lee before his passage of Beaver Creek. Marion did not succeed against Stewart.
Colonel Horry, one of his officers, cut off a few wagons; the only
advantage gained by the American corps. On the succeeding day
Sumter, Marion, and Washington joined Lee, when the united corps
advanced under Sumter a few miles toward Orangeburgh, convenient to the route of the American army. General Greene on the
subsequent day passed Beaver Creek, and, encamping contiguous to
the van troops, put himself at the head of his cavalry, commanded by
Washington and Lee, accompanied by his principal officers, for the
purpose of examining the enemy's position, with a view of forcing
it if possible. The reconnoissance was made with great attention,
and close to the enemy; for, being comparatively destitute of cavalry, Lord Rawdon had no means to interrupt it. After spending
several hours in examining the British position, General Greene
decided against hazarding an assault. The force of the enemy was
about sixteen hundred, infantry and artillery, without horse;
Greene's army, comprehending every sort, was rated at two thousand, of which near a moiety was militia. Cruger had not joined,

being engaged in his march, and in depositing his loyalists in their new homes; but he was daily expected, and would add at least fourteen hundred infantry and some few dragoons to the British force. If, therefore, any attempt was to be made against Rawdon, delay became inadmissible. Some of the officers attending upon Greene, and in whose opinions he properly confided, did not consider the obstacles to assault so serious; and believed that it was necessary to strike the enemy, in order to induce him to relinquish his design of establishing a post at Orangeburgh, with the view of holding all the country south of the Edisto and west of the Santee.

But the majority concurred with the general, and the contemplated attack was abandoned.* Two powerful reasons led to this deci-

* *Extract of a letter, dated "* 16th *July, 1781, camp High Hills, Santee" from Adjutant-General Williams to Major Pendleton, aid-de-camp to General Greene.*

"Dear Pendleton,—After you left us at Ninety-six we were obliged to retrograde as far as the cross-roads above Winnsborough. Lord Rawdon's return over Saluda induced the general to halt the army, and wait for intelligence respecting his further manœuvres, and hearing a few days after that his lordship was on his march to Fort Granby, our army was ordered to march toward that place by way of Winnsborough. Before we could arrive at Congaree, Lord Rawdon retired to Orangeburgh, and, as he had left a considerable part of his army at Ninety-six, General Greene detached the cavalry and light infantry to join General Marion, and endeavor to intercept Colonel Stewart, who was on his march from Charleston, with the third regiment, &c., consisting of about three hundred, convoying bread, stores, &c., of which Lord Rawdon's troops were in great want. Stewart, however, joined his lordship at Orangeburgh; and General Greene, from the information he had received, was encouraged to expect success from an attack upon the British army at that post. Accordingly he collected his troops, and called together the militia and State troops under Generals Sumter and Marion (General Pickens being left to watch the motions of Colonel Cruger). A junction of the whole formed a very respectable little army, which marched to a small branch of North Edisto, within four miles of Orangeburgh, where we halted, and lay the 12th instant from about nine o'clock in the morning till six in the afternoon.

"General Greene reconnoitred the position of the enemy, and found it materially different from what it had been represented. The ground is broken, and naturally strong, from the court-house (which is two stories high and built of brick), to a bridge four or five hundred yards distant, the only pass over the Edisto within many miles. The general had every reason to believe, what he had soon afterward confirmed, that Colonel Cruger had evacuated Ninety-six, and was on his march to join Lord Rawdon, which might possibly be done before we could force his lordship (if he could be forced at all) to a general action— the issue of which was not certain. These considerations induced the general rather to offer than to give battle. The enemy declined the opportunity, and put up with the insult. General Greene, therefore, ordered our troops to retire in the afternoon to Colonel Middleton's plantation, from whence we have proceeded by slow, easy marches to this place, and not without leaving behind sufficient detachments to intercept their convoys from below, and to create such a diversion at Monk's Corner, Dorchester, &c., as will very probably oblige his lordship to march to their relief. Indeed I am encouraged to hope that the

sion. One, that the British general was not only in a strong position, but that he had secured his retreat across the Edisto, by occupying with musketry a large brick prison and several other houses commanding the river, to the southern banks of which he could readily retire uninjured, should he think proper to avoid battle until Lieutenant-Colonel Cruger should join. Thus only could partial success be attained, if any, and that no doubt with severe loss. The second, that the cavalry, from the nature of the ground and the disposition of the enemy, could not be brought to take its part in the action; and as ours formed an essential portion of the American army, it was deemed unwise to seek for battle when deprived of this aid. It was very desirable to compel the enemy to relinquish his desire of holding the country south of the Edisto, by establishing a post at Orangeburgh; but other means might be resorted to productive of this end. One very obvious, was adopted by the American general when about to decamp, and which did completely effect his views.

We had often experienced in the course of the campaign want of food,* and had sometimes seriously suffered from the scantiness of our supplies, rendered more pinching by their quality; but never did we suffer so severely as during the few days' halt here. Rice furnished our substitute for bread, which, although tolerably relished by those familiarized to it from infancy, was very disagreeable to Marylanders and Virginians, who had grown up in the use of corn or wheat bread. Of meat we had literally none; for the few meagre cattle brought to camp as beef would not afford more than one or two ounces per man. Frogs abounded in some neighboring ponds, and on them chiefly did the light troops subsist. They became in great demand from their nutritiousness; and, after conquering the existing prejudice, were diligently sought after. Even the alligator was used by a few; and, very probably, had the army been much longer detained upon that ground, might have rivalled the frog in the estimation of our epicures.

---

garrison at Charleston will not be undisturbed. Mischief is meditated against them in other quarters; and I sanguinely trust the issue of this campaign will permanently fix the exalted idea the world has justly conceived of the eminent abilities of our general, and secure durable advantages to the country."

* Tacitus (de Moribus Germanorum) observes that they had a plentiful table instead of pay,—"Nam epulæ, et quanquam incompti largi tamen apparatus pro stipendio redunt." This cannot be said of us *in toto*. Like the Germans we had no pay; and instead of plentiful tables, in lieu of pay, our table was not often plentiful, and seldom agreeable.

The heat of the season had become oppressive, and the troops began to experience its effect in sickness. General Greene determined to repair to some salubrious and convenient spot to pass the sultry season; and having selected the High Hills of Santee, a place so called from the eminence of its ground, it became very opportune, while directing his march with the main body to his camp of repose, to detach his light troops against the British posts in the vicinity of Charleston, now uncovered by the concentration of all the enemy's disposable force in Orangeburgh. When, therefore, he decamped on the 13th of July, he ordered Sumter, Marion, and Lee to move rapidly toward Charleston; and, after breaking up the posts at and about Dorchester, to unite at Monk's Corner, for the purpose of dislodging the nineteenth regiment stationed there under Lieutenant-Colonel Coates. This service performed, their several corps would rendezvous at the High Hills of Santee, for which position the general now commenced his march.

The corps took distinct routes, concealing their march, and prepared to fall at the same moment, in different directions, upon the country lying between the Ashley and Cooper rivers. The small post at Dorchester was broken up, and some trivial successes gained by the several corps; among which the most important was achieved by Lieutenant-Colonel Hampton, commanding Sumter's cavalry, who falling in with some mounted refugees, dispersed the whole body, and made forty or fifty prisoners. A party of the Legion horse was pushed below the quarter-house in the Neck, from the confidence that in a place so near Charleston an advantageous stroke might be made. But it so happened that on that day none of the usual visits to the quarter-house took place, nor was even a solitary officer picked up in their customary morning rides.

Sumter hastened toward Monk's Corner, where lay the nineteenth regiment—an adequate prize for our previously disappointed exertions. Marion joined him on the same day, and Lee, having called in his parties from the Neck, followed on the subsequent morning. This officer expected that General Sumter would have seized the bridge over the Cooper River, near Monk's Corner, which afforded a direct route to the militia camp. But Lieutenant-Colonel Coates had very prudently occupied it with a detachment from his regiment, which compelled Lee to take a very circuitous route through deep sands, in the heat of July, to reach Sumter, then ready to fall upon Coates as soon as he should be joined by Lee. Late in the evening the desired junction took place, and the next morning

Monk's Corner was to have been assaulted.   Coates had three routes
of retreat, either of which led directly to Charleston.   Two lay on
the east of Cooper River, and one to the west.   The western offered
the readiest route ; for by passing the bridge in his possession, he
would place Cooper River on his left, and become relieved from
water obstruction in his whole progress.   It was, however, deemed
safer to take the two routes on the east of the river ; one of which
led over the Cooper, some miles below Monk's Corner, intersecting
the western route in Charleston Neck, and the other continued on
the east of the river, crossing the same river opposite to the town.
The head-waters of Cooper River make several branches about
Monk's Corner, all having bridges over them.   Brigadier Sumter
took the precaution to hold by a detachment from his corps the
bridge over that water-course in the way of Lieutenant-Colonel
Coates, should he take the eastern route, and calculated that the
resistance at that bridge would give him time to come up with the
enemy.   During the night Coates decamped in silence, setting fire
to the church which had been used as a magazine, for the purpose
of destroying stores which could not be withdrawn, and which he
did not choose to leave for the accommodation of his enemy.   The
fire in the course of some hours penetrated through the roof, and,
making then a wide illumination, was descried from our camp.

No doubt existed but the British colonel had fired the house, and
of course that he had considerably advanced in his retreat, notwithstanding the presumed possession of a bridge over which he must
pass.   The troops were called to arms, and with great celerity
moved upon Monk's Corner, where it was discovered that the enemy,
for the purpose of consuming his stores, had burnt the church, and
that he had retreated on the eastern side of the Cooper.   In this
direction Sumter pursued, preceded by the Legion, which was supported by the State cavalry under Lieutenant-Colonel Hampton.
To our surprise and mortification, no opposition at the bridge had
taken place ; and indeed our inquiries terminated in the conviction
that the detachment destined to occupy that post had abandoned it
a few hours after they had been sent to possess it.   Hence arose our
ignorance of Coates's movement, which could not have occurred
had the militia party continued at their post, and to which ignorance
the foe owed his escape.   Continuing to press the pursuit, the cavalry became considerably advanced before the infantry and the
mounted militia under Brigadier Marion.   When they had reached
the point where the roads separate, the British horse (not more than

a troop) had taken the route nearest to Cooper River. Expecting that it might be overtaken before it could pass, having only the ferry boats for its transportation, a detachment from the militia was ordered to pursue. But the attempt proved abortive, the British dragoons having crossed the river some hours before our detachment reached it.

Lee with the cavalry pursued the main body, and drew near to it in the neighborhood of Quinby Bridge, about eighteen miles from Monk's Corner. It was much wished to come up with Coates before he crossed that bridge, as it was well known that the stream, without a circuit, was only passable at the bridge, which it was certain the enemy would secure or destroy. As soon as the officer in advance announced view of the enemy, Lee inquired of his guides the distance from the bridge, and heard with great pleasure that it was at least three miles in front. The Legion cavalry was now directed to take close order; and Captain Eggleston with one troop was detached in the woods to the left to turn the enemy's right, while the squadron under Lee, supported by the cavalry under Lieutenant-Colonel Hampton, advanced along the road directly toward him. These in our view appeared to be Coates's rear-guard, charged with his baggage-wagons, and not to exceed one hundred men, and to be all infantry. Upon the approach of the horse in two directions, the commanding officer formed in line; his left on the road, and his right in the woods opposite to Eggleston. This disposition was the very one desired; as a deep swamp lined the margin of the road, in which Lee apprehended the enemy would take post to cover the road and wagons. To obviate this apprehended measure, formed the principal reason for throwing Eggleston to the left. The instant the enemy had formed, the charge was sounded, and the horse rushed upon them with drawn swords in full gallop. On our approach the enemy's order to fire was distinctly heard from right to left, which not taking place caused some inquietude, lest it was intentionally reserved to render it more fatal.

Contrary to expectation this was not the case. The suppression of their meditated fire was not a feint; but the line,* terrified at the

---

* The nineteenth regiment, of which this detachment was a part, was one of the three lately arrived from Ireland, and had not seen service. It is probably such submission would not have ensued had the troops been veteran. Generally speaking, infantry, unless surpassing greatly in number, or aided by the ground, will fall when vigorously charged by horse. If they discharge *in toto*, they are gone. Holding up he front file fire with charged bayonets, and pouring in the rear fire, best aids their chance of success.

novel and menacing attitude of the horse close upon it, hoped to secure their safety by this inoffensive conduct; and, without discharging a single musket, threw down their arms and begged for quarters. Their supplication was cheerfully granted, and like ourselves they escaped unhurt. Not doubting but that the Quinby Bridge was yet at least one mile in front, the cavalry were brought to order, and, leaving the captured rear in care of a few of the militia horse, hastened to strike the last blow.

They had not proceeded far when a courier was dispatched to Lieutenant-Colonel Lee with information that Captain Campbell had ordered his men to resume their arms, and this recalled Lee for a few minutes.

At this instant Armstrong with the leading section came in sight of Coates, who, having passed the bridge was carelessly reposing, expecting his rear-guard—having determined to destroy the bridge as soon as his rear and baggage should have passed it. With this view the planks were mostly raised from the sleepers, lying on them loosely, ready to be thrown into the stream when the rear should get over. Seeing the enemy, with the bridge interposed, which he knew to be contrary to his commandant's expectation, this gallant officer drew up, and sent back for orders—never communicating the unexpected fact that the bridge intervened. Lee, sending his adjutant to the captain, warmly reminded him of the order of the day, which was to fall upon the foe without respect to consequences. Stung with this answer, the brave Armstrong put spur to his horse at the head of his section, and threw himself over the bridge upon the guard stationed there with a howitzer. So sudden was this charge that he drove all before him—the soldiers abandoning their piece. Some of the loose planks were dashed off by Armstrong's section, which, forming a chasm in the bridge, presented a dangerous obstacle. Nevertheless the second section, headed by Lieutenant Carrington, took the leap and closed with Armstrong, then engaged in a personal combat with Lieutenant-Colonel Coates, who, placing himself on the side of a wagon which with a few others had kept up with the main body, effectually parried the many sabre strokes, aimed at his head. Most of his soldiers, appalled at the sudden and daring attack, had abandoned their colonel, and were running through the field, some with, some without arms, to take shelter in the farm-house.

Lee now got up to the bridge, where Captain O'Neal with the third section had halted; and seeing the howitzer in our possession, and the whole regiment flying in confusion (except the lieutenant-colonel, who, with a few, mostly officers, were defending themselves with their swords, and calling upon their soldiers for assistance), he used every effort to recover and replace the planks. The gap having been enlarged by Carrington's section throwing off more planks, O'Neal's horses would not take the leap; and the creek was deep in water and deeper in mud, so that the dragoons, who had dismounted for the purpose of getting the plank, could not, even though clinging to the studs of the bridge, stop from sinking—there being no foothold to stand upon; nor was it possible to find any firm spot from whence to swim the horses across. In this perplexing condition the victory gained by the gallantry of one troop of dragoons was wrested from them, when to complete it only a passage across the creek, not twenty yards wide, was wanting. Discerning the halt of the horse, the enemy took courage, and the bravest of the soldiers hastening back to their leader soon relieved him. Armstrong and Carrington, compelled to abandon the unequal contest, forced their way down the great road, turning into the woods up the stream to rejoin the corps Lee continued struggling to replace the planks, until Coates (relieved from Armstrong) repaired with the few around him to defend the bridge, where remained his deserted howitzer. Having only sabres to oppose to the enemy's fire, and those sabres withheld from contact by the interposing chasm, Lee was forced to draw off from the vain contest, after several of his dragoons had been wounded, among whom was Doctor Irvin, surgeon of the Legion cavalry.*

As soon as he had reached the enemy, Lee dispatched the intelligence to Brigadier Marion, and to the Legion infantry, urging their approach; and now foiled at the bridge, he communicated to Marion his movement some distance up the creek to a ford, which, from the information derived from his guides, would afford a ready passage. To this place he urged the brigadier to direct his march, assuring him that by their united effort the enemy might still be destroyed.

---

* Such was Doctor Skinner's unvarying objection to Irvin's custom of risking his life, whenever he was with the corps going into action, that, kind and amiable as he was, he saw with pleasure that his prediction, often communicated to Irvin to stop his practice (which contrasted with his own, Skinner felt as a bitter reproach), was at length realized, when Irvin was brought in wounded; and he would not dress his wound, although from his station he had the right of preference, until he had finished all the privates—reprehending with asperity Irvin's custom, and sarcastically complimenting him, every now and then, with the honorable scar he might hereafter show.

Marion pressed his march with diligence, bringing with him the Legion infantry; and, having passed the creek, united with Lee late in the evening, in front of the house, which, in their panic, had been so eagerly sought by the flying British soldiers, and which was now possessed by Lieutenant-Colonel Coates, who had repaired to it with his wagons and howitzer: affording, as it did, the most eligible position he could assume. Posted in the house, the outhouses, and along the yard and garden fences, with his howitzer in front and under cover of the house, Lieutenant-Colonel Coates found himself safe. Marion and Lee, seeing that no point of his position was assailable with probable hope of success (destitute, as they were, of artillery), reluctantly gave up this regiment; and being low down in the Neck, within striking distance from Charleston, after all the fatigue of the day they deemed it necessary to retire fifteen miles before they could give rest to their troops.

At this moment Armstrong and Carrington, whose suspended fate had excited painful sensations in the breasts of their friends, happily joined with their shattered sections. Both the officers were unhurt, only one horse killed and one wounded, but some few of the bravest dragoons were killed and more wounded.

Sending the captain with a detachment to the ground of action, for the purpose of bringing off the dead and wounded, Lee followed Marion; who, having detached a party to replace the planks of the bridge, took the direct course to it through the field. While we halted here with the Legion cavalry until Armstrong should rejoin, one of our wounded dragoons came hobbling out of the swamp, into which he had scrambled when his horse had fallen by the same ball which had shattered the rider's knee. Armstrong now came up, bringing with him sad evidences of his intrepid charge. Some of his finest fellows had fallen in this honorable, though unsuccessful attempt; soldiers who had passed from early life through the war, esteemed and admired. Placing the wounded in the easiest posture for conveyance, and bearing the dead on the pummels of our saddles, we concluded a toilsome sixteen hours in the sadness of grief; not for the loss of brave soldiers, nobly dying in their country's cause, but because they fell in an abortive attack, rendered so by unforeseen incidents. Had the bridge near Monk's Corner (over which the British passed) been held in conformity to Sumter's plan and order, Coates would have been overtaken before he arrived at Quinby's. Had the guides been correct in their estimation of the distance of the bridge, when we first saw the enemy's rear, Lee (having taken the rear-guard) would have found out some other route to the main body, and avoided the fatal obstacle. Had Armstrong, referring for further orders, communicated the interposition of the bridge, the warm reply would never have been made, but a cool examination of our relative situation would have followed; the result of which must have been propitious. Coates and his regiment must have fallen; giving increase of fame to our army, with solid good to our cause; and the sad loss would not have occurred. To produce a discomfiture, this series of omission and error was necessary and did take place. Soldiers may and must struggle,—but unless fortune smile, they often struggle in vain.*

As soon as we reached our quarters, one common grave was prepared for the dead, and at the dawn of light the rites of sepulture were performed.

The prisoners and baggage which had been taken were instantly sent off under a proper escort, and safely delivered to Brigadier Sumter. With the baggage was taken the regimental-military chest, whose contents being divided among the troops, by the brigadier's order, gave to each soldier one guinea. We reached, on the following day, the neighborhood of Nelson's Ferry, where the troops were permitted to repose for twenty-four hours. Resuming our march, we crossed the Santee, and by easy marches joined in a few days the army at the High Hills. Incomplete as was the expedition, the zeal and vigor uniformly exhibited reflected credit on all employed in it; and the general, always disposed to honor merit, testified his grateful approbation in very flattering terms. Armstrong, Carrington, and their gallant band, were, as they deserved, distinguished. The troops were placed in good quarters, and the heat of July rendered tolerable by the high ground, the fine air, and good water of the selected camp. Disease began to abate, our wounded to recover, and the army to rise in bodily strength. Enjoying this period of rest, the first experienced since Greene's assumption of the command, it was natural to meditate upon the past scenes. Nor was the conclusion of such meditations less instructive than agreeable. The wisdom of the general was manifest; and the zeal, patience, and firmness exhibited by the troops could not be denied. It is true, that untoward occurrences

* The author forgot to relate that, after his retreat from this position of Coates, it was attacked by Sumter and Marion, with considerable spirit, and some loss; but without success, in consequence chiefly of Sumter's failure to bring up his artillery.—Ed.

had deprived us of two victories, and lost us Ninety-six; but it was no less true, that the comprehensive views of the general, with his inflexible perseverance, and unvarying activity, had repaired these mortifying disappointments, and had closed the campaign with the successful execution of his object. Defeat had been changed by its consequences into victory, and our repulse had been followed by accession of territory. The conquered States were regained, and our exiled countrymen were restored to their deserted homes,—sweet rewards of toil and peril. Such results can only be attributed to superior talents, seconded by skill, courage, and fidelity. Fortune often gives victory; but when the weak, destitute of the essential means of war, successfully oppose the strong, it is not chance but sublime genius which guides the intermediate operations, and controls the ultimate event.

CHAPTER XXX.

Adventure of Sergeant-Major John Champe.

LATELY John Champe, Sergeant-Major of the Legion cavalry, who had been for several months considered by the corps as a deserter, returned. This high-minded soldier had been selected to undertake a very difficult and perilous project, the narration of which is due to his merit, as well as to the singularity of his progress.*

The treason of Brigadier Arnold—the capture of André—with intelligence received by Washington, through his confidential agents in New York, communicating that many of his officers, and especially a major-general named to him, were connected with Arnold—could not fail to seize the attention of a commander less diligent and zealous than Washington. It engrossed his mind entirely, exciting reflections the most anxious as well as unpleasant. The moment he reached the army, then under the orders of Major-General Greene, encamped in the vicinity of Tappan, he sent for Major Lee, posted with the light troops some distance in front. The officer repaired to head-quarters with celerity, and found the general in his marquee alone, busily-engaged in writing. As soon as Lee entered, he was requested to take a seat, and a bundle of papers, lying on the table, was given to him for perusal. In these much information was de-

---

* This retrospect carries the reader back to the northern campaign of 1780, where the author held the rank of major, and was serving under General Washington on the Hudson.—ED.

tailed, tending to prove that Arnold was not alone in the base conspiracy just detected, but that the poison had spread; and that a major-general, whose name was not concealed, was certainly as guilty as Arnold himself. This officer had enjoyed, without interruption, the confidence of the commander-in-chief throughout the war; nor did there exist a single reason in support of the accusation. It altogether rested upon the intelligence derived from the papers before him. Major Lee, personally acquainted with the accused, could not refrain from suggesting the probability, that the whole was a contrivance of Sir Henry Clinton, in order to destroy that confidence between the commander and his officers on which the success of military operations depends. This suggestion, Washington replied, was plausible, and deserved due consideration. It had early occurred to his own mind, and had not been slightly regarded; but his reflections settled in a conclusion not to be shaken; as the same suggestion applied to no officer more forcibly than a few days ago it would have done to General Arnold, known now to be a traitor.

Announcing this result of his meditations with the tone and countenance of a mind deeply agitated, and resolved upon its course, Lee continuing silent, the general proceeded: "I have sent for you, in the expectation that you have in your corps individuals capable and willing to undertake an indispensable, delicate, and hazardous project. Whoever comes forward upon this occasion, will lay me under great obligations personally, and in behalf of the United States I will reward him amply. No time is to be lost; he must proceed, if possible, this night. My object is to probe to the bottom the afflicting intelligence contained in the papers you have just read; to seize Arnold, and by getting him to save André. They are all connected. While my emissary is engaged in preparing means for the seizure of Arnold, the guilt of others can be traced; and the timely delivery of Arnold to me, will possibly put it into my power to restore the amiable and unfortunate André to his friends. My instructions are ready, in which you will find my express orders that Arnold is not to be hurt; but that he be permitted to escape if to be prevented only by killing him, as his public punishment is the sole object in view. This you cannot too forcibly press upon whomsoever may engage in the enterprise; and this fail not to do. With my instructions are two letters, to be delivered as ordered, and here are some guineas for expenses."

Major Lee replying, said, that he had little or no doubt but that his Legion contained many individuals daring enough for any operation, however perilous; but that the one in view required a combination of qualities not easily to be found unless in a commissioned officer, to whom he could not venture to propose an enterprise, the first step to which was desertion. That though the sergeant-major of the cavalry was in all respects qualified for the delicate and adventurous project, and to him it might be proposed without indelicacy, as his station did not interpose the obstacle before stated; yet it was very probable that the same difficulty would occur in his breast, to remove which would not be easy, if practicable.

Washington was highly pleased at finding that a non-commissioned officer was deemed capable of executing his views, as he had felt extreme difficulty in authorizing an invitation to officers, who generally are, and always ought to be, scrupulous and nice in adhering to the course of honor. He asked the name, the country, the age, the size, length of service, and character of the sergeant.

Being told his name—that he was a native of London County in Virginia, about twenty-three or twenty-four years of age—that he had enlisted in 1776—rather above the common size—full of bone and muscle; with a saturnine countenance, grave, thoughtful, and taciturn—of tried courage and inflexible perseverance, and is likely to reject an overture coupled with ignominy as any officer in the corps; a commission being the goal of his long and anxious exertions, and certain on the first vacancy;—the general exclaimed, that he was the very man for the business; that he must undertake it; and that going to the enemy by the instigation and at the request of his officer, was not desertion, although it appeared to be so. And he enjoined that this explanation, as coming from him, should be pressed on Champe; and that the vast good in prospect should be contrasted with the mere semblance of doing wrong, which he presumed could not fail to conquer every scruple. Major Lee assured the general, that every exertion would be essayed on his part to execute his wishes; and taking leave returned to the camp of the light corps, which he reached about eight o'clock at night. Sending instantly for the sergeant-major, he introduced the business in the way best calculated, as he thought, to produce his concurrence; and dilated largely on the very great obligations he would confer on the commander-in-chief, whose unchanging and active beneficence to the troops had justly drawn to him their affection, which would be merely nominal, if, when an opportunity should offer to any individual of contributing to the promotion of his views, that opportunity was not zealously embraced. That the one now presented to him had never before occurred, and in all probability never would occur again, even should the war continue for ages ; it being most rare for three distinct consequences, all of primary weight, to be comprised within a single operation, and that operation necessarily to be intrusted to one man who would want but one or two associates in the active part of its execution. That the chance of detection became extremely narrow, and consequently that of success enlarged. That by succeeding in the safe delivery of Arnold, he not only gratified his general in the most acceptable manner, but he would be hailed as the avenger of the reputation of the army, stained by foul and wicked perfidy; and what could not but be highly pleasing, he would be the instrument of saving the life of Major André, soon to be brought before a court of inquiry, the decision of which could not be doubted, from the universally known circumstances of the case, and had been anticipated in the general's instructions. That, by investigating with diligence and accuracy the intelligence communicated to him, he would bring to light new guilt, or he would relieve innocence (as was most probable) from distrust ; quieting the torturing suspicions which now harrowed the mind of Washington, and restoring again to his confidence a once honored general, presenting it at present only ostensibly, as well as hush doubts affecting many of his brother soldiers.

In short, the accomplishment of so much good was in itself too attractive to be renounced by a generous mind ; and when connected with the recollection of the high honor which the selection shed upon him as a soldier, he ought not—he must not pause. This discourse was followed by a detail of the plan, with a wish that he would enter upon its execution instantly. Champe listened with deep attention, and with a highly-excited countenance ; the perturbations of his breast not being hid even by his dark visage. He briefly and modestly replied that no soldier exceeded him in respect and affection for the commander-in-chief, to serve whom he would willingly lay down his life; and that he was sensible of the honor conferred by the choice of him for the execution of a project all over arduous ; nor could he be at a loss to know to whom was to be ascribed the preference bestowed, which he took pleasure in acknowledging, although increasing obligations before great and many.

That he was charmed with the plan ; even its partial success would lead to great good, as it would give peace to the general's mind, and do justice, as he hoped, to innocence; while full success would add powerful and delicious personal excitements, as well as the gratification of the general and army. He was not, he said, deterred by the danger and difficulty which was evidently to be encountered, but he was deterred by the ignominy of desertion, to be followed by the hypocrisy of enlisting with the enemy, neither of which comported with his feelings, and either placed an insuperable bar in his way to promotion.

He concluded by observing, that if any mode could be contrived, free from disgrace, he would cordially embark in the enterprise. As it was, he prayed to be excused, and hoped that services, always the best in his power to perform, faithfully performed, entitled his prayer to success. The objections at first apprehended, now to be combated, were extended to a consequence which had not suggested itself. Lee candidly admitted that he had expected the first objection made, and that only; which had been imparted to the general, who gave to it full consideration, and concluded by declaring that the crime of desertion was not incurred; as no act done by the soldier at the request of the commander-in-chief, could be considered as a desertion; and that an action so manifestly praiseworthy as that to be performed, when known, would dissipate by its own force the reflections excited by appearances, leaving the actor in full enjoyment of the rich rewards of his virtue. That the reflecting mind ought not to balance between the achievement of so much good, and the doing wrong in semblance only; to which Major Lee subjoined, that he had considered himself and corps highly honored by the general's call upon him for a soldier capable and willing to execute a project so tempting to the brave; and that he should feel himself reduced to a mortifying condition, if the resistance to the undertaking compelled him to inform the general that he must recur to some other corps to provide an agent to execute this bold and important enterprise.

He entreated the sergeant to ask himself what must be the reflections of his comrades, if a soldier from some other corps should execute the attempt; when they should be told that the glory transferred to the regiment of which he was one, might have been enjoyed by the Legion, had not Sergeant Champe shrunk from the overture made to him by his general, rather than reject scruples too narrow and confined to be permitted to interfere with grand and virtuous deeds. The *esprit de corps* could not be resisted; united to his inclination it subdued his prejudices, and he declared his willingness to conform to the wishes of the general, relying, as he confidently did, that his reputation would be protected by those who had induced him to undertake the enterprise, should he be unfortunate.

The instructions were read to him, and each distinct object presented plainly to his view, of which he took notes so disguised as to be understood only by himself. He was particularly cautioned to use the utmost circumspection in delivering his letters, and to take care to withhold from the two individuals, addressed under feigned names, knowledge of each other; for although both had long been in the confidence of the general, yet it was not known by either that the other was so engaged.

He was further urged to bear in constant recollection the solemn injunction, so pointedly expressed in the instructions to Major Lee, of forbearing to kill Arnold in any condition of things.

This part of the business being finished, their deliberation was turned to the manner of Champe's desertion, for it was well known to them both that to pass the numerous patrols of horse and foot crossing from the stationary guards, was itself difficult, which was now rendered more so by parties thrown occasionally beyond the place called Liberty Pole, as well as by swarms of irregulars, induced sometimes to venture down to the very point at Paulus Hook, with the hope of picking up booty. Evidently discernible as were the difficulties in the way, no relief could be administered by Major Lee, lest it might induce a belief that he was privy to the desertion, which opinion getting to the enemy would involve the life of Champe. The sergeant was left to his own resources and to his own management, with the declared determination, that in case his departure should be discovered before morning, Lee would take care to delay pursuit as long as practicable.

Giving to the sergeant three guineas, and presenting his best wishes, he recommended him to start without delay, and enjoined him to communicate his arrival in New York as soon as he could. Champe pulling out his watch, compared it with the major's, reminding the latter of the importance of holding back pursuit, which he was convinced would take place in the course of the night, and which might be fatal, as he knew that he should be obliged to zig-zag in order to avoid the patrols, which would consume time. It was now nearly eleven. The sergeant returned to camp, and taking his cloak, valise, and orderly book, he drew his horse from the picket, and mounting him put himself upon fortune. Lee, charmed

with his expeditious consummation of the first part of the enter
prise, retired to rest. Useless attempt! the past scene could not be
obliterated; and, indeed, had that been practicable the interruption
which ensued would have stopped repose.

Within half an hour Captain Carnes, officer of the day, waited
upon the major, and with considerable emotion told him that one
of the patrol had fallen in with a dragoon, who, being challenged,
put spur to his horse and escaped, though instantly pursued. Lee,
complaining of the interruption, and pretending to be extremely
fatigued by his ride to and from head-quarters, answered as if he did
not understand what had been said, which compelled the captain to
repeat it. "Who can the fellow that was pursued be?" inquired the
major, adding, "a countryman, probably." "No," replied the cap
tain, "the patrol sufficiently distinguished him to know that he was
a dragoon; probably one from the army; if not, certainly one from
our own." This idea was ridiculed from its improbability, as during
the whole war but a single dragoon had deserted from the Legion.
This did not convince Carnes, so much stress was it now the fashion
to lay on the desertion of Arnold, and the probable effect of his example. The captain withdrew to examine the squadron of horse,
whom he had ordered to assemble, in pursuance of established usage
on similar occasions. Very quickly he returned, stating that the
scoundrel was known, and was no less a person than the sergeant-major, who had gone off with his horse, baggage, arms, and
orderly book—so presumed, as neither the one nor the other could
be found. Sensibly affected at the supposed baseness of a soldier
extremely respected, the captain added that he had ordered a party
to make ready for pursuit, and begged the major's written orders.

Occasionally this discourse was interrupted, and every idea suggested which the excellent character of the sergeant warranted, to
induce the suspicion that he had not deserted, but had taken the
liberty to leave camp with a view to personal pleasure; an example, said Lee, too often set by the officers themselves, destructive
as it was of discipline, opposed as it was to orders, and disastrous
as it might prove to the corps in the course of service.

Some little delay was thus interposed; but it being now announced that the pursuing party was ready, Major Lee directed a
change in the officer, saying that he had a particular service in
view, which he had determined to intrust to the lieutenant ready
for duty, and which probably must be performed in the morning.
He therefore directed him to summon Cornet Middleton for the

present command. Lee was induced thus to act, first to add to the delay, and next from his knowledge of the tenderness of Middleton's disposition, which he hoped would lead to the protection of Champe, should he be taken. Within ten minutes Middleton appeared to receive his orders, which were delivered to him made out in the customary form, and signed by the major. "Pursue so far as you can with safety Sergeant Champe, who is suspected of deserting to the enemy, and has taken the road leading to Paulus Hook. Bring him alive, that he may suffer in the presence of the army ; but kill him if he resists, or escapes after being taken."

Detaining the cornet a few minutes longer in advising him what course to pursue ; urging him to take care of the horse and accoutrements if recovered, and enjoining him to be on his guard, lest he might, by his eager pursuit, improvidently fall into the hands of the enemy, the major dismissed Middleton, wishing him success. A shower of rain fell soon after Champe's departure, which enabled the pursuing dragoons to take the trail of the horse, knowing as officer and trooper did, the make of their shoes, the impression of which was an unerring guide.*

When Middleton departed it was a few minutes past twelve; so that Champe had only the start of rather more than an hour, by no means as long as was desired. Lee became very unhappy ; not only because the estimable and gallant Champe might be injured, but lest the enterprise might be delayed ; and he spent a sleepless night. The pursuing party during the night, was, on their part, delayed by the necessary halts to examine occasionally the road, as the impression of the horse's shoes directed their course. This was, unfortunately, too evident, no other horse having passed along the road since the shower. When the day broke, Middleton was no longer forced to halt, and he pressed on with rapidity. Ascending an eminence before he reached the Three Pigeons, some miles on the north of the village of Bergen, as the pursuing party reached its summit, Champe was descried not more than half a mile in front. Resembling an Indian in his vigilance, the sergeant at the same moment discovered the party, whose object he was no stranger to, and giving spur to his horse he determined to outstrip his pursuers. Middleton at the same instant put his horses to the top of

* The horses being all shod by our own farriers, the shoes were made in the same form ; which, with a private mark annexed to the fore shoes, and known to the troopers, pointed out the trail of our dragoons to each other, which was often very useful.

their speed, and being as the Legion all were well acquainted with the country, he recollected a short route through the woods to the bridge below Bergen, which diverged from the great road just after you gain the Three Pigeons. Reaching the point of separation, he halted, and dividing his party, directed a sergeant with a few dragoons to take the near cut, and possess with all possible dispatch the bridge, while he with the residue followed Champe, not doubting but that Champe must deliver himself up, as he would be closed between himself and his sergeant. Champe did not forget the short cut, and would have taken it himself, but he knew it was the usual route of our parties when returning in the day from the neighborhood of the enemy, properly preferring the woods to the road. He consequently avoided it; and persuaded that Middleton would avail himself of it, wisely resolved to relinquish his intention of getting to Paulus Hook, and to seek refuge from two British galleys lying a few miles to the west of Bergen.

This was a station always occupied by one or two galleys, and which it was known now lay there. Entering the village of Bergen, Champe turned to his right, and disguising his change of course as much as he could by taking the beaten streets, turning as they turned, he passed through the village and took the road toward Elizabethtown Point. Middleton's sergeant gained the bridge, where he concealed himself, ready to pounce upon Champe when he came up; and Middleton, pursuing his course through Bergen, soon got also to the bridge, when, to his extreme mortification, he found that the sergeant had slipped through his fingers. Returning up the road, he inquired of the villagers of Bergen whether a dragoon had been seen that morning ahead of his party. He was answered in the affirmative, but could learn nothing satisfactory as to the route he took. While engaged in inquiries himself, he spread his party through the village to strike the trail of Champe's horse, a resort always recurred to. Some of his dragoons hit it just as the sergeant, leaving the village, got in the road to the Point. Pursuit was renewed with vigor, and again Champe was descried. He, apprehending the event, had prepared himself for it, by lashing his valise (containing his clothes and orderly book) on his shoulders, and holding his drawn sword in his hand, having thrown away the scabbard. This he did to save what was indispensable to him, and to prevent any interruption to his swimming, should Middleton, as he presumed, when disappointed at the bridge, take the measures adopted by him. The pursuit was rapid and close, as the stop occasioned by the sergeant's preparations for swimming had brought Middleton within two or three hundred yards. As soon as Champe got abreast of the two galleys he dismounted, and running through the marsh to the river, plunged into it, calling upon the galleys for help. This was readily given. They fired upon our horse, and sent a boat to meet Champe, who was taken in and carried on board, and conveyed to New York, with a letter from the captain of the galley, stating the circumstances he had seen.

The horse, with his equipments, the sergeant's cloak and scabbard, were recovered; the sword itself being held by Champe until he plunged into the river, was lost, as Middleton found it necessary to retire without searching for it.

About three o'clock in the evening our party returned, and the soldiers seeing the well-known horse in our possession, made the air resound with acclamations that the scoundrel was killed.

Major Lee, called by this heart-rending annunciation from his tent, saw the sergeant's horse led by one of Middleton's dragoons, and began to reproach himself with the blood of the high-prized, faithful, and intrepid Champe. Stifling his agony he advanced to meet Middleton, and became somewhat relieved as soon as he got near enough to discern the countenance of his officer and party. There was evidence in their looks of disappointment, and he was quickly relieved by Middleton's information that the sergeant had effected his escape, with the loss of his horse, and narrated the particulars just recited.

Lee's joy was now as full as, the moment before, his torture had been excruciating. Never was a happier conclusion; the sergeant escaped unhurt, carrying with him to the enemy undeniable testimony of the sincerity of his desertion, cancelling every apprehension before entertained, unless the enemy might suspect him of being what he really was.

Major Lee imparted to the commander-in-chief the occurrence, who was sensibly affected by the hair-breadth escape of Champe, and anticipated with pleasure the good effect sure to follow the enemy's knowledge of its manner.

On the fourth day after Champe's departure, Lee received a letter from him, written the day before, in a disguised hand, without any signature, and stating what had passed after he got on board the galley, where he was kindly received.

He was carried to the commandant of New York as soon as he

arrived, and presented the letter addressed to this officer from the captain of the galley. Being asked to what corps he belonged, and a few other common questions, he was sent, under care of an orderly sergeant to the adjutant-general, who, finding that he was sergeant-major of the Legion horse, heretofore remarkable for their fidelity, began to interrogate him. He was told by Champe that such was the spirit of defection which prevailed among the American troops, in consequence of Arnold's example, that he had no doubt if the temper was properly cherished, Washington's ranks would not only be greatly thinned, but that some of his best corps would leave him. To this conclusion the sergeant said he was led by his own observations, and especially by his knowledge of the discontents which agitated the corps to which he had belonged. His size, place of birth, form, countenance, hair, the corps in which he had served, with other remarks, in conformity to the British usage, was noted down. After this was finished, he was sent to the commander-in-chief, in charge of one of the staff, with a letter from the adjutant-general. Sir Henry Clinton treated him very kindly, and detained him more than one hour, asking him many questions, all leading—first, to know to what extent this spirit of defection might be pushed by proper incitements ; what the most operating incitements ; whether any general officers were suspected by Washington as concerned in Arnold's conspiracy, or any other officers of note ; who they were, and whether the troops approved or censured Washington's suspicions ; whether his popularity in the army was sinking, or continued stationary. What was Major André's situation ; whether any change had taken place in the manner of his confinement ; what was the current opinion of his probable fate, and whether it was thought that Washington would treat him as a spy. To these various interrogations, some of which were perplexing, Champe answered warily ; exciting, nevertheless, hopes that the adoption of proper measures to encourage desertion (of which he could not pretend to form an opinion) would certainly bring off hundreds of the American soldiers, including some of the best troops, horse as well as foot. Respecting the fate of André, he said he was ignorant, though there appeared to be a general wish in the army that his life should not be taken ; and that he believed it would depend more upon the disposition of Congress than on the will of Washington.

After this long conversation ended, Sir Henry presented Champe with a couple of guineas, and recommended him to wait upon General Arnold, who was engaged in raising an American Legion in the service of his majesty. He directed one of his aids to write to Arnold by Champe, stating who he was, and what he had said about the disposition in the army to follow his example; which, being soon done, the letter was given to the orderly attending on Champe to be presented with the deserter to General Arnold. Arnold expressed much satisfaction on hearing from Champe the manner of his escape, and the effect of Arnold's example; and concluded his numerous inquiries by assigning quarters to the sergeant,—the same as were occupied by his recruiting sergeants.

He also proposed to Champe to join his Legion, telling him he would give him the same station he had held in the rebel service, and promising further advancement when merited. Expressing his wish to retire from war, and his conviction of the certainty of his being hung if ever taken by the rebels, he begged to be excused from enlistment; assuring the general, that should he change his mind, he would certainly accept his offer. Retiring to his quarters, Champe now turned his attention to the delivery of his letters, which he could not effect until the next night, and then only to one of the two incogniti to whom he was recommended. This man received the sergeant with extreme attention, and, having read the letter, assured Champe that he might rely on his faithful co-operation in every thing in his power consistent with his safety, to guard which required the utmost prudence and circumspection. The sole object in which the aid of this individual was required, regarded the general and others of our army, implicated in the information sent to Washington by him. To this object Champe urged his attention; assuring him of the solicitude it had excited, and telling him that its speedy investigation had induced the general to send him to New York. Promising to enter upon it with zeal, and engaging to send out Champe's letters to Major Lee, he fixed the time and place for their next meeting, when they separated.

Lee made known to the general what had been transmitted to him by Champe, and received in answer directions to press Champe to the expeditious conclusion of his mission; as the fate of André would be soon decided, when little or no delay could be admitted in executing whatever sentence the court might decree. The same messenger who brought Champe's letter, returned with the ordered communication. Five days had nearly elapsed after reaching New York, before Champe saw the confidant to whom only the attempts against Arnold was to be intrusted. This person entered with

promptitude into the design, promising his cordial assistance. To
procure a proper associate for Champe was the first object, and
this he promised to do with all possible dispatch. Furnishing a
conveyance to Lee, we again heard from Champe, who stated what
I have related, with the additional intelligence that he had that
morning (the last of September) been appointed one of Arnold's
recruiting sergeants, having enlisted the day before with Arnold ;
and that he was induced to take this afflicting step, for the purpose
of securing uninterrupted ingress and egress to the house which the
general occupied ; it being indispensable to a speedy conclusion of
the difficult enterprise which the information he had just received
had so forcibly urged. He added, that the difficulties in his way were
numerous and stubborn, and that his prospect of success was by no
means cheering. With respect to the additional treason, he asserted
that he had every reason to believe that it was groundless; that
the report took its rise in the enemy's camp, and that he hoped
soon to clear up that matter satisfactorily. The pleasure which
the last part of this communication afforded, was damped by the
tidings it imparted respecting Arnold, as on his speedy delivery
depended André's relief. The interposition of Sir Henry Clinton,
who was extremely anxious to save his aid-de-camp, still continued ;
and it was expected the examination of witnesses and the defence of
the prisoner, would protract the decision of the court of inquiry,
now assembled, and give sufficient time for the consummation of
the project committed to Champe. A complete disappointment
took place from a quarter unforeseen and unexpected. The honorable and accomplished André, knowing his guilt, disdained defence,
and prevented the examination of witnesses by confessing the character in which he stood. On the next day (the 2d of October)
the court again assembled ; when every doubt that could possibly
arise in the case having been removed by the previous confes-
sion, André was declared to be a spy, and condemned to suffer
accordingly.

The sentence was executed on the subsequent day in the usual
form, the commander-in-chief deeming it improper to interpose any
delay. In this decision he was warranted by the very unpromis-
ing intelligence received from Champe,—by the still existing impli-
cation of other officers in Arnold's conspiracy,—by a due regard to
public opinion,—and by real tenderness to the condemned.

Neither Congress nor the nation could have been with propriety
informed of the cause of the delay, and without such information it

must have excited in both alarm and suspicion. André himself could not have been intrusted with the secret, and would consequently have attributed the unlooked-for event to the expostulation and exertion of Sir Henry Clinton, which would not fail to produce in his breast expectations of ultimate relief: to excite which would have been cruel, as the realization of such expectation depended upon a possible but improbable contingency. The fate of André, hastened by himself, deprived the enterprise committed to Champe of a feature which had been highly prized by its projector, and which had very much engaged the heart of the individual chosen to execute it.

Washington ordered Major Lee to communicate what had passed to the sergeant, with directions to encourage him to prosecute with unrelaxed vigor the remaining objects of his instructions, but to intermit haste on the execution only as far as was compatible with final success.

This was accordingly done by the first opportunity. Champe deplored the sad necessity which had occurred, and candidly confessed that the hope of enabling Washington to save the life of André (who had been the subject of universal commiseration in the American camp) greatly contributed to remove the serious difficulties which opposed his acceding to the proposition when first propounded. Some documents accompanied this communication, tending to prove the innocence of the accused general; they were completely satisfactory, and did credit to the discrimination, zeal, and diligence of the sergeant. Lee inclosed them immediately to the commander-in-chief, who was pleased to express the satisfaction he derived from the information, and to order the major to wait upon him the next day; when the whole subject was re-examined, and the distrust heretofore entertained of the accused was forever dismissed.* Nothing now remained to be done, but the seizure and safe delivery of Arnold. To this subject Champe gave

---

* Copy of a Letter from General Washington to Major Lee, in his own Handwriting.

October 13, 1780.

Dear Sir,—I am very glad your letter, of this date, has given strength to my conviction of the innocence of the gentleman who was the subject of your inquiry.

I want to see you on a particular piece of business. If the day is fair, and nothing of consequence intervenes, I will be at the marquis's quarters by ten o'clock to morrow. If this should not happen, I shall be glad to see you at head-quarters.

I am, dear sir, your obedient servant,   G. Washington.

his undivided attention; and, on the 19th October, Major Lee received from him a very particular account of the progress he had made, with the outlines of his plan. This was, without delay, submitted to Washington; with a request for a few additional guineas. The general's letter,* written on the same day (20th October), evinces his attention to the minutiæ of business, as well as his immutable determination to possess Arnold alive, or not at all. This was his original injunction, which he never omitted to enforce upon every proper occasion.

Major Lee had an opportunity in the course of the week of writing to Champe, when he told him that the rewards which he had promised to his associates would certainly be paid on the delivery of Arnold; and in the mean time small sums of money would be furnished for casual expenses, it being deemed improper that he should appear with much, lest it might lead to suspicion and detection. That five guineas were now sent, and that more would follow when absolutely necessary.

Ten days elapsed before Champe brought his measures to conclusion, when Lee received from him his final communication, appointing the third subsequent night for a party of dragoons to

---

* COPY OF A LETTER FROM GENERAL WASHINGTON TO MAJOR LEE, IN HIS OWN HANDWRITING.

HEAD-QUARTERS, *October* 20, 1780.

DEAR SIR,—The plan proposed for taking A——d (the outlines of which are communicated in your letter, which was this moment put into my hands without date) has every mark of a good one. I therefore agree to the promised rewards; and have such entire confidence in your management of the business, as to give it my fullest approbation; and leave the whole to the guidance of your own judgment, with this express stipulation and pointed injunction, that he (A——d) is brought to me alive.

No circumstance whatever shall obtain my consent to his being put to death. The idea which would accompany such an event, would be that ruffians had been hired to assassinate him. My aim is to make a public example of him; and this should be strongly impressed upon those who are employed to bring him off. The sergeant must be very circumspect; too much zeal may create suspicion, and too much precipitancy may defeat the project. The most inviolable secrecy must be observed on all hands. I send you five guineas; but I am not satisfied of the propriety of the sergeant's appearing with much specie. This circumstance may also lead to suspicion, as it is but too well known to the enemy that we do not abound in this article.

The interviews between the party in and out of the city, should be managed with much caution and seeming indifference; or else the frequency of their meeting, &c., may betray the design, and involve bad consequences; but I am persuaded you will place every matter in a proper point of view to the conductors of this interesting business, and therefore I shall only add, that

I am, dear sir, &c., &c.,
G. WASHINGTON.

meet him at Hoboken, when he hoped to deliver Arnold to the officer. Champe had, from his enlistment into the Americ n Legion (Arnold's corps) every opportunity he could wish, to attend to the habits of the general. He discovered that it was his custom to return home about twelve every night, and that previous to going to bed he always visited the garden. During this visit the conspirators were to seize him, and being prepared with a gag, intended to have applied the same instantly.

Adjoining the house in which Arnold resided, and that in which it was designed to seize and gag him, Champe had taken off several of the palings and replaced them, so that with care and without noise he could readily open his way to the adjoining alley. Into this alley he meant to have conveyed his prisoner, aided by his companion, one of two associates who had been introduced by the friend to whom Champe had been originally made known by letter from the commander-in-chief, and with whose aid and counsel he had so far conducted the enterprise. His other associate was with the boat prepared, at one of the wharves on the Hudson River, to receive the party.

Champe and his friend intended to have placed themselves each under Arnold's shoulder, and to have thus borne him through the most unfrequented alleys and streets to the boat; representing Arnold, in case of being questioned, as a drunken soldier, whom they were conveying to the guard-house.

When arrived at the boat the difficulties would be all surmounted, there being no danger nor obstacle in passing to the Jersey shore. These particulars, as soon as known to Lee, were communicated to the commander-in-chief, who was highly gratified with the much-desired intelligence. He directed Major Lee to meet Champe, and to take care that Arnold should not be hurt. The day arrived, and Lee with a party of dragoons left camp late in the evening, with three led horses; one for Arnold, one for the sergeant, and the third for his associate, never doubting the success of the enterprise, from the tenor of the last-received communication. The party reached Hoboken about midnight, were they were concealed in the adjoining wood, Lee with three dragoons stationing himself near the river shore. Hour after hour passed, no boat approached. At length the day broke and the major retired to his party, and with his led horses returned to camp, when he proceeded to head-quarters to inform the general of the disappointment, as mortifying as inexplicable. Washington having perused Champe's plan and communication, had indulged the presumption that at length the object of his keen and constant pursuit was sure of execution, and did not dissemble the joy such conviction produced. He was chagrined at the issue, and apprehended that his faithful sergeant must have been detected in the last scene of his tedious and difficult enterprise.

In a few days Lee received an anonymous letter from Champe's patron and friend, informing him that on the day previous to the night fixed for the execution of the plot, Arnold had removed his quarters to another part of the town, to superintend the embarkation of troops, preparing (as was rumored) for an expedition to be directed by himself; and that the American Legion, consisting chiefly of deserters, had been transferred from their barracks to one of the transports; it being apprehended that if left on shore until the expedition was ready, many of them might desert. Thus it happened that John Champe, instead of crossing the Hudson that night, was safely deposited on board one of the fleet of transports, from whence he never departed until the troops under Arnold landed in Virginia! Nor was he able to escape from the British army until after the junction of Lord Cornwallis at Petersburg, when he deserted; and proceeding high up into Virginia, he passed into North Carolina near the Saura towns, and keeping in the friendly districts of that State, safely joined the army soon after it had passed the Congaree in pursuit of Lord Rawdon.

His appearance excited extreme surprise among his former comrades, which was not a little increased when they saw the cordial reception he met with from Lieutenant-Colonel Lee. His whole story soon became known to the corps, which reproduced the love and respect of officer and soldier, heightened by universal admiration of his daring and arduous attempt.

Champe was introduced to General Greene, who cheerfully complied with the promises made by the commander-in-chief, as far as in his power; and having provided the sergeant with a good horse and money for his journey, sent him to General Washington, who munificently anticipated every desire of the sergeant, and presented him with a discharge from further service,* lest he might in the

---

* When General Washington was called by President Adams to the command of the army, prepared to defend the country from French hostility, he sent to Lieutenant-Colonel Lee to inquire for Champe; being determined to bring him into the field at the head of a company of infantry.

Lee sent to Loudon County, where Champe settled after his discharge from the army; and learned that the gallant soldier had removed to Kentucky, and had soon after died.

vicissitudes of war, fall into the enemy's hands; when if recognized he was sure to die on a gibbet.*

CHAPTER XXXI.

Cornwallis advances upon Virginia.—Death of Gen. Phillips at Petersburg.—La Fayette retreats behind the Chickahominy.—Is followed by Cornwallis.—Retreats across the Pamunkey.—Is joined by Col. Mercer.—Is overtaken by a detachment under Tarleton.—La Fayette continues his retreat.—Steuben and Tarleton at Charlottesville.—Escape of the Assembly and Governor.—La Fayette is joined by Wayne, and by Col. Campbell.—Cornwallis retires to Richmond, followed by La Fayette.—Movements of Cornwallis.—La Fayette and Tarleton.—Battle of Green Spring.—Conclusion of the summer campaign in Virginia.—Reflections thereon.—The British forces concentrated at York and Gloucester.

LORD CORNWALLIS, whom we left at Wilmington, in pursuance of his ultimate decision moved on the 25th of April; eighteen days after Greene had advanced upon Camden. Previous to his march, he communicated to Major-General Phillips his intention, and his route; designating Petersburg as the place of junction between himself and Phillips. Proceeding toward Halifax on the Roanoke, the British general preserved (by the rigidness with which he enforced his orders) the country from devastation and private property from spoliation, hoping, by the exercise of his natural moderation and humanity, to give effect to his unremitted exertions to bring all the loyalists of North Carolina into active co-operation with his army. But wisely and perseveringly as he endeavored to realize this favorite object, his success was very partial. The severe chastisement so often experienced by these men, the unceasing vigilance of government, and the force of Greene's operations in South Carolina, were irresistible in

---

* Washington is reported to have returned to the head-quarters of the army at Tappan on the 26th September, 1780, and it is stated in the preceding chapter that Champe left camp that night.

The fourth day after this departure, Lee received his first communication stating what occurred after he had reached the galley. On the last day of September, Lee heard from him again. After the execution of André, which took place on the 2d October, Lee was ordered to communicate the occurrence to Champe with directions to him to "prosecute with unrelaxed vigor the remaining objects of his instructions" and, on the 12th or 13th of October, Lee received from him the communication which proved the innocence of the accused general. On the 14th of October, Lee received the outline of the plan for the capture of Arnold, another object of Champe's enterprise. The sergeant sent into the British lines by Major Lee on the 21st October, also for the purpose of capturing Arnold and with the approval of Washington (see pp. 546-7, Appendix to Washington's writings, vol. vii.), could not, therefore, have been Champe, unless, as Mr. Sparks observes, "in the lapse of time the transactions in which they were both engaged had become confounded in the writer's memory."

their effect.   Happily for themselves, happily for their country, these
deluded people adhered to a state of quiescence.   In this condition
of things, the militia were ordered to the field, and some portions
of them actually embodied, well disposed (as militia always are) to
sustain the common cause; but (as militia thus organized always
are and ever will be) incapable of executing their wish, or the will
of government.   Lieutenant-Colonel Tarleton led, as usual, the advance of Cornwallis, supported by Lieutenant-Colonel Hamilton
(of the North Carolina regiment), well known in that Státe, and
universally esteemed and respected.   To the influence and efforts
of this officer may, in a great degree, be ascribed the moderation
exhibited by the advanced corps * on their march; alike repugnant
to the principles, the temper, and habits it had heretofore displayed.
During the tedious progress from Cape Fear to the Roanoke, the
enemy met no interruption.   Even his foraging parties were undisturbed; and the marauders accompanying his army passed and
repassed in security, unless detected and apprehended by British
guards and British patrols.   A general torpor † prevailed throughout the country through which the British general took his course;
ascribable, not to the languor of the inhabitants, but to the impo-
tency of government.   After reaching Halifax, the British army
halted.   Here the restrained licentiousness of the unprincipled
burst out, and shocking outrages were committed upon our unprotected fellow-citizens—disgraceful to British arms, and degrading
to the name of man.‡

* Colonel Hamilton had, before the war, resided in Norfolk; where his goodness, hospitality, and urbanity had attracted universal esteem.   His business
leading him into much acquaintance with the inhabitants of North Carolina,
he acquired there, as in Norfolk, the general regard.   Believing the Mother
Country right in the dispute which led to the war, Hamilton took part with
Great Britain, and became a soldier.   He raised a regiment of North Carolinians, and both in the field and in the cabinet performed essential services to
his general: serving in the South, first under Prevost, afterwards under Sir
Henry Clinton, and lastly under Lord Cornwallis, in whose confidence he stood
very high.   Not only the native goodness of his heart set Hamilton against those
destructive proceedings too often practised by the corps of Tarleton; but he was
particularly desirous to preserve the inhabitants of North Carolina safe from
insult and injury; in consequence as well of his own acquaintance with many
of them, as of his solicitude to bring the mass of the people into support of the
royal measures.

† At Swift Run, and at Fish Creek, parties of our militia skirmished with the
British van, but these attempts were slight and soon crushed.   They were the
only ones essayed between Wilmington and Halifax, where a more serious
effort ensued; but this too was quickly overpowered.

‡ These enormities being discovered by Lord Cornwallis, he halted the light
troops about four miles beyond the Roanoke.

General Phillips took possession of Petersburg on the 9th of May, extremely ill with a bilious fever, which had afflicted him for several days; and, in spite of all medical exertions, it put a period to his life on the 13th; by which event the command of the army devolved upon Brigadier Arnold.

Cornwallis, leaving Halifax, passed the Roanoke, whence he detached Lieutenant-Colonel Tarleton with his Legion to the Meherrin, to hold the fords across the river: Lieutenant-Colonel Simcoe, with his rangers, being at the same time sent forward by General Arnold to the Nottoway, for the like purpose. No interruption was attempted against either detachment: all the force assembled for the protection of the State being with La Fayette in his position near Richmond. Following the advanced corps, Cornwallis passed the Meherrin, then the Nottoway, and on the 20th entered Petersburg.

One month of the best season of the year for military operations had been nearly expended in the march from Wilmington by one army; while the other, during the like period, occupied itself in the trivial expeditions heretofore described—as inoperative to effect the great object in view, as they were disgraceful to the British government, and oppressive to private individuals.

The union of the two armies gave to the British general a force so far superior to his enemy, as to threaten the destruction of Virginia. Cornwallis did not excel in numbers only; his troops were excellent, with the exception of Arnold's corps. Exclusive of the garrison of Portsmouth, two battalions of light infantry, the Queen's Rangers (horse and foot) under Lieutenant-Colonel Simcoe, the seventy-sixth and eightieth British regiments, with that of Hesse, two companies of yagers, and Arnold's American Legion, with a well-appointed detachment of artillery, composed the force lately under Phillips, and were now united to the tried troops of the South. In addition, a re-enforcement was in James River from New York under General Leslie, consisting of the seventeenth and forty-third regiments, British, and two battalions of Anspach. The seventeenth regiment and the Anspach battalions were ordered to

" On the arrival of some country people, Earl Cornwallis directed Lieutenant-Colonel Tarleton to dismount his dragoons and mounted infantry, and to form them into a rank entire for the convenient inspection of the inhabitants, to facilitate the discovery of the villains who had committed atrocious outrages the preceding evening. A sergeant and one private dragoon were pointed out, and accused of rape and robbery; they were conducted to Halifax, where they were condemned to death by martial law. The immediate infliction of the sentence, exhibited to the army and manifested to the country the discipline and justice of the British general."—(See *Tarleton's Campaigns.*)

Portsmouth, the command of which post was confided to General Leslie, while the forty-third was destined to join Cornwallis. About this time the British general received a dispatch from Lord Rawdon, communicating his victory at Hobkirk's Hill; and as if nothing should be wanting to stimulate the exertions of his lordship, he was also officially advised of the sailing of a fleet from Cork in Ireland, with three regiments, destined for South Carolina.

The success of Rawdon, and the re-enforcement from Ireland, calmed the disquietude heretofore excited in the breast of Cornwallis by General Greene's return to South Carolina; and reproduced the fallacious hope, that while he prostrated Virginia, Rawdon would maintain undiminished his late conquests.

La Fayette still held his position near Richmond, occasionally strengthened by detachments of militia brought into the field by the unceasing efforts of Governor Jefferson.

Baron Steuben, with six hundred levies, was on the south of James River, proceeding to South Carolina to re-enforce Greene; and Brigadier Wayne, with the Pennsylvania line (now reduced to eight or nine hundred), was on his march from the Northern army to unite with La Fayette.

The baron was recalled, and directed to take post at the Point of Fork, the depot of most of our remaining military stores; and General Nelson, with two thousand militia in the field, continued with La Fayette; while General Weedon, of the Continental line (now at home, in consequence of the diminution of our force), was requested to collect a corps of the militia in the vicinity of Fredericksburg for the purpose of covering the most important and well-conducted manufactory of arms in the State established at Falmouth, a small village on the north of the Rappahannock, one mile above Fredericksburg, and under the direction of Mr. John Strode—a gentleman singularly adapted, by his genius and habits, for its superintendence.

La Fayette's force, in his camp below Richmond, did not exceed four thousand, of which three fourths were militia. But in conformity to the system adopted by Governor Jefferson, Continental officers were substituted in the higher commands, for those of the militia: which, although not very well relished by those who retired, was highly grateful to the soldiers, who, perceiving the perils before them, rejoiced in being led by tried and experienced men. Such will always be the effect of acknowledged danger on the mind of man.

La Fayette selected seven hundred and fifty of his best militia marksmen, and dividing them into three corps of light infantry, of two hundred and fifty each, he placed them respectively under the orders of Majors Call, Willis, and Dick, regular officers.   This arrangement was judicious, and during the campaign its beneficial effect was often felt.

Could the American general have united to this body of infantry an adequate corps of cavalry, he would have very much increased its utility; but of this species of force he was unfortunately almost destitute, although the two States of Maryland and Virginia furnish horses of the best quality.   Only the remnant of Armand's corps (not more than sixty), and a troop of volunteer dragoons, under Captain Carter Page, late of Baylor's regiment, were with him.

Sir Henry Clinton states the force in Virginia, previous to the arrival of Lord Cornwallis, to be five thousand three hundred and four.   Since his lordship's assumption of the command, General Leslie (as has been mentioned) joined with three regiments from New York, of which the forty-third was added to the army.   The field force under Cornwallis cannot be estimated under eight thousand—more than double of that acting with his adversary.   What added vastly to this superiority was the enemy's strength in horse. His dragoons were rated at four hundred, to which were united seven or eight hundred mounted infantry.   During four days' halt in Petersburg, which period of rest was necessary to the army from Wilmington, the British general communicated his situation, strength, and views to his commander-in-chief and gave all requisite directions to the corps of Leslie occupying Portsmouth—that of Craig, in possession of Wilmington—and to Lord Rawdon, commanding the army of defence in the two Southern States.   On the 24th of May, his lordship moved, taking the route on the south of the Appomattox, with a determination of passing the James River at Westover, the seat of the late Colonel Byrd; where he not only could avail himself of maritime aid in the transportation of his army across the river, but might with facility draw to him the forty-third regiment, not yet disembarked.   Here General Arnold, having obtained permission to return to New York, left the army.   This step has been ascribed to two motives, each of which probably had its influence: the first was a prospect of a very active campaign, in the vicissitudes whereof he might fall into our hands; and the last, his own unpleasant situation among the British officers,—always irksome to him from their objections to his company and control, and

now considerably increased by the reluctance of the officers who
had served with so much glory and effect in the Carolinas, to
receive orders from a traitor.

Nearly three days were occupied in the passage of James River;
although unobstructed by any attempt on our side, and although
facilitated by every exertion on the part of the British navy, and
though all the horses belonging to the army swam the river, more
than two miles wide.

As soon as the rear division had passed, the main body proceeded
to White Oak Swamp, to which place the light troops under Tarleton and Simcoe had moved the day previous. La Fayette, well informed of the enemy's motions, and prepared for retreat, broke up
from his position below Richmond, and fell back behind the Chickahominy River, in the direction toward Fredericksburg, for the
double purpose of approximating Brigadier Wayne on his march
from the north, and of covering the manufactory of arms in the
vicinity of Falmouth.

The British general followed with zeal and rapidity, and crossed
the Chickahominy at Bottom Bridge, manifesting his determination
to force La Fayette into battle before his junction with Wayne;
which certainly ought to have been his primary object, and might
have been effected by his decided superiority in cavalry, augmented
by mounted infantry.

La Fayette felt his extreme inferiority, and used every means in
his power to draw to his aid additional re-enforcements in horse and
foot. To the governor, to Steuben, to Nelson, and to Weedon, he
applied with zeal bordering on importunity; and his applications
received, as they merited, due respect. But the preparations had
been improvidently delayed, and the loss of our military stores at
Westham, during Arnold's invasion, deprived us of the necessary
arms and equipments; which, with the removal of families and of
property, practised now in every direction, very much limited the
effect of the various exertions made to comply with his requests.

During the invasion of Leslie, which succeeded that under Matthews, Governor Jefferson (in pursuance of the full powers with
which he had been invested by the General Assembly) had brought
into the field some legionary corps, under the most approved Continental officers of the Virginia line.

Brigadier Lawson, who commanded one of the two brigades of
Virginia militia which behaved so handsomely at the battle of Guilford Court-House, was at the head of the strongest of these corps,

having under him the Lieutenant-Colonels Monroe,[*] Banister, and Mercer.[†] As soon as Leslie abandoned Virginia to join Cornwallis, in South Carolina, Lawson's corps had been disbanded; by which means the horse commanded by Banister was lost to the State, when our situation now so pressingly required cavalry.

On receiving La Fayette's request, Brigadier Weedon applied to Lieutenant-Colonel Mercer, who had served from the first year of the war in the third regiment of Virginia, until the battle of Monmouth. He was then one of the aids of Major-General Lee; and believing his general's suspension from his command both unjust and unwise, he retired from the profession of arms, for which he was well qualified, and in which he had acquired, by severe and active service, considerable proficiency with personal distinction. This gentleman instantly complied with Weedon's application; and in a few days raised a troop of dragoons, composed of the youth of the best families in his neighborhood, mounted and equipped at their own expense. With this troop Mercer hastened to the retiring army,—a small but acceptable aid.

La Fayette, adhering to the example and instructions of Greene, continued to retreat; and before Cornwallis reached the Chickahominy, had passed the Pamunkey, the southern branch of York River.

In this position he was overtaken by a detachment of the light troops under Lieutenant-Colonel Tarleton, whose sudden approach compelled him to form his army for battle. Had this movement of Tarleton been intended as a serious operation, it would have been adequately supported, and must have terminated in the destruction or dispersion of the American force; an event full of ill, not only to the suffering State but to the Union.

Wayne and Steuben never could have formed a junction but by crossing the Blue Ridge, and uniting on its western side. Cornwallis seems to have been sure of his meditated victim, if we may judge of his expectation from a paragraph of a letter of his, published in Doctor Ramsay's history of the revolution in South Carolina, wherein he says, " the boy cannot escape me." Like all soldiers over confident, he contrived to foil himself. The realization of this hope was not, indeed, difficult; as La Fayette had not preserved, on his retreat, the distance from his enemy required by his great inferiority.

---

[*] James Monroe, now Secretary of State.
[†] John Mercer, late Governor of Maryland.

He was often not more than twenty miles from the British general, who had at his disposal at least one thousand horse and mounted infantry. Putting one soldier behind each of those mounted, he could by an easy exertion, in any twenty-four hours, have placed two thousand veterans, conducted by skilful and experienced officers, close to his enemy; whose attempt to retreat would have been so embarrassed and delayed as to have given time for the main body to approach. Then La Fayette's destruction would have been as easy as inevitable. Why this plain mode of operation was overlooked and neglected by Cornwallis, did then and does still excite the surprise of all intelligent soldiers conversant with the transaction. Lieutenant-Colonel Mercer, with his small corps of horse, joined La Fayette in this critical situation, and was very instrumental in discovering that the corps under Tarleton was only a large patrol. The communication of this intelligence repressed those afflicting reflections which this apparent danger could not fail to create in an officer less penetrating and less anxious than the gallant La Fayette.

Tarleton did not continue long in his front, during which time one of his exploring parties was so fortunate as to intercept a courier conveying letters from the American general to Greene, Steuben, and Governor Jefferson. In the letter to Jefferson, the marquis, as Lieutenant-Colonel Tarleton informs us, " prophetically declared that the British success in Virginia resembled the French invasion and possession of Hanover * in the preceding war, and was likely to have similar consequences, if the government and country would exert themselves at the present juncture."

---

* It is well known that the Marshal D'Estrées was opposed, in 1757, to the Duke of Cumberland in Germany; and that passing the river Weser, he followed the duke step by step; overtook him at Hastenbek, fought him and beat him.

Marshal Richelieu now succeeded D'Estrées, and pressing the late victory, drove the duke upon the mouth of the Elbe, when he surrendered his army by convention; by which means the Electorate of Hanover fell into the possession of the French.

The great Frederick, already in the greatest distress, was in consequence of the surrender of the Duke of Cumberland, more oppressed, as it enabled the Prince of Soubise, at the head of one of the armies closing upon Frederick to draw a considerable re-enforcement from Marshal Richelieu. Nevertheless, the King of Prussia fell upon Soubise at Rosbach, and gained a signal victory. The Hanoverians, encouraged by this event, exerted themselves greatly; and, as the French monarch had not ratified the convention of Closterseven, the army of the duke was considered as relieved from its conditions, and joined the Hanoverians. Richelieu was speedily forced out of Hanover with considerable loss; and the electorate restored to the King of England.

As soon as the British patrol drew off, La Fayette broke up, and abandoning the protection of Fredericksburg, and the manufactory of arms in its neighborhood, hastened by forced marches through the western part of Spottsylvania County, across the head waters of the Mattapony, the northern branch of York River, to gain the road on which Wayne was advancing. This unavoidable departure from his original system was executed with indefatigable diligence; nor did he ever again, during his retreat, risk himself within twenty miles of his antagonist; so thoroughly had Tarleton's late approach convinced him of the peril to which he would be exposed.

Cornwallis persevered in pursuit; but finding that the distance between his adversary and himself daily increased, he halted and turned his mind to inferior objects.   He had in the former campaign experienced the inefficacy of pursuing Greene; and forgetting his then and present condition, as well as that of Greene and of La Fayette, he determined to struggle no longer to stop the junction of the latter with Wayne, but to employ his force in cowering the mind of the State, and in destroying all its remaining resources for the maintenance of armed resistance.

To this decision he seems to have been led by his conviction that Wayne, united to La Fayette, diminished so little his own relative superiority as to forbid his inattention to other objects deemed by himself important, while it would increase the chance of striking his meditated blow against both. Two considerations entitled to weight, supported this decision. The first grew out of the character of Wayne, which, after junction with La Fayette could not but mix itself in the subsequent operations, he being second in command; and the last arose from the increase of difficulty in movement, as well as in the procurement of necessary food for man and horse. He therefore turned his attention to the execution of such plans, as would manifest to the inhabitants their defenceless condition, and inflame their passions against those intrusted with their safety, who had thus abandoned them to the enemy.

Although the course adopted by the British general varied materially from that which a just estimate of the conjuncture and of his own force seemed to dictate, yet it was supported by cogent reasons.

Cornwallis might have pursued his flying enemy with increased vigor, as has been before explained; and this he ought to have done, especially after being informed by Tarleton of the effect of his approach. Pressing La Fayette by forced marches, his two thousand mounted veterans must have overtaken him before Wayne joined; and in the attempt to overtake, by understanding the situation of Wayne, it is possible he might have so operated on La Fayette's anxiety to avoid battle (by adhering to the intermediate route between Fayette and Wayne), as to have induced the former to fall off to his left, placing himself behind the little mountains of Orange County, and yielding up as well his junction with Wayne, as Wayne and his detachment. This heavy sacrifice would have been justified by the consequent salvation of the army of La Fayette. But should La Fayette's judgment and intelligence have enabled him to avoid the keen pursuit, and to have made good his junction with Wayne, his united force was still so inadequate, that he must persevere in retreat, when that operation would not only be rendered more difficult than before from his augmentation in force, but also from the peculiar character of Wayne and the brave corps under his command.

General Wayne had a constitutional attachment to the decision of the sword, and this cast of character had acquired strength from indulgence, as well as from the native temper of the troops he commanded. They were known by the designation of the line of Pennsylvania; whereas they might have been with more propriety called the line of Ireland.

Bold and daring they were impatient and refractory; and would always prefer an appeal to the bayonet, to a toilsome march.

Restless under the want of food and whiskey; adverse to absence from their baggage; and attached to the pleasures of the table; Wayne and his brigade were more encumbered with wagons than any equal portion of the army.

The general and his soldiers were singularly fitted for close and stubborn action, hand to hand, in the centre of the army; but very little adapted to the prompt and toilsome service to which La Fayette was and must be exposed, so long as the British general continued to press him.

Cornwallis therefore did not miscalculate when he presumed that the junction of Wayne would increase, rather than diminish, his chance of bringing his antagonist to action.

Had the British general pressed forward, determining never to stop until he forced his enemy to the last appeal, La Fayette or Wayne must have fallen if severed from each other; and if united both might have been destroyed. The Rappahannock lay in their rear; this river must be passed, and was in various points fordable, unless swelled by fall of rain. If the American army made good its retreat over the Rappahannock, it never could reach the Potomac without a blow; and that blow, from the enemy's vast superiority of horse, must have been fatal.

The destruction of La Fayette being accomplished, the British general had only to take post on the heights above Stafford Court-House, with his left resting on the village of Falmouth, to secure all the plentiful country in his rear between the two rivers, as well as that on the southern margin of the Rappahannock ; and to establish a convenient communication with such portion of his fleet as he might require to be sent up the Potomac.

This course of operations was however happily omitted, and another was adopted, very unlike the adventurous and decisive policy which had heretofore uniformly distinguished Lord Cornwallis.

It appears as if Sir Henry Clinton had contemplated ordering the Virginia army to the head of the Chesapeake, to which, it seems, he was encouraged by a confidence that in Maryland, in Pennsylvania, and in a portion of Virginia on the upper Potomac, he should find a large body of determined friends.

The evidence which supported this impression remains unascertained. As far as American information can be relied upon, we may venture to conclude that the British commander-in-chief was very much misinformed. Some trifling districts in parts of Maryland, and a small portion of the county of Hampshire in Virginia, were believed to be well affected to Great Britain ; but if all the disaffected in both States had been united in any one spot, they would have presented but an inconsiderable allurement to the formation of a plan like that supposed to be entertained by Sir Henry Clinton.

Whatever might have been the British general's intelligence and views, it is very evident, from his letters to Lord Cornwallis, that he inclined very much to hold his lordship near to Hampton Roads, for the protection of such of the British navy as should be employed within the capes of Virginia, and with the design of pushing solid operations at the head of the Chesapeake, as soon as every apprehension of interruption from the French navy should cease.

Considerations, drawn from due respect to the plan of his chief, no doubt contributed to turn Lord Cornwallis from the splendid prospect before him.

The British general having decided on his course, made two considerable detachments from his army while encamped in the county of Hanover, for the purpose of destroying our magazines at the Point of Fork,* under the protection of Baron Steuben with the raw levies under him, and of seizing the governor and the members of the General Assembly of the Commonwealth convened at Charlotteville, a small town on the western side of the Rivannah, the northern branch of James River.

Lieutetant-Colonel Simcoe commanded one of these detachments, composed of the Queen's Rangers (horse and foot) and the yagers, amounting to five hundred men; while the other, consisting of the Legion and one company of the twenty-third regiment, was placed under the orders of Lieutenant-Colonel Tarleton.

Simcoe was directed to fall upon the baron if practicable; at all events to force him across the Fluvannah, the southern branch of James River, and to destroy our magazines; while Tarleton was charged with interception of the governor and General Assembly, and with the destruction of all military stores and other resources necessary for the maintenance of the war on his route.

These enterprising officers took their parts with their accustomed vigor.

Recrossing the two branches of the Pamunkey, Simcoe proceeded on the direct route to the Point of Fork, and Tarleton moved on the road to Louisa Court-House.

Cornwallis, with the main body, followed on the route of Simcoe.

The latter officer conducted his march with the utmost secrecy; and, by detaining as prisoners all whom he overtook, he concealed his advance from the baron. Although unapprised of the intended attack upon his own post, Steuben became acquainted with the movement of Tarleton. In consequence of this information he engaged with diligence in removing our stores of every sort to the southern banks of Fluvannah: which being done, he passed the river with his corps, securing all the boats on its south side. Simcoe reached the Point of Fork about the conclusion of the baron's passage over the river, and captured a few of our troops waiting for the return of some of the boats. Chagrined at this disappointment, the British commander determined to recover by stratagem what he

---

* The Point of Fork is the tongue of land made by the Rivannah and Fluvannah rivers at their confluence, when the united streams take the name of James River. James River above the Rivannah no longer retains its old name of Fluvannah, and which belonged to it at the period of the expedition here spoken of.—See *Gerardin's History*, or *Howe's Virginia*, Fluvanna County.—ED.

had lost by his enemy's foresight. He encamped on the heights opposite to our camp, and by the number of his fires suggested to the baron the probability that the whole British army was only divided from him by the river. Thus impressed, and knowing that the corps of Tarleton was on his left, Steuben believed himself to be in imminent danger, and decided on saving his corps by the sacrifice of his stores. During the night the baron drew off, and, marching diligently, placed himself thirty miles from his foe. As soon as Simcoe perceived the next morning that the baron had decamped, he detached Captain Stevenson with a section of light infantry and Cornet Wolsey with four dragoons across the river in canoes; the first to destroy our stores, and the second, by mounting his dragoons on such horses as he could procure, to patrol some miles on the route of the baron to preserve the appearance of continuation of pursuit. Wolsey's advance had the desired effect. One of the baron's exploring parties fell in with him, and presuming that he was the precursor to the light corps, retired precipitately to the baron with information of the occurrence. Our corps was immediately put in motion, and retired still farther from the river. Nor would the baron have halted until he reached General Greene, but for orders from Greene directing him to return to La Fayette. Most of the arms found were muskets out of repair: they were however destroyed, as were the other military stores, except some brass cannon and mortars, which were mounted on carriages and conveyed to the British head-quarters.*

Lieutenant-Colonel Tarleton leaving the neighborhood of Louisa Court-House about two in the morning, having rested his corps only three hours, pursued his march with vigor.

Unluckily for Greene's distressed army, Tarleton overtook twelve wagons laden with clothing, under a weak guard, proceeding south. These were instantly taken and burned. The British lieutenant-colonel, knowing that his success depended on his activity, continued his march with diligence; but hearing that some of our influential citizens,—refugees from the lower country,—resided at Dr. Walker's and at Mr. John Walker's, whose houses were near his route, he injudiciously determined to spare the time necessary for the capture of all who might be found at the two houses. Detaching Captain Kinloch with one troop for the purpose of securing those at Mr.

* This account of Simcoe's expedition, Mr. Jefferson evidently misapprehended ; as it agrees with his own. See his letter of the 15th and 30th May, ante.—ED.

John Walker's, he went himself to the doctor's, where he made prisoner Mr. John Simms, of Hanover, brother to Patrick Henry (a member of the senate, and first governor of the State), with other gentlemen.

Captain Kinloch was equally successful.* He surprised and took three of our citizens,—Francis Kinloch, a member of Congress, from South Carolina, and William and Robert Nelson, brothers to General Nelson, all influential citizens; and who, suspecting the approach of parties of the enemy, had taken measures for their safety, which, by the address and rapid advance of the British captain, were rendered unavailing. This waste of time saved the members of the Assembly. Before the British cavalry reached Walker's, Mr. Jouitte a private gentleman, luckily descried them; and hastened by a disused road to Charlotteville to alarm the General Assembly, believing their capture to be the enemy's object.

Tarleton spent some time in resting his horses, and in paroling such of his prisoners as he chose to indulge with their paroles. Then resuming his march, he advanced with ardor upon Charlotteville; not doubting, as he had marched seventy miles in twenty-four hours, that his success would be complete.

Nor could he have been disappointed, had he not halted at Walker's: for, active and anxious as was Mr. Jouitte to outstrip the enemy, he would probably have failed but for Tarleton's diversion to a secondary object; or, even if he had been so fortunate as to precede the British colonel, the few minutes' notice would have been insufficient to secure a general escape.

As soon as Tarleton's van reached the Rivannah, it pressed forward in full charge through the river, followed by the main body. A small guard posted on the western bank was overpowered, and the enemy with concurring celerity fell upon the town. Jouitte had previously arrived, and the Assembly adjourning immediately, its members hastened away. A few of these gentlemen were nevertheless taken, as were several officers and soldiers. All our stores at this place, consisting of four hundred pounds of powder, one thousand stand of arms (manufactured in the armory near Falmouth), a quantity of tobacco, and some clothing provided for the Southern army, were destroyed. The British troops taken at

---

* This officer was a near relation to Francis Kinloch, member of Congress. When he left England for America he told their common relations, that he should certainly capture his cousin; which prediction was now verified, improbable as it was.

Saratoga were cantoned in the neighborhood of this village, and many of the soldiers were permitted to labor for their own emolument in the vicinity of the barracks. Of these twenty joined the British lieutenant-colonel in the few hours he continued in Charlotteville.

The attempt to take the governor, who was at his house in sight of the town, failed. Apprised of the approach of the dragoons, he very readily saved himself by taking shelter in an adjacent spur of the mountains.

Lieutenant-Colonel Tarleton leaving Charlotteville in the afternoon, proceeded down the Rivannah toward the Point of Fork, in the neighborhood whereof Lord Cornwallis had arrived with the main body.

La Fayette did not intermit retreat until he passed the Rapidan, the southern branch of the Rappahannock. In a few days afterward the corps under Wayne, between eight and nine hundred strong, joined him.

Soon after Tarleton's return to Lord Cornwallis, his corps was re-enforced by the seventy-sixth regiment, commanded by Major Needham, and the lieutenant-colonel received orders to mount the seventy-sixth, and to prepare for another expedition.* By refer-

---

* COPY OF A LETTER FROM EARL CORNWALLIS TO LIEUT.-COLONEL TARLETON.

JEFFERSON'S PLANTATION, *June 9th*, 1781.

DEAR TARLETON—You will proceed with the detachment of cavalry and mounted infantry under your command, before daybreak to-morrow morning, to Albemarle Old Court-House, where you will destroy any stores you may find. If you then hear of no other stores of any consequence on this side the Fluvannah, and the Baron Steuben should still be on the other side, you will cross that river, and make it your principal object to strike a blow at Baron Steuben; as the corps under his command consists of part of the new levies, and is the foundation on which the body of the eighteen-months' men, lately voted by the province of Virginia, will be formed. It will be of the utmost importance to defeat and destroy it; I shall, therefore, wish you to take every means in your power of effecting this service, if you should see a probability of success. I likewise recommend it to you to destroy all the enemy's stores and tobacco between James River and the Dan; and if there should be a quantity of provisions or corn collected at a private house, I would have you destroy it, even although there should be no proof of its being intended for the public service, leaving enough for the support of the family; as there is the greatest reason to apprehend that such provisions will be ultimately appropriated by the enemy to the use of General Greene's army, which, from the present state of the Carolinas, must depend on this province for its supplies.

I shall proceed by easy marches to Richmond, and it will probably be a business of eight or nine days from this time before I can get up my boats to that place to receive you; so that you may very well employ that time on your expedition. As it is very probable that some of the light troops of General Greene's army may be on their march to this country, you will do all you can to pro-

ence to Lord Cornwallis's instructions published in "Tarleton's Campaigns," the destruction of our stores at Albemarle Old Court-House,
the pursuit and dispersion of the corps of Steuben, and the interception of some light troops believed to be on their march from the
army of Greene to re-enforce La Fayette, constituted the objects of
the intended interprise. Lieutenant-Colonel Tarleton was directed,
after completing his expedition, to take the route on the south side
of James River to the town of Manchester, where boats would be
provided to transport himself and corps across the river to Richmond,
to which place the British general intended to proceed.

La Fayette, having effected his junction with Wayne, lost no
time in recrossing the Rapidan, and advancing toward the enemy—of whose proceedings he was regularly advised, and whose
present position was ascertained. Penetrating into the most prominent of his lordship's designs, the American general took the
resolution of interrupting their execution. With this view he moved
toward Albemarle Old Court-House, holding himself convenient
to the upper country. Cornwallis, apprised as well of the junction
of Wayne as of the direction of La Fayette's course of march, did
not doubt but that the preservation of the stores at Albemarle Old
Court-House, and the safety of the corps of Steuben, alike engaged
his adversary's intention. Willing that he should proceed on
his experiment, the British general held back Lieutenant-Colonel,
Tarleton, who was now ready for the intended expedition, and
continued in his position at Jefferson's plantation, convenient to his
adversary's presumed route, with a detachment to fall upon him in
his progress. La Fayette's discernment and activity baffled completely these views. Turning into a difficult and unfrequented road,
which not only shortened his distance to the point in view, but
threw him farther from the enemy, he crossed the Rivannah before
the British general was acquainted with his having reached it ; and
taking post behind Mechunk Creek, sat down on the direct route
from the British camp to Albemarle Old Court-House. Here he
was re-enforced by Colonel Campbell, one of the heroes of King's

cure intelligence of their route. I need not tell you of what importance it will
be to intercept them, or any prisoners of ours from South Carolina.

I would have all persons of consequence, either civil or military, brought to
me before they are paroled. Most sincerely wishing you success, and placing
the greatest confidence in your zeal and abilities, I am, with great truth and
regard,

Dear Tarleton,

Most faithfully yours,

CORNWALLIS.

Mountain, with his brave rifle militia. The expedition, for the execution of which Tarleton was prepared, was relinquished ; and the British general, drawing in his van troops, fell back on the ensuing day toward Richmond.

Notwithstanding the junction of Wayne, and the re-enforcement under Campbell, the British general continued to possess a decided superiority of force, not only in quality but in number. Steuben was still at a distance from La Fayette, and the destruction of the last would not fail in being followed by that of the first.

What reasons operated on Lord Cornwallis to induce him now to retire, when so many considerations urged his advance, remain un-ascertained. Certainly he must have acted in obedience to orders which have never yet been fully promulgated.

He was the same general who attacked Gates at the head of a very superior army, and who afterward fought Greene, though nearly double his number. In both instances he risked his own destruction, and, although victorious in the issue, was upon both occasions on the threshold of ruin.

Now, when victory was certain, when serious injury to himself was impracticable, and when his vast power in horse assured to him the complete improvement of success, he resigns his spirit of enterprise, and permits his inferior foe to enjoy undisturbed repose.

This change in conduct must be ascribed to the interference of his superior ; and Cornwallis's letter of the 26th of May,* to the British commander-in-chief satisfactorily evinces that his present operations were intended to be extremely limited, being subordinate

* Copy of a Letter from Earl Cornwallis to Sir Henry Clinton.

Byrd's Plantation, James River, 26th May, 1781.

The arrival of the re enforcement has made me easy about Portsmouth for the present. I have sent General Leslie thither with the seventeenth regiment and the two battalions of Anspach, keeping the forty-third with the army. I shall now proceed to dislodge La Fayette from Richmond ; and, with my light troops, to destroy any magazines or stores in the neighborhood, which may have been collected either for his use or General Greene's army. From thence I propose to move to the neck of Williamsburg, which is represented as healthy, and where some subsistence may be procured ; and keep myself unengaged from operations which might interfere with your plan for the campaign, until I have the satisfaction of hearing from you. I hope I shall then have an opportunity to receive better information than has hitherto been in my power to procure, relative to a proper harbor and place of arms. At present I am inclined to think well of York. The objections to Portsmouth are, that it cannot be made strong, without an army to defend it ; that it is remarkably unhealthy, and can give no protection to a ship of the line. Wayne has not yet joined La Fayette ; nor can I positively learn where he is, nor what is his force. Greene's cavalry are said to be coming this way ; but I have no certain accounts of it.

to some grand design conceived by Sir Henry Clinton to be executed within the year.* The retreat of the British general was soon known in the American camp, and La Fayette put his army in motion. Pleasing as was this unexpected turn in the enemy's course, the American general followed him with great circumspection, holding his main body between twenty and thirty miles in the rear of the foe, and feeling his way in front and flank with his cavalry and riflemen. Lieutenant-Colonel Tarleton, with the Legion, strengthened by the seventy-sixth regiment, was charged with the rear and one flank of the retiring army, while its other flank was committed to Simcoe at the head of the Queen's Rangers.

Cornwallis, secure from insult or surprise, had the force and views of La Fayette encouraged such attempts, proceeded by slow and convenient marches, without making a single effort to strike his enemy. On the 15th of June the British general reached Westham, and on the subsequent day entered Richmond, where he halted.

La Fayette, preserving his usual distance, continued to follow in the British rear; and, during the enemy's halt in Richmond, took a strong position on Allen's Creek, in the county of Goochland, twenty-two miles from Cornwallis, detaching his light troops close to the enemy's advanced posts—the one at Westham, commanded by Simcoe, and the other at the Meadow Bridge, under the orders of Lieutenant-Colonel Tarleton. On the 18th, Tarleton believing, from the intelligence he had acquired, the position of the corps under Brigadier Muhlenbergh—posted some little distance in front and to the left of the main body—vulnerable, made a sudden movement from the Meadow Bridge to beat up his quarters. But, although his advance was secret, the brigadier gained timely information of his approach; and, falling back upon La Fayette, met a detachment under General Wayne sent to his support. As soon as Tarleton discovered the movement of Muhlenbergh, he returned to his post. While engaged in this operation, Lieutenant-Colonel Mercer with his troop of horse passed in the enemy's rear, and reconnoitred, by order of his general, the position of Lord Cornwallis, encamped on the heights of Richmond. On his return Mercer fell

---

* Sir Henry Clinton, apprehending a combined attack by the American and French forces on his own position at New York, had required of Lord Cornwallis a re-enforcement of three thousand men; and had advised him to occupy and fortify a post on the Chesapeake.—See his letter to Lord G. Germain, 12th May, 1781.—Ed.

in with one of Tarleton's patrols of horse, which was taken, and conveyed to the American camp.

This was the only advantage of the sort as yet obtained by our army during these active operations.

The British general halted but a few days in Richmond, and resumed his march for Portsmouth, in pursuance of Sir Henry Clinton's instructions, as are plainly to be inferred from the letter of Lord Cornwallis of the 26th of May. Taking the direct route to Williamsburg, and consulting, as heretofore in his progress, the ease of his troops, he encamped in that city on the 25th.

La Fayette, while in his camp above Richmond, was joined by the baron with his corps of levies, about six hundred. This accession of force increased his army to between four and five thousand, of which two thousand one hundred were regulars, and fifteen hundred of these were veteran troops. The residue were composed of different corps of militia, better fitted for service than usual, as most of the higher grades were filled by Continental officers. Still we were inferior in numbers to the enemy by a third, and very deficient in cavalry, in which the British general continued to excel. Informed of Lord Cornwallis's continued retreat, La Fayette followed, and passing Richmond reached on the third evening New Kent Court-House, from which place the British general had moved in the morning of the previous day.

Hence the American head-quarters were transferred to Tyre's plantation, twenty miles from Williamsburg.

During this march no attempt was made by either general to disturb the other; a game of all others the most to be desired by La Fayette, as the campaign was wasting without improvement by his superior foe. While in his camp before Williamsburg, the British general learned that we had some boats and stores on the Chickahominy River. Hither he detached Lieutenant-Colonel Simcoe with his corps and the yagers to destroy them. This service was promptly performed; but the American general, having discovered from his exploring parties the march of Simcoe, detached on the 26th Lieutenant-Colonel Butler, of the Pennsylvania line, the second and rival of Morgan at Saratoga.* The rifle corps under the Majors Call and Willis, and the cavalry, which did not in the whole exceed one hundred and twenty effectives, composed Butler's van.

---

* This excellent officer passed through the war with distinction. He was employed by General Washington as next in command to St. Clair, in whose fatal defeat he fell.—Ed

Major McPherson, of Pennsylvania, led this corps; and having mounted some infantry behind the remnant of Armand's dragoons, overtook Simcoe on his return near Spencer's plantation, six or seven miles above Williamsburg. The suddenness of McPherson's attack threw the yagers into confusion; but the Queen's Rangers quickly deployed, and advanced to their support.

Call and Willis had now got up to McPherson with their riflemen, and the conflict became fierce. Lieutenant Lollar, at the head of a squadron of Simcoe's hussars, fell on Armand's remnant and drove it out of line, making Lieutenant Breso and some privates prisoners. Following his blow, Lollar turned upon our riflemen, then pressing upon the Queen's Rangers, and at the same moment Captain Ogilvie, of the Legion cavalry,—who had been sent that morning from camp with one troop for the collection of forage,—accidently appeared on our left flank. The rifle corps fell back in confusion upon Butler, drawn up in the rear with his Continentals. Satisfied with the repulse of the assailing troops, Lieutenant-Colonel Simcoe began to retire: nor was he further pressed by Butler, as Cornwallis had moved with the main body on hearing the first fire, to shield Simcoe. La Fayette claimed the advantage in this rencounter, and states his enemy's loss to be sixty killed and one hundred wounded; whereas Lord Cornwallis acknowledges the loss of only three officers and thirty privates, killed and wounded. Among the former was Lieutenant Jones, a much-admired young officer.

Our loss in killed and wounded does not appear in the report of La Fayette; but three officers and twenty-eight privates were taken.

Here was a second opportunity presented of attacking our army, and like the first it was not seized. Nothing was more feasible, as Cornwallis had moved his whole force, than for him to have turned Simcoe's horse and foot upon Butler. Following close in the rear, La Fayette must have sacrificed this corps, or risked battle. The latter would have taken place, as Wayne had moved to support Butler, and would have reached our advance about the time of the suggested movement upon our light corps.[*]

The British general returned to Williamsburg, preparing for his passage of James River; and La Fayette resumed his position at Tyre's plantation, waiting the motions of Cornwallis.

Sir Henry Clinton, from the moment he perused Washington's

---

[*] No doubt the intention of re-enforcing Sir Henry Clinton produced this suspense and inactivity.—ED.

letters, imparting to Congress the result of his conference with Count Rochambeau (which had been intercepted by one of the British general's parties), seems to have been persuaded that a formidable combined attack upon New York by the allies was not only contemplated, but certain; and as early as the 11th of June, he communicated his conviction of such an intention to Earl Cornwallis, and required him to occupy some salubrious situation about Williamsburg or Yorktown, calculated for the defensive, and convenient to desultory maritime expeditions up the rivers of Virginia, for the destruction of our remaining stores and resources. As soon as this was accomplished, Earl Cornwallis was ordered to return to Sir Henry the Queen's Rangers, the remnant of the seventeenth dragoons, two battalions of light infantry, two of Anspach, the forty-third and seventy-sixth or eightieth regiments.

It appears that subsequent to the issue of this order, the British commander-in-chief,[*] availing himself of water conveyance, contemplated striking at Philadelphia with the corps to be detached by Cornwallis, as it proceeded to New York, for the purpose of destroying the Continental supplies collected in that city.

No doubt Earl Cornwallis, feeling himself bound to give effect to his general's views, did not risk any operations which might produce delay in his movement to Portsmouth, which seems to have been the place preferred by himself for the embarkation of the troops demanded; whereas Sir Henry Clinton's instructions pointed out Williamsburg or York as the place of arms in his judgment best calculated to answer the intended purposes. Certainly Lord Cornwallis might and ought to have adopted the plan proposed by Clinton; as it was very easy to have withdrawn the garrison from Portsmouth, a post held contrary to his lordship's advice; to have brought it up to him either on James or York River, and in the same transports to have forwarded the required corps to New York. Nor would this operation have consumed the time which his passage of James River and march to Portsmouth required. He might, too, have combined with this system the destruction of La Fayette, hitherto omitted, though required by the most powerful considerations.

Believing the course originally adopted as that most likely to effect with celerity the object of the commander-in-chief, Cornwallis, after some deliberation as to its change, persevered.

---

[*] See his letter, page 440.

Halting eight or nine days in Williamsburg, his lordship decamp-ed on the 4th of July, having, after examining the river at Burwell's Ferry and James City Island, decided to pass it at the latter place. On the same evening he reached the island, and the British advance, consisting of the Queen's Rangers under Lieutenant-Colonel Simcoe, passed the river. On the 5th, the wheel carriages of every sort were transported across; as were, on the subsequent day, the baggage and bathorses. Cornwallis meant to have passed with the army on the 7th.

La Fayette did not doubt the intention of his adversary, and was much inclined to fall upon his rear when a major part of the army should have passed or was passing the river. To enable him to manage this delicate manœuvre with accuracy and precision, every effort was essayed by La Fayette's exploring parties to understand distinctly the steps taken by his lordship. Lieutenant-Colonel Mercer being, among others, employed with his dragoons in this service, made, during the night of the 3d, a circuitous march, and gained by the dawn of day the right flank of the enemy. Mercer discovered that the British general had just moved, and very quickly advised his commander of the event.

La Fayette put his army in motion on the same afternoon, and discontinuing his former caution, sat down on the evening of the 5th within eight miles of the foe; a dangerous adventure, but in its issue safe, so turned was Cornwallis from his former habit.

On the morning of the 6th the American general prepared to advance, believing that the hour was at hand for his meditated blow, as he had been accurately informed of the passage of troops on the 4th, and the continued crossing and recrossing of the boats ever since.

Mercer, with a party of his troops, was in advance for the purpose of procuring intelligence; and coming suddenly upon the mansion of Greenspring,* saw a negro, by whom he was told that Lieu-tenant-Colonel Tarleton quartered there, and was in the spring-house in the yard; and that Lord Cornwallis was at the church, not more than one mile in front. Satisfied from what he had learned of the negro, as well of the danger which awaited his party, as of the proximity of the British army, Mercer turned his horse to retire, when he found himself nearly closed up by a party of the enemy's

* The seat of Sir William Berkeley, formerly governor of Virginia; and afterward of Philip Ludwell, one of the king's council, from whom it descended to the late William Lee, sheriff of London, under the famous Wilkes.

dragoons pressing forward to intercept him. By changing his course, however, he avoided his pursuers, and in a few minutes rejoined his troop, concealed in a distant wood—whence he repaired toward the army, to communicate the intelligence to the general.

About eleven o'clock he met him advancing at the head of his troops, prepared for battle, and sanguine in the expectation that he should get up in time to fall upon the remains of the enemy on this side of the river.

The intelligence derived from Mercer produced a pause, and excited doubts as to the conduct to be pursued. At length La Fayette determined to proceed as far as Greenspring, the place which Mercer had visited in the morning, and where he acquired the information just imparted.

On approaching the house he learned that the enemy had moved toward the island; and two intelligent young dragoons now rejoined, who had been sent to the river with glasses, to attend to the passage of the enemy across it.* Their report concurred in supporting the opinion heretofore entertained; and which, though suspended by Mercer's intelligence, still existed. In fact, it comported with the inclination of officers and soldiers; and Brigadier Wayne, disquieted as he always was by losing a chance of battle, declared his conviction that the intelligence received from Lieutenant-Colonel Mercer applied only to a covering party, which would not fail to escape if our advance was longer delayed.

The American commander, indulging his desire to finish his toilsome and cautious operations by a happy blow, came into the opinion of Wayne, and began to make his final arrangements for close pursuit.

The British general, sage and experienced, had presumed that the opportunity which his crossing James River could not fail to present, would be seized by his enemy for the indulgence of that ardor natural to the season of youth, and which the enterprising La Fayette never ceased to feel, although he had for a time controlled it. He heard with pleasure that his adversary was drawing near, and took his measures to encourage the adventurous spirit which seemed now to sway him, with the resolution of turning it to his advantage. Holding his troops compact, covering as little ground as possible in his march and in his camp, he gave orders

* Bushrod Washington, now judge, and Ludwell Lee, late speaker of the Senate of Virginia.

for his pickets to fall back with the appearance of alarm and confusion, as soon as they should be seriously struck.

The ground in front of Greenspring, where by this time the whole American army had arrived, is low, wet, and sunken, reclaimed by ditches which intersect it in various directions. This sunken ground extends for a considerable distance above and below the house, and is nearly a quarter of a mile wide. As soon as you pass through it you enter the road from Williamsburg, on which the enemy marched, and which runs for a considerable distance parallel with the low ground. From the house to the road, across the low ground, a causeway* had been formed by the proprietor of Greenspring, and presented the only practicable route for troops. La Fayette must pass along this causeway on his advance to the island; and every step he proceeded after leaving it, put him more and more in the power of his prepared enemy.

The American general, by design probably, did not move from Greenspring until the hour of three in the afternoon; inasmuch as the remaining part of the evening gave sufficient daylight for the execution of his plan, if only a strong covering party of the enemy should be found on this side of the river; and the quicker darkness approached the more acceptable, should he stumble upon Cornwallis and his army.

The rifle corps under Call and Willis, preceded by a patrol of dragoons, formed our front, and after crossing the low ground, halted in a wood contiguous to the road. The cavalry of Armand and of Mercer, led by Major McPherson, followed the rifle corps, supported by the Continental infantry under Wayne.

Steuben, with the militia, formed the reserve, and continued on the ground at Greenspring, severed from the acting corps by the low ground. This disposition manifests that La Fayette calculated only on meeting with a covering party easy of conquest; as otherwise he would never have interposed the difficult defile just mentioned between the two divisions of his force.

As soon as the column reached the road, the rifle corps were thrown upon our flanks, and the horse continued to advance on the road.

We had not moved a mile before our van patrol of horse received

* La Fayette moved from Greenspring at three; and so much time was consumed in passing this defile, that his main body did not get up with the enemy, encamped not more than one mile and a half distant, until near sunset; which effect shows, in a military point of view, the disadvantages eventually accruing from the interposition of this defile.

a desultory fire from the enemy's yagers, and fell back upon McPherson. This officer communicated the occurrence to the commander, who answered by ordering Lieutenant-Colonel Mercer and himself to leave the cavalry and to take charge of the rifle corps. Mercer led that on the right, and McPherson that on the left. We very soon approached the enemy's pickets, which were briskly attacked, and losing some of their men killed, wounded, and taken, fell back in confusion upon the Legion horse, drawn up in an open field three hundred yards behind the front pickets. Our cavalry now came up; that of Armand joined McPherson, and the Virginia troop joined Mercer.

Emboldened by their successful onset, Mercer and McPherson continued to advance, and took post in a ditch under cover of a rail fence. From hence was plainly discerned a line of infantry posted on the flanks of the horse. Our rifle corps recommenced their fire, and were soon afterward joined by Major Galvan, with a battalion of the Continental infantry, who was followed by Major Willis, of Connecticut, with another battalion of infantry, and Captain Savage, with two field pieces. Galvan, Mercer, and McPherson maintained the conflict with spirit against the enemy, now advancing in body under Lieutenant-Colonel Yorke, supported by three pieces of artillery.

The conflict was keenly maintained for some minutes, when the rifle corps broke. Lieutenant-Colonel Mercer having his horse killed, remounted another, and drawing off his troop of dragoons, fell back upon Wayne, who was formed in close order in the adjacent wood. Galvan and Willis, with their light infantry, retired soon after the rifle corps dispersed; as did also Captain Savage, with our two pieces. Cornwallis pressed forward in two lines, his right wing under Lieutenant-Colonel Yorke, pushing the light infantry; while his left, under Lieutenant-Colonel Dundas, advanced upon Wayne, who, never indisposed to try the bayonet, gave orders to charge, which, though often repeated, was from the thickness of the wood, and his own close order, unexecuted, and the battle continued warmly maintained by a close fire. La Fayette, early in the action, began to apprehend that the expected covering party would turn out to be the British army, and took his measures to ascertain the fact. He became soon convinced from his own examination that he had been entirely mistaken, and immediately hastened to draw off his troops. Wayne was now closely engaged, and his flanks nearly enveloped. He was ordered to fall back to our second line of Continentals, arrayed half a mile in his rear. This was instantly executed through the favor of a dark night, with the loss of our two field-pieces; and Wayne having joined the second line, our whole detachment continuing to retire, recrossed the ravine, and proceeded with the reserve six miles in the rear of Greenspring, where La Fayette, finding the enemy did not pursue, encamped for the night.

We lost of our Continentals one hundred and eighteen, in killed, wounded, and prisoners, of which ten were officers. Our loss of rifle militia was never ascertained. The British suffered much less, having lost only five officers and seventy privates.

The marquis's postponement of his march to the evening was in its effect most fortunate. One hour more of daylight must have produced the most disastrous conclusion. Lord Cornwallis, in his official letter, considers one half hour only, to have been enough for his purpose. No pursuit was even attempted on the part of the conqueror, but he returned immediately, after the action terminated, to his camp. At the break of day Lieutenant-Colonel Tarleton, with his cavalry and some mounted infantry, by the order of the general, followed our army; and Captain Champagne, with three companies of light infantry, moved to support him.

After passing the defile in front of Greenspring, Tarleton fell in with one of our patrols of mounted riflemen, which he drove in upon La Fayette, killing some and wounding others. The marquis was still in the position he had taken the night before; and had Cornwallis moved at the same hour with his cavalry, he might have inflicted the heavy blow from whose crush we had so happily escaped the evening before. But after some consultation, after the action, upon the course to be pursued, he concluded it expedient to pass the river and hasten to Portsmouth, for the purpose of embarking the troops called for by the commander-in-chief. During the 7th and 8th, the British army crossed to the southern shore; and on the 9th, Lord Cornwallis detached Lieutenant-Colonel Tarleton, with his cavalry and eighty mounted infantry, to New London, in the county of Bedford, adjoining the Blue Ridge, and at least two hundred miles from any possible support. This perilous expedition was planned for the purpose of destroying some collections of stores said to be in that district for the army of Greene, and for the interception of some of the light troops believed to be moving from the southern army to the assistance of La Fayette. Tarleton passed through Petersburg on the 9th, and proceeded with expedition to

Prince Edward, where he expected to find our principal magazines. He was disappointed; all our stores at this place had been for some time forwarded to the south.

Continuing his march, he soon reached Bedford County, where he halted for two days, but met with no stores of any consequence, nor could he learn of the advance of any of the light troops from the south. On the contrary, he was informed that General Greene was before Ninety-six, pursuing with his whole force the object of his movement into South Carolina.

Turning toward the sea-board, the British officer returned unhurt on the fifteenth day from his departure, and joined Lord Cornwallis at Suffolk, where his lordship, having detached the re-enforcement required by the commander-in-chief to Portsmouth for embarkation, waited for the rejunction of the light corps. As soon as this took place, the British general moved to Portsmouth, and encamped with his infantry in front of his works; the cavalry passed Elizabeth River, and were cantoned in the county of Princess Ann, where wholesome and abundant subsistence for man and horse was to be found on every plantation.

La Fayette received, on the day after his repulse, a handsome squadron of dragoons, under Captain Moore, from the town of Baltimore, and retired with most of his army to the forks of York River, having dismissed all his militia.

Thus was concluded the summer campaign of Lord Cornwallis in Virginia. For eight or nine weeks he had been engaged in the most active movements, at the head of an army completely fitted for the arduous scenes of war, warmly attached to its general, conscious and proud of its own ability, and ready to encounter every danger and difficulty to give success to his operations. The inferiority of La Fayette in number, in quality, in cavalry, in arms and equipment, has been often recurred to and cannot be doubted.

Yet strange, when the primary object of the British general must have been the annihilation of our army in Virginia, he never struck it in whole or in part, although manoeuvring in his face in an open country, and remote from support of every sort except occasional aids of militia.

This omission on the part of Lord Cornwallis is inexplicable. More than once he had a fair opportunity to force an action; and that only was necessary, with his vast superiority, to produce the ruin of his antagonist.

The American general had great difficulties to surmount, as well as to guard against his formidable foe, pressing him on his retreat. Wayne, directing his most efficient aid, was far to his right, and the Baron Steuben, with the Virginia levies, was as far on his left. The public stores deposited in several magazines accessible to the enemy, and the great body of the inhabitants of the lower country flying from their homes with their wives, their children, and the most valuable of their personal property, to seek safety in the mountains. The State authorities, executive and legislative, like the flying inhabitants, driven from the seat of government; chased from Charlottesville; and at length interposing the Blue Ridge between themselves and the enemy to secure a resting-place at Staunton. In this period of gloom, of disorder, and of peril, La Fayette was collected and undismayed. With zeal, with courage, and with sagacity, he discharged his arduous duties; and throughout his difficult retreat was never brought even to array but once in order of battle.

Invigorating our counsels by his precepts; dispelling our despondency by his example; and encouraging his troops to submit to their many privations, by the cheerfulness with which he participated in their wants, he imparted the energy of his own mind to the country, and infused his high-toned spirit into his army. His efforts were crowned with success; and even the erroneous determination to risk the *élite* of his force for the purpose of capturing a supposed covering party of the hostile army, when occupied in passing James River, was repaired by the celerity with which he discovered his mistake, and with which he curtailed its consequences. To La Fayette, to his able second, to General Nelson, to his cavalry, to his rifle corps, to his officers, and to his soldiers, much praise is due; nor was it withheld by their comrades in arms, by their enemy, or by the nation.

Now, for the first time throughout the war, did ever doubt attach to the merits of the British general. In the North and in the South, in the cabinet and in the field, he stood pre-eminent: the bulwark of Great Britain—the dread of America.

When in command of mighty means, and in the heart of that State whose prostration he uniformly viewed as the first prerequisite to the subjugation of the South, that he should content himself with burning tobacco, destroying a portion of our scattered stores, and chasing our governor from hill to hill, and our legislature from town to town, comported neither with his fame nor his duty. The destruction of La Fayette ought to have been his sole object.

To it every other good appertained; and this was certainly in his power during his retreat, and even when he covered himself behind Mechunk Creek, to save the stores at Albemarle Old Court-House. But admit that this presumption is extravagant; we cannot err when we assert that by following up the blow at James's Island, he must have renewed the catastrophe of Camden in the lawns of Greenspring. A second army would have been annihilated; and that, too, when on its fate hung the safety of Virginia, of the South, if not of the United States.

Had Cornwallis acted as he always had done until he took command of the army at Petersburg, he would have moved after snatching some refreshments and a few hours' repose; he would have fallen upon the left flank of La Fayette; he would have forced him upon the Chickahominy, which for many miles skirted his right, and compelled him to surrender or to die in the last effort. For some cause not yet clearly known, a very different conduct was pursued; as derogatory to the high fame of this distinguished soldier, as it was in its consequences injurious to his country and destructive to himself and his army.

A careful examination of the commander-in-chief' and Lord Cornwallis's correspondence exhibits two facts: first, that Sir Henry Clinton was very much disposed to pursue, with the army of Virginia, operations at the head of the Chesapeake in the neighborhood of Baltimore, or in the Delaware Neck; and, secondly, that Earl Cornwallis did not accord with his chief in such application of the force under his orders, preferring the destruction of Virginia to any other object. This material difference in view and judgment laid the foundation for that languor in exertion which marks every step of Cornwallis in Virginia, until his manly resolve to take care of his army by crossing York River, when he found Clinton's promise of relief illusory.

Knowing it to be his duty to support, and not to direct, the serious intention expressed by Sir Henry Clinton of pressing solid operations in the upper Chesapeake, which we may fairly infer (from his letter written six days after he reached Virginia) was known to his lordship before he left Westover, induced him to adopt a contracted scale of conduct, lest he might delay, if not mar, his chief's design. He found himself now the mere puppet of the commander-in-chief, and not the carver and executor of his own plans, limited by general principles necessary to secure unity in design and correspondency in execution. This change in official character produced the subsequent change so apparent in his conduct. In his letter above alluded to, of the 26th of May, dated "Byrd's plantation, north of James River," is the following paragraph : "I shall now proceed to dislodge La Fayette from Richmond, and with my light troops destroy any magazines or stores in the neighborhood, which may have been collected either for his use or for General Greene's army. From thence I propose to move to the neck of Williamsburg, which is represented as healthy, and where some subsistence may be procured, and keep myself unengaged from operations which might interpose with your plan of the campaign, until I have the satisfaction of hearing from you."

It is evident from this letter that it was an answer to instructions found among General Phillips's papers, delineating the plan of the campaign ; or to a letter which met Cornwallis at Petersburg, explaining the views of the commander-in-chief.

To the tenor of this answer, Cornwallis's conduct corresponded. He did dislodge La Fayette from Richmond; he did destroy all the stores in that neighborhood, and even some more remote ; and he did afterward return to Williamsburg.

It is true that he employed some few days in pursuit of La Fayette; but confining himself in point of time, he did not persevere in pressing that object, lest it might consume more time than was compatible with the ulterior views of the commander-in-chief. In Sir Henry Clinton's letter of the 11th of June,* when comparing the

---

* EXTRACT OF A LETTER FROM SIR HENRY CLINTON TO EARL CORNWALLIS, DATED, NEW YORK; JUNE 11, 1781.

"Respecting my opinions of stations in James and York rivers, I shall beg leave only to refer your lordship to my instructions to, and correspondence with, Generals Phillips and Arnold ; together with the substance of conversations with the former, which your lordship will have found among General Phillips's papers, and to which I referred you in my last dispatch. I shall, therefore, of course, approve of any alteration your lordship may think proper to make in these stations.

"The detachments I have made from this army into the Chesapeake, since General Leslie's expedition in October last, inclusive, have amounted to seven thousand seven hundred and twenty-four effectives, and at the time your lordship made the junction with the corps there, there were under Major-General Phillips's orders, five thousand three hundred and four ; a force which, I should have hoped, would be sufficient of itself to have carried on operations in any of the southern provinces of America ; where, as appears by the intercepted letters of Washington and La Fayette, they are in no situation to stand against even a division of that army.

"I have reason to suppose the Continentals, under La Fayette, cannot exceed one thousand ; and I am told by Lieutenant-Colonel Hill, of the ninth regiment, that about a fortnight ago he met at Fredericktown the Pennsylvania line, under Wayne, of about the same number ; who were so discontented, that their officers

force under Cornwallis and that under Fa Fayette, he says:—
"I should have hoped you would have quite sufficient force to
carry on any operation in Virginia, should that have been advisable at
this late season." The concluding words plainly show that he considered it too late to press operations in Virginia, as they would interfere
with what he deemed more important. In this same letter, the British
chief communicates the prospect of a combined attack upon New
York, and demands a re-enforcement from the army in Virginia.
"By intercepted letters inclosed to your lordship in my last
dispatch, you will observe I am threatened with a siege in this
post. My present effective force is only ten thousand nine hundred
and thirty-one. With respect to that the enemy may collect for such
an object, it is probable they may amount to at least twenty thousand, besides re-enforcements to the French (which, from pretty
good authority, I have reason to expect), and the numerous militia
of the five neighboring provinces. Thus circumstanced, I am

were afraid to trust them with ammunition. This, however, may have since
altered; and your lordship may possibly have opposed to you from fifteen hundred
to two thousand Continentals, and (as La Fayette observes) a small body of ill-
armed peasantry, full as spiritless as the militia of the Southern provinces, and
without any service.

"Comparing, therefore, the force now under your lordship in the Chesapeake,
and that of the enemy opposed to you (and I think it clearly appears that they
have for the present no intention of sending thither re-enforcements), I should
have hoped you would have quite sufficient to carry on any operation in Virginia, should that have been advisable at this advanced season.

"By the intercepted letters inclosed to your lordship in my last dispatch,
you will observe that I am threatened with a siege in this post. My present
effective force is only ten thousand nine hundred and thirty-one. With
respect to that the enemy may collect for such an object, it is probable they
may amount to at least twenty thousand, besides re-enforcements to the French
(which, from pretty good authority, I have reason to expect), and the numerous militia of the five neighboring provinces. Thus circumstanced, I am persuaded your lordship will be of opinion, that the sooner I concentrate my force
the better. Therefore (unless your lordship, after the receipt of my letters of the
29th of May, and the 8th instant, should incline to agree with me in opinion,
and judge it right to adopt my ideas respecting the move to Baltimore or the
Delaware Neck, &c.), I beg leave to recommend it to you, as soon as you have
finished the active operations you may now be engaged in, to take a defensive
station, in any healthy situation you choose (be it at Williamsburg or Yorktown); and I would wish, in that case, that, after reserving to yourself such
troops as you may judge necessary for ample defensive and desultory movements by water, for the purpose of annoying the communications, destroying
magazines, &c., the following corps may be sent to me in succession, as you
can spare them: two battalions of light infantry; forty-third regiment;
seventy-sixth or eightieth regiments; two battalions of Anspach; Queen's
Rangers, cavalry and infantry; remains of the detachment of the seventeenth
light dragoons; and such proportion of artillery as can be spared, particularly
men."

persuaded your lordship will be of opinion that the sooner I concentrate my force the better.

"Therefore (unless your lordship, after the receipt of my letters of
the 29th of May and 8th of June, should incline to agree with me
in opinion, and judge it right to adopt my ideas respecting the move
to Baltimore, or the Delaware Neck, &c.), I beg leave to recommend
it to you, as soon as you have finished the active operations you may
now be engaged in, to take a defensive station in any healthy
situation you choose (be it at Williamsburg or Yorktown); and
I would wish, in that case, that after reserving to yourself such
troops as you may judge necessary for ample defensive and desultory movements by water, for the purpose of annoying the enemy's
communications, destroying magazines, &c., the following corps
may be sent to me in succession as you can spare them."

The letters above mentioned, of the 29th May and 8th June,
were (as we infer from Lord Cornwallis's dispatches) never received,
or probably the confidence they breathed might have induced his
lordship to venture to appropriate his time and measures as his own
judgment should direct. In which case the army of La Fayette
would have experienced a more determined and persevering
pursuit.

Conforming his whole conduct to the plan of his commander-in-
chief, he followed his enemy only over the North Anna, a branch of
the Pamunkey; and as soon as he completed some secondary
objects he fell back to Williamsburg, and from thence interposed
the James River between himself and La Fayette, for the purpose
of hastening the required detachment to Clinton; the demand for
which was repeated by a letter dated the 28th of June. It results
clearly from this cursory review of facts, that Lord Cornwallis, from
the moment he assumed the command of the army in Virginia (20th
of May), considered himself as the mere executor of plans devised
by his principals; and that he consequently never ventured to
engage in measures, whose execution might in any degree interrupt
the completion of Sir Henry Clinton's designs. This control
paralyzed all his efforts, and he no longer displayed that decision and
fire which had before marked his military career.

After passing James River, Cornwallis seems to have indulged
his natural bias, by detaching Lieutenant-Colonel Tarleton to the
county of Bedford. This daring enterprise emanated from his
unceasing desire to cramp the exertions of Greene, by destroying
all the storesint ended to supply the pressing wants of our army in

the South; and from his determination never to permit any of Greene's light troops to join La Fayette, some of whom he now believed were approaching the Dan to re-enforce the army in Virginia.

It is very surprising that La Fayette, who had just manifested his anxiety to strike his adversary, even at the risk of the loss of his army, should not have now indulged the same propensity, when the present opportunity so forcibly invited the attempt; which was not only practicable, but exempt from much hazard.

The re-enforcement of horse just received under Captain Moore must have augmented his cavalry to two hundred; Tarleton had with him about the same number of dragoons. The bat and other horses with the army, and such as might be readily procured in the neighborhood of the camp, would have enabled La Fayette to mount four or five hundred infantry, two upon a horse. Tarleton had with him but eighty mounted infantry. With this force a skilful officer (and the American general had many) could not have been disappointed in intercepting the British detachment.

But La Fayette contented himself with sending a body of infantry under Brigadier Wayne across James River, whose corps was not fitted to the enterprise, and who therefore could not with his means effect the object, unless Lieutenant-Colonel Tarleton had improvidently thrown himself into his lap.

Sir Henry Clinton, discovering Lord Cornwallis's aversion to the establishment of a post on the Chesapeake, and determined to fix one there, countermanded the move of the re-enforcement heretofore required, and repeated his directions for the selection and fortification of a permanent post, convenient for desultory maritime expeditions up the Chesapeake and its numerous rivers, and capable of protecting line-of-battle ships.

It appears that the British admiral on the American station had experienced the disadvantages which flowed from the navy's occupying the usual stations during the freezing months, and was consequently anxious of wintering his fleet further south. He says, in his letter to Lord Cornwallis, dated 12th July, off Sandy Hook, " That there is no place for great ships, during the freezing months, on this side of the Chesapeake, where the great ships will be in security, and at the same time capable of acting; and in my opinion they had better go to the West Indies, than to be laid up in Halifax during the winter;" and he goes on to recommend Hampton Roads as the proper place.

Earl Cornwallis declining further opposition to the will of Sir Henry Clinton, sent his engineer and some captains of the navy to examine Old Point Comfort, which appears to have been the site preferred for the intended post, both by the general and admiral.

The report of these officers was unfavorable ;* and Lord Cornwallis, coinciding in the same opinion, selected York and Gloucester, not far above the mouth of York River, instead of Old Point Comfort.

To this place he repaired with the first division of his army ; and disembarking it early in August, took possession of both posts. After occupying these, his lordship directed Brigadier O'Hara, commanding at Portsmouth, to destroy the works there, and to join him with the rear division of the army. This was done with all convenient dispatch, and the whole British force concentrated in the position of York and Gloucester before the twenty-third. Cornwallis, as soon as he landed the first division of the army, engaged in tracing the lines of the necessary works on both sides of the river ; and

---

* COPY OF THE REPORT OF LIEUTENANT SUTHERLAND, ENGINEER, DATED BILLY, ORDNANCE TRANSPORT, HAMPTON ROADS, JULY 25, 1781.

MY LORD:—Agreeably to your orders, I have examined the ground on Old Point Comfort with as much accuracy as I possibly could ; and for your lordship's better information, I have made a survey of the ground, upon which is laid down the width and sounding of the channel.   I beg leave to offer what appears to me, respecting the situation of a work on that spot.

The ground where the ruins of Fort George lie is the fittest for a work, but, at the same time must be attended with many inconveniences.

The level of the ground there is about two feet higher than the high-water mark ; which, from its very short distance to the deep water, must soon be destroyed by a naval attack.

The great width and depth of the channel gives ships the advantage of passing the fort with very little risk.   I apprehend one thousand five hundred yards is too great a distance for batteries to stop ships, which is the distance here.   Ships that wish to pass the fire of the fort, have no occasion to approach nearer.

Nor do I imagine a fort built there could afford any great protection to an inferior and weak fleet, anchored near the fort, against a superior fleet of the enemy ; which must have it in their power to make their own disposition, and place our fleet between them and the fort ; the channel offering no bay for the security of ships under cover of a fort.

The time and expense to build a fort there must be very considerable, from the low situation of the ground, which must necessarily cause the soil to be moved from a great distance to form the ramparts and parapets ; and every other material must be carried there, as the timber on the peninsula is unfit for any useful purpose.

These are the remarks which have occurred to me on examining the ground and situation of a work on Old Point Comfort, for the protection of the harbor and fleet ; which I humbly submit to your lordship.

I have the honor to be, &c,
ALEXANDER SUTHERLAND.

committing the direction of the post of Gloucester to Lieutenant-Colonel Dundas, continued himself in that of York.

While with zeal and assiduity he pressed forward the completion of his fortifications with his infantry, and at the same time employed his cavalry in collecting cattle and forage, he held his army ready to move upon La Fayette, should he think proper to approach him.

The American general, as soon as he was advised of the posses sion of the post on York River by the enemy, broke up from his camp on Pamunkey, and recalled Wayne from the southern side of James River, whither he had been detached to intercept Tarleton, and where he had been continued in conformity to the orders of the commander-in-chief ; who, as soon as he decided to turn his force upon the enemy in Virginia, apprised La Fayette of his intention, and commanded him to take measures for the interruption of Lord Cornwallis's retreat, should that general discover the intended blow and attempt to elude it by gaining North Carolina.

The Queen's Rangers, under Simcoe, held the post of Gloucester ; while Lieutenant-Colonel Tarleton, with his Legion, occupied the front of that of York. These officers displayed their habitual activity in traversing and foraging the country on both sides of the river, and in dispersing all the militia collected in their neighborhood. They took extensive sweeps in pursuit of their objects ; there being no force nearer to Simcoe than a detachment of volunteer militia under Lieutenant-Colonel John Taylor, formerly of Hazen's regiment, who had established himself near Gloucester Court-House, for the protection of that quarter of the country ; and none nearer to Tarleton, than a small body of militia at Chiswell's Ordinary, on the Fredericksburg road. Taylor baffled every attempt to strike his corps ; but the officer at Chiswell's was not so fortunate. Tarleton fell upon him very unexpectedly, and broke up his post, but with very little loss.

Brigadier Weedon being again called to take command of a portion of the militia, repaired by order to Gloucester Court-House, early in September, with several small detachments, where he relieved Lieutenant-Colonel Taylor.

As there were among our militia many soldiers who had served out their terms of enlistment in the army, Weedon judiciously directed those individuals to be thrown into one corps, and placed it under the command of Lieutenant-Colonel Mercer ; who had, during the preceding period of the campaign, served with his troop of dragoons in the army of La Fayette. This officer* selected proper persons for the subordinate stations; and with two hundred effectives, rank and file, was detached in front of the militia.

Weedon having arranged his corps, advanced to Dixon's mills about the middle of the month, where he continued, exerting every means in his power to confine the enemy's forages to a small circle, the chief object in view on the Gloucester side of the river.

CHAPTER XXXII.

Plans of Greene.—Rudolph, of the Legion infantry detached to Wilmington.—Col. Hayne executed.—The American officers urge Greene to retaliate.—His proclamation.—Proceedings in the House of Lords on the subject.

THE period of tranquillity and of rest still continued in the camp of Greene, undisturbed by the din of war. Worn down as were the troops, nothing could be more comfortable than this interval of peace; and its enjoyment was not less grateful than universal, with the single exception of him who most required and most deserved it. Greene's anxious mind and faithful heart rejected participation in the comfort himself had given.

1781. August 1st.

Virginia was overpowered by the foe; North Carolina agitated by intestine feuds, promoted by the countenance and excitement of the British garrison still possessing Wilmington: and a portion of the two Southern States, with each metropolis, in the hands of the enemy, to be wrested from him only by battle.

With his small means, to sustain Virginia, to restore North Carolina, and confine the British force in South Carolina and Georgia, to Charleston and Savannah, called for unceasing efforts of mind and body. He gave both without reserve; and finally determined, first to liberate North Carolina, by carrying the garrison of Wilmington; then to pass into the enemy's country south of the Congaree, and compel him to give it up; afterward to hasten to Virginia with the *élite* of his force, uniting to it the army of La Fayette, and once more to face Lord Cornwallis. In pursuance of these arrangements, he gave orders on the 2d of August to Lieutenant-Colonel Lee to hold himself in readiness, with his Legion,

---

* Mercer having resigned his commission in the army (as has been mentioned), and not being an officer in the militia, the court of the county of Stafford, in which he was born, recommended him (as is required by the constitution of the State of Virginia) to the executive, who conferred on him the commission of lieutenant-colonel.

Kirkwood's Delawares, and Handy's Marylanders. To prevent suspicion of his intention, Washington, with his cavalry, was directed to pass the Wateree; Marion, with his militia, was detached to the country on the Combahee, which river makes the southern boundary of the Charleston district; and other demonstrations were made, indicating the design of entering into the territory occupied by the British. The general aimed his blow against Wilmington, upon the persuasion that the enterprise could not fail, if concealed to the moment of execution; and this he deemed practicable from its distant situation, in itself sufficient to lull the vigilance of the garrison; from the sultry season, forbidding military effort; from the attachment of the country through which the course selected for the march passed; and from the facility with which that attachment might be applied to subserve the object. Minute intelligence respecting the enemy and his defences, as well as boats for the passage of the Cape Fear River, remained to be procured before the expedition could commence. Lee dispatched Captain Rudolph, with a small party from the Legion infantry, to acquire the one and to collect the other.

This officer quitting camp in the night, soon reached the pine barrens; and continuing his course through the woods to the Pedee, passed that river and approached with celerity the country south of the Cape Fear. Concealing himself in the friendly family to which he was introduced, he engaged, with his usual diligence and caution, in the execution of his mission. So favorable was his report, as to confirm the sanguine expectations before entertained of complete success. Boats, though chiefly canoes, were procurable in sufficient number to pass the infantry, and the horse could swim. Major Craig still commanded the British garrison; an officer well qualified for the trust, being circumspect as well as brave; but his garrison consisted only of three hundred men, many of them in the hospital, and the whole inadequate to man his extensive works. With good reason, therefore, was it concluded, that a concealed and sudden approach was alone necessary to accomplish the object. The day was fixed for the march of Lee, and his final orders were made out. His movement was disguised by the ostensible pretext of hastening to secure a convoy, given out to be on its way from Virginia, which might be taken or destroyed by the loyalists of North Carolina, when passing through their neighborhood: in concurrence with which pretence, Lee was ordered to proceed in the direction of Camden until he reached the course carrying him through the pine barren into the tract of country inhabited by well-affected citizens. At this period information was received from General Washington, indicating the probability that the French West India fleet would visit our coast during the autumn, and intimating the propriety of being prepared in every quarter for instant co-operation; as its place of arrival was uncertain, and its continuance with us would be necessarily short. In consequence of this information, General Greene changed his plan, believing it most eligible to devote his means toward the accomplishment of the immediate liberation of South Carolina and Georgia; persuaded that as soon as the British general should be apprised of the probability of a visit from the French fleet, the garrison would be withdrawn from Wilmington, and thus the State of North Carolina would be relieved, without risk of repulse, or loss of life. This change in measures, too, was extremely agreeable to Governor Rutledge, just returned from the North to resume the duties of his station, delighted with the prospect of seeing his State completely freed by the expected naval assistance, and desirous that the force of Greene should be held for that end primarily.

The detachment under Lee, prepared for service, was discharged, and Captain Rudolph directed to return, holding nevertheless secret his visit to Cape Fear.

General Greene, though induced to depart from the minor object in his plan of operations, adhered to the general system, believing it the wiser policy to depend as little as possible on the aid of friends.

Repeating his orders to the Marquis de la Fayette, urging his unvarying adherence to the most cautious conduct, and communicating his intention of hastening to his support as soon as the state of affairs in South Carolina would permit—he now turned his entire attention to the British army, still encamped on the south of the Congaree, between Motte's and the Santee.

The season yet continued extremely hot; but our wounded were recovered, our sick restored to health, and the month of August wasting away. Orders were issued preparatory to movement, and on the 21st the American general decamped from the benign hills of Santee,* for the avowed purpose of seeking his enemy. Lieu-

---

* The soldiers of Greene's army may truly call these hills benignant. Twice our general there resorted, with his sick, his wounded, and worn-down troops; and twice we were restored to health and strength, by its elevated dry situation, its pure air, its fine water, and the friendly hospitality of its inhabitants.

tenant-Colonel Cruger joined at Orangeburgh, soon after Greene (finding Rawdon unassailable with hope of success) had retired from its vicinity. Lord Rawdon having accomplished the evacuation of Ninety-six, removed the loyalists of that quarter within the British lines; and concentrating his force at Orangeburgh, upon General Greene's retirement to his summer quarters, relinquished the command of the army to Lieutenant-Colonel Stewart, and returned to Charleston, with the view of embarking for England—long intended, but heretofore delayed by the critical posture of affairs.

Stewart did not establish a post, as was expected, at Orangeburgh; but moving his whole force toward the Santee, sat down near the confluence of its two branches, about fifteen miles from his adversary, on the opposite side of that river.

Previous to the breaking up from the High Hills of Santee, an occurrence had taken place in Charleston which deeply affected the feelings of the American general and army. The affair would probably have led to a war of extermination, had not the fast approach of peace arrested the progress of a system, deliberately adopted by Greene, and ardently maintained by every individual of his army.

Isaac Hayne,* a highly respectable citizen of South Carolina, had taken part with his country from the commencement of the war, and served as a private in the militia during the siege of Charleston. After the surrender of that place, Hayne returned to his seat west of the Edisto, under the protection of the fourth article of capitulation. " The militia now in the garrison," says the answer to that article, " shall be permitted to return to their respective homes as prisoners on parole; which parole, as long as they observe it, shall secure them from being molested in their property."

We have before mentioned the extraordinary proclamation of Sir Henry Clinton, which ordered all our militia prisoners on parole, not taken by capitulation, or in confinement, at the surrender of

---

* So extremely beloved was this citizen by his neighbors that, when a company of volunteers was levied near his residence in the beginning of the war, Hayne was called unanimously to the command of it.

He obeyed the call, and fulfilled the duties of his station honorably to himself, and beneficially to his soldiers.

The regiment to which the company was attached being destitute of field officers, Hayne was named as colonel. He did not succeed, owing to some intrigues believed to be practised in favor of his competitor, which so disgusted Captain Hayne that he resigned his commission and returned to the ranks, where by his exemplary zeal and obedience he very much advanced the discipline of the regiment, and highly contributed to its subsequent utility.

Lincoln, to become British subjects, or return instantly to the commandant of Charleston. Although the prisoners taken at the sur render of that city were excepted in the proclamation, the popularity and patriotism of Hayne notwithstanding marked him as the first victim of its tyranny.

Colonel Ballingall, of the royal militia in the district of Hayne's residence, waited on him from personal respect, and communicated the orders he had received. Hayne asserted his inviolability under the capitulation of Charleston ; represented that small-pox was then raging in his family ; that all his children were ill with the disease ; that one of them had already died, and his wife was on the verge of dissolution. Finding the remonstrance unavailing, he declared to Ballingall that no human force should remove him from the side of his dying wife. A discussion followed, which terminated in a written stipulation, by which Hayne engaged to " demean himself as a British subject, so long as the country should be covered by the British army."

In a civil war no citizen should expect or desire neutrality. Whoever attempts to place himself in that condition, misunderstands human nature, and becomes entangled in toils always dangerous— often fatal. By endeavoring to acquire, with the most virtuous motive, a temporary neutrality, Hayne was unwisely led into a compact which terminated in his ruin.

Pursuing his first object, the care of his sick wife and children, Hayne repaired to Charleston, presented himself to Brigadier Patterson with the written agreement of Ballingall, and solicited permission to return home. This indulgence he presumed could not be denied, being consistent with his late compact and his view to executing it. The request, however, was peremptorily refused ; and Hayne was told, that he " must either become a British subject, or submit to close confinement." The latter alternative was most agreeable to his inclination ; but the tender devotion to his family which had induced him to repair to Charleston urged his acceptance of the former. To his friend Dr. Ramsay, who was then a prisoner with the enemy, he communicated the conflicting emotions of his mind.* Tranquillized by the interview, he returned to the

---

* " If the British would grant me the indulgence, which we in the day of our power gave to their adherents, of removing my family and property, I would seek an asylum in the remotest corner of the United States, rather than submit to their government ; but as they allow no other alternative than submission or confinement in the capital, at a distance from my wife and family, at a time when they are in the most pressing need of my presence and support, I must

commandant, and completed his error by a formal acknowledgment of allegiance to the British king—openly excepting, however, to the clause which required his support of government with arms. Patterson the commandant, and Simpson the intendant of police, assured him, that such service would never be required; and added, "when the regular forces cannot defend the country without the aid of its inhabitants, it will be high time for the royal army to quit it." Thus this amiable citizen proceeded from delusion to delusion, until he placed himself in a fallacious security, which subsequent incidents turned to his destruction.

Hayne hastened to his family, happy in the expectation of preserving it through the prevailing pestilence. But in this hope he was sorely disappointed; for his wife and a second child soon fell victims to the fatal malady. These afflictions did not limit his misfortunes; inasmuch as he was interdicted from enjoying even the political quietude he had attempted to secure. He was occasionally required to bear arms in the regal service; and, uniformly refusing to obey, on the ground of his exception at the time of subscribing the declaration of allegiance, he was threatened with close confinement.

In this situation Mr. Hayne was found, when Greene had forced the enemy from the upper country, and restored to the Union the whole of Carolina east of the Santee, and north of the Congaree. A detachment of Marion's militia under Colonel Harden, passing to the west of the Edisto for the protection of their own homes, reached the neighborhood of Hayne. Well knowing his worth and influence, they were extremely anxious to procure his aid. Paul Hamilton,[*] one of this party, and an intimate friend of Hayne, called on him to solicit co-operation. Hayne frankly stated the change which had taken place in his political condition; and, believing himself bound by the declaration of allegiance, refused to concur with his friends in supporting a cause the success of which was the ardent wish of his heart. Hamilton then asked the accommoda-

for the present yield to the demands of the conquerors. I request you to bear in mind, that, previous to my taking this step, I declare that it is contrary to my inclination, and forced on me by hard necessity. I never will bear arms against my country. My new masters can require no service of me but what is enjoined by the old militia law of the province, which substitutes a fine in lieu of personal service. That I will pay as the price of my protection. If my conduct should be censured by my countrymen, I beg that you would remember this conversation, and bear witness for me, that I do not mean to desert the cause of America."

* Present Secretary of the Navy.

tion of a few horses, in which resources Hayne was known to abound. Hayne refused the request; and informed his friend, that the moment he heard of Harden's approach he ordered all his horses to be removed, lest assistance might be obtained in violation of his plighted faith. Yet he assured Hamilton, that whenever he should find the royal authority unable to afford its promised protection, he should consider himself absolved from the extorted allegiance, and would with joy enroll himself with the defenders of his country.

Thus did Hayne scrupulously adhere to a contract, which was never obligatory—having been coerced by the duress of power, and in palpable violation of the capitulation of Charleston.

Soon after this occurrence, the British were driven below the Edisto; and nearly the whole country between the river and the Stono Inlet fell under the protection of the American arms. Every person in the recovered country believed himself released from those obligations which the late condition of affairs had imposed; for it was justly thought that the allegiance due to a conqueror ceased with his expulsion from the subdued territory. Under this correct impression, Hayne with many others repaired to the American camp. His merit attracted immediate attention; and the militia of his district, by an election in camp, honored him with the command of a regiment.

Taking the field immediately, Colonel Hayne conducted an expedition in the enemy's territory. Some of his mounted militia penetrated the neck of Charleston, and, near the quarter-house, captured General Williamson; who had been as active in supporting the royal authority since the surrender of Lincoln, as he had been firm and influential in opposing it prior to that event. Lieutenant-Colonel Balfour, successor of Brigadier Patterson, put his cavalry in motion to recover Williamson. This detachment fell suddenly on the camp of Hayne; but was handsomely received and repelled by Colonel Harden, who did not deem it prudent to push his success by pursuit.* Colonel Hayne, attended by his second, Lieutenant-Colonel McLachlin, and a small guard, had unfortunately gone to breakfast with a friend, about two miles from camp. The house was on the Charleston road; and the negligent guard having left its post in search of fruit,† Colonel Hayne was unap-

---

* From the character of Major Harden it is to be presumed that the inferiority of his force forbade this measure, or it would have been resorted to.

† One of the thousand instances during the war of the waste of American life by confidence in militia, and among the numerous evidences in favor of a

prised of the enemy's approach until he saw them a few rods from the door. Being very active and resolute, he pushed for his horse, mounted, and forced his way through the foe. To pass a fence in his route, he put spur to his horse, which unfortunately fell in leaping, and the entangled rider was overtaken by his pursuers. McLachlin, being cut off from his horse, fell sword in hand, contending against the surrounding enemy. Colonel Hayne was conveyed to Charleston, and lodged in the prison of the provost. The purity of the prisoner's character, and his acknowledged kindness to the unfortunate in his power, pleaded against the severity which the commandant was disposed to exercise; nevertheless the most rigorous course was pursued with relentless pertinacity.

Soon after he was confined in the provost, Colonel Hayne received an official letter from the town-major, stating that "a board of general officers * would assemble the next day, for his trial." In the evening of the following day, the same officer informed him, that "instead of a counsel of general officers, a court of inquiry would be held to determine in what view he ought to be considered; and that he should be allowed pen, ink, and paper, and counsel." On the 29th of July, two days after this intelligence, the town-major directed his adjutant to acquaint Colonel Hayne, "that in consequence of the court of inquiry, held as directed, Lord Rawdon and Colonel Balfour have resolved on his execution, on Tuesday, the 31st instant, at six o'clock, for having been found under arms, and employed in raising a regiment to oppose the British government, after he had become a subject, and accepted the protection of government at the reduction of Charleston."

The prisoner, now for the first time informed of the charge exhibited against him, addressed the following letter to the two British officers, who were about to imbrue their hands in his blood :—

To Lord Rawdon and Colonel Balfour.

"My Lord and Sir,—On Thursday morning I had the honor of receiving a letter from Major Frazer, by which he informed me,

---

classification of our militia, by which measure we should obtain defenders worthy of the high trust reposed in them.

* This should probably be *staff officers*, as there were no British *general* officers then in Carolina. In a statement of this case submitted by Colonel Hayne to his counsel in Charleston, and published in the *London Political Magazine* for 1782, he says he received from Major Frazer, a notice in the following words—" a court of inquiry, composed of four *staff officers*, and five captains," &c.—Ed.

that a council of general officers would be assembled the next day
for my trial; and on the evening of the same day, I received
another letter from the same officer, acquainting me that instead of
that, a court of inquiry would sit for the purpose of deciding under
what point of view I ought to be considered. I was also told, that
any person whom I should appoint, would be permitted to accompany me as my counsel. Having never entertained any other idea
of a court of inquiry, or heard of any other being formed of it, than
of its serving merely to precede a council of war, or some other
tribunal, for examining the circumstances more fully, except in the
case of a spy; and Mr. Jarvis, lieutenant-marshal to the provost, not
having succeeded in finding the person who had been named for my
counsel, I did not take the pains to summon any witnesses, though it
would have been in my power to have produced many; and I presented myself before the court without any assistance whatever.
When I was before that assembly, I was further convinced that I
had not been deceived in my conjectures. I found that the members
of it were not sworn, and the witnesses were not examined upon
oath; and all the members, as well as every person present, might
easily have perceived, by the questions which I asked, and by the
whole tenor of my conduct, that I had not the least notion that I was
tried or examined upon an affair on which my life or death depended.

" In the case of spies, a court of inquiry is all that can be necessary, because the simple fact, whether the person is or is not a spy,
is all that can be the object of their researches; and his having
entered the lines of the enemy's camp or garrison, subjects him
to military execution. As that accusation neither is nor can be
made against me, I humbly conceive that the information I received, that the court would make inquiry concerning what point
of view I ought to be considered under, could not be taken as a
sufficient notice of their having an intention to try me then; but
could only be thought to signify, that they were to take it into consideration whether I ought to be looked upon as a British subject
or as an American; that in the first case I should undergo a legal
and impartial trial; in the second, I should be set at liberty on my
parole. Judge then, my lord and sir, of the astonishment I must
have been in, when I found they had drawn me by surprise into a
proceeding tending to judgment, without my knowing it to be such;
and deprived me of the ability of making a legal defence, which it
would have been very easy for me to have done, founded both in
law and in fact;—when I saw myself destitute of the assistance of

counsel and of witnesses; and when they abruptly informed me, that after the procedure of the court I was condemned to die, and that in a very few days. Immediately upon receiving this notice, I sent for the lawyer whom I had originally chosen for my counsel. I here inclose his opinion concerning the legality of the process held against me; and I beg that I may be permitted to refer myself to him. I can assure you with the utmost truth, that I had and have many reasons to urge in my defence, if you will grant me the favor of a regular trial; if not, which I cannot however suppose from your justice and humanity, I earnestly entreat that my execution may be deferred, that I may at least take a last farewell of my children, and prepare for the dreadful change. I hope you will return me a speedy answer; and am, with respect,

"ISAAC HAYNE."

To this representation the town major returned the following answer: " I have to inform you, that your execution is not ordered in consequence of any sentence from the court of inquiry; but by virtue of the authority with which the commander-in-chief in South Carolina and the commanding officer in Charleston are invested; and their resolves on the subject are fixed and unchangeable."

Disdaining further discussion with relentless power, Hayne merely solicited a short respite, to enable him for the last time to see his children. The request was granted in the following communication from the town major: " I am to inform you, that in consequence of a petition signed by Governor Bull and many others, as also of your prayer of yesterday, and the humane treatment shown by you to the British prisoners who fell into your hands, you are respited for forty-eight hours; but should General Greene offer to expostulate in your favor with the commanding officer, from that moment this respite will cease, and you will be ordered to immediate execution."

After the delivery of this message, the amiable American enjoyed the comfort of seeing his family and conversing with his friends. During this interesting—this awful—period, he exhibited a dignified composure; and in his last evening declared, that " he felt no more alarmed at death, than at any other occurrence which is necessary and unavoidable." Very different, indeed, were the feelings of his friends. Mrs. Peronneau, his sister, accompanied by his children, all clad in the deepest mourning, and manifesting the torture of their heart-rending agony, waited on Lord Rawdon, and on their knees supplicated him to spare their father and brother! But his lordship's "resolve was fixed and unchangeable!" Anxious to terminate a life of truth in the formalities of honor, Colonel Hayne solicited, in a second letter to the stern duumvirate, permission to die like a soldier. He then arranged the preceding correspondence; and on the morning of his execution presented the packet to his son (a boy of thirteen years) and directed him to "deliver it to Mrs. Edwards, with my request to forward it to her brother in Congress. Go, then, to the place of my execution,—receive my body, and see it decently interred with my forefathers." This done, he embraced him, imploring the divine blessing on his orphan children. Dressed with his accustomed neatness, accompanied by a few friends, he marched with unruffled serenity, through a weeping crowd, to the place of execution. He had flattered himself with the presumption that his last request would be granted : quickly the sight of the gibbet, announced the fallacy of this hope. For a moment he paused, but immediately recovering his wonted firmness, moved forward. At this instant, a friend whispered his confidence that "you will now exhibit an example of the manner in which an American can die." "I will endeavor to do so," was the reply of the modest martyr. Never was intention better fulfilled: neither arrogating superiority, nor betraying weakness, he ascended the cart, unsupported and unappalled. Having taken leave of his friends, and commended his infant family to their protection, he drew the cap over his eyes, and illustrated by his demeanor, that death in the cause of our country, even on a gallows, cannot appal the virtuous and the brave.

The proceedings in this case exhibit a prevarication and precipitance, no less disreputable to the authors, than repugnant to the feelings of humanity. The unfortunate captive is first informed, that a court-martial will be convened for his trial; next, that a court of inquiry will determine the proper mode of procedure, before whom he will be allowed the assistance of counsel ; then without this assistance that he is doomed to death in consequence of the deliberations of the latter tribunal ; and lastly, that the bloody sentence does not emanate from this authority, but is the inflexible decree of the two military commanders. Had the discovery of truth and execution of justice been the sole objects in view, those who well knew English law, liberty, and practice, could not have erred. Colonel Hayne was certainly either a prisoner of war, or a British subject. If the latter, he was amenable to the law, and indisputably entitled to the formalities and the aids of trial ; but if the former, he was not responsible to the British government, or its military commander, for his lawful conduct in the exercise of arms. Unhappily for this virtuous man, the royal power was fast declining in the South. The inhabitants were eager to cast off the temporary allegiance of conquest ; it was deemed necessary to awe them into submission by some distinguished severity, and Hayne was the selected victim !

As soon as this tragical event was known to General Greene, he addressed a letter to Colonel Balfour, demanding an explanation of the daring outrage. The commandant replied, that " the execution of Colonel Hayne took place by the joint order of Lord Rawdon and himself; but in consequence of the most explicit directions from Lord Cornwallis ' to put to death all those who should be found in arms, after being at their own request received as subjects, since the capitulation of Charleston, and the clear conquest of the province in the summer of 1780 ; more especially such as should have accepted of commissions, or might distinguish themselves in inducing a revolt of the country.' To his lordship, therefore, as being answerable for the measure, the appeal will more properly be made." *

---

* EXTRACT OF A LETTER FROM LIEUTENANT-COLONEL BALFOUR TO MAJOR-GENERAL GREENE, DATED CHARLESTON, SEPTEMBER 3, 1781.

" I come now to that part which has respect to the execution of Colonel Hayne ; on which head I am to inform you it took place by the joint order of Lord Rawdon and myself, in consequence of the most express directions from Lord Cornwallis to us, in regard to all those who should be found in arms, after being at their request received as subjects, since the capitulation of Charleston and the clear conquest of the province in the summer of 1780 ; more especially such as should have accepted of commissions, or might distinguish themselves in inducing a revolt of the country. To his lordship, therefore, as being answerable for this measure, the appeal will more properly be made, and, on such appeal, I must not doubt, every fit satisfaction will be tendered ; but as the threat in your letter is of a nature which may extend in its consequences to the most disagreeable and serious lengths, I cannot discuss this subject without some general remarks, still referring for the particular justification to the opinion and decision of Lord Cornwallis, immediately under whom I have the honor to act.

" And first, I must conceive, without adverting to the particular cause of dispute between Great Britain and this country, that on the subjection of any territory, the inhabitants of it owe allegiance to the conquering power (in the present case a voluntary acknowledgment was given, and consequent protection received) ; and that, on any account to recede from it, is justly punishable with death, by whatever law, either civil or military, is then prevalent.

" To justify retaliation, I am convinced you will agree, a parity of circumstances in all respects is required ; without such, every shadow of justice is removed, and vengeance only points to indiscriminate horrors."

The order of Lord Cornwallis, as avowed by the commandant of
Charleston, engaged the serious attention of Greene; who determined to resist, with all his power, the cruel and sanguinary system.
The officers of the American army entered with zeal into the views
of their leader; and urged, in a unanimous address, the propriety
of retaliation. " Permit us to add," says the concluding paragraph
of that manly paper, " that while we lament the necessity of such
a severe expedient, and commiserate the sufferings to which individuals will be necessarily exposed; we are not unmindful that such a
measure may, in its consequences, involve our own lives in additional danger. But we had rather forego temporary distinctions,
and commit our lives to the most desperate situation, than prosecute this just and necessary war on terms so unequal and dishonorable." Greene was highly gratified with the cordial support, spontaneously pledged by his army; and, soon after his departure from
the High Hills, issued a proclamation, severely arraigning the
execution of Colonel Hayne, declaring his determination to " make
reprisals for all such inhuman insults, and to select for the objects of
retaliation officers of the regular forces, and not the deluded Americans who had joined the royal army."

The inhabitants of Carolina, whom the enemy had expected to
intimidate by the wanton sacrifice of Hayne, discovering the generous and determined spirit of the American general and army, dis-
carded the apprehensions at first excited, and flocked to the standard
of their country. Emulating the ardor and decision of the regular
troops, they were ready to subject themselves to all the perils to
which they might be eventually exposed in the just cause of
retaliation.

The British officers and soldiers were not unmindful of the
changed condition of the war. The unpleasant sensations arising
from this state of things naturally produced a serious examination
of the cause; and the inquiry was not calculated to inspire confidence.

The feelings which it excited received a considerable addition
from the representation which by permission of the American general, was now made by two British subalterns, taken prisoners
shortly after the execution of Colonel Hayne was known in the
American camp; and who, as soon as captured, were committed to
the provost by order of General Greene. Apprehending that they
would become the first victims of the barbarous policy introduced
by their commanders, they addressed their friends in Charleston,

describing their condition, announcing their probable fate, and referring to that clause in the American general's proclamation, which confined his menaced retaliation to British officers only.

The honorable and reflecting of both armies perceived, that the justice of the sentence was at least questionable; that inconsistency and passion had marked the proceedings. Nor did it escape observation, that Colonel Balfour, when attempting to shield himself and coadjutor under cover of instructions, withheld their *date*. This suppression naturally excited a belief, that the orders of Lord Cornwallis were previous to Greene's recovery of that part of Carolina in which Hayne resided. Although his instructions might have comprehended the case of the ill-fated American, while the country around him was subject to the royal power; yet after the reconquest by Greene, they could not be applied with justice. The extraordinary condition which accompanied the respite, corroborated this conjecture. It was generally asked, if the decision be really conformable with the instructions of Cornwallis, why should Greene's expostulation be prohibited? The interposition of the American general could not prevent the execution of the sentence, if correct; but would lead to a discussion with his lordship, which might demonstrate its injustice—an event to be courted, not avoided, by honorable men dispensing death at their pleasure. It occasioned no little surprise, that Lord Rawdon, who had been deemed scrupulously observant of the nice bearings of honor, should have provoked a system of retaliation, in the unpleasant consequences of which he could not participate, being about to depart forever from the theatre of action! *

All these considerations, combined with the actual condition of two of their comrades, produced a meeting of the British officers in Charleston, who presented a memorial to the commandant, expressing their dissatisfaction at the changed condition of the war.

It was reported and believed that the memorial was answered by an assurance, that the late sanguinary precedent should never be repeated; which not only calmed the just apprehensions of the British army, but seems to have influenced the future conduct of British commandants.

When the execution of Hayne was known in England, it became a topic of animadversion. The Duke of Richmond introduced the

---

* The reader will find in the Appendix, Lord Rawdon's able justification of himself in a letter to the author.—ED.

subject in the House of Lords, by " moving an address to the king, praying that his Majesty would give directions for laying before the House the several papers relative to the execution of Isaac Hayne." His grace prefaced the motion with a succinct and correct narrative of the capture, condemnation, and execution of the American colonel; and charged the procedure with " illegality," " barbarity," and " impolicy." He read to the House an extract from the proclamation of General Greene, in which the execution was " reprobated as a cruel and unjustifiable murder, and severe retaliation was threatened on the persons of British officers. His grace called on the House to institute an immediate and effectual inquiry, as the only means of securing their own officers from the dangers which hung over them; and of rescuing the British nation from the opprobrious charges of cruelty and barbarity, under which it labored in all the states of Europe." The motion was strenuously opposed by the lord chancellor, the Lords Walsingham and Stormont. They argued that " as his majesty's ministers had declared that no information had been received relative to the facts alluded to, it was inconsistent with the dignity and gravity of the House to proceed to a formal inquiry on vague and uncertain surmises; that it was still less candid and equitable, on such slight grounds, to call in question the characters of brave, deserving, absent officers. But were the facts true and authentic, these lords contended that Colonel Hayne, having been taken in arms after admission to his parole, was liable to instant execution, without any other form of trial than that necessary to identify the person." The Earl of Huntingdon, uncle to Lord Rawdon, acquainted the House, that " he had authority from the Earl of Cornwallis to declare, that this had been the practice in several cases under his command in North Carolina." The doctrine of the ministerial lords was denied, with great confidence, by the Earls Shelburne and Effingham. It was asserted by the former, " from circumstances within his own knowledge, that the practice in the late war was totally different. A great degree of ignominy and stricter confinement were the consequences of a breach of parole, and the persons guilty of that offence were shunned by gentlemen; but it had never before entered into the head of a commander to hang them." The Earl of Effingham remarked, that " the practice of granting paroles was a modern civility of late date, not yet prevalent in all countries; and that the lord chancellor's quotation from Grotius related to spies, and not to prisoners who had broken their paroles." The motion of the Duke of Richmond was rejected by a large majority ; twenty-five lords voting in favor of the address, and seventy-three against it.

The arguments in opposition to the motion, are certainly feeble. Want of official information was a good reason for postponement, but not for rejection. If the principles of public law, relative to spies, can be applied to prisoners who violate their paroles, they were inapplicable to the case of Hayne; who was condemned for "being found in arms after he had become a subject." Nor is the doctrine of the Earl of Shelburne entirely correct. "Modern civility" has indeed meliorated the severities of war, by accommodating prisoners with paroles. Sometimes the indulged captive is permitted to return to his country ; at others, he is restrained to a particular town or district; and in either case, he is required to remain neuter until officially exchanged. Ignominy justly follows the violation of parole in regard to limits; but the breach of it by resumption of arms is invariably and rightly punished with death. Had Hayne been guilty of this offence, his execution would have been indisputably just; but the virtuous American neither was nor could be charged with infraction of parole by resumption of arms. The parole, under which he retired to his seat after the capitulation of Charleston, was completely revoked by the order to repair to that city, and by the surrender of his person to the British commandant. He was then permitted to return to his family, not as a prisoner on parole, but as a British subject; of which character the reconquest by Greene entirely divested him, and restored him to his country, his liberty, and duty.

The ship in which Lord Rawdon embarked for England, was captured by some of the French cruisers, and brought into the Chesa-peake. Soon afterward the propitious termination of the siege of York placed in our hands the Earl of Cornwallis. Washington had it now in his power to execute the intention of Greene ; but the change in the demeanor of the British commanders, and the evident and fast approach of peace, rendered the severe expedient unnecessary. He therefore indulged his love of lenity, and conformed his conduct to the mild temper of the United States; forgiving an atrocity, which at any other period of the war, would not have been overlooked.

Relieved as must have been Lord Rawdon and Colonel Balfour, not more by the decision of the House of Lords, than by the clemency of the American commander-in-chief, they could not, with propriety, infer from either circumstance, justification of their conduct. The rejection of the Duke of Richmond's motion grew out of considerations foreign to the real merits of the subject; and the lenity of Washington may be truly ascribed to an unwillingness to stain the era of victory and returning amity with the blood even of the guilty.

Had this principle, as amiable as wise, governed Lord Rawdon and Colonel Balfour, their fame would not have been tarnished by the blood of an estimable individual, wantonly and unnecessarily shed. How unlike the conduct of these commanders was that of the American chieftain to the unfortunate André! At a period of the war, when a strict and stern execution of martial law was indispensable, the interposition of Sir Henry Clinton in behalf of an acknowledged spy was received by Washington with patience and with tenderness; and every argument, which the British general and his commissioners could suggest, was respectfully weighed. But in the closing of the war, when true policy and the mild tenets of Christianity alike urged oblivion and good will, Lord Rawdon and Colonel Balfour hurried an innocent American to the gallows, and cruelly interdicted previous communication with the general!

CHAPTER XXXIII.

Greene approaches Stewart.—Disperses his proclamation in regard to Hayne.—Is joined by Pickens, Col. Henderson, and by Marion.—Battle of the Eutaws.—British take post at Monk's Corner.—Greene retires to High Hills.—Marion to protect the country south of the Congaree.—Leslie to command the British in the Carolinas and Georgia.

The deliberate resolve of Greene, guaranteed by the solemn and spontaneous pledge of his officers, changed the character of the war, and presented death to the soldier in the most ignominious form. Death, in the field of battle, has no terror for the brave; to expire on the gibbet shocks all the noble and generous feelings.

Major André's letter, when condemned as a spy, emphatically delineates this horror; and paints in vivid colors, sensations common to every soldier.*

* COPY OF A LETTER FROM MAJOR ANDRÉ TO GENERAL WASHINGTON, DATED TAPPAN, OCTOBER 1, 1780.

SIR: Buoyed above the terror of death, by the consciousness of a life devoted to honorable pursuits, and stained with no action that can give me remorse, I trust that the request I make to your excellency at this serious period, and which is to soften my last moments, will not be rejected.

Nevertheless the army exhibited on its march the highest spirit, with zealous anxiety to reach the foe; and conscious of the justice of the measure adopted by their general, with one feeling cheerfully submitted to its consequences.

Proceeding by easy marches, Greene crossed the Wateree near Camden; but still separated from the enemy by the Congaree, he was obliged to make a long and circuitous march to gain its southern bank, which placed him safe from the possibility of insult while in the act of passing the river.

Copies of the proclamation heretofore issued were distributed throughout the country, as well as forwarded to the hostile head-quarters, and to Charleston; that the enemy, being duly apprised of the determination of the American general, might without delay arrest its execution by suitable explanation and atonement. No attempt of this sort was made, and no doubt remained that the menaced retaliation would take effect as soon as fit subjects for its application should fall into our hands.

Having reached the neighborhood of Friday's Ferry, the army passed the Congaree at Howell's; having been joined by Brigadier Pickens, with his militia, and by Lieutenant-Colonel Henderson, of the South Carolina line, with a small body of State infantry lately raised.

The two armies being now on the same side of the river, Lieutenant-Colonel Lee, with his Legion and the corps of Henderson, was detached in advance, followed by the main body in supporting distance.

Greene continued to pursue his march with unvarying attention to the ease and comfort of his troops; preserving unimpaired their strength by witholding them from exposure to the midday sun, which continued to be keen and morbid.

As the van approached Motte's, the exploring cavalry under Captain O'Neal fell in with a light party of the enemy detached for the purpose of procuring intelligence. These were all killed or

Sympathy toward a soldier will surely induce your excellency, and a military tribunal, to adapt the mode of my death to the feelings of a man of honor.

Let me hope, sir, that if aught in my character impresses you with esteem toward me,—if aught in my misfortunes marks me as the victim of policy, and not of resentment,—I shall experience the operation of these feelings in your breast, by being informed that I am not to die on a gibbet.

I have the honor to be,
Your excellency's most obedient and most humble servant,
JOHN ANDRÉ,
Adjutant-General to the British army.

taken. From the prisoners we learned that Colonel Stewart, when informed of Greene's passage of the Wateree and movement toward Friday's Ferry, broke up from his position, and retired down the Santee for the purpose of meeting a convoy from Charleston, and of establishing himself near Nelson's Ferry on that river, which information was forthwith communicated to the general. Persevering in his plan of forcing the enemy to confine himself to the region bordering on the sea, after a few days' halt in the vicinity of Motte's, waiting for the junction of Brigadier Marion, then on his return from the Edisto, he again advanced. Lieutenant-Colonel Lee, still preceding the army, soon found that Stewart had sat down at the Eutaw Springs, forty miles below his late position, where the convoy from Charleston had arrived. This intelligence was dispatched to Greene, who was disposed to stimulate further retreat; his sole object being the recovery of the country, which, though determined to effect, he preferred doing without further waste of blood. Lee was accordingly instructed to announce rather than conceal the advance of the American army, in order that Stewart might, if he chose, fall back a second time. During our march on the 5th and 6th the van corps met with not a single individual, excepting two dragoons from the enemy's camp, one each day, bearing a flag, with dispatches for the American general. These dragoons successively confirmed the continuance of Stewart at the Eutaws; adding that there was no appearance of change in position, and that when they left camp, it was believed that General Greene was still near Motte's post. Instead of receiving the dispatches and sending them on as was customary. Lee ordered the British dragoons to proceed to the army, with the view that if General Greene continued to prefer annunciation of his approach to the enemy, the same might be effectually done by the immediate return of the flags, with orders for their proceeding to Stewart. Inasmuch as no attempt had been made to conceal the advance of the American army, Greene could not suppose that Stewart remained ignorant of the fact; and, therefore, in the course of the day dismissed the flags, sending them back to Lieutenant-Colonel Lee without any special directions; knowing from the discretion appertaining to the officer in advance, that he would be governed in his disposal of them by intervening occurrences. The same uninterrupted quietude continuing during the seventh, Lee became convinced, strange as it appeared, that the British commander was uninformed of our proximity; and therefore determined to retain the flags. This was accordingly done, and Greene having first halted at Laurens's farm,* encamped for the night at Burdell's plantation, within seven miles of the enemy, determining to advance at an early hour the ensuing morning. It was well ascertained that the British troops were forced to forage at a distance, and that occasionally parties were detached for the collection of vegetables as well as of forage; Lee consequently determined to take every precaution to prevent any communication during the night, believing it probable that he might in the morning fall in with some of the detachments employed in procuring supplies. The same dead calm continued: nobody was seen moving in any direction—a state of quiet never before experienced in similar circumstances. While Stewart spent the night perfectly at ease, from his ignorance of passing events, the American general was preparing for battle.

Our whole force, including the re-enforcements from North Carolina (which joined us at the High Hills) under General Sumner, the corps of Marion and of Pickens, with that lately formed in South Carolina under Lieutenant-Colonel Henderson, amounted to two thousand three hundred men, of which the Continentals (horse, foot, and artillery), made about sixteen hundred.

Lord Rawdon, as has been before mentioned, led to the relief of Ninety-six an army of two thousand,† to which was annexed the garrison of that place under Lieutenant-Colonel Cruger, part of which only was now with Stewart.

---

* This farm belonged to Henry Laurens, one of the most respectable, honorable, and distinguished statesmen of our country. He had for many years been a member of Congress, and was president of that body in a very trying period of the war. He was afterward appointed minister plenipotentiary to the United Provinces, and was unfortunately captured on his voyage by a British cruiser. On landing in England, he was sent to London, when he was immediately committed to the tower. From this confinement, and its eventual consequence, death upon a gibbet, he was relieved by the surrender of the army of Lord Cornwallis; from which era the enemy relinquished every hope of subjugation, and turned his attention with diligence to the conclusion of peace.

Laurens went from England to France, where he assisted in the negotiations which were terminated by the treaty of peace.

† Extract from "Tarleton's Campaigns"—"There appears to be an error in this statement of the force marched from Charleston. Lord Rawdon, in his letter of the 5th, to Earl Cornwallis, says, he should move on the 7th of June toward Ninety-six with the troops at Monk's Corner, and the flank companies of the three regiments lately arrived. Therefore it seems more probable that Lord Rawdon's whole force did not exceed two thousand men, viz.: the garrison withdrawn from Camden; Lieutenant Colonel Watson's corps; Major McArthur's re-enforcement; and the flank companies of Colonel Gould's brigade." Add to this the regulars of the garrison of Ninety-six (four hundred) and the flank companies under Majoribanks, between two and three hundred.

The effective force of the hostile armies may be fairly estimated as nearly equal, each about two thousand three hundred. A portion of both armies, and that too nearly equal, had never as yet been in action; so that in every respect the state of equality was preserved, excepting in cavalry, where the advantage, both in number and quality, was on our side.

The night passed in tranquillity; and, judging from appearances, no occurrence seemed more distant than the sanguinary battle which followed.

Greene advanced at four in the morning in two columns with artillery at the head of each, Lieutenant-Colonel Lee in his front, and Lieutenant Colonel Washington in his rear.

While moving with much circumspection, in the well-grounded expectation that we should fall upon the British pickets unperceived, Captain Armstrong, conducting the reconnoitring party, communicated to Lee the approach of a body of the enemy. This occurred about eight o'clock in the morning, four miles from the British camp. Forwarding this intelligence to the general, and presuming that the descried foe, consisting of horse and foot, must be the van of the enemy, Lee halted, waiting for the approximation of our main body.

The Legion infantry were drawn up across the road, the cavalry in open wood on its right, and Henderson with his corps in thick wood upon his left. Shortly the British appeared, following Armstrong. The action opened, and the enemy were soon forced in in front, while the horse, making a rapid movement under Major Eggleston gained the rear. The infantry was destroyed, several killed, and about forty taken with their captain; the cavalry, flying in full speed as soon as they saw the Legion dragoons pressing forward, saved themselves, as did the foraging party following in the rear, consisting of two or three hundred without arms.[*]

Pressing forward, we soon got in view of another body of the enemy, with whom the action recommenced. Lieutenant-Colonel Lee, advising the general of this occurrence, requested the support of artillery to counteract that of the enemy now opening. Quickly Colonel Williams, adjutant-general, brought up Captain Gains with his two pieces in full gallop, who unlimbering took his part with decision and effect.

---

[*] The rooting party, being unarmed, hastened back to the British camp upon the first fire, and therefore escaped.

During this rencounter both armies formed. The American having, as before mentioned, moved in two columns, each composed of the corps destined for its respective lines, soon arranged in order of battle.

The North Carolina militia under Colonel Malmedy, with that of South Carolina, led by the Brigadiers Marion and Pickens, making the first, and the Continentals making the second line; Lieutenant-Colonel Campbell with the Virginians on the right; Brigadier Sumner with the North Carolinians in the centre; * and the Marylanders, conducted by Williams and Howard, on the left, resting with its left flank on the Charleston road. Lee with his Legion was charged with the care of the right, as was Henderson with his corps with that of the left flank. The artillery, consisting only of two threes and two sixes, commanded by the Captains Gains and Finn, were disposed, the first with the front, and the last with the rear line; and Baylor's regiment of horse, with Kirkwood's infantry of Delaware, composed the reserve, led by Lieutenant-Colonel Washington.

The British army was drawn up in one line, a few hundred paces in front of their camp (tents standing), with two separate bodies of infantry and the cavalry posted in the rear, ready to be applied as contingencies might point out.

The Buffs † (third regiment), composed its right, resting with its flank on the Charleston road; the remains of several corps, under Lieutenant-Colonel Cruger, the centre; and the sixty-third and sixty-fourth (veterans), the left. On the Eutaw branch, which runs to the British camp, right of the Charleston road, was posted Major Majoribanks at the head of the grenadiers and light infantry, making

---

* This arrangement of Greene's second line is not correct in point of fact. The North Carolinians under Sumner were posted on the right, and Campbell with the Virginians in the centre. But when the militia of the first line gave way, the brigade of Sumner was ordered to support them, and by his advance, Campbell's brigade became the right of the second line. And after Sumner was driven back, the brigades of Virginia and Maryland, were brought up, the former on the right and in contact with the Legion infantry. In this order the most important part of the battle was fought, the charge was made, and Campbell killed; and Lee writing from memory rather than research, places Campbell on the right in the original order, because he remembered he was in that position when he fell by his side.—ED.

† This regiment was one of the three which had lately arrived from Ireland, and had never before been in action; yet, nevertheless, fought with the most determined courage. The regiment of Maryland, under Lieutenant-Colonel Howard, was opposed to it; and such was the obstinacy with which the contest was maintained, that a number of the soldiers fell transfixed by each other's bayonets.

one battalion, his right on the branch, and his left stretching in an oblique line toward the flank of the Buffs. This branch issued from a deep ravine, between which and the British camp was the Charleston road, and between the road and the ravine was a strong brick house. The artillery was distributed along the line, a part on the Charleston road, and another part on the road leading to Roache's plantation, which passed through the enemy's left wing.

The front line of the American army, following close in the rear of the two pieces under Captain Gains, began now to be felt by the van, who diverging to the right and left, firing obliquely, took post on the flanks agreeably to the orders of battle.

The militia advancing with alacrity, the battle became warm, convincing Lieutenant-Colonel Stewart, unexpected as it appears to have been, that Greene was upon him. The fire ran from flank to flank; our line still advancing, and the enemy, adhering to his position, manifested a determination to wait an approach.

The sixty-third and the Legion infantry were warmly engaged, when the sixty-fourth, with a part of the centre, advanced upon Colonel Malmedy, who soon yielding, the success was pushed by the enemy's left, and the militia, after a fierce contest, gave way, leaving the corps of Henderson and the Legion infantry engaged, sullenly falling back.

Greene instantly ordered up the centre of the second line, under Brigadier Sumner, to fill the chasm produced by the recession of the militia, who came handsomely into action, ranging with the infantry of the Legion and the corps of Henderson, both still maintaining the flanks with unyielding energy. The battle being reinstated grew hotter, and the enemy, who had before gained ground, fell back to his first position. Stewart now brought into line the corps of infantry posted in the rear of his left wing, and directed Major Coffin with his cavalry to take post on his left; evincing a jealousy of that flank where the woods were open, and the ground opportune for cavalry, in which we excelled. At this period of the action, Lieutenant-Colonel Henderson received a ball, which stopped his further exertion. His corps, however, soon recovered from the effect produced by his fall; and, led on by Lieutenant-Colonel Hampton, continuing to act well its part, the American line persevered in advance, and the fire became mutually destructive. Greene, determining to strike a conclusive blow, brought up the Marylanders and Virginians; when our line became dense, and pressing forward with a shout, the battle raged with redoubled fury.*

The enemy, sensible that the weight of our force was bearing upon him, returned our shout, and sustained himself nobly from right to left. Majoribanks now for the first time was put in motion, which being perceived, Lieutenant-Colonel Washington, with the reserve, was commanded to fall upon him, and at the same moment the line was ordered to hold up its fire and to charge with bayonet. The air again resounded with the shouts of the advancing Americans ; the enemy answering by pouring in a close and quickly repeated fire. As we drew near, Lieutenant-Colonel Lee, at the head of his infantry, discerning that we outstretched the enemy's line, ordered Captain Rudolph to fall back with his company, to gain the enemy's flank, and to give him a raking fire as soon as he turned it. This movement was executed with precision, and had the happiest effect. The enemy's left could not sustain the approaching shock, assailed in front as it was in flank, and it instantly began to give way, which quickly afterward took place along the whole line, in some parts of which the hostile ranks contended with the bayonet, individuals of the Marylanders and of the Buffs having been mutually transfixed.

The conquering troops pressed the advantage they had gained, pursuing the foe, and possessed themselves of his camp, which was yielded without a struggle. Washington promptly advanced to execute the orders he had received, and made a circuit to gain the rear of Majoribanks, preceded by Lieutenant Stuart† with one section. As he drew near to the enemy, he found the ground thickly set with black jack, and almost impervious to horse. Deranging as was this unlooked-for obstacle, Washington with his dauntless cavalry forced his way, notwithstanding the murderous discharge of the enemy, safe behind his covert. Human courage could not surmount the obstruction which interposed, or this gallant officer with his intrepid corps would have triumphed. Captain Watts, second in command, fell, pierced by two balls. Lieutenants King and Simmons experienced a similar fate ; and Washington's horse being killed, he became entangled in the fall, when struggling to extricate himself he was bayoneted and taken. Lieutenant Stuart was now dismounted, being severely wounded, and his horse killed close to

* Sumner's brigade had retreated before this took place, and was not in the charge.—Ed.
† Colonel Philip Stuart, from Maryland.

the hostile ranks; nor did a single man of his section escape, some being killed and the rest wounded. The gallant young Carlisle, from Alexandria, a cadet in the regiment, was killed, and half the corps destroyed; after which the residue was drawn off by Captain Parsons, assisted by Lieutenant Gordon.

This repulse took place at the time the British line gave way. Majoribanks, although victorious, fell back to cover his flying comrades; and Major Sheridan, with the New York volunteers, judiciously took possession of the brick house before mentioned for the same purpose; while, with the same view, Major Coffin, with the cavalry, placed himself on the left, in an open field west of the Charleston road.

In our pursuit we took three hundred prisoners and two pieces of artillery; one taken by Captain Rudolph, of the Legion infantry, and the other by Lieutenant Duval, of the Maryland line, who was killed—a young officer of the highest promise. As soon as we entered the field, Sheridan began to fire from the brick house. The left of the Legion infantry, led by Lieutenant Manning, the nearest to the house, followed close upon the enemy still entering it, hoping to force his way before the door could be barred. One of our soldiers actually got half way in, and for some minutes a struggle of strength took place—Manning pressing him in, and Sheridan forcing him out. The latter prevailed, and the door was closed. Here Captain Barré, Deputy Adjutant-General, the brother of the celebrated Colonel Barré,* and some few others, were overtaken and made prisoners. Lieutenant-Colonel Lee, finding his left discomfited in the bold attempt, on the success of which much hung, recalled it; and Manning so disposed of his prisoners, by mixing them with his own soldiers, as to return unhurt; the enemy in the house sparing him rather than risking those with him.

At this point of time Lieutenant-Colonel Howard, with a part of his regiment, passed through the field toward the head of the ravine, and Captain Kirkwood appeared approaching the house on its right. Majoribanks, though uninjured, continued stationary on the enemy's right, as did Coffin with the cavalry on the left. Sheridan, from a few swivels and his musketry, poured his fire in every direction without cessation.

During this period, Stewart was actively employed in forming his line; difficult in itself from the severe battle just fought, and ren-

---

* Member of Parliament.

dered more so by the consternation which evidently prevailed. The followers of the army, the wagons, the wounded, the timid, were all hastening toward Charleston ; some along the road in our view, others through the field back of the road, equally in view; while the staff were destroying stores of every kind, especially spirits, which the British soldiers sought with avidity.

General Greene brought up all his artillery against the house, hoping to effect a breach, through which he was determined to force his way; convinced that the submission of the enemy in the house gave him the hostile army. At the same moment Lieutenant-Colonel Lee (still on the right) sent for Eggleston and his cavalry, for the purpose of striking Coffin, and turning the head of the ravine ; which point was properly selected for the concentration of our force, too much scattered by the pursuit, and by the allurement which the enemy's camp presented. Here we commanded the ravine, and might readily break up the incipient arrangements of the rallying enemy ; here we were safe from the fire of the house, and here we possessed the Charleston road. While Lee was halted at the edge of the wood, impatiently waiting for the arrival of his horse, he saw Captain Armstrong (the leading officer for the day) approaching, and not doubting that the corps was following, the lieutenant-colonel advanced into the field, directing Armstrong to follow.

He had gone but a little way, when the captain told him that only his section was up, having never seen the rest of the corps since its discomfiture on the left some time before. This unlooked-for intelligence was not less fatal to the bright prospect of personal glory, than it was to the splendid issue of the conflict.* Not a single doubt can be entertained, had the cavalry of the Legion been in place, as it ought to have been, that Coffin would have been car-

---

* When Lieutenant-Colonel Lee took charge of his infantry, General Greene was pleased to direct that the cavalry of the Legion should be placed at his disposal. It accordingly followed, at a safe distance, in the rear of the infantry.

Being sent for at this crisis (as has been related) only one troop appeared. Major Eggleston had been previously ordered into action, and had been foiled, by encountering the same sort of obstacle experienced by Washington, as was afterward ascertained.

To this unfortunate and unauthorized order, may be ascribed the turn in this day's battle. Had the Legion cavalry been all up at this crisis Coffin would have been cut to pieces, the enemy's left occupied in force, the route already commenced completed, and Stewart would have been deprived, by the change in our position, of the aid derived from the brick house; and his army must in consequence have laid down their arms.

ried, which must have been followed by the destruction of the British army. Our infantry were getting into order, and several small bodies were sufficiently near to have improved every advantage obtained by the cavalry. Howard, with Oldham's company, had recommenced action between the house and the head of the ravine; and our troops on the right were in motion for the same ground, not doubting the destruction of Coffin, who only could annoy their flank. The recession of Lee, and the retirement of Howard, who was at this instant severely wounded, nipped in the bud measures of offence in this quarter; while, on the left, the house remained in possession of Sheridan, the weight of our metal being too light to effect a breach.

This intermission gave Stewart time to restore his broken line, which being accomplished, he instantly advanced, and the action was renewed. It soon terminated in the enemy's repossession of his camp, followed by our retreat, with the loss of two field-pieces and the recovery of one of the two before taken by us.

Satisfied with these advantages, Colonel Stewart did not advance further; and General Greene (after dispatching Lieutenant-Colonel Lee with a proposition to the British commander, the object of which was to unite with him in burying the dead) drew off; persuaded that he had recovered the country, the object in view, as well as that a more convenient opportunity for repetition of battle would be presented on the enemy's retreat, which he was convinced could not long be deferred.

The battle lasted upward of three hours, and was fiercely contested, every corps in both armies bravely supporting each other. The loss was uncommonly great—more than one-fifth of the British, and one-fourth of the American army being killed and wounded, as stated in the official returns, which intelligent officers of both armies considered short of the real loss sustained. The enemy made sixty prisoners, all wounded;—we took about five hundred, including some wounded left in his camp by Colonel Stewart when he retired. Of six commandants of regiments bearing Continental commissions, Williams and Lee were only unhurt. Washington, Howard, and Henderson were wounded; and Lieutenant-Colonel Campbell, highly respected and beloved, was killed.

This excellent officer received a ball in his breast, in the decisive charge which broke the British line, while listening to an interrogatory from Lieutenant-Colonel Lee, then on the left of the Legion infantry, adjoining the right of the Virginians, the post of Campbell. He dropped on the pummel of his saddle speechless,* and was borne to the rear by Lee's orderly dragoon, in whose care he expired, the moment he was taken from his horse.† Many of our officers of every grade suffered, militia as well as Continentals; among whom was Brigadier Pickens, who was wounded.

The conclusion of this battle was as unexpected to both armies as it was mortifying to ours. The splendor which its beginning and progress had shed upon our arms became obscured, and the rich prize within our grasp was lost. Had our cavalry contributed its aid, as heretofore it never failed to do, a British army must have surrendered to Greene on the field of battle. But they were unfortunately brought into action under difficulties not to be conquered; one corps cut to pieces, and the other dispersed, in effect the same; and the critical moment passed, before it concentrated. Had the infantry of the reserve preceded the cavalry of the reserve, Washington would have avoided the unequal contest to which he was exposed; and by patiently watching for the crisis, would have fallen upon Majoribanks when retiring to shield the enemy's broken line. Had Eggleston not been drawn from his post by orders officiously communicated to that officer as from the general, when in truth he never issued such orders, Lee would have been joined by his cavalry, ready to inflict the last blow, so clearly within his power. Both these untoward incidents were necessary to stop us from the signal victory courting our acceptance, and both occurred.

The honor ‡ of the day was claimed by both sides, while the benefits flowing from it were yielded to the Americans: the first belonged to neither, and the last to us.

Congress expressed their sense of the conduct of the general and of the merit of the army, presenting their thanks to Greene, and to every corps who fought under him on that day; presenting him at

---

* Doctor Ramsay has represented the death of this highly-respected officer differently, from information which no doubt the doctor accredited.

But as the writer was personally acquainted with the transaction, he cannot refrain from stating it exactly as it happened. The Virginians had begun to fire, which was not only against orders, but put in danger Rudolph and his party, then turning the enemy's left. To stop this fire, Lieutenant-Colonel Lee galloped down the line to Campbell, and while speaking to him on the subject, the lieutenant-colonel received his wound, of which he soon expired without uttering a word.

† Colonel Campbell, though in appearance dead, actually survived some hours after his fall, and on being told just before he expired, that the Americans were victorious, exclaimed with the heroic fervor of Wolfe, "Then I die contented." ED.

‡ See Appendix Q. and R.

the same time with a British standard, and a gold medal emblematical of the battle.*

Not a spring or a rivulet was near, but that in possession of the enemy; and the water in our canteens had been exhausted early in the battle. The day was extremely sultry, and the cry for water was universal.

Much as General Greene wished to avail himself of the evident advantage he had gained, by sitting down close to Stewart, he was forced to forego this desire, and to retire several miles to the first spot which afforded an adequate supply of water. There he halted for the night, determined to return and renew the battle.

* By the United States in Congress assembled, October 29th, 1781.

Resolved, That the thanks of the United States in Congress assembled, be presented to Major-General Greene, for his wise, decisive, and magnanimous conduct in the action of the 8th of September last, near the Eutaw Springs, in South Carolina; in which, with a force inferior in number to that of the enemy, he obtained a most signal victory.

That the thanks of the United States, in Congress assembled, be presented to the officers and men of the Maryland and Virginia brigades, and Delaware battalion of Continental troops, for the unparalleled bravery and heroism by them displayed, in advancing to the enemy through an incessant fire, and charging them with an impetuosity and ardor that could not be resisted.

That the thanks of the United States, in Congress assembled, be presented to the officers and men of the Legionary corps and artillery, for their intrepid and gallant exertions during the action.

That the thanks of the United States, in Congress assembled, be presented to the brigade of North Carolina, for their resolution and perseverance in attacking the enemy, and sustaining a superior fire.

That the thanks of the United States, in Congress assembled, be presented to the officers and men of the State corps of South Carolina, for the zeal, activity, and firmness by them exhibited throughout the engagement.

That the thanks of the United States, in Congress assembled, be presented to the officers and men of the militia, who formed the front line in the order of battle, and sustained their place with honor, propriety, and a resolution worthy of men determined to be free.

Resolved, That a British standard be presented to Major-General Greene, as an honorable testimony of his merit, and a golden medal emblematical of the battle and victory aforesaid.

That Major-General Greene be desired to present the thanks of Congress to Captains Pierce and Pendleton, Major Hyrne and Captain Shubrick, his aids-de camp, in testimony of their particular activity and good conduct during the whole of the battle.

That a sword be presented to Captain Pierce, who bore the general's dispatches, giving an account of the victory; and that the board of war take order herein.

Resolved, That the thanks of the United States, in Congress assembled, be presented to Brigadier-General Marion, of the South Carolina militia, for his wise, gallant, and decided conduct in defending the liberties of his country; and particularly for his prudent and intrepid attack on a body of British troops, on the 30th day of August last; and for the distinguished part he took in the battle of the 8th of September. Extract from the minutes,

CHARLES THOMPSON, Secretary.

Marion and Lee were to move on the 9th, and turn the enemy's left, with the view of seizing the first strong pass on the road to Charleston, below the Eutaw Spring, as well to interrupt Colonel Stewart when retreating, as to repel any re-enforcement which might be detached from the garrison of Charleston; while the general continued in his camp, actively engaged in preparing arrangements for the conveyance of the wounded to the High Hills, Marion and Lee approaching the enemy's left, discovered that he had been busily employed in sending off his sick and wounded, and that he was hastening his preparations to decamp. Dispatching a courier to Greene with this information, the light troops made a circuit to fall into the Charleston road near Ferguson's swamp, and to take post on its margin; being an eligible position for the accomplishment of the object in view.

In our march, we received intelligence that a detachment from Monk's Corner, led by Major McArthur, was hastening to join Stewart. It was now deemed advisable to recede from the original purpose, and by a rapid, though circuitous movement, to gain a more distant position, with the view of striking at McArthur so far below the Eutaws as to put him out of possibility of support from Stewart; the commencement of whose retreat was momently expected. To accomplish this arduous movement in time, every exertion was made. Fatigued as the troops were, by their active service the day before, with the long morning's march through deep sand and scorching heat, yet they gained the desired ground within the allotted time.

But this oppressive march was useless. Stewart hurried his preparations, and, commencing his retreat on the evening of the 9th, had brought his first division within a few miles of McArthur, when the light troops reached their destined point. Thus situated, to fight McArthur became rash; as it could not be doubted that he could and would maintain the action, until re-enforced by Stewart. Marion and Lee were compelled to desist, and taking post at some distance in the woods, on the right flank of Stewart, they waited until the main body passed, hoping to strike successfully his rearguard.

In the course of the morning of the 10th, the junction of McArthur was effected below Martin's tavern, and the British army continued moving toward Monk's Corner, which is one day's march from Charleston.

Gaining the rear of Stewart, the Legion dragoons were directed

to fall upon the cavalry attached to the rear-guard. This was handsomely executed by the van, under Captain O'Neal: he made most
of the rear party prisoners, two or three escaping to the infantry
by the fleetness of their horses.

So evident was the dismay* which prevailed, that Lieutenant-
Colonel Lee, not satisfied with this advantage, determined to persevere in pursuit with his cavalry; hoping to find an opportunity of
cutting off the rear-guard, with a portion of their wagons conveying
the wounded.

Following until late in the evening, picking up occasionally the
fatigued who had fallen behind, and the stragglers, he received
intelligence from some of the last taken, which determined him not
longer to postpone his blow. Detaching Eggleston with one troop
on his right, to fall upon the flank, Lee, at the head of the other two
troops, moved along the road to force the enemy in front. As soon
as Eggleston had gained the desired situation the charge was sounded, and the cavalry rushed upon the enemy. Unluckily the wood,
through which Eggleston passed to the road, was thickly set with
black jack. It became more difficult as you came nearer the road,
and the rear officer of the enemy forming his guard *en potence*, gave
the assailants a warm reception, flying the moment he delivered his
fire, yielding up several wagons.

Eggleston and his troop were roughly handled; his horse being
killed,—himself happily escaping although five balls pierced his
clothes and equipments; an unexpected issue, and which would not
have taken place had not the wood arrested his progress. Lee's
squadron was very little injured, having none of the impediments to
encounter, which accidentally interfered with Eggleston. The success turned out to be useless, for the miserable wounded supplicated

---

* After the battle, Lieutenant-Colonel Stewart ordered all the arms belonging
to the dead and wounded to be collected, which was accordingly done. When
the army had marched off the ground, this pile of arms was set on fire by the
rear-guard. Many of the muskets being loaded, an irregular discharge took
place, resembling the desultory fire which usually precedes battle. The retreating army at once presumed that Greene was up, and had commenced his attack
on the rear. Dismay and confusion took place; wagoners cut their horses from
the wagons and rode off, abandoning their wagons.

The followers of the army fled in like manner, and the panic was rapidly
spreading when the firing in the rear ceased. Colonel Washington, who had
been taken, though indulged with his parole, was accompanied by two officers.
These gentlemen abandoned the colonel and galloped off, not liking present
appearances; but as soon as the mistake was discovered, returned to their
prisoner. Washington, after his exchange, communicated these facts to his
friend Major Pendleton, aid-de-camp to General Greene.

so fervently to be permitted to proceed, that Lieutenant-Colonel Lee determined not to add to their misery, and to his trouble; but taking off his own wounded returned to Marion, leaving the wagons and the wounded to continue their route.

Greene did not reach the hostile camp in time to fall upon Stewart; and so expeditious was the progress of the latter, that every endeavor to come up with him with the main body, was nugatory.

The British army took post at Monk's Corner, and General Greene returned to Eutaw Spring. Here he found some of the enemy's wounded,—left because their condition forbade moving,—with some of his own in the same situation. The necessary arrangements being made for the care and comfort of these unfortunate individuals, the American general proceeded by easy marches to our favorite camp, the High Hills of Santee.

This retirement from the field became indispensable; not only because of our diminished force from the severe battle lately fought, but disease had resumed its wasting havoc, brought on by the forty-eight hours' hard service; throughout which we were exposed to the sultry sun during the day, and to the heavy dew during the night. Never had we experienced so much sickness at any one time as we did now; nor was it confined to new levies, as was customary, but affected every corps; even those most inured to military life, and most accustomed to the climate. Nearly one-half of the army was disabled by wounds or fever, and among the last some of the best officers who had escaped in the action. General Greene happily enjoyed his usual health, and softened our misery by his care and attention. Litters were provided for those most afflicted, and all the comforts which the country afforded were collected and reserved for the exclusive use of the sick and wounded. On the 18th we reached the High Hills, when permanent arrangements were adopted for the accommodation of the wounded, for checking the spread of disease, and for the plentiful supply of wholesome provisions. Marion and his militia, being habituated to the swamps of Pedee, were less affected by the prevailing fever, and continued on the south of the Congaree, to protect the country from the predatory excursions of the enemy.

The British army did not escape the insalubrity of the season and climate, and, like its adversaries, was held quiet in quarters their chief attention, too, being called to the restoration of the sick and wounded.

Upon Lord Rawdon's sailing for Europe, Cornwallis appointed

Major-General Leslie, then serving under him in Virginia, to the command of the British troops in the Carolinas and Georgia; but this officer did not reach Charleston for some weeks after the battle of the Eutaws.

CHAPTER XXXIV.

De Grasse informs Washington of his intended co-operation.—Depressed state of our resources.—Robert Morris made superintendent of finance.—A National Bank established.—Credit restored.—Junction of the French and American armies at Dobb's Ferry.—They prepare to strike at New York.—Washington turns his attention toward Cornwallis.—De Barras sails for the Chesapeake. Also De Grasse. —Battle between the French and English fleets.

A NEW scene now opened upon the American theatre. The expectation announced by the commander-in-chief to the general in the South, previous to our decampment from the High Hills of Santee, became confirmed in the course of the last month. Admiral Count De Barras, the French naval commander on this station, communicated officially to General Washington, the resolution taken by the Count De Grasse, commanding the French fleet in the West Indies, of sailing from Cape François, in St. Domingo, for the Chesapeake, on the 3d of August with a powerful fleet, having on board three thousand land forces. Charmed with the prospect of being enabled at length to act with the vigor congenial with his disposition, Washington hastened his preparations to invest New York, as soon as the fleet of his most Christian majesty should arrive. Nothing was wanting but one decisive stroke to put an end to the war, which his daily experience of the embarrassments attendant upon all the measures of Congress, convinced him was at this time indispensable to our final success. The nation was absolutely wearied out; voluntary enlistments to fill up our ranks, had long since yielded to the enrolment of drafts from the militia for short periods of service, and this last resort had proved very inadequate. Reduced as had been our number of regiments, in consequence of the insufficiency of the annual supply of men, yet they remained incomplete. When Washington took the field in June, his whole force (including the army under La Fayette, the garrison of West Point, and a detachment of the New York line under Brigadier Clinton, posted on the frontier of that State) amounted to something more than eight thousand. His effective force, ready to act under his immediate orders, is rated at four thousand five hundred.

Such was the humble condition of the main army, after the most judicious, active, and persevering efforts of the commander-in-chief throughout the winter and spring, supported by Congress, to bring into the field a respectable force.

Diminutive as our army was, yet our capacity to subsist it was more so. Occasionally its separation became inevitable, to secure daily food; and therefore we may congratulate ourselves that our ranks were not crowded. The four Eastern States, upon this, as upon many previous urgent occasions, took effectual measures to provide and to transport all the necessary supplies within their reach; these consisted of meat, salt, and liquor. Bread was still wanting; and this was procurable only from Pennsylvania and Maryland, so completely exhausted were the two States of New York and New Jersey; having been, from 1776, the continued seat of war.

The wicked and stupid system of coercion had been pushed to its extreme, and was at length necessarily abandoned; having become as unproductive as it had always been irritating. We had no money; as our paper notes (so called) had lost every semblance of coin, except the name, and the credit of the United States had become the general topic of derision.

Tender laws had been enacted to support it; but the more we attempted to compel the coy dame, the faster she withdrew from our embrace. Our credit became extinct; and having nothing but depreciated paper to offer in payment, poverty and distrust overspread the land.

In this distressing crisis, Congress came to the wise resolution of stopping the emission of paper, and substituted an annual requisition on the States for the means of supporting the war. Even this last resource failed to produce the intended effect, the States neglecting the calls of the federal head. Confusion and disorder had reached its height; and Washington himself, the last to despond, began to apprehend that we should fail in profiting from the effectual and timely aid proffered by our ally, through our own incapacity and impotence.

Soon after Congress adopted the resolution above mentioned, the finances of the nation were committed to the superintendence of an individual,—a wise reform too long delayed.

Robert Morris, of Philadelphia, a member of Congress from Pennsylvania, possessing a mind penetrating and indefatigable,— who had passed from early life through the various grades of commercial pursuits, as distinguished by his enterprise and system, as by the confidence which his probity and punctuality had established,—was happily selected to fill this arduous station.

Compelled by the confusion and want which everywhere existed, he entered upon the duties of his office sooner than he intended; having on his acceptance stipulated for a limited suspension, with the view of completing satisfactorily the various prerequisite arrangements.

Discarding considerations forcibly applying to his own reputation in this threatening conjuncture, he immediately assumed his new station, giving his entire attention to the restoration of credit. Promulgating his determination to meet with punctuality every engagement, he was sought with eagerness by all who had the means of supplying the public wants. The scene changed; to purchase now, as heretofore to sell, was considered the favor bestowed. Faithfully performing his promise, our wants began to disappear, and the military operations no longer were suspended by the want of necessary means.

To facilitate his efforts he very soon proposed to Congress the formation of a national bank, which expedient was immediately adopted; and this institution became a powerful engine to smooth the difficulties in his way. Nor was he less sagacious than fortunate in his measures to bring into use the annual contribution of Pennsylvania to the federal treasury, by undertaking to pay for the State the requisitions of Congress, on being authorized to receive the taxes imposed by the legislature to meet the demand. This masterly negotiation secured bread to the troops, the last important supply yet wanting, after the patriotic and successful efforts of the four New England States to furnish the other articles.

Strong in his personal credit, and true to his engagements, the superintendent became firmer every day in the public confidence; and unassisted, except by a small portion of a small loan* granted by the court of Versailles to the United States, this individual citizen gave food and motion to the main army; proving by his conduct, that credit is the offspring of integrity, economy, system, and punctuality.

The apprehensions which had retarded for a time the contemplated movements of the army vanishing, Washington crossed from the western to the eastern side of the Hudson River, having pre-

* Six millions of livres tournais, a part of which was applied to the purchase of clothing for our army, and the balance was obtained by bills on Paris.

viously directed the Count de Rochambeau, commanding the French army, to move from Rhode Island. As the count approached the confines of the State of New York, an officer was dispatched to him, changing his direction with a view to bring him in timely support of an enterprise on the eve of execution against some of the enemy's posts on York Island. The French general very cordially and zealously pressed forward to contribute the desired aid; but the projected plan proving abortive, Washington fell back to the North River, where he was joined by the French army at Dobb's Ferry on the 6th of July.

It having been settled to strike at New York, in a conference which ensued between the allied generals, soon after the decision of the cabinet of Versailles to co-operate by sea in the course of the following autumn, was known, all the measures hitherto adopted pointed to this object. Of themselves they were sufficiently significant to attract the attention of Sir Henry Clinton; and he accordingly sent orders to Lord Cornwallis, to detach a considerable portion of his army to his support. Before this order was executed, Sir Henry Clinton received a re-enforcement of three thousand men from England, which induced him to counteract his requisition for a part of the army in Virginia, and to direct Cornwallis to place himself safe in some strong post on the Chesapeake during the approaching equinox, ready to resume offensive operations as soon as it should blow over. Deficient as Washington was in the strength of his army, and apprised that Sir Henry Clinton, although holding in New York only four thousand five hundred regulars (exclusive of his late re-enforcement), could augment his force with six thousand of the militia in the city and its environs; he began to turn his attention to a secondary object, lest he might find the first impracticable. The army of Cornwallis was the next in order as in consequence. He therefore advised La Fayette, in Virginia, of the probability of this result; directing him to take his measures in time to prevent Cornwallis's return to North Carolina, should his lordship, apprehending the intended blow, attempt to avoid it by the abandonment of Virginia.

Washington, now at the head of the allied army, for the first time during the war, held a force capable of continued offence.

His effective strength was not more than nineteen thousand;[*]

---

[*] Congress had demanded from the States an army of thirty-seven thousand men, to assemble in January. In May our whole force, from New Hampshire to

but this body might be greatly augmented by the militia of New Jersey, New York, and Connecticut, as well as by the garrison of West-Point, and by the corps under Brigadier Clinton, still on the frontiers of the State. Nor can it be doubted that he would have received every possible aid to his operations, as the great boon for which he fought came into our possession by the fall of New York. Fixed in his resolution to bring to submission the first or second army of the enemy, he pressed forward his preparations for carrying New York (the object preferred) as soon as the naval co-operation appeared. With this view, he took his measures with the governors of the adjacent States for obtaining such auxiliary force as he might require; and he placed his army in convenient positions to act in unison either against New York or Staten Island. The latter was certainly that which claimed primary attention; as its possession by the allies gave a facility for naval co-operation against the city and harbor, as important to a combined effort, as tending to hasten the surrender of the British army.

Sir Henry Clinton was not inattentive to the course selected by his enemy. He strengthened his corps on Staten Island, he strengthened his post at Paulus Hook, and he held in the city a portion of his disposable force ready to re-enforce either station which the progress of his adversary might render expedient. Washington, persevering in his decision to bring to his aid the navy of our ally

Georgia, did not exceed ten thousand; nor had we adequate supplies of provisions and clothing even for this small force.

"Instead of having magazines filled with provisions, we have a scanty pittance scattered here and there in the different States. Instead of having our arsenals well supplied with military stores, they are poorly provided, and the workmen all leaving them. Instead of having the various articles of field equipage in readiness to deliver, the quartermaster-general is but now applying to the several States (as the *dernier ressort*) to provide these things for their troops respectively. Instead of having a regular system of transportation established upon credit—or funds in the quartermaster's hands to defray the contingent expenses of it—we have neither the one nor the other; and all that business, or a great part of it, being done by military impressment, we are daily and hourly oppressing the people, souring their tempers, alienating their affections. Instead of having the regiments completed to the new establishments (and which ought to have been so by the ——— day of ———, agreeably to the requisitions of Congress), scarce any State in the Union has, at this hour, one-eighth part of its quota in the field; and there is little prospect, that I can see, of ever getting more than half. In a word, instead of having every thing in readiness to take the field, we have nothing; and instead of having the prospect of a glorious offensive campaign before us, we have a bewildered and gloomy prospect of a defensive one; unless we should receive a powerful aid of ships, land troops, and money from our generous allies, and these at present are too contingent to build upon."—Extract from Washington's Journal, published in MARSHALL'S *Life of Washington.*

in the commencement of his assault, determined first to possess Staten Island. He therefore drew large bodies of his troops from the east of the Hudson, and pushed all the preliminary preparations for vigorous operations against that island. Connecticut, always true to her principles, with the virtuous Trumbull at her head, was ready to fill up with her hardy sons, the chasm in the line of force east of the Hudson; and Washington had so often experienced the zeal and fidelity of that brave and virtuous people, that he did not hesitate in reducing his force opposite to York Island in order to strengthen himself in New Jersey.

This State had been roused to a higher pitch of enthusiasm in our just cause, by the predatory incursions often repeated in the sound since the expedition of Sir Henry Clinton for the relief of Rhode Island. She sent her fat beeves to feed us, and her willing sons to fight by our sides.

Safe on the east of the Hudson, Washington continued to augment his strength on the west.

This course of action was not only adapted to his present object, but was supported by the consideration that if events should compel him to relinquish his design on New York, he would be more conveniently situated to press the destruction of the enemy in Virginia.

In accordance with his original design, the commander-in-chief continued to increase his means of commencing his operations with the reduction of Staten Island. Magazines of flour had been collected in the vicinity of Springfield, in Jersey; to which place, about the middle of August, the line of that State, with Hazen's regiment, was detached, to cover the depot, and to hasten the completion of houses and ovens then preparing to supply bread for the troops moving toward the Hudson, for the purpose of crossing into Jersey to the scene of action. The boats destroyed by Simcoe had been replaced; and all others which could be procured were now collected at places convenient to Staten Island, mounted on wheels, ready for instantaneous conveyance, when August. requisite to transport the army to the intended attack. The last division of the allies crossed the Hudson on the 25th, and assembling in the neighborhood of Paramus, halted, waiting apparently only for the arrival of the French fleet to advance upon Staten Island.

Late communications with Admiral Count de Barras evincing that the Chesapeake had been selected by the Count de Grasse as his

point of destination, and the short period allotted by that officer for
his continuance on our coast, more and more impressed Washington
with the probability that he might be compelled to relinquish his
first object, and content himself with the second.   Therefore, while
seriously preparing to strike at New York, he never lost sight of
placing himself in the most eligible position to hasten to Virginia,
should he be compelled to abandon that design.

The force to be employed in the South, in the event of such a
change in his plan, had now passed the Hudson, with its van near
Springfield—detached thither, as has been mentioned, for the ostensible purpose of protecting our magazine of flour; but in case
Washington decided to turn his arms against Cornwallis, the advance of this corps had the double effect of confirming the apprehensions of Sir Henry Clinton as to New York, and of placing it
nearer to Virginia.   He repeated his orders to La Fayette to take
measures to arrest Cornwallis, should he attempt to retreat to the
South; and at the same time addressed Governor Jefferson, urging
him to exert all his powers in preparing certain specified aids of
men, provisions, wagons, and implements, which the conjuncture
demanded.

Never was a game better played; and the final decision taken by
the commander-in-chief to proceed against Cornwallis, grew out of
three considerations, every one of which was weighty.   The French
admiral preferred the unfortified bay of Chesapeake to the fortified
basin of New York for co-operation; the time appropriated for the
absence of his fleet from the West Indies comported more with
undertaking the facile enterprise against Lord Cornwallis, than
the stubborn operation against New York; and the expected re-enforcements of the army had in a great degree failed.   When too
the situation of the United States was brought into view—which
was thoroughly understood by Washington—no doubt could remain of the propriety of changing the scene of action from New York
to Virginia.   Year after year had the hope been indulged of receiving
adequate naval aid: at length its approach was certain.   To apply
it unsuccessfully would be productive of every possible ill; and our
debility forbade hazarding such an issue, great as might be the gain.
Necessarily, therefore, did the commander-in-chief relinquish his
first object.

This change was communicated to Count de Barras, who, keeping
his fleet in readiness, sailed on the 25th with his squadron for the
Chesapeake, expecting to find there the Count de Grasse, having in

his care all the heavy ordnance and military stores for the intended operations.

Pursuant to his plan, the Count de Grasse left Cape François early in August with twenty-nine sail of the line, taking under convoy a very large fleet of merchantmen, richly laden, destined for Europe. As soon as the French admiral had placed his charge in safety, he steered with twenty-eight sail of the line for the Chesapeake, trusting the fleet of merchantmen to the protection of one of his ships of the line and a few frigates.*

The British admiral in the West Indies, Sir G. B. Rodney, had, by his activity, courage, and success, acquired considerable distinction; but although advised by the British ministry of the intended visit of the French fleet to the coast of America, he seems to have neglected or underrated its effect. He was led to this conclusion probably by the persuasion that De Grasse never would trust the rich fleet in his care across the Atlantic to a single ship of the line and a few frigates; but that he would guard it with an adequate convoy, which would necessarily bring his force to a size within the control of the squadron under Admiral Graves, re-enforced by that now committed by Sir George to Admiral Hood, with orders to hasten to the Chesapeake; thus evincing his knowledge of the intention of his adversary. Hood lost not a moment in executing his orders, and with press of sail shaped his course, at the head of fourteen sail of the line, for the Chespeake, where he arrived on the 25th—the very day Count de Barras left Rhode Island, and the last division of the American army, intended to act against Cornwallis, crossed the Hudson.

Finding the Chesapeake empty, he continued along our coast, looking, as he passed, into the Delaware, which, like the Chesapeake, was unoccupied and on the 28th arrived at Sandy Hook. Admiral Graves, thus strengthened, although he had with him but five ships of the line fit for service, put to sea on the same day; hoping either to fall in with Count de Barras—of whose departure from Rhode Island he was just apprised—or with the French West-India fleet,

---

* To this admirable and judicious decision of the Count de Grasse, we owe the propitious event which followed, and which led to peace and independence.

Very properly did Congress take care of the relatives of the count when lately so oppressed with adversity. Sir G. B. Rodney was completely deceived, for he would not for a moment believe that the French admiral would risk such a valuable fleet with such slight protection, and therefore detached only fourteen sail of the line to our coast, which secured to our ally the naval ascendency so essential to our success.

before the intended junction could be effected.   Most ruinous would have been the consequence had fortune favored his attempt ; De Barras, conducting not only a very inferior squadron, but having in his care all the military supplies requisite for the attempt on the British army in Virginia.

He met with neither—De Barras having very judiciously avoided him by going far out to sea, and De Grasse having arrived in the Chesapeake on the 30th, long before the British admiral reached the latitude of the capes of Virginia.

As soon as he anchored he was boarded by an officer from La Fayette, announcing his situation and that of the enemy.   The count immediately detached four ships of the line to block up York River, and employed some of his frigates in conveying the Marquis St. Simon, with the French re-enforcement under his orders, up James River, for the purpose of joining La Fayette.

On the 5th of September the van of the British fleet appeared off Cape Henry.   De Grasse waited only to ascertain its character, doubtful whether it might not be the French squadron from Rhode Island.   Signals unanswered demonstrated that the fleet was British, and every moment brought into view additional strength.

The doubt as to character being removed, the French admiral took his part with decision and gallantry.   He slipped cable and put to sea, determined to bring his enemy to battle.   This was not declined, although Graves had but nineteen ships of the line to contend against twenty-four.

The opinion of the day was unfavorable to the conduct of the British admiral, reprehending with asperity his mode of entering into battle.   Hood, with the van division leading handsomely in a compact body, was closing fast with the adverse fleet, when the admiral hoisted the signal to tack, throwing Hood off and putting Drake with the rear division ahead.   It was contended that, excelling in seamanship, and inferior in number of ships, he ought to have supported Hood, inasmuch as he would thus have brought on action close in with the coast, which would have lessened the effect of the superior strength to which he was opposed ; whereas, by the course adopted, he indulged his adversary in gaining sea-room, the object in view, indispensable to the full application of his superior force.

If the suggestion be correct, the heavy disaster which ensued may be truly ascribed to this deviation from the track of genius. It is thus on sea as well as on land, that nations suffer by not searching for superior talents when they stake themselves on the conduct of an individual.

France and England have for centuries fought by sea and by land. Each preserves its ancient system, improved by experience, adhering, however, to first principles long established. At sea the French strive to disable the vessel by destroying the masts and rigging. The English, on the contrary, aim at the hull and press into close action, boarding as soon as possible.

The French theory seems to be supported by reason. For by diminishing the means of motion, which appears material, the ship is rendered unfit for effective action and thrown out of line; we are consequently led to conclude that victory ought to follow the French system; but experience, the corrector of human calculations, proves the fallacy of this conclusion.

England has always beaten France at sea, and for a century past a drawn battle upon that element, with equality of force, seems to be the utmost glory attainable by the latter. The English possess an advantage growing out of their extensive commerce, which must ever secure to that nation naval superiority, so long as such a state of commerce shall continue. The British sailor is unequalled in Europe, nor will he ever be matched but by the American seaman, who is formed in the same manner.

It is singular, but true, that the British genius seems latterly more to excel on the water than on the land. Whether this be the result of her insular situation, which points to the ocean as the proper theatre for private and public exertion, or whether it be accident, remains wrapt in doubt; but for a long period there has been a striking disparity in the achievements of her admirals and generals, and this disparity has become more striking during the present war.*

Formerly she could boast of her Marlborough, her Peterborough, and her Wolfe: latterly not a single soldier has appeared entitled to the first rank. Yet she abounds in good officers, and her soldiers equal any on earth. Cornwallis stands first in the last age; but his exploits do not place him alongside of Marlborough. Lord Rawdon's early service gave high promise of future eminence; but he has been permitted to waste his talents in retirement.

France, on the other hand, shines on land. In every period of her history we find her marshals, consummate in the art of war, sustaining by their genius the splendor of her arms.

* This was written before the great victories of Wellington.—ED.

It is, perhaps, happy for the human race that neither nation is alike great on both elements, or the civilized world would again be brought under the yoke of one master.*

Both fleets were now standing on the same tack, the British holding what the sailors call the weather-gage. About four in the afternoon the leading divisions, with a few ships of the centre, bore down upon each other, and fought with that determined courage which rivalry and discipline seldom fail to produce. These were roughly handled, the remainder never exchanging a ball. The approach of night put an end to this partial engagement; which, although the adverse fleets continued for four days near each other, was not renewed. Drake's division suffered considerably, so much so as to be deemed incapable of further action until refitted. One ship was so much damaged as to be abandoned and burned. The French fleet did not suffer equally ; and, having the wind for four days after the battle, might have readily renewed it.

Drawing off, De Grasse returned into the bay on the 10th, where he found his squadron from Rhode Island safely moored, with the fleet of transports bearing the battering cannon and other necessary implements of war. Admiral Graves, notwithstanding his crippled condition, approached the capes, when, finding the bay occupied by the whole naval force of the enemy, he bore away for New York.

This battle, like most fought at sea, being indecisive, both sides, as is common in such cases, claimed the victory. The British supported their claim by the acknowledged fact, that the French admiral might at pleasure have renewed the action, and declining to do so, they contended he necessarily admitted his defeat. Whereas the French maintained their title by the equally acknowledged fact that they fought for the undisturbed possession of the Chesapeake ; its possession being necessary to the capture of a British army, the object which brought them to the American coast ; and that this possession was yielded by the enemy's return into port. Nor can a doubt exist, if title to victory rests upon the accomplishment of the end proposed by hazarding battle, that the French admiral's pretensions upon this occasion are completely supported ; and, with his superiority of force, it was scarcely to be expected that a different result could occur.

* " And it came to pass in those days there went out a decree from Cæsar Augustus that all the world should be taxed."—St. Luke, ii. 1. Give to the Emperor of France the British fleet, and we shall soon read and feel a similar decree.

CHAPTER XXXV.

Washington pushes South —Sir H. Clinton falls on Connecticut.—Critique on Sir Henry's arrangements—Washington visits De Grasse on board the Ville de Paris.—The allied armies arrive before Yorktown.—Cornwallis besieged.—Retires within the town.—Col. Scammel killed.—Gen. Choisé takes command of the allied troops.—Rigid blockade of Gloucester Point.—This post strengthened by Tarleton's Legion.—Trenches opened against Yorktown.—The British redoubts carried by storm.—Cornwallis resolves to attempt to escape.—Prevented by a storm.—His surrender.—Joy at the surrender of Cornwallis.—Thanks of Congress.

Pursuing in appearance, with unrelaxed effort, those measures which indicated an attempt upon Staten Island, and continuing to point the march of his troops toward that place to the last moment, Washington suddenly turned his back upon New York, directing his course for the Delaware—having under him a detachment from the American army, consisting of Scammel's light infantry of the New England line, Angel's regiment of Rhode Island, Hazen's regiment, two regiments from the line of New York, the residue of the Jersey line, and Lamb's regiment of artillery, amounting altogether to two thousand effectives, with the French army under Count Rochambeau.

Sir Henry Clinton seems to have been so thoroughly persuaded that New York was the sole object of Washington, as to adhere to this conviction until he was assured that the van division of the allied army had actually passed the Delaware. Then he discovered that the army in Virginia was the intended victim; but, instead of instantly taking measures for its relief, he fell with fury upon Connecticut,* vainly presuming that he would thereby recall Washington from the South.

* A strong corps was placed under General Arnold, who embarking at New York went up the sound. He landed at New London, where we had a considerable collection of naval stores. This town is situated on the west side of New Thames, and was defended by two forts, one called Fort Trumbull, and the other Fort Griswold. On the appearance of Arnold, Fort Trumbull was evacuated, and the garrison drawn into Fort Griswold, where Lieutenant-Colonel Ledyard commanded with only one hundred and sixty men.

Lieutenant-Colonel Eyre, at the head of nearly three regiments, summoned Ledyard to surrender, which being refused, Eyre advanced with fixed bayonets. Never during the war was more gallantry displayed than on this occasion, both by the assailant and the assailed. At length the British made a lodgment in our ditch, and forced their way by the bayonet through the embrasures. Eyre was killed, as was Major Montgomery, second in command, and nearly two hundred privates were killed and wounded. The intrepid Ledyard, being overpowered, delivered his sword to the conqueror, who, to his eternal disgrace, plunged it into the bosom of his conquered antagonist. This bloody example was followed, and the carnage was continued by the slaughter of the greater

Never was a military commander more completely deceived, whether we regard Sir Henry Clinton's conception of his enemy's design, or the measures adopted with the view of frustrating that design when discovered.

It did not require any great cast of mind to perceive that New York or Virginia must be the destined object, inasmuch as the only force which could effectually co-operate with the navy of our ally was the army of Washington and the army of Count Rochambeau ; one of which was encamped on the Hudson and the other at Rhode Island.   The meaning of naval aid was to bring into effectual action our land force.

That effectual co-operation could not take place in the South, for there our force was not adequate of itself, and could not be re-enforced in time by the march of troops from the Hudson.   The army in Virginia, though nearest to South Carolina, could not be moved without giving up the State.   This simple and concise view manifests that New York or Virginia only could be comprehended in the concerted plan ; and it could not be doubted, from our insufficient force, that one of the two, and not both, would employ our entire strength.

This being clearly settled, as it ought to have been, in the mind of the British general, what ought he to have suspected ? and what ought he to have done ?   Certainly to have prepared in both points to baffle the attempt.

Instead of being over anxious for his own security, he ought to have been less attentive to himself, and more regardful of Cornwallis.   The post of New York was by nature strong, and had been annually strengthened, since its possession, for six years, as experience directed or leisure permitted.

Lord Cornwallis had no fortifications but those which he could contrive in a few weeks with a diminished force ; obliged at the same time to attend to an enemy near him, now almost equal in number, and to procure food and forage.   He ought, therefore, to have commanded the primary attention of Clinton, at least so far as to have placed him as safe as was practicable, with due regard to those operations intended to be pursued as soon as the limited suspension should cease.

Instead of ordering Cornwallis to take post at Old Point Comfort,

part of the garrison.   The town and every thing in it was consumed by fire, believed by the Americans to be done intentionally, but ascribed to accident by the enemy.

or some other suitable position on the Chesapeake, he ought to have directed him to select a position on one of its rivers convenient to the resumption of offensive war upon the departure of the French fleet, and safe as to himself in case the naval ascendency of his enemy upon our coast should render retreat necessary. If necessary, this was only practicable by returning to North Carolina ; and, therefore, the southern margin of James instead of that of York River, was the ground to which Earl Cornwallis ought to have repaired, and very probably would have selected, had his instructions permitted him a choice. City Point was suitable for the renewal of offence, and was convenient to North Carolina whenever retreat became unavoidable. The force to be dreaded was that under Washington ; and as soon as Cornwallis learned that the combined army was passing the Delaware, he had only to fall back upon the Roanoke, and the mighty effort would have been baffled. La Fayette and the Marquis St. Simon never could have effected a junction—(Cornwallis at City Point)—but on the north side of James River ; and that junction was not very readily to be accomplished in the peninsula made by James and York rivers, his lordship having, as he would have, an easy and adequate boat conveyance across the James River.

The safe route of junction was circuitous. St. Simon landing at West Point on York River, from thence might, without chance of being struck, have united with La Fayette in the vicinity of Richmond ; or, passing the river there, proceeded to Petersburg, had the American general taken that position for the purpose of arresting Cornwallis's retreat. The progress of St. Simon could not have been concealed from the British general, nor could that of the commander-in-chief, as well as the disposition made by La Fayette. In his camp at City Point he would with ease have outstripped the two first, and, forcing La Fayette from his front, made good his passage of the Roanoke, before, strengthened by St. Simon, La Fayette could have approached him. Even had they closed upon him, he was nearly equal to them both, and at the head of troops inured to hard service, and familiar with battle.

Washington, finding the enemy out of reach,* would have retraced his steps ; and the French admiral, foiled in his expectations, would have returned as soon as St. Simon could reach the fleet.

---

* Washington's solicitude to take care of West Point was unceasing, and would have infallibly recalled him to its vicinity, as soon as he despaired of overtaking Cornwallis.

Had a Turenne or a Marlborough, a Condé or a Wolfe,[*] commanded at New York, City Point or Bermuda Hundred, and not Little York, would have been the position of the hostile army in Virginia.

The allied army pressed its march with all possible dispatch; and the van division reaching Elkton, embarked in transports collected for its conveyance. The centre division continued its march to Baltimore, where it also embarked; and the remainder of the troops and some of the baggage proceeded by land through Alexandria and Fredericksburg.

<small>September.</small>

Washington having finished his arrangements for the movement to Virginia, hastened to the theatre of action, accompanied by the Count Rochambeau.

He arrived at Williamsburg, now the head-quarters of La Fayette, on the fourteenth; and proceeded to Hampton, attended by the Generals Rochambeau, Knox, Chatelleux, and Du Portail, went on board the Ville de Paris, when the plan of siege was concerted with the Count de Grasse. Some difficulty occurred in preventing the count from quitting the Chesapeake to block up the enemy's fleet in the harbor of New York, a measure which seems to have fastened itself upon his mind.

This decision was founded upon information he had just received of the arrival of Admiral Digby with six ships of the line, which induced him to conclude that he should be soon visited a second time by his enemy; and, therefore, he determined to quit the Chesapeake, preferring to hold the hostile fleet in its own port, rather than to be shut up himself.

There seems to be a palpable contradiction in the conduct of the admiral when late close to his enemy off the capes of Virginia and his present decision. He held the wind, as has been mentioned, for four days after the action; which, though not a decisive circumstance, was certainly favorable to him, and yet he would not renew the battle, but wisely determining to avoid hazarding the great object in view, drew off from his crippled adversary, and regained the Chesapeake. Now when the preparations for the execution of

---

[*] This superior soldier fell in the important victory which he gained on the Heights of Abraham in the year 1759, when he was thirty-six years of age. Had he lived he would have been fifty-two in the beginning of our war, and very probably would have been placed at the head of the forces sent to America. His letter, written a few days before his death, portrays his vast genius, and it is inserted in the appendix for the edification of my military readers.—See Appendix S.

the concerted enterprise were concluding, and the commander-in-chief had reached the ground ready to begin his work, the count adopts the very measure he had before renounced, and goes in quest of his re-enforced enemy—vainly presuming that he would shut him up in port, putting to hazard the sure and splendid prospect before him, and converting eventually certain triumph into disgrace if the British admiral, by his superior seamanship, by the shift of wind or any other of the incidents common to war, should cut him off from the Chesapeake ; an event much to be apprehended, had the contemplated movement been attempted.

Washington received with surprise and regret the annunciation of the count's intention ; and, discerning in it every possible ill, with no probable good, resisted the project with his whole weight. He prevailed ; and the count, relinquishing imaginary naval triumph off Sandy Hook, took a permanent station with his fleet in the bay ; resolved not to hazard for the hope of success off New York a victory within his grasp, as splendid and as powerful in its effects. To strengthen his station the admiral, having disembarked a body of marines, commenced the erection of a battery for heavy ordnance on Old Point Comfort, which is the northern promontory of James River.

The weight of Washington's character, as well as the soundness of his judgment, are both illustrated by this circumstance. The count, from what followed, seems to have been peculiarly attached to the line of conduct then contemplated, and which he renounced in obedience to the judgment of Washington. Soon after his return to the West Indies, he invested (in conjunction with the Marquis de Bouillé, commanding the army of France) the Island of St. Christopher.

Having landed the marquis and his army, he anchored his fleet, consisting of thirty-two ships of the line, in Basseterre Road. Admiral Hood, who had fought him under Graves, hearing of the descent upon St. Christopher, sailed at the head of twenty-two ships of the line with a determination to relieve the island if practicable.

As soon as Hood appeared off Basseterre Road, De Grasse left his anchorage ground, standing out for sea to avail himself of his superior force. Hood delighted with the movement of his adversary, continued in line of battle, as if ready to engage ; drawing farther and farther from the shore until he had decoyed the French admiral to the desired distance, when with press of sail he passed him with his whole fleet unhurt, and seized the anchorage ground which De Grasse had left.

Thus actually happened what Washington's penetrating mind suggested as possible, and which, taking place in the Chesapeake, would have given safety to the falling army.

The last division of the allied army arrived on the 25th, four weeks from the day our rear passed the Hudson River, and embarking at Burwell's Ferry upon James River joined in the neighborhood of Williamsburgh.

Our whole force being now collected, moved, on the 28th, in four columns, and sat down in front of the enemy, two miles from him ; the Americans forming its right and the French its left.

Lord Cornwallis, adhering to his instructions, had directed his whole attention and labor to the completion of his fortifications in his position at York and Gloucester. These were by no means perfected, and consequently still engaged his unwearied exertions.

On the side of York, which is a small town on the southern banks of the river whose names it bears, more remarkable for its spacious and convenient harbor than for its strength of ground in a military point of view, batteries had been erected to co-operate with the naval force in the protection of the harbor, and a line of circumvallation had been cut in front of the town, beginning on a small gut which falls into the river on its upper side, and terminating in a deep ravine below the town. This line was defended by redoubts and batteries, united by communications and strengthened by fosses and abatis ; and the heights on the opposite side of the gut or creek were fortified, commanding thoroughly the gorge of land made by the river and the creek.

In front of the intrenchments surrounding the town, the last resort of the British general, was another line of redoubts and field-works, judiciously arranged to co-operate with the army in battle, should the allies determine to force it to withdraw from the field.

Gloucester Point, opposite to Yorktown, was also fortified ; not only as a necessary appendage to York, and contributing to the protection of the harbor, but as it was convenient to a fertile country where forage for the cavalry might be abundantly procured and afforded the most likely point of junction for the promised relief. Here the works were finished, and the post was committed to Lieutenant-Colonel Dundas, with a few infantry and all the cavalry.

Under cover of the outer range of protection Cornwallis was encamped, flattering himself in the presumption that his enemy, trusting to his superior numbers and solicitous to hasten his submission, would attempt by storm to dislodge him. He entertained the hope that, supported as he was by his redoubts and *flèches,* he should be able to withstand the assault; and might, by the intervention of some of those lucky incidents which often happen in battle, strike his enemy so seriously as to retard considerably, if not defer forever, his approaches. No opportunity was allowed for the indulgence of this expectation; and the character of Washington forbade much reliance on this hope, as he was never known to commit to the caprice of fortune what was attainable by obedience to the mandate of reason.

In the course of the evening a messenger arrived from Sir Henry Clinton with dispatches to his lordship, dated the 24th, communicating the result of a council of war, held on that day, consisting of the general and flag officers, wherein " it was agreed that upward of five thousand troops should be embarked on board the king's ships; that every exertion should be made both by the army and the navy to relieve him; and that the fleet, consisting of twenty-three sail of the line, might be expected to start on the 5th of October." Strong as was this assurance, it derived additional strength from the postscript, announcing the arrival of Admiral Digby, inasmuch as having determined to hazard the fleet and army, the determination became fortified by the accession of strength where it was most wanted.

Cornwallis, yielding to assurances too solemn to be slighted, as well as conforming to the spirit of his orders, renounced his intention of disputing the advance of his adversary; and, giving up his fortified camp, retired in the night to his town position, never doubting that the promised relief would " start"* on the appointed day,

---

* COPY OF A LETTER FROM SIR HENRY CLINTON TO EARL CORNWALLIS, DATED

NEW YORK, *September* 24, 1781.

MY LORD,—I was honored yesterday with your lordship's letter on the 16th and 17th instant; and, at a meeting of the general and flag officers held this day, it is determined that above five thousand men, rank and file, shall be embarked on board the king's ships, and the joint exertions of the navy and army made in a few days to relieve you, and afterward co-operate with you.

The fleet consists of twenty-three sail of the line, three of which are three-deckers. There is every reason to hope we start from hence the 5th of October. I have received your lordship's letter of the 8th instant.

I have the honor to be, &c.,

H. CLINTON.

P. S.—Admiral Digby is this moment arrived at the Hook, with three sail of the line.

and well assured that if it did, he should be able to sustain himself until it appeared; when, presuming that a general battle would ensue, he considered it to be his duty in the mean time to preserve rather than cripple his force.

His lordship's conclusion was certainly correct; disastrous as was the consequence of his mistaken confidence.

This nocturnal movement did not pass unperceived by our guards; and Lieutenant-Colonel Scammel, officer of the day, put himself at the head of a reconnoitring party with the dawn of light, to ascertain its character and extent. Advancing close to the enemy's position, he fell in with a detachment of the Legion dragoons, who instantly charged our party.

In the rencounter, Scammel was mortally wounded and taken. He soon expired. This was the severest blow experienced by the allied army throughout the siege: not an officer in our army surpassed in personal worth and professional ability this experienced soldier.

He had served from the commencement of the war in the line of New Hampshire;* and when Colonel Pickering, adjutant-general of the army, succeeded General Greene as quartermaster-general, Lieutenant-Colonel Scammel was selected by the commander-in-chief to fill that important and confidential station—from which post he had lately retired, for the purpose of taking an active part, at the head of a battalion of light troops, in the meditated operation.

When the allies moved from Williamsburgh, General Choisé (of the army of Count Rochambeau), attended by the infantry of the Duke de Lauzun's Legion, which had disembarked on the 23d, was detached across York River to take command of the corps in front of Gloucester Point, with orders to stop effectually the supplies still partially collected from the country by the enemy.

General Choisé reached on the next day the camp of Weedon, and took the command of the combined troops.

The Duke de Lauzun, with his cavalry, had re-enforced General Weedon some days before. Joined now by his infantry, and

---

At a venture, without knowing whether they can be seen by us, I request, that, if all is well, upon hearing a considerable firing toward the entrance of the Chesapeake, three large separate smokes may be made parallel to it; and if you possess the post of Gloucester, four.

I shall send another runner soon.   H. CLINTON.

* He was a native of Massachusetts.

strengthened by a select battalion under Lieutenant-Colonel Mercer, this corps composed (under the orders of the duke) the van of Choisé, who prepared forthwith to establish himself close to Gloucester. He was again re-enforced by one thousand of the French marines; which, added to the Legion of Lauzun (about seven hundred, horse and foot), and to the militia of Weedon, gave a total of three thousand five hundred effectives. On the evening of the 2d of October, the post of Gloucester was strengthened by Lieutenant-Colonel Tarleton, with his Legion and mounted infantry. Lieutenant-Colonel Dundas moved with the dawn on the morning of the 3d, at the head of a great portion of his garrison, to make a grand forage. The wagons and bathorses were loaded three miles from Gloucester before ten o'clock, when the infantry covering them commenced their return. On the same morning, and at an early hour, the corps of Choisé was put in motion, for the execution of his plan of close investiture. Count Dillon, with a squadron of Lauzun's dragoons and Mercer's infantry, took the York River road; while General Choisé, with the main body of his infantry, seconded by Brigadier Weedon, and preceded by the Duke de Lauzun with the remainder of his cavalry, moved on the Severn road. These two roads unite in a long lane, nearly four miles from Gloucester, with inclosed fields on each side. Passing through the lane, you arrive at an open field on your right and a copse of wood on your left, lining the road for half a mile, where it terminated at a small redoubt facing the road.

Choisé, in his advance, was informed that the enemy's cavalry were in front; and being desirous of striking them, he pressed forward with his horse, ordering Dillon and Lieutenant-Colonel Mercer to hasten their junction with him. The rapid push of the cavalry left the main body of our infantry far in the rear; Mercer's corps only was in supporting distance.

Dillon, with his cavalry, met the general, with the Duke de Lauzun, at the mouth of the lane. The united body of dragoons advanced down the lane, through which the British cavalry had just passed, proceeding leisurely toward camp, to give convenient time for the foraging party's return to Gloucester, when Lieutenant Cameron, commanding the rear-guard, communicated the appearance of the French dragoons. This was soon confirmed by the approach of our van; upon which the main body of the enemy's horse halted and formed in the wood. Lieutenant-Colonel Tarleton advanced with a part of his horse upon us, and was instantly charged by the

French cavalry, when one of the enemy's horses was wounded by a spear,* and plunging overthrew Tarleton's horse.

The main body of the British horse pressed forward to support their commandant, but could not force the French dragoons. Falling back they were pursued by our cavalry, and took shelter under cover of their infantry, arrayed in the wood on one side, and along a post and rail fence on the other side of the road.

This line of infantry opened their fire, and Choisé in his turn receded, but slowly, and in good order. The infantry pressing forward under cover of the wood, and incessantly delivering their fire, galled us considerably; when the French general discovering the corps of Mercer just emerging out of the lane, threw himself by a rapid evolution into its rear, and faced about to renew the conflict.

Tarleton having rallied his cavalry, hastened up to the infantry, still advancing in the woods, and, resting his right flank upon its left, came forward in point of time just as Mercer entered through the lane into the field. Mercer instantly deployed, stretching his left into the woods, and opened his fire upon the horse opposite to his right, and upon the infantry in front of his left.

No regular corps could have maintained its ground more firmly than this battalion of our infantry. It brought the enemy to pause, which was soon followed by his retreat. When Tarleton drew off, the corps of Mercer had expended nearly all its cartridges. Choisé established himself on the contested ground, and commenced a rigid blockade of the post of Gloucester, which continued to the end of the siege.

Lieutenant Moir, of the infantry, was killed within a few paces of our line; besides whom the enemy lost eleven rank and file, as stated by Lieutenant-Colonel Tarleton, who puts down our loss at two officers and fourteen privates.

Choisé's infantry not having yet got up, he did not think proper to renew the attack without them, inasmuch as the enemy's whole force might be readily brought to sustain the retreating crops.

General Washington, in his orders of the 4th, speaks in handsome terms of the behavior of this portion of the allied troops, and returns his thanks to the cavalry of the Duke de Lauzun, and to the grenadiers of Mercer, which constituted the whole of our force engaged. Lieutenant-Colonel Tarleton is extremely mistaken when

---

* A part of the Duke de Lauzun's regiment (called Hulans) were armed with spears.

he supposed that the main body of the investing corps was up. The infantry of Lauzun were the first which approached; they joined in thirty or forty minutes after the enemy retreated, followed by the marines and the militia under Weedon.

As soon as the retirement of Cornwallis from his outer position was discovered on the subsequent morning, Washington occupied by a forward movement the abandoned ground, ready to open his trenches whenever the ordnance and other requisite implements should arrive. Indefatigable as were his exertions to hasten their conveyance from the transports lying in James River, only six miles from him, it was not accomplished until the 6th of October, the day after that assigned by Sir Henry Clinton for the departure of the armament from Sandy Hook destined to relieve the besieged army.

The course of our first parallel being ascertained, his working detachment took its post with the fall of night, covered by the requisite guards. Commanded to preserve profound silence, which order, applying so forcibly to every man's safety, was implicitly obeyed, no discovery of our beginning labors took place until the light of day showed them, when by the zeal of the troops they had nearly covered themselves. Cornwallis now opened his batteries, but so well improved had been the night as to render his fire unavailing. Our soldiers sinking themselves lower and lower, we completed our first parallel with a loss short of thirty killed and wounded, which fell chiefly upon our left. Before the 10th our batteries and redoubts appeared along the fosse, many of them mounted, which opening in succession, soon began to manifest the superiority sure to accrue to the besieger possessing adequate means, and conducting those means with sagacity and diligence. The slender defences opposed to us began to tumble under the demolishing fire. The loss of time sustained in bringing our cannon six miles, was amply compensated by the effects of the wise determination to put the issue of the siege on heavy metal. Cornwallis still looked with undiminished confidence for the promised relief, and wisely adhered to his plan, saving his troops for the battle to be fought as soon as Sir Henry Clinton should reach him. Yet he exerted himself to counteract our approach, by repairing in the night the dilapidations of the day, and by opening new embrasures throughout his line in support of his defences. All our batteries on the first parallel being completed, and mounted in the true style (weight and not number the standard), the fire on the 11th and 12th tore to pieces most of the enemy's batteries, dismounting their ordnance in every direction.

So powerful was the effect of our first parallel, that our shells and red-hot balls in this range of destruction reached even the small navy in the harbor, setting fire to and destroying the Charon, the largest ship, a forty-four gun frigate, with three transports.

Cornwallis saw his fate from this first display of our skill and strength, and if left to his own means, would have resorted to his own mind for safety ; but not doubting that the promised relief must soon arrive, he determined, as was his duty, to wait the timely interposition of his commander.

Washington discovering the effect of his first parallel, could he have depended on the French superiority at sea, would probably have spared the labor which afterward ensued ; for Cornwallis was now destroyed, unless relieved, or unless his own genius could effect his deliverance. The American general therefore adhering to his system of leaving naught to fortune, which labor and judgment could secure, continued to urge his operations, and in the night of the 11th opened his second parallel. The same order was given, commanding silence ; and its observance being more cogent from the increased proximity to the enemy (now within three hundred instead of six hundred yards), our trench was nearly completed before the dawn of day ; manifesting to the British general how far we surpassed, in this second effort, that zeal displayed in our first attempt, great as it was. Surprised at the unexpected condition in which he found himself, he urged with redoubled vigor the repairs wherever requisite, and strengthened his advanced works. This was the morning of the seventh day since Sir Henry Clinton was to " start" with his relief " navy and army." Cornwallis continued to believe in the assurance, and with unappalled courage determined to maintain his lines. His battery and his two front redoubts opened, and during this day his fire most injured us. Many of our soldiers were killed and wounded. Nevertheless our parallel advanced, and our batteries began to show themselves, yet his two redoubts continued their fire with severe effect.

Washington determined to silence them with the bayonet, and accordingly on the 14th directed two detachments to be held ready ; the right from the corps of La Fayette, and the left as the Count de Rochambeau should designate. La Fayette conducted in person the assault on our right, and the Baron de Viomenil that of our left. Major Campbell, with sixty men (as was afterward ascertained),

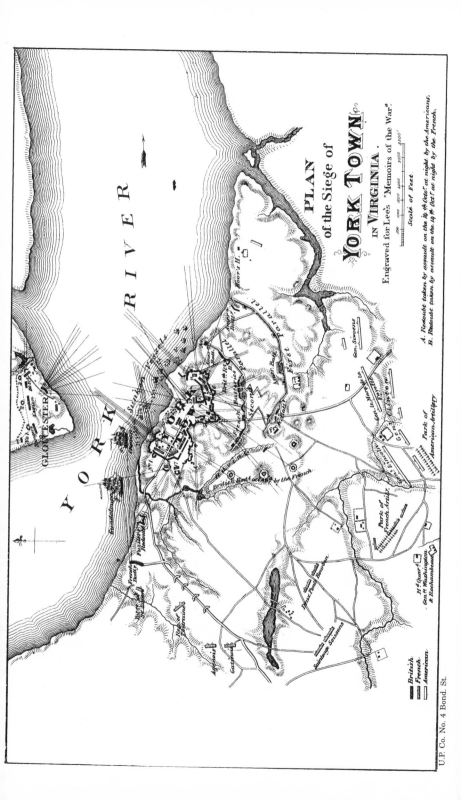

PLAN
of the Siege of
YORK TOWN
IN VIRGINIA.
Engraved for Lee's "Memoirs of the War".

Scale of Feet.
500   1000   2000   3000   4500′

A. Redoubt taken by assault on the 14th Oct.r at night by the Americans.
B. Redoubt taken by assault on the 14th Oct.r at night by the French.

GLOUCESTER

Y O R K   R I V E R

YORK

Nelson's H.s

Gen. Steuben.

Gen. La Fayette.

G.l Wayne Hill.

Park of
American Artillery.

British South attack by the French.

Park of
French Artillery.

H.d Quart.r
Gen.l Washington
& Rochambeau.

Duke Deux Ponts.

Montagne Soissons.

Agénois.

Gâtinais.

British
French
American

U.P. Co. No. 4 Bond. St.

defended the first, and Lieutenant-Colonel Johnson with one hundred and twenty men, defended the second redoubt. Lieutenant-Colonel Hamilton (formerly aid-de-camp to the commander-in-chief) * conducted the van of La Fayette, as did ———— that of Viomenil. Having removed to their respective posts as soon as it was dark, they advanced to the attack by signal at an early hour in the night.

Hamilton, with his own and Gimat's corps of light infantry, rushed forward with impetuosity. Pulling up the abatis and knocking down the palisades, he forced his way into the redoubt;

* An unhappy difference had occurred in the transaction of business between the general and his much-respected aid, which occasioned the latter to withdraw from his family. A few days previous to this time, Hamilton had been engaged all the morning in copying some dispatches, which the general, when about to take his usual rounds, directed him to forward as soon as finished.

Washington finding on his return the dispatches on the table, renewed his directions in expressions indicating his surprise at the delay ; and again leaving his apartment, found, when he returned, the dispatches where he had left them. At this time Hamilton had gone out in search of the courier, who had been long waiting, when accidentally he met the Marquis de la Fayette, who seizing him by the button (as was the habit of this zealous nobleman), engaged him in conversation ; which being continued with the marquis's usual earnestness, dismissed from Hamilton's mind for some minutes the object in view. At length breaking off from the marquis he reached the courier, and directed him to come forward to receive his charge and order. Returning he found the general seated by the table on which lay the dispatches. The moment he appeared, Washington, with warmth and sternness, chided him for the delay ; to which Hamilton mildly replied, stating the cause ; when the general, rather irritated than mollified, sternly rebuked him. To this Hamilton answered, " If your excellency thinks proper thus to address me, it is time for me to leave you." He proceeded to the table, took up the dispatch, sent off the express, packed up his baggage, and quitted head-quarters.

Although Washington took no measure to restore him to his family, yet he treated him with the highest respect ; giving to him the command of a regiment of light infantry, which now formed a part of La Fayette's corps.

In the arrangements for the assault of the redoubt, La Fayette had given his van to his own aid-de-camp, Lieutenant-Colonel Gimat ; but it being Hamilton's tour of duty, he remonstrated to the marquis upon the injustice of such preference. La Fayette excused himself by saying, that the arrangements made had been sanctioned by the commander-in-chief, and could not be changed by him. This no doubt was true ; but Washington did not know that any officer had been called to command out of tour.

Hamilton, always true to the feelings of honor and independence, repelled this answer, and left the marquis, announcing his determination to appeal to head-quarters. This he accordingly did, in a spirited and manly letter. Washington, incapable of injustice, sent for the marquis, and inquiring into the fact, found that the tour of duty belonging to Hamilton had been given to Gimat. He instantly directed the marquis to reinstate Hamilton, who consequently was put at the head of the van, which he conducted so advantageously to the service and so honorably to himself.

This anecdote was communicated to the writer by Lieutenant-Colonel Hamilton, during the siege of Yorktown.

having detached Lieutenant-Colonel Laurens (aid-de-camp to the commander-in-chief), with two companies of light infantry, to gain the rear, and enter in that quarter. The resistance of the enemy was instantly overpowered : the major, with every man of his guard, except six or seven, were killed or taken, and the prisoners experienced that marked humanity from the conqueror so uniformly displayed by the Americans in victory. This too when the horrid and barbarous outrage committed at Fort Griswold in Connecticut (in the late operations of Sir Henry Clinton in that State), was fresh in our memory. Only eight of the enemy were killed, while our own loss was nine killed and thirty-two wounded : among the latter was Captain Stephen Olney, of the Rhode Island regiment, whose zeal and intrepidity upon this, as upon every other occasion, had placed him high in the esteem of the general and army. La Fayette instantly dispatched Major Barbour, one of his aids, to the Baron de Viomenil, communicating his success. The baron, ready for the assault, was waiting to give time to the axe and fascine men to cut down the palisades and fill up the fosse ; when astonished at the intelligence received, he announced it in a loud voice to his troops, ordering them to advance. This was done with the ardor of Frenchmen ; and although here the resistance was much more formidable—the enemy being double in number, and apprised of our approach—still the intrepidity of the assailants was irresistible. The commandant escaped, leaving half his force (about sixty) in our possession; of these eighteen were killed. Our loss was severe, being one hundred killed and wounded. Thus did Viomenil honor the bill drawn upon him by La Fayette.*

Washington was highly gratified with the splendid termination of this double assault, and was very liberal in his compliments to the troops engaged ; nor did he omit to avail himself of the opportunity which is presented of cherishing that spirit of concord, good will, and mutual confidence between the allied troops, so essential to the common cause. He thus concludes his order of thanks:

---

* Louis XV., after gaining the battle of Fontenoy, dispatched M. de la Tour with the intelligence to his ally the great Frederick. La Tour reached the King of Prussia passing at the head of his army the defiles of the mountains in Upper Silesia, near the village of Friedburgh; where in a few hours he attacked the Austrian army, and gained a signal victory, which he announced to the King of France by M. de la Tour in the following words: "The bill of exchange which you drew on me at Fontenoy, I have paid at Friedburgh."—VOLTAIRE.

" The general reflects with the highest degree of pleasure on the confidence which the troops of the two nations must hereafter have in each other. Assured of mutual support, he is convinced there is no danger which they will not cheerfully encounter,—no difficulty which they will not bravely overcome."

Nothing could exceed the vigor with which our operations were pushed, so completely had Washington infused into the mass of the troops his own solicitude to bring the siege to a conclusion. Before daylight the two redoubts were included in our second parallel, which was now in great forwardness.

Cornwallis saw with amazement the fruit of our night's labor, and was sensible of his condition. Ten days had elapsed since the promised armament was to have sailed, and as yet it had not appeared off the capes, nor had his lordship been informed of the cause of the unexpected and torturing delay. Persuaded that his relief could not be remote, he determined for once to depart from the cautious system enjoined by his expectation of succor, and to resort to his habit of bold enterprise; hoping that by retarding our advance he should still give time for the arrival of succor. On the fifteenth of October he ordered Lieutenant-Colonel Abercrombie to hold himself in readiness with a detachment of three hundred and fifty men from the guards and light infantry, for the purpose of possessing himself of two of our redoubts nearly finished.

At four in the succeeding morning Abercrombie advanced upon our lines, detaching Lieutenant-Colonel Lake with the guards against one, and Major Armstrong with the light infantry against the other redoubt.

The British rushed upon us with determined courage, and both officers completely succeeded; driving out the French, who occupied the redoubts, with the loss of one hundred men killed and wounded.

This success was of short duration; for the support moving up from the trenches soon gained the lost ground, the enemy relinquishing the redoubts and hastening to his lines. We found our cannon spiked, but, being done in much hurry, the spikes were readily drawn, and before the evening the redoubts were finished and opened upon the enemy. Deriving no solid good from this his only sortie for the purpose of retarding our approach, and still ignorant of the cause of Clinton's delay, Cornwallis was brought to the alternative of surrendering or of attempting his escape. Incapable of submitting, so long as such an event might possibly be avoided, he prepared with profound secrecy to pass his army in the night to Gloucester, garnishing the works with his convalescents, leaving behind his baggage of every sort, his sick, wounded, shipping, and stores.

To Lieutenant-Colonel Johnson, the officer selected still to hold York, a letter was delivered addressed to General Washington, commending to his humanity his abandoned comrades.

As soon as he passed the river, the British general determined to envelop Choisé with his whole force, and seizing all the horses in his enemy's possession to mount his army and to press forward by forced marches, preceded by his numerous cavalry, the corps of Simcoe, and the Legion of Tarleton, about four hundred. Horses were to be taken everywhere as he passed, until his whole force was mounted. He intended to keep a direct course to the upper country, with the view of leaving it doubtful whether his ultimate object was New Jersey or North Carolina; hoping thus to distract the motions of his adversary, if not to draw him to one point of interception, when he might take his decision as circumstances should warrant.

This bold conception bespoke the hero, and was worthy of its author. Nor can it justly be deemed so desperate as was generally conceived. Washington could not possibly in time seize the northern and southern route; and without availing himself of horses, he never could overtake his foe. This aid could not have been instantly procured; and when procured, must have been limited to a portion of his force. It is probable he might, with all the horses in the camp and in the neighborhood, have mounted four thousand men in four days;* more could not have been collected in time. He could readily, by the aid of water-conveyance at his command, with prosperous gales, have transported his major force to the head of the Chesapeake, so as to have brought it in contact with the retreating foe on the confines of the Delaware, should Cornwallis have taken the northern route; but he must and would have calculated on the interposition of Sir Henry Clinton, who certainly would have moved through New Jersey to Easton, on the Delaware, ready to support the retreating army.

---

* This would have comprehended all the horses in camp to be spared from other indispensable services, as well as all to be afforded by the country; and no doubt, upon such an occasion, every horse in the neighborhood and along the route of march would have been proffered, but such a collection in four days could not be effected but by great exertions.

The American army under Heath would have followed Clinton, but in this condition of things our prospect could not be considered cheering. Clinton and Cornwallis marching in a straight line to each other, Heath upon their upper flank, and the army from the Chesapeake on the lower flank, placed our whole force in hazard. Washington would not have risked such a game.

No hope could be indulged that troops would assemble from the country through which the enemy passed, capable of serious opposition. We had seen Arnold the year before with nine hundred men seize the metropolis of Virginia, and return to his shipping, twenty-five miles below, uninjured. We had afterward seen Simcoe possess himself of the Point of Fork, high up James River, unhurt; and Tarleton in Charlotteville, not far from the Blue Ridge, almost capturing the governor and legislature of the State. What chance then could exist of stopping Cornwallis by any intermediate force from the country? Passing the Potomac, this expectation, faint always, considerably diminished. In the part of Maryland through which his course lay, a considerable portion of the people had been considered affected with an ardent attachment to the British government; and Pennsylvania, the next State in his progress, whose union with Maryland might have yielded a force, destructive to the enemy, held a population averse to war. A great body of its citizens, from religious principles, resist not at all; another portion was certainly inclined rather to aid than oppose the British general; the remainder, not more than one half, solid, sincere, and resolute in our cause, were scattered over that extensive State, and consequently could not have been embodied in season. It is therefore probable that the enemy could not have been stopped by the militia; for in addition to the above causes there was a want of arms and ammunition in all the lower country; and the riflemen west of the mountains were too remote to be brought to act in time.

Should the British general find his enemy's chief efforts directed to occlude him from the north, he would turn to the south; and what here stood in his way? In a very few days he would reach North Carolina, and in a few more he would encamp on the Cape Fear in the midst of his friends.

From this view of the country it is evident that Cornwallis would have made good his retreat, unless out-speeded by Washington. Every exertion would have been essayed by the commander-in-chief, and our willing countrymen would have contributed with alacrity to support the man of their heart. Yet difficulties stubborn and constant were to be surmounted. But we will presume that these were overcome, and that Washington, detaching Rochambeau with the army of France up to the Chesapeake, should be enabled to mount in time a superior force, and follow upon the heels of the British general.

This is the most flattering situation we could expect. He would not, could not, overtake him south of the Potomac, if shaping his course northwardly; nor could he overtake him north of the Dan, if proceeding to the south. Whenever he did approach him, action would ensue; and thus Cornwallis would be brought to a field battle, with a force rather inferior to his enemy. How much more to be desired was such change to him than his present condition. Victory gave him safety, and victory was not impossible. He fought and destroyed Gates; he fought and forced Greene out of the field with a greater disparity of force against him. The issue of the action would decide his fate. If adverse, he was destroyed; if successful, he was safe. Who, then, comparing his lordship's present condition with the worst that could befall him in the execution of his heroic decision, can withhold his admiration of a determination so bold and wise.

Early in the night the first division of the army passed unperceived to Gloucester, the other division ready to embark for the same shore as soon as the boats returned. This done, the arduous attempt would have commenced by falling upon De Choisé. But Providence had decreed otherwise: a furious storm suddenly arose, and forced the returning boats down the river considerably below the town. Day appeared before the boats reached their destination, and the forenoon was occupied in bringing back the division which had passed. Disconcerted by this uncontrollable difficulty, Cornwallis nevertheless continued to make head against his enemy with his divided force; cutting new embrasures to remount his dismounted guns, and expending his last shells in maintaining the unequal contest.

Our second parallel was now completed; and its numerous batteries, stored with heavy ordnance, opened with the day. The enemy's shattered defences, could not afford for many hours even shelter to the troops, much less annoyance to Oct. 17th the assailant. In every direction they were tumbling under our destructive fire; and it was evident that the town was no longer tenable. Washington had only to order his troops to advance to bring his foe to unconditional submission; nor would this measure

SURRENDER OF LORD CORNWALLIS

University Publishing Company

have been postponed longer than the next day had any event occurred, rendering it advisable. No intelligence was as yet received of the progress of Sir Henry Clinton; and it appeared from subsequent information that he was still in New York.

Without the hope of timely succor, and foiled in the bold attempt to cut his way to safety, the British general had no alternative left, but to surrender on the best terms he could obtain. Taking this mortifying decision, he beat a parley, and proposed by letter addressed to the commander-in-chief, a cessation of hostilities for twenty-four hours, that commissioners, mutually appointed, might meet and arrange the terms of surrender. Washington lost no time in reply; declaring his " ardent desire to spare the further effusion of blood, and his readiness to listen to such terms as were admissible;" but he added, that as he could not permit the waste of time in fruitless discussion, he required, that previous to the appointment of the commissioners, his lordship would submit in writing the basis of his proposed surrender; to give time for which, hostilities should continue suspended for two hours. Cornwallis acceded to the requisition of Washington, and without delay proposed the basis of his surrender of the two posts of York and Gloucester, with the naval force appertaining to them. This produced a correspondence,* which was concluded on the following

* COPY OF THE CORRESPONDENCE.

EARL CORNWALLIS TO GENERAL WASHINGTON.

YORK, VIRGINIA, *October* 17, 1781.

SIR,—I propose a cessation of hostilities for twenty-four hours; and that two officers may be appointed by each side, to meet at Mr. Moore's house, to settle terms for the surrender of the posts of York and Gloucester.

CORNWALLIS.

GENERAL WASHINGTON TO EARL CORNWALLIS.

CAMP BEFORE YORK, *October* 17, 1781.

MY LORD,—I have the honor of receiving your lordship's letter of this date.
An ardent desire to save the effusion of human blood will readily incline me to listen to such terms, for the surrender of your posts and garrisons at York and Gloucester, as are admissible.

I wish, previous to the meeting of the commissioners, that your lordship's proposals, in writing, may be sent to the American lines; for which purpose, a suspension of hostilities, during two hours from the delivery of this letter, will be granted.

G. WASHINGTON.

EARL CORNWALLIS TO GENERAL WASHINGTON.

YORK, *17th October*, 1781.

SIR,—I have been this moment honored with your excellency's letter dated this day.

day in accordance with the principles fixed by Washington.   Commissioners were immediately appointed: the Viscount de Noailles,

The time limited for sending my answer will not admit of entering into the detail of articles; but the basis of my proposals will be, that the garrisons of York and Gloucester shall be prisoners of war, with the customary honors; and for the convenience of the individuals which I have the honor to command, that the British shall be sent to Britain, and the Germans to Germany, under engagements not to serve against France, America, or their allies, until released, or regularly exchanged. That all arms and public stores shall be delivered up to you; but that the usual indulgence of side-arms to officers, and of retaining private property, shall be granted to officers and soldiers; and that the interest of the several individuals in civil capacities and connected with us, shall be attended to.

If your excellency thinks that a continuance of the suspension of hostilities will be necessary to transmit your answer, I shall have no objection to the hour that you may propose.

I have the honor to be, &c.
CORNWALLIS.

GENERAL WASHINGTON TO EARL CORNWALLIS.

CAMP BEFORE YORK, 18*th October*, 1781.

MY LORD,—To avoid unnecessary discussions and delays, I shall at once, in answer to your lordship's letter of yesterday, declare the general basis upon which a definitive treaty of capitulation may take place.

The garrisons of York and Gloucester, including the seamen, as you propose, shall be received prisoners of war. The condition annexed, of sending the British and German troops to the parts of Europe to which they respectively belong, is inadmissible. Instead of this they will be marched to such parts of the country as can most conveniently provide for their subsistence; and the benevolent treatment of the prisoners, which is invariably observed by the Americans, will be extended to them. The same honors will be granted to the surrendering army as were granted to the garrison of Charleston.

The shipping and boats in the two harbors, with all their guns, stores, tackling, furniture, and apparel, shall be delivered in their present state to an officer of the navy appointed to take possession of them.

The artillery, arms, accoutrements, military chest, and public stores of every denomination, shall be delivered, unimpaired, to the heads of the departments to which they respectively belong.

The officers shall be indulged in retaining their side-arms; and the officers and soldiers may preserve their baggage and effects, with this reserve, that property taken in the country will be reclaimed.

With regard to the individuals in civil capacities, whose interest your lordship wishes may be attended to, until they are more particularly described, nothing definitive can be settled.

I have to add, that I expect the sick and wounded will be supplied with their own hospital stores, and be attended by British surgeons, particularly charged with the care of them.

Your lordship will be pleased to signify your determination, either to accept or reject the proposals now offered, in the course of two hours from the delivery of this letter, that commissioners may be appointed to digest the articles of capitulation, or a renewal of hostilities may take place.

I have the honor to be, &c.,
G. WASHINGTON.

of the army of Rochambeau, and Lieutenant-Colonel Laurens, aid-de-camp to the commander-in-chief, on the part of the allies ; Lieutenant-Colonel Dundas, with Major Ross, aid-de-camp to Lord Cornwallis, on the part of the enemy. The commissioners met; but not agreeing definitively, a rough draft of the terms prepared were submitted to the respective generals-in-chief. Washington, always indisposed to risk the accidents of fortune, adhered to his decision already announced of preventing the waste of time ; and therefore transmitted the next morning a fair copy of the terms to Lord Cornwallis, declaring his expectation, that they would be ratified on the part of his lordship before the hour of eleven ; and that his troops would lay down their arms at two in the afternoon.

Perceiving that it was in vain longer to contend, the British general assented to the terms presented.* Two points had been

EARL CORNWALLIS TO GENERAL WASHINGTON, DATED,

YORK, 18th October, 1781.

SIR,—I agree to open a treaty of capitulation upon the basis of the garrisons of York and Gloucester, including seamen, being prisoners of war, without annexing the condition of their being sent to Europe; but I expect to receive a compensation in the articles of capitulation for the surrender of Gloucester in its present state of defence.

I shall, in particular, desire that the Bonetta sloop of war may be left entirely at my disposal, from the hour that the capitulation is signed, to receive an aid-de-camp to carry my dispatches to Sir Henry Clinton. Such soldiers as I may think proper to send as passengers in her, to be manned with fifty men of her own crew, and to be permitted to sail, without examination, when my dispatches are ready ; engaging on my part, that the ship shall be brought back and delivered to you, if she escapes the dangers of the sea ; that the crew and soldiers shall be accounted for in future exchanges; that she shall carry off no officer without your consent, nor public property of any kind. And I shall likewise desire that the traders and inhabitants may preserve their property, and that no person may be punished or molested for having joined the British troops.

If you choose to proceed to negotiation on these grounds, I shall appoint two field-officers of my army to meet two officers from you at any time and place that you think proper, to digest the articles of capitulation.

I have the honor to be, &c.,
CORNWALLIS.

* ARTICLES OF CAPITULATION.

ARTICLE 1ST. The garrisons of York and Gloucester, including the officers and seamen of his Britannic majesty's ships, as well as other mariners, to surrender themselves prisoners of war to the combined forces of America and France. The land troops to remain prisoners to the United States; the naval, to the naval army of his most Christian majesty.
Answer. Granted.

ARTICLE 2D. The artillery, arms, accoutrements, military chest, and public stores of every denomination, shall be delivered, unimpaired, to the heads of departments appointed to receive them.
Answer. Granted.

strenuously insisted on by Lord Cornwallis : the first, that his army
should be sent to Europe, upon the condition of not serving against

ARTICLE 3D. At twelve o'clock this day the two redoubts on the left flank
of York to be delivered; the one to a detachment of the American army, the
other to a detachment of French grenadiers.

Answer. Granted.

The garrison of York will march out to a place to be appointed in front of
the posts at two o'clock precisely, with shouldered arms, colors cased, and
drums beating a British or German march. They are then to ground their
arms, and return to their encampments, where they will remain until they are
dispatched to the places of their destination. Two works on the Gloucester
side will be delivered at one o'clock to a detachment of French and American
troops appointed to possess them. The garrison will march out at three
o'clock in the afternoon: the cavalry, with their swords drawn, trumpets
sounding; and the infantry in the manner prescribed for the garrison of York.
They are likewise to return to their encampments until they can be finally
marched off.

ARTICLE 4TH. Officers are to retain their side-arms. Both officers and soldiers
to keep their private property of every kind, and no part of their baggage or
papers to be at any time subject to search or inspection. The baggage and
papers of officers and soldiers taken during the siege to be likewise preserved
for them.

Answer. Granted.

It is understood, that any property, obviously belonging to the inhabitants
of these States, in the possession of the garrison, shall be subject to be
reclaimed.

ARTICLE 5TH. The soldiers to be kept in Virginia, Maryland, or Pennsylvania,
and as much by regiments as possible, and supplied with the same rations of
provisions as are allowed to soldiers in the service of America. A field-officer
from each nation, to wit, British, Anspach, and Hessian, and other officers on
parole in the proportion of one to fifty men, to be allowed to reside near their
respective regiments, to visit them frequently, and be witnesses of their treatment; and that their officers may receive and deliver clothing and other necessaries for them ; for which passports are to be granted when applied for.

Answer. Granted.

ARTICLE 6TH. The general, staff, and other officers not employed as mentioned in the above articles, and who choose it, to be permitted to go on parole
to Europe, to New York, or any other American maritime post at present in
the possession of the British forces, at their own option ; and proper vessels to
be granted by the Count de Grasse to carry them under flags of truce to New
York within ten days from this date, if possible ; and they to reside in a district, to be agreed upon hereafter, until they embark.

The officers of the civil department of the army and navy to be included in
this article. Passports to go by land, to be granted to those to whom vessels
cannot be furnished.

Answer. Granted.

ARTICLE 7TH. The officers to be allowed to keep soldiers as servants, according to the common practice of the service. Servants, not soldiers, are not to be
considered as prisoners, and are to be allowed to attend their masters.

Answer. Granted.

ARTICLE 8TH. The Bonetta sloop of war to be equipped, and navigated by
its present captain and crew, and left entirely at the disposal of Lord Cornwallis
from the hour that the capitulation is signed, to receive an aid-de-camp to carry
dispatches to Sir Henry Clinton, and such soldiers as he may think proper to

the United States or France until exchanged; and the second, security for our citizens who had joined the British army. Both were peremptorily refused; but the last was in effect yielded by permitting his lordship to send a sloop of war with his dispatches to Sir Henry Clinton free from search. Availing himself of this send to New York; to be permitted to sail without examination, when his dispatches are ready.

His lordship engages, on his part, that the ship shall be delivered to the order of the Count de Grasse, if she escapes the dangers of the sea; that she shall not carry off any public stores. Any part of the crew that may be deficient on her return, and the soldiers, passengers, to be accounted for on her delivery.

Answer. Granted.

ARTICLE 9TH. The traders are to preserve their property, and to be allowed three months to dispose of or remove them; and those traders are not to be considered as prisoners of war.

Answer. The traders will be allowed to dispose of their effects, the allied army having the right of pre-emption. The traders to be considered as prisoners of war upon parole.

ARTICLE 10TH. Natives or inhabitants of different parts of this country, at present in York or Gloucester, are not to be punished on account of having joined the British army.

Answer. This article cannot be assented to, being altogether of civil resort.

ARTICLE 11TH. Proper hospitals to be furnished for the sick and wounded. They are to be attended to by their own surgeons on parole; and they are to be furnished with medicines and stores from the American hospitals.

Answer. The hospital stores now in York and Gloucester shall be delivered for the use of the British sick and wounded. Passports will be granted for procuring them further supplies from New York, as occasion may require; and proper hospitals will be furnished for the reception of the sick and wounded of the two garrisons.

ARTICLE 12TH. Wagons to be furnished to carry the baggage of the officers attending the soldiers, and to surgeons when travelling on account of the sick, attending the hospitals at public expense.

Answer. They are to be furnished if possible.

ARTICLE 13TH. The shipping and boats in the two harbors, with all their stores, guns, tackling, and apparel, shall be delivered up in their present state to an officer of the navy appointed to take possession of them, previously unloading the private property, part of which had been on board for security during the siege.

Answer. Granted.

ARTICLE 14TH. No article of capitulation to be infringed on pretence of reprisals: and if there be any doubtful expressions in it, they are to be interpreted according to the common meaning and acceptation of the words.

Answer. Granted.

Done at York in Virginia, October 19th, 1781.

CORNWALLIS.
THOMAS SYMONDS.

Done in the trenches before Yorktown, in Virginia, October 19th, 1781.

G. WASHINGTON.·
LE COMTE DE ROCHAMBEAU.
LE COMTE DE BARRAS,
   en mon nom et celui du Comte de Grasse.

asylum for the individuals with him, obnoxious to our government, they were safely conveyed to New York.

At two o'clock in the evening the British army, led by General O'Hara, marched out of its lines with colors cased, and drums beating a British march.

The author was present at this ceremony; and certainly no spectacle could be more impressive than the one now exhibited. Valiant troops yielding up their arms after fighting in defence of a cause dear to them (because the cause of their country), under a leader who, throughout the war, in every grade and in every situation to which he had been called, appeared the Hector of his host. Battle after battle had he fought; climate after climate had he endured; towns had yielded to his mandate, posts were abandoned at his approach; armies were conquered by his prowess; one nearly exterminated, another chased from the confines of South Carolina beyond the Dan into Virginia, and a third severely chastised in that State on the shores of James River. But here even he, in the midst of his splendid career, found his conqueror.

The road through which they marched was lined with spectators, French and American. On one side the commander-in-chief, surrounded by his suite and the American staff, took his station; on the other side, opposite to him, was the Count de Rochambeau in like manner attended. The captive army approached, moving slowly in column with grace and precision. Universal silence was observed amidst the vast concourse, and the utmost decency prevailed; exhibiting in demeanor an awful sense of the vicissitudes of human fortune, mingled with commiseration for the unhappy. The head of the column approached the commander-in-chief;— O'Hara, mistaking the circle, turned to that on his left for the purpose of paying his respects to the commander-in-chief, and requesting further orders; when quickly discovering his error, with much embarrassment in his countenance, he flew across the road, and advancing up to Washington, asked pardon for his mistake, apologized for the absence of Lord Cornwallis, and begged to know his further pleasure. The general feeling his embarrassment, relieved it by referring him to General Lincoln for his government. Returning to the head of the column, it moved under the guidance of Lincoln to the field selected for the conclusion of the ceremony.

Every eye was turned, searching for the British commander-in-chief, anxious to look at that man, heretofore so much the object of their dread. All were disappointed. Cornwallis held himself back from the humiliating scene; obeying emotions which his great character ought to have stifled. He had been unfortunate, not from any false step or deficiency of exertion on his part, but from the infatuated policy of his superior, and the united power of his enemy, brought to bear upon him alone. There was nothing with which he could reproach himself; there was nothing with which he could reproach his brave and faithful army; why not then appear at its head in the day of misfortune, as he had always done in the day of triumph? The British general in this instance deviated from his usual line of conduct, dimming the splendor of his long and brilliant career.

The post of Gloucester, falling with that of York, was delivered up on the same day by Lieutenant-Colonel Tarleton, who had succeeded to the command on the transfer of Lieutenant-Colonel Dundas to the more important duties assigned to him in the defence of York. Previous to the surrender, Tarleton waited upon General Choisé, and communicated to that officer his apprehensions for his personal safety if put at the disposal of the American militia. This conference was sought for the purpose of inducing an arrangement which should shield him from the vengeance of the inhabitants. General Choisé did not hesitate a moment in gratifying the wishes of Tarleton. The Legion of Lauzun and the corps of Mercer were selected by the general to receive the submitting enemy, while the residue of the allied detachment was held back in camp. As soon as the ceremony of surrender was performed, Lieutenant-Colonel Hugo, of the Legion of Mercer, with his militia and grenadiers, took possession of the redoubts, and protected the hostile garrison from those outrages so seriously, though unwarrantably, anticipated by the British commandant. It would have been very satisfactory to give the reasons which induced this communication from Lieutenant-Colonel Tarleton, but Choisé did not go into the inquiry, and they remained unascertained.

Indubitably they did not grow out of the American character or habit. Rarely in the course of the war were the rights of humanity violated, or the feeling of sympathy and commiseration for the unfortunate suppressed by the Americans; and a deviation from our general system ought not now to have been expected, as the commander-in-chief was present, and the solemnity of a capitulation had interposed. We look in vain to this quarter for the cause of this procedure; and therefore conclude that it must have arisen from events known to the lieutenant-colonel himself, and applying to the corps under his command.

By the official returns it appears that the besieging army, at the termination of the siege, amounted to sixteen thousand men—five thousand five hundred Continentals, three thousand five hundred militia, and seven thousand French. The British force *in toto* is put down at seven thousand one hundred and seven; of which only four thousand and seventeen, rank and file, are stated to have been fit for duty.

The army, with every thing belonging to it, fell to the United States; while the shipping and all its appurtenances were allotted to our ally. The British loss, including officers, amounted to five hundred and fifty-eight; while ours did not exceed three hundred.

We obtained an excellent park of field artillery, all of brass. At any other period of the war no acquisition could have been more acceptable.

The commander-in-chief, in his orders of congratulation on the happy event, made his cordial acknowledgments to the whole army, which was well deserved; as in every stage of the service it had exemplified unvarying zeal, vigor, and intrepidity. On the Count de Rochambeau, the Generals Chatelleux and Viomenil, high applause was bestowed for the distinguished support derived from them throughout the siege; and Governor Nelson of Virginia received the tribute of thanks so justly due to his great and useful exertions. The Generals Lincoln, La Fayette, and Steuben, are named with much respect. General Knox, commanding the artillery, and General Du Portail, chief of engineers, in the American army, are particularly honored for their able and unremitting assistance.

On the very day in which Lord Cornwallis surrendered, Sir Henry Clinton left Sandy Hook, with the promised relief; originally put down at four thousand, afterward at more than five thousand, now seven thousand; made up of his best corps, escorted by Admiral Digby who had succeeded Graves, with twenty-five sail of the line, two ships of fifty guns, and eight frigates. Such want of precision must always blast military enterprise. Why it happened, remains unexplained; but there seems to have been, in all expeditions of the same sort, either from English ports or from those of the colonies, the same unaccountable dilatoriness, uniformly producing deep and lasting injury to the nation.

After a fine passage the fleet appeared on the 24th off the capes of Virginia, where Sir Henry Clinton received intelligence of the surrender. Continuing some days longer off the mouth of the Chesapeake to ascertain the truth, his information became confirmed; when further delay being useless he returned to New York.

In the mean time De Grasse continued on his anchorage ground with thirty-six sail of the line, and the usual proportion of frigates, hastening preparations for his departure.

Why Sir Henry Clinton should have ever encouraged his general in Virginia to expect relief, seems unaccountable. The project adopted, too late, by Cornwallis of escaping north or south, was much more feasible than the plan of relief so confidently relied upon by the British general-in-chief. How were twenty-five ships of the line to force their way into the bay of Chesapeake, occupied by a superior hostile fleet? But, admitting the improbable event; what then would ensue? Sir Henry, with his seven thousand men, would disembark up the bay so as to approach Gloucester Point, or he would land in the vicinity of Hampton; from whence the road to York is direct, and the distance not more than one day's march. To land at the former place would be absurd, unless the French fleet was annihilated—an indecisive action, though unfavorable to France, could not produce the desired end. It was scarcely possible for such inferiority of naval force to strike a blow so decisive.

The route to Gloucester was therefore not eligible; as the York River intervening, sure to be occupied by the French fleet, would sever the two armies. That by the way of Hampton, or from James River, was occluded by only one obstacle, and that obstacle was insurmountable: sixteen thousand bayonets interposed; twelve thousand five hundred of which were in the hands of regulars, all chosen troops.

Cornwallis, with his small force, could not leave his lines; if he did, Washington, moving toward Clinton, would have only to turn upon his lordship as soon as he ventured from his intrenched camp, and in one hour he must have destroyed him. Clinton next in order must infallibly fall. Acting upon the opposite principle, Cornwallis would continue in his position, and Washington would attack Clinton on his advance, midway between Hampton and York, or between his point of debarkation on James River and our lines; the issue would be the same, though the order would be reversed: Clinton would be first destroyed, and Cornwallis would then surrender.

The further the inquiry is pursued the more conspicuous will the want of due foresight and wise action in the British commander-in-chief appear. The moment he was informed by his government that he might expect a French fleet upon our coast in the course of the autumn, he ought to have taken his measures as if he had been assured of the maritime superiority which happened. Thus acting, should the presumed event happily fail, he was safe; should it unhappily be realized, he would have been prepared to meet it.

Relying upon the superiority of the British navy, he seems never to have reflected that the force of accidents might give that superiority to his enemy. Had he for a moment believed that the care of the spoils of Saint Eustatius could have benumbed the zeal of Sir G. B. Rodney, commander-in-chief of the naval force of Great Britain in our hemisphere, he might have pursued a safer course. Or, if he had conceived it possible that a storm might have torn to pieces one fleet, injuring but little the other (an occurrence which sometimes happens), he would have discerned the wisdom of relying upon himself for safety; and consequently would have ordered Cornwallis to take post on the south of James River, ready to regain North Carolina should it become necessary. But never presuming upon the interposition of any incident giving to France a naval ascendency upon our coast, he took his measures upon commonplace principles, following the beaten track, and fell an easy prey to his sagacious adversary; who, to prevent the interference of any occurrence impeding the progress of his views, made ready in time to take his part as circumstances might invite, and to press forward to his end with unslackening vigor. Sir Henry Clinton was—like most of the generals who appeared in this war—good, but not great. He was an active, zealous, honorable, well-bred soldier; but Heaven had not touched his mind with its ethereal spark. He could not soar above the ordinary level; and though calculated to shine in a secondary sphere, was sure to twinkle in the highest station. When presidents, kings, or emperors confide armies to soldiers of common minds, they ought not to be surprised at the disasters which follow. The war found General Gage in chief command in America; confessedly better fitted for peace. He was changed for Sir William Howe; who, after two campaigns, was withdrawn, or withdrew. Sir Henry Clinton succeeded; and when peace became assured, Sir Guy Carleton, afterward Lord Dorchester, took his place. By a strange fatality the soldier best qualified for the arduous duties of war, was reserved to conduct the scenes of returning peace. This general was and had been for many years Governor of Canada. He defended Quebec against Montgomery; where he gave strong indications of a superior mind by his use of victory. Instead of detaining his enemy (fellow-subjects, as he called them), in prisonships, committing them to the discretion of mercenary commissaries for food and fuel, and to military bailiffs for safe-keeping, Carleton paroled the officers, expressing his regret that they should have been induced to maintain a cause wrong in principle, and fatal to its abettors in issue; and sent home the privates, giving to all every requisite aid for their comfortable return, enjoining them never to take up arms a second time against their sovereign; as thereby they would forfeit the security and comfort which he had presented, as well as violate their own peace of mind, by cancelling a contract founded in the confidence of their truth.

Commiserating the delusion under which they had acted, he encouraged their abandonment of the new doctrines; anathematizing with bitterness the arts, intrigues, and wickedness of their rebellious leaders, against whom, and whom only, the thunderbolt of power ought, in his judgment, to be hurled.

The effect of such policy was powerful. General Greene, from whom the information is derived, expressed his conviction that the kindness of Carleton was more to be dreaded than the bayonet of Howe; and mentioned as an undeniable fact, that in the various districts to which our captured troops returned, not excepting the faithful State of Connecticut, the impressions made by the relation of the treatment experienced from him, produced a lasting and unpropitious effect. Here is exhibited deep knowledge of the human heart—the groundwork of greatness in the art of war. When we add the honorable display of patriotism evinced by the same officer, in his support of the expedition under General Burgoyne, intruded by the minister into an important command which the governor of Canada had a right to expect, and subjoin that when a colonel at the head of a regiment in the army under Wolfe, before Quebec, he was the only officer of that grade intrusted by that great captain with a separate command, America may justly rejoice in the misapplication of such talents, and Great Britain as truly lament the infatuation of her rulers, who overlooked a leader of such high promise.*

Cornwallis, in his official letter, representing his fall, gave serious umbrage to Sir Henry Clinton; so difficult is it to relate the truth without offence, when communicating disaster resulting from the improvidence or incapacity of a superior. That the reader may

* See Appendix S.

judge of this last act of the most distinguished general opposed to us in the course of the war, his lordship's letter has been annexed.*

General Greene, as has been mentioned, hoping that as soon as the army of Virginia was brought to submission, the French admiral might be induced to extend his co-operation farther south, had sent to the commander-in-chief Lieutenant-Colonel Lee, with a full and minute description of the situation and force of the enemy in the Carolinas and Georgia.

This officer arrived a few days before the surrender; and having executed his mission, was detained by the commander-in-chief to accompany the expedition, which he anxiously desired to forward conformably to the plan of General Greene.

The moment he finished the great work before him, he addressed himself to the Count de Grasse, urging his further aid if compatible with his ulterior objects. The French admiral was well disposed to promote the views of Washington; but the interest of his king and his own engagements forbade longer delay on our coasts. Failing in the chief object of his address, Washington informed the admiral of his intention to re-enforce the army in the South, dilating upon the benefits inseparable from its speedy junction with General Greene, and his hope that the conveyance of the re-enforcements to Cape Fear River would not be inconvenient. This proposition was cheerfully adopted, and the corps destined for the South, were put under the direction of the Marquis La Fayette, with orders to possess himself of Wilmington, situated fifteen miles up the Cape Fear, still held by Major Craig, and from thence to march to the southern head-quarters. It so happened, that the count found it necessary to recede from his promise; so that General Greene, much as he pressed naval co-operation, which could not fail in restoring the three Southern States completely, was not only disappointed in this, his fond expectation, but was also deprived of the advantage to be derived from the facile and expeditious conveyance of his re-enforcement as at first arranged.

The army of Rochambeau was cantoned for the winter in Virginia; the brigades of Wayne and Gist were detached to the South under Major-General St. Clair; the remainder of the American army was transported by water to the head of the Chesapeake, under Major-General Lincoln, who was ordered to regain the Hudson River; and the detachment with St. Simon re-embarked, when the French admiral returned to the West Indies.

* See Appendix T.

Thus concluded the important co-operation of the allied forces; concerted at the Court of Versailles, executed with precision on the part of the Count de Grasse, and conducted with judgment by the commander-in-chief. Great was the joy diffused throughout our infant empire. Bonfires, illuminations, feasts, and balls, proclaimed the universal delight; congratulatory addresses, warm from the heart, poured in from every quarter, hailing in fervid terms the patriot hero; the reverend ministers of our holy religion, the learned dignitaries of science, the grave rulers and governors of the land, all tendered their homage; and the fair, whose smiles best reward the brave, added, too, their tender gratitude and sweet applause.

This wide acclaim of joy and of confidence, as rare as sincere, sprung not only from the conviction that our signal success would bring in its train the blessings of peace, so wanted by our wasted country, and from the splendor with which it encircled our national name, but from the endearing reflection that the mighty exploit had been achieved by our faithful, beloved Washington. We had seen him struggling throughout the war with inferior force against the best troops of England, assisted by her powerful navy; surrounded with difficulties; oppressed by want; never dismayed, never appalled, never despairing of the commonwealth. We had seen him renouncing his own fame as a soldier, his safety as a man; in his unalloyed love of country, weakening his own immediate force to strengthen that of his lieutenants; submitting with equanimity to his own consequent inability to act, and rejoicing in their triumphs, because best calculated to uphold the great cause intrusted to his care; at length by one great and final exploit under the benign influence of Providence, lifted to the pinnacle of glory, the merited reward of his toils, his sufferings, his patience, his heroism, and his virtue. Wonderful man! rendering it difficult by his conduct throughout life to decide whether he most excelled in goodness or in greatness.

Congress testified unanimously their sense of the great achievement.* To Washington, De Grasse, Rochambeau, and to their

* By the United States, in Congress assembled, October 29th, 1781.

Resolved, That the thanks of the United States, in Congress assembled, be presented to his excellency General Washington, for the eminent services which he has rendered to the United States, and particularly for the well-concerted plan against the British garrison in York and Gloucester; for the vigor, attention, and military skill with which the plan was executed; and for the wisdom and prudence manifested in the capitulation.

That the thanks of the United States, in Congress assembled, be presented to his excellency the Count de Rochambeau, for the cordiality, zeal, judgment,

armies, they presented the thanks of the nation, the most grateful reward which freemen can bestow, or freemen receive ; and pass :d a resolution to erect a monument of marble on the ground of vic-

and fortitude, with which he seconded and advanced the progress of the allied army against the British garrison in York.

That the thanks of the United States, in Congress assembled, be presented to his excellency Count de Grasse, for his display of skill and bravery in attacking and defeating the British fleet off the bay of Chesapeake ; and for his zeal and alacrity in rendering, with the fleet under his command, the most effectual and distinguished aid and support to the operations of the allied army in Virginia.

That the thanks of the United States, in Congress assembled, be presented to the commanding and other officers of the corps of artillery and engineers of the allied army, who sustained extraordinary fatigue and danger, in their animated and gallant approaches to the lines of the enemy.

That General Washington be directed to communicate to the other officers and the soldiers under his command the thanks of the United States, in Congress assembled, for their conduct and valor on this occasion.

Resolved, That the United States, in Congress assembled, will cause to be erected at York, in Virginia, a marble column, adorned with emblems of the alliance between the United States and his most Christian Majesty, and inscribed with a succinct narrative of the surrender of Earl Cornwallis to his excellency General Washington, commander-in-chief of the combined forces of America and France, to his excellency the Count de Rochambeau, commanding the auxiliary troops of his most Christian Majesty in America, and his excellency the Count de Grasse, commanding in chief the naval army of France in the Chesapeake.

Resolved, That two stands of the colors taken from the British army under the capitulation of York, be presented to his excellency General Washington, in the name of the United States, in Congress assembled.

Resolved, That two pieces of field ordnance, taken from the British army under the capitulation of York, be presented by the commander-in-chief of the American army to Count de Rochambeau ; and that there be engraved thereon a short memorandum, that Congress were induced to present them from consideration of the illustrious part which he bore in effectuating the surrender.

Resolved, That the Secretary of Foreign Affairs be directed to request the minister plenipotentiary of his most Christian Majesty, to inform his Majesty, that it is the wish of Congress that Count de Grasse may be permitted to accept a testimony of their approbation, similar to that to be presented to Count de Rochambeau.

Resolved, That the Board of War be directed to present to Lieutenant-Colonel Tilghman, in the name of the United States, in Congress assembled, a horse properly caparisoned, and an elegant sword, in testimony of their high opinion of his merit and ability.*

November 7th, 1781.

Resolved, That the Secretary of Foreign Affairs be directed to prepare a sketch of emblems of the alliance between his most Christian Majesty and the United States, proper to be inscribed on the column to be erected in the town of York, under the resolution of the 29th day of October last.

Resolved, That an elegant sword be presented in the name of the United

* Lieutenant-Colonel Tench Tilghman had served from the year 1776 in the character of aid-de-camp to the commander-in-chief, was highly beloved and respected, and was honored by Washington with bearing to Congress his official report of the surrender of the British army in Virginia.

tory, as well to commemorate the alliance between the two nations, as this the proud triumph of their united arms. Nor did they stop here. Desirous that the chiefs of the allied forces should carry with them into retirement some of the trophies of their prowess, they presented to the commander-in-chief two of the standards taken from the enemy, to the admiral two field-pieces, and a like number to the general of the French troops. They concluded, by dedicating the 30th of December for national supplication and thanksgiving to Almighty God in commemoration of his gracious protection, manifested by the late happy issue of their councils and efforts, themselves attending in a body divine worship on that day.

CHAPTER XXXVI.

The main army proceeds to the Four Holes.—Greene moves against Dorchester.—The enemy withdraw to the Quarterhouse.—Greene's army moves to the Round O.—Marion detached to the eastern side of the Ashley, and Lee to the western.—The main army moves to Pompon.—Irruption of the Cherokees.—Enterprise against St. John's Island defeated.—Capture of Capt. Armstrong.—Wayne ordered to Georgia. —Scarcity of supplies.—Assembly of South Carolina convened.—Speech of Governor Rutledge.—Reply of the Senate.—Capture of a British galley.—Treason in the camp of Greene.—Crushed by his decisive conduct.

As soon as it was ascertained that the Count de Grasse would not take under convoy the troops destined to re-enforce the Southern army, General St. Clair was ordered to prepare for immediate motion; and Lieutenant-Colonel Lee was directed to return with the dispatches of the commander-in-chief. Hastening to the South, the lieutenant-colonel proceeded with expedition to the High Hills of Santee,—still the head-quarters of the Southern army. General Greene finding himself baffled in the expectation he had indulged, of being sufficiently strengthened to complete the restoration of the South, which he had so happily, in a great degree, accomplished; determined, nevertheless, though reduced by battle and by disease, to remain inactive no longer than the season rendered it necessary. The autumn in South Carolina is extremely debilitating as well as prolific of disease. Prepared to move, he only waited for the commencement of the cool season. The general was well apprised

---

States, in Congress assembled, to Colonel Humphreys, aid-de-camp of General Washington, to whose care the standards taken under the capitulation of York were consigned, as a testimony of their opinion of his fidelity and ability, and that the Board of War take order therein.

Extract from the minutes.

CHARLES THOMPSON, Secretary.

of the effect of the late hard-fought battle; which, notwithstanding the enemy's claim to victory, had broken the force and spirit of the British army. Nor was he unmindful in his calculations of the relative condition of the two armies, that this operative battle had been fought by his infantry only; the horse under Washington, although very much shattered, had not in the smallest degree contributed to the issue of the action; while that of the Legion had by a manœuvre only aided the van in the morning rencounter; a circumstance well known to the enemy, and which could not be overlooked in his estimate of the past and of the future. The American general being convinced that he was in effect the conqueror, conformed his plan and measures to this character.

In the severe contention of the last ten months, the districts between the Santee and the Pedee, and between the Watcree and Congaree, having been successively the seat of war, their cultivation had been neglected. The product of the soil was scanty, and of that little, all not concealed for the subsistence of the inhabitants had been taken by the armies. The only country from which Greene could draw supplies was that on the lower Pedee, and this was so distant as to render the conveyance to camp extremely inconvenient, which, added to the insecurity of the route of transportation, from its exposure to the enemy's maritime interruption, forbade resort to that district. It fortunately happened that subsistence for man and horse was most abundant in the quarter of the State to which the general was desirous of transferring the war. Although he had confidently expected that the commander-in-chief would have succeeded in prevailing on the French admiral to continue in our waters long enough for the execution of the plan submitted by him to Washington, nevertheless he sedulously applied himself in preparing for the partial accomplishment of his object with his own means, in case of disappointment. In North Carolina, Wilmington remained in the possession of the enemy. In South Carolina, he had only Charleston and the contiguous islands, and the isthmus formed by the rivers Cooper and Ashley, with a portion of the country lying between the last river and the Edisto. But in Georgia, Savannah, with a larger space of country, was in his uncontrolled possession.

With the requested aid the American general could not have been disappointed in the entire liberation of the three States; without this aid, he flattered himself with being able, by judicious and vigorous operations, to relieve North Carolina and Georgia.

To this object he turned his attention, and for this purpose he determined to place himself intermediate to Charleston and Savannah. The district south of the Edisto fitted his views in point of locality; and having been since 1779 exempt in a great degree from military operations, agriculture had been cherished, and the crops of rice in particular were tolerably abundant. This substitute for bread, however unpalatable to Marylanders and Virginians, of whom Greene's army was principally composed, is nourishing to man, and with the Indian pea, which grows luxuriantly in South Carolina and Georgia, affords nutritious forage for horse. He put his army in motion (on the 18th of November), and soon after, when he crossed the Congaree, left the main body under the orders of Colonel Williams, who was directed to advance by easy and stated marches to the Four Holes, a branch of the Edisto, while the general himself, at the head of the light troops, took a circuitous route to the same place. Correspondence in the movements of the two corps being preconcerted, Williams proceeded on the direct route to the Four Holes; and Greene advanced by forced marches upon Dorchester, where the enemy had established a post, garrisoned at present by four hundred infantry, all the cavalry, not exceeding one hundred and fifty, and some militia. This post (if surprised) could be readily carried, and such a result was not improbable. If not surprised, the general flattered himself, unless the enemy had recovered from the despondency which followed the battle of the Eutaws, that he would abandon it; and if disappointed in both these expectations, he considered himself as amply compensated for this movement, by his own view of a part of the country to which he meant to extend his operations.

The cavalry, preceding the light infantry in various directions, occupied an extensive front, for the purpose of precluding communication of our approach; which it was intended to conceal from the inhabitants as well as from the enemy, lest some of the disaffected might inform him of our advance. We marched in paths through woods and swamps seldom trod by man; and wherever we could not avoid settlements, all the inhabitants capable of conveying information were secured. Notwithstanding these precautions, and our active cavalry, the enemy received advice of our approach sometime in the night previous to the morning intended for the meditated blow.

The commanding officer drew in his outposts, and concentrated his force in Dorchester, keeping in his front a few patrols to ascertain and report our progress. Lieutenant-Colonel Hampton, at the head of the State horse (a small corps which had, with honor to itself and effect to its country, shared in the dangers of the latter part of the campaign with our army), fell in with one of these, and instantly charging it, killed some, wounded others, and drove the rest upon the main body. The British cavalry sallied out in support, but declining combat, soon retired.

Disappointed in the hoped-for surprise, the general continued to examine the enemy's position, desirous of executing by force, what he hoped to have accomplished by stratagem. In the course of the day the presence of Greene became known to the foe, who instantly prepared for departure. He destroyed his stores of every sort, fell back in the night down the isthmus, and before daylight (the return of which he seemed to have dreaded) established himself at the Quarterhouse, seven miles from Charleston. General Greene pursued his examination of the country at his leisure, which being finished, he returned to the army, now encamped on the Four Holes.

After a few days he passed the Edisto, and sat down at the Round O, which is situated between that river and the Ashepoo, about forty or fifty miles from Charleston, and seventy miles from the confluence of the Wateree and Congaree; fifteen miles beyond which, on the east of the Wateree, in a straight line, are the High Hills of Santee.

Taking immediate measures for the security of the country in his front, he detached Brigadier Marion with his militia to the east of Ashley River, with orders to guard the district between that river and the Cooper; and he sent Lieutenant-Colonel Lee down the western side of the Ashley, directing him to approach by gradual advances St. John's Island, and to place himself in a strong position within striking distance of it.

Previous to this the enemy had evacuated Wilmington, by which North Carolina became completely restored to the Union. Shut up as were the British troops in Charleston and its isthmus, Major Craig, with the garrison from Wilmington, some additional infantry and the cavalry, had been detached to St. John's Island, where most of the cattle collected for the British army were at pasture, where long forage was procurable for the cavalry, where co-operation with the garrison of Charleston was convenient, and whence infantry might be readily transported along the interior navigation to Savannah.

To repress incursions from this post, as well as to inhibit the conveyance of supplies from the main to the island, became the principal object of Lee's attention.

The advance of Marion and Lee being, by the general's order, simultaneous, they gave security to their contiguous flanks from any attempt by land, although they were divided by the Ashley; it being not inconvenient to apprise each other of any movement of the enemy on either side of the river. This co-operation was enjoined by the general, and punctually executed by the two commandants. The first day's march brought these detachments to the country settled by the original emigrants into Carolina. The scene was both new and delightful. Vestiges, though clouded by war, everywhere appeared of the wealth and taste of the inhabitants. Spacious edifices, rich and elegant gardens, with luxuriant and extensive rice plantations, were to be seen on every side. This change in the aspect of inanimate nature, could not fail to excite emotions of pleasure, the more vivid because so rare. During our continued marches and countermarches, never before had we been solaced with the prospect of so much comfort. Here we were not confined to one solitary mansion, where a few, and a few only, might enjoy the charms of taste and the luxury of opulence. The rich repast was wide spread; and when to the exterior was added the fashion, politeness, and hospitality of the interior, we became enraptured with our changed condition, and the resolve of never yielding up this charming region but with life, became universal. To crown our bliss, the fair sex shone in its brightest lustre. With the ripest and most symmetrical beauty, our fair compatriots blended sentimental dignity and delicate refinement, the sympathetic shade of melancholy, and the dawning smile of hope; the arrival of their new guests opening to them the prospect of happier times.

The rapture of these scenes was as yet confined to the light troops. The general continuing in his position at the Round O, subsisting upon the resources of the country in that neighborhood and in his rear, reserved all the surplus food and forage within the advanced posts for the future support of his army. Decamping from the Round O, he moved on the route taken by his van; when the main body participated in the gratifications which this pleasing district, and its more pleasing possessors, so liberally bestowed. After some marches and countermarches, Brigadier Marion took post between Dorchester and Biggin's Bridge, and Lieutenant-Colonel Lee at McQueen's plantation, south of Ashley River. The main body encamped at Pompon, in the rear of Lee. Here General Greene began to enter more particularly into his long-meditated design of relieving the State of Georgia, by forcing the enemy to evacuate Savannah.

We have before mentioned that Major, now Lieutenant-Colonel Craig, had taken possession of St. John's Island, with a respectable detachment. Lee was ordered, when detached toward that island, to take measures for ascertaining with exactness the strength and position of Craig, with his customary precautions against surprise, and his manner of discharging the duties which his situation imposed. This service was undertaken with all that zeal and diligence which the mandates of a chief so enlightened and so respected, and an enterprise more brilliant than all the past exploits in the course of the Southern war, could claim. Some weeks were assiduously de-voted to the acquiring of a clear comprehension of this arduous and grand design, with an exact knowledge of the complicated means necessary to its execution ; in the mean time demonstrations were made and reports circulated, exhibiting a settled plan in the general of passing Ashley River, to be ready to fall upon Charleston as soon as the re-enforcement under St. Clair, now approaching, should arrive.

About this time Greene's attention to the leading object of his measures was diverted by accounts from the West, announcing an irruption of the Cherokee tribe of Indians on the district of Ninety-six ; which having been as sudden as it was unexpected, had been attended with serious injury. Several families were mas-sacred, and many houses were burnt. Brigadier Pickens (whose name we have often before mentioned, and always in connection with the most important services), had, after his long and harassing campaign, returned home with his militia. The moment he heard of the late incursion, he again summoned around him his well-tried warriors. To this officer the general resorted, when he was informed of his new enemy. Among the first acts of General Greene's com-mand in the South, was the conclusion of a treaty with this tribe of Indians, by which they had engaged to preserve a state of neu-trality so long as the war between the United States and Great Britain should continue. What is extraordinary, the Cherokees rigidly complied with their engagement during the past campaign, when the success of Lord Cornwallis, with the many difficulties Greene had to encounter, would have given weight to their inter-ference. Now, when the British army in Virginia had been forced to surrender, and that acting in South Carolina and Georgia had been compelled to take shelter in the district of country protected by forts and ships, they were so rash as to listen to the exhortations often before applied in vain. Pickens followed the incursors into their own country; and having seen much and various service, judiciously determined to mount his detachment, adding the sword * to the rifle and tomahawk. He well knew the force of cavalry, having felt it at the Cowpens, though it was then feebly exemplified by the enemy. Forming his mind upon experience, the straight road to truth, he wisely resolved to add to the arms, usual in Indian wars, the unusual one above mentioned.

In a few days he reached the country of the Indians, who, as is the practice among the uncivilized in all ages, ran to arms to oppose the invader, anxious to join issue in battle without delay. Pickens, with his accustomed diligence, took care to inform himself accurately of the designs and strength of the enemy; and, as soon as he had ascertained these important facts, advanced upon him. The rifle was only used while reconnoitring the hostile position. As soon as this was finished, he remounted his soldiers, and ordered a charge: with fury his brave warriors rushed forward, and the astonished Indians fled in dismay. Not only the novelty of the mode, which always has its influence, but the sense of his incapacity to resist horse, operated upon the flying forester.

Pickens followed up his success, and killed forty Cherokees, took a great number of prisoners of both sexes, and burned thirteen towns. He lost not a soldier, and had only two wounded. The sachems of the nation assembled in council; and thoroughly satisfied of their inability to contend against an enemy who added the speed of the horse† to the skill and strength of man, they determined to implore

---

* John Rogers Clarke, colonel in the service of Virginia against our neighbors the Indians in the revolutionary war, was among our best soldiers, and better acquainted with the Indian warfare than any officer in our army. This gentleman, after one of his campaigns, met in Richmond several of our cavalry officers, and devoted all his leisure in ascertaining from them the various uses to which horses were applied, as well as the manner of such application. The information he acquired determined him to introduce this species of force against the Indians, as that of all others the most effectual.

By himself, by Pickens, and lately by Wayne, was the accuracy of Clarke's opinion justified; and no doubt remains, but in all armies prepared to act against the Indians, a very considerable proportion of it ought to be light cavalry.

† The Indian, when fighting with infantry, is very daring. This temper of mind results from the consciousness of superior fleetness; which, together with his better knowledge of woods, assures to him extrication out of difficulties,

forgiveness for the past, and never again to provoke the wrath of their triumphant foe. This resolution being adopted, commissioners were accordingly appointed, with directions to wait upon General Pickens, and to adjust with him the terms of peace. These were readily listened to, and a treaty concluded, which not only terminated the existing war, but provided against its renewal, by a stipulation on the part of the Cherokees, in which they engaged not only to remain deaf to the exhortations of the British emissaries, but that they would apprehend all such evil-doers, and deliver them to the Governor of South Carolina, to be dealt with as he might direct.

The object of the expedition being thus happily accomplished, General Pickens evacuated the Indian territory, and returned to South Carolina, before the expiration of the third week from his departure, without losing a single soldier.

Pickens's dispatches, communicating the termination of the Cherokee hostilities, were·received by Greene just as he was about to enter upon the execution of his meditated enterprise. All the requisite intelligence had been acquired, the chances calculated, the decision taken, the plan concerted, and the period proper for execution* was fast approaching.

Lieutenant-Colonel Craig, with his infantry, was posted at a plantation not far from the eastern extremity of the island. The cavalry were cantoned six or seven miles from the infantry, at different farm-houses in its western quarter. At low water the inlet dividing St. Johns from the main was passable by infantry at two points only, both familiar to the enemy. That at the western extremity of the island was full of large rocks, and could be used only in the day, it being necessary carefully to pick your route, which in the deep water was from rock to rock. About midway between the eastern and western extremities was the other, where no natural difficulty occurred, and in the last of the ebb tide the depth of water was not more than *waist high*. This was guarded by two galleys, the one above and the other below it, and within four hun-

though desperate. This temper of mind is extinguished, when he finds that he is to save himself from the pursuit of horse, and with its extinction falls that habitual boldness.

* Only one or two nights in a month suited, as it was necessary that the tide of ebb should be nearly expended about midnight, the proper hour of passing to the island ; and it was desirable to possess the advantage of moonlight after we entered the island. Besides, then the galley crews were most likely to be at rest; and we had sufficient time before daylight to execute our various arrangements.

dred yards of each other, as near to the ford as the channel would permit.

Lee's examination of their position, together with his observations of the manner in which the captains of the galleys performed night duty, suggested the practicability of passing between the galleys with infantry unperceived. As soon as General Greene became satisfied that this difficulty could be surmounted, he determined to hazard the attempt, if a proper place for the cavalry to swim across could be ascertained. But the deep marshes which lined the shores seemed at first likely to prevent the approach of the horse. At length Major Eggleston, commanding the Legionary cavalry, discovered a practicable route some distance below the galleys. He ordered one or two of his dragoons to swim to the opposite shore in the night to select firm ground, and to erect small stakes as beacons to guide the cavalry where first to strike the shore of the island. This was duly executed, and reported accordingly to the general.

The day was now fixed for making the attempt, and preparatory orders were issued. Lieutenant-Colonel Lee, with the light corps acting under him, being insufficient in strength, a detachment of infantry from the army was made ready and placed under Lieutenant-Colonel Laurens, who was ordered to join Lee at a given point, when on his march to the theatre of action.

The plantation on which Lieutenant-Colonel Craig had encamped was intersected by many ditches, as was usual in the cultivated grounds of South Carolina near the sea. One of these stretched along the front of the British camp, about one hundred yards distant from it, which afforded sufficient space for the infantry of Craig to display in line, and which the assailants did not doubt the Lieutenant-Colonel would seize as soon as he should discover their advance.

To compensate in some measure for the advantage which the ground afforded to the enemy, the infantry of the attacking corps was rendered superior by one-fifth to that to be assaulted.

Lieutenant-Colonel Craig, although to all appearance protected from annoyance by his insulated situation, did not neglect the necessary precautions for his safety; nor did he permit any relaxation in discipline, or any diminution of vigilance. The chance of surprising him was not encouraging; but being very desirable and possible, it was determined that it should be attempted. On the road leading from the ford, protected by the galleys, Craig had

placed a picket, about a mile from the galleys; and two miles
farther on was another, at the point where the road last mentioned
intersected another which ran longitudinally through the island;
on the left of this point of intersection, Craig was encamped,
three or four miles from it toward Charleston; and on the right
of the same point were the cavalry, a few miles distant toward
the western extremity of the island. Our plan was as follows: As
soon as the infantry should effect its passage to the island, an
officer of cavalry, who had been directed for the purpose to
accompany Lieutenant-Colonel Lee, was then to return to Major
Eggleston with orders for the cavalry to pass over, and wait for
the infantry near the road of march, which took a direction inclining to the landing-place of the horse.

The first picket was to be approached with the utmost secrecy,
and then to be forced with vigor by the van, which was ordered
to spread itself for the purpose of preventing the escape of any
individual; and the cavalry had directions to take measures to
intercept every person who might endeavor to pass in their direction. We flattered ourselves with possessing the picket without
much resistance; and knowing that Craig was too remote to hear
the firing, should any occur, we hoped by the interception of every
fugitive to stop communication with him.

The second picket was to be avoided, which with proper care
was feasible; when the infantry supported by one troop of horse,
was to advance upon Craig, while Eggleston with the residue of
the dragoons would fall upon the enemy's cavalry. Succeeding in
both preliminary points, the main body could not escape the meditated surprise, which would give us an easy victory: failing in
arresting every individual of the post, or in evading the last
picket, Craig would be advised of our approach, and would be prepared to receive us. In the latter event, we intended, by turning
one of his flanks, in case he threw himself into the ditch,—of which,
from our knowledge of his character, no doubt could exist,—to
force him to change his front; and we were so thoroughly satisfied
with the character of our troops as to assume it as a fact, that no
corps, even of equal force, could execute the manœuvre in their
face without being destroyed. In this opinion Greene concurred,
and on its accuracy was rested the issue of the enterprise. However such a conclusion may wear the appearance of arrogance, it
does not merit the reproach. The veteran troops in the Southern
army had attained the highest state of discipline. Every soldier as

well as officer was conscious of his acquirements, and had experienced their good effect. They also knew that victory ,was not only the sure reward of every man's doing his duty in battle, but they were convinced that each man's personal safety was promoted by the same course.

Thus persuaded, they were habitually actuated by the determination of confiding entirely in their leader, their discipline, and their valor. Such troops will generally succeed, and, upon this occasion, could scarcely fail : for the major part of Craig's infantry had long been in garrison at Wilmington, where they never had seen an enemy in arms ; and his cavalry were known to be very inferior to the American horse, and were separated from the infantry. To reckon, therefore, upon victory, did not manifest presumption ; but only showed that Lee and Laurens duly appreciated the advantages they possessed, and were willing to stake their reputation and lives on the correctness of the estimate they had formed of them.*

The day appointed for the execution of the enterprise now arrived (28th December). Lieutenant-Colonel Laurens moved with his detachment from the main body toward the Ashley River, for the ostensible purpose of passing the river and taking post in the neighborhood of Dorchester. Halting near Bacon's Bridge until

---

* The delicacy of the calculation on which this enterprise was founded, and the confidence with which minute estimates of character, position, and of time were relied upon, afford happy illustrations of that branch of the art military, which has little relation to technicalities, and springs from the highest powers of the mind. Bonaparte divides military genius into that which is divine, and that which is terrestrial. ("Mémoires, vol. 5, p. 76, Montholon.") "Achille était fils d'une déesse et d'un mortel; c'est l'image du génie de la guerre; la partie divine c'est tout ce qui dérive des considérations morales du caractère, du talent, de l'intérêt de votre adversaire ; de l'opinion, de l'esprit du soldat, qui est fort et vainqueur, faible et battu, selon qu'il croit l'être ; la partie terrestre c'est les armes, les retranchements, les positions, les ordres de bataille, tout ce qui tient à la combinaison des choses matérielles." He afterward relates the following anecdote of Turenne, and exclaims—"voilà qui tient à la partie divine de l'art."

In 1653 Turenne in reconnoitring the position of the Archduke Leopold, who with the great Condé, was besieging Arras, passed so near the Spanish lines as to have several of his attendants killed by discharges of grape-shot. To his friends who remonstrated against this exposure of his person, and apprehending a more serious attack upon him, he replied—"This step would be imprudent it is true, if it was taken in front of the quarter where Condé commands. But it is important that I should observe their position closely, and *I am sufficiently acquainted with the Spanish service to know, that before the archduke will be informed of it, and can take the advice of Condé, I shall be safe in my own camp.*" The next day he attacked the besieging army, forced its intreuchments, defeated it with great slaughter, and saved Arras.—ED.

late in the evening, he countermarched, as if returning to camp, when after nightfall he turned to his left, taking the route prescribed for his junction with Lee. The latter officer moved in the same evening from his position at McQueen's plantation, and about nine P. M. reached the rendezvous, where he was met with precision by Laurens. The troops halted, and took the last meal for twenty-four hours; after which they were called to arms and were made acquainted with the destined object. They were told, that the enterprise before them was replete with difficulties; that the most powerful of the many which attended it would be met at the threshold; that this was to be encountered by the infantry, and could be overcome only by profound silence and strict obedience to orders. Success in the first step would in all probability lead to complete victory; inasmuch as the enemy was inferior in number, divided in position, and safe, in his own presumption, from his insular situation. That the plan of operations had been approved by the general; and the troops now united had been honored by his selection of them for the purpose of concluding the campaign in a manner worthy of the zeal, courage, and patience displayed by the army in all preceding scenes. They were assured that every difficulty had been well weighed; the best intelligence with the best guides had been procured; and that they could not be disappointed in reaping a rich harvest of glory unless the commandants had deceived themselves in their estimate of their intrepidity and discipline. A burst of applause ensued from the ranks, evincing the delight which all felt in knowing that victory was certain, unless lost by their misbehavior.

The disposition for battle was now made. The infantry was arrayed in two columns; that of Lee forming the right, that of Laurens the left. The cavalry were also divided into two squadrons: one-third under Armstrong was attached to the infantry; while the other two-thirds, under Eggleston, were appropriated to strike at the enemy's dragoons, with orders as soon as they were secured to hasten to the support of the infantry.

Every necessary arrangement having been made, we resumed our march; and, after a few miles, the cavalry filed to our left to gain its station on the river. Within an hour from this separation, we got near to the marsh, which on this side lines the river in the place where the infantry was to pass. Here the infantry again halted and deposited their knapsacks, and the officers, dismounting, left their horses. Dr. Skinner, of the Legion infantry, who considered fighting as no part of his business, was indulged in his request of being intrusted with the charge of the baggage. The detachment again moved ; every man in his place ; and every officer enjoined to take special care to march in sight of his leading section, lest in the darkness of the night a separation might happen.

After some time our guides informed us that we were near the marsh. This intelligence was communicated from section to section, and the columns were halted, as had been previously concerted, that every officer and soldier might pull off boots and shoes to prevent the splashing which they produced when wading through water, to be resumed when we reached the opposite shore. The order was instantly and cheerfully executed by the troops. Entering on the marsh, we moved very slowly, every man exerting himself to prevent noise. The van, under Rudolph, reached the shore, and proceeded, in conformity to orders, without halting into the river. Lee coming up with the head of the column, accompanied by Lieutenant-Colonel Laurens, halted and directed a staff officer to return and see that the sections were all up. We now enjoyed the delight of hearing the sentinels from each galley crying "*all's safe*," when Rudolph with the van was passing between them.

No circumstance could have been more exhilarating, as we derived from it a conviction that the difficulty most to be apprehended would be surmounted, and every man became persuaded, from the evidence of his own senses, that an enemy assailable only in this way would be found off his guard, and, therefore, that victory was certain. At this moment the staff officer returned with information that the rear column was missing. Laurens immediately went back to the high land with some of the guides and staff officers to endeavor to find it. The affliction produced by this communication is indescribable. At the very moment when every heart glowed with anticipations of splendid glory, an incident was announced which menaced irremediable disappointment.

Hour after hour passed ; messengers occasionally coming in from Laurens, and no intelligence gained respecting the lost column. At length the tide, which was beginning flood when the van passed, had now risen so high as to compel the recall of Rudolph, even had not the morning been too far advanced to admit perseverance in the enterprise. A sergeant was sent across the inlet with orders for the return of the van, and the column retired.

Rudolph found the water, which had not reached the waist as he passed, up to the breast as he returned. Nevertheless every man

got back safe; the tallest assisting the lowest, and the galley sentinels continuing to cry "all's safe." We soon regained our baggage,
where large fires were kindled, and our wet troops dried themselves. Here we met General Greene, who had, in conformity with
his plan, put his army in motion to draw near to the theatre of action, lest a body of troops might be pushed across the Ashley to
intercept the attacking corps in its retreat from the island; and with
a view of compelling the galleys to abandon their station, that Lee
might retire on the next low tide where he had passed, it being the
most convenient route. He received with regret the unexpected
intelligence, rendered the more so, as he was well assured that the
enemy would learn the intended enterprise, and, therefore, that it
could never be again attempted.

As soon as the day broke, the last column—which had been completely bewildered, and was, if possible, more unhappy at the occurrence than its chagrined comrades—regained the road taken in the
night, and was now discerned by those who had been searching for
it. Laurens returned with it to our baggage-ground, most unhappy
of the unhappy.

On inquiry it was ascertained that the leading section, instead of
turning into the marsh, continued along the road, which lead to a
large plantation. Here the error was discovered, to which was added
another. Instead of retracing his steps, the senior officer, from his
anxiety to rejoin without delay, took through the fields under the
guidance of a negro, it being the nearest route, and again got lost,
so very dark was the night; nor was he even able to reach the road
until directed by daylight.

Thus was marred the execution of an enterprise surpassed by
none throughout our war in grandeur of design, and equalled by
few in the beneficial effects sure to result from its successful termination. Censure attached nowhere; for every precaution had been
adopted to guard against the very incident which did occur, and
dark as the night was, the troops had nearly completed the most
difficult part of the march without the least interruption. The
officer of the leading section of Laurens's column was among the
most attentive and trust-worthy in the army, and yet the blunder
was committed by him which led to our disappointment. The
whole corps lamented the deranging occurrence, especially Laurens,
who reproached himself with having left his column, presuming
the accident would not have happened had he continued in his
station. This presumption may be correct, as that officer was sin-

gularly attentive to his duty; and yet his absence being necessary, it could not be better supplied than it was. The passage of the river was the essential point, that on which the expedition hung, and Laurens being second in command, it was deemed prudent—as Lieutenant-Colonel Lee would necessarily pass with the front column for the purpose of directing those measures intended to be applied against the enemy's picket the moment our rear reached the island —that Lieutenant-Colonel Laurens should repair to the river, and there continue to superintend the troops as they entered into the water: lest the sections might crowd on each other and thus increase the noise, a consequence to be dreaded and guarded against; or, by entering too high up or too low down the stream, miss the ford and get into deep water.

Laurens left his column by order to give his personal superintendence to this delicate operation; and, therefore, was entirely exempted from any participation in the production of the unlucky accident which occurred.

General Greene assuaged the sorrow which the baffled troops so keenly felt, by thanking them as they arrived, for the exemplary manner in which they had conducted themselves, and for the ardent zeal they had displayed in the abortive attempt to execute the enterprise committed to their skill and courage. He lamented the disappointment which had occurred, but declared it to be owing to one of those incidents which so often take place in war, and against which upon this occasion every precaution had been adopted which prudence could suggest. He attributed the accident to the darkness of the night, and by commending all, forbade the censure of any. Not satisfied with this oral declaration to the troops, the general, on his return to camp, addressed a letter to each of the lieutenant-colonels, repeating his thanks to them and to their respective corps.

How often do we find military operations frustrated by the unaccountable interposition of accident, when every exertion in the power of the commander has been made to prevent the very interruption which happens? No doubt these incidents generally spring from negligence or misconduct; and, therefore, might be considerably diminished, if not entirely arrested, by unceasing attention. When the van turned into the marsh, Lee, as has been mentioned, halted to give a minute or two for taking off boots and shoes, and did not move until Lieutenant-Colonel Laurens, who had been sent for, came up and informed him that every section was in place. From this time Laurens continued with Lee, and in the very short space which occurred before the leading section of Laurens reached the point of turning into the marsh did the mistake occur which put an end to our much-desired enterprise. Lieutenant-Colonel Lee, believing the intervention of mistake impracticable, as the sections were all up, and as the march through the marsh would be slower than it had been before, did not direct one of his staff as he had done heretofore, to halt at the point where the change in the course of the route occurred. This omission cannot be excused. The precaution, although now neglected in consequence of the official communication then received that the sections were all in place, and the short distance to the marsh, ought still to have been observed; the experience of this night proves that however satisfactorily the march may have been conducted, and however precisely in place the troops may be, yet that no preventive of mistake should be neglected. Had the practice been followed at the last change of course, which had uniformly taken place during the previous march, the fatal error would not have been committed, nor this concluding triumph to our arms in the South been lost.

The State of Georgia might probably have been recovered by the effects of this severe blow; as the northern re-enforcement soon after joined us, and General Leslie would have found it necessary for the security of Charleston to replace the troops lost on St. John's Island, which could not be so conveniently done as by drawing to him the garrison of Savannah. Hitherto Greene had struggled to recover the country far from the ocean; now he contemplated its delivery even where British troops were protected by British ships, but was baffled by this night's accident. The spirit of disaffection,* which had always existed among the inhabitants of Charleston, had been vigilantly watched by the British commander, as he was no stranger to its prevalence. When Lord Rawdon evacuated Camden, this spirit became so formidable in consequence of the success of the American arms in the South, as to induce his lordship to continue with his army at Monk's Corner until the arrival of three regiments

---

* Lord Rawdon to Earl Cornwallis, May 24th, 1781.—"Lieutenant-Colonel Balfour was so good as to meet me at Nelson's. He took this measure that he might represent his circumstances to me. He stated that the revolt was universal, and that, from the little reason to apprehend this serious invasion, the old works in Charleston had been in part levelled, to make way for new ones, which were not yet constructed; that its garrison was inadequate to oppose any force of consequence; and that the disaffection of the town's people showed itself in a thousand instances. I agreed with him in the conclusion to be drawn from thence, that any misfortune happening to my corps might entail the loss of the province."

from Ireland enabled him to leave behind an adequate force for the security of that city during his resumption of offensive operations. Subsequent events promoted this disposition, and the capture of the army under Earl Cornwallis, gave it full energy. Nor can it be doubted that, had Greene succeeded in destroying the corps under Lieutenant-Colonel Craig, this spirit would have been turned to his co-operation, in case General Leslie had been so imprudent as to rely upon his reduced garrison for the defence of Charleston after the junction of our re-enforcement from the North. We may, therefore, safely pronounce that General Greene did not err in his calculation of restoring Georgia to the Union in the event of his success against Craig, and we sincerely lament that his bold design should have been frustrated by the derangement which occurred.

The army resumed its position at Pompon, and the light corps returned to its camp at McQueen's. In a very few days our intended enterprise became suspected by the enemy, and excited merited attention. The British general made a change in his position; and reducing his force in St. John's Island, drew it near the eastern point.

Greene, baffled unfortunately in his well-digested plan, began to take other measures for the purpose of effecting his favorite object. He meditated a movement into the isthmus, on which stands Charleston, connected with an attempt to float a detachment down the Ashley in the night to enter the town in that quarter at the hour fixed for an assault upon the enemy's lines.

As the scheme presented great and numerous difficulties, it was not to be executed unless a more attentive examination should justify the attempt. A British galley, for some purpose not known to us, was stationed high up the Ashley, and obstructed the desired inspection of that part of the rivers. Greene expressed his wish that it should be destroyed, if to be done without too great a sacrifice. Captain Rudolph, of the Legion infantry, was advised by his commandant of the general's wish, and requested to discover the state of discipline on board the galley, and to devise a plan for its seizure. This officer gave his immediate attention to the project. While Rudolph was pursuing his object, Lieutenant-Colonel Lee became informed of the enemy's design to beat up his quarters at McQueen's. As soon as this information was received he drew in all his parties, including Rudolph, and fell back in the night three miles nearer to the army, where he established himself in a position so well secured by rice ditches as to place the corps safe from nocturnal attack. The hostile detachment moved from Charleston about noon, drawing near to Ashley River before sunset. Early in the night it resumed its march, but did not reach McQueen's, having lost its way in consequence of the darkness of the night. Lee returned early in the morning to his relinquished position, presuming that he should find his disappointed adversary retreating hastily; and hoping that he should be able to derive some advantage from the perplexity to which he would be soon driven by fresh and vigorous troops. Finding that the enemy had not advanced as far as McQueen's, he proceeded toward Bacon's Bridge, where halting, he learnt their misdirection, and returned to his former position.

The country between Dorchester and the Quarterhouse had been occasionally visited by our light parties, which infringed upon the domain claimed by the once army of South Carolina, now garrison of Charleston. A well-concerted enterprise was projected by the commandant to repress the liberties taken by our light parties. Infantry was detached in the night to occupy specified points, and cavalry followed in the morning, some for co-operation with the infantry, and others for the seduction of our light parties. It so happened that Captain Armstrong, of the Legion cavalry, had been sent to Dorchester by General Greene the night before, for the purpose of conferring with a spy from Charleston. On the approach of morning Armstrong advanced to Dorchester; and meeting the party of dragoons sent forward for the purpose of decoying any of the American detachments traversing this quarter, he rushed upon it. In obedience to order the enemy, though superior in number, fled. Armstrong was one of the most gallant of the brave, too apt to bury in the confidence he reposed in his sword, those considerations which prudence suggested. Eager to close with his flying foe, he pursued vehemently, and fell into the snare spread for his destruction. The moment he discovered his condition he turned upon his enemy and drove at him in full gallop. The bold effort succeeded so far as to open a partial avenue of retreat, which was seized by his subaltern and some of the dragoons. They got off; but Armstrong and four privates were taken, the first and only horse-officer of the Legion captured during the war.*

Previous to this the Northern re-enforcement under Major-General St. Clair having arrived, Brigadier Wayne was ordered to Georgia; having under him Lieutenant-Colonel White, who had lately joined

* How he was admired, and how handsomely he was treated by his captors, see GARDEN'S *Anecdotes*, page 125.

the army with the remains of Moylan's regiment of dragoons. Wayne proceeded without delay, and in a few days crossed the Savannah River at the Two Sisters' Ferry. A small corps of Georgia militia, encamped in the vicinity of Augusta, was directed to fall down to Ebenezer, the station selected by the brigadier for the rendezvous of his troops. Here he was shortly re-enforced by Lieutenant-Colonel Posey,* of the Virginia line, at the head of three hundred Continentals from the army of General Greene.

The immediate object of this motion into Georgia was to protect the country from the incursions of the garrison of Savannah. With that design was connected the expectation that the insufficiency of the British force in that town to man its extensive works would probably present an opportunity of carrying the post by a nocturnal assault. Wayne was accordingly ordered, while engaged in executing the first, to give due attention to the accomplishment of the last object.

As soon as the advance of the American detachment was known in Savannah, Brigadier-General Clarke, who commanded the royal forces in Georgia, directed his officers charged with his outposts to lay waste the country with fire, and to retire with their troops and all the provisions they could collect into Savannah. This order was rigidly executed, and the district circumjacent to the capital was devastated. In consequence whereof Wayne found it necessary to draw his subsistence from South Carolina, which added to the difficulties daily experienced in providing for the main army.

The country, heretofore the seat of war in South Carolina, was literally without food; and its distressed inhabitants, with the utmost difficulty, procured enough for bare support. That into which Greene had advanced was relatively well supplied; but still it might be justly considered a gleaned country. It had furnished the British post at Orangeburgh during the summer; it had also supplied the army of Lord Rawdon when advancing upon Ninety-six, and when retiring thence, and had always contributed considerably to the maintenance of the troops and inhabitants in Charleston.

The crop, originally small in consequence of the habitual neglect of agriculture in a state of war, had been much exhausted by the

* The same officer who so gallantly seconded Brigadier Wayne in his assault of Stony Point.

Posey commanded the column with which the brigadier marched in person, and was by his side when Wayne received the ball which fortunately only grazed the crown of his head, but which laid him prostrate for a few moments.

previous drains from it before the arrival of Greene, and was, after that event, the sole resource of our army in South Carolina, and the principal one of that sent to Georgia under Wayne. This real scarcity was increased by the waste which always accompanies compulsory collection of subsistence; a practice yet necessarily continued, as the civil authority had been but lately restored.

The battle of the Eutaws evidently broke the force and humbled the spirit of the royal army; never after that day did the enemy exhibit any symptom of that bold and hardy cast which had hitherto distinguished them.

Governor Rutledge being persuaded that the happy period had at length arrived for the restoration of the government, issued a proclamation in a few weeks after the battle of the Eutaws, convening the General Assembly at Jacksonborough, a small village upon the Edisto River, about thirty-five miles from Charleston. Invested with dictatorial powers, the governor not only issued writs for the intervening elections, but also prescribed the qualifications of the electors.

The right of suffrage was restricted to those inhabitants who had uniformly resisted the invader, and to such who, having accepted British protections, had afterward united with their countrymen in opposition to the royal authority before the 27th day of September; in the early part of which month the battle of the Eutaws had been fought. The exchange of prisoners which had previously taken place, liberated many respectable and influential characters too long lost to the State.

These citizens had now returned, and were ready to assist with their counsel in repairing the desolation of war. This period presents an interesting epoch in the annals of the South. From all quarters were flocking home our unfortunate maltreated prisoners. The old and the young, the rich and the poor, hastened to their native soil; burying their particular griefs in the joy universally felt in consequence of the liberation of their country.

They found their houses burnt, their plantations laid waste, their herds and flocks destroyed, and the rich rewards of a life of industry and economy dissipated. Without money, without credit, with debilitated constitutions, with scars and aches, this brave and patriotic group gloried in the adversity they had experienced, because the price of their personal liberty and of national independence. They had lost their wealth, they had lost their health, and had lost the props of their declining years in the field of battle; but they had established the independence of their country; they had secured to themselves and posterity the birthright of Americans. They forgot past agony in the delight of present enjoyment, and in the prospect of happiness to ages yet unborn. From this class of citizens the senators were chiefly selected. On the appointed day the Assembly convened at Jacksonborough, when Governor Rutledge, in an interesting and eloquent speech, opened the session. The incipient proceedings of the Assembly present authentic information of the havoc of the war and of the distress of the country, and convey the pleasing testimony of the mild and amiable disposition which swayed, even in this day of wrath and irritation, the legislature of South Carolina.

The length of the governor's speech forbids its entire insertion; extracts of it are given, with the answer of the Senate, which will sufficiently exemplify the justice of these observations, as do the consequences of the amiable policy pursued by the legislature demonstrate that beneficence in the sovereign is the readiest cure which can be applied to heal the wounds of discord and of war.

" *Honorable Gentlemen of the Senate, Mr. Speaker,*
  and Gentlemen of the House of Representatives :—

" Since the last meeting of a General Assembly, the good people of this State have not only felt the common calamities of war, but from the wanton and savage manner in which it has been executed, they have experienced such severities as are unpractised, and will scarcely be credited, by civilized nations.

" The enemy, unable to make any impression on the Northern States, the number of whose inhabitants, and the strength of whose country had baffled their repeated efforts, turned their views to the Southern, which a difference of circumstances afforded some expectation of conquering, or at least of distressing. After a long resistance, the reduction of Charleston was effected by the vast superiority of force with which it had been besieged. The loss of that garrison, as it consisted of the Continental troops of Virginia and the Carolinas, and of a number of militia, facilitated the enemy's march into the country, and the establishment of strong posts in the upper and interior parts of it; and the unfavorable issue of the action near Camden induced them vainly to imagine, that no other army could be collected which they might not easily defeat. The militia commanded by the Brigadiers Marion and Sumter, whose enterprising spirit and unremitted perseverance under many diffi--

culties are deserving of great applause, harassed and often defeated
large parties; but the numbers of those militia were too few to
contend effectually with the collected strength of the enemy. Regardless therefore of the sacred ties of honor, destitute of the
feelings of humanity, and determined to extinguish, if possible,
every spark of freedom in the country, they, with the insolent
pride of conquerors, gave unbounded scope to the exercise of their
tyrannical disposition, infringed their public engagements, and violated the most solemn capitulations. Many of our worthiest citizens were, without cause, long and closely confined, some on board
of prison ships, and others in the town and castle of St. Augustine.

"But I can now congratulate you, and I do so most cordially, on
the pleasing change of affairs, which, under the blessing of God,
the wisdom, prudence, address, and bravery of the great and gallant
General Greene, and the intrepidity of the officers and men under
his command, has been happily effected; a general who is justly
entitled, from his many signal services, to honorable and singular
marks of your approbation and gratitude. His successes have been
more rapid and complete than the most sanguine could have expected. The enemy compelled to surrender or evacuate every post
which they held in the country, frequently defeated and driven from
place to place, are obliged to seek refuge under the walls of Charleston, or in the islands in its vicinity. We have now the full and absolute possession of every other part of the State; and the legislative, executive, and judicial powers, are in the free exercise of their
respective authorities. The interest and honor, the safety and
happiness of our country, depend so much on the result of your
deliberations, that I flatter myself you will proceed in the weighty
business before you, with firmness and temper, with vigor, unanimity, and dispatch.   JOHN RUTLEDGE."

The address of the honorable the Senate in answer to the
governor's speech.

"*May it please your Excellency :—*

"We beg leave to return your Excellency the thanks of this House
for your speech.

"Any words which we might adopt would convey but a very faint
idea of the satisfaction we feel on the perfect re-establishment of
the legislative, executive, and judicial powers in this State.

"It is with particular pleasure that we take the earliest opportunity to present to your Excellency our unfeigned thanks for your unwearied zeal and attention to the real interest of this country, and to testify our entire approbation of the good conduct of the executive since the last meeting of the General Assembly.

" We see and revere the goodness of Divine Providence in frustrating and disappointing the attempts of our enemies to conquer the Southern States; and we trust that, by the blessing of the same Providence on the valor and intrepidity of the free citizens of America, their attacks and enterprises will continue to be repelled and defeated.

" We reflect with pleasure on the steady resolution with which Charleston was defended by a small body of brave men against such a vast superiority of force; and we gratefully acknowledge the meritorious conduct and important services of the officers and privates of the militia, who stood forth in the hour of danger; whose coolness, perseverance, and ardor, under a complication of difficulties, most justly entitle them to the applause of their country.

"We flatter ourselves that the blood which the enemy spilled, the wanton devastation which has marked their progress, and the tyrannical system that they have invariably pursued, and which your Excellency hath so justly and pathetically described to us, will rouse the good people of this State, and will animate them into a spirit to protect their country, to save their rights and liberties, and to maintain at all hazards their independency.

" It is with inexpressible pleasure that we receive your Excellency's congratulations upon the great and glorious measures of the campaign, on the happy change of affairs and the pleasing prospect before us; and we assure your Excellency that we concur most sincerely with you in acknowledging and applauding the meritorious zeal, and the very important services which have been rendered to this State by the great and gallant General Greene, and the brave and intrepid officers and men under his command, and to whom we shall be happy to give the most grateful and singular testimonies of our approbation and applause.

"We are truly sensible of the immense advantage which the United States derive from the magnanimous prince, their ally. We have the most perfect confidence on his royal word, and on the sincerity of his friendship; and we think ourselves much indebted to that illustrious monarch for the great and effectual assistance which he hath been pleased to give the Confederated States, and by whose means they have been enabled to humble the pride of

Britain, and to establish their independency upon the most permanent basis.

"The importance of the several matters which your Excellency hath communicated to our consideration is so evident that we shall proceed to deliberate upon them with all possible dispatch; and we flatter ourselves that our business will be carried on with temper, firmness, and unanimity.

"J. L. GERVAIS, President."

During this session a law was passed, prescribing a mode of providing for the subsistence of the army by the civil authority. No regulation was more requisite; as the military process was grating to our fellow-citizens, wasteful of the resources of the country, inconvenient to the army, and repugnant to the feelings of soldiers, who believed themselves to be in heart as in name the defenders of liberty. Resort to compulsion had been forced upon the general by necessity, though in every way objectionable; and which ought never to be tolerated for a moment when avoidable. In pursuance of power invested by this law, the governor appointed William Hiot agent for the State. This gentleman executed the duties of his station with intelligence, zeal, and diligence; and very much contributed to our support, without offence to to the husbandmen, and with very little aid from the army.

But such was the real scarcity of the primary articles of subsistence, that with all the exertions (and they were great) of the agent, want continued to haunt the camp, which compelled General Greene to contribute, upon some occasions, his assistance to the authority of the laws.

Brigadier Marion, although a colonel in the line of South Carolina, had been chosen a member of the legislature; and before he set out for Jacksonborough, had selected a station for his militia, near the Santee River, remote from Charleston. His absence from his command, notwithstanding the distance of his selected position, inspired the enemy with a hope that a corps which had heretofore been invulnerable might now be struck. A detachment of cavalry was accordingly prepared for the meditated enterprise, and placed under the orders of Lieutenant-Colonel Thompson. This officer having passed the Cooper River near Charleston, late in the evening, proceeded toward the Santee. Observing the greatest secrecy, and pushing his march with diligence, he fell upon the militia camp before the dawn of day, and completely routed the corps. Some were killed, some wounded, and the rest dispersed, with little or no loss on the part of the British. Major Benson, an active officer, was among the killed.

Thompson hastened back to Charleston with his detachment; and Marion, returning from Jacksonborough, reassembled his militia.

Captain Rudolph, who had been charged with the destruction of the British galley in the Ashley River, although often interrupted by other duties, had never intermitted his attention to that object. Early in March, some time after the dispersion of the militia near the Santee, the captain presented his plan to Lieutenant-Colonel Lee, who communicated it to the general. It was founded on the facility he had discovered with which boats going to market with provisions passed the galley.

Rudolph proposed to place in one of these boats an adequate force, disguising himself in a countryman's dress, and disguising three or four of his soldiers in the garb and color of negroes. The boat was to be stored with the usual articles for Charleston market, under the cover of which he concealed his armed men, while himself and his four negroes should conduct the boat. His plan was approved; and Lieutenant Smith, of the Virginia line, who had been very instrumental in acquiring the intelligence on which the project was grounded, was united to the captain in its execution. Every thing being prepared with profound secrecy, Rudolph and Smith embarked with their parties at a concealed landing-place, high up the Ashley, on the night of the 18th of March. Between three and four in the morning, Rudolph got near to the galley, when the sentinel hailed the boat. He was answered in the negro dialect that it was a market boat going to Charleston, and asked permission to proceed. In reply, the boat was ordered to hale alongside, as the captain of the galley wished to purchase some provisions. Rudolph obeyed; and as soon as he got alongside threw some of his poultry on deck, his disguised negroes at the same time taking fast hold of the galley.

On a signal from Rudolph, Smith and his soldiers rose and boarded the galley. The sentinel and a few others were killed; some escaped in the darkness of the night by throwing themselves into the river; and the captain with twenty-eight sailors were captured.

The galley mounted twelve guns besides swivels, and was manned with forty-three seamen. Rudolph did not lose a man; and after

35

taking out such stores as he found on board the galley, he burnt her and returned to his place of embarkation.

Thus the tone of enterprise continued high and vigorous on our side, while low and languishing with the enemy. The novelty of this successful attempt attracted notice in Charleston; and such was the state of despondency which prevailed in its garrison, as to give currency to opinions calculated still further to depress the humbled spirit of the British soldier. When it was found that even their floating castles, the pride and bulwark of Englishmen, were successfully assailed by landsmen, the quarter of the town, which was accessible by water, necessarily became an object of jealousy. Every alarm in the night excited dire apprehensions; sometimes Greene was moving to force their lines, at other times he was floating down the Ashley; and in one way or other he was ever present to their disturbed imaginations.

But such fears were illusory. After a critical examination of the enemy's situation, no point was found vulnerable; and the general was obliged to relinquish any attempt on Charleston. He nevertheless indulged a hope that Wayne might discover an opening to strike the post of Savannah, where the garrison amounted scarcely to one thousand men, too small for the extensive works before that town; and he held ready therefore a chosen corps to re-enforce Wayne whenever requisite.

At this juncture treason had found its way into our camp. The inactivity which had succeeded the series of bold and vigorous service was a fit season for recollection of grievances long endured, and which, being severely felt, began to rankle in every breast. Hunger sometimes pinched, at other times cold oppressed, and always want of pay reminded us as well of the injustice of our government as of our pressing demands upon it. The Pennsylvania line had joined the army; the soldiers of which, being chiefly foreigners, were not so disposed to forget and to forgive as our native troops. Even heretofore this line had pushed their insubordination so far as to abandon in a body the commander-in-chief, to drive off their officers, to commit the eagles to base hands, and to march under the orders of leaders elected by themselves.

They justified this daring mutiny by referring to their contract of enlistment, which they alleged had been violated; and it must be admitted that this allegation was too well founded. Soldiers who had enlisted for three years had been detained after the period of their service expired, under the pretext that they had enlisted for the war. As soon as this injustice was redressed, and some pecuniary accommodation rendered, all not entitled to their discharge returned to their duty.

The violation of contract is always morally wrong; and however it may sometimes yield present good, it is generally overbalanced by subsequent injury. The government which is under the necessity of resorting to armed men, enlisted for a term of service, to protect its rights, ought to take care that the contract of enlistment is fair as well as legal, and that it be justly executed; or they afford a pretext for incalculable ills, which, though often avoided from the force of circumstances, are sometimes productive of irreparable misfortunes to the nation. Every effort was made at the time by the enemy to turn this menacing occurrence into the deepest injury; but the fidelity of the revolting troops remained invulnerable; the best possible apology for their previous conduct.

The present mutiny was marked by a very different character. It was grounded on the breach of allegiance, and reared in all the foulness of perfidy. Greene himself was to be seized and delivered to the enemy. How could treason ascend higher?

A sergeant in the Pennsylvania line took the lead in this daring conspiracy; a soldier heretofore much esteemed, and possessing talents adapted to the enterprise. No doubt exists but that he and his associates held continued correspondence with the enemy, and that a plan had been concerted for the protection of the mutineers by the co-operating movements of the British force.

The vigilance and penetration of Greene could neither be eluded nor overreached. He well knew that the soldiers were discontented; nor was he insensible to the cause of their complaints. But he confided in the rectitude of Congress, and in the well-tried fidelity of that portion of the army which had so often fought by his side. He nevertheless dreaded the effects of the wiles of the artful and wicked, when applied to the inflammable mass around him.

To the enemy's camp and to that description of his troops most likely to forget self-respect and patriotism, he directed his close and vigorous attention. From both he drew information which convinced him that his apprehensions were not groundless. Redoubling his exertions, as well to discover the plan and progress of the conspirators as to thwart their designs, he learned that the sergeant, supposed to be the leader, had, by indulging unwarily the free declaration of his sentiments, subjected himself to martial law, and alarmed all the faithful soldiers, who, though prone to unite in the declaration of the wrongs they had suffered, and of their determination to obtain redress, had never entertained a thought of executing their views by the prostitution of military subordination, much less by the perpetration of the blackest treason, of the basest ingratitude. Greene, acting with his usual decision, ordered the arrest and trial of the sergeant. This order was immediately executed, and the prisoner being by the court-martial condemned to die, the sentence of the court was forthwith carried into effect. (23d April.)

Some others, believed to be associates with the sergeant, among whom were Peters and Owens, domestics in the general's family, were also tried; but the testimony was not deemed conclusive by the court. Twelve others deserted in the course of the night, and got safe to Charleston.

Thus the decisive conduct of the general crushed instantly this daring conspiracy; and the result proved, as often happens, that although the temper of complaint and of discontent pervaded the army, but few of the soldiers were in reality guilty of the criminal intentions which were believed at first to have spread far through the ranks.

While the arrests and trials were proceeding in our camp, and while General Greene continued to watch the movements of the enemy, they disclosed a spirit of adventure, which had been for some months dormant. Large bodies of horse and foot were put in motion; some of which, in the course of the night, approached us with unusual confidence. This boldness tended to confirm the suspicions before entertained that the enemy was not only apprised of the intentions of our mutineers, but had prepared to second their designs. General Greene, feeling his critical situation, contented himself for the present with detaching select parties to hover around the enemy for the purpose of observing his motions, with the determination to strike his adversary as soon as he should find his army restored to its pristine discipline and character. On the

April 24th. morning after the execution of the traitor, Captain O'Neal of the Legion cavalry fell in with a body of the enemy's horse under Major Frazer.

O'Neal, being very inferior in strength to his antagonist, retired, and was vigorously pursued by Frazer. During his flight he perceived a second body of the enemy in possession of his line of retreat. He was now compelled to change his course; and with the utmost difficulty escaped himself, after losing ten of his dragoons. Frazer had advanced as high as Stan's Bridge, the place assigned for the reception of that portion of the conspirators who had undertaken to betray the person of their general. On his return he was met by O'Neal, not far from Dorchester. This was the sole advantage resulting to the enemy in a conjuncture from which he expected to derive signal benefit.

CHAPTER XXXVII.

England determines upon peace with America.—A cessation of hostilities proposed.— The war degenerates into one for supplies.—Discontent of the Legion.—Operations in Georgia—Remarkable expedition of Guristersigo.—His battle with Wayne.—Is defeated and killed.—Savannah evacuated by the British.—War closed in Georgia. —Leslie repeats his pacific overture.—Death of Col. Laurens.—Correspondence between Gen. Leslie and Governor Matthews.—Nakedness of the American army. —Contract for clothing.—Charleston evacuated, and peace restored to the South.

THE unexpected events which had occurred in the preceding campaign, when known in England, attracted universal attention, and produced a determination to put a period to the war in America. In accordance with this resolution instructions were forwarded to the commander-in-chief of the royal forces, who conformed his subsequent measures to the change in the system of administration; further waste of life being in his opinion unnecessary. His lieutenant in South Carolina, Major-General Leslie, proposed to General Greene a cessation of hostilities. This proposition was rejected by the American general, as his powers did not reach the subject. He consequently communicated the same to Congress, who alone could give the requisite authority.

General Leslie, finding his pacific overture unavailing, was compelled to pursue measures to obtain supplies for his troops, although sure to produce the sacrifice of individuals in both armies; a sacrifice which he anxiously desired to avoid. For this purpose incursions into our territory were occasionally attempted; sometimes with success, but generally the British detachments were forced to regain their lines without the accomplishment of their views.

This little warfare, always irksome, unless the prelude to grand operations, was peculiarly so to troops inured to the most interesting scenes of war, and conscious that those scenes could never be renewed. Men of the sword only can appreciate this condition of war, the most revolting to every real soldier. Inquietude and ill-humor could not fail to prevail, especially in the American camp; where want of clothes, want of food, and empty purses, were super-added. Amid these a new cause of uneasiness was excited. Lieu-tenant-Colonel Laurens, who became a prisoner on the fall of Charleston, had been exchanged by Congress out of course, which was much disrelished by our officers in the hands of the enemy; as they considered every departure from the usage of war not only unjust in principle, but cruel to themselves in application. This usage secures to every prisoner his exchange in turn; and un-doubtedly, as a general rule, is unexceptional. Deviations from it ought rarely to be admitted, and then only from a strong cause. In support of the present deviation, it was contended that the war raged in South Carolina, Laurens's native country; that his ac-knowledged talents would therefore be singularly useful in that theatre; and, moreover, that he was aid-de-camp to the commander-in-chief, and consequently was an exception to the general rule. No doubt these reasons are forcible, and will always have weight with the sovereign. They did not however tranquillize the feelings which the occurrence had excited. Lieutenant-Colonel Laurens, after joining the Southern army, continued in the family of General Greene, waiting for some change of circumstances which might enable the general to fix him permanently in the line of service. This Greene was very desirous of effecting; not only because the resolution of Congress authorizing his exchange called indirectly for it, but the commander-in-chief required it from his own conviction of the worth and capacity of this excellent officer.

Notwithstanding these high authorities, notwithstanding his own inclination and Laurens's reputation, stubborn difficulties interposed, not to be readily vanquished. Officers of the highest merit, who had served under himself from his accession to the command of the Southern army, to whom he owed, and to whom he felt, every obli-gation which a general can owe or feel, must be supplanted or over-looked to make way for the desired appointment.

Lieutenant-Colonel Lee had become incapable from ill-health of continuing in command of the light troops, and had obtained leave of absence. This contingency produced a vacancy which the general had the clear right of supplying at his will. The occurrence offered some relief to the embarrassment into which the resolution of Con-gress and the wishes of the commander-in-chief had involved Gen-eral Greene; but as the vacant station was the most desirable within his gift, because the most honorable, the preferment of an officer who had not shared in the arduous struggle just closed, to the many who had in every vicissitude of his eventful campaign, covered themselves with glory, did not comport with justice, and could not escape animadversion. To smooth the difficulties which intervened, the general had associated Laurens with Lieutenant-Colonel Lee in the expedition against St. John's Island, hoping that the brilliancy of success, would cover the substitution of the second for the first, as soon as that officer should retire. But unfortunately the attempt failed, and the general lost the aid which he expected to derive from the magic power of victory. In this perplexing situation some of General Greene's confidential advisers did not hesitate to urge him to recede from his purpose, upon the ground of the superior pretensions of officers, whose services imposed upon him primary attention. Nor would this counsel have been unavailing, had not the general been persuaded that his omission to employ Lieutenant-Colonel Laurens would be considered as disrespectful to the commander-in-chief. One of Greene's aid-de-camps had been for some time at head-quarters; and from this gentleman was derived the information which led to the above conclusion. He had heard insinuations in the family of Washington which lisped these sentiments. It was more than once suggested that the general of the South had been less communicative than was expected; and even allusion to the conduct and fate of Gates were occasionally made, which clearly imported the possibility, if not the probability, that the conqueror in the South, like the conqueror in the North, might become the rival of the commander-in-chief. In justice to General Washington it was acknowledged that sentiments of this sort never fell from his lips, or in his presence. Nevertheless when those around him ventured to hold such language, it could not but inspire unpleasant feelings in the breast of Greene.

General Greene determined at every hazard, to afford no just cause for such unjust suspicions. He declared his conviction that Washington himself would spurn such insinuations, unless his mind should have been previously poisoned by artful and designing men, possessing his esteem and confidence.

He lamented that the motives which actuated his conduct must, from their nature, be concealed; as he was persuaded that the very officers themselves, whom he apparently neglected, would approve the course in the then stage of the war, when every opportunity for the acquirement of military reputation was probably finally closed.

In consequence of this resolution, as soon as Lieutenant-Colonel Lee took leave, the general new modelled the light corps,* giving it additional strength. By this arrangement he was warranted in calling a general officer to its direction, and consequently avoided those just complaints which must have arisen among his lieutenant-colonels, had the command been continued in that grade, and had any other than a lieutenant-colonel of his own army been honored with it. Brigadier Gist, of the Maryland line, who had lately reached head-quarters, was placed at the head of the augmented corps, having under him Colonel Baylor, of the third regiment of dragoons, who had also lately joined, and Lieutenant-Colonel Laurens. The first commanded the cavalry, and the last the infantry.

However judicious the course adopted by General Greene to give effect to the wishes of the commander-in-chief had been, disagreeable consequences nevertheless ensued. In the reorganization of the light corps, the cavalry of the third regiment and of the Legion had been united; as had been the infantry of the Legion with Kirkwood's Delawares, for the purpose of forming a command for Lieutenant-Colonel Laurens.

The separation of the horse and foot of the Legion now for the first time took place, and gave considerable umbrage and inquietude to the officers and soldiers. The first considered the constitution of the corps sacrificed, and the last had been so long habituated to fight side by side, that they were very unwilling to commute approved and beloved comrades for any other, however brave.

The Legion officers gave vent to their feelings in a remonstrance to the general, couched in terms not the most loyal. Greene replied with moderation, firmness, and dignity, and adhered to his

---

* HEAD-QUARTERS CAMP NEAR BACON'S BRIDGE.

General Gist will take command of the light troops, which will consist of the following corps, viz. :—

The cavalry of the Legion, and the cavalry of the third and fourth regiments, under the command of Colonel Baylor.

The infantry of the Legion, the dismounted dragoons of the third regiment, the Delaware regiment, and one hundred men properly officered, fit for light infantry service, under Major Beall, to be immediately detached from the line, and the whole of the infantry to be commanded by Lieutenant-Colonel Laurens.

General Gist will make such further arrangements as he may find necessary ; but that the service may be accommodated as much as possible to the constitution of the cavalry corps, whenever the cavalry of any corps are ordered out, and infantry are wanted, the infantry belonging to such corps will march with it.

Extract from the general orders of the 13th June, 1782.

JOS. HARMAR,
Lieutenant-Colonel, Deputy Adjutant-General.

adopted system. This was followed by the resignation of every officer in the Legion, a result as unexpected as inconvenient. The general lamented the rash step, but did not condescend by any relaxation in his measures, or remodification of the light troops, to avert it. He, however, reminded the remonstrants of their right of appeal to Congress, who would no doubt correct the proceedings of their generals, whenever they might invade the rights or cancel the privileges of any portion of the troops submitted to their direction. The officers had acted under the impulse of first impressions, which, though honest, are not always correct. Passion had now subsided, and the temerity of their conduct became exposed to their view. They cheerfully seized the opportunity presented by the general's suggestion, withdrew their resignations, and committed their case to the controlling power of Congress.

The inhabitants of the State of South Carolina had been for several months in the peaceable enjoyment of legal government, with the exception of the metropolis, and a small range of country upon the Little Pedee River. A Major Ganey, with his band of royalists, resided here; and, insulated as they were, still resisted. Brigadier Marion had, in June, 1781, entered into a formal treaty with Ganey and his associates, by which they were pardoned for past offences (both numerous and atrocious),* secured in their estates and in the rights of citizenship, upon the condition that they would return to the rightful owners all plundered property, that they would renounce forever allegiance to his Britannic majesty, and demean themselves hereafter as became peaceable citizens. This treaty was now renewed, with the condition that such of the royalists as preferred removing into the British lines might do so, and take with them their property.

The wise and forgiving policy which dictated the course pursued by Marion, was attended with the happiest consequences. Bitter enemies were converted into warm friends; and many of these reclaimed citizens enrolled themselves in the corps of Marion, ready to fight by the sides of their countrymen, whose lives they had sought by night and by day from the fall of Charleston to the period of this treaty.

* Among the many murders and burning of houses perpetrated by this banditti, that of Colonel Kobb was singularly atrocious. A party of them, led by a Captain Jones, surprised the colonel on a visit to his family. He defended his house, until he was induced, by the promise of personal safety, to surrender as a prisoner of war; when he was immediately murdered in the presence of his wife and children, and his house burnt.

During these transactions in South Carolina, Brigadier Wayne pursued with vigor his operations in Georgia. At the head of a force equal only to half of that opposed to him, he nevertheless exhibited that daringness of character which marked his military life. The signal chastisement inflicted by Major-General Grey at the Paoli, in the campaign of 1777, with some minor admonitions, had, it is true, subjected this natural propensity in some degree to the control of circumspection. While in command before Savannah, his orders, his plans, his motions, all bespoke foresight and vigilance; and although he played a hazardous game, he not only avoided detriment or affront, but added to the honor of our arms. The pacific policy lately adopted by the British general, and to which Brigadier Clarke invariably adhered, contributed not a little to a result so favorable to our views.

The British general rarely sent detachments into the country, and only once in considerable force; never with a view of provoking resistance, but always with the expectation of accomplishing his object by the secresy and celerity of his measures. About the middle of May he received information of an intended trading visit from some of his Indian friends, then considerably advanced on their route to Savannah. To protect this party from the corps under Wayne, to which it would be exposed in its progress, Lieutenant-Colonel Browne (who had been exchanged soon after his surrender of Augusta) was detached by Brigadier Clarke on the 19th, with three hundred and fifty infantry and a squadron of cavalry. Browne advanced as far as Ogeechee to meet the Indians; but being disappointed, he moved early in the morning of the 21st, to regain Savannah. It appears that a dispute having arisen between the warriors of the Overhill Creeks, from which tribe this trading party came, had occasioned a delay for a few weeks; otherwise the Indians would have reached the Ogeechee the very evening Browne arrived there.

Wayne discovered, on the 20th, that a detachment of the enemy had passed from Savannah to the Ogeechee; and he took his measures forthwith to intercept it on its return. With this view his corps (about five hundred effectives, mostly infantry, with three grasshoppers) were put in motion. The van consisted of one company of light infantry and a section of dragoons, under the orders of Captain Alexander Parker. This officer was directed to hasten his march through woods and swamps, and to seize a causeway on which Browne must necessarily pass. Parker was ordered, whenever he met the enemy, to reserve his fire, and to fall back upon him with sword and bayonet. Wayne followed with the main body, to support his van. About ten in the forenoon Captain Parker reached the causeway, when he discovered a small patrol of cavalry in his front. Each advancing, the two parties soon met, when Captain Parker accosted the leading file, and demanded the countersign. Confounded or deceived, the British officer, instead of falling back upon Browne, approached Parker in the attitude of friendship. He now discovered his mistake, but too late to extricate himself, and was with his patrol taken, except one dragoon, who got back to Colonel Browne, moving in column to sustain his van, with his cavalry in front.

Lieutenant Bowyer, who commanded our horse, was ordered to charge, which was executed with decision. Bowyer was supported by Parker with his infantry. The British cavalry were thrown into confusion; and as Browne's whole force was in column on the causeway, from whence there was no moving, to the right or left, the substitution of his infantry for his cavalry became impracticable, and the British colonel was obliged to fall back. This was accomplished without loss, as General Wayne did not get up in time to improve the advantage gained by Parker. Two of our van were killed and three were wounded. We took Major Alexander, second in command, and eighteen dragoons, with their horses and furniture. Wayne had been delayed by the swamps, which in the South invariably presented stubborn difficulties to the march of troops.

As soon as he reached Parker he pursued the enemy; but all his endeavors to renew the action proved abortive, and Browne made good his retreat to Savannah.

The Indians, whom Lieutenant-Colonel Browne expected to meet, would have rendered his corps superior to that under Wayne, when the encounter might have terminated differently. General Wayne seems either to have been unapprised of this intended junction, or to have disregarded it; for he pressed forward to strike his foe, regardless of ground or number. The fortuitous success of such conduct, encourages the ardent soldier to put himself upon his fortune and his courage,—overlooking those numerous, sure, and effectual aids to be drawn from accurate intelligence and due circumspection. Fortune at length forsakes him, no prop remains to support him but his courage, and he falls a victim of his own presumption; honored for his bravery, but condemned for his temerity.

Some weeks before General Clarke made this attempt to secure the safe entry of his Indian friends into Savannah, Wayne had intercepted a trading party of the Creeks on their way to the British garrison. Of these the American general detained a few as hostages, and permitted the rest to return to their own country. This generous treatment seems to have inspired apprehensions in Savannah, that its effect would diminish the British influence among the Creeks; an event deprecated by the enemy in case of continuance of the war, which, though improbable, might nevertheless happen. Therefore it was thought proper to prevent, by suitable succor, the interruption of this second visit. To that end Browne had been detached. Not only, as has been seen, did the effort fail, but it was followed by a disaster very unpleasant to the enemy, and in its conclusion pregnant with cause of regret to ourselves.

Guristersigo, a principal warrior among the Creeks, conducted the party of Indians lately expected by Clarke. Although he did not arrive at the appointed rendezvous so as to meet Browne, he reached in the latter part of the succeeding month.

This warrior, accompanied by his white guides, passed through the whole State of Georgia unperceived, except by two boys, who were taken and killed; and having reached the neighborhood of Wayne on the 23d of June, he determined to strike at a picket of the American corps stationed, as he was informed, at Gibbons's plantation, directly on the route to and not far distant from Savannah.

There were two plantations, so called, in the same range of country, both of which were occasionally stations for our troops. At this time Wayne himself with the main body occupied one, while the other was on the same day (22d) held by a picket guard. Not only to avoid Wayne, but to carry this picket, became the object of Guristersigo; and he acquired through his white conductors the requisite intelligence, with negro guides for the execution of his purpose.

Wayne, in pursuance of a system adopted to avoid surprise (of which the Indian chief was uninformed), moved every night; and consequently the calculation that he would be on the 23d where he had been on the 22d, was unfounded. The reverse was the fact which would undoubtedly have been perceived by Guristersigo had he been acquainted with the custom of the American general, and his plan of attack would have been modified accordingly. Decamping from Gibbons's late in the evening of the 22d, Wayne exchanged positions with his picket, and thus fortunately held the very post against which the Indian warrior had pointed his attack.

Here the light infantry under Parker (who had been for several days close to Savannah) joined, and being much harassed by the late tour of duty, was ordered by the brigadier to take post near his artillery, in the rear. Knowing but one enemy, the garrison of Savannah, Wayne gave his entire attention to that quarter; and conscious, from his precautions, that no movement could be made by the enemy in Savannah without due notice, he forbore to burden his troops with the protection of his rear, because in his opinion unnecessary. A single sentinel only from the quarter-guard was posted in the rear, on the main road leading through the camp to Savannah, and the very road which Guristersigo meant to take.

Soon after nightfall the Indian chief at the head of his warriors emerged from the deep swamps, in which he had lain concealed, and gained the road. He moved in profound silence, and about three in the morning reached the vicinity of our camp; here he halted, and made his disposition for battle. Believing that he had to deal with a small detachment only, his plan of attack was simple and efficient. Preceded by a few of the most subtle and daring of his comrades, directed to surprise and kill the sentinel, he held himself ready to press forward with the main body upon the signal to advance. This was not long delayed. His wily precursors having encompassed our sentinel, killed him, when Guristersigo, bounding from his stand, fell with his whole force upon our rear. Aroused from sleep, the light infantry stood to their arms, and the matrosses closed with their guns.

But the enemy was amongst them; which being perceived by Parker, he judiciously drew off in silence and joined the quarter-guard behind Gibbons's house at head-quarters. The general had about this time mounted, and, concluding that the garrison of Savannah was upon him, he resorted to the bayonet, determined to die sword in hand. Orders to this effect were given to Parker and dispatched to Lieutenant-Colonel Posey, commanding in camp, distant a few hundred yards. Captain Parker, seconded by the quarter-guard, advanced upon the foe; and Posey moved with all possible celerity to support the light troops, but did not arrive in time to share in the action. Wayne, participating with his light corps in the surrounding dangers, was now dismounted, his horse being killed; the light troops, nevertheless, continued to press forward, and Parker drove all in his way back to our cannon,.

where the Indian chief with a part of his warriors was attempting
to turn our guns to his aid. Here Guristersigo renewed the conflict,
and fought gallantly ; but the rifle and tomahawk are unavailing
when confronted by the bayonet in close quarters. We soon recovered our artillery, and Guristersigo, fighting bravely, was killed.
Seventeen of his warriors and his white guides fell by his side, and
the rest fled.*

* The narrative in the text is founded chiefly on information contributed by
Captain Parker (the late General Alexander Parker, of Virginia.) who was personally and conspicuously engaged in the rencounter. Soon after the appearance of the Memoirs, General Posey, who was then in the Senate of the United
States, sent to the author, the following statement, with a letter from General
Parker, attesting its correctness. The veracity of Posey was as unquestioned
as his courage, and it is satisfactory to be able to render him justice in his own
words.—ED.

*A statement in Lee's Memoirs of the War in the Southern Department of the Uni-
ted States, corrected, relative to the encounter which General Wayne had with
the Creek Indians, in the State of Georgia, on the night of the 23d of June,
1782.*

The army on that night was disposed agreeably to general orders in the following manner. The artillery, the cavalry, and the light infantry of Posey's
regiment, commanded by Captain Alexander Parker, were arranged in proper
order, at the lower Mrs. Gibbons's (distinguished in that way, there being two
widow ladies of the same name, where the troops were encamped alternately),
with a guard and chain of sentinels in the rear, and Posey's regiment posted a
few hundred yards on the road leading by Mrs. Gibbons's to Savannah, with a
proper disposition of guards, and a chain of sentinels in front. Major Samuel
Findley was with the regiment, Posey having received orders to remain with
General Wayne that night, the regiment being within so short a distance. The
whole of the troops had for several weeks been doing hard duty, every night
lying down in their ranks with their clothes and accoutrements on, and their
arms by their sides, and almost worn out with fatigue in watching and loss of
rest, in constant expectation that the British would either come out of Savannah in force for action, or that we might have an opportunity of falling in with
foraging parties. The account General Lee gives until he commences with the
attack made by Guristersigo is correct, except as to the disposition of the troops
above stated.

When the attack was made, it was with such fury and violence, at a dead
time of the night when the men were in profound sleep (except the guards),
with yelling and the use of their tomahawk, spears, scalping-knives, and guns,
that our men were thrown into disorder. Wayne and Posey had thrown their
cloaks about them and lay down close to each other, the alarm soon roused
them, and they had proceeded but a few steps when Captain Parker met Colonel Posey, and informing him that the suddenness of the attack had confused his
men, wished to know if the colonel had any particular orders. Posey immediately ordered that the light infantry should be rallied behind the house, and
his exertions, united with Parker's, in a short space of time collected the men.
Posey then placed himself with Parker at their head, and ordered a charge
through the enemy to the regiment; the charge was made with celerity and
firmness, though the conflict was severe, many of the Indians falling by the force
of the bayonet. One or more of the enemy fell by Posey's own arm, and unfortunately for Sergeant Thompson of Parker's light infantry (who contrary to

Now it was discovered that the assailing foe was not from Savannah. Although surprised at the extraordinary occurrence, Wayne adopted with promptitude his measures to the occasion, and scattering his troops in every direction, pursued the flying Indians. Twelve of them were taken, and after a few hours' captivity were put to death by order of the general. One hundred and seventeen pack-horses, laden with peltry, fell into our hands; and although every exertion was made to capture the surviving Indians, they all got back to their distant country. Our loss was small, not exceeding twelve killed and wounded.

This bold and concluding scene, though highly honorable to the unlettered chief, did not surpass those which preceded it in the

orders had taken off his coat and tied up his head with a handkerchief, but who was manfully engaged, and had immediately next to Posey fired at an Indian), Posey took him, from his appearance with his coat off and head tied up, for an Indian, and thrusting his sword through his body, laid him at his feet. But he greatly lamented the circumstance when he visited the hospital the next morning, and learned from the brave but incautious sergeant the particulars of his wounds. General Wayne with the cavalry followed Posey, who had filed off to the right to gain his regiment, which he met on its march to the scene of action, and placing himself at the head, charged immediately upon the rear of the enemy and put them to flight. General Wayne filed off to the left where he fell in with a considerable body of Indians, and compelled them to retreat after a severe conflict. Thus, with the united force and much bravery of both officers and soldiers, the whole of the Indians were defeated and routed. Posey then sent to Wayne for orders, and informed him that he should be found on his march toward Savannah, whither he was proceeding, with a view to ascertain the situation of the British. When the regiment reached the forks of the road (within one mile of the town), a small party was detached to examine the British guards, and ascertain whether they retained their usual positions, who soon returned and reported that they did. Shortly after this a trooper brought information that within half a mile in our rear he had discovered a large body of men, but that it was too dark to distinguish whether they were Indians or British. Posey immediately marched, ordering the trooper to show him where he had discovered the enemy. On approaching them it was light enough to see they were a body of Indians. They were standing in a road leading through a large swamp. While the regiment was preparing for action, several of the chiefs advanced about twenty or thirty steps and halted, looking very earnestly and apparently at a loss to know whether we were the enemy or British troops, as we were marching directly out from toward Savannah. Posey discovering that all retired and hid in the swamp except those few that had advanced, waved his sword for them to come up; they accordingly came to him; he ordered them under guard, and made search in the swamp for the others, but could not find any of them. He then returned to the forks of the road, and shortly after General Wayne joined with the balance of the troops. The general appeared in a good humor until he discovered the Indian prisoners, his countenance then changed, and he asked Posey in a very peremptory manner, how he could think of taking those savages prisoners. Posey related the circumstance of the manner in which they were decoyed, and observed that he thought it wrong to put them to death after they became prisoners; he said they should not live, and they were accordingly put to death.

progress of his daring enterprise. The accuracy of the intelligence obtained respecting the interior of Georgia, the geographical exactitude with which he shaped his course, the control he established over his rude band—repressing appetite for plunder when opportunity for gratification hourly occurred—and the decision with which he made his final arrangements, alike merit applause. Guristersigo died as he had lived, the renowned warrior of the Overhill Creeks.[*]

Wayne behaved with his accustomed gallantry. Not doubting but that General Clarke with his whole force from Savannah was upon him, he determined to cut his way to victory, or to die in the midst of his enemy. To this end was his order to Captain Parker; to this end was his order to Lieutenant-Colonel Posey; and to this end was his own conduct and example. It is true the American general was surprised; but if a surprise can be overlooked, this is the one. Who could suppose that an Indian warrior would be found bold enough to relinquish his safe and distant forests to traverse longitudinally the State of Georgia, and to force his entry through an investing army into Savannah. If the comprehensive and searching mind had, in its prying into all possible adventures, presumed upon such an attempt, it would scarcely have been brought to conclude, that the enterprise could remain undiscovered until the edge of the Indian tomahawk was felt in our camp.

However military critics may be disposed to withhold censure in consequence of the novelty and singularity of the late enterprise, yet, like every other incident in war, it demonstrates that the general who is contented with the inadequate protection of his camp, not only places himself at the disposal of fortune, but invites disaster. This would probably have been the result now, had not the Indian chief been turned from his right course by taking our cannon, and thus gave time to recover by valor, what had been lost by want of due caution.

---

[*] As it will probably not be long before the liberal part of the civilized world will seek eagerly for information respecting this perishing race of men, so remarkable for a strange mixture of cunning and fortitude, of secresy and violence, of patience and impetuosity, I have thought proper to subjoin the account which General Parker, as an eye-witness, gave of the conduct and fate of this bold and sagacious warrior of the woods. "He was the largest and bravest of the warriors—six feet, three inches high—weighing about two hundred and twenty pounds—of a manly and expressive countenance, and thirty years of age. After receiving an espontoon and three bayonets in his body, encouraging his warriors all the while, he retired a few paces, composedly laid himself down, and died without a groan or struggle."—ED.

As soon as General Wayne had buried the dead, and taken care of the wounded, he changed his ground as usual ; and finding that he had an enemy in the rear as well as in front, he became more circumspect in his future arrangements.

This was the last rencounter in Georgia. General Clarke held his troops safe within his fortifications, prepared to evacuate Savannah whenever he should receive orders to that effect, which he knew could not be long deferred.

Wayne continued in the neighborhood of the enemy pursuing his desultory game, and watching with unceasing vigilance his adversary's motions. Early in July he was visited by a deputation of merchants from Savannah, under the protection of a flag of truce, for the purpose of ascertaining on what conditions the British subjects would be permitted to remain with their property for a given term after the evacuation of the city, which event might be daily expected in consequence of orders recently received.

General Wayne informed the deputation, that whenever the British garrison should withdraw, he would protect the persons and property of all who might remain ; but that the ultimate disposal of the one and of the other belonged to the civil authority of the State, to which he would communicate the purport of their application. This answer being made known to the merchants and other inhabitants wishing to remain in Savannah, they, by permission of the British general, sent a second deputation to the American headquarters, with the view of fixing definitely the conditions on which they might be indulged in their desire.

In the mean time General Wayne had consulted Governor Martin, who, soon after the American detachment entered Georgia, removed with his council of state to Ebenezer, for the purpose of extending the limits of the civil authority. In pursuance of the governor's instructions, the American general gave assurances to the inhabitants, that all who chose to remain should be protected in person and property, and should be allowed sufficient time to dispose of their property and to adjust their affairs, when they might depart in manner and form most agreeable to themselves. Major Habersham, a respectable officer in the line of Georgia, was employed by General Wayne in the conclusion of this business, and seems to have afforded facility to the arrangements, by the confidence reposed in his personal character.

Satisfied with the assurance given, many of the British subjects discontinued their preparations for removal, and were found in the town when entered by Wayne. They received the promised protection, and pursued, without molestation, their customary occupations. As soon as the loyalists had finished their arrangements with the American general, Brigadier Clarke completed his evacuation (on the 11th July), and General Wayne on the same day took possession of Savannah, which had been for more than three years occupied by the enemy.

The spontaneous restoration of Georgia to the United States confirmed the expectation which prevailed, that the further prosecution of the war in America had been relinquished by his Britannic majesty, and would necessarily be soon followed by the recall of the royal army and fleet.

Previous to this event Lieutenant-Colonel Carrington rejoined. While at the High Hills of Santee, this officer, although at the head of the quartermaster-general's department, was permitted by the general to repair to the main army, in consequence of a vacancy in the line of artillery by the resignation of Colonel Proctor, of Pennsylvania. Carrington was considered as entitled to the vacancy, and took command of the regiment on its arrival in Virginia, with part of the allied army. But inasmuch as Congress had not established the mode of promotion in the cavalry and artillery, his continuance in the command of the regiment was uncertain; and therefore General Greene determined that, though absent, he should govern the department through his deputy, for the purpose of securing his future services, should his expectation of promotion fail. On Captain Crump, of the Virginia line, second in the department, the important trust devolved during the absence of his principal, and he discharged its various duties with intelligence and effect. When the siege of York terminated, Carrington, disappointed in his expected promotion, repaired to Philadelphia by order of General Greene, for the purpose of concerting measures with the superintendent of finance, for the future subsistence and clothing of the Southern army. Mr. Morris entered with alacrity into the proposed application of a portion of the funds under his direction to this desirable object. In pursuance whereof General Greene was empowered to contract for the requisite supplies, payable in specie; by which arrangement, the irksome and wasteful system heretofore pursued was superseded, and the cheering prospect of regular subsistence and comfortable clothing was presented to the long-suffering army of the South.

The evacuation of Savannah was followed in the same month

(August) by the meeting of the General Assembly of Georgia at Augusta, when the exercise of the civil authority was completely re-established throughout the State. Brigadier Wayne having, soon after the departure of the royal forces, detached Lieutenant-Colonel Posey to the main army, now proceeded to South Carolina with his corps. General Greene concentrating his troops, drew nearer to Charleston, and directed his operations to the single object of preventing the enemy from deriving any subsistence from the country. The intention of evacuating Charleston was now announced in general orders by the British commander; ^{August.} who, however, continued to exert his force in procuring the provisions necessary not only for the daily support of the army and loyalists, but also for their maintenance until the first should be established in their future quarters, and the last transplanted to their intended settlements. Small parties were therefore occasionally detached from Charleston in various directions through those parts of the country remote from the American army, for the purpose of collecting and transporting rice, corn, and meat, to the British head-quarters. Sometimes these parties succeeded; but generally they were compelled to return without effecting the object of their incursion.

Major-General Leslie soon perceived the precariousness of this resource; to remedy which, and to stop the further effusion of blood, now unnecessary as to the main object of the war, notwithstanding the rejection of his pacific overture some time before, addressed General Greene by letter (August), expressing the motives and object of his military inroads, and proposing to discontinue them, on condition of being permitted to purchase from the country such supplies as might be necessary during his continuance in Charleston. The civil authority was necessarily consulted on Leslie's proposition by the American general. So manifold and interesting were the advantages to our army from agreeing to the enemy's proposal, that deliberation seemed to border upon absurdity. The American soldiers were covered by tattered garments, destitute of shoes, and scarcely furnished with blankets. Winter was approaching, when privations now tolerable would become intolerable; and every effort had been vainly essayed to procure clothing on the credit of the specie funds appropriated by the superintendent of finance in the preceding spring to the use of the Southern army, which, by the proposed intercourse, might have been readily obtained from Charleston. Imperiously as the general was urged by these considerations to

avail himself of the opportunity within his grasp, he was constrained
to forego it.   The government of South Carolina entertained the
belief, that the British army, on the evacuation of Charleston, would
be transferred to the West Indies.   Connected with this opinion
was the conviction that the proposed purchase of provisions was
not so much intended to meet present wants, as to amass magazines
for the support of the British forces contending against our ally in
that quarter.   To accommodate the enemy in the accomplishment
of this object was deemed dishonorable and perfidious ; therefore it
was determined to endure present ills rather than tarnish the
national character : the proposition of General Leslie was accordingly rejected.

Sensibly as the American army felt this unexpected termination
of the enemy's overture, not a murmur was heard in its ranks.
Trained to suffer when required so to do by authority, the officers
and soldiers exemplified upon this occasion their immutable disposition to forget their own wants in their zeal to uphold the cause
and character of their country.

The punctilious observance of the obligations of treaties and
scrupulous obedience to the injunctions of honor cannot be too
much applauded ; yet it will scarcely be contended that compliance
with the proposal of General Leslie either violated the treaty
between the United States and his Most Christian Majesty, or
trenched upon the principles of honor ; nor can it be denied that it
subserved the cause of humanity.   The British general's letter
candidly expressed his situation, amicably showed his unwillingness to shed more blood, now culpable because useless, but at
the same time frankly announced, that unless he could be supplied
with provisions in the manner proposed, he must obtain them by
force.

How easy would it have been for the governor and general, with
their just solicitude, to observe the stipulations of treaties, and to
avoid even in appearance the violation of honor, to accept the enemy's proposition on the express condition that the subsistence to
be procured should be limited to present support, and to that of
the approaching voyage, declaring that any attempt to transcend the
specified limits should cancel the contract.   The limitations which
a temperate examination of the enemy's overture would have suggested never came into view ; and in the overstrained anxiety to
avoid possible injury to France, the absolute advantages, comfort
to our suffering soldiers, and stoppage to human slaughter, were

neglected. This mistaken decision was soon followed by its natural, and with us deeply lamented, consequences.

Foiled in accomplishing his object in the way desired, the British general prepared to resume his suspended incursions into the country, determined to effect by force the procurement of those supplies which he had flattered himself with obtaining by purchase.   Supported by marine co-operation applicable with readiness to all the circumjacent country by the facilities of its interior navigation, and possessing the contiguous islands, with strong detachments from his army, General Leslie proceeded to the execution of his determination, fearless of consequences, but lamenting the necessity of wasting human life.

A detachment of light infantry, attended by armed vessels, passed along the interior navigation, and having reached Combahee River, began to collect and convey provisions to the transports which accompanied the expedition for the purpose of transporting to Charleston whatever might be procured.   General Greene, never doubting Leslie's execution of his menace, held his light corps ready to counteract any attempt he might make.   As soon, therefore, as he became apprised of the movement of the British detachment, he directed Brigadier Gist to advance in pursuit.   Gist was soon in motion, and after a long and rapid march gained the neighborhood of the enemy, then at Page's Point, on the Combahee.   At this moment, Lieutenant-Colonel Laurens, commanding the infantry under Gist, joined, having, as soon as informed of the march of the light troops, left his sick-bed to hasten to the field of battle.   Laurens no sooner overtook the corps than, by permission of the brigadier, he put himself at the head of the American van.   Discovering that the enemy were preparing to retire, he determined, with his inferior force, though out of supporting distance, to commence the attack.   This bold decision was gallantly executed ; but incapable of making any serious impression from the inadequacy of his force, he fell in the vain attempt at the head of his intrepid band, closing his short and splendid life in the lustre of heroism.   Gist now got up with the main body, and took one of the vessels from the enemy returning to Charleston.

The British general finding himself foiled in his expectations, henceforward discontinued these predatory inroads, and confined his exertions in the collection of provisions to the islands along the coast, and to the country contiguous to the interior navigation, remote from the American camp.

Preparations for the evacuation of Charleston proceeded, but not with the celerity expected. This excited apprehensions among the owners of the numerous bodies of negroes within the enemy's lines, that with the removal of the army would be carried off their slaves. They made known their apprehensions to Governor Matthews, who addressed a letter to General Leslie on the subject, and reminded him of the act of confiscation passed by the legislature, from the operation of which had been exempted all debts due to British merchants, and claims on real estates by marriage settlement. These two funds, added to that arising from the confiscation of estates, furnished a valuable resource ; and the governor assured General Leslie that he would apply them in remunerating his fellow-citizens for their negroes, if removed with the retiring army.

This annunciation seriously affected the loyalists in Charleston, and especially the mercantile portion of them, ever alive to the feelings of interest. They soon beset the British general, who was always inclined to do right and to diminish the evils of war. Leslie, in reply to the governor, proposed negotiation, with the view of reconciling the opposite interests of the adverse parties. Commissioners were accordingly appointed with full powers to treat upon the subject. The honorable William Gerrard, on the part of the State, and Alexander Wright and James Robertson, on the part of the loyalists. The discussion which ensued terminated in a compact on the 10th of October, to the following effect :—

" That all the slaves of the citizens of South Carolina now in the power of the honorable Major-General Leslie shall be restored to their former owners as far as is practicable; except such slaves as may have rendered themselves particularly obnoxious on account of their attachment and services to the British troops, and such as had specific promises of freedom. That the faith of the State is hereby solemnly pledged that none of the debts due to British merchants, or to persons who have been banished, or whose estates have been confiscated, or property secured by family settlements fairly made, or contracts relative thereto, shall now, or at any time hereafter, be arrested or withheld by the executive authority of the State; that no act of the legislature shall hereafter pass for confiscating, or seizing the same, in any manner whatever, if it is in the power of the executive to prevent it; and that its whole power and influence within its public and private capacity shall at all times be exerted for that purpose.

" That the same power shall be allowed for the recovery of the debts and property hereby protected and secured, by the parties or their representatives in the courts of justice or otherwise, as the citizens of the State may be or at any time were entitled to, notwithstanding any act of confiscation or banishment, or any other disability whatsoever; and that the same may be remitted to any part of the world they may think proper, under the same and no other regulations than the citizens of the State may be subject to.

"That no slaves, restored to their former owners by virtue of this agreement, shall be punished by the authority of the State for having left their masters and attached themselves to the British troops; and it will be particularly recommended to their respective owners to forgive them for the same.

"That no violence or insult shall be offered to the persons or houses of the families of such persons as are obliged to leave the State for their adherence to the British government, when the American army shall take possession of the town, or at any time afterward, as far as it is in the power of those in authority to prevent it.

"That Edward Blake and Roger Parker Saunders, Esqs., shall be permitted to reside in Charleston on their parole of honor to assist in the execution of the first article of this compact."—*Ramsay.*

In pursuance of this contract all minor measures were punctiliously adopted for its consummation. The two American commissioners were duly accredited and received in Charleston.

But the very first embarkation of the retiring enemy evinced that matured consideration of the preceding compact produced its violation by the party which had proposed it. Leslie began to remove the loyalists; for a portion of whom St. Augustine had been selected as a retreat. A fleet for their transportation was accordingly prepared; and when they embarked, two hundred negroes accompanied them. The American commissioners remonstrated against this infraction of the compromise entered into, to superintend the honorable fulfilment of which they not only had been appointed by the governor of the State, but had been admitted into Charleston by the general. The remonstrance produced the disembarkation of a small part of the negroes on board; but when the commissioners asked for permission to restore this small part to their owners, by forwarding them to the assigned post for their reception without the British lines, the request was denied, and justified by the following letter :—

"To Edward Blake and Roger P. Saunders, Esquires.

"Head-quarters, *October* 18, 1782.

"Gentlemen,—General Leslie was much surprised on finding that a large patrol from General Greene's army, two days ago, came down so near our advanced post on Charleston Neck, as to carry off three soldiers, who were a little way in the front. At the time this little act of hostility was committed, Mr. Ferguson and another person were at Accabee; where, I believe, they still remain, in expectation of the negroes to be delivered up, without any sanction but that of the agreement entered into. I am directed to observe, that if a line of conduct on the part of General Greene, so different from ours, is adopted, it must of course put an end to the pacific intentions General Leslie means to follow in regard to this province, during the short time he is to remain in it.

"He wishes you will inform Governor Mathews that he expects the soldiers taken away will be returned, and that the governor will take proper measures to have this requisition complied with. Until this is done, General Leslie must be under the necessity of putting a stop to the further completion of the agreement."

"(Signed)   S. Weyms, deputy adjutant-general."

The inability of the British general to secure the faithful execution of the compact might have been perceived by him before its ratification; inasmuch as the effectuation of its material conditions depended on the will of the State legislature, more apt to oppose than to fulfil executive recommendations. If, however, this inability was not discovered until after ratification, better would it have been to declare the fact, then to resort to a flimsy and irrelevant pretext for abrogation of a contract.

However, the British general seems to have preferred resorting for his justification to an expedient not less defective in reason than incompatible with his fair and honorable character.

No suspensions of military operations had ever been suggested, much less stipulated. How then the capture of British soldiers, by an American patrol, could be construed into a violation of the contract entered into with the governor of the State, is not discernable.

But pretexts, the most trival, will be embraced by power when disposed to forget right, in furtherance of its will. Such appears to have been the present temper of the British general; and the contract lately sought by himself, and well calculated to stop the spread of injustice, was annulled.

The American commissioners forwarded the letter received from the British adjutant-general to Governor Matthews, who replied as follows:—

"*October* 19*th*, 1782.

"SIR,—I was a few minutes ago favored with a letter from Messrs. Blake and Saunders, inclosing one to them from Major Weyms, written by your authority. As I do not like a second-hand correspondence, I therefore address myself immediately to you. I addressed a letter to you this morning, by which you will find that I was not even then without some apprehension of the intended evasion of the compact entered into on the 10th instant; but on the receipt of Major Weyms's letter, no room was left me for doubt; which obliges me, without giving further trouble to those engaged in the business, and introducing further altercation between us, to declare that I look upon that agreement as dissolved, and have accordingly ordered my commissioners immediately to quit your lines. But before I take my final leave of you, permit me to make one or two observations on Major Weyms's letter, as probably the whole correspondence between us may one day be brought to public view.

"On the 12th instant I wrote to you, to know whether persons going to Accabee to bring off the negroes when brought there, should be protected from your armed parties; and, further, to permit me to send a party of militia to guard the negroes remaining unclaimed to some part of the country where they could be supplied with provisions. To this letter I have received no answer, which has obliged me to use the precaution of giving flags to all persons who have applied to go to Accabee; as I could on no principle look on that ground as neutral, until it had been mutually agreed on as such. Indeed I was led to believe the contrary was intended on your part, both by your tedious silence and detachments from your army making excursions as far as Ashley Ferry; which was absolutely the case the morning of the day that the party from General Greene's army took the soldiers you so peremptorily demanded of me; and if I am rightly informed, hostilities were commenced by your party. Be that as it may, I conceive it of little consequence, as either party had a right to commence hostilities on hostile ground; and between enemies every spot must be considered as such, until mutually agreed upon to be otherwise. Besides, it is a well-known fact, that there is not a day but some of your armed parties are on that very ground which you affect to hold neutral.

"With regard to Messrs. Ferguson and Waring remaining at Accabee unmolested, I hold myself under no manner of obligation to you for this forbearance; as I informed you they were there under the sanction of a flag; that they were to remain there for the purpose of receiving the negroes sent out by the agents in Charleston. They were therefore authorized to continue there, till you signified the contrary to them. Flags from you have remained within half a mile of our lines for several days on private business, without the least molestation whatever. Besides, sir, if your reasoning, as far as it applies to those gentlemen, prove any thing, it proves too much; because on the same principle, the other two commissioners being in Charleston, ought to make that neutral ground also, notwithstanding no stipulation for that purpose had been entered into. I never interfere with General Greene's military plans, therefore the paragraph which relates to his operations ought to have been addressed to him; but I believe he pays as little regard to threats as I do."

With this letter ceased every effort to give effect to the contract between the governor and General Leslie. The American commissioners.returned home, and the negroes seduced and taken from the inhabitants of South Carolina in the course of the war, remained subject to the disposal of the enemy. They were successively shipped to the West Indies; and it is asserted, upon the authority of the best-informed citizens of South Carolina, that more than twenty thousand slaves were lost to the State in consequence of the war; of which not an inconsiderable portion was appropriated by British officers, and sold for their benefit in the West Indies.

Preparations for the embarkation of the enemy continued, but so tardily, that General Greene himself, who never yielded entirely to the opinion that peace was near at hand, began to doubt the sincerity of those pacific professions which accompanied General Leslie's annunciation of his intended evacuation of Charleston. His presumption of the enemy's perseverance in the war, and intimate knowledge of the distressed condition of his army for clothing of every sort, could not fail more and more to excite the sensibility of a commander justly regarded as the father of his soldiers.

From the return of Lieutenant-Colonel Carrington, after his visit to the superintendent of finance, General Greene had endeavored without intermission to negotiate a contract for the supply of the army with provisions, and to secure winter clothing for the troops, the want of which became every day more pressing. Vain were all his efforts to accomplish the first, although supported by the executive authority of the State, and seconded by the active exertions of the quartermaster-general; who was authorized by the general to pledge the specie funds appropriated by the superintendent of finance to the Southern service, to those who might contract for the supply either of provsions or clothing.

The devastation of the country, the neglect of the culture of the soil, and the bankrupt condition of the numerous class of individuals heretofore opulent and influential, prevented the acceptance of his overtures by any, although repeatedly proffered and zealously pressed. But however disinclined to relax his endeavors to substitute the regular and cheap system of feeding his troops by special contract, instead of the wasteful mode of requisition by the State agent, who was occasionally compelled to resort to military aid, Greene was reluctantly compelled to yield to the general inability, and to rely on the precarious and ruinous old mode, adopted through necessity and continued from the same cause. The evacuation of Charleston would of course change the state of the country, and give vigor to enterprising individuals. Then, and not till then, could he indulge the hope of effecting the discreet change in subsisting his army; and he was obliged to rely upon the same event for procuring the requisite clothing, rendered more and more necessary by the approach of winter.

Exclusively, therefore, of the importance of the expected event, in a military and national view, it became the peculiar object of anxious solicitude with the American general, as it presented the only resource to relieve his army from difficulties, which must, unless surmounted, lead to its dissolution.

General Leslie had declared, in his orders of the 7th of August, his intention of withdrawing his army; but September had passed away, and Charleston still remained in possession of the enemy.

In the course of the preceding month, Governor Matthews had contrived, through his influence with some of the royalists in Charleston, who had resolved to throw themselves on the mercy of their country, to procure a small quantity of the most necessary articles of clothing. This fortunate acquisition, added to a supply forwarded from Philadelphia by means of the superintendent of finance, enabled the general to cover the most naked of his army; and the unceasing exertions of the State commissary, aided by the co-operation of the quartermaster-general, produced an agreeable change in the quantity and quality of provisions. Still the situation of the army was deplorable, and much remained to be done to give durable comfort to the troops, whose past distress is thus described by General Greene in an official letter written on the 13th of August. "For upward of two months, more than one-third of our army was naked, with nothing but a breech-cloth about them, and never came out of their tents; and the rest were as ragged as wolves. Our condition was little better in the articles of provision. Our beef was perfect carrion; and even bad as it was, we were frequently without any. An army thus clothed and thus fed may be considered in a desperate situation."

The delay and uncertainty in evacuating Charleston, however productive of gloomy forebodings in the American camp, did not stop the enterprise of adventurous individuals, who, believing the event at hand, seized, as they presumed, the sure opportunity of advancing their fortunes. Many of these procured admittance into Charleston, and entered into contracts with the British merchants, whom they found as desirous of selling their stock on hand, as they were eager to buy it.

Among the adventurers who, about the end of August or beginning of September, made their way into Charleston, was Mr. John Banks from Virginia. This gentleman (no doubt with permission), after a short stay in town, visited the American army. Here he was introduced to General Greene. Well knowing the naked condition of his countrymen in arms, and convinced of the general solicitude to relieve their sufferings, he offered to procure and deliver whatever might be wanted. Greene having been, as before mentioned, authorized by the superintendent of finance to enter into contracts for supplying his army, did not hesitate in accepting Banks's proposal, and a contract was arranged with him for the requisite clothing to be delivered on the evacuation of Charleston. This was the first opportunity which had presented of effecting the long-wished and much-desired object. It was embraced with avidity, and Mr. Banks completely executed his contract at the designated period, to the great joy of the general and army.

The preparations for evacuating Charleston began now to assume a determinate character; and the doubts heretofore entertained on that subject to be dissipated. The American general held still his position at Ashley Hill, shutting up every avenue to intercourse between town and country. The enemy no longer attempted to interrupt this operation, but fixed in his design of withdrawing from South Carolina, he avoided unavailing conflict. Thus passed the autumn, and General Leslie, although never intermitting his preparations to retire, still continued with his army in Charleston. At length, early in December, the embarkation of the military stores, ordnance, and baggage commenced. When this was completed, the troops followed, and on the 14th the embarkation was finished. General Wayne, with the Legion and light infantry, had for some days previous, by order of Greene, placed himself near the Quarterhouse for the purpose of entering the town as soon as it should be evacuated. To this officer, Leslie informally intimated his wish to prevent injury to the town, in which he presumed on the cordial coincidence of the American general, and which he insinuated was only to be effected by prohibiting every attempt to interrupt the embarkation of the retiring army.

Wayne communicated to the general the intimation he had received from Leslie, who directed him to conform to it.

Accordingly no effort was made to disturb the enemy's embarkation, which took place without the smallest confusion or disorder; the light troops under Wayne entered into town close after the retirement of the British rear.

Thus was the metropolis of South Carolina restored to the United States, after having been in the possession of the enemy from its surrender to Sir Henry Clinton. (12th May, 1780.)

The governor with his suite was escorted into the capital on the same day. On the next the civil authority resumed its former functions, and the din of arms yielded to the innocent and pleasing occupations of peace.

APPENDIX.

A.—Page 83.

LIEUTENANT-GENERAL BURGOYNE had been a soldier from early life, and very much distinguished himself in the campaign of 1762, under the Count de la Lippe Schomburg, in Portugal, where he established his reputation in arms, signalizing himself particularly by his surprise of the Spaniards at Valentia de Alcantera, and afterward with Colonel Lee at Villavelha. He was an accomplished gentleman, with the advantage of respectable family connections, and a highly finished education.

B.—Page 83.

MAJOR-GENERAL GATES, like his antagonist, had been bred to arms, and served in America during the war of 1755. His course seems to have been *mediocre*.

After the peace of 1763 he settled in Virginia, where the revolutionary war found him. Unprovided as were the States with soldiers of experience, General Gates was called forth by the Congress of 1775, and was appointed adjutant-general, with the rank of brigadier, to the army assembled before Boston in our first campaign.

C.—Page 113.

MAJOR-GENERAL CHARLES LEE was born in England, and entered very young into the army—the profession most congenial to his mind. He served in America, in Portugal, and in Turkey, always respected, and sometimes distinguished.

Like his unfortunate friend, Lieutenant-General Burgoyne, he possessed the confidence and esteem of Count de la Lippe, under whose orders, with Lieutenant-Colonel Burgoyne, he was detached to strike at a detached camp of the enemy in the village of Villavelha, during the campaign of 1762, in Portugal; which service was handsomely performed.

In the dispute between the colonies and the mother country, Lee espoused with warmth the cause of the colonies, whose rights he believed to be despotically invaded; and some time after came over to America. When convinced that the sword must be drawn, he resigned his commission in the British army, and accepted the third station in the American staff, proffered to him by Congress. He possessed a sublime genius, highly improved by books and travel; but was eccentric from freedom of thought, which he uttered without reserve; sarcastic without malignity of heart, but with asperity of tongue; and imprudent, from an indisposition to guard himself by cramping mental independence.

D.—Page 186.

MAJOR-GENERAL BARON DE KALB was a German by birth;* and, from the best information obtainable, must have served during the war of 1755 in some

---

* Colonel Howard thinks he was from Alsace or Lorraine—German provinces, ceded to France; and that he served in the French army in conjunction with that of the Imperialists in 1755. It is very probable the French had in this country the regiment of Deux Ponts, a German corps—but raised from a district then belonging to France.

of the inferior stations of the quartermaster-general's department, in the imperial army operating with that of his most Christian majesty; it being well ascertained by his acquaintances in our army that he was intimately versed in the details of that department. Toward the close of that war he must have been dispatched by the French court to North America, as he has himself often mentioned his having traversed the then British provinces in a concealed character; the object of which tour cannot be doubted, as the baron never failed, when speaking of the existing war, to express his astonishment, how any government could have so blundered as to efface the ardent and deep affection which, to his own knowledge, existed on the part of the colonies to Great Britain previous to the late rupture,—a preference equalled only by their antipathy to the French nation, which was so powerful as to induce the baron to consider it, as he called it, "instinctive."

Just before the peace our incognitus, becoming suspected, was arrested; and for a few days he was imprisoned. On examination of his baggage and papers, nothing could be found confirming the suspicion which had induced his arrest, and he was discharged.

Such discovery was not practicable; as during this tour the baron himself declared, that he relied entirely upon his memory, which was singularly strong; never venturing to commit to paper the information of others or his own observations. On the restoration of peace the baron returned to Europe, and came once more to America in 1777 or 1778, recommended to Congress as an experienced soldier, worthy of confidence. A brigadier in the service of France, he was honored by Congress with the rank of major-general, and repaired to the main army, in which he served at the head of the Maryland division very much respected.

Possessing a stout frame, with excellent health, no officer was more able to encounter the toils of war. Moderate in mental powers, as in literary acquirements, he excelled chiefly in the practical knowledge of men and things, gained during a long life by close and accurate investigation of the cause and effect of passing events.

We all know that the court of France has been uniformly distinguished by its superior address and management in diving into the secrets of every nation, whether friend or foe, with whom it has relation.

The business of espionage has been brought in France to a science, and a regular trained corps, judiciously organized, is ever in the service of the court. Of this body there is strong reason to believe that the baron was a member, and probably one of the chief confidants of that government in the United States. No man was better qualified for the undertaking. He was sober, drinking water only: abstemious to excess; living on bread, sometimes with beef soup, at other times with cold beef; industrious, it being his constant habit to rise at five in the morning, light his candle, devote himself to writing, which was never intermitted during the day but when interrupted by his short meals, or by attention to his official duty; and profoundly secret. He wrote in hieroglyphics, not upon sheets of paper as is customary in camps, but in large folio books; which were carefully preserved, waiting to be transmitted to his unknown correspondent whenever a safe opportunity might offer. He betrayed an unceasing jealousy lest his journals and mystic dictionary might be perused; and seemed to be very much in dread of losing his baggage; which, in itself was too trifling to be regarded, and would only have attracted such unvarying care from the valuable paper deposit. He never failed to direct his quartermaster to place him as near the centre of the army as was allowable, having an utter aversion to be in the vicinity of either flank, lest an adventuring partisan should carry off his baggage. What became of his journals is not known; but very probably he did not venture to take them into South Carolina; what is most probable, he placed such as remained in the hands of the French minister for transmission to Paris, when he was ordered to the South.

If he continued to write when marching to South Carolina, his progress must have been slow, as he was necessarily much engaged in the duties of his command, which became multiplied by the extreme difficulty with which subsistence was procurable. Whether his baggage was captured is not known to me; but it cannot be doubted, that his papers did not fall into the possession of the enemy; as in such event we should probably have heard not only of the fact, but also of their contents. No man surpassed this gentleman in simplicity and condescension; which gave to his deportment a cast of amiability extremely ingratiating, exciting confidence and esteem. Although nearer seventy than sixty years of age, such had been the temperance of his life, that he not only enjoyed to the last day the finest health, but his countenance still retained the bloom of youth; which circumstance very probably let to the error committed by those who drew up the inscription on the monument, erected by order of Congress. This distinguished mark of respect was well deserved, and is herewith presented to the reader.

"*Resolved*, That a monument be erected to the memory of the deceased Major-General Baron de Kalb, in the town of Annapolis, in the State of Maryland, with the following inscription:—

"'Sacred to the memory of the Baron de Kalb, Knight of the Royal Order of military merit, Brigadier of the armies of France, and Major-General in the service of the United States of America. Having served with honor and reputation for three years, he gave a last and glorious proof of his attachment to the liberties of mankind, and to the cause of America, in the action near Camden, in the State of South Carolina; where, leading on the regular troops of Maryland and Delaware against superior forces, and animating them by his example to deeds of valor, he was wounded in several places, and died the 19th of August following, in the forty-eighth year of his age. The Congress of the United States of America, in acknowledgment of his zeal, of his services, and of his merit, hath erected this monument.'"

E.—Pages 176, 192.

WILLIAM RICHARDSON DAVIE, of North Carolina, was born in the village of Egermont, near White Haven, in England, on the 20th of June, 1756.

His father, visiting South Carolina soon after the peace of 1763, brought with him this son; and, returning to England, confided him to the care of the Reverend William Richardson, his maternal uncle; who, becoming much attached to his nephew, not only took charge of his education, but adopted him as his son and heir. At the proper age William was sent to an academy in North Carolina; whence he was, after a few years, removed to the college of Nassau Hall, in Princeton, New Jersey, then becoming the resort of most of the Southern youth under the auspices of the learned and respectable Doctor Witherspoon. Here he finished his education, graduating in the autumn of 1776, a year memorable in our military as well as civil annals.

Returning home, young Davie found himself shut out for a time from the army, as the commissions for the troops just levied had been issued. He went to Salisbury, where he commenced the study of the law. The war continuing contrary to the expectation which generally prevailed when it began, Davie could no longer resist his ardent wish to place himself among the defenders of his country. Inducing a worthy and popular friend, rather too old for military service, to raise a troop of dragoons, as the readiest mode of accomplishing his wish, Davie obtained a lieutenancy in this troop. Without delay the captain joined the Southern army, and soon afterward returned home on furlough. The command of the troop devolving on Lieutenant Davie, it was at his request annexed to the Legion of Count Pulaski, where Captain Davie continued, until promoted by Major-General Lincoln to the station of brigade major of cavalry. In this office Davie served until the affair of Stono, devoting his leisure to the acquirement of professional knowledge, and rising fast in the esteem of the general and army. When Lincoln attempted·to dislodge Lieutenant-Colonel Maitland from his intrenched camp on the Stono, Davie received a severe wound, and was removed from camp to the hospital in Charleston, where he was confined for five months.

Soon after his recovery, he was empowered by the government of North Carolina to raise a small Legionary corps, consisting of one troop of dragoons and two companies of mounted infantry ; at the head of which he was placed with the rank of major.

Quickly succeeding in completing his corps, in whose equipment he expended the last remaining shilling of an estate bequeathed to him by his uncle, he took the field, and was sedulously engaged in protecting the country between Charlotte and Camden from the enemy's predatory incursions. On the fatal 16th of August, he was hastening with his corps to join the army, when he met our dispersed and flying troops. He nevertheless continued to advance toward the conqueror ; and by his prudence, zeal, and vigilance, saved a few of our wagons and many of our stragglers. Acquainted with the movement of Sumter, and justly apprehending he would be destroyed unless speedily advised of the defeat of Gates, he dispatched instantly a courier to that officer, communicating what had happened, performing in the midst of distress and confusion, the part of an experienced captain. The abandonment of all the southern region of North Carolina, which followed the signal overthrow, and the general despondency which prevailed, have been recorded in the body of this work ; nor have the fortunate and active services of Major Davie been overlooked. So much was his conduct respected by the government of North Carolina, that he was, in the course of September, promoted to the rank of colonel-commandant of the cavalry of the State.

In this station he was found by General Greene on assuming the command of the Southern army; whose attention had been occupied from his entrance into North Carolina, in remedying the disorder in the quartermaster and commissary departments. To the first Carrington had been called ; and Davie was now induced to take upon himself the last, much as he preferred the station he then possessed. At the head of this department Colonel Davie remained throughout the trying campaign which followed ; contributing greatly by his talents, his zeal, his local knowledge, and his influence, to the maintenance of the difficult and successful operations which followed. While before Ninety-six, Greene foreseeing the difficulties again to be encountered in consequence of the accession of force to the enemy by the arrival of three regiments of infantry from Ireland, determined to send a confidential officer to the legislature of North Carolina, then in session, to represent to them his relative condition, and to urge their adoption of effectual measures for the collection of magazines of provisions, and the re-enforcement of his army. Colonel Davie was selected by Greene for this prominent mission, and immediately repaired to the seat of government, where he exerted himself to give effect to the views of his general.

The events of the autumn assuring the quick approach of peace, Colonel Davie returned home; and having shortly after married Miss Sarah Jones, daughter of General Allen Jones, of North Carolina, he selected the town of Halifax, on the Roanoke, for his residence; where he resumed the profession with the practice of law.

F.—Page 103.

SIMEON THAYER was born in the town of Mendon, in the county of Worcester, in the State of Massachusetts, on the 21st of April, 1738; and early in life removed from thence to the town of Providence, in Rhode Island, where a few years afterward he married, and permanently established himself.

No man more uniformly possessed the esteem of his neighbors and acquaintances than this gentleman did, being distinguished for unvarying goodness of heart, rendered peculiarly agreeable by the modesty of his demeanor, and the simplicity of his manners. Bottomed on this solid foundation, his popularity extended as he advanced in life. And when in his thirty-seventh year, resistance to Great Britain became necessary, the determination of Thayer to take the field was anticipated by the spontaneous offer of the command of a company in Colonel Hilchcork's regiment of Rhode Island, about to be detached to the American army before Boston. Thayer's merit soon attracted attention: and when Washington projected the arduous enterprise against Quebec, committed to the direction of Colonel Arnold for the purpose of co-operating with Montgomery, the choice spirits of his army were selected for the expedition. Thayer could not of course be overlooked: he marched under Arnold at the head of a company, exhibiting, throughout the operation, peculiar fitness in mind and body to meet danger and difficulty. The fall of Montgomery being soon followed by our repulse, Thayer was made prisoner, bravely struggling to carry the second barrier, and experienced in common with his comrades the beneficence extended by Sir G. Carleton to the American prisoners,—so truly honorable to the heart and to the head of the British general. Captain Thayer rejoined his regiment as soon as he was exchanged, and went through the war, adding to his early stock of military reputation whenever opportunity offered. He served generally under Washington, by whom he was highly respected.

His conduct in the defence of Mud Island has been briefly touched in the course of this work. It is but justice to add, that the assumption of the command in the desperate condition to which the island was reduced, was in consequence of the voluntary request of Major Thayer, displaying as much magnanimity as gallantry.

It was known that the island must soon fall : to defend it to the last moment, and then to save the garrison, was the best which could be done. Few presumed this practicable ; and fewer were disposed to undertake the hazardous task. Thayer offered himself to Brigadier Varnum, commanding our force in New Jersey, which was joyfully accepted ; and the gallant major as joyfully repaired to his post.

In the battle of Monmouth the corps to which Thayer was attached was closely engaged ; he was wounded by a cannon-ball, which deprived him of the sight of the eye on the side it passed.

Concluding his military life with the war, he returned to Providence ; carrying with him the esteem of his fellow-soldiers, the gratitude of his country, the admiration of the witnesses of his exploits, and the immutable approbation of the commander-in-chief. Here he continued to deck the laurels he had acquired in the field of battle by his benevolence, his sincerity, his constancy in virtue, and his modesty in deportment.

The legislature of Rhode Island honored him with the commission of major-general in her militia, which he held to his death. In 1796 General Thayer removed from Providence to his farm in the township of Cumberland, where he spent his last years in the exclusive occupation of agriculture. Enjoying good health, with universal esteem, he closed his honorable life, after a short illness, at home, on the 21st day of October, 1800, in the sixty-third year of his age, leaving one son and one daughter. His remains were brought to Providence and interred in the north Presbyterian burying-ground. His grave is distinguished by a plain white marble slab; emblematic of his deportment through life, and spotless as his virtue.

G.—Page 85.

BRIGADIER-GENERAL DANIEL MORGAN, of the Virginia line on Continental establishment, deservedly ranked among the best and most efficient soldiers of the United States, was born in New Jersey ; from whence he emigrated to

Virginia in 1755. Like many of the greatest men of every country, his native condition was indigent, so much so as to render it necessary for young Morgan to enter into service as a laborer for daily wages.

Soon after his arrival in Virginia, he obtained employment from farmer Roberts, near Charleston, in the county of Jefferson (then Berkeley). Afterward he was engaged to drive a wagon for John Ashley, overseer for Nathaniel Burrell, Esq., at his estate on the Shenandoah River, in Frederick County, near Berry's Ferry. When he left Ashley, Morgan had by his care and industry amassed enough cash to purchase a wagon and team; which purchase he made, and soon afterward entered with it into the employment of Mr. John Ballantine, at his establishment on Occoquan Creek. At the expiration of his year, Braddock's expedition was spoken of as an event certainly to take place in the course of the ensuing summer. Morgan reserved himself, wagon, &c., for this expedition, and joined the army, but in what character is not known.

He received, during his military service, a severe wound in the face; the scar of which was through life very visible. We do not understand in what affair this happened; but it was from a rifle or musket, aimed, as he said himself, by an Indian. The bullet entered the back of his neck, and passed through his left cheek, knocking out all his jaw teeth on that side.

In the course of the campaign he was unjustly punished, by being brought to the halbert under a charge of contumely to a British officer, where he received five hundred lashes. The officer being afterward convinced of his cruel error, made every amends in his power to the maltreated Morgan; who, satisfied with the contrition evinced by the officer, magnanimously forgave him. Nor did the recollection of this personal outrage operate in the least to the prejudice of the British officers in the late war. Many of them, as is well known, fell into the hands of Morgan, and invariably received from him compassionate and kind treatment.

The general would often, among his intimate friends, recur to this circumstance; the narrative whereof he generally concluded, by saying, in a jocular way, that "King George was indebted to him one lash yet; for the drummer miscounted one, and he knew well when he did it; so that he only received four hundred and ninety-nine, when he promised him five hundred."

In this period of life, from twenty to thirty years of age, Morgan was extremely dissipated; and spent much of his time in vulgar tippling and in gambling-houses. However, although habituated to the free use of ardent spirits, he was never considered as a drunkard; and though enamored with cards and dice, he was a cautious player, increasing rather than diminishing his cash fund. This course of life subjected him to many affrays and furious pugilistic combats. The theatre of these exploits was Berryville, a small village in the county of Frederick, commonly called Battletown; named, as is generally supposed, from the fierce combats fought on its soil under the banners of Morgan.

Whatever may have been the cause, it is certain that he spent much of his leisure at this place; that he fought there many severe battles; and that though often vanquished he never was known to omit seizing the first opportunity which presented, after return of strength, of taking another bout with his conqueror; and this he repeated from time to time, until at length victory declared in his favor.

Such was the innate invincibility of young Morgan—which never forsook him—when, by the strength of his unimproved genius, and the propitiousness of fortune, he gained an extended theatre of action; as replete with difficulty as to him with glory. When he returned from Braddock's expedition he reassumed his former employment, and drove his own wagon. In a few years his previous savings, added to the little he earned in the campaign, enabled him to purchase a small tract of land from a Mr. Blackburn, in the county of Frederick; on which, during our war, he erected a handsome mansion-house, with suitable accompanying improvements, and called it Saratoga,—in commemoration of the signal victory obtained by General Gates, to which he had himself principally contributed. On this farm Morgan, having married shortly after his return from his military tour, resided when the revolutionary war broke out.

The smattering of experience gained during Braddock's expedition, pointed him out to the leading men of Frederick as qualified to command the first company of riflemen, raised in that county in defence of our country. He speedily completed his company, as all the finest youth of Frederick flocked to him; among whom was Lieutenant, afterward Colonel, Heth, and many others, who in the course of the war became approved officers. With this company Morgan hastened to the American army encamped before Boston, in 1775, and soon afterward was detached by the commander-in-chief under Arnold, in his memorable expedition against Quebec.

The bold and disastrous assault, planned and executed by the celebrated Montgomery, against that city, gave opportunity for the display of heroism to individuals, and furnished cause of deep regret to the nation by the loss of the much-beloved Montgomery. No officer distinguished himself more than Captain Morgan. Arnold commanded the column to which Morgan was attached, and became disabled by a ball through his leg early in the action, and was carried off to a place of safety.

Our troops having lost their leader, each corps pressed forward as the example of its officer invited. Morgan took the lead, and preceded by Sergeant, afterward Lieutenant-Colonel, Porterfield, who unfortunately fell at the battle of Camden, when his life might have saved an army, mounted the first barrier, and rushing forward, passed the second barrier, Lieutenant Heth and Sergeant Porterfield only before him. In this point of the assault a group of noble spirits united in surmounting the obstacles opposed to our progress; among them were Greene and Thayer, of Rhode Island, Hendricks, of Pennsylvania, and Humphreys, of Virginia, the last two of whom were killed.

Vain was this blaze of glory. Montgomery's fall stopped the further advance of the principal column of attack; and the severity of the raging storm, the obstacles of nature and of art in our way, and the combined attack of the enemy's force, no longer divided by attention to the column under Montgomery, overpowered all resistance. Morgan (with most of the corps of Arnold) was taken, and, as heretofore mentioned, experienced a different treatment from Sir Guy Carleton, than was at that period customary for British officers to dispense to American prisoners. The kindness of Carleton, from motives of policy, applied more forcibly to the privates than the officers, and produced a durable impression.

While Morgan was in confinement at Quebec, the following anecdote, told by himself, manifests the high opinion entertained by the enemy of his military talents from his conduct in this assault. He was visited occasionally by a British officer, to him unknown; but from his uniform, he appeared to belong to the navy, and to be an officer of distinction. During one of his visits, after conversing upon many topics, he asked Morgan if he did not begin to be convinced that the resistance of America was visionary; and he endeavored to impress him with the disastrous consequences which must infallibly ensue if the idle attempt was persevered in, and very kindly exhorted him to renounce the ill-advised undertaking. He declared, with seeming sincerity and candor, his admiration of Morgan's spirit and enterprise, which he said were worthy of a better cause; and told him if he would agree to withdraw from the American and join the British standard, he was authorized to promise him the commission, rank, and emoluments of a colonel of the royal army. Morgan rejected the proposal with disdain, and concluded his reply by observing, "That he hoped he would never again insult him in his distressed and unfortunate situation, by making him offers which plainly implied that he thought him a rascal." The officer withdrew, and the offer was never repeated.

As soon as our prisoners were exchanged, Morgan hastened to the army, and by the recommendation of General Washington was appointed to the command of a regiment. In this station he acted under the commander-in-chief in 1777, when a select rifle corps was formed out of the others in the army, and committed to his direction, seconded by Lieutenant-Colonel Richard Butler, of Pennsylvania, and Major Morris, of New Jersey, two officers of high talents, and especially qualified for the enterprising service to which they were assigned. Morgan and his riflemen were singularly useful to Washington; but our loss of Ticonderoga, and the impetuous advance of Burgoyne, proclaimed so loudly the gloomy condition of our affairs in the North, that the general, who thought only of the public good, deprived himself of Morgan and sent him to Gates, where he was persuaded his services were most required.

The splendid issue of the subsequent campaign, and the triumph of Gates, have been mentioned, as well as the instrumentality of Morgan in producing the glorious issue. Great and effectual as were his exertions, General Gates did not even mention him in his official dispatches. The cause of this cruel omission was then known but to a few.

General Morgan himself says that immediately after the surrender of Burgoyne he visited Gates on business, when he was taken aside by the general, and confidentially told that the main army were extremely dissatisfied with the conduct of the war by the commander-in-chief, and that several of the best officers threatened to resign unless a change took place. Morgan perfectly understood the views of Gates in this conference, although he was then a stranger to the correspondence which he had held with Conway and others; and sternly replied, "that he had one favor to ask of him, which was, never to mention that detestable subject to him again; for under no other man than Washington as commander-in-chief would he ever serve." From that moment all intimacy between himself and Gates ceased; and when, a few days afterward, the latter gave a dinner to the principal officers of the British army, among which, of course, some of ours were mixed, Morgan was not invited.

It so happened that this meritorious officer found it necessary to call upon General Gates the same evening on military business. He was introduced into the dining-room, and, as soon as he spoke with Gates, withdrew, unannounced to his guests. The British officers inquired his name, seeing from his uniform that he was a field officer; and upon being informed that it was Colonel Morgan, they arose from the table, overtook him in the yard, and made themselves severally known to him; having, as they ingenuously declared, severely felt him in the field. Thus the slight of Gates recoiled poignantly on himself.

After the return of Morgan to the main army, he continued actively employed by the commander-in-chief, and never failed to promote the good of the service by his sagacity, his vigilance, and his perseverance. In 1780 his health became much impaired, and he obtained leave of absence, when he returned to his family in Frederick, where he continued until after the fall of Charleston.

When General Gates was called to the chief command in the South, he visited Morgan, and urged the colonel to accompany him. Morgan did not conceal his dissatisfaction at the treatment he had heretofore received, and proudly spoke of the important aid he had rendered to him, and the ungrateful return he had experienced. Being some few weeks afterward promoted by Congress to the rank of brigadier-general by brevet, with the view of detaching him to the South, he repaired to the army of Gates, but did not reach Carolina in time to take a part in the battle of Camden. He joined Gates at Hillsborough, and was sent under Smallwood to Salisbury with all the force fitted for service. Gates, as soon as he had prepared the residue of his army, followed, and gave to Morgan, in his arrangements for the field, the command of the light troops.

Greene now arrived as the successor of Gates, which was followed by that distribution of his force which led to the battle of the Cowpens; the particulars of which have been related, and the influence of which was felt in every subsequent step of the war in the Carolinas.

*Morgan, when overtaken by Greene on his retreat with the prisoners, had decided upon passing the mountains; a resolution no doubt salutary in its effect, if applied to the safety of his own corps and of the prisoners, but fatal to the operations of Greene, which ought to have guided the deliberations of Morgan, but which seems not to have had its due weight. Greene forbade the measure; which produced a declaration from Morgan, that he would be no longer responsible for consequences; to which the restorer of the South amicably and firmly replied—" Neither shall you, for the measure is my own."

Morgan continued at the head of the light troops until the two divisions of the army united at Guilford Court-House. There every persuasion and excitement were essayed to induce him to retain his command until the army made good its retreat, but the effort was vain. He left us, and left impressions with many not very favorable to that purity of patriotism essential to round the character of a great soldier. Returning home, he continued in tranquillity with his family, bestowing his attention on the improvement of his farm and his fortune.

When the infatuated transmontane inhabitants of Pennsylvania menaced by force of arms to prostrate the majesty of the laws, and consequently reduced President Washington to the mortifying necessity of arresting their folly and wickedness by the bayonet, Morgan was summoned by the executive of Virginia to the field, at the head of the militia of that State, ordered on this service; having been some years before appointed senior major-general in the commonwealth.

On the advance of the army from Fort Cumberland and Bedford to pass the Alleghany mountains, General Morgan was charged with the direction of the light troops of the left column.

The ill-treatment which his old friend Colonel Neville had experienced from a party of the insurgents, the exile of his son-in-law, Presley Neville, and his innate abhorrence of opposition to the laws of his country, whose government he admired in theory and in practice, gave to the mind of Morgan an indignant irascibility which occasionally manifested itself on the expedition, to the disquietude of those against whom it pointed. Nevertheless he bridled this adventitious fierceness, and conformed his conduct to the regulations prescribed for the government of the army.

Upon the retreat of the main body, Morgan was left at the head of a respectable corps in the bosom of the insurgents until the ensuing spring, when, by order of the president, his corps was withdrawn.

The part he took upon this occasion seems to have inspired the general with a desire for political distinction. He was baffled in the first, and succeeded in the second attempt to obtain a seat in the House of Representatives of the United States, from the district of Frederick. Having served the constitutional period, he returned to his family, and declined offering as a candidate at the ensuing election.

About this time his health was much impaired, and the robustness of his constitution was gradually sinking. He had previously removed from Saratoga to a farm near his juvenile ground, Berryville (Battletown), and after a few years he retired from thence to the town of Winchester for the benefit of his health, which more and more declined. Languishing for some years, he at length closed his eventful life at Winchester.

Morgan was stout and active, six feet in height, strong, not too much encumbered with flesh, and was exactly fitted for the toils and pomp of war. His mind was discriminating and solid, but not comprehensive and combining. His manners plain and decorous, neither insinuating nor repulsive. His conver-

* This anecdote is considered by Colonel Howard to be derived from erroneous information. Before he reached the Catawba, and before he was joined by Greene, Morgan often told Howard that "if it was necessary to save the prisoners he would cross the mountains with them;" but when he was joined by Greene they were three or four days' march ahead of him, and out of the enemy's reach.—ED.

sation grave, sententious, and considerate, unadorned and uncaptivating. He reflected deeply, spoke little, and executed with keen perseverance whatever he undertook. He was indulgent in his military command, preferring always the affections of his troops to that respect and awe which surround the rigid disciplinarian.

No man better loved this world, and no man more reluctantly quitted it. He was in the habit of expressing this feeling to his intimates without reserve, and used to say that he would agree to pass much of his life as a galley-slave rather than exchange this world for that unknown. He was the reverse of the great Washington in this respect, whom he very much resembled in that happy mixture of caution and ardor which distinguished the American hero. For the latter, when speaking upon the subject of death, would often declare that he would not repass his life were it in his option. Yet no man, contradictory as it may appear, valued life less than Morgan, when duty called him to meet his foe. Stopped neither by danger nor by difficulty, he rushed into the hottest of the battle, enamored with the glory which encircles victory.

General Morgan, like thousands of mortals when nearly worn out by the hand of time, resorted for comfort to the solace of religion. He manifested great penitence for the follies of his early life; this was followed by joining the Presbyterian Church in full communion, with which he continued to his last day. When his remains were interred, an eloquent and appropriate sermon was delivered, to a crowded audience, by the Reverend Mr. William Hill.

H.—Page 203.

FRANCIS MARION, colonel in the regular service, and brigadier in the militia of South Carolina, was born at his father's plantation, in the vicinity of Georgetown, in South Carolina, in the year 1733. His ancestors were Huguenots, and fled from France to British America upon the revocation of the edict of Nantes.

They settled on Cooper River, near Charleston, from whence the father of General Marion moved to the neighborhood of Georgetown, where he resided during his life, occupied in the culture of his plantation.

He had five sons, of whom Francis was the youngest, who, with his brothers, received only a common country education. As his three eldest sons arrived at the age of manhood, they successively obtained a portion of their father's property, after which the old gentleman became embarrassed in his affairs, and was, in consequence, deprived of the means of extending similar aid to his two youngest sons. They had to depend upon their own exertions for support and comfort.

Francis, at the age of sixteen, entered on board a vessel bound to the West Indies, with a determination to fit himself for a seafaring life. On his outward passage the vessel was suddenly upset in a gale of wind, when the crew took to their boat without water or provisions, it being impracticable to save any of either. A dog jumped into the boat with the crew, and upon his flesh eaten raw did the survivors of these unfortunate men subsist for seven or eight days, in which period several died of hunger.

Among the few who escaped was young Marion. After reaching land, Marion relinquished his original plan of life, and engaged in the labors of agriculture. In this occupation he continued until 1759, when he became a soldier, and was appointed a lieutenant in a company of volunteers, raised for an expedition against the Cherokee Indians, commanded by Captain William Moultrie (since General Moultrie). This expedition was conducted by Governor Lyttleton; it was followed in a year or two afterward by another invasion of the Cherokee country by Colonel Grant, who served as major-general in our war, under Sir William Howe.

In the second expedition Lieutenant Marion also served, having been promoted to the rank of captain. As soon as the war broke out between the colonies and mother country, Marion was called to the command of a company in the first corps raised by the State of South Carolina. He was soon afterward promoted to a majority, and served in that rank under Colonel Moultrie in his intrepid defence of Fort Moultrie against the combined attack of Sir Henry Clinton and Sir H. Parker, on the 2d of June, 1776. He was afterward placed at the head of a regiment as lieutenant-colonel commandant, in which capacity he served during the siege of Charleston, when having fractured his leg by some accident, he became incapable of military duty, and fortunately for his country, escaped the captivity to which the garrison was, in the sequel, forced to submit.

When Charleston fell into the enemy's hands, Lieutenant-Colonel Marion abandoned his State and took shelter in North Carolina. The moment he recovered from the fracture of his leg, he engaged in preparing the means of annoying the enemy, then in the flood tide of prosperity. With sixteen men only, he crossed the Santee, and commenced that daring system of warfare which has been related in the course of the preceding memoirs.

General Marion was in stature of the smallest size, thin as well as low. His visage was not pleasing, and his manners not captivating. He was reserved and silent, entering into conversation only when necessary, and then with modesty and good sense.

He possessed a strong mind, improved by its own reflection and observation, not by books or travel. His dress was like his address—plain, regarding comfort and decency only. In his meals he was abstemious, eating generally of one dish, and drinking water mostly.

He was sedulous and constant in his attention to the duties of his station, to which every other consideration yielded. Even the charms of the fair, like the luxuries of the table and the allurements of wealth, seemed to be lost upon him.

The procurement of subsistence for his men, and the contrivance of annoyance to his enemy, engrossed his entire mind. He was virtuous all over; never, even in manner, much less in reality, did he trench upon right. Beloved by his friends, and respected by his enemies, he exhibited a luminous example of the beneficial effects to be produced by an individual, who, with only small means at his command, possesses a virtuous heart, a strong head, and a mind devoted to the common good. After the war the general married, but had no issue. He died in February, 1795, leaving behind him an indisputable title to the first rank among the patriots and soldiers of our revolution.

I.—Page 195.

WILLIAM DAVIDSON, lieutenant-colonel commandant in the North Carolina line, and brigadier-general in the militia of that State, was the youngest son of George Davidson, who removed with his family from Lancaster County, in Pennsylvania, in the year 1750, to Rowan County in North Carolina.

William was born in the year 1746, and was educated in the plain country manner at an academy in Charlotte, the county town of Mecklenburg, which adjoins Rowan.

Like most of the enterprising youth of America, Davidson repaired to the standard of his country on the commencement of our war, and was appointed a major in one of the first regiments formed by the government of North Carolina.

In this character he marched with the North Carolina line under Brigadier Nash, to the main army in New Jersey, where he served under the commander-in-chief, until the North Carolina line was detached in November, 1779, to re-enforce the Southern army, commanded by Major-General Lincoln. Previous to this event, Major Davidson was promoted to the command of a regiment, with the rank of lieutenant-colonel.

As he passed through North Carolina, Davidson obtained permission to visit his family, from which he had been absent nearly three years. The delay produced by this visit saved him from captivity, as he found Charleston so closely invested when he arrived in its neighborhood, as to prevent his joining his regiment.

Soon after the surrender of General Lincoln and his army, the loyalists of North Carolina not doubting the complete success of the royal forces, began to embody themselves for the purpose of contributing their active aid in the field to the subsequent operations of the British general. They were numerous in the western parts of the State, and especially in the Highland settlement about Cross Creek. Lieutenant-Colonel Davidson put himself at the head of some of our militia, called out to quell the expected insurrection. He proceeded with vigor in the execution of his trust; and in an engagement with a party of loyalists near Calson's Mill, he was severely wounded; the ball entered at the umbilical region, and passed through his body near the kidneys. This confined him for eight weeks; when recovering, he instantly took the field, having been recently appointed brigadier-general by the government of North Carolina, in the place of Brigadier Rutherford, taken at the battle of Camden. He exerted himself in conjunction with General Sumner and Colonel Davie to interrupt the progress of Lord Cornwallis in his advance toward Salisbury, and throughout that eventful period, gave unceasing evidences of his zeal and firmness in upholding his falling country.

After the victory obtained by Morgan at the Cowpens, Davidson was among the most active of his countrymen in assembling the militia of his district to enable General Greene, who had joined the light corps under Morgan, to stop the progress of the advancing enemy, and was detached by Greene on the night of the last day of January to guard the very ford selected by Lord Cornwallis for his passage of the Catawba River on the next morning. Davidson possessed himself of the post in the night at the head of three hundred men; and having placed a picket near the shore, stationed his corps at some small distance from the ford.

This was a deviation from the orders of General Greene, who directed the brigadier to post his whole force close to the shore, under cover of the nearest trees. The cause of this change from the ordered position is not known, though very probably some justifiable reason produced it, as Davidson was in the habit of executing his orders with the utmost precision. The rencounter which ensued in the morning has been related, with its disastrous termination.

The loss of Brigadier Davidson would have been always felt in any stage of the war. It was particularly detrimental in its effect at this period; as he was the chief instrument relied upon by Greene for the assemblage of the militia; an event all important at this crisis, and anxiously desired by the American general. The ball passed through his breast, and he instantly fell dead.

This promising soldier was thus lost to his country, in the meridian of life, and at a moment when his services would have been highly beneficial to her. He was a man of popular manners, pleasing address, active, and indefatigable. Devoted to the profession of arms, and to the great cause for which he fought, his future usefulness may be inferred from his former conduct.

The Congress of the United States, in gratitude for his services, and in commemoration of their sense of his worth, passed the following resolution:—

"*Resolved*, That the governor and council of the State of North Carolina be desired to erect a monument, at the expense of the United States, not exceeding the value of five hundred dollars, to the memory of the late Brigadier-General Davidson, who commanded the militia of the district of Salisbury, in the State of North Carolina, and was killed on the first day of February last, fighting gallantly in the defence of the liberty and independence of these States."

J.—Page 154,

WILLIAM WASHINGTON, lieutenant-colonel commandant of a Continental regiment of dragoons during the revolutionary war, was the eldest son of Baily Washington, Esq., of Stafford County, in the State of Virginia.

First among the youth of Virginia who hastened to the standard of his country, on the rupture between Great Britain and her colonies, he was appointed to the command of a company of infantry in the third regiment of the Virginia line, commanded by Colonel, afterward Brigadier-General Mercer. In no corps in our service was the substantial knowledge of the profession of arms more likely to be acquired.

Here young Washington learned the rudiments of war. He fought with this gallant regiment at York Island, and on the retreat through New Jersey, sharing with distinguished applause in that disastrous period, its difficulties, its dangers, and its glory. When afterward the commander-in-chief struck at Colonel Ralle, stationed with a body of Hessians in Trenton, Captain Washington was attached to the van of one of the assailing columns, and in that daring and well-executed enterprise, received a musket-ball through his hand, bravely leading on his company against the enemy.

The commander-in-chief having experienced the extreme difficulties to which he had been exposed during the preceding campaign, by his want of cavalry, was, shortly after this period, in consequence of his suggestions to Congress, authorized to raise three regiments of light dragoons. To the command of one of these he appointed Lieutenant-Colonel Baylor one of his aid de-camps. To this regiment Captain Washington was transferred with the rank of major, and returned to Virginia for the purpose of assisting in recruiting the regiment.

As soon as the corps was completed, Baylor joined the main army; his regiment was, in 1778, surprised by a detachment of the British, led by Major-General Gray, and suffered extremely. Washington fortunately escaped; and in the course of the succeeding year, or early in 1780, he was detached with the remains of Bland's, Baylor's, and Moylan's regiments of horse to the army of Major-General Lincoln in South Carolina, where he was constantly employed with the light troops, and experienced, with some flashes of fortune, two severe blows; first at Monk's Corner, where he commanded our horse, and last, at Lenew's Ferry, where he was second to Lieutenant-Colonel White of Moylan's regiment. These repeated disasters so reduced our cavalry, that White and Washington retired from the field and repaired to the eastern confines of North Carolina for the purpose of repairing their heavy losses. It was here that they applied to General Gates for the aid of his name and authority to expedite the restoration and equipment of their regiments, that they might be ready to take the field under his orders. This salutary and proper request was, as has been mentioned, injudiciously disregarded; from which omission very injurious consequences seem to have resulted in the sequel.

After the defeat of General Gates on the 16th of the following August, it will be recollected that the American general retired to Hillsborough from whence he returned to Salisbury.

Lieutenant-Colonel Washington, with his cavalry, now accompanied him, and formed a part of the light corps placed by Gates under the direction of Brigadier Morgan. He resumed his accustomed active and vigorous service, and was highly useful in the execution of the trust confided to Morgan.

During this period he carried, by an extraordinary stratagem, the post at Rudgley's; which drew from Lord Cornwallis the following letter to Lieutenant-Colonel Tarleton; "Rudgley will not be made a brigadier. He surrendered, without firing a shot, himself and one hundred and three rank and file, to the cavalry only. A deserter of Morgan's assures us that the infantry never came within three miles of the house."

Greene now succeeded Gates, when Brigadier Morgan, with the light corps was detached to hang upon the enemy's left flank, and to threaten Ninety-six.

The battle of the Cowpens ensued, in which Washington at the head of our horse, acquired fresh laurels. He continued with the light corps, performing with courage and precision the duties assigned him until the junction of the two divisions of the American army, at Guilford Court-House. Soon after this event a more powerful body of horse and foot was selected by General Greene and placed under Colonel Williams, of which Washington and his cavalry were a constituent part.

In the eventful and trying retreat which ensued, Lieutenant-Colonel Washington contributed his full share to the execution of the measures of Williams, which terminated so propitiously to our arms, and so honorably to the light troops and commander. After our repassage of the Dan, Washington and his horse were again placed in the van, and with Howard and Lee, led by Williams, played that arduous game of marches, countermarches, and manœuvres, which greatly contributed to baffle the skilful display of talents and enterprise exhibited by Lord Cornwallis in his persevering attempt to force Greene, at the head of an inferior army, to battle, or to cut him off from his approaching re-enforcements and supplies.

We have seen the distinguished part this officer successively bore in the battles of Guilford, Hobkirk's Hill, and Eutaws; and we have found him throughout the arduous campaign of 1781, always at his post, firm and brave, courting danger, and contemning difficulty. His eminent services were lost to the army from the battle of Eutaw, where, to its great regret, he was made prisoner; nor did he afterward take any part in the war, as from the period of his exchange nothing material occurred, the respective armies being confined to minor operations, produced by the prospect of peace. While a prisoner in Charleston, Washington became acquainted with Miss Elliot, a young lady, in whom concentrated the united attractions of respectable descent, opulence, polish, and beauty. The gallant soldier soon became enamored of his amiable acquaintance, and afterward married her.

This took place in the spring of 1782; and he established himself in South Carolina at Sandy Hill, the ancestral seat of his wife.

Washington seems to have devoted his subsequent years to domestic duties, rarely breaking in upon them by attention to public affairs; and then only as a member of the State legislature.

He possessed a stout frame, being six feet in height, broad, strong, and corpulent. His occupations and his amusements applied to the body, rather than to the mind; to the cultivation of which he did not bestow much time or application, nor was his education of the sort to excite such habits, being only calculated to fit a man for the common business of life. In temper he was good-humored; in disposition amiable; in heart upright, generous, and friendly; in manners lively, innocent, and agreeable.

His military exploits announce his grade and character in arms. Bold, collected, and persevering, he preferred the heat of action to the collection and sifting of intelligence, to the calculations and combinations of means and measures, and was better fitted for the field of battle than for the drudgery of camp and the watchfulness of preparation. Kind to his soldiers, his system of discipline was rather lax, and sometimes subjected him to injurious consequences, when close to a sagacious and vigilant adversary.

The Washington family emigrated from England, and settled in Virginia, always respectable and respected. The consanguinity of its numerous ramifications is involved in doubt; but it is generally believed that they sprang from the same source.

Lieutenant-Colonel Washington was selected by his illustrious relation, when he accepted the command of the army during the presidency of Mr. Adams, as one of his staff, with the rank of brigadier-general, a decided proof of the high value attached by the best judge in America to his military talents.

Leading a life of honor, of benevolence, and hospitality, in the bosom of his family and friends, during which, until his last two years, he enjoyed high health, this gallant soldier died, after a tedious indisposition, leaving a widow, with a son and daughter, the only issue of his marriage.

K.—Page 98.

CHRISTOPHER GREENE, lieutenant-colonel commandant of one of the Rhode Island regiments in the service of Congress during the revolutionary war, was born in the town of Warwick in the State of Rhode Island, in the year 1737. His father, Philip Greene, Esq., was descended from Jonathan Greene, Esq., one of the earliest settlers of Massachusetts Bay. The latter gentleman emigrated from England in the year 1637, and settled in Salem, now a well-improved opulent commercial town. Mr. Greene, soon after his arrival, purchased from the Indian sachems Micantenomon and Socononeo, a part of the township of Warwick called Occupassatioxet, which property is still possessed by some of his descendants. He left three sons, the progenitors of a numerous and respectable race of men, successively distinguished as well by the highest offices in the gift of their country, as by their talent, their usefulness, and goodness.

Philip Greene, the father of the lieutenant-colonel, was a gentleman of the first respectability in the State, beloved for his virtues, and admired for his honorable discharge of the duties of the various stations to which he was called, the last of which placed him upon the bench as judge of the common pleas in the county of Kent.

A father so situated could not but cherish the intellectual powers of his progeny with the most careful attention.

Christopher received all the advantages in the best line of education procurable in our country, which he took care to improve by the most assiduous application.

He was particularly attached to the study of mathematics, in which he made great proficiency, and thus laid up a stock of knowledge exactly suitable for that profession to which he was afterward unexpectedly called.

Exhibiting in early life his capacity and amiability, he was elected, by his native town when very young, to a seat in the colonial legislature, which he continued to fill by successive elections until the commencement of the revolutionary war. At this period the legislature wisely established a military corps, styled "Kentish guards," for the purpose of fitting the most select of her youth for military office. In this corps young Greene was chosen a lieutenant, and in May, 1775, he was appointed by the legislature a major in what was then called "an army of observation"—one brigade of one thousand six hundred effectives, under the orders of his near relation, Brigadier Greene, afterward so celebrated.

From this situation he was promoted to the command of a company of infantry, in one of the regiments raised by the State for Continental service. The regiment to which he belonged was attached to the army of Canada, conducted by General Montgomery, in the vicissitudes and difficulties of which campaign Captain Greene shared, evincing upon all occasions that unyielding intrepidity which marked his military conduct in every subsequent scene. In the attack upon Quebec, which terminated as well the campaign as the life of the renowned Montgomery, Captain Greene belonged to the column which entered the lower town, and was made prisoner.

His elevated mind ill brooked the irksomeness of captivity, though in the hands of the enlightened and humane Carleton; and it has been uniformly asserted, that, while a prisoner, Greene often declared that "he would never again be taken alive;" a resolution unhappily fulfilled.

As soon as Captain Greene was exchanged he repaired to his regiment, with which he continued without intermission, performing with exemplary propriety the various duties of his progressive stations, when he was promoted to the majority of Varnum's regiment. In 1777 he succeeded to the command of the regiment, and was selected by Washington to take charge of Fort Mercer (commonly called Red Bank), the safe-keeping of which post, with that of Fort Mifflin (Mud Island), was very properly deemed of primary importance.

The noble manner in which Colonel Greene sustained himself against a superior force of veteran troops, led by an officer of ability, has been particularly related in the body of this work, as also the well-earned rewards which followed his memorable defence. Consummating his military fame by his achievements on that proud day, he could not be overlooked by the commander-in-chief, when great occasions called for great exertions. Greene was accordingly attached with his regiment to the troops placed under Major Sullivan, for the purpose of breaking up the enemy's post on Rhode Island, soon after the arrival of the French fleet under Count d'Estaing, in the summer of 1778; which well-concerted enterprise was marred in the execution by some of those incidents which abound in war, and especially when the enterprise is complicated and intrusted to allied forces, and requiring naval co-operation. Returning to head-quarters, Colonel Greene continued to serve under the commander-in-chief whose confidence and esteem he invariably enjoyed.

In the spring of 1781, when General Washington began to expect the promised naval aid from our best friend the ill-fated Louis the XVI., he occasionally approached the enemy's lines on the side of York Island. In one of these movements, Colonel Greene, with a suitable force, was posted on the Croton River, in advance of the army. On the other side of this river lay a corps of refugees (American citizens who had joined the British army), under the command of Colonel Delancey. These half citizens, half soldiers, were notorious for rapine and murder; and to their vindictive conduct may be justly ascribed most of the cruelties which stained the progress of our war, and which at length compelled Washington to order Captain Asgil, of the British army, to be brought to head-quarters, for the purpose of retaliating, by his execution, the murder of Captain Huddy, of New Jersey, perpetrated by a Captain Lippincourt of the refugees. The commandant of these refugees (Delancey was not present), having ascertained the position of Greene's corps, which the colonel had cantoned in adjacent farm-houses, probably with a view to the procurement of subsistence, took the resolution to strike it. This was accordingly done by a nocturnal movement on the 13th of May. The enemy crossed the Croton before daylight, and hastening his advance, reached our station with the dawn of day, unperceived. As he approached the farm-house in which the lieutenant-colonel was quartered, the noise of troops marching was heard, which was the first intimation of the fatal design. Greene and Major Flagg immediately prepared themselves for defence, but they were too late, so expeditious was the progress of the enemy. Flagg discharged his pistols, and instantly afterward fell mortally wounded; when the ruffians (unworthy the appellation of soldiers), burst open the door of Greene's apartment. Here the gallant veteran singly received them with his drawn sword. Several fell beneath the arm accustomed to conquer, till at length, overpowered by numbers, and faint from the loss of blood streaming from his wounds, barbarity triumphed over valor. "His right arm was almost cut off in two places, the left in one, a severe cut on the left shoulder, a sword thrust through the abdomen, a bayonet in the right side, and another through the abdomen, several sword-cuts on the head, and many in different parts of the body."

Thus cruelly mangled fell the generous conqueror of Count Donop, whose wounds, as well as those of his unfortunate associates, had been tenderly dressed as soon as the battle terminated, and whose pains and sorrows had been as tenderly assuaged. How different was the relentless fury here displayed!

The commander-in-chief heard with anguish and indignation the tragical fate of his loved and faithful friend and soldier, in which 'feelings the army sincerely participated. On the subsequent day the corpse was brought to head-quarters, and the funeral was solemnized with military honors and universal grief.

Lieutenant-Colonel Greene was murdered in the meridian of life, being only forty-four years old. He married, in 1758, Miss Anne Lippit, a daughter of J. Lippit, Esq., of Warwick, whom he left a widow with three sons and four daughters. He was stout and strong in person, about five feet ten inches high, with a broad round chest, his aspect manly, and demeanor pleasing; enjoying always a high state of health, its bloom irradiated a countenance, which significantly expressed the fortitude and mildness invariably displayed throughout his life.

L.—Page 227.

John Eager Howard, lieutenant-colonel commandant of the second regiment of Maryland, was born on the 4th of June, 1752, on the farm settled by his grand-father, Joshua Howard, in the county of Baltimore. This gentleman, when very young, had left his father residing in the vicinity of the town of Manchester, in England, to join the army of King James, moving to quell the insurrection headed by the Duke of Monmouth. The object being effectually accomplished, young Howard, conscious of having excited the displeasure of his father, by his unauthorized departure from home, determined not to return, but to seek his fortune in America. He embarked for Maryland, where arriving, he purchased the tract of land above mentioned, on which he established himself, having married Miss Joanna O'Carroll, whose father and family had lately settled in the same colony from Ireland. Mr. Howard had a numerous progeny. One of his sons Cornelius, married Miss Ruth Eager, the daughter of John Eager, the son of George Eager, who possessed an estate adjoining to, and now part of, the city of Baltimore.

John Eager Howard, the son of Cornelius, was educated in the customary manner of our country, being intended for no particular profession. The dispute between the colonies and the mother country issuing in an appeal to the sword, one of the first measures of defence adopted by the colonies, was the assemblage of the bodies of the militia, denominated flying camps. The first of these in Maryland was formed in June, 1776, when young Howard, then twenty-three years of age, offered his services, and received the commission of captain in a regiment commanded by Colonel Josias C. Hall. Engaged for a few months only, this corps was discharged in December, before which period Congress had prepared a system of defence, requiring from each of the Confederate States its proportion of men to be enlisted, organized, and disciplined as regular soldiers. The State of Maryland furnished seven regiments, in one of which Captain Howard, in obedience rather to the wishes of the State Commissioners, empowered to appoint officers, than to his own inclination, was retained. Shortly afterward these regiments were organized, and Captain Howard was promoted to a majority in the fourth regiment, at the head of which was placed the same Colonel Hall. In the summer of 1779 he was appointed lieutenant-colonel of the fifth; in the spring of 1780 he was transferred to the sixth, commanded by Colonel Williams; and after the battle of Hobkirk's Hill, he succeeded to the command of the second, in consequence of the death of Lieutenant-Colonel Ford, who never recovered from the wound received in that battle.

In this station Howard continued until the army was disbanded, when he returned to his native State, married Miss Margaret Chew, daughter of Benjamin Chew, Esq, of Philadelphia, and settled on his patrimonial farm near Baltimore, where he now resides, enjoying " otium cum dignitate."[*]

This officer was one of the five lieutenant-colonels, on whom Greene rested

---

[*] He has since been governor of Maryland, and served in Congress.

throughout the hazardous operations to which he was necessarily exposed, by his grand determination to recover the South, or die in the attempt.

We have seen him, at the battle of the Cowpens, seize the critical moment, and turn the fortune of the day ;—alike conspicuous, though not alike successful, at Guilford and the Eutaws; and at all times, and on all occasions, eminently useful. He was justly ranked among the chosen sons of the South.

Trained to infantry service, he was invariably employed in that line, and was always to be found where the battle raged, pressing into close action to wrestle with fixed bayonet. Placid in temper, and reserved in deportment, he never lessened his martial fame by arrogance or ostentation, nor clouded it with garrulity or self-conceit.

Granting to all the applause due to their merits, he enjoyed that due to himself with universal assent.

General Greene, whose discriminating mind graduated, with nice exactitude, the merit of all under him, thus speaks of this officer, in a private letter to his friend in Maryland, dated the 14th of November, 1781:—

" This will be handed to you by Colonel Howard, as good an officer as the world affords. He has great ability and the best disposition to promote the service. My own obligations to him are great—the public's still more so. He deserves a statue of gold no less than the Roman and Grecian heroes. He has been wounded, but has happily recovered, and now goes home to pay a little attention to his private affairs, and to take charge of the Fifth Maryland regiment recruiting in your State. With esteem and respect, I am, dear sir, yours,

" N. GREENE."

M.—Page 237.

OTHO HOLLAND WILLIAMS was descended from the English stock, his ancestors having emigrated soon after Lord Baltimore became proprietor of the colony of Maryland.

His father settled in the county of Prince George, where Otho, his eldest son, was born in the year 1748. His father soon afterward removed from Prince George to Frederick County and settled near the mouth of Conogocheaque Creek, where himself and wife died, leaving one daughter, and two sons, the elder son not more than twelve years old. A Scotch gentleman by the name of Rosa, having married his sister, Otho was taken under his protection, and was bred up in the clerk's office of the county, a profession which presented better prospects to a young man, than any other office then procurable under the colonial government of Maryland. Ross dying, Colonel Steele of Hagerstown, married his widow, and continued to patronize his wife's brothers. In this situation Williams continued until he was removed, just before the war broke out, to the clerk's office in the county of Baltimore, of which he had the principal direction, and the business of which he conducted with exemplary propriety. Anxious to draw his sword in defence of his oppressed country, as soon as the last resort became inevitable, Williams was appointed lieutenant in the company of riflemen raised in the county of Frederick, commanded by Captain Price, and marched in 1775 to the American camp before Boston. In 1776 a rifle regiment was formed, of which Stephenson was appointed colonel, Rawlings lieutenant-colonel, and Williams major.

Stephenson soon dying, the command of the regiment devolved upon Rawlings, who, with his regiment, formed part of the garrison of Fort Washington, in the State of New York, when assailed by Sir William Howe, pushing Washington over the North River. In this attack, the rifle regiment opposed the Hessian column, and behaved to admiration, for a long time holding victory in suspense, and severely crippling its adversary. The fort was nevertheless carried by capitulation, and its garrison became prisoners of war. After the surrender of Burgoyne's army, Colonel Wilkinson, adjutant-general to General Gates, who was personally attached to Major Williams, procured his exchange for Major Ackland, wounded in the first action between the Northern armies, and left on the ground, with many others, to the mercy of the American general. While in captivity, Williams became entitled to the command of a regiment, and as soon as he was exchanged, he was placed at the head of the Sixth Maryland. The Maryland and Delaware lines having been detached to South Carolina, soon after the reduction of Charleston, Colonel Williams accompanied the Baron de Kalb, and after General Gates took command of the army, he was called to the important station of adjutant-general to the same. He bore a distinguished part in the battle of the 16th of August, and shared with the general in the bitter adversity of that disastrous day.

When Greene took command of the Southern army, Colonel Williams was retained in the station he then occupied, which he held to the end of the war, enjoying the uninterrupted confidence of his commander, and the esteem of his fellow-soldiers.

Throughout the important campaign which followed, he acted a conspicuous part, and greatly contributed by the honorable and intelligent discharge of the duties of the station which he held, to the successful issue of Greene's operations. At the head of the light troops, during our difficult retreat, he was signally efficient, in holding the army safe until it effected its passage across the Dan; and after Greene's return into North Carolina, when to save that State, the American general was constrained to put to hazard his inferior force, he was not less useful in thwarting the various attempts of Lord Cornwallis to strike his antagonist. We have seen with what vigor and effect he seconded his general in the fields of Guilford, of Hobkirk, and of Eutaws, invariably exciting by his impressive example, officer and soldier to the animated display of skill and courage.

Returning, upon peace, to his native State, the government desirous (a sentiment *at that time* common through America) to reward, whenever it had the power, those officers and soldiers who continued in service to the last, bestowed upon this distinguished patriot the collectorship of the port of Baltimore, the most lucrative office within its gift.

On the adoption of the present government of the Union, Washington was called to the presidency, and of course continued Williams, with whose merit he was particularly acquainted, in his office.

Previous to this epoch he married Miss Mary Smith, daughter of William Smith, Esq., one of the most respectable inhabitants of the town, by whom he had four sons, all of whom survived their parents. General Williams's health had, for many years before his death, been very delicate, resulting from the hardships incident to military life, increased in his case by the severe treatment experienced while a prisoner in New York, which was peculiarly oppressive while Sir William Howe commanded the British forces in America. Vainly attempting by change of climate, and every other advisable measure, to stop the menacing disease, he, unhappily for his country, his family and friends, fell a victim to a pulmonary complaint in July, 1794, on his way to the Sweet Springs. His amiable and disconsolate widow soon fell the victim of grief, exhibiting a rare display of the tenderness and ardor of conjugal love.

Brigadier-General Williams was about five feet ten inches high, erect and elegant in form, made for activity rather than strength. His countenance was expressive, and the faithful index of his warm and honest heart. Pleasing in his address, he never failed to render himself acceptable, in whatever circle he moved, notwithstanding a sternness of character, which was sometimes manifested with too much asperity. He was cordial to his friends, but cold to all whose correctness in moral principle became questionable in his mind. As a soldier, he may be called a rigid, not cruel, disciplinarian, obeying strictly his superior, he exacted obedience from his inferior. He possessed that range of mind, although self-educated, which entitled him to the highest military station, and was actuated by true courage which can refuse as well as give battle.

Soaring far above the reach of vulgar praise, he aimed singly at promoting the common weal, satisfied with the consciousness of doing right, and desiring only that share of applause, which was justly his own.

There was a loftiness and liberality in his character, which forbade resort to intrigue and hypocrisy in the accomplishment of his views, and rejected the contemptible practice of disparaging others to exalt himself.

In the field of battle he was self-possessed, intelligent, and ardent; in camp circumspect, attentive, and systematic; in counsel sincere, deep, and perspicacious. During the campaign of General Greene, he was uniformly one of his few advisers, and held his unchanged confidence. Nor was he less esteemed by his brother officers, or less respected by his soldiery.

Previous to the disbandment of the army, Congress manifested their sense of Williams's merit and services, by promoting him to the rank of brigadier-general, of which event we have his own account, in a letter to his friend, Major Pendleton, written in Philadelphia, and dated May 18, 1782.

"My Dear Pendleton:—

"Your laconic epistle of the 20th April was handed to me by General St. Clair, in the situation you wished. Involved in a scene of the most agreeable amusements, I have scarcely had time for reflection; therefore, if I have been guilty of any omission toward you, or any other of my Southern friends, I hope it will be imputed to the infatuating pleasures of the metropolis.

"My promotion (for which I am principally indebted to my invaluable friend, General Greene), might prove the efficacy of making a short campaign to court (especially as it had been once rejected), if the circumstances'which attended it, did not too evidently discover how much the greatest men are actuated by caprice, and how liable the most respectable bodies are to inconsistencies. Upon the application of General Greene, seconded by the recommendation of Washington, the votes of Congress were taken, whether I should or should not be made a brigadier, in consequence of former resolves, which very clearly, in my opinion, gave me a right to promotion. It was resolved in the negative. Upon the second motion in Congress, the same letters were reconsidered, and the man whose legal claim was rejected (because it was inconvenient, or might give umbrage to others), is promoted in consideration of his distinguished talent and services. I wish I may be always able to justify and maintain an opinion that does me so much honor. If Congress will please to wink at my imperfections, I will be careful not to meddle with theirs."

N.—Pages 222, 414.

General ANDREW PICKENS was born in Paxton township, Pennsylvania, on the 19th September, 1739. His parents were from Ireland—his ancestors from France. When he was a child his father removed to the county of Augusta, in Virginia, and in 1752, to the Waxhaw settlement in South Carolina. Bred on the Indian frontiers, his first occupations were hunting and war, those in which our best patriots have been nursed. In the French war which was concluded by the peace of 1763, he served as a volunteer in Grant's expedition against the Cherokees. In the revolutionary contest he took an early and spirited part— was captain, major, colonel, and brigadier-general successively in the militia of South Carolina; and by his constant and gallant exertions contributed in an equal degree with Sumter and Marion, to the liberation of the Southern States. The reader will have noticed his activity and valor at the Cowpens, at Haw River, at Augusta, and at Eutaw, at which last place a musket-ball which struck his breast was prevented from proving mortal by the buckle of his sword-belt. He commanded in chief in several Indian expeditions. In 1779, at Kettle Creek, he defeated Colonel Boyd, a very brave officer, at the head of a body of tories and Indians, double his own force in numbers. This action, in which Boyd was killed, dispersed and greatly dispirited the tories in the western parts of South Carolina and Georgia, and gave an ascendency to the whigs. In 1781, he was equally efficient and successful in an expedition against the Cherokees, which is recorded, in the body of this work. He served in the legislature of South Carolina from the close of the war until 1794, when he was elected to Congress. In 1795 he retired from Congress, and then was re-elected to the State legislature until he declined that office also. He was unanimously elected major-general of the first division of South Carolina militia; and was repeatedly appointed by the federal government a commissioner to treat with the Southern Indians, in conjunction with Colonel Hawkins, with Governor Blount, and with General Wilkinson. President Washington offered him a brigade of light troops under General Wayne against the Northern Indians, which service he declined. In all his public stations his conduct was faithful and efficient, satisfactory to his country, and honorable to himself. In 1765 he married Miss Calhoun, the aunt of the present Vice-President of the United States. She bore him three sons and six daughters, all of whom survived their parents. This great and good *military chieftain* died on the 11th of August, 1817, at Tennessee, in Pendleton District, South Carolina, a seat at which he had long resided, and which was peculiarly interesting to him from having been the scene of one of his earliest Indian battles. He was a sincere believer in the Christian religion, and a devout observer of the Presbyterian form of worship. His frame was sinewy and active; his habits were simple, temperate, and industrious. His characteristics were taciturnity and truth, prudence and decision, modesty and courage, disinterestedness and public spirit. His letter to the author of this work, which details the chief particulars of his life, closes with sentiments which harmonize so perfectly with his character, that they form a suitable conclusion to a sketch of his life. "At the sieges of Augusta and Ninety-six, at the battle of Eutaw, and in other services with the army, you know whether I did my duty. And I leave it to my country to say whether I have been a humble instrument in the hands of Providence to its advantage. But whatever the public sentiment may be, I have a witness within myself that my public life and conduct have been moved and actuated by an ardent zeal for the welfare and happiness of my beloved country."- ED.

ANTHONY WAYNE was born in the year 1745, in Westchester County, Pennsylvania, of parents who were respectable in character and condition. His grandfather was a captain under William III., at the battle of the Boyne. In 1773 he was a member of the provincial legislature of Pennsylvania, and as soon as the dispute between England and America commenced he took part with the latter. In 1775 he commanded a regiment, served under Montgomery, and was wounded at the siege of Quebec. During the next year, he acted under Gates at Ticonderoga, and was promoted to the rank of brigadier. He was distinguished at the battles of Brandywine, Germantown, and Monmouth. But his most shining exploit was the storming of Stony Point, where he received a wound in the head, and exhibited a love of glory far stronger than the love of life; for, supposing his wound to be mortal, he desired to be carried forward that he might die in the enemy's works. Congress rewarded him by the vote of a gold medal, in those days an honor equal to a Roman triumph. He was second to La Fayette in 1781, in his Virginia campaign, and bore a conspicuous part in the perils and honors of the siege of York. After the surrender of that place he was detached with the Pennsylvania line to join General Greene, and under his orders completed, as the reader has seen, the liberation of Georgia. After the war he served in Congress, as a member of the House of Representatives. In 1792, he was selected by President Washington as commander-in-chief against the Western Indians, who, having defeated St. Clair, had become formidable. His operations were conducted with great skill and prudence, and after gaining a decisive victory over their troops, he forced them to conclude a treaty of peace. In December, 1796, he died, leaving behind him the reputation of having been one of the most distinguished and meritorious officers of the revolution. His person was robust; his presence commanding; his manners graceful; his temper frank, fiery, and generous. His military conduct was characterized perhaps too much by a love of fighting; but fierce and formidable as he was in battle, his excessive courage never destroyed his self-possession, nor obscured the excellent judgment which he possessed, and had cultivated by much reading and experience.—ED.

O.—Page 283.

General Greene's Official Report of the Battle of Guilford, to the President of Congress.

CAMP AT THE IRON WORKS, *March* 16, 1781.

SIR,—On the 10th, I wrote to his excellency General Washington from the High Rock Ford, on the Haw River (a copy of which I inclosed your excellency), that I had effected a junction with the Continental regiment of eighteen months' men, and two considerable bodies of militia, belonging to Virginia and North Carolina. After this junction, I took the resolution of attacking the enemy without loss of time, and made the necessary disposition accordingly, being persuaded, that if we were successful, it would prove ruinous to the enemy, and, if otherwise, it would only prove a partial evil to us.

The army marched from the High Rock Ford on the 12th, and on the 14th arrived at Guilford. The enemy lay at the Quaker meeting-house on Deep River, eight miles from our camp. On the morning of the 15th, our reconnoitring party reported the enemy advancing on the great Salisbury road. The army was drawn up in three lines. The first line was composed of North Carolina militia, under the command of Generals Butler and Eaton. The second line of Virginia militia, commanded by Generals Stevens and Lawson, forming two brigades, one of Virginia, and one of Maryland Continental troops, commanded by General Huger and Colonel Williams. Lieutenant-Colonel Washington, with the dragoons of the first and third regiments, a detachment of light infantry, composed of Continental troops, and a regiment of riflemen under Colonel Lynch, formed a corps of observation for the security of our right flank. Lieutenant-Colonel Lee, with his Legion, a detachment of light infantry, and a corps of riflemen, under Colonel Campbell, formed a corps of observation for the security of our left flank.

The greater part of this country is a wilderness, with a few cleared fields interspersed here and there. The army was drawn up on a large hill of ground, surrounded by other hills, the greatest part of which was covered with timber and thick underbrush. The front line was posted with two field-pieces, just on the edge of the woods, and the back of a fence which ran parallel with the line, with an open field directly in their front. The second line was in the woods, about three hundred yards in the rear of the first, and the Continental troops about four hundred yards in the rear of the second, with a double front, as the hill drew to a point where they were posted; and on the right and left were two old fields. In this position we waited the approach of the enemy, having previously sent off the baggage to this place appointed for our rendezvous in case of a defeat. Lieutenant-Colonel Lee, with his Legion, his infantry, and part of his riflemen, met the enemy on their advance, and had a severe skirmish with Lieutenant-Colonel Tarleton, in which the enemy suffered greatly. Captain Armstrong charged the British Legion, and cut down thirty of their dragoons; but as the enemy re-enforced their party, Lieutenant-Colonel Lee was obliged to retire, and take his position in the line.

The action commenced by cannonade, which lasted about twenty minutes; when the enemy advanced in three columns; the Hessians on the right, the guards in the centre, and Lieutenant-Colonel Webster's brigade on the left. The whole moved through the old fields to attack the North Carolina brigades, who waited the attack until the enemy got within one hundred and forty yards, when part of them began to fire, but a considerable part left the ground without firing at all. The general and field officers did all they could to induce the men to stand their ground; but neither the advantages of the position, nor any other consideration could induce them to stay. General Stevens and General Lawson and the field-officers of those brigades were more successful in their exertions. The Virginia militia gave the enemy a warm reception, and kept up a heavy fire for a long time; but being beat back, the action became general almost everywhere. The corps of observation, under Washington and Lee, were warmly engaged, and did great execution. In a word the engagement was long and severe, and the enemy only gained their point by superior discipline.

They having broken the second Maryland regiment, turned our left.flank, and got into the rear of the Virginia brigade, and appearing to be gaining on our right, which would have encircled the whole of the Continental troops, I thought it most advisable to order a retreat. About this time Lieutenant-Colonel Washington made a charge with the horse upon a part of the brigade of guards, and the first regiment of Marylanders, commanded by Colonel Gunby, and seconded by Lieutenant-Colonel Howard, followed the horse with their bayonets; near the whole of the party fell a sacrifice. General Huger was the last that was engaged, and gave the enemy a check. We retreated in good order to the Reedy Fork River, and crossed the ford about three miles from the field of action and then halted, and drew up the troops, until we collected most of the stragglers. We lost our artillery, and two ammunition wagons, the greater part of the horses being killed before the retreat began, and it being impossible to move the pieces but along the great road. After collecting our stragglers, we retired to this camp, ten miles distant from Guilford.

From the best information I can get the enemy's loss is very great; not less, in killed and wounded, than six hundred men, besides some few prisoners that we brought off.

Inclosed I send your excellency a return of our killed, wounded, and missing —most of the latter have gone home, as it is but too customary with the militia after an action. I cannot learn that the enemy has got any considerable number of prisoners. Our men are all in good spirits, and in perfect readiness for another field-day.

I only lament the loss of several valuable officers, who are killed and wounded in the action. Among the latter are General Stevens, shot through the thigh, and General Huger in the hand; and among the former is Major Anderson, one of the Maryland line.

The firmness of the officers and soldiers, during the whole campaign, has been unparalleled. Amidst innumerable difficulties they have discovered a degree of magnanimity and fortitude that will forever add a lustre to their military reputation.

P.—Page 283.

Earl Cornwallis to Lord George Germain.

My Lord,— Guilford, *March* 17, 1781.

I have the satisfaction to inform your Lordship, that his majesty's troops under my command obtained a signal victory on the 15th instant, over the rebel army commanded by General Greene.

In pursuance of my intended plan, communicated to your lordship in my dispatch No. 7, I had encamped on the 13th instant at the Quaker's meeting-house, between the forks of Deep River. On the 14th I received information that General Butler, with a body of North Carolina militia, and the expected re-enforcements from Virginia, said to consist of a Virginia State regiment, a corps of Virginia eighteenmonths' men, three thousand Virginia militia and recruits for the Maryland line, had joined General Greene; and the whole army, which was reported to amount to nine or ten thousand men, was marching to attack the British troops. During the afternoon, intelligence was brought, which was confirmed in the night, that he had advanced that day to Guilford, about twelve miles from our camp. Being now persuaded that he had resolved to hazard an engagement, after detaching Lieutenant-Colonel Hamilton with our wagons and baggage, escorted by his own regiment, a detachment of one hundred infantry and twenty cavalry, toward Bell's mill, on Deep River, I marched with the rest of the corps at day-break on the morning of the 15th, to meet the enemy, or attack them in their encampment. About four miles from Guilford our advanced guard, commanded by Lieutenant-Colonel Tarleton, fell in with a corps of the enemy, consisting of Lee's Legion, some back-mountain men and Virginia militia, which he attacked with his usual good conduct and spirit, and defeated; and continuing our march, we found the rebel army posted on rising grounds, about a mile and a half from the court-house. The prisoners taken by Lieutenant-Colonel Tarleton having been several days with the advanced corps, could give me no account of the enemy's order or position, and the country people were extremely inaccurate in their description of the ground. Immediately between the head of the column and the enemy's line was a considerable plantation; one large field of which was on our left of the road, and two others, with a wood of about two hundred yards broad, between them, on our right of it; beyond these fields the wood continued for several miles to our right. The wood beyond the plantation in our front, in the skirt of which the enemy's first line was formed, was about a mile in depth, the road then leading to an extensive space of cleared ground about Guilford Court-House. The woods on our right and left were reported to be impracticable for our cannon; but as that on our right appeared the most open, I resolved to attack the left wing of the enemy; and whilst my disposition was making for that purpose, I ordered Lieutenant McCleod to bring forward the guns and cannonade their centre.

The attack was directed to be made in the following order. On the right the regiment of Bose and the seventy-first regiment, led by Major-General Leslie, and supported by the first battalion of guards; on the left, the twenty-third and thirty-third regiments, led by Lieutenant-Colonel Webster, and supported by the grenadiers and second battalion of guards, commanded by Brigadier O'Hara; the yagers and light infantry of the guards remained in the wood on the left of the guns, and the cavalry in the road, ready to act as circumstances might require. Our preparations being made, the action began at about half an hour past one in the afternoon. Major-General Leslie, after being obliged, by the great extent of the enemy's line, to bring up the first battalion of guards to the right of the regiment of Bose, soon defeated every thing before him; Lieutenant-Colonel Webster having joined the left of Major-General Leslie's division, was no less successful in his front; when, on finding that the left of the thirty-third was exposed to a heavy fire from the right wing of the enemy, he changed his front to the left; and, being supported by the yagers and light infantry of the guards, attacked and routed it; the grenadiers and second battalion of the guards moving forward to occupy the ground left vacant by the movement of Lieutenant-Colonel Webster.

All the infantry being now in the line, Lieutenant-Colonel Tarleton had directions to keep his cavalry compact, and not to charge without positive orders, except to protect any of the corps from the most evident danger of being defeated. The excessive thickness of the woods rendered our bayonets of little use, and enabled the broken enemy to make frequent stands, with an irregular fire, which occasioned some loss, and to several of the corps great delay, par-

ticu'arly on our right, where the first battalion of the guards and regiment of
Bose were warmly engaged in front, flank, and rear, with some of the enemy
that had been routed on the first attack, and with part of the extremity of their
left wing, which, by the closeness of the woods, had been passed unbroken.
The seventy-first regiment, and grenadiers, and second battalion of the guards,
not knowing what was passing on their right, and hearing the fire advance on
their left, continued to move forward, the artillery keeping pace with them on
the road, followed by the cavalry. The second battalion of guards first gained
the clear ground near Guilford Court-House, and found a corps of Continental
infantry, much superior in number, formed in the open field on the left of the
road. Glowing with impatience to signalize themselves, they instantly attacked
and defeated them, taking two six pounders: but pursuing into the wood with
too much ardor, were thrown into confusion by a heavy fire, and immediately
charged and driven back into the field by Lieutenant-Colonel Washington's dragoons, with the loss of the six-pounders they had taken. The enemy's cavalry
was soon repulsed by a well-directed fire from two three-pounders, just
brought up by Lieutenant McCleod, and by the appearance of the grenadiers, of
the guards, and the seventy-first regiment, which, having been impeded by
some deep ravines, were now coming out of the wood on the right of the guards
opposite to the court-house. By the spirited exertions of Brigadier-General
O'Hara, though wounded, the second battalion of the guards was soon rallied,
and, supported by the grenadiers, returned to the charge with the greatest
alacrity. The twenty-third regiment arriving at that instant from our left, and
Lieutenant-Colonel Tarleton having advanced with part of the cavalry, the
enemy were soon put to flight, and the two six-pounders once more fell into our
hands; two ammunition wagons, and two other six-pounders, being all the
artillery they had in the field, were likewise taken. About this time, the thirty-
third regiment and light infantry of the guards, after overcoming many difficulties, completely routed the corps which was opposed to them, and put an
end to the action in this quarter. The twenty-third and seventy-first regiments,
with part of the cavalry, were ordered to pursue; the remainder of the cavalry
was detached with Lieutenant-Colonel Tarleton to our right, where a heavy
fire still continued, and where his appearance and spirited attack contributed
much to a speedy termination of the action. The militia with which our right
wing had been engaged, dispersed in the woods; the Continentals went off by
the Reedy Fork, beyond which it was not in my power to follow them, as their
cavalry had suffered but little. Our troops were excessively fatigued by an
action which lasted an hour and a half, and our wounded dispersed over an
extensive space of country, required immediate attention. The care of our
wounded, and the total want of provisions in an exhausted country, made it
equally impossible for me to follow the blow the next day. The enemy did
not stop until they got to the iron works on Troublesome Creek, eighteen
miles from the field of battle.

From our observation, and the best accounts we could procure, we did not
doubt but the strength of the enemy exceeded seven thousand men; their militia composed their line, with parties advanced to the rails of the field in their
front; the Continentals were posted obliquely in the rear of their right wing.
Their cannon fired on us whilst we were forming from the centre of the line of
militia, but were withdrawn to the Continentals before the attack.

I have the honor to inclose to your lordship the list of our killed and wounded. Captain Schutz's wound is supposed to be mortal; but the surgeons assure
me that none of the other officers are in danger; and that a great number of
the men will soon recover. I cannot ascertain the loss of the enemy, but it
must have been considerable: between two and three hundred dead were left
upon the field; many of their wounded that were able to move, whilst we were
employed in the care of our own, escaped and followed the routed enemy; and
our cattle drivers, and forage parties, have reported to me that the houses, in a

circle of six or eight miles around us, are full of others. Those that remained we have taken the best care of in our power. We took few prisoners, owing to the excessive thickness of the wood facilitating their escape, and every man of our army being repeatedly wanted for action.

The conduct and action of the officers and soldiers that compose this little army will do more justice to their merit than I can by words. Their persevering intrepidity in action. their invincible patience in the hardships and fatigues of a march of above six hundred miles, in which they have forded several large rivers and numberless creeks, many of which would be reckoned large rivers in any other country in the world, without tents or covering against the climate, and often without provisions, will sufficiently manifest their ardent zeal for the honor and interest of their sovereign and their country.

I have been particularly indebted to Major-General Leslie for his gallantry and exertion in the action, as well as his assistance in every other part of the service. The zeal and spirit of Brigadier-General O'Hara merits my highest commendations; for, after receiving two dangerous wounds, he continued in the field whilst the action lasted; by his earnest attention on all other occasions, seconded by the officers and soldiers of his brigade. His majesty's guards are no less distinguished by their order and discipline than by their spirit and valor.

The Hessian regiment of Bose deserves my warmest praises for its discipline, alacrity, and courage, and does honor to Major Du Buy, who commands it, and who is an officer of superior merit. I am much obliged to Brigadier-General Howard, who served as a volunteer, for his spirited example on all occasions.

Lieutenant-Colonel Webster conducted his brigade like an officer of experience and gallantry. Lieutenant-Colonel Tarleton's good conduct and spirits, in the management of his cavalry, were conspicuous during the whole action; and Lieutenant McCleod, who commanded the artillery, proved himself upon this, as well as all former occasions, a most capable and deserving officer.

The attention and exertions of my aids-de-camp, and of all the other public officers of the army, contributed very much to the success of the day.

I have constantly received the most zealous assistance from Governor Martin during my command in the Southern district; hoping that his presence would tend to incite the loyal subjects of this province to take an active part with us, he has cheerfully submitted to the fatigues and dangers of our campaign; but his delicate constitution has suffered by his public spirit; for, by the advice of the physicians, he is now obliged to return to England for the recovery of his health.

This part of the country is so totally destitute of subsistence, that forage is not nearer than nine miles, and the soldiers have been two days without bread. I shall therefore leave about seventy of the worst of the wounded cases at the New Garden Quaker meeting-house, with proper assistance, and move the remainder with the army to-morrow morning to Bell's mill. I hope our friends will heartily take an active part with us, to which I shall continue to encourage them; still approaching our shipping by easy marches, that we may procure the necessary supplies for further operations, and lodge our sick and wounded where proper attention can be paid to them.

This dispatch will be delivered to your lordship by my aid-de-camp, Captain Brodrick, who is a very promising officer, and whom I beg leave to recommend to your lordship's countenance and favor, &c.

Q.—Page 473.

HEAD-QUARTERS, MARTIN'S TAVERN, NEAR FERGUSON'S SWAMP, SOUTH CAROLINA, *September* 11, 1781.

SIR,—In my last dispatch, of the 25th of August, I informed your excellency that we were on our march for Friday's Ferry, to form a junction with the State troops, and a body of militia, collecting at that place, with an intention to make an attack upon the British army lying at Colonel Thompson's, near McCord's Ferry. On the 27th, on our arrival near Friday's Ferry, I got intelligence that the enemy were retiring.

We crossed the river at Howell's Ferry, and took post at Motte's plantation. Here I got intelligence that the enemy had halted at Eutaw Springs, about forty miles below us; and that they had a re-enforcement, and were making preparations to establish a permanent post there. To prevent this, I was determined rather to hazard an action, notwithstanding our numbers were greatly inferior to theirs. On the 5th we began our march, our baggage and stores having been ordered to Howell's Ferry under a proper guard. We moved by slow and easy marches, as well to disguise our real intention, as to give General Marion an opportunity to join us, who had been detached for the support of Colonel Harden, a report of which I transmitted in my letter of the 5th, dated Maybrick's Creek. General Marion joined us on the evening of the 7th, at Burdell's plantation, seven miles from the enemy's camp.

We made the following disposition, and marched at four o'clock the next morning to attack the enemy. Our front line was composed of four small battalions of militia, two of North and two of South Carolinians; one of the South Carolinians was under the immediate command of General Marion, and was posted on the right, who also commanded the front line; the two North Carolina battalions, under the command of Colonel Malmedy, were posted in the centre; and the other South Carolina battalion, under the command of General Pickens, was posted on the left. Our second line consisted of three small brigades of Continental troops—one from North Carolina, one from Virginia, and one from Maryland. The North Carolinians were formed into three battalions, under the command of Lieutenant-Colonel Ash, Majors Armstrong and Blount; the whole commanded by General Sumner, and posted upon the right. The Virginians consisted of two battalions, commanded by Major Snead and Captain Edmonds, and the whole by Lieutenant-Colonel Campbell, and posted in the centre. The Marylanders also consisted of two battalions, commanded by Lieutenant-Colonel Howard and Major Hardman, and the brigade by Colonel Williams, deputy adjutant-general to the army, and were posted upon the left. Lieutenant-Colonel Lee, with his Legion, covered our right flank; and Lieutenant-Colonel Henderson with the State troops, commanded by Lieutenant-Colonels Hampton, Middleton, and Polk, our left. Lieutenant-Colonel Washington with his horse, and the Delaware troops under Captain Kirkwood, formed a corps de *reserve*. Two three-pounders under Captain-Lieutenant Gaines, advanced with the front line, and two sixes under Captain Browne, with the second.

The Legion and State troops formed our advance, and were to retire upon the flanks upon the enemy's forming. In this order we moved on to the attack. The Legion and State troops fell in with a party of the enemy's horse and foot, about four miles from their camp, who, mistaking our people for a party of militia, charged them briskly, but were soon convinced of their mistake by the reception they met with. The infantry of the State troops kept up a heavy fire, and the Legion in front, under Captain Rudolph, charged them with fixed bayonets: they fled on all sides, leaving four or five dead on the ground, and several more wounded. As this was supposed to be the advance of the British army, our front line was ordered to form and move on briskly in line, the Legion and State troops to take their position upon the flanks. All the country is covered with timber from the place the action began to the Eutaw Springs. The firing began again between two and three miles from the British camp. The militia were ordered to keep advancing as they fired. The enemy's advanced parties were soon driven in, and a most tremendous fire began on both sides from right to left, and the Legion and State troops were closely engaged. General Marion, Colonel Malmedy, and General Pickens conducted the troops with great gallantry and good conduct; and the militia fought with a degree of spirit and firmness that reflects the highest honor upon that class of soldiers. But the enemy's fire being greatly superior to ours and continuing to advance, the militia began to give ground. The North Carolina brigade, under General Sumner, was ordered up to their support. These were all new levies, and had been under discipline but little more than a month; notwithstanding which they fought with a degree of obstinacy that would do honor to the best of veterans; and I could hardly tell which to admire most, the gallantry of the officers or the bravery of the troops. They kept up a heavy and well-directed fire, and the enemy returned it with equal spirit, for they really fought worthy of a better cause, and great execution was done on both sides. In this stage of the action, the Virginians under Lieutenant-Colonel Campbell, and the Marylanders under Colonel Williams, were led on to a brisk charge, with trailed arms, through a heavy cannonade and a shower of musket-balls. Nothing could exceed the gallantry and firmness of both officers and soldiers upon this occasion. They preserved their order, and pressed on with such unshaken resolution that they bore down all before them. The enemy were routed in all quarters. Lieutenant-Colonel Lee had, with great address, gallantry, and good conduct, turned the enemy's left flank, and was charging them in rear at the same time the Virginia and Maryland troops were charging them in front. A most valuable officer, Lieutenant-Colonel Henderson, got wounded early in the action; and Lieutenant-Colonel Hampton, who commanded the State cavalry, and who fortunately succeeded Lieutenant-Colonel Henderson in command, charged a party of the enemy, and took upward of one hundred prisoners. Lieutenant-Colonel Washington brought up the corps *de reserve* upon the left, where the enemy seemed disposed to make further resistance; and charged them so briskly with the cavalry and Captain Kirkwood's infantry, as gave them no time to rally or form. Lieutenant-Colonels Polk and Middleton, who commanded the State infantry, were no less conspicuous for their good conduct than for their intrepidity; and the troops under their command gave a specimen of what may be expected from men, naturally brave, when improved by proper discipline. Captain-Lieutenant Gaines, who commanded the three-pounders with the front line, did great execution until his pieces were dismounted. We kept close at the enemy's heels after they broke, until we got into their camp, and a great number of prisoners were continually falling into our hands, and some hundreds of the fugitives ran off toward Charleston.

But a party threw themselves into a large three-story brick house, which stands near the spring; others took post in a picketed garden, while others were lodged in an impenetrable thicket, consisting of a cragged shrub, called a black jack. Thus secured in front, and upon the right by the house and a deep ravine, upon the left by the picketed garden and in the impenetrable shrubs, and the rear also being secured by the springs and deep hollow ways, the enemy renewed the action. Every exertion was made to dislodge them. Lieutenant-Colonel Washington made most astonishing efforts to get through the thicket to charge the enemy in the rear; but found it impracticable, had his horse shot under him, and was wounded and taken prisoner. Four six-pounders were ordered up before the house—two of our own, and two of the enemy's, which they had abandoned—and they were pushed on so much under the command of the fire from the house and the party in the thicket, as to render it impracticable to bring them off again when the troops were ordered to retire. Never were pieces better served; most of the men and officers were either killed or wounded. Washington failing in his charge upon the left, and the Legion baffled in an attempt upon the right, and finding our infantry galled by the fire of the enemy, and our ammunition mostly consumed, though both officers and men continued to exhibit uncommon acts of heroism, I thought proper to retire out of the fire of the house, and draw up the troops at a little distance in the woods; not thinking it advisable to push our advantages further, being persuaded the enemy could not hold the post many hours, and that our chance to attack them on the retreat was better than a second attempt to dislodge them, in which, if we succeeded, it must be attended with considerable loss.

We collected all our wounded, except such as were under the command of the fire of the house, and retired to the ground from which we marched in the morning, there being no water nearer. and the troops ready to faint with the heat, and want of refreshment, the action having continued near four hours. I left on the field of action a strong picket, and early in the morning detached General Marion and Lieutenant-Colonel Lee with the Legion horse between Eutaw and Charleston, to prevent any re-enforcements from coming to the relief of the enemy; and also to retard their march, should they attempt to retire, and give time to the army to fall upon their rear and put a finishing stroke to our success. We left two pieces of our artillery in the hands of the enemy, and brought off one of theirs. On the evening of the 9th, the enemy retired leaving upward of seventy of their wounded behind them, and not less than one thousand stand of arms that were picked up on the field, and found broken and concealed in the Eutaw Springs. They stove between twenty and thirty puncheons of rum, and destroyed a great variety of other stores, which they had not carriages to carry off. We pursued them the moment we got intelligence of their retiring. But they formed a junction with Major McArthur at this place. General Marion and Lieutenant-Colonel Lee not having a force sufficient to prevent it: but on our approach they retired to the neighborhood of Charleston. We have taken five hundred prisoners, including the wounded the enemy left behind; and I think they cannot have suffered less than six hundred more in killed and wounded. The fugitives that fled from the field of battle spread such an alarm that the enemy burned their stores at Dorchester, and abandoned the post at Fair Lawn; and a great number of negroes and others were employed in felling trees across the road for some miles without the gates of Charleston. Nothing but the brick house, and the peculiar strength of the position at Eutaw, saved the remains of the British army from being all made prisoners.

We pursued them as far as this place; but not being able to overtake them, we shall halt a day or two to refresh, and then take our old position on the High Hills of Santee. I think myself principally indebted for the victory we obtained to the free use of the bayonet made by the Virginians and Marylanders, the infantry of the Legion, and Captain Kirkwood's light infantry: and though few armies ever exhibited equal bravery with ours in general, yet the conduct and intrepidity of these corps were peculiarly conspicuous. Lieutenant-Colonel Campbell fell as he was leading his troops to the charge, and though he fell with distinguished marks of honor, yet his loss is much to be regretted: he was the great soldier and the firm patriot.

Our loss in officers is considerable, more from their value than their number; for never did either men or officers offer their blood more willingly in the service of their country. I cannot help acknowledging my obligations to Colonel Williams for his great activity on this and many other occasions in forming the army, and for his uncommon intrepidity in leading on the Maryland troops to the charge, which exceeded any thing I ever saw. I also feel myself greatly indebted to Captains Pierce and Pendleton, Major Hyrne and Captain Shubrick, my aids-de-camp, for their activity and good conduct throughout the whole of the action.

This dispatch will be handed to your excellency by Captain Pierce, to whom I beg leave to refer you for further particulars.

I have the honor to, &c.,

NATH. GREENE.

His Excellency the President of Congress.

R.—Page 473.

Extract of a Letter from Lieutenant-Colonel Stewart to Earl Cornwallis.

EUTAW, *September* 9, 1781.

With particular satisfaction I have the honor to inform your lordship that, on the 8th instant, I was attacked by the rebel General Greene with all the force he could collect in this province and North Carolina; and after an obstinate engagement, which lasted near two hours, I totally defeated him, and took two six-pounders. Soon after I had the honor of writing your lordship from Thompson's, I received information of Greene's having moved with the rebel army toward Camden, and crossed the Wateree at that place, and, from the best intelligence I could collect, was on his march to Friday's Ferry, on the Congaree. The army under my command being much in want of necessaries, and there being at the same time a convoy with provisions on their march from Charleston, which would necessarily have obliged me to make a detachment of at least four hundred men—which at that time I could ill afford, the army being much weakened by sickness—to meet the convoy at Martin's, fifty-six miles from the camp. The distance being so great, a smaller escort was liable to fall by the enemy's cavalry, which are very numerous. I therefore thought it advisable to retire by slow marches to the Eutaws, where I might have an opportunity of receiving my supplies, and disencumber myself from the sick, without risking any escorts, or suffer myself to be attacked at a disadvantage, should the enemy have crossed the Congaree. Notwithstanding every exertion having been made to gain intelligence of the enemy's situation, they rendered it impossible by waylaying the by-paths and passes through the different swamps, and even detained different flags of truce which I had sent on public business on both sides. About six o'clock in the morning I received intelligence by two deserters, who left General Greene's camp the preceding evening about seven miles from this place; and from their report the rebel army consisted of near four thousand men and four pieces of cannon. In the mean time I received intelligence by Major Coffin, whom I had previously detached with one hundred and forty infantry and fifty cavalry, in order to gain intelligence of the enemy, that they appeared in force in his front, then about four miles from my camp. Finding the enemy in force so near me, I determined to fight them; as from their numerous cavalry a retreat seemed to me to be attended with dangerous consequences. I immediately formed the line of battle, with the right of the army to Eutaw's branch, and its left crossing the road leading to Roche's plantation, leaving a corps on a commanding situation to cover the Charleston road, and to act occasionally as a reserve. About nine o'clock the action began on the right, and soon after became general. Knowing that the enemy were much superior in numbers, and at the same time finding that they attacked with their militia in front, induced me not to alter my position, unless I saw a certain advantage to be gained by it; for by moving forward I exposed both flanks of the army to the enemy's cavalry, which I saw already formed to take that advantage, particularly on the left, which obliged me to move the reserve to support it.

By an unknown mistake the left of the line advanced and drove their militia and North Carolinians before them; but unexpectedly finding the Virginia and Maryland lines ready formed, and at the same time receiving a heavy fire, occasioned some confusion. It was therefore necessary to retire a little distance to an open field, in order to form; which was instantly done, under cover of a heavy, well-directed fire from a detachment of New York volunteers, under the command of Major Sheridan, whom I had previously ordered to take post in the house to check the enemy, should they attempt to pass it. The action was renewed with great spirit; but I was sorry to find that a three-pounder, posted on the road leading to Roche's, had been disabled, and could not be orought off when the left of the line retired. The right wing of the army being composed of the flank battalion, under the command of Major Majoribanks, having repulsed and drove every thing that attacked them, made a rapid move to the left, and attacked the enemy in flank; upon which they gave way in all quarters, leaving behind thom two brass six-pounders, and upward of two hundred killed on the field of action, and sixty taken prisoners, among whom is Colonel Washington, and from every other information, about eight hundred wounded, although they contrived to carry them off during the action. The enemy retired with great precipitation to a strong situation about seven miles from the field of action, leaving their cavalry to cover their retreat. The glory of the day would have been more complete, had not the want of cavalry prevented my taking the advantage which the gallantry of my infantry threw in my way.

I omitted to inform your lordship in its proper place of the army's having for some time been much in want of bread, there being no old corn or mills near me. I was, therefore, under the necessity of sending out rooting parties from each corps, under an officer, to collect potatoes every morning at day-break; and unfortunately that of the flank battalion and buffs, having gone too far in front, fell into the enemy's hands before the action began, which not only weakened my line, but increased their number of prisoners.

Since the action, our time has been employed in taking care of the wounded; and, finding that the enemy have no intention to make a second attack, I have determined to cover the wounded as far as Monk's Corner with the army. My particular thanks are due to Lieutenant-Colonel Cruger, who commanded the front line, for his conduct and gallantry during the action; and Lieutenant-Colonel Allen, Majors Dawson, Stewart, Sheridan, and Coffin, and to Captains Kelly and Campbell, commanding the different corps and detachments; and every other officer and soldier fulfilled the separate duties of their stations with great gallantry. But to Major Majoribanks, and the flank battalion under his command, I think the honor of the day is greatly due. My warmest praise is due to Captain Barry, deputy adjutant-general, Major Brigade Coxon, Lieutenant Ranken, assistant quartermaster-general, and to acting Major of Brigade Roebuck, for the great assistance rendered me during the day.

I hope, my lord, when it is considered that such a handful of men, attacked by the united force of Generals Greene, Sumter, Marion, Sumner, and Pickens, and the Legions of Colonels Lee and Washington, driving them from the field of battle, and taking the only two six-pounders they had, deserve some merit. Inclosed is the return of the killed, wounded, and missing of his majesty's troops. From the number of corps and detachments, which appear to have been engaged, it may be supposed our force is great; but your lordship will please to observe, that the army was much reduced by sickness and otherwise. I hope your lordship will excuse any inaccuracy that may be in this letter, as I have been a good deal indisposed by a wound which I received in my left elbow, which, though slight, from its situation is troublesome. It would give me most singular pleasure if my conduct meets with the approbation of his majesty, that of your lordship, and my country.

Return of Killed, Wounded, and Missing.

3 commissioned officers, 6 sergeants, 1 drummer, 75 rank and file, killed.

16	ditto	20	ditto	2	ditto	313	ditto	wounded.
10	ditto	15	ditto	8	ditto	224	ditto	missing.

S.—Page 492.

HEAD-QUARTERS AT MONTMORENCI, ON THE RIVER ST. LAWRENCE, SEPTEMBER 2, 1759.

SIR,—

I wish I could, upon this occasion, have the honor of transmitting to you a more favorable account of his majesty's arms; but the obstacles we have met with, in the operations of the campaign, are much greater than we had reason to expect, or could foresee; not so much from the number of the enemy (though superior to us), as from the natural strength of the country, which the Marquis de Montcalm seems wisely to depend upon.

When I learned that succors of all kinds had been thrown into Quebec; that five battalions of regular troops, completed from the best of the inhabitants of the country, some of the troops of the colony, and every Canadian that was able to bear arms, besides several nations of savages, had taken the field in a very advantageous situation; I could not flatter myself, that I should be able to reduce the place. I sought, however, an occasion to attack their army, knowing well, that with these troops, I was able to fight, and hoping that a victory might disperse them.

We found them encamped along the shore of Beauport, from the river St. Charles to the Falls of Montmorenci, and intrenched in every accessible part. The 27th of June we landed upon the Isle of Orleans; but receiving a returning message from the admiral, that there was reason to think the enemy had artillery, and a force upon the Point of Levi, I detached Brigadier Monckton, with four battalions, to drive them from thence. He passed the river the 29th, at night, and marched the next day to the point; he obliged the enemy's irregulars to retire, and possessed himself of that post: the advanced parties, upon this occasion, had two or three skirmishes with the Canadians and Indians, with little loss on either side.

Colonel Carleton marched with a detachment to the westernmost part of the Isle of Orleans, from whence our operations were likely to begin.

It was absolutely necessary to possess these two points, and fortify them; because from either the one or the other, the enemy might make it impossible for any ship to lie in the basin of Quebec, or even within two miles of it.

Batteries of cannon and mortars were erected, with great dispatch, on the Point of Levi, to bombard the town and magazines, and to injure the works and batteries. The enemy perceiving these works in some forwardness, passed the river with 1,600 men, to attack and destroy them. Unluckily they fell into confusion, fired upon one another, and went back again; by which we lost an opportunity of defeating this large detachment. The effect of this artillery has been so great (though across the river), that the upper town is considerably damaged, and the lower town entirely destroyed.

The works for the security of our hospitals and stores, on the Isle of Orleans, being finished, on the 9th of July, at night, we passed the North Channel, and encamped near the enemy's left, the Montmorenci between us. The next morning Captain Dank's company of rangers, posted in a wood to cover some workmen, were attacked and defeated by a body of Indians, and had so many killed and wounded, as to be almost disabled for the rest of the campaign. The enemy also suffered in this affair, and were in their turn driven off by the nearest troops.

The ground to the eastward of the falls seemed to be (as it really is), higher than that on the enemy's side, and to command it in a manner which might be useful to us. There is, besides, a ford below the falls, which may be passed for some hours in the latter part of the ebb and beginning of the flood tide; and I had hopes, that possibly means might be found of passing the river above, so as to fight the Marquis de Montcalm, upon terms of less disadvantage than directly attacking his intrenchments. In reconnoitring the river Montmorenci, we found it fordable at a place about three miles up; but the opposite bank was intrenched, and so steep and woody, that it was to no purpose to attempt a passage there. The escort was twice attacked by the Indians, who were as often repulsed; but in these rencounters, we had forty (officers and men) killed and wounded.

The 18th of July, two men of war, two armed sloops, and two transports with some troops on board, passed by the town without any loss, and got into the upper river. This enabled me to reconnoitre the country above, where I found the same attention on the enemy's side, and great difficulties on ours, arising from the nature of the ground and the obstacles to our communication with the fleet. But what I feared most was, that if we should land between the town and the river, on Cape Rouge, the body first landed could not be re-enforced before they were attacked by the enemy's whole army.

Notwithstanding these difficulties, I thought once of attempting it at St. Michael's, about three miles above the town; but perceiving that the enemy were jealous of the design, were preparing against it, and had actually brought artillery and a mortar (which being so near to Quebec, they could increase as they pleased), to play upon the shipping; and as it must have been many hours before we could attack them, even supposing a favorable night for the boats to pass by the town unhurt, it seemed so hazardous, that I thought it best to desist.

However, to divide the enemy's force, and to draw their attention as high up the river as possible, and to procure some intelligence, I sent a detachment under the command of Colonel Carleton, to land at the Point de Trempe, to attack whatever he might find there, bring off some prisoners, and all the useful papers he could get. I had been informed that a number of the inhabitants of Quebec had retired to that place, and that probably we should find a magazine of provisions there.

The colonel was fired upon, by a body of Indians, the moment he landed, but they were soon dispersed and driven into the woods; he searched for magazines, but to no purpose; brought off some prisoners, and returned with little loss.

After this business I came back to Montmorenci, where I found that Brigadier Townshend had, by his superior fire, prevented the French from erecting a battery on the bank of the river, from whence they intended to cannonade our camp. I now resolved to take the first opportunity which presented itself of attacking the enemy, though posted to great advantage, and everywhere prepared to receive us.

As the men-of-war cannot (for want of sufficient depth of water) come near enough to the enemy's intrenchments to annoy them in the least, the admiral had prepared two transports (drawing but little water), which, upon occasion, could be run aground to favor a descent. With the help of these vessels, which I understood would be carried by the tide close in shore, I proposed to make myself master of a detached redoubt, near to the water's edge, and whose situation appeared to be out of musket-shot of the intrenchment upon the hill. If the enemy supported this detached piece, it would necessarily bring on an engagement, what we most wished for; and if not, I should have it in my power to examine their situation, so as to be able to determine where we could best attack them.

Preparations were accordingly made for an engagement. The 31st of July in the forenoon, the boats of the fleet were filled with grenadiers, and a part of Brigadier Monckton's brigade from the Point of Levi. The two brigades under the Brigadiers Townshend and Murray were ordered to be in readiness to pass the ford, when it should be thought necessary. To faciliate the passage of this corps, the admiral had placed the Centurion in the channel, so that she might check the fire of the lower battery, which commanded the ford. This ship was of great use, as her fire was very judiciously directed. A great quantity of artillery was placed upon the eminence, so as to batter and enfilade the left of their intrenchments.

From the vessel which ran aground, nearest in, I observed that the redoubt was too much commanded, to be kept without very great loss, and the more, as the two armed ships could not be brought near enough to cover both with their artillery and musketry, which I at first conceived they might. But as the enemy seemed in some confusion, and we were prepared for an action, I thought it a proper time to make an attempt upon their intrenchments. Orders were sent to the brigadier-generals to be ready with the corps under their command. Brigadier Monckton was to land, and the Brigadiers Townshend and Murray to pass the ford.

At a proper time of the tide, the signal was made, but in rowing toward the shore, many of the boats grounded upon a ledge that runs off a considerable distance. This accident put us into some disorder, lost a great deal of time, and obliged me to send an officer to stop Brigadier Townshend's march, whom I then observed to be in motion. While the seamen were getting the boats off, the enemy fired a number of shells and shot, but did no considerable damage. As soon as this disorder could be set a little to rights, and the boats were ranged in a proper manner, some of the officers of the navy went in with me, to find a better place to land; we took one flat-bottomed boat with us to make the experiment, and as soon as we had found a fit part of the shore, the troops were ordered to disembark, thinking it not yet too late for the attempt.

The thirteen companies of grenadiers, and two hundred of the second royal American battalion, got first on shore. The grenadiers were ordered to form themselves into four distinct bodies, and to begin the attack, supported by Brigadier Monckton's corps, as soon as the troops had passed the ford, and were at hand to assist. But whether from the noise and hurry at landing, or from some other cause, the grenadiers, instead of forming themselves as they were directed, ran on impetuously toward the enemy's intrenchments in the utmost disorder and confusion, without waiting for the corps which were to sustain them, and join in the attack. Brigadier Monckton was not landed, and Brigadier Townshend was still at a considerable distance, though upon his march to join us in very great order. The grenadiers were checked by the enemy's first fire, and obliged to shelter themselves in or about the redoubt which the French abandoned upon their approach. In this situation they continued for some time, unable to form under so hot a fire, and having many gallant officers wounded, who (careless of their persons) had been solely intent upon their duty, I saw the absolute necessity of calling them off, that they might form themselves behind Brigadier Monckton's corps, which was now landed, and drawn up on the beach, in extreme good order.

By this new accident, and this second delay, it was near night; a sudden storm came on, and the tide began to make; so that I thought it most advisable not to persevere in so difficult an attack, lest (in case of a repulse) the retreat of Brigadier Townshend's corps might be hazardous and uncertain.

Our artillery had a great effect upon the enemy's left, where Brigadiers Townshend and Murray were to have attacked; and it is probable that if those accidents I have spoken of had not happened, we should have penetrated there, whilst our left and centre (more remote from our artillery) must have borne all the violence of their musketry.

The French did not attempt to interrupt our march. Some of their savages came down to murder such wounded as could not be brought off, and to scalp the dead, as their custom is.

The place where the attack was intended, has these advantages over all others hereabout: our artillery could be brought into use; the greater part, or even the whole of the troops, might act at once; and the retreat (in case of repulse) was secure, at least for a certain time of the tide. Neither one nor the other of these advantages can anywhere else be found. The enemy were indeed posted upon a commanding eminence; the beach, upon which the troops were drawn up, was of deep mud, with holes, and cut by several gullies; 'the hill to be ascended very steep, and not everywhere practicable; the enemy numerous in their intrenchments, and their fire hot. If the attack had succeeded, our loss must certainly have been great, and theirs inconsiderable, from the shelter which the neighboring woods afforded them. The river St. Charles still remained to be passed, before the town was invested. All these circumstances I considered; but the desire to act in conformity to the king's intentions, induced me to make this trial, persuaded that a victorious army finds no difficulties.

The enemy have been fortifying ever since with care, so as to make a second attempt still more dangerous.

Immediately after this check, I sent Brigadier Murray above the town with one thousand two hundred men, directing him to assist Rear-Admiral Holmes in the destruction of the French ships (if they could be got at), in order to open a communication with General Amherst. The brigadier was to seek every favorable opportunity of fighting some of the enemy's detachments, provided he could do it upon tolerable terms, and to use all the means in his power to provoke them to attack him. He made two different attempts to and upon the north shore without success; but in a third was more fortunate. He landed unexpectedly at De Chambaud, and burned a magazine there, in which were some provisions, some ammunition, and all the spare stores, clothing, arms, and baggage of their army. Finding that their ships were not to be got at, and little prospect of bringing the enemy to a battle, he reported his situation to me, and I ordered him to join the army.

The prisoners he took informed him of the surrender of the fort of Niagara, and we discovered, by intercepted letters, that the enemy had abandoned Carillon and Crown Point, were retired to the Isle aux Noix, and that General Amherst was making preparations to pass the Lake Champlain, to fall upon M. de Burlemaque's corps, which consist of three battalions of foot, and as many Canadians as make the whole amount to three thousand men.

The admiral's dispatches and mine would have gone eight or ten days sooner, if I had not been prevented from writing by a fever. I found myself so ill, and am still so weak, that I begged the general officers to consult together for the public utility. They are all of opinion, that (as more ships and provisions have now got above the town) they should try, by conveying up a corps of four or five thousand men (which is nearly the whole strength of the army, after the Points of Levi and Orleans are left in a proper state of defence), to draw the enemy from their present situation, and bring them to an action. I have acquiesced in their proposal, and we are preparing to put it in execution.

The admiral and I have examined the town, with a view to a general assault; but after consulting with the chief engineer, who is well acquainted with the interior parts of it, and after viewing it with the utmost attention, we found, that though the batteries of the lower town might be easily silenced by the men-of-war, yet the business of an assault would be little advanced by that, since the few passages that lead from the lower to the upper town are carefully intrenched, and the upper batteries cannot be affected by the ships, which must receive considerable damage from them and from the mortars. The admiral would readily join in this, or in any other measure, for the public service; but I could not propose to him an undertaking of so dangerous a nature, and promising so little success.

To the strength of the country, the enemy have added (for the defence of the river) a great number of floating batteries and boats. By the vigilance of these and the Indians around our different posts, it has been impossible to execute any thing by surprise. We have had almost daily skirmishes with these savages; in which they are generally defeated, but not without loss on our side.

By the list of disabled officers (many of whom are of rank) you may perceive, sir, that the army is much weakened. By the nature of the river, the most formidable part of this armament is deprived of the power of acting, yet we have almost the whole force of Canada to oppose. In this situation, there is such a choice of difficulties, that I own myself at a loss how to determine. The affairs of Great Britain, I know, require the most vigorous measures; but the courage of a handful of brave men should be exerted only where there is some hope of a favorable event. However, you may be assured, sir, that the small part of the campaign which remains, shall be employed (as far as I am able) for the honor of his majesty, and the interest of the nation, in which I am sure of being seconded by the admiral and by the generals. Happy if our efforts here can contribute to the success of his majesty's arms in any other parts of America.

I have the honor to be, &c..

JAMES WOLFE.

T.--Page 512.

Earl Cornwallis to Sir Henry Clinton, K. B.

YORKTOWN, *October* 20, 1791.

SIR,—

I have the mortification to inform your excellency, that I have been forced to give up the posts of York and Gloucester, and to surrender the troops under my command, by capitulation, on the 19th instant, as prisoners of war, to the combined forces of America and France.

I never saw this post in a very favorable light; but when I found I was to be attacked in it, in so unprepared a state, by so powerful an army and artillery, nothing but the hopes of relief would have induced me to attempt its defence; for I would either have endeavored to escape to New York by rapid marches from the Gloucester side, immediately on the arrival of General Washington's troops at Williamsburgh; or I would, notwithstanding the disparity of numbers, have attacked them in the open field, where it might have been just possible that fortune would have favored the gallantry of the handful of troops under my command. But being assured by your excellency's letters, that every possible means would be tried by the navy and army to relieve us, I could not think myself at liberty to venture upon either of those desperate attempts. Therefore, after remaining for two days in a strong position, in front of this place, in hopes of being attacked, upon observing that the enemy were taking measures which could not fail of turning my left flank in a short time, and receiving on the second evening your letter of the 24th of September, informing me that the relief would sail about the 5th of October, I withdrew within the works on the night of the 29th of September, hoping by the labor and firmness of the soldiers to protect the defence until you could arrive. Every thing was to be expected from the spirit of the troops; but every disadvantage attended their labor, as the work was to be continued under the enemy's fire; and our stock of intrenching tools, which did not much exceed four hundred when we began to work in the latter end of August, was now much diminished.

The enemy broke ground on the night of the 30th, and constructed on that night and the two following days and nights two redoubts, which, with some works that had belonged to our outward position, occupied a gorge between two creeks or ravines, which came from the river on each side of the town. On the night of the 6th of October they made their first parallel, extending from its right on the river to a deep ravine on the left, nearly opposite to the centre of this place, and embracing our whole left, at a distance of six hundred yards. Having perfected this parallel, their batteries opened on the evening of the 9th, against our left; and other batteries fired at the same time against a redoubt over a creek upon our right, and defended by about one hundred and twenty men (of the twenty-third regiment and marines), who maintained that post with uncommon gallantry. The fire continued incessant from heavy cannon, and from mortars and howitzers, throwing shells from eight to sixteen inches, until all our guns on the left were silenced, our work much damaged, and our loss of men considerable. On the night of the 11th they began their second parallel, about three hundred yards nearer to us. The troops being much weakened by sickness, as well as by the fire of the besiegers, and observing that the enemy had not only secured their flanks, but proceeded in every respect with the utmost regularity and caution, I could not venture so large sorties, as to hope from them any considerable effect; but otherwise I did every thing in my power to interrupt their work, by opening new embrasures for guns, and keeping up a constant fire with howitzers and small mortars that we could man. On the evening of the 14th, they assaulted and carried two redoubts that had been advanced about two hundred yards for the purpose of delaying their approaches and covering our left flank, and included them in their second parallel, on which they continued to work with the utmost exertion. Being perfectly sensible that our works could not stand many hours after the opening of the batteries of that parallel, we not only continued a constant fire with all our mortars, and every gun that could be brought to bear upon it, but a little before day-break on the morning of the 16th, I ordered a sortie of about three hundred and fifty men, under the direction of Lieutenant-Colonel Abercrombie, to attack two batteries which appeared to be in the greatest forwardness, and to spike the guns. A detachment of guards, with the eightieth company of grenadiers, under the command of Lieutenant-Colonel Lake, attacked the one; and one of light infantry, under the command of Major Armstrong, attacked the other; and both succeeded, by forcing the redoubts that covered them, spiking eleven guns, and killing or wounding about one hundred of the French troops who had the guard of that part of the trenches, and with little loss on our side. The action, though extremely honorable to the officers and soldiers who executed it, proved of little public advantage; for the cannon having been spiked in a hurry, were soon rendered fit for service again; and before dark the whole parallel batteries appeared to be nearly complete.

At this time we knew that there was no part of the whole front attacked on which we could show a single gun, and our shells were nearly expended. I therefore had only to choose between preparing to surrender next day, or endeavoring to get off with the greatest part of the troops; and I determined to attempt the latter, reflecting that, though it should prove unsuccessful in its immediate object, it might, at least, delay the enemy in the prosecution of farther enterprises. Sixteen large boats were prepared, and, upon other pretexts, were ordered to be in readiness to receive troops precisely at ten o'clock. With these I hoped to pass the infantry during the night; abandoning our baggage, and leaving a detachment to capitulate for the town's people, and the sick and wounded, on which subject a letter was ready to be delivered to General Washington.

After making my arrangements with the utmost secrecy, the light infantry, greatest part of the guards, and part of the twenty-third regiment, landed at Gloucester; but at this critical moment, the weather from being moderate and calm, changed to a violent storm of wind and rain, and drove all the boats, some of which had troops on board, down the river. It was soon evident that the intended passage was impracticable; and the absence of the boats rendered it equally impossible to bring back the troops that had passed, which I had ordered about two in the morning. In this situation, with my little force divided, the enemy's batteries opened at day-break. The passage between this place and Gloucester was much exposed; but the boats having now returned, they were ordered to bring back the troops that had passed during the night, and they joined in the forenoon without much loss. Our works in the mean time were going to ruin; and not having been able to strengthen them by abatis, nor in any other manner than by a slight fraising, which the enemy's artillery were demolishing whenever they fired, my opinion entirely coincided with that of the engineer and principal officers of the army, that they were in many places assailable in the forenoon, and that by the continuance of the same fire for a few hours longer, they would be in such a state as to render it desperate, with our numbers, to attempt to maintain them. We at that time could not fire a single gun; only one eight-inch and a little more than one hundred Cohorn shells remained. A diversion by the French ships of war which lay at the mouth of York River, was to be expected. Our numbers had been diminished by the enemy's fire, but particularly by sickness; and the strength and spirits of those in the works were much exhausted by the fatigue of constant watching and unremitting duty.

Under all these circumstances, I thought it would have been wanton and inhuman to the last degree to sacrifice the lives of this small body of gallant soldiers, who had ever behaved with so much fidelity and courage, by exposing them to an assault, which, from the numbers and precaution of the enemy, could not fail to succeed. I therefore proposed to capitulate; and I have the honor to inclose to your excellency the copy of the correspondence between General Washington and me on that subject, and the terms of capitulation agreed upon. I sincerely lament that better could not be obtained; but I have neglected nothing in my power to alleviate the misfortune and distress of both officers and soldiers.

The men are well clothed and provided with necessaries, and I trust will be regularly supplied by the means of the officers that are permitted to remain with them. The treatment, in general, that we have received from the enemy since our surrender, has been perfectly good and proper. But the kindness and attention that have been shown to us, by the French officers in particular—their delicate sensibility of our situation, their generous and pressing offer of money, both public and private, to any amount—have really gone beyond what I can possibly describe; and will, I hope, make an impression on the breast of every officer, whenever the fortune of war should put any them into our power.

Although the event has been so unfortunate, the patience of the soldiers in bearing the greatest fatigues, and their firmness and intrepidity under a persevering fire of shot and shells, that I believe have not often been exceeded, deserve the highest admiration and praise. A successful defence, however, in our situation, was, perhaps, impossible; for the place could only be reckoned an intrenched camp, subject in most places to an enfilade, and the ground in general so disadvantageous, that nothing but the necessity of fortifying it as a post to protect the navy, could have induced any person to erect works upon it. Our force diminished daily by sickness and other losses, and was reduced when we offered to capitulate, on this side, to little more than three thousand two hundred rank and file fit for duty, including officers, servants, and artificers; and at Gloucester about six hundred, including cavalry. The enemy's army consisted of upward of eight thousand French, nearly as many Continentals, and five thousand militia. They brought an immense train of heavy artillery, mostly amply furnished with ammunition, and perfectly well-manned.

The constant and universal cheerfulness and spirit of the officers, in all hardship and dangers, deserve my warmest acknowledgments; and I have been particularly indebted to Brigadier-General O'Hara and Lieutenant-Colonel Abercrombie, the former commanding on the right, and the latter on the left, for their attention and exertion on every occasion. The detachment of the twenty-third regiment and of the marines, in the redoubt on the right, commanded by Captain Apthorpe, and the subsequent detachments commanded by Lieutenant-Colonel Johnston, deserve particular commendation. Captain Rochfort, who commanded the artillery, and indeed every officer and soldier of that distinguished corps, and Lieutenant Sutherland, the commanding engineer, have merited in every respect my highest approbation: and I cannot sufficiently acknowledge my obligations to Captain Symonds, who commanded his majesty's ships, and to the other officers and seamen of the navy, for their active and zealous co-operation.

I transmit returns of our killed and wounded. The loss of seamen and town's people was likewise considerable.

I trust your excellency will please to hasten the return of the Bonetta, after landing her passengers, in compliance with the articles of capitulation.

Lieutenant-Colonel Abercrombie will have the honor to deliver this dispatch, and is well qualified to explain to your excellency every particular relating to our past and present situation.

I have the honor to be, &c.,
CORNWALLIS.

U.—Page 459.

Letter from the Marquis of Hastings, formerly Lord Rawdon, and then Earl of Moira, in justification of his conduct in relation to the execution of Colonel Isaac Hayne.

AT SEA, 24*th June*, 1813.

SIR :—

The letters which you did me the honor to write to me, with the copy of your Memoirs of the War in the Southern Provinces of America, reached me at a time when the arrangements for my immediate embarkation left me not a moment to peruse the work.

I had proposed myself to begin the study of it as soon as we should put to sea; but a farther delay occurred. The box containing the book was accidentally placed in the hold, under such a quantity of other packages, as till lately rendered it impracticable for me to retrieve it.

I must undoubtedly feel flattered by your procedure in writing to me, as well as by the tenor of your letters; and I beg leave to return thanks for your politeness. One consideration alone, the conviction of your not having interiorily credited a particular statement, which you have promulgated on the faith of its currency among your party, could prevent my expressing astonishment, that you should profess any sort of estimation, or offer a complimentary attention toward a person represented in that narrative as capable of an atrocious act. No gentler description would befit the measure ascribed to me in that statement, of sacrificing to any views of general policy, an individual not truly standing within the scope of capital punishment, or even of inflicting that punishment where justly incurred, if public duty did not exact the enforcement.

It is the most disgusting of the circumstances attending civil war, that men, holding themselves aloof from its dangers, always endeavor by virulence and hardihood of imputation against their adversaries, to disguise from themselves and others, the nothingness of spirit which restrains them from taking efficient part in the conflict. The slanders thus raised cannot be met. They acquire substance by uncontradicted circulation, as every successive propagator feels pledged to maintain the verity of the assertion. And when the contest is over, while the successful faction has not either interest or inclination (perhaps not the means) to retract the calumny, the individuals of the subdued party are cautious not to entail on themselves outrage by controverting any charges which their victors may have pleased to fabricate. The misrepresentations thus become articles of political creed; and the most generous mind will be apt, unconsciously, to satisfy itself that it may remain exempt from the necessity of scrutinizing a statement; when the consequences of exposing its inaccuracy, would be to revolt popular prejudice, to incur the appearance of want of ardor in the general cause, and above all to overthrow some favorite position of the person himself. Hence it is, as I think, that you have been led to receive implicitly a representation, which with very little trouble you could have proved to be incorrect.

I well know that your honorable disposition, judging from all I have heard of your character, would not deliberately advance so serious a charge as you have published against me, had you believed it to be erroneous. But to affix the brand of injustice in the execution of Isaac Hayne, was a ground-work necessary for your giving due credit to the gallant devotion which you state to have been displayed by the American officers, in reference to that measure; and you have hence been betrayed into too easy a credence of the recital you were sure to receive from all of the party in Carolina (your only informants), to which the unfortunate man belonged.

The strange want of reflection with which you must have listened to every story palmed upon you, cannot be more strikingly exemplified than in the communications from the town major to the prisoner, which you have retailed. To have supposed the town major capable of informing the prisoner that he was to appear before a board of general officers, you must have imagined a principal staff officer of ours ignorant of that which you, and every man in your army, and every other individual in the province, knew; namely, that we had not a single general officer in South Carolina.

Admitting unfeignedly that much of excuse, I still cannot but feel extraordinary surprise, that when you entered into a long argumentative detail (founded on an assumption quite novel) to prove that the conduct of Hayne ought not to have been treated as guilt, you avoided perceiving he could not be brought within your own hypothesis. Were your position tenable (which your better reflection would hardly contend), that the inroad of a skulking party gives a manumission from every tie of allegiance to the inhabitants of any district through which it passes, your advertence to period, to locality, and to particulars would have satisfied you, that the treason of Hayne could not be so extenuated; and I only wonder how the recollection could escape presenting itself. In truth, you must have indistinctly surmised that there would be a difficulty about the applicability of your principle when you deemed it requisite to urge another vindication; a vindication totally inconsistent with the former, because it acknowledges the criminality which the other denies, and only labors to lessen its degree. I allude to the situation in which you suppose Hayne to have been placed by the proclamation of Sir Henry Clinton. Not having an opportunity to consult any copy of that proclamation, I can only say that I never had the impression of its bearing the sense you ascribe to it, and that I have no remembrance of its being so understood by others. Could, however, that proclamation have had the effect of annulling any of the conditions on the faith of which Charleston was surrendered, it would have stamped indelible disgrace on him who issued it, and would have been deeply disreputable to the country which in that act he represented; but how was it to bear on the case of Hayne? The part which he had to take, as a prisoner on parole under the capitulation, was clear. He had only to repair to Charleston, and surrender himself, till the remonstrance of Congress could be exerted with Sir Henry Clinton, upon so gross an infraction of public faith.

The non-existence of any such reclamation on the part of Congress, whose view would not be restricted to the single case of Hayne, sufficiently rebuts the construction you put upon the proclamation. Still, supposing for the sake of giving you the utmost advantage your assumption (if valid) would claim, that the proclamation did so press upon the unhappy man, I repeat that the fit course for him was to submit himself a prisoner. If from any private considerations he preferred any other alternative, he made his choice with all the obligations inseparable from it, and spontaneously rendered himself liable to all the penalties attached to a breach of those obligations. The slightest inquiry would have satisfied you that all who exchanged the character of prisoner on parole under the capitulation, for that of a British subject, did so voluntarily, in order to enjoy the benefits of disposing of the produce of their plantations, in a lucrative course of trade, not allowed to prisoners. And when you represent Hayne as having plighted only a conditional fidelity, it is wonderful you should not have at once detected the imposition that was attempted upon you, by those who made such an assertion. Where was the British officer to be found, who could have inducement, or disposition, or competence, to allow of a limited oath of allegiance to his sovereign! The tale carried falsity on the very face of it. Your penetration might, therefore, have been expected to see through the flimsy pretext, and to perceive, that this was an excuse which Hayne would naturally make to his former comrades, to mitigate the reproach attached by them to his having taken the oath of allegiance, and to soften the unfavorable construction which he must imagine would, even in their opinions, attend his perfidy under so solemn a compact. But your cause would gain nothing were this observation not irrefragable. Were the possibility admitted of his having established the stipulation to which you allude, it would not alter his criminality. When summoned to bear arms (if he ever were so), he would have to say that he had made a condition, that he abided by the reservation, and that he was prepared to meet any consequence of adhering to it. If, instead of that course, he chose to enter into secret negotiation with the enemy, he did it knowingly under all the peril connected with the act. Nay, had he at once broken his engagement, and repaired to General Greene's army, though it would have been treason, it would not have been treason of so deep and complicated a dye, as that in which he involved himself.

Before I proceed further on this head, it is expedient that a material point should be cleared up to you. You mistake entirely in supposing that the province of South Carolina was under my command. Lieutenant-Colonel Balfour was my senior in the army list; and my provincial rank of Colonel, held for the purpose of connection with the regiment raised by me, did not alter that relation, as the colonels on the provincial establishment were subordinate to the youngest lieutenant-colonels of the line. Sir Henry Clinton, in order to give me the management of affairs in South Carolina, subsequently promoted me, as a brigadier of provincials; but we had no intimation of this till the commission arrived, after I had actually embarked for England; Lieutenant-Colonel Balfour would, therefore, at all events have commanded me. A still more particular limitation of my powers existed. Lord Cornwallis, on intrusting me with the management of the troops on the frontier, had specially allotted the whole track within the Santee, Congaree, and Saluda rivers, to Lieutenant-Colonel Balfour, as commandant of Charleston. Camden had always been reprobated by me as a station; not merely from the extraordinary disadvantages which attended it, as an individual position; but from its being on the wrong side of the river and covering nothing; while it was constantly liable to have its communication with the interior district cut off. Lord Cornwallis did not consider how much he augmented this objection, often urged by me to him, by an arrangement whence I was debarred from any interference with the district, from which alone I could be fed: the country in front of Camden, as well as that between the Wateree and Broad rivers, being so wasted as to afford nothing beyond precarious and incidental supplies. Fixed at Camden, with seven hundred men (Lieutenant-Colonel Watson's corps never having formed part of my garrison, and the residue of the force with which I encountered General Greene, having been introduced by me into Camden three days after he sat down before it), I was completely dependent on Lieutenant-Colonel Balfour for subsistence, for military stores, for horses, for arms, and for those re-enforcements which were indispensable from the expenditure of men, in the unceasing activity of our service. With his posts at Motte's house, Congaree, and Ninety-six, I had no concern, further than their occasional danger obliged me to make movements for their protection; an assistance which I had peculiar difficulty in rendering to the two former, from the works having unaccountably been so placed as not to command the ferries, through which blunder succors could not be thrown across the river to the garrisons when invested by an enemy. Hence it happened that, on the abandonment of Camden in the hope of saving those posts, and protecting the interior country, I was forced to pass the Santee by the circuitous route of Nelson's Ferry. From this delay arose the circumstance, that on the day after my crossing the river, I received an account of the fall of the two redoubts, pompously denominated Fort Motte and Fort Granby. The event by throwing into your hands the only magazines of provisions in the country utterly incapacitated me from advancing: for, destitute of cavalry to face yours, I must have been unable to glean daily food for my troops; and could not think so lightly of the talents of General Greene, as to indulge the visionary expectation that he would put his fortune to the hazard of a battle, when he might reduce me to the extreme of distress by a policy unattended with risk to himself.

These particulars are not stated so much for the purpose of conveying any information which will be interesting to you in explaining much of the campaign, as to show, that I had not in the interior district, any immediate interest, or any course of management, the interruption of which could excite in me irritation against Hayne, or indeed call my attention to his crime. And you well know there was not any peevish acrimony in our warfare. In fact, I never heard of the insurrection which he instigated, till its suppression was communicated to me by Lieutenant-Colonel Balfour.

The way I came to have any part in the affair was this. When Lord Cornwallis suddenly marched into North Carolina, he wrote to me (then through accidental circumstances at Camden), to assign to me the very unexpected charge of maintaining that post, and the frontier beyond the rivers. In the same letter he entreated me, as a proof of friendship to himself, that I would act cordially with Lieutenant-Colonel Balfour, between whom and me his lordship knew there had been some estrangement. In answer, I assured him, that he might depend on my giving Lieutenant-Colonel Balfour, in every particular, the most zealous support.

Shortly after we had withdrawn from Ninety-six and the upper country, Lieutenant-Colonel Balfour wrote to apprise me, that an insurrection had taken place in the rear of my army, but had luckily been crushed. He stated the imperious necessity of repressing the disposition to similar acts of treachery, by making an example of the individual who had planned, as well as headed the revolt, and who had fallen into Lieutenant-Colonel Balfour's hands. He solicited my concurrence (absolutely ineffective in any other point of view, in a district where I was wholly under his control) that it might vouch to Sir Henry Clinton, with whom he was on ill terms, for the public policy of the measure. On the justice of it, there was not then a conception, that in possibility a question could be raised. I replied that there could be no doubt as to the necessity for making the example, to which I would readily give the sanction of my name.

Collateral circumstances were then unknown to me. Immediately on my arrival at Charleston, application was made to me by a number of ladies (principally of your party) to save Hayne from the impending infliction. Ignorant of the complicated nature and extent of the crime, I incautiously promised to use my endeavors toward inducing Lieutenant-Colonel Balfour to lenity. A petition to be signed by the ladies, was drawn up as a step gratifying to me, by one of the officers of the staff (I believe by Major Barry, the deputy adjutant-general) to serve as a basis for my address to the commandant. When I opened the matter to him he appeared much astonished; detailed to me circumstances of the case with which I had been completely unacquainted; requesting me to inform myself more minutely upon them; and earnestly begged me to ponder on the effect, which forbearance from visiting such an offence with due punishment (sure to be ascribed to timidity) must unavoidably produce on the minds of the inhabitants. It was a grievous error in me that I did not at once yield to the reasoning, and to the conviction which it could not but impress, instead of still attempting to realize the hope, which I had suffered the ladies so loosely to entertain. I unluckily persevered in the effort to reconcile a pardon with some appearance of propriety. At this time I saw a lady connected with Hayne; I suppose it must have been the Mrs. Perroneau mentioned by you. I frankly told her what had passed between me and Lieutenant-Colonel Balfour, stating the embarrassment in which I found myself, from the enormity of the transgression, and the objections too justly urged, but adding, that, unless there should be intervention from General Greene, I would still try if the difficulty could be surmounted. This point, I understand, was most profligately wrested, as if Lieutenant-Colonel Balfour and I had held forth a sort of implied condition to the unfortunate man, that he should be spared if General Greene did not interfere; and that the latter was thence withheld from exertions which might have been effectual. Lieutenant-Colonel Balfour was never privy to the conversation between Mrs. Perroneau and me; nor could it in any case have been imagined possible, that such a communication should reach General Greene, when the attempt at any correspondence with him would have been a capital offence. It was simply an expression of my fears, that a circumstance might occur which would at once destroy all chance of my being useful. Any interposition on the part of General Greene must have been in irritating terms, and would infallibly have precluded an excuse which I hoped to obtain, and which would afford a decent pretence for a lenity, felt by me to be liable to great and well-founded censure. As a mode of gaining time, I had solicited Lieutenant-Colonel Balfour to have the particulars of the case ascertained by a court of inquiry for my satisfaction, alleging the chance (though I could not really believe the existence of any such), that circumstances might have been distorted by the animosity of Hayne's neighbors. This step, although a court of inquiry was the same form of investigation as had been used in the case of Major André, was an indiscretion on my part; because it afforded a color for perversion, by seeming to imply that there might be a doubt as to the amount of guilt; whereas by all the recognized laws of war, nothing was requisite in the case of Hayne, but to identify his person previous to hanging him on the next tree. Before that court (the proceedings of which were unavoidably thrown overboard with my other papers, when I was taken by the French at sea), he produced documents to establish his claim of being treated as an American officer, but which only more distinctly substantiated his criminal correspondence with the enemy. So that the case, had it admitted of aggravation, would have been made worse by the result of that inquiry. He was, from his correspondence with the enemy, while within our posts, a spy in the strictest sense of the word; and to that guilt was added the further crime of his having debauched a portion of our enrolled militia, at the head of which he menaced with death all persons of the vicinage, who would not join him in arms against us, and actually devastated the property of those who fled from participation in the revolt. Such were the difficulties of the task in which I had improperly entangled myself; I notwithstanding persevered. Mr. Alexander Wright and Mr. Powell (I think his Christian name was Charles), in compliance with my wishes, undertook to try whether a petition for pardon to Hayne might not be procured from a respectable number of loyalists; though they gave me little encouragement to hope success, from even their known and just influence with that body. They first applied to Lieutenant-Governor Bull, who consented to sign the petition, provided the Attorney-General, Sir Egerton Leigh, would do so. The answer of Sir Egerton Leigh was, *that he would burn his hand off rather than do an act so injurious to the king's service.* Lieutenant-Governor Bull's conditional promise of course fell to the ground, though he subsequently, from some dupery practised upon his age, joined his name with those of certain of your most active and avowed partisans; and not one loyalist of repute could be persuaded to put his name to the petition. There then remained no possible excuse for a remission of the punishment; under which circumstances, it would have been baseness in me toward Lieutenant-

Colonel Balfour, and a forfeiture of my plighted assurance to Lord Cornwallis, had I withheld my name from the measure, when, after what had passed, I could but be conscious it was deeply necessary for the public service.

The enterprise which Hayne had planned and achieved when he was intercepted and taken, had an object of singular malignity. I allude to the seizure of Mr. Williamson; and the insulting triumph with which Mr. Williamson was told, that the purpose in capturing him, was to have been hanged in the camp of General Greene, had naturally roused the indignation of all the friends of the British Government. Mr. Williamson, as you know, had been a brigadier-general of the American militia at the time of our invading South Carolina. When the rest of the province submitted, Mr. Williamson also adopted that line. He had not taken up arms against you, nor was he intermeddling in politics, but quietly residing in the neighborhood of Charleston. The attempt, therefore, to carry him off, and to exhibit in his person, a proof that even mere submission to our rule should detail the utmost severity of infliction, caused great ferment in the minds of the loyalists. This was extraordinarily augmented by a dreadful impolicy on the part of the unfortunate prisoner. The number of individuals professedly of your party, to whom the capitulation had given the right of remaining in Charleston, afforded to Hayne a communication most mischievous for him. For those persons, intoxicated by an apparent change of tide in their favor, not only themselves, held the language that the British Government would not dare to execute Hayne, but misled the unhappy man to use the same tone of defiance to the loyalists. To have been swayed by their resentment would have been unworthy; but they had a claim very distinct from that of passion, to a consideration of their opinions, from those intrusted with the conduct of the general concern. When their fortunes and their lives were risked in the cause of Britain, they had a right to demand that the joint stake should be so managed, as to give them their fair chance for success in the contest; and it was obvious, that if in an hour when the highest peril was to be encountered by those who remained faithful, no terrors were to impend over a breach of the sacred ties by which they were individually bound to each other and to government, a premium should in fact be held forth to treachery, and the dissolution of the common interest would be inevitable. If we were to maintain a claim on their fidelity, it could only be by showing a just sensibility for their welfare.

You prove yourself perfectly aware of the nature of the period, and of the urgent pressure under which we labored, when you mention the expectation you were authorized to entertain, that a French army would land in the Southern provinces. We had received from the Secretary of State, an intimation which led us to believe, that Beaufort was its probable destination. Advertence to this contingency, and the necessity of making provision against the event, had materially influenced the conduct of the campaign. It was the reason why, when I undertook the relief of Ninety-six, I was furnished with but barely seventeen hundred men. Even of that force, a principal proportion was composed of Hessians, or of troops just landed from Ireland, so little suited to bear the rapidity of march which our circumstances exacted, that we left numbers of them (very many dead from the heat) along the road. The crisis may be estimated by my being obliged to risk such an enterprise with a strength, on any ordinary calculation, so inadequate to the object. In this exigency, we found ourselves surrounded by defection and treachery on all sides. The perfidy had gone so far, that soon after my crossing the Santee, I had to communicate to Lieutenant-Colonel Balfour the necessity for his immediately disarming a portion of his town militia, designated by me; as I knew from information not questionable, that they were in correspondence with General Greene, and had engaged to seize the gates for him, if he could slip by me, and present himself suddenly before Charleston. In such extremities, those administering the interest of their country (if they were not to bow their heads to the defection, and abjectly sacrifice the important trust reposed in them) had no option but to exert against the mischief that strenuous resistance which their duty required, and the purest justice authorized.

Such, sir, are the real features of a case, which you hold forth in unfavorable contrast with the tenderness of sentiment displayed in the proceedings against Major André! It is not my wish to enter into a discussion of the latter case; and it would be most unfair to doubt the dispositions of General Washington, or the irresistible pressure which rendered them abortive. Yet thus far I must remark. Had there been so much solicitude to save that unfortunate officer as you represent, this ostensible plea might have been advanced for him: That his entering in disguise within your fortress, was by the direction and with the invitation of your officer commanding there. For the guilt of Hayne no shadow of palliation could be found. The story of remonstrance from the British officers to Lieutenant-Colonel Balfour shows how lamentably you were deceived in every respect by the fabrications in the province. That recurrence of the British officers to the commandant, was for the purpose of urging him to secure objects for retaliation, in case of General Greene's carrying into effect his outrageous threat. They needed not to have given themselves the trouble; and though I have no disposition to depreciate the spirit which dictated it, the proffered devotion of your American officers was equally superfluous. General Greene sagaciously comprehended that it was necessary to counteract the impression which the execution of Hayne was calculated to produce. Hence it was his policy to declaim against it as an undue infliction, the repetition of which in any similar case, should be prevented by retaliation. But he was too wise not to know, that the matter would not bear scrutiny, and that it must not for his ends be driven to minute question.

Having mentioned retaliation, let me say, that Lieutenant-Colonel Balfour and I had severally, direct orders from Lord Cornwallis to check by retaliation the merciless severity with which your civil governments treated the loyalists who fell into their power. With numbers in our hands justly amenable to rigor, each of us had taken it upon himself to dispense with that injunction: not from any doubt of its equity, but from a fear that our obedience would only extend the calamity, and from a hope, that the difference of our procedure would be the best corrective of the inhumanity. So far were the British officers from having such feelings, as the fallacious representations practised upon you have led you to suppose, that I had been informed by particular friends, of the extraordinary dissatisfaction testified by those officers, at the seeming hesitation respecting the fate of Hayne. They viewed it as a feebleness, and a dishonest desertion of the interests which our army was bound to uphold. This sentiment was so strong, that at a dinner which Lieutenant-Colonel Balfour gave to the staff and principal officers on the eve of my embarkation, I thought myself bound in justice toward the commandant, to address the company, to confess that the apparent demur was imputable to me alone, to own that I had sought to find grounds to excuse a remission of the punishment, and to admit that I had been wrong in the endeavor. The acknowledgment was conscientious: and at no period since, has my reflection made me regard myself as otherwise than culpable, in not having at once given the just weight to the considerations, which so imperiously called for the example.

That the punishment of Hayne may appear an unnecessary severity, you state, that at this juncture the British cause was evidently lost in America. The opinion of an enemy, especially of an enemy so zealous and energetic as you, would be no very rational guide for an officer's conduct. There was not at that period any reason for our entertaining such a notion; nor would duty have allowed a relaxation of the exertions, which the trust demanded, upon any personal conception of the sort. No apprehension existed of inability to cope with your joint force, should the French land in South Carolina, though the necessity of keeping the British troops in a position to be readily collected into one body, gave you for the time apparent advantages. Your circumstances were still critical. The situation must not be argued from subsequent occurrences, not then within the foresight of any one; and there were measures which would at once have altered the relative condition of affairs. Had Lord Cornwallis, with his army refreshed, re-equipped, and re-enforced, originally marched from Wilmington to the upper country of North Carolina, the step must have been decisive against you. Its consequences were so clear, that, ignorant of the uncontrollable obstacles, which doubtless must have existed to forbid his lordship's pursuing that policy, we every day expected to hear of his being in Hillsborough.

If, leaving Virginia occupied in self-defence against such a portion of troops as he might think proper to allot for the purpose, he had proceeded to raise and organize the loyalists of North Carolina in your rear, cutting off all your supplies and re-enforcements from the northward, it appeared to us that the destruction of General Greene's army was almost inevitable. We were sufficiently on the watch to prevent a junction between you and any French force that might be landed at Beaufort; and for the ends of co-operation, instructions from Lord Cornwallis would undoubtedly have caused the field army in South Carolina to be put on a footing of efficiency, which it did not possess during my service.

Fortunate it would have been had this movement, so confidently reckoned upon by us, taken place. While it must have so seriously affected General Greene's army, it would have removed Lord Cornwallis from a position, where he was an object for the concentration of force by the Americans and French, and it would of course have precluded that fatal operation. The wisdom of Providence decreed it otherwise; and the judgment of Lord Cornwallis was not left unfettered.

This letter has run into inordinate length; though you will readily understand that I have forborne to dilate on many points connected with the subject. Its prolixity has arisen from the wish to furnish you with full means of forming a sure judgment on the case. Be assured that I have not a suspicion of your having given any color to your narrative, but what you really believed to be the true one. After the promulgation of so invidious a charge against me, I know not how it can be in your power to make me any reparation: but of this I will remain persuaded; that if my statement shall lead you to a conviction of your having done me injustice, you will sincerely regret the facility with which you credited representations, so likely to be warped by the interests and the passions of those from whom you received them.

I have the honor, sir, to be your most obedient humble servant,

MOIRA.

Major-General HENRY LEE.